KINGS, BARONS AND JUSTICES

The Making and Enforcement of Legislation in Thirteenth-Century England

This book is a study of two important and related pieces of thirteenth-century English legislation – the Provisions of Westminster of 1259 and the Statute of Marlborough of 1267 – and is the first on any of the statutes of this period of major legislative change.

The Provisions of Westminster were the first major legislation enacted in England after Magna Carta. They were the product of political upheaval, when Henry III surrendered control of government to a baronial council with an agenda of institutional reform. The Provisions were revised and reissued by the king in 1263, and a further revision in 1267 produced the Statute of Marlborough. Exceptionally good surviving documentation is used to follow the evolution of the individual clauses from initial suggestions for reform, through a series of drafts, to the various versions of the final texts. The book also places each clause in the context of the prior development of the Common Law. A wide range of surviving (and mainly unpublished) sources are then used to trace the enforcement and interpretation of legislation between 1259 and 1307. Three appendices provide a modern text and translation of the legislation.

PAUL BRAND is a Senior Research Fellow at All Souls College, Oxford. His other publications include *Origins of the English Legal Profession* and *The Making of the Common Law*. He is a Fellow of the British Academy.

Cambridge Studies in Medieval Life and Thought
Fourth Series

The series Cambridge Studies in Medieval Life and Thought was inaugurated by G. G. Coulton in 1921; Professor D. E. Luscombe now acts as General Editor of the Fourth Series, with Dr Christine Carpenter and Professor Rosamond McKitterick as Advisory Editors. The series brings together outstanding work by medieval scholars over a wide range of human endeavour extending from political economy to the history of ideas.

For a list of titles in the series, see end of book.

KINGS, BARONS AND JUSTICES

The Making and Enforcement of Legislation in Thirteenth-Century England

PAUL BRAND

All Souls College, Oxford

CAMBRIDGE
UNIVERSITY PRESS

CAMBRIDGE UNIVERSITY PRESS
Cambridge, New York, Melbourne, Madrid, Cape Town, Singapore, São Paulo

Cambridge University Press
The Edinburgh Building, Cambridge CB2 2RU, UK

Published in the United States of America by Cambridge University Press, New York

www.cambridge.org
Information on this title: www.cambridge.org/9780521372466

First published 2003
Reprinted 2005
This digitally printed first paperback version 2006

A catalogue record for this publication is available from the British Library

ISBN-13 978-0-521-37246-6 hardback
ISBN-10 0-521-37246-1 hardback

ISBN-13 978-0-521-02585-0 paperback
ISBN-10 0-521-02585-0 paperback

In memory of the late Derek Hall

CONTENTS

Appendixes

TABLES

PREFACE

This book has had a long genesis. In 1967 I started work on an Oxford D.Phil. thesis under the supervision of the late G.D.G. Hall. My original intention was to work on the *Leges Henrici Primi*, but Derek did not think it was a suitable topic for a postgraduate thesis and suggested that there was another topic I might like to work on. It was a problem that had arisen out of his own current work on dating registers of writs for the Selden Society edition of *Early Registers* which had been begun by Elsa de Haas but which he was then completing. This was the extent to which the Provisions of Westminster of 1259 (or the reissues of 1263 and 1264) had ever been enforced in the courts or in other ways between 1259 and the final reissue of the Provisions as the Statute of Marlborough in 1267. This turned out to be a little too narrow a focus for a doctoral thesis. So we agreed to broaden it out to a more general consideration of the genesis and background of the legislation and its enforcement not just between 1259 and 1267 but also between 1267 and the end of the reign of Edward I in 1307. There was much less pressure then to finish doctoral theses within a three-year period and I did in fact not complete and submit the thesis until 1974. The thesis benefited considerably from the delay. In 1970 I had been appointed an Assistant Keeper at the Public Record Office. I profited from the opportunities this offered me to explore much more fully the riches of the Record Office after working hours and especially while working as overnight Duty Officer. The eventual thesis owed much to the more thorough archival research I was able to do between 1970 and 1974. When the thesis was examined in 1974 my two examiners (S.F.C. Milsom and Barabara Harvey) encouraged me to publish material from it, though not the entire thesis as it stood. I am now sure that their judgement was correct. The thesis as it stood was well-researched and thorough but somewhat rebarbative and lacking in a clear overall argument. After 1974 I put the thesis on one side, though I continued to note additional material relevant to the matters discussed in the thesis as I encountered it in the course of other research. In 1988 Professor J.C. Holt encouraged me to transform the original thesis into a publishable book for the present series and I agreed to do so. Work on other projects prevented any rapid progress until comparatively recently. Those who have read the original 1974 thesis will see just how much it has been transformed in the interim. This book contains almost all the material contained in the original thesis but also a great deal of other original material produced by subsequent research in the plea rolls and contemporary law reports. It has also been completely reorganised and reconceptualised to provide much clearer answers to three basic questions: why was the legislation of 1259–67 necessary and what effect was it intended to produce? What effect did the legislation have during its initial period of operation between 1259 and 1267? How was the legislation enforced and interpreted by the courts between 1267 and 1307?

In the course of its long gestation this book and its author have accumulated many debts, more than can easily be mentioned here. The greatest is acknowledged in its dedication. Derek Hall taught me directly and by example what it is to be a legal historian. The topic he suggested to me back in 1967 was not one which would have occurred to me on my own but it has turned out to be one of the best possible introductions I could have had to the study of English thirteenth-century legal history. I have also benefited over the years from the friendship and assistance of two other scholars who were being supervised by Derek Hall at the same time as me, Paul Hyams and Alexandra Nicol. I am grateful to S.F.C. Milsom and Barbara Harvey for their helpful comments on the original thesis and to Jim Holt for encouraging me to resume work on the thesis and to transform it into a book. My more recent debt is to All Souls College, Oxford for providing me with an excellent working environment in which to complete work on this book, and to my colleagues there for friendship and intellectual stimulation. I am also grateful to Bill Davies of Cambridge University Press for his patience and forbearance in awaiting the completion of this book.

I owe a twofold debt to the Public Record Office and its staff: both for providing me with the opportunity to finish my original thesis while employed there between 1970 and 1974 and for subsequent assistance while working as a researcher in the public search-rooms. I am also grateful to the staff of various other institutions, especially the British Library (and its Students' Room), the Cambridge University Library and the Bodleian Library in Oxford, for their assistance in my work on various manuscripts in their custody.

Of my London friends I would single out David Carpenter for special mention in encouraging me to continue work on this project and Jim Bolton for friendship and help over the years. Of my American friends I would single out Bob Palmer and Joseph Biancalana for their friendship and stimulation over the many years of our friendship.

My parents did not live to see the appearance of this book but were always supportive of my scholarly endeavours during their lifetimes and I remain grateful to them for this. The book also owes more than I can say to the wise criticism and continued support of my wife, Vanessa, and I am happy to take this opportunity to thank her publicly for this.

ABBREVIATIONS

Unless otherwise noted, all references to unpublished manuscripts are to documents in the Public Record Office, London.

BL	British Library
BNB	*Bracton's Note Book: A Collection of Cases decided in the King's Courts during the Reign of Henry the Third, annotated by a Lawyer of that Time, seemingly by Henry of Bratton*, ed. F.W. Maitland (3 vols., London, 1887)
Bracton	Bracton, *De Legibus et Consuetudinibus Angliae*, ed. G.E. Woodbine and transl. (with revisions and notes) by Samuel E. Thorne (4 vols., Cambridge, Massachusetts, 1968–77)
Brand, 'Contribution'	P.A. Brand, 'The Contribution of the Period of Baronial Reform (1258–1267) to the Development of the Common Law in England' (Oxford D.Phil. thesis, 1974)
Brand, *MCL*	Paul Brand, *The Making of the Common Law* (London, 1992)
Brand, *OELP*	Paul Brand, *The Origins of the English Legal Profession* (Oxford, 1992)
Britton	*Britton*, ed. and transl. F.M. Nichols (2 vols., Oxford, 1865)
CCR	*Calendar of the Close Rolls preserved in the Public Record Office: Edward I* (5 vols., London, 1900–8)
CIPM	*Calendar of Inquisitions Post Mortem and other analogous Documents,* vol. I (Henry III), vols. II–IV (Edward I) (London, 1904–13)
CLRO	Corporation of London Records Office

Coke, *Second Institutes*	Edward Coke, *The Second Part of the Institutes of the Laws of England* (2 vols., continuously paginated, London, 1809) [pages cited from older marginal page numbers]
CPR	*Calendar of the Patent Rolls preserved in the Public Record Office: Henry III* (4 vols., London, 1906–13); *Calendar of the Patent Rolls preserved in the Public Record Office: Edward I* (4 vols., London, 1893–1901)
CR	*Close Rolls of the reign of Henry III* (14 vols., London, 1902–38)
CRR	*Curia Regis Rolls* (18 vols., London, 1923–)
CUL	Cambridge University Library
DBM	*Documents of the Baronial Movement of Reform and Rebellion, 1258–1267*, selected by R.F. (misprinted as R.E.) Treharne and edited by I.J. Sanders (Oxford, 1973)
Early Registers	*Early Registers of Writs*, ed. Elsa de Haas and G.D.G. Hall (Selden Society vol. 87, 1970)
EELR	*The Earliest English Law Reports*, ed. Paul A. Brand (2 vols., Selden Society vols. 111 and 112, 1996)
Fleta	*Fleta*, volumes II, III and IV [vol. I not published], ed. H.G. Richardson and G.O. Sayles [vol. IV by Sayles alone] (3 vols., Selden Society vols. 72, 89 and 99, 1955, 1972 and 1984]
Glanvill	*Tractatus de legibus et consuetudinibus Anglie qui Glanvilla vocatur*, ed. G.D.G. Hall (London, 1965)
IT	Inner Temple, London
J.	Justice
LAL	*Liber de Antiquis Legibus*
LI	Lincoln's Inn, London
Maitland, *Collected Papers*	*The Collected Papers of Frederic William Maitland*, ed. H.A.L. Fisher (3 vols., Cambridge, 1911)
Meekings, *Crown Pleas*	*Crown Pleas of the Wiltshire Eyre, 1249*, ed. C.A.F. Meekings (Wiltshire

	Archaeological and Natural History Society, Records Branch vol. 16, 1960)
NN	*Novae Narrationes*, ed. Elsie Shanks and S.F.C. Milsom (Selden Society vol. 80, 1963)
P&M	F. Pollock and F.W. Maitland, *The History of English Law before the Time of Edward I*, 2nd edition (2 vols., Cambridge, 1898)
PKJ	*Pleas before the King or his Justices,* vols. I and II (1198–1202), vols. III and IV (1198–1212), ed. D.M. Stenton (4 vols., Selden Society vols. 67, 68, 83 and 84, 1953, 1952, 1967 and 1967)
Plucknett, *Legislation*	T.F.T. Plucknett, *Legislation of Edward I*, revised edition (Oxford, 1962)
PRO	Public Record Office, Kew, London
Reg. Omn. Brev.	*Registrum Omnium Brevium, tam Originalium quam Judicialium . . .* (London, 1595)
RH	*Rotuli Hundredorum*, ed. W. Illingworth and J. Caley (2 vols., London, 1812–18)
SCKB	*Select Cases in the Court of King's Bench under Edward I*, ed. G.O. Sayles (3 vols., Selden Society vols. 55, 57 and 58, 1936, 1938 and 1939)
SR	*Statutes of the Realm*, ed. A. Luders and others (11 vols., London, 1810–28)
SSC	*Select Charters and other Illustrations of English Constitutional History*, ed. W. Stubbs, 9th edition revised by H.W.C. Davis (Oxford, 1913)
VCH	Victoria History of the Counties of England (1900–)
YB	Year Books
YB 20 & 21 EI	*Year Books 20 & 21 Edward I: Year Books of the Reign of King Edward the First: Years XX and XXI*, ed. A.J. Horwood (Rolls Series, London: 1866)
YB 21 & 22 EI	*Year Books 21 & 22 Edward I: Year Books of the Reign of King Edward the First: Years XXI and XXII*, ed. A.J. Horwood (Rolls Series, London: 1873)

YB 30 & 31 EI	*Year Books 30 & 31 Edward I: Year Books of the Reign of King Edward the First*, ed. A.J. Horwood (Rolls Series, London: 1863)
YB 32 & 33 EI	*Year Books 32 & 33 Edward I: Year Books of the Reign of King Edward the First: Years XXXII–XXXIII*, ed. A.J. Horwood (Rolls Series, London: 1864)
YB 33–35 EI	*Year Books 33–35 Edward I: Year Books of the Reign of King Edward the First: Michaelmas Term, Year XXXXIII and Years XXXXIV and XXXV*, ed. A.J. Horwood (Rolls Series, London: 1879)

INTRODUCTION

When the lawyers who taught the English common law in the Inns of Court in the later Middle Ages constructed a lecture course for apprentices which consisted of an exposition of, and commentary on, the most important legislation of the thirteenth and early fourteenth centuries, most of the legislation they chose came from the reign of King Edward I.[1] That course also, however, included three statutes that belonged to the reign of Edward's father, King Henry III. These were the 1225 reissue of Magna Carta,[2] the Provisions of Merton of 1236 and the Statute of Marlborough of 1267. The singling out of these three particular pieces of legislation from Henry III's reign as of enduring importance parallels their treatment within the textual tradition of the statute books. Statute books were beginning to be copied in large numbers by the final decade of the thirteenth century and the first decade of the fourteenth century and contained mainly the major and minor statutes of the reign of Edward I and various other non-statutory but useful texts.[3] Magna Carta, the Provisions of Merton and the Statute of Marlborough were not quite the only statutes of the reign of Henry III to be included in such volumes. It was not uncommon to include the quasi-statutory Dictum of Kenilworth of 1266 and the Leap Year ordinance of 1256 as well. Sometimes other statutory texts are found there too. These three statutes, however, were always included and they almost always stood at the very beginning of the volume. This was not just sentimental antiquarianism. They were included because they were statutes of continuing legal importance whose texts any practising lawyer needed to have.

[1] J.H. Baker, *Readers and Readings in the Inns of Court and Chancery* (Selden Society Supplementary series vol. 13, 2000), pp. 3–5; Brand, *MCL*, pp. 70–2.

[2] The text they used is, however, likely to have been that of the confirmation issued in 1300.

[3] Don C. Skemer, 'Reading the Law: Statute Books and the Private Transmission of Legal Knowledge in Late Medieval England' in *Learning the Law: Teaching and the Transmission of Law in England, 1150–1900*, ed. Jonathan A. Bush and Alain Wijffels (London, 1999), pp. 113–31; Paul Brand, 'English Thirteenth Century Legislation' in '*. . . Colendo iustitiam et iura condendo . . .*': *Federico II Legislatore del Regno di Sicilia nell'Europa del Duecento*, ed. A. Romano (Rome, 1997), pp. 325–44 at pp. 342–3.

Successive generations of legal and constitutional historians have worked on the origins and development of the text of Magna Carta, starting with the political crisis of 1215 and its roots in the prior events of John's reign and those of his brother and father and leading through to the definitive text of the 1225 reissue.[4] They have also worked on its later history and shown how the Charter was used and interpreted in practice both in the courts and elsewhere.[5] Less work has been done on the two other major pieces of legislation belonging to Henry III's reign. The detailed investigations of a series of historians over the past century have at least revealed the composite nature of what later passed for the Provisions of Merton and shown that it is not just a single piece of legislation enacted at Merton in 1236. They have also revealed something of the background and context of the individual clauses.[6] Some work has also been done on the subsequent use and interpretation of those clauses, though there is as yet no comprehensive modern account of this available.[7]

The story of the origins and evolution of the Statute of Marlborough of 1267 is an even more complex one. The Statute was, as will be seen, in effect a final reissue, in an amended and expanded form, of the Provisions of Westminster. Those Provisions had originally been promulgated in 1259 and had then been reissued with amendments and additions in 1263 and (in a virtually identical text) in 1264. There also survive a number of different draft texts which lie behind the Provisions as issued in 1259 and texts of some of the requests for legal changes which provoked that legislation and which form part of the 1258 Petition of the Barons. The rediscovery of these various texts lying behind the eventual Statute of Marlborough and recovery of the wider contemporary political and legal context of the legal changes of this period has been a gradual process. The starting-point for modern scholarship on the origins and evolution of the Statute of Marlborough seems to have been the rediscovery of the Provisions of Westminster of 1259 by Serjeant Hawkins, who printed them in the Appendix to the sixth volume of his edition of the *Statutes at*

[4] The classic modern work is J.C. Holt, *Magna Carta* (Cambridge, 2nd edition, 1992).

[5] Faith Thompson, *The First Century of Magna Carta: Why It Persisted as a Document* (Minneapolis, 1925); Faith Thompson, *Magna Carta: Its Role in the Making of the English Constitution, 1300–1629* (Minneapolis, 1948); J.C. Holt, *Magna Carta and Medieval Government* (London, 1985).

[6] G.J. Turner, 'Some Thirteenth Century Statutes', *Law Magazine and Review* 4th series 21 (1896), 300–16, and 22 (1897), 240–50; H.G. Richardson, 'Glanville Continued', *Law Quarterly Review* 54 (1938), 381–99; F.M. Powicke, *King Henry III and the Lord Edward: the Community of the Realm in the Thirteenth Century* (Oxford, 1966), pp. 148–52, 769–70; *Early Registers*, p. ciii.

[7] J.L. Barton, 'The Mystery of Bracton', *Journal of Legal History* 14, no. 3 (1993), 1–142, especially 5–20; Paul Brand, '"Time out of Mind": the Knowledge and Use of the Eleventh and Twelfth-Century Past in Thirteenth-Century Litigation', *Anglo-Norman Studies* 16 (1994), 37–54, especially 40–1.

Large in 1735–6.[8] They had needed to be rediscovered because texts of the Provisions of Westminster of 1259 and of the reissues of 1263 and 1264 had not been included in most later manuscript collections of statutes and so had not made their way into any of the earlier printed editions of the statutes. The editors of the official edition of *Statutes of the Realm* published between 1810 and 1822 printed the same text in their volume I and also included variants from the 1263 and 1264 reissues in their footnotes.[9] Of the various texts which lie behind the Provisions of Westminster, the 'Petition of the Barons' has been in print (albeit in a version derived from only one of the three surviving texts) since William Fulman's edition of the Burton Annals in 1684. This was re-edited by H.R. Luard in his Rolls Series edition of the Burton Annals in 1864 and reached a much wider public through Bishop Stubbs' *Select Charters and Other Illustrations of English Constitutional History from the Earliest Times to the Reign of Edward the First* in 1870.[10] Of the various drafting stages, the penultimate French text of the Provisions of Westminster, apparently as prepared for the Westminster parliament of October 1259, has also been in print since 1684 as one text formed part of the Burton Annals and was also re-edited by Luard in 1864.[11] The Latin draft text of part of the Provisions known as the *Providencia Baronum* was first published (from two of the four surviving texts) by E.F. Jacob in 1922; the French draft text which lies behind this was first published (from the only known surviving text, now in Philadelphia) only in 1990.[12]

The first coherent general account of the background to, and evolution of, the Provisions of Westminster and the Statute of Marlborough was that provided by William Stubbs in volume II of his *Constitutional History of England*.[13] It was Stubbs who was first to discuss the series of grievances presented to the Oxford parliament of the summer of 1258. He is also responsible for giving it the name of the 'Petition of the Barons'. Stubbs saw it as a list of the grievances of Henry III's baronial opposition produced during the interval between Henry III's agreement to the 'project of reform' in May and the session of parliament at Oxford. Stubbs knew nothing of the various intermediate drafts of the Provisions of 1259 and so did not discuss them. His account of the Provisions of Westminster

[8] Hawkins was not, however, followed in this by either of his main successors, Ruffhead and Pickering.

[9] *SR*, I, 8–11. Somewhat confusingly for later scholars, the numbers printed in the margin of their edition were the numbers of the corresponding clauses of the Statute of Marlborough. The 1259 Provisions are not called the 'Provisions of Westminster' in this text. They are captioned merely as 'Provisions made by the King and his Council'.

[10] Brand, *MCL*, pp. 327–8. [11] Ibid., pp. 349–51. [12] Ibid., pp. 335–8, 359–61.

[13] William Stubbs, *The Constitutional History of England*, 2nd edition (3 vols., Oxford, 1874–8), II, 73–97.

misunderstands the relationship between the 'administrative' decisions reached there and the legislation enacted there and says very little about that legislation. Stubbs knew of the reissues of the Provisions of 1263 and 1264, though he did not note, and so did not discuss, the significant differences between these reissues and the original 1259 Provisions. His lack of interest in the details of legal reform also emerges from his brief discussion of the Statute of Marlborough, which he characterises simply as a statutory re-enactment of the Provisions of 1259.[14] The first scholar to note the existence of the Latin draft version of a text of part of the Provisions of Westminster published in March 1259 (the *Providencia Baronum*) and to discuss its contents was E.F. Jacob in his *Studies in the Period of Baronial Reform and Rebellion*, published in 1925.[15] Jacob also distinguished, in a way that Stubbs had not, between the 'administrative' decisions taken at Westminster and the proposed arrangements for the forthcoming special eyre and the permanent legislation enacted there.[16] Jacob was also the first scholar to discuss various of the texts of the 1263 and 1264 reissues of the Provisions and correctly to note that they represented a revised version of the original Provisions of 1259 with various additions.[17] But Jacob's main interest was in local administrative reform during this period and the remedying of local grievances. He did not attempt to give anything like a coherent account of the gradual evolution of the legislation of this period over time or even a full account of the immediate political context of the reforms; and his interest in legislative texts did not extend as far as the Statute of Marlborough of 1267. There is a much more detailed account of the immediate political context of the baronial take-over of royal government in 1258, of the drafting of the 'Petition of the Barons' and of the relationship between the 'Petition' and the Provisions of Westminster of 1259 in R.F. Treharne's *The Baronial Plan of Reform, 1258–1263*, first published in 1932 and originally envisaged as the first part of a two-part study, of which the second part was never published.[18] Treharne also discussed the *Providencia Baronum* and the different published texts of the Provisions of Westminster and gave the first more general account of the contents of the Provisions of Westminster, though one which inevitably suffered from Treharne's lack of detailed knowledge of the earlier legal context. The one major contribution to our knowledge of the 'Petition of the Barons' (noting the existence of

[14] Ibid., II, 97.

[15] E.F. Jacob, *Studies in the Period of Baronial Reform and Rebellion, 1258–1267* (Oxford Studies in Social and Legal History 8, 1925), pp. 72, 78–83.

[16] Ibid., pp. 86–101. [17] Ibid., pp. 76–7, 121–5.

[18] R.F. Treharne, *The Baronial Plan of Reform, 1258–1263* (Manchester, 1932). For Treharne's plan to write a second volume see pp. viii–ix.

three separate and different texts) and of what can now be seen as three different draft texts that lie behind the Provisions of Westminster that has been published since was an article by the present writer originally published in 1990, which has since been reprinted in a collection of my essays.

There has also been some work on the use and later interpretation of this legislation. E.F. Jacob noted in passing some of the evidence on the plea rolls for the enforcement of various of the individual clauses of the Provisions of Westminster between 1259 and 1263,[19] and Treharne was able to add to this with further evidence drawn from the Chancery Rolls.[20] G.D.G. Hall was able to add materially to what was already known (and to look beyond 1263) in a brief discussion in his introduction to a jointly edited volume of *Early Registers of Writs* in 1970.[21] For the use and interpretation of the provisions of the Statute of Marlborough after 1267 the modern literature begins with the passing references to the provisions of the Statute in Plucknett's *Statutes and their Interpretation in the First Half of the Fourteenth Century*, first published in 1922.[22] Plucknett also dealt in rather more depth with the enforcement and interpretation of many of the clauses of the Statute of Marlborough in his Ford Lectures of 1947, first published in 1949 and subsequently reissued in a revised form in 1962.[23] The main weakness of Plucknett's work, however, was that it was based wholly on the material then in print. The only reported cases of the reign of Edward I known to him were those published by Horwood in the Rolls Series edition of *Year Books of Edward the First*.[24] Nor did he look at any one of the voluminous surviving plea rolls of the royal courts for the reign of Edward I which, as will be seen, provide an invaluable source of information on this subject.

In Part I of this book I make a fresh attempt to explore the background and contemporary context of the Statute of Marlborough. Chapter 1 looks at the immediate political context of the Provisions of Westminster of 1259 as part of the reform programme of the baronial opposition which came to power in the summer of 1258. It also examines the various surviving texts which allow us to trace the gradual evolution of the Provisions

[19] Jacob, *Studies*, pp. 110, 113, 115–16, 123.

[20] Treharne, *Baronial Plan*, pp. 209–10.

[21] *Early Registers*, pp. xlv–xlvii.

[22] T.F.T. Plucknett, *Statutes and their Interpretation in the First Half of the Fourteenth Century* (Cambridge, 1922). There is also an older scholarship on the enforcement and interpretation of the Statute to be found in Sir Edward Coke's *The Second Part of the Institutes of the Laws of England*, first published after his death in 1642, at pp. 101–55.

[23] T.F.T. Plucknett, *Legislation of Edward I* (Oxford, 1949 and revised edition of 1962).

[24] For the many other surviving reports see Paul Brand, 'The Beginnings of English Law Reporting' in *Law Reporting in England*, ed. Chantal Stebbings (London, 1995), pp. 1–14.

between the first suggestions for reform contained in the so-called 'Petition of the Barons', presented to the Oxford parliament of that same summer, and the final promulgation of the first version of the reforming legislation at the autumn parliament held at Westminster in the summer of 1259. Chapters 2 and 3 look in greater depth than has been previously attempted at the social and legal context of the individual clauses of the Provisions in the development of the common law prior to 1259, and try to explain why reform in these particular terms was thought necessary in 1259. They also analyse the ways in which the individual clauses changed during the course of drafting and what these changes meant and why they were made. Chapter 2 focuses on three different groups of clauses. A first group are those clauses which reformed aspects of the lord–tenant relationship: regulating distraints made to enforce performance of suit of court, preventing abuses of the lord's rights at succession and giving lords a right to control alienations to the religious made by their tenants. The second group of clauses are those giving landholders additional powers to control and bring to account the temporary managers of their lands, whether lessees or bailiffs or the trustee guardians of lands held in socage. The third group of clauses examined in this chapter are those which speeded up the process used by the king's court in securing the appearance of recalcitrant defendants and allowed those courts to override charters of exemption from jury service. Chapter 3 also looks at three different groups of clauses. A first section examines those clauses which were intended to reform the criminal justice system, eliminating abuses in the levying of *murdrum* fines and other kinds of unjustified amercements plus various kinds of beaupleder fine and exempting various categories of person from attendance at the sheriff's tourn. A second section looks at other clauses intended to eliminate grievances relating to attendance at sessions of royal courts held in the localities but not connected with the hearing of criminal pleas. The third group of clauses confirmed existing rules restricting the use of the right of distraint, gave clear authority for the release of distresses held within franchises when the franchise-holders failed to act and confirmed and strengthened various royal franchisal monopolies.

Chapter 4 considers the evidence for the enforcement of the Provisions of Westminster during their initial period of operation prior to the first reissue of the Provisions early in 1263. It looks at the evidence for the creation of new forms of action by Chancery and their subsequent use by litigants; for the enforcement of the legislation by means of plaints; for the citation and observance of the legislation in pre-existing forms of litigation; for the observance of the legislation relating to crown pleas fines and amercements; and for the observance of the legislation in relation to initial and mesne process to secure the appearance of defendants and in authorising shorter adjournments between procedural stages in various kinds of action. It also analyses the degree of correlation that exists between observance of the legislation and the current political climate during this period. Much of the evidence used in this chapter has not previously been known to scholars and it allows a more accurate and more finely nuanced picture to be drawn of the enforcement of the legislation during this first period than has hitherto been possible. Chapter 5 examines the evidence for the reissuing of the Provisions in 1263 and 1264. It argues for there having been two reissues in 1263 (in January and again in June) as well as a single reissue in 1264. It discusses the changes made for the 1263 reissue, particularly in the preamble to the Provisions and in a number of minor amendments elsewhere, and looks at the four clauses added to the Provisions. The most important of these was a clause allowing the issue of writs of entry 'outside the degrees', which allowed writs of entry to be used in a wider range of situations than had hitherto been possible. The chapter also examines the surviving unofficial texts of the 1264 reissue and the minor changes made in the text of the 1263 reissue for this reissue under the Montfortian regime. Chapter 6 then focuses on the evidence for the enforcement of the Provisions as amended between the early months of 1263 and the winter of 1267, when the Provision of Westminster received their final revision and reissue as part of the Statute of Marlborough. Again the full range of possible ways of applying the legislation are considered: the use of remedies specifically authorised by the Statute, both those invented between 1259 and 1263 and the new remedies authorised by the clauses added in 1263; the enforcement of the legislation through pre-existing common law actions or in crown pleas sessions; the application of the legislation through modified process to secure appearances in court or through the shortening of adjournments; and the evidence for the enforcement of the one clause (on mortmain alienations) omitted from the 1263 and 1264 reissues of the Provisions. Although the poor survival of records makes our picture necessarily an incomplete one, more evidence survives than has hitherto been known to historians and it casts interesting light on the divergent attitudes towards the Provisions held and expressed during the period prior to their confirmation and re-enactment in 1267.

Chapter 7 concludes the first part by exploring in detail the final expanded revision and reissue of the Provisions in 1267 as the Statute of Marlborough. It examines the evidence for what this revision contained and what it omitted, together with the context of the eight new chapters added at the beginning of the legislation. The first four chapters were a restatement and reaffirmation of some of the basic norms of the thirteenth-century legal system and were intended to provide ideological and practical support for the reassertion of royal power after the civil war. Chapters 5 and 8 were also in effect reaffirmations of existing law. Chapters 6 and 7 were the most obviously innovatory chapters. Chapter 6 dealt with devices which deprived lords of their rights of wardship. Previous writers have seen the chapter as intended to deal with a major social problem but it is argued that the chapter was probably a reaction to two specific cases then pending in the courts. Chapter 7 provided a further modest instalment of statutory procedural reform along the lines initiated in 1259 and continued in 1263: allowing the awarding of judgment by default in the action of wardship, but with various procedural safeguards.

Part II looks at the rather different story of the enforcement and interpretation of the Statute of Marlborough during the first four decades after its enactment, down to the end of the reign of Edward I, a period when the validity of the legislation had ceased to be in question and legislators had ceased to look for ways of improving or amending its text. The chief interest of the story in this period is in seeing how the courts dealt with the prescriptions of the legislation and how useful they proved to be to individual litigants. This is the first time that the evidence of the unprinted plea rolls and unpublished law reports of the reign (as well as that of the Year Books of the reign of Edward I already in print) has been used for this purpose. These new sources, as will be seen, make a major contribution to our understanding of how the legislation was enforced and interpreted in practice and also provide us with significant information on those parts of the legislation which do not seem to have been much used or cited.

Chapter 8 traces the post-1267 history of the one form of action specifically created by the Provisions of Westminster (and which received continuing authorisation from the Statute of Marlborough) in order to give effect to the new rules about the use of distraint to enforce the performance of suit to lords' courts laid down in the legislation, the action of *contra formam feoffamenti*. A thorough examination of the plea roll evidence indicates that it was in regular, but not common, use during this period and various reasons are suggested for why this might have been so. Also examined are the various ways in which the courts seem consciously to have departed from the specific provisions of the Statute during this period: in respect of the process used in the action; through altering or allowing the alteration of the limitation date used in the action, the date before which defendants had to show regular seisin of suit to make a good title to distrain for it; through refusing to give its natural meaning to the clause exempting those with charters specifying a fixed service 'for all service' from suit other than in a single case brought by a special writ. There is also an analysis of the types of plaintiff and defendant involved in such cases, the types of court to which suit was claimed and the counties involved.

Chapter 9 starts by looking at the evidence for enforcement of the same chapter of the Statute of Marlborough through actions other than *contra formam feoffamenti:* at whether or not the lord's action authorised by the chapter ever came into existence; at the enforcement of the rules about liability to perform suit and other services contained in the chapter in the non-statutory action of replevin; and at the creation of various new actions specifically invoking that Statute to enforce the rules about liability for suit in respect of divided tenements which it laid down. It then focuses briefly on the enforcement of the clause protecting tenants against lords abusing their rights of wardship and primer seisin by awarding them damages in the short period before this was superseded by the more general provisions of the Statute of Gloucester of 1278. The chapter ends by looking at the enforcement of two measures intended for the benefit of lords: the new chapter 6 of the Statute of Marlborough protecting the rights of wardship enjoyed by lords against devices whose effect, if not intention, was to deprive them of this; and the clause of the original Provisions of Westminster which required the consent of the lord of whom land was held for any grant of that land to the religious which was omitted from all subsequent reissues, including the Statute of Marlborough, but which was being cited from the later 1270s as though it was legislation still validly in force and enforced through specially drafted writs citing its provisions.

Chapter 10 examines the evidence for the enforcement of the various provisions relating to abuses within the criminal justice system. The statements of county custom on the presentment of Englishry provide a good source for the extent to which individual counties picked up on the legislation confining the adjudging of *murdrum* fines to felonious homicides and specifically cited it, tacitly adopted it, or simply continued to state their previous liability to present Englishry in respect of accidental deaths as well. Examination of the actual practice of the justices in eyre in making judgments of *murdrum* provides, however, a much better guide to the actual extent of observance of the legislation by those in the best position to ignore or observe it and also to just how much difference the legislation made in practice to the communities who were liable to payment of the fine. The contrasting fate of two of the other clauses on crown pleas amercements is then traced: the continuing observance after 1267 of the clause exempting from amercement the sureties of clergy charged with felonies who pleaded their clerical status, and the effective repeal in 1267 of the clause exempting villages from amercement for failing to attend inquests 'fully' by a proviso that took coroners' inquests into homicides outside its scope. The chapter also looks at the post-1267 enforcement of the chapter exempting various categories of person from attendance at the sheriff's tourn through prohibitions issued by both Exchequer and Chancery; at the post-1267 extension of the statute's provisions to attendance at the private, franchisal view of frankpledge and their enforcement through litigation; and at the enforcement of the rules about attendance at the tourn and at view of frankpledge through a variety of common law actions. The chapter concludes by considering the evidence for the enforcement of the clause abolishing beaupleder fines, unless they had become fixed prior to 1230, and the variety of different ways this was enforced in practice: through prohibitions, through special actions based on the litigation, through plaints, through presentments and through citation in the common law action of replevin.

Chapter 11 investigates the effectiveness of the various chapters of the Statute relating to the procedures of the king's courts. It looks at the evidence for their compliance with the prescriptions of chapter 12 of the Statute of Marlborough on the abbreviation of adjournments in actions of dower and actions of *quare impedit* and darrein presentment and the telescoping of mesne process in *quare impedit* and in personal actions generally; at the enforcement of the provisions for the awarding of judgment by default in *quare impedit* and the various technical problems this posed for the courts, and the use of the similar provisions (but with a much more complicated preliminary process) in the action of wardship and why this seems to have been rather less successful in practice. The chapter also looks at the post-1267 history of the writ of *monstravit de compoto*, an action of account employing a special initial process: at the different forms of this writ; at the procedures required of those who wished to use the writ (and at the evidence suggesting that initially it was only available to a limited group of persons enjoying privileged access to Chancery); at the initial process which the writ authorised and the subsequent process used when that initial process failed to produce the defendant in court; at the different types of defendant against whom the writ could be brought; and at the remedies available against its improper use and the various technical problems of statutory interpretation these raised for the courts. It concludes by considering briefly the fragmentary evidence on three other clauses: that authorising the courts to override charters of exemption from jury service; that prohibiting the amercement of warrantors resident in a county who were not in court when vouched to warranty in the eyre; and one limiting the justices with authority to amerce for default of common summons.

Chapter 12 surveys the remedies authorised by the Provisions of Westminster and Statute of Marlborough whose common feature is that they bear no trace on their face of the fact that they had received this statutory authorisation. One whole group of remedies of this kind are the writs of entry in the *post*, whose creation had been first authorised in 1263 and which had all come into existence by 1272, which extended quite materially the scope of the availability of the writ of entry. The chapter uses statistics drawn from eyres in selected counties and selected Common Bench terms to track the rise in the use of writs of entry and the decline in the use of the writ of right between *c.* 1250 and 1290 that reflects this extension of the ambit of writs of entry. A second, and much less popular, extension of existing remedies was the extension of the remedies available to ecclesiastical tenants first authorised in the revised Provisions of Westminster of 1263 and confirmed by the Statute in 1267. Evidence is examined for the direct use of that part of chapter 28 of the Statute of Marlborough which extended the availability of the action of trespass to allow successors to recover property taken from their immediate predecessors and also of its occasional citation to support the availability of other actions. The evidence is also surveyed for the use of the second part of the chapter which authorised the creation and use of actions to allow prelates to recover land taken from their ecclesiastical institution during a vacancy. A third extension of an existing remedy was that authorised by clause 20 of the Provisions (chapter 23 of the Statute) allowing an action of waste against lessees. The evidence is examined for the use of this provision during the relatively brief period prior to the general overhaul of the action of waste by the Statute of Gloucester in 1278.

Chapter 13 reviews the evidence for the enforcement of the obligation of guardians in socage to account to their wards once those wards had come of age, as prescribed by clause 12 of the Provisions and restated by chapter 17 of the Statute. The chapter looks at the creation of a writ specifically reciting the Statute, intended to compel a socage guardian to render account in the king's court, at the creation of a non-returnable form of the same writ, allowing the initiation of an action of account in the county court, and also at the enforcement of the obligation to account by local courts and at eyre sessions without the use of writs. Only the recorded cases in the Common Bench and the eyre are available for detailed analysis. The chapter analyses the frequency of recorded actions; the value of the tenements held in wardship for which an account was required; the length of the periods of wardship concerned and the time elapsed between the ending of the period of wardship and the bringing of the litigation; the possible defences to such claims and the way they reveal that the action had been extended to cover not just tenure of the wardship by the guardian of right but also usurpation of the wardship by third parties, especially by the lords of whom the land was held.

Chapter 14 focuses on the enforcement of various of the chapters of the Statute which were intended to control the use of distraint. The possibility of a connexion between two of the different types of trespass writ alleging wrongful distraint and the provisions of chapters 1–4 of the Statute is investigated, as is also the connexion between these chapters of the Statute and one of the articles for which presentments were sought that were added to the articles of the eyre in 1278. The origins of a different trespassory writ alleging wrongful distraint outside a lord's fee or in the highway and specifically reciting the provisions of chapter 15 of the Statute are traced and an analysis offered of the pleaded cases brought by such writs found on the Common Bench plea rolls. The pleading in these cases also demonstrates the existence of a number of interesting exceptions to the general rule prohibiting distraints made outside the fee or in the king's highway. Allegations of distraint in the highway are also found frequently in common law actions of replevin in this period, as are allegations of distraint outside a lord's fee (though the latter come up at a different stage in pleading), but neither seems to owe anything to the statutory provisions.

Chapter 15 is concerned with a variety of provisions relating to the operation of local courts and, not surprisingly, it has proved much more difficult to find much evidence for the working and observance of these provisions in such courts. Special writs specifically invoking the legislation have been found for some of the clauses, though in no case did the use of these writs ever become common; for others it is possible to find articles of the eyre asking for presentments for breaches of the rules or other presentments which show their non-observance; and some of the rules can be shown to have been invoked in ordinary litigation. For some of the clauses no evidence at all can be found. The most likely explanation seems to be that they were observed without the need for special mechanisms to punish their breach.

PART I

Politics and the legislative reform of the common law: from the Provisions of Westminster of 1259 to the Statute of Marlborough of 1267

Chapter 1

THE MAKING OF THE PROVISIONS OF WESTMINSTER: THE PROCESS OF DRAFTING AND THEIR POLITICAL CONTEXT

On 24 October 1259, towards the end of a session of parliament, the Provisions of Westminster were read out in Westminster Hall in the presence of King Henry III, many of his earls and barons and a large number of other people.[1] The Provisions of Westminster were, by any reckoning, a major piece of legislation. No contemporary text of the Provisions numbers its clauses, but in the conventional modern enumeration first devised by William Stubbs and still used by scholars the Provisions consist of twenty-four clauses.[2] The final text of the Provisions, as subsequently copied and sent out to the counties, and probably also as initially read out at Westminster, makes no direct mention of the session of parliament. It does, however, ascribe the making of the legislation to a meeting of the king and his magnates at Westminster (meaning a parliament) held a fortnight after Michaelmas (the week beginning 13 October) in the year of grace 1259 and in Henry III's forty-third regnal year.[3] The date is probably the date parliament opened.

The Provisions directly reflect the exceptional political situation which existed at the time of their enactment, and the degree to which the king had agreed, or been compelled, to surrender the control of his administration to a group of his opponents, drawn from the baronage. They do this by speaking (in the preamble) of this legislation as having been 'made' and 'published' not just by the king but also by his magnates, and by ascribing them not just to the 'common counsel' but also to the common 'consent' of both king and magnates.[4] This language does more than just reflect the political and administrative situation at the time of the enactment of the Provisions. It is also a faithful reflexion of the

[1] *De Antiquis Legibus Liber: Cronica Maiorum et Vicecomitum Londoniarum*, ed. Thomas Stapleton (Camden Society original series vol. 34, 1846), p. 42.

[2] *SSC*, pp. 390–4. This is the enumeration used in the text of the Provisions edited and translated below in Appendix I at pp. 413–27.

[3] See the preamble to the text of the Provisions in Appendix I at pp. 414–15. The quindene of Michaelmas (13 October and perhaps the following week) was when the parliamentary session opened.

[4] Appendix I, preamble, at pp. 414–15.

circumstances which underlay their genesis and the prolonged process of drafting and revising successive versions of the legislation prior to their eventual official promulgation in October 1259. The Provisions of Westminster were, as will be seen, the end product of a process which had begun over a year and half earlier, in May 1258, when the king had agreed to the reform of his realm by a Committee of Twenty-four. This chapter locates the Provisions of Westminster within their immediate political context as part of the reform process and tracks the process by which the final text of the Provisions of Westminster as published in October 1259 emerged. The following two chapters will then look at the content of the individual clauses of the Provisions and place them in their wider social and legal context and also trace the way in which the texts of the individual clauses changed and developed during the course of the drafting process.

THE ESTABLISHMENT OF THE COMMITTEE OF TWENTY-FOUR

On 2 May 1258 Henry III had issued letters patent announcing that he had promised the magnates of England by means of an oath taken on his behalf by Robert Walerand that

> the state of our kingdom shall be put in order, corrected and reformed by twelve of our subjects belonging to our council who have already been chosen and by twelve other of our subjects, chosen by the magnates . . . as seems to them to be most fitting to the honour of God, our faith and the benefit of our kingdom . . . and that whatever shall be decided by the twenty-four chosen by both sides and sworn for this purpose, or by a majority of them, we will observe inviolably, wishing and ordering that their decisions be observed inviolably by all others.[5]

It was this concession made by Henry III to his magnates which marks the beginning of the process that was to lead some eighteen months later to the enactment of the Provisions of Westminster of 1259. A second set of letters patent issued on the same day appears to explain its context.[6] Henry had summoned his magnates to a parliament in London in early April and

[5] *DBM*, pp. 74–6 (I have modified their translation at various points). The Tewkesbury annalist suggests that the oath had been taken on 31 April: *Annales Monastici*, ed. H.R. Luard (5 vols., Rolls Series, London, 1864–9), I, 164. For a suggestion that this part of the Tewkesbury annals was written from a news-letter received from an eye-witness and as to the possible identity of this eye-witness see D.A. Carpenter, 'What Happened in 1258?' in *War and Government in the Middle Ages: Essays in Honour of J.O. Prestwich* (Woodbridge, 1984), pp. 106–19 at pp. 110–12. It is Matthew Paris' account of the parliament which provides the additional detail that the oath was sworn at the altar and on the bones of Henry III's favourite saint, St Edward: *Matthaei Parisiensis Chronica Majora*, ed. H.R. Luard (7 vols., Rolls Series, London, 1872–84), V, 689.

[6] *DBM*, pp. 72–5.

had asked them for their assistance in furthering the *negocium Sicilie*, the papally sponsored plan to displace the Hohenstaufen and place Henry's younger son, Edmund, on the throne of Sicily. For this Henry needed both money and soldiers.[7] The magnates had eventually promised that they would indeed support a royal request for financial aid to be submitted to the 'community of the realm' (*communitas regni*), an expression which apparently refers here to a body including representatives of the counties, but they had imposed two conditions which had to be met before they would do so. The pope would have to agree to some modification of the agreement he had made with Henry for the *negocium Sicilie*. The king would have to agree to the establishment of a Committee of Twenty-four to make necessary reforms in the 'state of the kingdom' (*status regni*) and would have to wait until this Committee had completed its work before making his request.[8] This second set of letters patent also makes it plain that it was envisaged that the work of the Committee would be completed no later than Christmas 1258.[9] Until recently, historians have generally accepted the picture presented by these letters patent at face value. They have explained the king's capitulation in terms of his desperate need for money to avoid the personal excommunication and the interdict of his kingdom threatened by Pope Alexander IV for failure to meet the financial terms agreed for the *negocium Sicilie* in 1254.[10] It has, however, recently been suggested that Henry may well have known that Alexander was likely in practice to be more flexible than he sounded. The papal threats were, it is argued, aimed not so much at the king as at his subjects and were intended primarily to loosen their purse-strings.[11] If this really was the case, then it is unlikely that it was the papal threats which forced the king's agreement to the Committee of Twenty-four and it is much more likely to have been something else. It was really force, or at least the threat of force, it is argued, that brought about the king's surrender.[12] This reading of the evidence relating to the three-cornered relationship between king, pope and barons is by no means implausible. It also seems quite possible that the threat of force did play some part in

[7] For the literature on the *negocium Sicilie* see Carpenter, 'What Happened in 1258?', p. 107. The Tewkesbury annalist mentions a royal request for a third of both movables and immovables and suggests that this demand was put to the magnates on around 28 April: *Annales Monastici*, I, 163.

[8] This latter condition is only spelled out in the first set of letters patent: *DBM*, pp. 76–7.

[9] They also make it clear that if a papal legate came to England during this period he was to play a part in the Committee's deliberations.

[10] Treharne, *Baronial Plan*, pp. 59–65; Powicke, *Henry III and the Lord Edward*, pp. 371–7.

[11] Carpenter, 'What Happened in 1258?', pp. 107–9. Carpenter also suggests that Henry must have known that the conditional nature of the magnates' agreement to support the king's request for a subsidy made it unlikely that any subsidy would in fact be granted, so that the king obtained little, if anything, in return for his concession: p. 109.

[12] Ibid., pp. 109–12.

securing the king's agreement to the Committee of Twenty-four. But it is also difficult, in view of the letters patent of 3 May, not to believe that the king's wish to place his second son on the throne of Sicily also played at least as important a part in that decision. Henry knew that he needed the financial and military support of his subjects if the kingdom of Sicily was to be conquered for Edmund. He may even have been willing to pay the high price of agreeing to the Committee of Twenty-four in the hope that, if he did so, that support would indeed be forthcoming.

There is also a puzzle about the magnate demand for the reforming Committee of Twenty-four. It has been suggested that it was intense magnate dislike of the king's Poitevin half-brothers that was the real motor driving the demand for a reforming Committee. During the years prior to 1258 they had monopolised royal patronage and had behaved in a manner both arrogant and violent and had relied on the king's tacit support in doing so.[13] There can be little doubt that dislike of the Lusignans was a major factor in creating a united magnate opposition that included many *curiales* in April and May 1258. Yet the demand for a reforming Committee and the supposed reason for it seem ill-matched. A general reform of the *status regni* was hardly required if all that was needed was the downfall, and perhaps the exile, of the Lusignans. It seems rather more likely that the demand is to be explained by something else. There was perhaps already some kind of commonly understood linkage between reform of the *status regni*, through the remedying of general grievances and abuses, and the granting of taxation by the *communitas regni*, of a kind that is certainly observable in later medieval parliamentary practice. The magnates may have warned the king that there was no chance of getting the *communitas regni* to agree to the subsidy he was seeking unless he agreed to some such arrangement. If that is so, then the magnates may well not themselves have had any particular grievances or abuses in mind when they made the demand but may simply have been pointing out to the king that the remedying of grievances was a *sine qua non* for getting the county representatives to agree to taxation.

THE WORK OF THE COMMITTEE OF TWENTY-FOUR

The Committee of Twenty-four did not set to work immediately. The first set of royal letters patent issued on 2 May make it clear that their first meeting had by then already been arranged. It was not, however, to take place until the second week of June and in Oxford.[14] It was also arranged

[13] Ibid., pp. 112–17.

[14] The date fixed for the meeting was one month after Whitsunday (9 June) but this should not perhaps be taken too literally.

either then or soon afterwards that the session of parliament meeting in London should also be adjourned to Oxford to resume at about the same date.[15] Once it had met, the Committee of Twenty-four quickly agreed to a number of significant changes in the machinery of central royal administration.[16] First in time (by the third week of June) came the revival of the office of justiciar, albeit in a significantly altered form and with rather different responsibilities from those which the holder of the post had previously possessed. Hugh Bigod was appointed the first holder of the newly revived post and was probably appointed by the Committee of Twenty-four itself. Then came the replacement (by the end of the first week of July) of the existing members of the king's council who had been chosen by the king himself with a fifteen-man royal council whose members were chosen by four electors nominated by the Committee of Twenty-four,[17] and the establishment of the responsibility not just of the justiciar but also of the chancellor and of the treasurer to this new council. There was also a new limitation on the period during which each of these major office-holders could hold their offices and the imposition of additional restrictions on the chancellor's power of independent initiative. The Committee of Twenty-four also provided for the holding of regular parliaments at three fixed times each year and for the attendance at those parliaments not just of the new royal councillors but also of a group of twelve men apparently chosen on the spot by those attending the Oxford parliament and who were henceforth to represent the wider *communitas regni* at these regular meetings of parliament.

The Committee of Twenty-four also began the process of reform of local government and administration and the creation of a machinery to remedy grievances against local officials. The sheriffs of individual counties were in future, they decided, to be drawn solely from the 'vavassours' of those counties; they were to hold office for no longer than a year; and they were to be paid expenses by the king. The existing castellans of royal castles were replaced by new men chosen by the Twenty-four. To ensure continuing conciliar control of castles for the next twelve years, these

[15] *Matthaei Parisiensis Chronica Majora*, v, 688–9, 695–6. The adjournment was from 5 May to the feast of St Barnabas (11 June).

[16] The most detailed account of these decisions is still that given by Treharne in *Baronial Plan* at pp. 72–6. For the text of these decisions (with cross-references to some of the other relevant documents) see *DBM*, pp. 97–113.

[17] Two of these electors were chosen from among the twelve members of the Committee of Twenty-four who had been nominated by the magnates but they were to be chosen by the twelve members of the Committee of Twenty-four who had been chosen from the existing king's council. The other two electors were similarly chosen from the twelve nominated by the king's council but by the twelve chosen by the magnates. Their choices had to be approved by a majority of the Twenty-four.

men were only to surrender their castles to men whose appointment had been approved by a majority of the new council. The Twenty-four also decided to appoint four knights in each county to receive and enrol complaints against sheriffs, bailiffs and others and to make all the necessary preparations for these to be heard and determined by the justiciar when he visited their county.

The Committee of Twenty-four seems also to have noted down a number of areas where reform was clearly needed but which required further investigation and thought before specific measures could be put in place. These were the affairs of the Church, the running of the Exchequer (and the management of royal finances more generally), the affairs of the Jewish community and the Exchequer of the Jews, the running of the London mint, the city of London and other towns and cities, the household of the king and of the queen. In almost all these areas what was required was administrative reform, not a change in legal rules, and none of the accounts of decisions made at Oxford mentions even a general decision in favour of making necessary or desirable reforms in the common law.[18]

THE 'PETITION OF THE BARONS'

There is, however, other evidence to suggest that reform of the law was among the matters considered, or at least among the matters on the agenda for consideration, by the Committee of Twenty-four under the general rubric of reform of the *status regni* at the parliament of Oxford and that the absence of any mention of law reform in accounts of the decisions reached at Oxford may merely indicate that the Committee knew that such matters needed detailed and careful consideration before any specific reforms could be introduced. This is the so-called 'Petition of the Barons' of which three independent, but related, texts survive.[19] It

[18] The so-called 'Coke' roll mentions a 'remembrance that Relligious persons purchase not so much': H.G. Richardson and G.O. Sayles, 'The Provisions of Oxford: a Forgotten Document and Some Comments', *Bulletin of the John Rylands Library* 17 (1933), 291–321 at 317. This decision can be seen as a foreshadowing of what eventually became clause 14 of the Provisions of Westminster which required the religious to obtain the assent of lords before acquiring property from their tenants. It is, however, reasonably clear from the note that no specific decision was taken to enact legislation along the lines eventually adopted and not even clear that the Twenty-four were even agreed that it was legislation that was needed to cope with the perceived problem. See further below, pp. 58–62.

[19] Brand, *MCL*, pp. 327–9, 354–5. Each version has a different number of clauses. The 'standard' text taken from a version of the Burton Annals has the largest number and in citing invididual clauses in the following discussion I will refer to them by the numbers assigned to individual clauses by Stubbs (in *SSC* at pp. 373–8) which were also followed by Treharne and Sanders in their edition and translation of the Petition (*DBM*, pp. 76–91).

was apparently drawn up for the meeting of the Committee of Twenty-four at Oxford in June and in some sense 'published' at their meeting. What exactly 'publication' means here and elsewhere is not entirely clear. It almost certainly means, as a minimum, read out publicly; it may also imply making available for copying.[20]

By no means all of the clauses of the Petition seem to be asking, whether explicitly or implicitly, for changes in the law. Some seem only to be looking for a change in government policy, either changes in the way in which the king exercised his rights,[21] or acceptance by him of restraints on the kinds of claim he made,[22] or in the way he granted rights to others.[23] Others seek only the proper enforcement of what are claimed to be the existing law or pre-existing rules.[24] A number of clauses describe grievances but do not suggest any specific remedy for them. It is reasonable, for example, to suppose that the framers of clauses 10, 17 and 18 had some kind of legislative remedy in mind when they complained of the religious acquiring lands without the consent of the lords of whom those lands were held (clause 10) and of sheriffs demanding the personal attendance of earls and barons and of the tenants of small parcels of land at the sheriff's tourn (clauses 17 and 18), even though they do not specifically ask for legislation. It is less clear, but still quite possible, that this was the case with several other clauses of the Petition. Clause 13, for example, complained of the amercement of earls and barons for default of the common summons (failing to appear when a general summons was issued) at sessions of the general and forest eyres when several such eyres were taking place simultaneously in different parts of the country. The complaint might have been answered either by a standing royal instruction to the justices concerned to excuse the absence of those attending eyres elsewhere or by more formal legislation to the same effect.[25] Other clauses, however, leave no room for doubt that they are calling for changes in the law which could be achieved only through legislation. This is clearly the case with clause 1 which asked that the law be amended to prevent lords from taking seisin of their tenants' holdings after their deaths unless they were entitled to wardship and to punish any waste they committed if they did so. Clause 3 was likewise clearly asking for a change in the law to reduce the king's right of prerogative wardship to a right to wardship over the person of the heir and the lands held by him in chief but not over his other lands. A change in the law

[20] Brand, *MCL*, p. 326.
[21] E.g. clauses 4 and 5, clause 6, clause 16 (part) and clause 23.
[22] E.g. clauses 2 and 11.
[23] E.g. clauses 9 and 15.
[24] E.g. that part of clause 1 relating to the exaction of queen's gold on the reliefs paid by tenants-in-chief, and clauses 7, 12, 16 (part), 20, 24, 25 and 29.
[25] Other similar clauses are clauses 14, 19, 21, 22 and 28.

was also what was requested by clause 27. Here the grievance was that when land had been granted in *maritagium* to a husband and wife and the heirs of their bodies the wife was able after the death of her husband to validly grant away the land even when no such issue had been born. The suggestion was to provide the grantor or his heir with a suitable remedy through either a new form of writ of entry or some other kind of writ to secure the reversion after her death. For these reasons it is difficult to estimate with absolute certainty the number of clauses of the Petition of the Barons which either directly or indirectly sought legislation. There were at least six and perhaps as many as twelve. Even if these are less than half the total number of clauses contained in the Petition they do clearly indicate that legal reform was on the agenda almost from the beginning of the reform process in 1258.

Who placed it there? Treharne thought that the Petition as a whole was the work of the twelve baronial members of the Committee of Twenty-four or at least of those members of the twelve who had been in England during the interval between the king's agreement to the Committee of Twenty-four and the beginning of the Committee's work at Oxford in June, and that it was intended as a 'memorandum of definite grievances in administrative and legal matters and in judicial procedure, noted for correction when the barons should have set up the necessary machinery of governmental control'.[26] There is, however, no evidence to support this suggestion and it seems inherently improbable. The baronial twelve had not yet been chosen when the king issued his letters patent agreeing to abide by the decisions of the Committee of Twenty-four on 2 May and it seems quite likely that they were only chosen after parliament met in Oxford in the second week of June. They can hardly have drawn up the Petition in advance of being chosen. Even if the twelve were chosen before the Oxford parliament there is still no evidence to suggest that they were holding meetings in advance of the session at Oxford. There is also the negative evidence of what the otherwise well-informed Burton annalist says, and does not say, about the Petition. If it had been the work of the baronial twelve he might have been expected to mention this. He does not do so. Stubbs believed that the Petition was compiled by an undefined group of 'barons' as a 'list of grievances' for redress by the Committee of Twenty-four.[27] There is rather more support for this hypothesis. Several clauses of the Petition do indeed state that they are the complaints or suggestions of the 'earls and barons'[28] or just of the 'barons'.[29] With the

[26] Treharne, *Baronial Plan*, pp. 69–70. By 1973 he sounded less confident about this ascription: *DBM*, pp. 4–5.

[27] Stubbs, *Constitutional History*, II, 74–5.

[28] See clauses 1, 10, 11, 13, 17 and 20.

[29] See clause 3.

exception of clause 1, these clauses do indeed seem to represent specifically magnate grievances and might suggest that the Petition was indeed the work of the magnates present at the Oxford parliament, perhaps much the same group as those who chose the twelve 'baronial' members of the Committee of Twenty-four.[30] However, most of the clauses are not put forward specifically in the name of the 'earls and barons' and a number of them seem most unlikely to have been the work of members of this group. Clause 19, for example, is clearly stating a grievance of the 'knights and free tenants', not of the barons or earls, about amercements for non-attendance at sessions of assize justices. Clause 25 is a complaint about the misconduct of certain magnates and potentates (*magnates et potentiores regni*) in acquiring Jewish debts and then refusing to accept payment from creditors who are described as 'lesser men' (*minores*) and is clearly voicing a grievance of the latter group against some of the earls and barons. It was evidently also such lesser men who were behind clause 18 relating to demands for attendance at the sheriff's tourn from those who held small parcels of land without houses on them, for the earls and barons had their own more general grievance about demands for their attendance at the tourn which was voiced in clause 17. Nor were lesser rural landowners the only non-magnate group to find a voice in the Petition. Clause 26 reads like a complaint of the native merchants of the city of London against the Cahorsins. The co-existence within the Petition of these several different voices, especially when taken in conjunction with the heterogeneity in form of the individual clauses,[31] suggests that the Petition is probably a general collection of complaints assembled from a variety of sources, which expresses the interests and grievances of a number of different groups. It looks, however, as though the 'earls and barons', perhaps at their meeting in the parliament at Oxford, may have added some kind of collective *imprimatur* to this collection of petitions. This might explain why the demand for legislation to punish the commission of waste during primer seisin, the main demand of clause 1, is presented as having been made in the name of the 'earls and barons', despite the fact that (as drafted) it was of no significance to them other than as a threat to their existing rights.[32] The scribe charged with bringing the various complaints together may have begun by making this

[30] The Burton Annals text of the Provisions of Oxford records the names of eleven of the twelve men so chosen under the heading 'Chosen on behalf of the earls and barons' (*Electi ex parte comitum et baronum*): *DBM*, p. 100.

[31] Brand, *MCL*, pp. 328–9.

[32] The suggested punishment of such waste by amercement and the awarding of damages was clearly irrelevant to the commission of such waste by the king (the 'chief lord' of all 'earls and barons') and his officials, for neither would be a deterrent in their case.

demand conform to the overall format of a demand by the 'earls and barons', the group formally submitting the Petition. But he clearly tired of his work and thus failed to disguise the heterogeneous origins of the constituent elements of the final document. The general point, however, is a significant one. The Petition of the Barons is not the work of the small, politically involved group who comprised the baronial members of the Committee of Twenty-four. It expresses the grievances of a number of different, and in some cases much less powerful, groups and their desire for legislative and other changes.

THE CONTINUATION OF THE REFORM PROCESS AFTER THE PARLIAMENT OF OXFORD

The first stage: up to the Michaelmas parliament of 1258

The session at Oxford was the last, as well as the first, meeting of the Committee of Twenty-four.[33] This did not, however, mean a premature end to the process of central and local administrative reform, legal reform and the remedying of grievances, merely that they were to be continued after early July 1258 by other means and by other agencies.

From the first it had been envisaged that it would be part of the role of the new justiciar to go round the country, county by county, hearing individual complaints against sheriffs and other local officials.[34] The four knights who were to be appointed in each county to receive such complaints do not, however, seem to have been appointed until late July or early August and by then there had been a change of plan. They were now required actively to conduct enquiries in their counties rather than just passively to receive complaints. They were also now to bring a record of what they had discovered to Westminster for delivery to the council at the octaves of Michaelmas (early October) 1258, in time for the first session of parliament to be held under the new arrangements made at Oxford.[35] Even before their work had been completed, Bigod had begun hearing some individual local complaints, though not in any kind of systematic fashion.[36]

33 Treharne, *Baronial Plan*, pp. 75–6. 34 *DBM*, p. 98.

35 *DBM*, pp. 112–15. The articles of enquiry given to the four knights are to be found in *Matthaei Parisiensis Chronica Majora*, VI, 397–400. It is not, however, clear whether they were meant to be exhaustive or whether the four knights still had (as their commission suggests) a wider power to enquire into 'all excesses, trespasses and wrongs . . . done to whatever persons by anyone'.

36 Andrew N. Hershey, 'Success or Failure? Hugh Bigod and Judicial Reform during the Baronial Movement, June 1258–February 1259' in *Thirteenth Century England V*, ed. P.R. Coss and S.D. Lloyd (Woodbridge, 1995), pp. 65–87.

Administrative and legal reform became the responsibility of the new king's council.[37] Some preparatory work on legal reform may well have been done in advance of the Michaelmas parliament. The London chronicle of Arnulf fitzThedmar mentions the Earl Marshal, Simon de Montfort, John fitz Geoffrey (all members of the new council) and unspecified others who had been part of the baronial twelve on the Committee of Twenty-four visiting the Guildhall on 22 July to demand the adherence of the city to the Provisions. He then goes on to speak of the 'said barons' (*predicti barones*) – possibly, but not certainly, the same men as had visited the Guildhall earlier – subsequently conducting daily discussions, sometimes at the New Temple and sometimes elsewhere, 'on the reform of the usages and customs of the realm' (*super usibus et consuetudinibus regni in melius conformandis*).[38] Further work was probably also done in advance of the parliament on the reforms proposed at Oxford in the office of sheriff. A detailed code of conduct was drawn up to govern the behaviour of sheriffs while in office and the decision taken that all sheriffs should be required on appointment to promise on oath to observe it.[39] The council may also have done some work on the reform of the Jewry. A royal mandate of 8 July talks of their intention to make some such reform on the following 28 July, though no enactment of any kind now survives.[40]

Little is known to have been achieved at the Michaelmas parliament of 1258 itself. The baronial council meeting in parliament did take care to draw up for publication in each county in both French and English a document in the king's name dated 18 October confirming the transfer of responsibility for reform of the *status regni* from the Committee of Twenty-four to the new king's council. The same document also ordered all the king's subjects to take a promise on oath to observe and maintain all the provisions (*establissements*) already made and to be made by the council.[41] The document suggests that the council was already aware of

[37] The memoranda of the decisions made by the Committee of Twenty-four at Oxford (the so-called 'Provisions of Oxford') specifically note that the new council was to have the power not just to advise the king 'on the government of the realm and all things touching the king and kingdom' but also 'to amend and redress all matters that seem to them to need redress and amendment': *DBM*, pp. 110–11.

[38] *De Antiquis Legibus Liber*, pp. 38–9. It is worth noting that the chronicler uses similar terms when describing the Provisions of Westminster themselves: they were, he says, 'composicionem factam per barones . . . super usibus et legibus regni emendandis': p. 42. John Maddicott doubts whether the reference is to the same group and suggests that the reference is to the whole of the baronial twelve during an afterlife extending beyond the appointment of the council of fifteen: J.R. Maddicott, *Simon de Montfort* (Cambridge, 1994), p. 166, note 41.

[39] The wording of the oath is given in the so-called 'Ordinance of Sheriffs': *DBM*, pp. 120–3. The form of the oath is also given in PRO E 159/32, m. 2 and in BL MS. Additional 15668 at f. 32r.

[40] *CR 1256–1259*, p. 318.

[41] *DBM*, pp. 116–17. The document was issued in French and English and possibly also in Latin.

the need to manipulate public opinion in the counties in support of the baronial council. That this was indeed the case is suggested even more strongly by a second document also clearly a product of the same session and misleadingly known as the 'Ordinance of Sheriffs'. This was issued in the king's name to the men of each county on 20 October.[42] It apologised for the failure of the reformers to redress grievances as quickly as they would have liked and excused their not having done so. It also held out the promise that from the 'first amendments which will be made in the first counties to which we will send our justiciar and other wise men', the men of the county being addressed would be able to derive the 'certain hope that you will have the like done for you as soon as possible'. They were also told of the new form of oath that the sheriffs were being made to swear and the punishment which awaited those who broke their oath, that sheriffs were now being allowed their reasonable expenses by the king and that none was to remain in office for more than a year. The changes in local administration were thus not just being made but also being publicised, evidently in an attempt to gain favour with lesser men in the localities.

It may also have been at this parliament that a decision was reached which is recorded in the 'Coke' roll, that 'The Justices *et autres sages homes* (and other wise men) are summoned that between that and the next Parlement they should consider of what ill Lawes and need of reformation there were, and that they meet eight days before the Parlement beginne againe, at the place where it shall be appointed to treat etc.'[43] Unfortunately, this item comes from a portion of the roll which contains material of various dates between 10 July 1258 and February 1259. The material is in no particular order and the item is itself undated.[44] The parliament referred to could have been this parliament and the decision one taken at the parliament of Oxford or at its continuation at Winchester, as Treharne and Sanders suggest.[45] But Powicke is probably right in thinking that this was a decision reached at the October parliament.[46]

42 *DBM*, pp. 118–23. 43 Richardson and Sayles, 'The Provisions of Oxford', 321.

44 For the dating of items 23–33 on the roll see ibid., 6–12 (and note that item 24 belongs to 22 February 1259; item 25 to 28 July 1258 (and succeeding days); item 28 to 4 August 1258).

45 *DBM*, p. 12. They attempt to link this with the fact that the parliament actually opened (according to the Winchester annalist) only on the feast of the Translation of St Edward (13 October), suggesting that the opening of parliament was delayed so that the information on abuses brought by the knights to Westminster on 6 October could be 'analysed by "the judges and wise men" to prepare the way for reforms to be enacted in the coming parliament': *DBM*, p. 14. But the clause as reported by the Coke roll says nothing of the use of such information. Richardson and Sayles also seem to hint at a similar date for this clause: 'The Provisions of Oxford', 295–6 and note 1 on 296.

46 Powicke, *Henry III and the Lord Edward*, p. 397. It is, perhaps, relevant that the three justices of the Common Bench (Thirkleby, Preston and Hadlow) were only confirmed in office or appointed

This shows that from a fairly early stage not only were legal experts involved in the technical business of drafting the future legislation to be promulgated in the king's name by the baronial council but also that they were being given an input into the content of that legislation as well. Although the 'Coke' roll does not say this, it may also from the first have been intended that the justices and others should draw not just on their own experience but also on the written enrolments of complaints collected in the counties and brought to the Michaelmas parliament. It is difficult to see why arrangements should have been made to bring the complaints to the meeting of parliament unless it was envisaged that some such use would be made of them. In practice less than half the counties of England sent returns.[47] Even so these may have supplied useful material for the reforming legislators.[48]

The second stage: from the Michaelmas parliament of 1258 to the Candlemas parliament of 1259

During the period between the Michaelmas parliament of October 1258 and the Candlemas parliament of February 1259 (more specifically, during the period between the end of Michaelmas term 1258 and the beginning of Hilary term 1259),[49] Hugh Bigod dealt with presentments from Surrey and Kent and also held sessions in London to deal with individual complaints.[50] It was also probably during this period that the main work was done on the drafting of the initial, French-language, version of the '*Providencia Baronum*'. This survives only in a single MS. now in Philadelphia.[51] It consists of some eleven clauses. Nine represent initial

just prior to the October parliament: *CPR 1247–58*, p. 652. The council is more likely to have trusted the advice of the men whom it had itself just appointed or confirmed than the men appointed by the previous regime.

[47] Hershey, 'Success or Failure?', p. 79 and note 90.

[48] It is unfortunate that only a fragment of one return survives, that published by Jacob in *Studies* at pp. 337–44, but we also know of some of the material contained in the returns for Kent and Surrey from the records of the justiciar's visitations of those counties. There are also some individual entries on Bigod's rolls which deal with presentments made in other counties: Hershey, 'Success or Failure?', pp. 79–81 and note 91 on p. 79.

[49] Bigod seems to have presided in the court *coram rege* during term time as the court dealt with its normal term-time business.

[50] Hershey, 'Success or Failure?', pp. 66, 69–70, 83–4.

[51] Philadelphia Free Library, Hampton L. Carson Collection, MS. LC 14.3, fols. 202r–v. For descriptions of this MS. see J.H. Baker, *English Legal Manuscripts in the United States of America, part 1: Medieval and Renaissance* (Selden Society, 1985), no. 162, pp. 57–8 and Brand, *MCL*, p. 337. The text itself is undated, but for the arguments for supposing that it is a preliminary draft of the Latin version of the *Providencia Baronum* published in March 1259 and therefore most probably produced for discussion at the February 1259 session of parliament see Brand, *MCL*, pp. 337–44. The text is printed in Brand, *MCL*, pp. 359–61.

drafts of nine of the twenty-four clauses which were to constitute the Provisions of Westminster as eventually enacted in October 1259. There is also a draft of a clause on the extension of writs of entry omitted from that enactment but included in the Provisions as reissued in 1263 and 1264 and of a clause on the extension of the availability of the assize of mort d'ancestor which was likewise omitted from the Provisions as eventually enacted but not subsequently revived.[52]

The Petition of the Barons was plainly the most important single source of inspiration for this draft legislation. It is, however, clear that the drafters saw their task as being much more than simply turning the grievances and demands for remedies contained in the various clauses of the Petition of the Barons into legislation. In most cases they took them as no more than a starting-point for the legislation they drafted. Clause 5 of the draft legislation, for example, on exemptions from attendance at the sheriff's tourn, while clearly related to clauses 17 and 18 of the Petition of the Barons, is much more than simply a translation of those complaints into draft legislation. Clause 17 had complained only about demands for attendance at the tourn by earls and barons. Clause 5 proposed the exemption from attendance not just of members of these two groups but also of abbots and priors and more generally of the tenants of all other sizeable holdings. Where clause 18 of the Petition had complained only of demands for attendance at the tourn by those who possessed small holdings without any residence attached, clause 5 of the draft proposed a much wider exemption. The proposed clause covered not just all of those not resident in the hundred when the sheriff's tourn was held but also those who were resident but who were prevented by sickness or other good cause from attending it. A different kind of change is observable between clause 14 of the Petition and clause 6 of the draft legislation. Clause 14 had complained only about the exaction of beaupleder fines by the justices in eyre. Clause 6 of the draft legislation transformed this into a proposal to prohibit the exaction of beaupleder fines by 'any bailiff', an expression which seems not to cover the fines against which the original complaint had been directed but vastly extends it in other directions. The closest correspondence is between clause 28 of the Petition and clause 8

[52] Clauses 1 and 2 are preliminary drafts of clauses 1 and 2 of the Provisions; clauses 3 and 4 of clause 3; clauses 5 and 6 of clauses 4 and 5; clause 7 of clauses 6 and 7; clause 8 of clause 8; clause 9 of the clause on writs of entry in the *post* only included in the reissued Provisions; clause 10 of clause 15; clause 11 of a proposal to allow the use of the assize of mort d'ancestor against the alienees of guardians which was not in the end carried out. Thus the draft text has clauses corresponding to each of the first eight clauses of the Provisions as eventually enacted plus clause 15, the additional clause on writs of entry in the *post* and the clause on the extension of mort d'ancestor eventually abandoned.

of the draft legislation. Clause 28 had asked for a remedy for the difficulties posed for the choice of knights for the grand assize by the king's granting of charters of exemption from jury service. Clause 8 proposed the overriding of such charters and again specifically only in the case of grand assizes. It is also just possible that there is also some connexion between clauses 1–4 of the draft legislation and clause 24 of the Petition. Clause 24 had asked for some remedy against suits newly demanded to county, hundred and liberty courts (*tam ad comitatus et hundreda quam ad curias libertatis*). Clauses 1–4 of the draft legislation were likewise concerned with demands for suit of court. However, they said nothing about suit to county or hundred courts and their concern was with non-franchisal seignorial courts rather than franchisal ones, the type of court apparently singled out in the Petition.[53] There is also another and much more plausible source of inspiration for these same clauses. One of the complaints made by the clergy at their council held in the summer of 1258 just prior to the parliament of Oxford had been that ecclesiastics who had been granted land to hold in free alms were being forced to perform suit of court to the courts of the king, of magnates and other lords for the lands they had been given, contrary to the terms of such gifts, unless they could produce evidence of the original gifts and the charters concerned. The council established that if distraints were made in future by the donors or founders concerned or by their heirs or successors they were to face ecclesiastical censures. Similar measures were also to be taken if such suits were demanded by superior lords which had not customarily been performed.[54] Here we find the same concern with the exaction of suit of court to ordinary seignorial courts and also specifically with the use of distraint to secure its performance. We also find a concern with the rules governing the obligation, and the relationship between the obligation and the terms of the tenant's charter of feoffment. The draft legislation is certainly not a direct borrowing from the ecclesiastical legislation, but the latter makes a more intelligible starting-point for the development of these clauses than does the Petition of the Barons. They were probably intended to provide a secular counterpart to the spiritual remedies that had been proposed by the church council and one that was available to laymen as well as clerics.

[53] The term *curias libertatis* is a curious one (one might have expected *curias libertatum*) but the reading is supported by all three texts of the Petition. Were it not for the unanimity it would have been tempting to amend the text to *curias liberas*, which might indeed refer to seignorial courts. Dr Carpenter (personal communication) suggests that the clause may just have been badly drafted and have been intended to refer to seignorial courts.

[54] *Councils and Synods with Other Documents Relating to the English Church*, vol. II (in two parts) (1205–1313), ed. F.M. Powicke and C.R. Cheney (Oxford, 1964), I, p. 584. A similar complaint had been made in the previous year: ibid., p. 546.

Of the remaining four clauses, two (clauses 7 and 9) relate to technical legal improvements of precisely the kind we might expect to have been suggested by the judges and other legal experts consulted on matters in need of reform.[55] Legal experts may also have suggested clause 11 on the extension of the availability of the assize of mort d'ancestor. Clause 10 about the warranting of essoins was, however, concerned with a problem which only arose in local courts and seems unlikely to have been suggested by the legal experts. It looks like a response to a grievance similar to some of the grievances expressed in the Petition of the Barons. Perhaps it was one of the matters brought to the attention of the drafters by the presentments brought to parliament in October 1258.

The third stage: the Candlemas parliament of 1259 and its aftermath

It seems likely that there was a detailed discussion of this draft legislation at the Candlemas parliament of February 1259 and probable that we can ascribe to this parliament a number of the detailed substantive changes which are observable in the revised draft text of the same eleven clauses published in Latin as the *Providencia Baronum* in March 1259.[56] The most radical amendment and reshaping went into clause 5. As redrafted, it included two additional provisions at the end. One emphasized that even at the tourn amercements were only to be imposed in accordance with Magna Carta. The other stipulated that no more men were to be required to attend the tourn from among the unfree of each village than was necessary for the holding of inquisitions into the articles of the tourn. There were also significant changes in the portion of clause 5 inherited from the earlier draft. There had clearly been an inconclusive discussion about the position of those who possessed large holdings but did not belong to one of the status categories exempted from attendance at the tourn. Some thought, with the framers of the earlier draft, that they should also gain automatic exemption from attendance unless specially needed. Others thought they should only be exempt if absent from the area where the tourn was being held or prevented by illness or other good cause from attendance. The more general exemption for those with these excuses for non-attendance was also omitted from this revised draft. Two

[55] These are clause 7 on the shortening of the length of adjournments in cases of dower *unde nichil habet*, darrein presentment and *quare impedit*, and clause 9 on the extension of the writ of entry outside the degrees.

[56] For the two related MSS. which contain a text of the *Providencia Baronum* and the two other MSS. which contain incomplete copies of the same document see Brand, *MCL*, pp. 335–7, 355–9. Other changes were, however, probably only made in connexion with that process of publication itself: see below, p. 33.

other significant changes made were those to clause 6, turning it into a general prohibition of beaupleder fines (where the earlier draft apparently only applied to beaupleder fines in local courts), and to clause 8, to allow the overriding of royal charters of exemption from jury service more widely than for grand assizes alone. Most other clauses remained much the same in substance in the revised draft even where the wording had been radically revised.[57]

It is only from an unrelated document coming from the same parliamentary session that we learn that other matters were also already under consideration for legislation as well. Letters patent sealed by the members of the king's council and the twelve representatives of the community at parliament dated 22 February 1259 mention legislation already contemplated not just on suit of court (clearly corresponding to clauses 1–4 of the *Providencia Baronum*) but also on amercements (too imprecise to identify), socage wardship (*gardes socages*) (probably a reference to what was to become clause 12 of the Provisions of Westminster) and '*ses fermes et autre manere de franchises*' (also too imprecise to identify).[58] Evidently there was as yet no draft of all of the relevant clauses to place before parliament but the letters patent also indicate that there was some kind of commitment to finalise the process of drafting and enact the legislation by All Saints' Day following (1 November 1259).

The context of these letters patent seems to have been the first real attempt by the king, or by others acting on his behalf, to put the council, which he had been forced to accept, on the defensive, to appeal over their heads to the wider world of the *communitas regni* for support against the magnates. The document clearly sets out each of the reforming commitments which the king had himself already made: that any wrongs committed by his bailiffs should be redressed; that he and his bailiffs would observe Magna Carta; that he would accept the legislation already enacted and the other legislation yet to be promulgated on the subjects already mentioned; that his sheriffs and other bailiffs would take an oath promising to observe the new standards of conduct promulgated at the Michaelmas parliament of 1258. Side by side with these it places parallel commitments which the king's council and the representatives of the community were only now themselves making, and implicitly only

[57] Clause 1 was revised to make it clear that tenants without charters of feoffment because they had been enfeoffed at or soon after the Conquest could benefit from subsequent quitclaims of any suit they or their ancestors had once performed. In clause 9 the specimen writ of entry in the *post* was revised to make use of three actual names in place of the *cely*, B. and *celuy* of the earlier draft. These were Roger de Mortimer, Peter de Montfort and Roger de St John. It is probably not a coincidence that the first two were themselves members of the king's council.

[58] *DBM*, pp. 132–3.

at the king's prompting: that wrongs done by them and their bailiffs both to their own tenants and to their neighbours should similarly be redressed by the justiciar or others and by plaints unless they involved title to free tenement and they would not attempt to obstruct the process in any way or take any revenge for it subsequently; that they would accept the limitations imposed by Magna Carta both in their relationships with their tenants and with their neighbours and in their franchises as well as in their own demesnes; that they too would accept both the legislation already enacted and that yet to come into force; that they would make their bailiffs take a similar oath to that sworn by sheriffs and other royal bailiffs setting out the rules of their conduct while in office and agree that those bailiffs should be liable to similar punishment if they broke the rules.[59] The reformers were being made to live up to the standards they had imposed on the king. They were also (and perhaps at least as significantly) being cast in an unfavourable light for not having done so already.

Although these letters patent had been sealed on 22 February, it was not until 28 March that they were issued with a covering letter from the king ordering that they were to be read out in every county and hundred court.[60] It is just possible that the Candlemas parliament of 1259 continued until late March and that a decision to circulate and publicise the letters patent of the council and the twelve was made at the very end of the parliament. The evidence of the king's movements during February and March 1259, however, suggests that the meeting of parliament was probably over by 26 February, for it was then that the king left Westminster for Windsor, travelling on to Wallingford and Reading and only returning to Westminster by way of Windsor, Chertsey and Merton on 20 March.[61] The Latin text of the *Providencia Baronum*, in the form we now have, probably also belongs to the end of March. There is also the contemporary testimony of Matthew Paris in the heading to his incomplete copy of the *Providencia Baronum* in his *Liber Additamentorum* to indicate that the text was 'published' with the king's consent at the New Temple in London in March 1259 and late March (when the king returned to Westminster and when other business done in the Candlemas parliament was also deliberately publicised) seems the most likely time for this to have occurred.[62] The text had probably been translated during

[59] They were even made to agree on oath not to promise to support any man who was not their tenant against their lord or their neighbours or others.

[60] *DBM*, pp. 130–7.

[61] The information about Henry's movements is derived from the published calendars of Chancery enrolments.

[62] On the dating of the Latin text of the *Providencia Baronum* see Brand, *MCL*, pp. 340–1.

the interval between the ending of the Candlemas parliament and publication. It was also probably during this period that care was taken to insert into the text a number of separate phrases making it clear that this was only draft legislation, not legislation that was intended to come into immediate effect, and removing other phrases in the French draft which might have appeared to imply the opposite.[63] What does 'publication' mean here?[64] Treharne thought it meant no more than 'read out for discussion'.[65] This seems unlikely for, as we have seen, the text had probably been discussed a month earlier and translation from French into Latin was a positive impediment to easy discussion of the text. There was probably some formal reading of the Latin text at the New Temple and perhaps a formal announcement that the text was available for copying to anyone who wished to have copies of it or informal arrangements made to allow access to it. It is just possible that there was some formal circulation of the text to the counties. The wording of Matthew Paris' heading to his copy of the text certainly sounds as if it could be repeating in part the wording of a writ sent out with such a text, though there is no other evidence for this.[66] The purpose of publication was presumably to show that real progress had been made with the drafting of legislation, even if the legislation was not yet quite ready for promulgation. If we can trust Matthew Paris' heading, it may also have been intended to associate the king, and not just his council, with the drafting of the reforming legislation. Thus publication of the *Providencia Baronum* in March 1259 may also fit the context of a king determined to reassert himself against his baronial council: the same context which also explains his publication in late March of the letters patent committing the council and the twelve representatives of the community to abiding by similar standards to those they had already imposed on the king.

The fourth stage: from March to October 1259

As has been seen, the French draft text prepared for the Candlemas parliament of 1259 contained draft versions of only nine of the twenty-four clauses which were to constitute the Provisions of Westminster as eventually enacted in October 1259. It seems probable that a similar draft was also prepared of the remaining clauses and of the two other clauses which appear in the penultimate French draft of the Provisions but were dropped from the final Latin text. This was probably prepared for, and discussed

63 Ibid., pp. 337–8, 342.

64 For previous discussions of this point see Jacob, *Studies*, p. 80; Treharne, *Baronial Plan*, pp. 133, 135; *DBM*, p. 17.

65 Treharne, *Baronial Plan*, p. 135.

66 Brand, *MCL*, p. 357.

at, the June parliament of 1259.[67] However, no text of this draft is known to survive and there is no evidence this time of any second attempt to translate and publish the amended draft. Nor is there any other surviving evidence to suggest significant reform activity at this parliament.[68]

The next stage in the process of legislative drafting that is represented by surviving evidence is the production of a penultimate French draft of the whole of the Provisions. This seems to have been produced for discussion, amendment and approval at the Michaelmas parliament of 1259 and thus in time for a production of a final text of the legislation in time to meet the promised deadline of All Saints' Day, 1259.[69] Four independent copies of this penultimate French draft survive plus one crude related translation of the French text into Latin.[70] Of the sixteen 'new' clauses of which no prior draft survives,[71] six are clearly related to grievances or demands voiced in the Petition of the Barons. Only one (clause 13 requiring seignorial assent for mortmain acquisitions by the religious) is a direct response to a clause in the Petition (clause 10), simply translating the request for legislation into actual legislation. The other five clauses all go some way beyond the suggestions or requests made in the Petition, in a way already familiar from the *Providencia Baronum*.[72] Clause 10, for example, was clearly in some sense a response to the main part of clause 1 of the Petition. However, the legislation proposed allowed a general remedy (through the awarding of damages in the assize of mort d'ancestor) against any lord who ejected or refused to admit an heir of full age as to whose identity there was no question, not just if that lord committed waste. It also extended the same remedy to the case of the underage heir who had been in wardship to a lord if that heir was then refused entry into his lands by his former guardian, a situation that goes unmentioned in the Petition.[73] Two other clauses (clauses 23 and 25) may also be linked to the general complaint in clause 14 of the Petition about the 'many

[67] This seems more plausible than my earlier suggestion that it was prepared for a 'parliament' said by two chroniclers to have been held in April 1259: Brand, *MCL*, p. 353.

[68] The only business known to have been discussed at this parliament was the arrangements for peace with France: Treharne, *Baronial Plan*, p. 141. However, for the possible survival of part of the draft prepared for this parliament see below, chapter 5, p. 159.

[69] The draft probably took the form of a roll: see the reference forward in clause 1 to a later clause 'sicum il est purveu en est roule' in one MS. of this draft: Brand, *MCL*, p. 361.

[70] Brand, *MCL*, pp. 349–51, 361–7.

[71] Clauses 9–13, 15–25 in the composite text printed in *MCL* at pp. 361–7.

[72] This was also the case, as has been seen, with most other clauses related to the Petition of which we do have earlier draft versions: above, pp. 28–9.

[73] Brand, *MCL*, p. 364; *SSC*, p. 373. Other examples are clause 12 of the draft text which is clearly a response to clause 19 of the Petition (protesting at the summoning and amercing for non-attendance of all the free men of a locality for sessions before justices of assize) but also covered the summoning of jurors for sessions held by escheators, holders of enquiries, justices of oyer and terminer and all others other than the justiciar and the justices of the general eyre; clauses

other grievances of the pleas of the crown' for they prohibit amercement for particular specified causes arising out of the hearing of crown pleas.[74] Clause 24 shared with them the characteristic of prohibiting a type of amercement which was probably considered unduly harsh and unfair. It was, however, a form of amercement that was associated with civil pleas, rather than crown pleas, and again had not been mentioned in the Petition.[75] Clause 11, which provided for an action of account against guardians in socage, probably made good on the promise made in February 1259 of legislation on socage wardship. The need for this legislation may have been suggested by the consideration of complaints from the county of Kent, the county which contained the largest concentration of socage tenants, although the record of Bigod's visitation of the county in January 1259, during which he dealt with presentments and complaints, suggests that the usurpation of socage wardships by lords (of which the legislation has nothing to say) was much more of a problem than abuses committed by next-of-kin acting as socage guardians which is the subject of the legislation.[76] It is also conceivable, though by no means certain, that clause 19 of this draft (making lessees liable for waste unless they had written permission from the lessor) made good on another of the pieces of legislation promised in February 1259.[77] Another of the new clauses (clause 17), allowing the use of attachment by the body against landless bailiffs in the action of account, was even more clearly a measure favouring the interests of magnates and the greater men, just the kind of measure one might expect a magnate-dominated council to suggest. The remaining four new clauses (clauses 9, 15, 16 and 18) are perhaps the most surprising. All are concerned with asserting the rights of the king and of royal justice against seignorial usurpation and directed specifically against seignorial wrongdoing.[78] They suggest that the king and others acting with his interests in mind did indeed have a significant input into

20 and 21 which are clearly a response to that part of clause 14 of the Petition (which protested at the practice of heavily amercing vills summoned for coroners' inquests into homicides if all those aged twelve or more did not attend the inquest) but make it clear that only the justices in eyre can impose such amercements, extend the rule to cover other types of coroners' inquest and make it clear that there was still a requirement that enough men of the four nearest villages appear to allow the inquest to proceed; and clause 22 which is clearly a response to clause 21 of the Petition (which had protested at the practice of imposing *murdrum* fines for the death of unknown strangers dying from hunger) but which established the more general principle that the *murdrum* fine was not to be payable in the case of any accidental death: Brand, *MCL*, pp. 365–6; *SSC*, pp. 375–7.

[74] Brand, *MCL*, pp. 366–7; *SSC*, p. 375. [75] Brand, *MCL*, p. 366.

[76] For examples see JUST 1/873, mm. 16, 16d, 22d, 23.

[77] The legislation promised was on 'ses fermes' which should refer to royal leases but might perhaps be a garbled reference to leases in general: above, p. 31.

[78] Clause 11 reasserted the traditional prohibition against distraints made outside the fee or in the highway other than by the king; clause 16 asserted the king's traditional monopoly over pleas of

the drafting of the legislation. They also help to confirm the picture of a king taking a much more active role in the business of government that can already be seen in the events of February and March 1259.[79]

The penultimate draft omits two of the clauses which had been included in both the French draft of February 1259 and the published Latin draft of March 1259: the proposal to extend writs of entry outside the degrees (clause 9) and the proposal to allow the use of the assize of mort d'ancestor against the alienees of guardians (clause 11). The former was to be revived and incorporated in the 1263 reissue of the Provisions;[80] the latter disappeared entirely. There had also been a radical revision of some of the other clauses to be found in those earlier drafts. Clause 1 (on the basis of the obligation to perform suit of court) was among these. It had been significantly watered down in a direction that made it more favourable to lords and much less favourable to their tenants.[81] The only balancing change (and that one of much less significance) was the amendment to clause 4 about the lord's action for recovery of suit of court which removed the possibility of lords recovering suit by default in this new action. Clause 5 had also been watered down, but mainly in a way that favoured the interests of the king and the royal revenue. The exemption from attendance at the tourn of those with extensive lands who did not belong to one of the exempt groups was now to apply only in the case where attendance at the tourn was demanded from them on the basis of a holding that had no house on it. This is significantly less generous than either of the proposals made in March 1259.[82] The sub-clauses specifically referring to amercements being made in accordance with Magna Carta and exempting from attendance at the tourn those of the unfree who were not required for the making of presentments are represented in this draft by a much less specific (and therefore much weaker) sub-clause referring in general terms to the tourn being held in

false judgment; clause 17 confirmed the sheriff's right to release animals taken in distraint even if taken within franchises; clause 18 confirmed the traditional rules that a royal writ was required to make a tenant answer for his free tenement and to force free tenants to serve as jurors.

[79] Above, pp. 31–3. [80] Below, pp. 151–60.

[81] Lords now only had to be able to prove either that suit was specifically stipulated in the tenant's charter of feoffment or that it had been done before 1230. Tenants who possessed 'service certain' charters stipulating performance of a certain service 'for all service' were no longer automatically exempt from performing suit; and lords no longer had to prove in the case of all tenants other than those whose obligation to perform suit was included in the charter of feoffment that they had performed the suit continuously since time out of mind (much more difficult to prove than that the suit had been done prior to 1230). The 'service certain' provision was revived and extended in the Statute of Marlborough of 1267: below, pp. 189–90. There was also a minor change in clause 3 (about the tenant's action for the recovery of suit), inserting an additional stage of process before the tenant could recover against the lord by default which favoured lords, but this was much less important.

[82] Above, p. 30.

accordance with Magna Carta and the way tourns had been held under kings Richard and John. There were also significant changes in clauses 7 and 8 of the draft Provisions, as compared with the same clauses in the draft versions of February and March. It is probable that we owe both these changes to the practical influence of the judiciary on the drafting process. Clause 7 no longer required that adjournments in pleas of dower *unde nichil habet* be made for further hearing after a three-week interval, which seems likely to have been an impossibly brief period in practice. The courts were simply required to ensure that such cases be adjourned from term to term so that there be at least four court-days in such cases each year and more than that, if practicable. The interval between stages in darrein presentment and *quare impedit* was now reduced to three weeks or even two and authority given for the abbreviation of mesne process (to secure the appearance of the defendant) in the latter form of action. Clause 8 allowed the overriding of royal charters of exemption from jury service not just in the grand assize but also in other assizes and more generally whenever the royal justices thought it necessary.[83] The remaining changes seem to have been only minor ones, intended primarily to clarify rather than change the proposed legislation.[84]

The fifth stage: the Michaelmas parliament of 1259 and the promulgation of the Provisions of Westminster

This penultimate draft formed the basis for one final discussion of the text of the legislation at the Michaelmas parliament of 1259. During this discussion a number of further changes were evidently made to the legislation for the Provisions of Westminster as finally enacted are rather more than just a straight translation into Latin of the penultimate French text.[85] The most significant of the changes was the omission of two complete clauses (clauses 21 and 23). Also significant is the amendment of clause 7 to allow judgment by default in actions of *quare impedit*. There is also evidence of still further tinkering with clause 5 of the draft text (clause 4 of the Provisions) to exempt those with extensive holdings

83 The clause gave as specific examples of other types of situation where it might be necessary the making of perambulations, attaint juries and cases where the charter-holder was among the witnesses to a charter. The list was clearly not intended to be exhaustive.

84 Clause 2 now spelled out the liability of the eldest of the coheirs of an inheritance to perform the single suit owed by the coheirs as a group and their obligation to contribute to his expenses in doing so. Clause 6 now spelled out the courts where beaupleder fines were not to be demanded: the eyre, the county court, the courts of barons and of free men, franchisal courts and any other court. Clause 14 now spelled out that the demand for the warranting of essoins on oath was not to be made either in the county court or elsewhere.

85 For a detailed discussion of these differences see Brand, *MCL*, pp. 351–2.

from attendance at the sheriff's tourn except in the areas where they were resident.[86] After final amendment and approval the legislation was translated into the official Latin of legislation and read out in public, as we have seen, in Westminster Hall on 24 October 1259.[87]

A text of the Provisions was subsequently sent to the Exchequer and copied into the Red Book of the Exchequer; and another text was copied on to the Close Roll.[88] The justices of the special eyre which was arranged at this same parliament were also to receive copies of the Provisions and have them proclaimed in the counties they visited;[89] and copies were also probably sent to the justices of the Common Bench and King's Bench as well as to each county, as was normally the practice with major legislation.[90]

The same parliamentary session also saw a resumption of the process of reform of central and local government and administration and a major change in the machinery already established for the remedying of local grievances against royal (and baronial) officials.[91] One significant change was made in the workings of the king's council itself. A decision was taken to ensure that in future two or three of the lesser men (*mesne gent*) on the council be chosen at each session of parliament to be in continual attendance on the king, evidently to advise him on routine business.[92] Their decisions and advice were then to be subject to review at the following parliament when their successors were also to be chosen.[93] The Exchequer and the Exchequer of the Jews had still not been reformed, although it had been among the decisions taken at the Oxford parliament that they should be, and, as has been seen, reform of the latter institution had also been promised in July 1258.[94] The justiciar and the treasurer were now delegated the task of choosing a sub-committee which was to meet during Advent and the subsequent festive season prior to the next (Candlemas) parliament to decide what changes were required in these two institutions and also what remuneration the officials of the two institutions were to receive in future. A separate sub-committee was given the task of settling the vexed question of the queen's gold and on what

86 For two other less significant changes see Brand, *MCL*, p. 352.

87 Above, p. 15.

88 Brand, *MCL*, p. 347; *CR 1259–1261*, pp. 146–50.

89 *DBM*, pp. 148–9.

90 Brand, 'Contribution', pp. 31–2.

91 The changes made are noted (together with other decisions on matters of current concern) in the document printed in *DBM*, pp. 148–57 under the title 'The Provisions of Westminster [Administrative and Political Resolutions]'.

92 Any major, non-routine but urgent business that arose between sessions of parliament was to lead to the summoning of the whole of the council. Any councillor who was called to court by the king's order or came on his own business was to join the group in their activities for as long as he was at court.

93 *DBM*, pp. 150–1.

94 Above, pp. 20, 25.

proffers she was entitled to claim this.[95] It was probably envisaged that both committees would report back to the next parliament. It was also decided, though there seems to be no evidence that the decision was ever carried out, that two men of discretion (*prodes homes*) who were outsiders not belonging to the council should start sitting in the Exchequer to see that justice was done there and that a similar arrangement should also apply to the Common Bench.[96]

Another committee was established at this parliament to appoint sheriffs for the current year and reminded that they were only to be chosen from among the vavassours of the county concerned, but the decision was also taken that for the following year (and perhaps subsequent years) sheriffs were to be chosen by the Exchequer from among four candidates chosen by the county itself at the last county court prior to Michaelmas.[97] There was also a plan, apparently subsequently abandoned before it was carried into effect, to appoint groups of four knights in each county with a watching brief over the behaviour of the sheriff. They were to have power to warn the sheriff to amend any misbehaviour and, if he failed to do this, to record his misconduct on a roll which would be routinely handed over to the justiciar at the end of the year, when the sheriff left office and had to account at the Exchequer. Preparations were also made for the reform of another area of local administration, the forest. Two further groups were appointed with the remit not just of enquiring into the state of the king's forests north and south of the Trent but also of discovering abuses in forest administration which were to be reported back to king and council.[98]

There was a drastic revision of the arrangements previously made for the remedying of grievances in the localities, probably because the justiciar, who had been meant to deal with them, had as yet managed to deal with the grievances of only two counties. It looks, however, as though the revised arrangements were themselves subject to amendment, possibly during the course of the parliament. The initial plan seems to have been for such grievances to be deal with mainly through a visitation of the general eyre. This was to possess not only the ordinary powers of itinerant justices but also additional power to determine plaints about any wrongs that had been committed within the previous seven years and to enquire (through presentment juries) into the conduct of sheriffs and their bailiffs

[95] *DBM*, pp. 152–5. The sub-committee consisted of the justiciar, the treasurer, Master Thomas of Wymondham, Roger of Thirkleby and Henry of Bath. One type of claim for the queen's gold which was considered unjustified had been mentioned in clause 1 of the Petition of the Barons: *DBM*, pp. 78–9.

[96] *DBM*, pp. 152–3, 156–7. It was provided that these two men might be drawn from the twelve individuals chosen to represent the wider *communitas regni* at parliament.

[97] *DBM*, pp. 154–5. [98] *DBM*, pp. 154–5.

and magnates and their bailiffs since the enactment of the legislation governing their behaviour at the Michaelmas parliament of 1258 and the Candlemas parliament of 1259. The justices were to be accompanied (in a manner reminiscent of the arrangements made for the Exchequer and the Common Bench) by one outsider who was to see that justice was done to complainants and others. The justices were not, however, to go to those counties where an eyre had recently been held. In those counties men of discretion (*prodes homes et sages*) of an unspecified number were to be appointed to exercise only the additional powers given to the itinerant justices, the determination of plaints of recent wrongs and the making of enquiries into the conduct of sheriffs and their bailiffs and magnates and their bailiffs.[99] It was subsequently decided to treat all counties alike and to hold special sessions at six (or perhaps seven)[100] locations in England to remedy complaints of any wrongs committed within the previous seven years and any misconduct by sheriffs and their officials or magnates and their officials; to receive presentments on various matters (including the usurpation of franchises by magnates); and to hear not only petty assizes and attaints but also pleas of dower *unde nichil habet* and assizes of darrein presentment.[101] There were to be six groups of commissioners to conduct these sessions and, as originally envisaged, each group was to consist of one regular royal justice, one member of the king's council and one member of the twelve chosen on behalf of the *communitas regni* to attend parliaments. The timetable envisaged was also a tight one. There was to be an initial session on 8 December for the submission of complaints and for the delivery of the articles of enquiry to the jury, and a second and final session beginning on 7 January 1260 to determine the complaints and receive the presentments. Still further modifications had taken place by the time the justices were actually appointed and the counties notified of their appointment on 28 November 1259.[102] Some groups of counties were still to get three commissioners, but others only two. No attempt was made to arrange visitations for the counties north of the Trent. The plan of a single session for each group of counties was abandoned and

[99] *DBM*, pp. 148–52. The memorandum only spells out the details of the plan to appoint men of discretion with limited powers in those counties where eyres had recently been held and says very little about the remit of the justices who are to be appointed 'to go round the country'. My reconstruction of the original plan with regard to these justices is a deduction from the details that are given for the counties where eyres have recently been held.

[100] The original mention of six groups of commissioners acting probably omits the justiciar who is mentioned as dealing himself with a group of counties at the end of the same document.

[101] *DBM*, pp. 158–65. That the modification took place during the session of parliament may be suggested by clause 18 of the so-called 'Administrative Provisions of Westminster' (*DBM*, pp. 152–3).

[102] *CR 1259–1261*, pp. 141–5.

separate sessions in each of the counties substituted, with only the first county in each group being dealt with in the initial sessions.

The reforming impulse was thus clearly not yet exhausted in the autumn of 1259; indeed there are signs in some of these measures that the reforming movement itself was becoming more radical, more intent on ensuring that the holders of power become responsible to a wider group both nationally and at a local level. Even legal reform was by no means considered finished for the memoranda of decisions taken at the Michaelmas parliament indicate that at least one other reform (of mesne process in personal actions) was under consideration and referred to a special sub-committee for consideration, even as the Provisions of Westminster themselves were being finalised and promulgated.[103] But with the enactment of those Provisions the first stage in the process of reforming the law was brought to a successful close.

[103] *DBM*, pp. 152–3. The members of this sub-committee were to be the justiciar, the treasurer, Master Thomas of Wymondham and the royal justices Roger of Thirkleby and Henry of Bath. A reform of mesne process in such actions was carried out in one of the clauses added to the Provisions when they were reissued in 1263: below, p. 148.

Chapter 2

THE MAKING OF THE PROVISIONS OF WESTMINSTER: THE SOCIAL AND LEGAL CONTEXT AND THE EVOLUTION OF THE INDIVIDUAL CLAUSES: I

The previous chapter located the Provisions of Westminster of 1259 within their immediate context, as one of the products of the 'reform movement' of 1258–9, and traced in general terms the stages by which the legislation developed from the first requests for legislation in the Petition of the Barons of the summer of 1258 through three separate drafts of part or all of the legislation to the final published text of October 1259. This chapter and the next locate the Provisions within a rather different broader contemporary setting by looking at the social and legal context of the individual clauses and the changes in the law which they were intended to produce. Only in this way is it possible to gauge the importance and significance of the changes which the Provisions were attempting to make. These two chapters will also trace the ways in which the proposals for legislation and individual clauses changed during the course of the drafting process, reflecting the care and effort that went into it. This chapter deals with those reforms which were concerned with different facets of the relationship between lords and their tenants and with the relationship between landowners and those who managed their lands, and those which made improvements in the procedures of the king's central courts. The following chapter examines reforms in the workings of the criminal justice system and the remedying of other grievances relating to the functioning of royal justice in the counties together with reforms whose apparent aim was to strengthen royal justice against seignorial encroachment. It also deals with the one reform intended to bring procedures in local courts into line with those followed in the king's court.

REFORMS IN THE LORD–TENANT RELATIONSHIP

From the very beginning of the common law as an organised and centralised system of royal justice in the second half of the twelfth century, the king's courts had been involved in regulating the relationships between lords and their free tenants and in enforcing the rights and duties of both parties to such relationships. The lord–tenant relationship itself, however, remained a problematic one, a frequent source of conflict and litigation. Its difficulties were almost certainly magnified by the fact that lords continued to enjoy extensive rights of self-help for the enforcement of their rights and their tenants' duties. These included the right of distraint, the right to seize movable property, generally animals, belonging to a tenant and to impound it until the tenant had performed his duties, or what the lord considered to be his duties, to the lord. It is therefore, in general terms, hardly surprising that a significant part of the Provisions of Westminster of 1259 was concerned with further regulation and adjustment of the rights of lords and tenants against each other and of the mechanisms for the enforcement of those rights. It is, perhaps, more surprising that, despite the origins of the process of 'baronial reform' as a distinctly magnate political movement, the legal reforms that were enacted in this area on balance favoured tenants against their lords, and were therefore contrary to the interests of the magnates as a group. Of the relevant clauses, those concerned with suit to seignorial courts (clauses 1–3) and with the succession of tenants to their holdings (clauses 9–10) all in broad terms favoured tenants against their lords, even if, as will be seen, the clauses relating to suit of court were significantly amended in the course of drafting in a way that made them much less favourable to tenants than they had been in their original draft form. They were only partially balanced by the clause about seignorial consent to mortmain alienations (clause 14) which certainly favoured lords. Nor did the reforms favouring tenants provide any counterbalancing advantages to the magnates in their relationship with the king, for neither the legislation on suit of court nor the legislation on succession applied in the case of tenants-in-chief holding of the crown.

SUIT OF COURT

The Provisions of Westminster begin with three clauses about the obligation to perform suit to seignorial courts. These clauses provide the longest, the most detailed and the most elaborate treatment of any of the topics covered in the legislation. Their position, their detail and the care which went into their drafting all suggest that they dealt with a matter of major contemporary importance and thus that suit of court was a significant matter of contention between lords and tenants in 1259.[1] To understand why this should have been the case we need to examine the nature of suit of court and the reasons why lords may have wished to

[1] This renders the omission of any mention of suit of seignorial courts from the Petition of the Barons all the more puzzling. For one possible explanation see above, p. 29 and note 53.

secure it from their tenants and why those tenants may have wished to avoid it. We also need to look at the evidence to suggest the existence of very different views about the proper incidence of the obligation during the years immediately prior to 1259. This also provides an essential part of the context for the legislation.

Suit of court was the obligation to attend a lord's court in order to play a role in its proceedings as one of the court's non-professional judges.[2] The lord or his representative, whether a steward or a bailiff, presided over the court. It was the suitors, those who owed suit of court, who made the court's judgments. Their relationship was similar in this respect to that between a sheriff or a hundred bailiff and the suitors who owed suit to a county or hundred court. Many, if not most, seignorial courts possessed suitors of two different kinds. Some suitors were obliged to attend the court whenever it was held. Others were obliged to attend only when the court dealt with the more important types of business. During the first three decades of the thirteenth century the minimum interval between sessions of seignorial courts had been two weeks,[3] but in 1234 legislation lengthened this to three weeks.[4] Most seignorial courts seem in practice in the first half of the thirteenth century to have met as often as was legally permissible. Regular suit thus normally meant, during the years prior to 1259, a duty to attend the court every three weeks.[5] Those who owed suit only when the court was dealing with more important business generally owed suit only when the court was sitting in judgment on a thief caught red-handed,[6] when there was a case before the court initiated by the king's writ (the writ of right) or, more generally, whenever the court had a difficult case to decide and their attendance was needed for the 'afforcement' of the court. Although both types of suitor might also be specially required and distrained by the lord to attend the court to answer the lord, one of their fellow-tenants or even a stranger, on any plea legitimately within the court's jurisdiction, the general view was that the lord possessed this power over all of his tenants and not just over those who owed suit to his court. There was thus no direct connexion between this obligation ('justiciability') and suit of court.

[2] '. . . those who owe suit, by whom pleas are held and judgments made' ('. . . illi qui sectas debent, per quos teneantur placita et fiant judicia'): *CR 1231–1234*, p. 589. cf. P&M, I, 548–53.

[3] For pre-1234 cases in which suit every two weeks to a seignorial court is mentioned see JUST 1/801, m. 1d (1227 Staffordshire eyre); *CRR*, XIII, no. 1994 (1229); *BNB*, pl. 531 (1231); JUST 1/62 m. 14d (1232 Buckinghamshire eyre).

[4] *CR 1231–1234*, pp. 588–9. The legislation arose out of a misunderstanding of the significance of the clause in Magna Carta relating to the sheriff's tourn: see *CR 1231–1234*, pp. 592–3 and JUST 1/801 m. 15 (1227 Staffordshire eyre).

[5] A few seignorial courts met on a less regular basis. For the Sussex court of the abbot of Fecamp which met no more than four, five or six times a year see JUST 1/912A m. 15 (1262 Sussex eyre).

[6] By virtue of the not uncommon seignorial franchise of infangenetheof.

Suit of court was of no direct financial benefit to the lord. Having free suitors performing suit to his court was, however, probably essential if the lord's court was legitimately and successfully to exercise any jurisdiction over cases involving the lord's free tenants.[7] Although the second half of the twelfth century and the first half of the thirteenth had witnessed a great extension of royal jurisdiction and an increase in the business of royal courts and of county courts at the expense of seignorial courts,[8] those courts still retained, in addition to their jurisdiction over the unfree, an exclusive jurisdiction as a court of first instance in land actions brought by the writ of right for tenements held of the lord of the court.[9] They also possessed a jurisdiction over such personal actions as could be brought without writ against the lord's free tenants. These included cases of debt and detinue, cases of covenant, and cases of trespass where no breach of the peace was involved.[10] Lords or their representatives might even claim such cases for hearing in their courts if brought against their tenants in the courts of other lords or in hundred courts.[11] Running an active court for free tenants was partly a matter of status. It was an obvious, tangible and continuing sign of the lord's lordship and superiority over those tenants who attended the court and had to answer litigation brought there. It was also a profitable right. An active exercise of jurisdiction brought the lord income from the fines and amercements arising out of proceedings in the court. Suit of court was, thus, at least indirectly, of financial benefit to the

[7] For this understanding of the requirement of 'judgment by peers' see the 1284 Norfolk case cited in Brand, *MCL*, p. 296.

[8] *Select Pleas in Manorial and other Seignorial Courts*, vol. 1, ed. F.W. Maitland (Selden Society vol. 2, 1888), pp. liii–lx.

[9] See the assertion made in a Yorkshire case heard in the 1248 Surrey eyre that 'such is the custom and common right throughout the kingdom that every knight and even every free man have his court for his free tenants when they are impleaded by writ of right' ('talis est consuetudo et commune jus per totum regnum quod quisque miles et eciam liber homo habet curiam suam de suis libere tenentibus quando implacitantur per breve de recto'): *Alice of Staveley v. Roger de Mowbray*: JUST 1/871 m. 8d. The defendant did not attempt to deny this but seems to have asserted that, as a tenant in drengage, the plaintiff was outside the scope of the common law rule: see KB 26/135 m. 18 (Michaelmas term 1249).

[10] For a clear later statement of the extent of this jurisdiction see John S. Beckerman, 'The Forty-Shilling Jurisdictional Limit in Medieval English Personal Actions' in *Legal History Studies, 1972*, ed. Dafydd Jenkins (Cardiff, 1975), pp. 110–17 at pp. 115–16.

[11] For later evidence relating to seignorial courts see *Master of Templars v. the bailiffs of John de Warenne of Grantham*: CP 40/163 m. 94 (Easter term 1307) and *RH*, I, 484. For later evidence relating to hundred courts see the false judgment case brought by the earl and countess of Gloucester against the suitors of the royal hundred of Holt in Norfolk for refusing to allow them such a case when it was claimed: CP 40/149 m. 316 (Michaelmas term 1304). Evidence suggesting that such claims may also have been common prior to 1259 comes from the legislation of 1234 which authorised the appointment of attorneys by suitors owing suit of court to seignorial, hundred or county court who desired to do so. This specifically stated that such an attorney should be allowed also to bring and defend actions without writ in the court to which the suit was owed and claim his lord's court and his lord's liberties in that court: *CR 1231–1234*, p. 551.

lord. It might also be directly profitable if and when the suitor failed to attend the court or to send a legitimate excuse for his absence through an essoiner, since the suitor was then liable to an amercement. Lords are also known to have accepted payments from some of those who owed suit to their courts to be free of the obligation for limited periods (often for a year or half a year at a time),[12] perhaps because they had enough suitors for the court or because the court itself was already moribund. Occasionally they even accepted a lump sum for total remission of the obligation.[13]

For free tenants who owed suit to their lord's court, suit probably constituted a constant and humiliating reminder of their subordination to their lords, an anomalous survival from a world where the link between lords and their tenants had been much closer into a world where in most other respects tenants had achieved a considerable degree of independence. Homage and fealty, which were also expressions of this same subordination, were performed only at long intervals, at the succession of the tenant and at the succession to the lordship of a new lord. Suit of court, by contrast, was still performed relatively frequently. In that earlier world the lord's court had made important decisions affecting the lord's tenants and their tenancies. Suit of court must then have seemed as much a privilege, a right to share in the making of those decisions, as an onerous obligation. With the transfer of the most important areas of seignorial jurisdiction and decision-making to the king's courts this had ceased to be the case. Suit of court had become for most an irksome obligation. It might, of course, be no more than that, a regular inconvenience. For

[12] In several MSS. of the pleading manual *Brevia Placitata* the lord's defence in an action of *ne vexes* asserts that his ancestor had been seised of suit of court both through amercements for default and through fines to be quit of the suit for a year: *Brevia Placitata*, ed. G.J. Turner and completed by T.F.T. Plucknett (Selden Society vol. 66, 1951), pp. 134, 219. From subsequent argument in the same specimen pleading it is clear that this part of the treatise was written prior to 1259. For a later reference to such payments see *YB 2 & 3 Edward II*, ed. F.W. Maitland (Selden Society vol. 19, 1904), p. 94. In the early fourteenth century fines of between three shillings and four pence and ten shillings a half year were being paid by suitors wishing to escape suit to the honour of Clare: *Court Rolls of the Abbey of Ramsey and of the Honor of Clare*, ed. W.O. Ault (New Haven, 1928), pp. xxvii–xxviii. In 1314 a figure of two or three shillings a year is mentioned as the fine paid for freedom from suit to a local court at Little Bavington, Northumberland: CP 40/205 m. 169d. The yearly valuations of suit of court mentioned in a number of inquisitions probably also reflect the amounts charged for such fines. In 1289 the three-weekly suit owed by John de Lithegrenes for his manor of Lazenby to the bishop of Durham's court of Northallerton was valued by the jurors of an inquisition *ad quod dampnum* at half a mark a year: C 143/12, no. 20. A similar inquisition in 1284 valued the three-weekly suit owed by Geoffrey Arsick for his lands in Ashley and Silverley, Cambridgeshire, to the earl of Oxford's court at Cheveley at only twelve pence a year: C 143/7, no. 24.

[13] For an example see *Sir Christopher Hatton's Book of Seals*, ed. L.C. Loyd and D.M. Stenton (Northamptonshire Record Society vol. 15, 1950), no. 209: forty shillings paid in 1288 for quittance from the suit due every three weeks from a tenement in Old, Northamptonshire, to the earl of Oxford's court of Yeldham in Essex.

those tenants who owed suit of court but who were not in a position to fulfil the obligation, perhaps because they lived at an inconvenient distance from the court concerned or were simply too busy with other matters, suit of court might also represent a continuing financial burden. Legislation of 1234 had conferred on all those who owed suit to seignorial as well as other types of local court the right to appoint substitutes (attorneys) to perform the suit in their place.[14] It was, however, sometimes, and perhaps even commonly, necessary to obtain a royal writ from Chancery which recited the terms of the statute before lords or their officials would admit such substitutes,[15] and any substitute would expect some form of remuneration for his activity. The only alternatives were to pay regular amercements for absence or to fine with the lord of the court for short-term freedom from suit.

The conflict of interest between lords and tenants about suit of court was one obvious reason for it to be a matter of contention between them. What almost certainly made things much worse was the legal position with regard to the obligation. Suit was not one of the incidents of tenure which all tenants owed to their lord merely by virtue of the existence of the tenurial bond between them like homage, fealty, aids, relief and justiciability. Nor was it owed merely by virtue of the existence of a particular kind of tenurial bond between them, as wardship was automatically an incident of tenure by knight service, though not of other forms of tenure. Instead, suit was treated like one of those other obligations, such as rent or the performance of knight service or payment of scutage, where liability to perform the service in question was established, in case of dispute, simply on the basis of whether or not the lord, or more rarely one of his ancestors, had been seised of the service concerned at the hands of the tenant, or more rarely one his ancestors.[16] In the case of most other types of service the tenant would generally possess a charter of feoffment specifying the quantity of service agreed between lord and tenant at the time of the feoffment.[17] The tenant could no longer use such a charter as an absolute bar to claims for additional service, as he had been able to do

[14] *CR 1231–1234*, p. 551. This is the legislation inaccurately summarised in chapter 10 of the Statute of Merton.

[15] For evidence that such a writ was already in use prior to 1259, but also that it might turn out to be ineffective, see JUST 1/1188, m. 11d (Bigod's 1259 session at Winchester: a plaint relating to a demand for suit to the court of Aymer, bishop-elect of Winchester at Winchester).

[16] Brand, *MCL*, pp. 312–17; Brand, 'Contribution', pp. 57–68.

[17] Plucknett is wrong to suggest (*Legislation*, p. 52) that charters of feoffment were only just becoming common and that they were often 'vague and uninformative' about services. The use of charters of feoffment was very well established by 1259, so well established that litigants in 1238 and 1249 thought it necessary to demonstrate the existence of local customs to the contrary, allowing enfeoffments without charter within the towns of South Molton in Devon and Petersfield in Hampshire: JUST 1/174, m. 23; JUST 1/997, m. 17. Nor were they anywhere

for at least a generation prior to *c.* 1240,[18] but he could still show it to a jury in an attempt to convince them that any seisin of additional services which the lord might have possessed had been wrongful.[19] In the case of suit of court, however, this was generally not possible. The obligation to perform suit of court had not traditionally been something spelled out in the tenant's charter of feoffment, though clause 1 of the Provisions of Westminster suggests that this practice may have been becoming more common during the years immediately prior to 1259 and may even have become standard practice immediately prior to the enactment of the legislation.

There seems, moreover, to have been continuing uncertainty as to whether seisin alone was the proper basis for establishing whether or not a tenant was liable to perform suit of court. The king's courts themselves had formerly accepted that the obligation to perform suit of court was an incident of tenure. This was not true of regular suit of court, only of 'special' suit, the obligation to attend the lord's court for matters of direct concern to the king: when a thief was to be judged or the king's writ of right to be heard there. Such is the doctrine of *Bracton*.[20] It is also the doctrine applied in a number of decided cases recorded on the plea rolls between 1223 and 1241.[21] Thereafter, however, seisin became the basis of all claims to suit of court, as far as the king's courts were

near as uninformative as Plucknett suggests about services other than suit of court. There was of course a special problem with those tenants who had no charters of feoffment, but, as the drafters of clause 1 of the Provisions suggested, these were generally tenants (evidently a fairly small minority) whose tenancies could be traced back directly to the 'time of the Conquest or other ancient feoffment'.

18 Brand, 'Contribution', pp. 68–70.

19 For direct evidence of such a use of a charter of feoffment see *Geoffrey of Newton v. Alard of Horswell et al.*: JUST 1/175, m. 7d (1244 Devon eyre). This would normally not have been recorded on the plea roll.

20 *Bracton*, fol. 35 (II, 112): 'ad iusticiam faciendam per breve de recto, et ad pacem sicut de latrone judicando, et pro aforciamento curiae in predictis'. It is not clear why the author distinguishes the third category, since he seems to allow for 'afforcement' of the court only for these two kinds of case, rather than generally. He seems also to be referring to the same three kinds of occasion in the 'tres sectae prenominate ad curias' of fol. 37 (II, 117). For other evidence of 'afforcement' being limited to just these two kinds of case see *Hamon of Acastre v. Jocelin of Hele* (JUST 1/175, m. 29: 1244 Devon eyre): 'et faciendo ei sectam ad curiam suam predictam bis in anno et pro afforciamento curie, scilicet quando breve domini regis fuerit ibi placitandum vel latro fuerit judicandus'. But for equally clear evidence that 'afforcement' could mean more than this see *Maud Pecche v. Reginald of Ilsley* (KB 26/143, m. 24: Michaelmas term 1250): 'debet facere sectam . . . quando aliquis implacitatur ibi per breve domini regis de recto et quando latro fuerit ibi judicandus et similiter ad efforciamentum curie'.

21 *CRR*, XI, no. 1101 (1223); *Richard of Draycote v. William of Cheteltun*: JUST 1/801, m. ld (1228 Staffordshire eyre); *CRR*, XIV, no. 480 (1230); *BNB*, pl. 531 (1231); *Robert de Bello Alneto v. Nicholas of Haversham*: JUST 1/62 m. 14d (1232 Buckinghamshire eyre); *Vincent of Wyrham v. Walter of Wyrham*: KB 26/120 m. 25 (Trinity term 1239); *John of Shawford v. Robert Blund and his wife Gunnora, guardians of John de Bures*: JUST 1/868 m. 15 (1241 Surrey eyre).

concerned. This view may not have been shared by all lords, nor by all tenants. Several pieces of evidence from the 1230s seem to indicate that some lords thought that regular suit was simply an incident of tenure.[22] This is also the view of suit which the compiler of an elaborate set-piece argument about the basis of the obligation contained in several texts of the pleading manual *Brevia Placitata* sets out specifically to rebut.[23] The argument must have been written prior to 1259 for it makes no mention of the Provisions but it seems likely that it was written not long before and it must indicate that this was indeed a view that some lords took. Lords may also have gone further and acted on this view by distraining tenants to perform suit of court even though they had not previously performed this obligation, on the basis that as the lord's tenants they owed suit of court unless they could prove from their charters of feoffment that they were specifically exempted. When in January 1264 the king's opponents compiled an account of the matters which had needed reforming in England in 1258 for submission to King Louis IX of France as part of the preliminaries to the Mise of Amiens, one grievance or abuse they specifically mentioned was that the king's alien relatives, his courtiers and nobles and their bailiffs had made their tenants perform suit of court even when they had not customarily performed it unless the tenants could show charters specifically exempting them from it.[24] There is also the evidence of the decrees of a clerical council which met in the summer of 1258. This spoke of the king, magnates and others and their bailiffs compelling churches and the religious to perform suit of court even for lands they held in frankalmoin unless the tenants concerned were able to show the original charters exempting them from suit of court.[25] Some tenants may well have successfully resisted their lords in their attempts to secure suit of court from those who had not hitherto performed it; other tenants must have succumbed. The *Providencia Baronum* may thus

[22] When William Maudut assigned the rent of certain of his tenants to Westminster abbey by final concord in 1234 he was careful to reserve to himself the 'suits, reliefs and other incidents owed from the tenements' ('salvis sectis et releviis et omnibus aliis eschaetis de predictis tenementis'): CP 25(1)/146/9, no. 111. A specific connexion with military tenure is suggested by the final concord of 1236/7 in which a tenant acknowledged owing the rent of a penny a year and the service of one-tenth of a knight's fee 'for all service, so that the said Walter and his heirs cannot demand wardship or relief of the heirs of Nicholas or suit from Nicholas and his heirs to the court of Walter and his heirs for the said tenements by reason of the said forinsec service' ('pro omni servicio, ita tamen quod predictus Walterus nec heredes sui habere potuerunt de heredibus ipsius Nicholai custodiam nec relevium nec sectam de ipso Nicholao et heredibus suis ad curiam ipsius Walteri et heredum suorum pro predictis tenementis occasione predicti forinseci servicii'): CP 25(1)/263/30, no. 21. It is also implied in the claim of a Yorkshire plaintiff in the 1235 Surrey eyre for the services of half a knight's fee 'as in scutages and suits to his court of Aiskew' ('ut in scutagiis et sectis ad curiam suam de Eykesco'): *Rannulph fitzHenry v. Everard le Fraunceis*: JUST 1/864, m. 6d.

[23] *Brevia Placitata*, pp. 135–6, 220–1. [24] *DBM*, pp. 274–5. [25] *Councils and Synods*, II, i, 584.

be referring to a real and genuine phenomenon when it talks of 'those who have not customarily performed suit of court but who have recently been forced to perform suit by the distraint and will of magnates and others' ('Illi autem qui nec sectam facere consueverunt nisi quidam noviter per districcionem et voluntatem magnatum aut aliorum ad ipsam sectam faciendam sunt coacti').[26] Such a view of suit, seeing it as an incident of tenure, also had a further corollary. This was that when a tenement was divided between coheirs each of those coheirs became obliged to perform suit to the lord's court. There is less evidence that lords had commonly acted on this assumption before 1259. But the abbot of Ramsey certainly had. A 1253 chirograph issued by Abbot Ranulph of Ramsey shows him quitclaiming the suit he had previously been claiming from the junior coheir of a tenement to his court of Broughton on the basis of the homage he had performed to the abbot for his portion of the inheritance, but equally careful to preserve his right to suit if the tenement then held by the senior coheir should come into the hands of the same junior coheir.[27] This suggests some feeling that the junior coheir's tenement should be exempt from suit but the lord's view that the performance of homage alone made him liable for it. That other lords too had made a similar claim is suggested by the argument about suit of court in *Brevia Placitata* where the wider discussion of suit of court arises out of just such a claim by a lord.[28] It is also suggested by the care which the framers of the legislation on suit of court took to deal with precisely this kind of situation.

There is also some evidence to suggest that tenants, though perhaps only in response to the new aggressiveness of lords, had begun to develop their own dissenting view about the proper basis for this obligation. The same set-piece argument in *Brevia Placitata* may also provide us with an insight into this opposing view. Suit of court is only due, it is here argued on the tenant's behalf, when tenant and feoffor have specifically agreed (in writing) that the tenant perform suit of court, or when a tenant has come into possession of land already owing suit, either as the result of an ancient feoffment, or as the result of some later agreement to perform suit attested by a charter or some other writing.[29] As will be seen, this is fairly close to one view of suit represented in the legislation as originally drafted in February and March 1259. That same draft legislation, however, also hints at the prior existence of a second and less radical tenant's view of suit. This would have exempted from suit only those with a specific

[26] Jacob, *Studies*, p. 366. cf. Brand, *MCL*, p. 358 and for the earlier French draft version of the same passage see Brand, *MCL*, p. 359.

[27] E 40/5449 (calendared in *Catalogue of Ancient Deeds preserved in the Public Record Office* (6 vols., London, 1890–1915), III, 180).

[28] *Brevia Placitata*, pp. 134–5, 219–20.

[29] *Brevia Placitata*, pp. 136, 220.

written exemption from it plus those who had been enfeoffed to hold for a specific service 'for all service'.[30]

It was because this continuing uncertainty about the proper basis of the obligation to perform suit of court was at the heart of the problem that the draft legislation brought to the Candlemas (February) parliament of 1259 began by suggesting general rules about the basis of the obligation that were to be applicable in future.[31] Clause 1 adopts in its first and third sub-clauses the most radical tenant view of suit of court.[32] Suit is to be owed only if the tenant's charter specifically obliges him to perform it or if the tenant's ancestors have performed it continuously since the Conquest or over a long period of time since then. The logical deduction from these two sub-clauses is then spelled out in the fourth and final sub-clause. Tenants who have recently been forced to perform suit of court but who do not owe it are not to be obliged to perform it. The lord's seisin of such suit, however long continued, will not confer any title to claim it. The second sub-clause, however, as has already been suggested, belongs to a different and much less radical scheme. It stipulates only that tenants are to be exempt from suit where they have been enfeoffed to hold by a specific service 'for all service'. Discussion at the Candlemas parliament improved the drafting of the third sub-clause,[33] but did not resolve the apparent contradiction between the different sub-clauses.[34]

The second clause of the draft legislation dealt with a subsidiary issue related to the more general issue tackled in the first clause. This was what was to happen to the obligation of suit of court when the tenement for which it was owed came to be divided between coheirs.[35] In future, it suggested, only one suit was to be owed for such a divided inheritance. It did not establish who was to be obliged to perform that suit but it did make clear that all the coheirs and any alienees who held the shares of such coheirs were to 'aid' in its performance.[36] No significant changes were made to this clause at the Candlemas parliament itself.

The third and fourth clauses of the draft legislation proposed the creation of two entirely new forms of action for the enforcement of the new rules relating to suit of court.[37] Clause 3 prescribed the characteristics of

[30] It is unclear where this theory left tenants who had no charter of feoffment. Perhaps they too were entitled to exemption if they had not customarily performed suit.

[31] For this draft legislation see above, pp. 27–30. [32] Brand, *MCL*, p. 359.

[33] It spelled out that the 'long time' of the original draft meant 'from a time beyond which action is not allowed', that is 'time out of mind'. It also specified that any subsequent quittance of such suit by the lord or his ancestors would bar any claims to the suit.

[34] Jacob, *Studies*, p. 366; Brand, *MCL*, pp. 357–8. [35] Brand, *MCL*, p. 359.

[36] The alienee of such a share might, however, be exempted from having to contribute if he could show that his feoffor had promised to acquit him.

[37] Brand, *MCL*, pp. 359–60.

the new action for tenants to use against lords who distrained them for suit which they did not owe. The proposed action resembled the existing common law action of replevin. It, too, was to test whether or not the lord's distraint had been justified. In it, too, the tenant was to secure the release of his animals which had been taken in distraint pending the outcome of his suit. The tenant was also to be able to recover damages for any wrongful distraint, just as he could in replevin. Where it differed from the existing action, however, was in allowing the tenant immediate access to the king's court rather than sending him to the county court to commence his action; in establishing an abbreviated mesne process beginning with attachment to secure the lord's appearance in court; and in allowing the awarding of judgment by default if the lord refused to appear after all the stages of the abbreviated mesne process had been used. Clause 4 proposed the establishment of a matching action for lords if their tenants withdrew suit to which those lords were entitled. They too were to enjoy the benefits of an abbreviated mesne process in securing the attendance of their tenants in the king's court to answer the lord's action and were to be able in the case of continued refusal to appear to secure judgment by default. They too were to be able to recover damages. It is not, however, entirely clear why this second form of action was proposed. There is little reason to suppose that the withdrawal of suit by tenants had been a major problem prior to 1259. The drafters of the legislation may have thought it only proper to balance the new tenant's action by creating this second action for lords. It is also conceivable that they hoped to discourage lords from using their power of distraint by offering an easy and attractive alternative.

The draft legislation had been heavily revised by the time a penultimate draft of these same clauses was presented to the Michaelmas parliament of October 1259.[38] The most important of the revisions were to the first clause. The second sub-clause, as has been seen, really belonged to an alternative and incompatible solution to the problem of stating a set of general rules about liability to suit of court. It now simply disappeared. So too did the fourth sub-clause spelling out the corollary of the rules about suit contained in the first and third sub-clauses. This must have been omitted because it was considered unnecessary. Even more significant was the drastic modification of the third sub-clause. This now established that the duty of suit, where not specified in the charter of feoffment, was to be inferred not from proof of continuous performance ever since time out of mind but simply from proof that suit had been customarily

[38] For the process of revision see above, p. 34. For the text of the penultimate version of these clauses see Brand, *MCL*, pp. 361–2.

performed before Henry III's first voyage into Brittany (in 1230). The new rule would, of course, still offer tenants protection against the consequences of the recent usurpation of suit, the main avowed object of the reform. It would also, however, make it much easier for lords to establish their entitlement to suit. The same clause also lost its rider specifying the continued validity of quitclaims. This was probably omitted simply because it too was thought to be superfluous.

The other amendments were of a more technical nature. Clause 2 preserved the main principle of not allowing the multiplication of suits on the division of an inheritance between coheirs but now spelled out what had probably always been intended by the clause. Suit was to be performed by the coheir holding the share of the eldest coparcener with the others contributing to his or her costs. Clause 3 added an additional stage of mesne process, where the writ of *facias venire* was to be used, before the tenant could gain a judgment by default in his new action against his lord; and since the same process was also to apply in the new lord's action created by clause 4 it also effectively lengthened the stages of process in the lord's action too. Another amendment significantly extended the potential use of the new lord's action. It was now to be available not just in respect of suits withdrawn after the enactment of the legislation but also for any suit withdrawn by a tenant since 1230.

There were yet further modifications before the legislation reached its final form in clauses 1–3 of the Provisions of Westminster of 1259.[39] Clause 1 was redrafted without changing its meaning. Clause 2 was substantially revised and extended. It now covered not only the division of inheritances through partition between coheirs but also their division through alienation. The same general principle was to apply in both cases. Only a single suit was to be owed for any divided tenement. The redrafters did not apparently have a ready solution for the problem of which of the alienees of a divided inheritance was to be responsible for the suit, so this question was left open. In clause 3 (which covered both the new tenant's action and the new lord's action) the main change was to remove any possibility of lords recovering suit by default in their new action. This removed one of the main potential attractions to lords of using the new form of action.[40] It was in this modified form that the legislation came into force.

[39] Above, p. 37. For the text see Appendix I: below, pp. 414–17.

[40] Redrafting of this clause also introduced an ambiguity as to whether or not the new lord's action was to be available only for suit withdrawn after the enactment of the legislation itself (as originally proposed in February and March 1259) or also for any suit withdrawn after 1230 (as proposed in the penultimate French text of the Provisions). In the first part of the relevant sub-clause the formulation is that the action is to be available if tenants withdraw the suit they owe 'after this constitution', ('post hanc constitucionem') but the sub-clause goes on to say that damages are to be

SEIGNORIAL RIGHTS AT SUCCESSION

There was a second area where the Provisions of Westminster made adjustments in the lord–tenant relationship which favoured tenants. This was in dealing with what were seen as abuses of seignorial rights exercised in connexion with hereditary succession to land. The king's courts had been involved in the enforcement of the heir's right of succession and, more specifically, of the heir's right to succeed to all the property his ancestor had held on the day of his death, ever since the enactment of the Assize of Northampton of 1176.[41] Heirs had been provided with a special remedy (the assize of mort d'ancestor) to enforce this right, though the assize was only available if the heir claiming was a close relative of the deceased: a son or daughter, brother or sister, nephew or niece.[42] During the 1230s Chancery had begun to make available additional remedies for those heirs who could not bring the assize because their deceased ancestor had been a more distant relative but who still wished to make a claim in the king's court based on the seisin of that ancestor at the time of his death.[43] After some initial resistance,[44] these new remedies, the writ of aiel (for claims based on the seisin of a grandfather or grandmother) and cosinage (for claims based on the seisin of some other relative not covered by the assize), became a permanent addition to the standard property actions available in the king's courts.[45]

recoverable only in respect of withdrawals made 'in the time of these lords and not in the time of their predecessors' ('de subtractionibus sibi factis et non de subtractionibus factis predecessoribus ipsorum') and to explain that the existing common law is to apply to suits 'withdrawn before the said time' ('de sectis autem que ante tempus supradictum') which could mean prior to 1230. In practice, as will be seen, the courts were not required to resolve this difficulty: below, pp. 115, 251.

41 *SSC*, pp. 179–80. On the background and significance of this provision see Brand, *MCL*, pp. 213–8, 224; Joseph Biancalana, 'For Want of Justice: Legal Reforms of Henry II', *Columbia Law Review* 88 (1988), 484–514.

42 Biancalana, 'For Want of Justice', 507.

43 The earliest writ of cosinage (claiming on the basis of the seisin of a kinsman whose precise relationship is unstated) so far noted is one brought for lands in Lincolnshire in the 1235 Cambridgeshire eyre: *Thomas Bluet (guardian of Juliana of Gevesby) v. William Motkin* (JUST 1/80, m. 14). The earliest writ of aiel so far noted is that brought in the Common Bench in 1239: *Hosee v. Hosee* (*SCKB*, II, clvi).

44 *BNB*, pl. 1215 (February 1237); *SCKB*, II, clvi.

45 There long remained, however, some uncertainty about just how broad the category of kinsmen covered by cosinage should be. In a Common Bench case of Trinity term 1254 there was doubt as to whether its use was proper where the kinsman concerned was the brother of some of the plaintiffs, the uncle of one of the others, and the great-uncle of two others but the writ was upheld: *Maud of Wytham et al. v. Robert of Hafford et al.* (KB 26/154, m. 19d). In a Common Bench case of Easter term 1260 there was doubt about whether it could properly be used where the common ancestor was four generations removed from the claimant: *John le Sauser v. John Renger* (KB 26/165, m. 19). In two Common Bench cases heard in Michaelmas term 1261 there was doubt as to whether it could properly be used when claimants were the descendants of siblings of the 'kinsman' concerned: *Nicholas of Freton v. John Juete* (KB 26/171, m. 32d) and *Simon le*

These remedies were primarily intended for use against the lord of whom the heir claimed to hold the land, not against a rival heir. The Assize of Northampton is couched in terms which suggest that the lord is the only possible defendant to the assize of mort d'ancestor,[46] and the argument offered in defence of the newly invented actions of aiel and cosinage in 1237 seems to assume that the lord is the most likely defendant to these actions as well.[47] There were good reasons why this should have been the case. By the time *Glanvill* was written, and most probably from the time the assize itself was invented, mort d'ancestor could not be used against someone who claimed to hold the land 'by the same descent'.[48] The same rule was also applied in the actions of aiel and cosinage.[49] Mort d'ancestor was, moreover, the appropriate action to bring against the lord not just when he was claiming the land in his own right (for example, when he claimed that the ancestor was just a life tenant and he was entitled to the reversion or that the land had escheated to him at the ancestor's death) but also when the lord had been holding the land in wardship and lord and tenant disagreed about whether or not the wardship ought by now to have ended. The likelihood of the lord being defendant in the action was also increased by the fact that although the Assize of Northampton had acknowledged (or created) the right of the tenant to take possession of his ancestor's holding if he was on the tenement at the time of the ancestor's death or managed to enter it before the lord could do so,[50] it had also preserved the lord's right to take possession if he was first on the scene. By the second quarter of the thirteenth century, and quite probably earlier, he was entitled to retain this possession until he was satisfied as to the identity of the heir and that the heir was of age and had also been offered homage and fealty by the new tenant and an appropriate surety for the payment of the tenant's relief.[51]

The one major deficiency in the heir's remedies, however, was that when he succeeded in them he only secured possession of the inheritance. He was not entitled to any damages in respect of the period he had been

Parmenter of Stortford v. Robert of Thorley (KB 26/171, m. 31). During the 1250s it could not apparently be used for a claim based on the seisin of a great-grandfather: *Brevia Placitata*, p. 119; *Casus Placitorum and Reports of Cases in the King's Courts (1272–8)*, ed. W.H. Dunham, jr. (Selden Society vol. 69, 1952), p. 9/39. This seems still to have been the case in 1271: see the argument in *Ediva daughter of Hugh Attehelde v. Hamon of Betlescumbe et al.*: JUST 1/365, m. 31d (1271 Kent eyre). It had probably ceased to be the case by 1278 when the line was being drawn at its use for a claim based on the seisin of a great-great-grandfather: *Robert and William of Eglingham v. William de la Chaumbre and others*: JUST 1/648, m. 5 (1278 Northumberland eyre).

46 *SSC*, p. 180. 47 *BNB*, pl. 1215. 48 *Glanvill*, xiii, 11 (p. 155).

49 *Bracton*, fols. 282b–283 (III, 322–3).

50 This was certainly the rule by the time *Bracton* was written: *Bracton*, fol. 252 (III, 245).

51 *Bracton*, fols. 252b–253b (III, 246–8).

prevented from taking possession or for any deterioration in the value of his land caused by the lord's actions during the period he had retained the land in his possession.[52] This must have seemed particularly anomalous because the tenant was entitled to recover damages as well as his land through the assize of novel disseisin if he had managed to take possession of the land before the lord and the lord then attempted to do more than take a 'simple', nominal seisin of the land.[53] The heir's misfortune in not being first to take possession of the land therefore not only might require him to bring a legal action (mort d'ancestor) to secure his inheritance but also would allow his lord to retain the land with impunity until the tenant had succeeded in his action, however clear the heir's title to succeed might be. What must have seemed still more anomalous was that, even if the lord had caused a lasting deterioration in the value of the land while he held on to it through committing waste, the heir was still not entitled to damages, since the heir's action of waste (in which he would recover damages) was only available in respect of waste committed by a lord while the heir was under age and the land in his wardship.[54] That this was felt to be a particularly hard case is evident from *Bracton*. The treatise says that, if a chief lord takes first seisin and maliciously delays handing over seisin to the heir even though the heir's identity (and entitlement) are clear, and commits waste and destruction, he is to restore the tenements with damages just as in the assize of novel disseisin. The treatise admits, however, that this is 'not a remedy currently in use' ('liceat non habeatur in usu') and the failure to cite any cases where damages had been awarded may suggest that they never had been, but that the author of this passage thought that they ought to have been.[55]

A change in the law relating to succession was the first of the demands made in the Petition of the Barons of 1258. Clause 1 of the Petition called for the awarding of damages if a lord committed waste of any kind while he was in possession of land at a succession.[56] But it also contained what looks like a much more radical proposal. This was that, at least where the heir was a close relative,[57] the lord should only ever in future be entitled to a 'simple' seisin without any right to receive any of the issues of the land or rents owed to the heir, provided the heir was of age and ready to perform all his obligations to the lord and apparently irrespective of whether the lord or the heir had entered the land first.

[52] *Glanvill*, xiii, 2–17 (pp. 149–60); *Bracton*, fols. 252–84 (III, 245–326).

[53] The existence of such a rule can be inferred from *Glanvill*, vii, 9 (p. 82). It is specifically stated in *Bracton*, fol. 252 (III, 245).

[54] *NN*, p. cxci. [55] *Bracton*, fol. 253b (III, 248). [56] *DBM*, pp. 76–9.

[57] The relationships specified in the clause are those covered by the assize of mort d'ancestor.

There is no early draft of this clause in the French text prepared for the Candlemas parliament of 1259 or in the published text of the *Providencia Baronum* of March 1259. The earliest draft text that does survive is that contained in the penultimate French draft of the Provisions of Westminster produced for the Michaelmas parliament of 1259.[58] The draft clause consists of two sub-clauses.[59] One deals with the situation envisaged in the Petition, where an heir had already come of age by the time his ancestor died. It proposed that, if the lord kept such an heir from taking possession and forced him to bring either the assize or an action of cosinage,[60] the heir should in future be entitled to recover damages. It did not specifically mention waste, but damages awarded in such actions would also have covered any waste the lord had committed. The same sub-clause also mentioned the case of the heir apparent who was the first to take possession. Here it simply confirmed the existing position. In such a case the lord was only to be entitled to take 'simple' seisin and could not eject the heir or take anything from his property.[61] The other sub-clause dealt with a second kind of situation and one which had not been mentioned in the Petition. This was that of an heir who had been in wardship to his lord and whose lord then refused to surrender the land. Again an obvious injustice was involved. By taking the land in wardship with the heir, the lord had already acknowledged the heir's entitlement to succeed to the land. Nor was the lord entitled to any relief after a wardship. It proposed that in this case too the heir should be entitled to recover damages as from the time he had come of age.[62] With only minor amendments these proposals became law as clauses 9 and 10 of the Provisions of Westminster at the end of October 1259.[63]

SEIGNORIAL CONTROL OF MORTMAIN ALIENATIONS

The third area of lord–tenant relations where the Provisions of Westminster made a significant change was in relation to seignorial controls

[58] Above, p. 34. [59] Brand, *MCL*, p. 364.

[60] This was probably intended also to cover the action of aiel. The discussion of cosinage in *Bracton* also covers this second action and it was probably considered at this time as no more than a special case of cosinage: *Bracton*, fols. 281–281b (III, 318–9).

[61] It is conceivable that this part of the sub-clause does not owe its presence to any desire on the part of the drafters to deal with all possible situations that might occur but that it is a reminder of a more radical scheme (perhaps on the lines of the original proposal) reducing lord's rights in all cases to 'simple' seisin which had been watered down in the course of prior amendment.

[62] It is probably only careless drafting that appears to restrict this to the assize of mort d'ancestor, since damages under the provisions of the other sub-clause were also available in the action of cosinage. There was no such restriction in the clause as eventually enacted into law.

[63] For the text see Appendix I: below, pp. 420–1.

over alienations into mortmain made by their tenants. An alienation 'into mortmain' occurred whenever a layman gave or sold land or other property either to an ecclesiastical institution or corporation such as an abbey, priory, hospital or college or to the holder of a particular ecclesiastical dignity or benefice such as a bishop, a canon, the rector of a parish church or the priest serving a chantry, if the property was to pass at his death to his successor rather than his heir. Special legal rules applied to property held once it had passed into ecclesiastical hands. Even if, for many purposes, the property held by ecclesiastical institutions was treated as though the property of the head of that institution (the abbot, prior or warden) and even if secular services such as knight service or rent were owed by him for the property, his death would not normally give the lord of whom the property was held any right to claim a relief from his successor,[64] and often no right even to custody of the property during the interval between his death and the election of his successor.[65] The same was also true of property held by individual ecclesiastical tenants. The tenure of property by individual ecclesiastics or ecclesiastical institutions also brought an end to any hope on the lord's part that the property might escheat. There was no prospect that such a tenant would ever die without a successor. Even his conviction for felony would not mean the forfeiture of the property. The mere fact that property was held by an individual ecclesiastic or ecclesiastical institution did not of itself automatically mean that the property was held in frankalmoin and free of all secular service, but such tenants normally preferred, if at all possible, to acquire land on such terms and might work over time to ensure that not only the immediate lord but also superior lords freed the land from the burden of service.

Alienations into mortmain were, not surprisingly, widely seen in thirteenth-century England as damaging to the interests of the lord of whom the property was held.[66] If the grant or sale took the form of a subinfeudation, with the new ecclesiastical tenant holding the property he had been given of the grantor and his heirs, this safeguarded the original lord's right to any relief due from the heir of his original tenant as this was

64 But see Brand, *MCL*, p. 302 for exceptions.

65 Susan Wood, *English Monasteries and Their Patrons in the Thirteenth Century* (Oxford, 1955), pp. 75–100. It is probably no coincidence that clause 11 of the Petition of the Barons (the clause immediately following clause 10 which is concerned with mortmain alienations) complained of the king's usurpation of the custody of religious houses founded in the fees of others where the earls and barons were mesne lords between the religious houses and the king: *DBM*, pp. 82–3. There was a close connexion between the two complaints.

66 J.M.W. Bean, *The Decline of English Feudalism, 1215–1540* (Manchester, 1968), pp. 40–2; Donald W. Sutherland, *The Assize of Novel Disseisin* (Oxford, 1973), pp. 86–8; Sandra Raban, *Mortmain Legislation and the English Church, 1279–1500* (Cambridge, 1982), pp. 4–5.

still payable in full. Normally, however, it would significantly diminish the value of the much more profitable right of wardship the lord might exercise over the heir's holding and of the even more profitable, but much less common, right of escheat over the holding, if the tenant died without heirs or was convicted of felony, since these could only be exercised over the land the tenant retained and would only give the lord a right to any services the grantor had reserved when making the mortmain grant. These were generally nominal or non-existent.[67] It would also diminish the value of any right of wardship over the person of the tenant's heir and the associated right to arrange a marriage for the heir since the value of that marriage bore a direct relationship to the value of the lands he was due to inherit. The lord's right to the services owed by his tenant was in theory wholly unaffected by any subinfeudation he might make, but in practice, if the grant was for nominal or purely spiritual services, the subinfeudation might seriously impair the tenant's ability to perform them. In theory, the lord had the right to secure performance of his services by the seizure and impounding of animals or other possessions belonging not only to his tenant but also to any sub-tenant of his,[68] but if he attempted to exercise this right against an ecclesiastical sub-tenant he might find himself subjected to ecclesiastical sanctions for doing so.[69] If the alienation took the form of a substitution, with the new ecclesiastical tenant becoming the direct tenant of the grantor's own lord, this provided full protection for the lord's right to his services but it would still mean the loss of all feudal incidents in respect of the land which had been so alienated. Those lords who were themselves religious institutions had additional reasons for objecting to other religious institutions acquiring lands which were held of them by their tenants. Many seem to have considered themselves entitled to a monopoly in acquiring lands from their own tenants. During the 1240s and 1250s a number of such institutions obtained standing royal prohibitions against other specified institutions (or exceptionally all other institutions) 'entering their fees',[70] that is, acquiring lands held of them. In 1246 and 1268 we find a bishop and a religious house agreeing to particular acquisitions of lands belonging to their fees

[67] If the land had been granted to another layman the lord could hope for a wardship by reason of wardship over the sub-tenant's land: that the sub-tenant would die leaving an heir under age while he held the tenant's lands in wardship. This was not a possibility where the land had been granted in mortmain.

[68] Brand, *MCL*, pp. 302, 308.

[69] *Councils and Synods*, II, i, 584.

[70] *CR 1242–1247*, pp. 50–1 (1243: for the abbot of Westminster against the abbot of Pershore), 404 (1246: for the abbot of Reading against the abbot of Boxley or others); *CR 1251–1253*, pp. 52 (1252: for the hospital of St John the Baptist, Oxford against the prior of St Frideswide's, Oxford), 106 (1253: for the same against the abbot of Biddlesden); *CR 1254–1256*, p. 124 (1255: for the same against the prior of Luffield and all other religious houses).

by other religious houses but only in return for an acknowledgement of their right to control any further such acquisitions.[71] There were also other, non-material objections to at least some mortmain acquisitions. A widespread perception existed that many, if not all, of the older religious houses were already well-enough endowed and had no need to go on accumulating property. The existence of such a perception only emerges clearly after the enactment of the Statute of Mortmain in 1279. In the 1280 clerical *gravamina* the assembled clergy suggested amendments to the Statute of Mortmain prohibiting all alienations in mortmain which would make it plain that it was only to apply to religious institutions 'sufficiently well-endowed and wealthy' ('sufficienter dotatis pariter et ditatis').[72] The clerical *gravamina* of 1285 likewise presumably attempted to appeal to existing lay sentiment in seeking that the legislation be amended to exempt generally all gifts to hospitals and chantries, for the construction of new religious houses and for the support of the necessary expenses of parish churches.[73] Such an attitude can also be glimpsed in the comments of the king's council endorsed on an inquisition *ad quod damnum* into a proposed grant to Worcester cathedral priory in 1291 noting that 'It seems to the council that the king can, if he wishes, give his consent without damage to anybody, as is clear from the inquisition. But the request is for land worth ten pounds a year and they are rich enough already.'[74] Such views had almost certainly also existed prior to 1279.

None of these considerations suggested any need for a total prohibition on alienations into mortmain. Such a total ban would probably always have been impracticable anyway. What they did suggest was the need for lords to exercise control over such alienations. The power of veto over such grants would allow a lord to obtain compensation either of a financial or of a spiritual nature for his material losses. A power of control would also allow religious institutions to prevent other religious institutions entering their fees. Seignorial controls could also ensure that only deserving institutions were allowed to make further acquisitions. However, the legal system as it stood in 1258–9 seems to have given lords only a limited degree of control over mortmain alienations.[75] They could probably as a matter of practice exercise a power to reject or accept any

[71] *The 'Registrum Antiquissimum' of the Cathedral Church of Lincoln*, ed. C.W. Foster (8 vol., Lincoln Record Society vols. 27–9, 32, 34, 41, 42 and 46, 1931–53), III, 277 (no. 938) (by the prior and convent of Clattercote); BL MS. Cotton Cleopatra C vii, fols. 131v–132r (by Merton priory in favour of the canons of Beaulieu). The latter mentions an alleged general custom of the county of Kent that the religious may not enter the fee of other religious without their consent.

[72] *Councils and Synods*, II, ii, 885–6. [73] *Councils and Synods*, II, ii, 958.

[74] C 143/15, no. 29. The king none the less overrode their advice because the grant was in honour of St Wulfstan and in augmentation of the alms of the house.

[75] Brand, *MCL*, pp. 234–8.

alienations by way of substitution. Against subinfeudations their powers were much weaker. The 1217 reissue of Magna Carta had contained two clauses, one prohibiting subinfeudations where too great a proportion of the tenant's land was granted away and the other subinfeudations to religious houses as part of an arrangement designed to deprive the lord of his incidents. Neither clause seems to have been much cited or used in practice. From *c.* 1247 onwards vigilant and strong lords possessed a recognised right to prevent damaging subinfeudations by immediate seizure of the alienated property. They could also seek compensation for any losses they suffered by summoning new ecclesiastical sub-tenants to their courts to answer for entering their fees without their consent. A few weaker lords obtained the assistance of the king and his local officials in controlling mortmain alienations within their fees. But there was no general rule allowing lords to control such alienations nor any general remedy available from the royal courts assisting them in doing so.

It is in this context that clause 10 of the Petition of the Barons of 1258 needs to be read.[76] This did not ask for the prohibition of all mortmain alienations but only for some measure to prevent the religious (*religiosi*), that is abbeys and priories, 'entering the fees' of earls, barons and others against their wishes. It cited as the adverse consequence of their doing so the loss of 'wardships, marriages, reliefs and escheats'.[77] The demand was thus, at least implicitly, for lords to be given a general power to control such alienations and the justification offered was primarily a financial one. However, the singling out of the 'religious' for special attention suggests that there may also have been mingled with this a particular concern with further acquisitions by those least deserving of doing so. That the reformers themselves were at least as much concerned with the further acquisition of property as with lords' losses from such acquisitions is suggested by the wording of a decision from the Oxford parliament of the summer of 1258 recorded on the so-called 'Coke' roll to the effect 'that Relligious persons purchase not so much'.[78] No early draft of the clause on mortmain alienation survives. Clause 13 of the penultimate French draft of the Provisions is close in spirit to the original demand of clause 10 of the Petition but even more restricted in its scope.[79] The legislation proposed would have required the consent of the immediate lord for mortmain alienations. This was, however, only to apply to acquisitions made by the religious (*hom de religiun*) and was apparently only to apply to purchases they made (*ne puise nule tere achater*) and not to gifts. Here again

[76] *DBM*, pp. 80–1.

[77] Reliefs should not have featured on this list since they were not lost by subinfeudations.

[78] Richardson and Sayles, 'The Provisions of Oxford', 317.

[79] Brand, *MCL*, p. 365.

we can probably see the influence of the sentiment against acquisitions by the older and wealthier religious houses. They were the purchasers of land par excellence as opposed to the recipients of pious benefactions. The original formulation of the Petition was, however, restored in the final text. Under clause 14 of the Provisions of Westminster the lord's consent was in future to be required for any of the religious 'entering the fee' of a lord. This covered gifts as well as purchases.[80] The clause did not specify how the requirement was to be enforced.

LEGAL RELATIONSHIPS BETWEEN LANDOWNERS AND THE TEMPORARY MANAGERS OF THEIR LANDS

By 1259 tenants had long possessed satisfactory remedies against lords attempting to abuse their rights over their lands while those lands were in the lord's wardship: an action of waste where lords attempted to over-exploit the opportunities for profit that a wardship offered them,[81] and a writ of entry to recall any purported alienation of the tenant's land made by the guardian.[82] Clauses 9 and 10 of the Provisions of Westminster, as has been seen, were intended in part to create satisfactory remedies against lords who exploited their rights to possession of the tenant's lands at a succession or at the end of a wardship.[83] Royal justice had, however, in general been much slower and more reluctant to get involved on any kind of regular basis in regulating the relationships between landowners and others who held their lands on a temporary basis, whether as lessees, as bailiffs or as non-seignorial, family guardians. The main exceptions had been where lessees had attempted to retain the lands after the end of their lease or purported to grant them to third parties or where bailiffs had purported to grant the lands they managed to third parties. In all these situations a writ of entry had been made available to secure the return of the land.[84] It had also been possible to use a writ of entry to secure the return of land which had been held in wardship by a socage guardian and which that guardian had purported to convey to a third party.[85] A second set of clauses in the Provisions attempted to set in place

[80] For the text see Appendix I: below, pp. 422–3. [81] Above, p. 56.

[82] The earliest example seems to be a case of 1220: *CRR*, VIII, 230. [83] Above, p. 57.

[84] The writ of entry *ad terminum qui preteriit*, apparently originally invented for use against creditors who had been given land as surety for repayment of loans and held on to it, had been modified for use against lessees and those whose title derived from them by 1196 at latest: see *CRR*, VII, 332. It was in regular use thereafter. The earliest action for the recovery of land purportedly alienated by a bailiff seems to be *CRR*, XIII, no. 159 (1227). It never became common.

[85] For an early example of the writ of entry 'through a guardian' used against a tenant who allegedly derived his title to the land through a socage guardian see *CRR*, I, 182, 249–50 (1200).

additional rules governing the conduct of parties to relationships of this sort or enhancing the enforcement of the existing rules in this area.

Lessees

The action of covenant had existed since at least the last decade of the twelfth century.[86] One of its main uses was to enforce the obligations of lessor and lessee towards each other: to provide the lessee with some protection against ejection by the lessor,[87] and to provide the lessor with a way of enforcing payment of the rent due under the lease and enforcing the other conditions of the lease. The action was not, however, brought with any frequency in the royal courts during the first half of the thirteenth century as a way of enforcing obligations under leases. This may partly have been because of its limitations as a way of regulating the behaviour of the parties to a lease. Its normal method of enforcing compliance with the terms of a lease was indirect, through the awarding of retrospective damages. It did not attempt to secure direct enforcement of the terms. It is perhaps even more likely that the reason that such actions appear so rarely on the plea rolls of the king's courts is that during this period the action was one heard normally in the county court.[88]

It is thus against the largely unknown, and unknowable, context of the practice and custom of county courts whose records for this period do not survive that the legislation of 1259 relating to the conduct of lessees needs to be placed. Understanding its precise context is made more difficult by the fact that this is not one of the clauses which corresponds to any of the complaints contained in the Petition of the Barons, so that document provides no clues to its understanding. Even more frustratingly, the only draft version of the relevant clause is that which appears in the penultimate French draft of the Provisions (as clause 19) and this differs in no significant particulars from the clause as enacted.[89] What clause 20 of the Provisions said was that lessees were not to commit waste during the period of their lease without a special clause in their lease permitting them to do so.

[86] David J. Ibbetson, 'Words and Deeds: the Action of Covenant in the Reign of Edward I', *Law and History Review* 4, no. 1 (1986), 71–94.

[87] From *c.* 1234 the lessee was also provided with a remedy (*quare ejecit infra terminum*) against third parties who gained possession of the land and whose title was derived from the same lessor: for an early example where the writ was used against a second lessee of the same lessor see *CRR*, XV, no. 1263.

[88] The only forms of the writ which appear in the earliest registers of writs are for the initiation of litigation in the county court: *Early Registers*, pp. 16, 27 (Hib. 49; CA 36); Maitland, *Collected Papers*, II, 146 (CB 77).

[89] Brand, *MCL*, p. 366.

If it were proved that lessees had committed waste without such prior authorisation they were to pay damages.[90]

The wording of the clause seems to suggest that there may have been some real doubt about the interpretation of the terms of leases during the years prior to 1259 and that some county courts may have been giving lessees the benefit of the doubt if waste was not explicitly prohibited by the terms of their leases. Yet this seems inherently implausible.[91] An alternative possibility is that the real purpose of the clause was to provide statutory authority for the creation of a new variant on the action of waste, to cover waste committed by lessees, and thus to allow lessors to recover damages for waste through a separate action in the king's courts (where actions of waste were determined) rather than through the action of covenant in the county court.[92] There is other evidence to suggest that there may have been a wider discussion of the areas in which the common law and the king's courts failed to provide adequate protection against the commission of waste.[93] If this is correct, the real underlying purpose of the clause was to secure a jurisdictional transfer of such cases and a specialised action of waste for use under these circumstances. But if so, it is strange that the legislation itself makes no direct mention of any such action. There is also a third possibility. This is that the clause did not change anything and was not intended to do so. It may have been merely exhortatory, a confirmation of existing law and custom, perhaps even a reaffirmation of the law after some recent incident where a lessee had committed waste.[94] As will be seen, there are a number of other clauses of the Provisions of Westminster which do not change the law but merely confirm the existing legal position.[95]

90 For the text see Appendix I: below, pp. 424–5.

91 But note that in a covenant case brought in the 1241 Kent eyre alleging waste committed in woods during the lease of a knight's fee with its appurtenances the defendant pleaded that the covenant had said nothing about waste, sale or 'exile' of woods and that there had been no mention of woods in it at all. Although judgment was given against the plaintiff on other grounds the argument must have had some plausibility: see *Alan de Legh v. Reginald of Cobham* (JUST 1/359, m. 18d).

92 But there is some evidence to suggest that a writ of waste covering waste committed by lessees already existed before 1259. A judgment dismissing a covenant case brought in the 1241 Kent eyre alleging waste by a lessee in the woods belonging to a manor was partly based on the fact that there existed a specific alternative remedy by writ in such a case ('et aliud breve formatum est in curia domini regis quod vocatur breve de vasto, vendicione et exilio. Et quia aliud breve jacet in casu isto'): *Alan de Legh v. Reginald of Cobham* (JUST 1/359, m. 18d).

93 Below, p. 68.

94 In the early fourteenth century it was apparently believed that the prohibition on the commission of waste by lessees, unless they had specific prior authority for doing this, was a common law rule, not a statutory one: see Bereford's rhetorical question in BL MS. Harley 25, fol. 196r (report of a covenant case of 1304: *Robert Turgys and Willelma v. John de la Rokele of Wymondham*: CP 40/149, m. 257d).

95 Below, pp. 95, 99–101.

Bailiffs

An action of account had also existed since at least the final decade of the twelfth century.[96] Its purpose was to secure the appearance of a bailiff to render his account for the period during which he had managed the property (both lands and movables) of a landowner and to pay any arrears found due once the accounting process had been concluded. Bailiffs would, it seems, normally render such accounts at the end of their period of administering the landowner's property without the landowners having to bring litigation against them. Something had already gone wrong in the relationship if the landowner needed to bring an action against his bailiff for this purpose. Thus the fact that the action is found only comparatively rarely in the king's courts during the first half of the thirteenth century may simply mean that most landowners were able to secure accounts from their bailiffs without the need for royal assistance.[97] It is, in any case, probable that most actions of account during this period were brought in county courts rather than in the king's courts. Thus the action may have been much more common than the evidence of the surviving plea rolls of the king's courts would by itself appear to suggest.[98]

It is thus again the almost total absence of material to shed light on the activities of county courts during this period that makes it impossible to gauge just how widespread a problem it was that clause 19 of the Provisions of Westminster was intended to redress.[99] The clause was concerned with absconding bailiffs whom the normal processes of the courts would not reach because they had no significant land holdings. It authorised the use of 'attachment by the body' (in effect, arrest and imprisonment) as a way of securing their appearance in court and it was probably from the first intended that this be used as the very first stage in the process in such cases.[100] It is conceivable that the legislation was

[96] For the earliest plea roll reference to the action of account see *Memoranda Roll 10 John etc.*, ed. R. Allen Brown (Pipe Roll Society new series vol. 31, 1957), p. 105 (1198) and for a still earlier Pipe Roll reference to an action of account see *The Great Roll of the Pipe for the thirty-first year of the reign of King Henry the Second, AD 1184–1185* (Pipe Roll Society original series vol. 34, 1913), p. 17.

[97] For other early cases see *Ranulph clerk of the archbishop of Canterbury v. Ralph son of Anketil* (*CRR*, I, 191, 249) (1200); *Sampson de Pomeroy v. William of Upton* (*CRR*, IV, 64, 145) (1206); *John of Stowe v. Hubert son of William son of Gery* (*CRR*, XII, no. 605) (1225); *Theobald Hautein v. John of Preston* (*CRR*, XIV, nos. 930, 1442, 2004) (1230–2).

[98] The earliest register of writs in which the writ of account appears (CB) gives only a non-returnable form for initiating litigation in the county court: Maitland, *Collected Papers*, II, 146 (CB 83).

[99] The only draft version of this clause is in clause 17 of the penultimate French version of the Provisions (Brand, *MCL*, p. 365) and this is virtually identical. The Petition of the Barons does not mention the matter.

[100] For the text see Appendix I: below, pp. 424–5. That this was probably intended to be used as the initial process is clear only from the sequel: below, pp. 117–19.

dealing with a common problem, that many bailiffs were indeed landless and did abscond at the end of their period of office before they had rendered an account. It is, however, equally possible that the legislation did not deal with a widespread problem but was prompted by just one or two recent instances of landless bailiffs absconding without rendering an account and that it was those instances alone which prompted this general legislation.

There is no mistaking, however, just how drastic the solution proposed was. The normal mesne process in personal actions like the action of account did not involve any measure nearly as severe an infringement of the personal liberty of the defendant as 'attachment by the body' and started with nothing more threatening than a summons.[101] The only action in which 'attachment by the body' seems regularly to have been used prior to 1259 as the first stage in securing the appearance of a defendant was the appeal of homicide.[102] The absconding bailiff was now being equated with a defendant accused of one of the most serious criminal offences. The drastic nature of the process now being made available to landowners against their bailiffs is perhaps partly explicable in terms of the social differential which normally existed between lords and their bailiffs and the large sums of money which might be involved in such cases.

Socage guardians

The general rule about the wardship rights associated with lands and other property held by socage tenure, land for which the only service owed was a rent in money or in kind, as it is stated both by *Glanvill*[103] and by *Bracton*,[104] was that both the person and the land of a tenant in socage who was under age were in the wardship of the nearest relation of the tenant, whether male or female, who was incapable of inheriting that land. Thus in the most common case, where lands descended to such a tenant from his father, the wardship of both his person and his lands would go to his mother. If she was already dead, they went instead to her next of kin. If the lands descended from his mother, and his father was still living, he would be entitled to hold them for life, but as curtesy tenant rather than guardian. If the father was dead, the wardship would go to the nearest paternal relation. Local custom seems sometimes, however,

[101] For this process see Brand, 'Contribution', pp. 309–13.

[102] *Bracton*, fol. 149 (II, 420); *Early Registers*, pp. 12, 24 (Hib. 34, CA 23). For examples of the use of this process see KB 26/173, m. 25 (Trinity term 1263); KB 26/196, m. 2 (Hilary term 1270); KB 26/202, m. 8 (Easter term 1271).

[103] *Glanvill*, vii, 11 (pp. 84–5).

[104] *Bracton*, fol. 87b (II, 254).

to have allowed the dying socage tenant to treat that wardship as among the chattels available for his disposal and thus to bequeath the wardship of child and land by will to whomsoever he liked.[105] Local custom (or, more precisely, the custom of certain lordships) also sometimes gave the wardship even of socage tenants and their lands to the lord of the fee of whom the land was held.[106] *Brevia Placitata* suggests that socage wardships might also on occasion have been the subject of grants by seignorial courts.[107]

Where the wardship went to the non-inheriting next of kin, and perhaps also where it was left by will, it seems to have been the general assumption that the 'guardian' held the land and exercised his rights over the person of the heir only as a trustee, as someone bound to act in the best interests of his ward. In some areas that trust was enforced by allowing the heir when he came of age to require the guardian to account for his management. During Bigod's visit to Kent early in 1259 he was told that local gavelkind custom gave wardship of the heir's land and person to the closest relation incapable of inheriting the land 'to manage it to the heir's profit and to answer for the profits of the land to the heir when he came of age'.[108] In the city of London, too, city custom, as explained to the justices in the eyre of 1244, was that, whether the guardianship had been bequeathed by will or whether it had fallen by intestacy to the next of kin incapable of inheriting the heir's land, the guardian was held responsible 'to the heir when he came of age for all the profits of

[105] *William son of Walter v. William de Huntercombe* (KB 26/148, m. 13: Berkshire 1253); *Alice wife of Philip son of Richard le Constable v. Richard Manyword* (JUST 1/300C, m. 3: 1256 Herefordshire eyre). For an assize of mort d'ancestor in the 1231 Yorkshire eyre in which a lord tried unsuccessfully to plead that he had been bequeathed the wardship of socage land and a socage heir by the tenant, who was also a relation of his, 'that he might be raised better in his custody than in any other's' ('ut melius nutritetur in custodia sua quam in alia') see *John son of Robert son of Peter v. Saer of Sutton*: JUST 1/1042 m. 14d. For evidence of the disposal of a gavelkind wardship in Kent by will (though it is not entirely clear whether this is a wardship already in existence or one just coming into existence) see *Roger of Tylmanston et al. (executors of Malemeins) v. Stephen of Penchester et al.*: KB 27/24, m. 29. London tenants also had the power to leave the wardship of their lands by will: *The London Eyre of 1244*, ed H.M. Chew and M. Weinbaum (London Record Society vol. 6, 1970), p. 74.

[106] (i) The bishopric of Hereford: *CRR*, XI, nos. 1436 (= *BNB*, pl. 990), 2191; (ii) the bishopric of Winchester: *Bracton*, fol. 88 (II, 225); (iii) the bishopric of Durham (though this was contested in a series of cases): see KB 26/142 m. 28 (1250); KB 26/171, m. 78d (1261); JUST 1/1194, m. 3d (1265); (iv) the barony of Roger de Mortimer: KB 26/169 m. 10 (1260).

[107] *Brevia Placitata*, pp. 135, 220.

[108] '... ad appruandum et ad respondendum de exitibus ejusdem terre predicto heredi cum ad etatem pervenerit': JUST 1/873 m. 23 (a presentment from the hundred of Middleton about the exaction of heavy fines by sheriffs to allow such tenants to succeed); cf. JUST 1/873, m. 18d: a complaint of fines exacted for wardship of gavelkind lands by the bailiffs of William de Say 'although no wardship belongs to the profit of the lords of fees, only to the profit of the heir' ('nulla custodia pertinet ad opus dominorum feodorum nisi tantum ad comodum heredis').

the inheritance'.[109] What, however, did not exist before 1259 was any general common law rule enforcing that responsibility or any form of action, either in the county court or in the king's courts, to facilitate its enforcement.

There was no demand for the enforcement of the accountability of such guardians in the Petition of the Barons. Nor is there any early draft of legislation on this subject among the draft clauses produced for the Candlemas (February) parliament of 1259 or published in the *Providencia Baronum* of March 1259. It is, however, clear that legislation on this subject was already under contemplation by the time of the Candlemas parliament for it is one of the subjects on which the king's council promised legislation by the following All Saints' Day in the letters patent they sealed during the course of that parliament.[110] How legislation on socage wardships came to be taken up by the reformers is not entirely clear. It may have arisen during the course of discussion of clause 1 of the Petition. Discussion of the abuse of the lord's rights at succession could easily have led on to a discussion of the abuse by others of their rights and to a realisation that heirs to tenements held in socage were also badly protected by the common law against abuses committed by their guardians. An alternative, but related, possibility is that it was the specific raising of the topic of waste and demonstration of the existence of one area where the common law offered inadequate protection against this that led on to a more general consideration of the topic and to other kinds of situation where landowners were currently unprotected against waste. Thus the legislation may have started specifically as legislation against the commission of waste by socage guardians and only in the course of discussion have been broadened to legislation that enforced more generally the accountability of socage guardians. This would explain why the legislation as eventually enacted specifically prohibits waste first and only then goes on to stipulate the accountability of guardians in socage, though the latter might be thought to be an adequate mechanism in itself to prevent waste without the need for a separate, specific prohibition. A third possibility is that the need for legislation on this subject was first suggested by complaints made to the justiciar, Hugh Bigod, during his visit to Kent in January 1259. Gavelkind tenants were the largest and most concentrated group of socage tenants in any county in England. However, Kent custom, as has been seen, seems to have required socage guardians to account even prior to 1259,[111] and the plea roll which records complaints made to Bigod during this visit contains only complaints against the usurpation of such wardships by the lords of the tenements to the exclusion of the next

[109] *London Eyre of 1244*, p. 74. [110] Above, p. 31. [111] Above, p. 67, note 108.

of kin, and nothing of abuses by the next of kin themselves.[112] Bigod may none the less have picked up the idea of accountability of socage guardians from his visit to Kent and then suggested to his fellow members of the king's council that it might be a good idea to make this a general rule applicable to all guardians in socage.

The earliest draft version of the legislation on socage guardians and their responsibilities is that contained in clause 11 of the penultimate, French draft version of the Provisions of Westminster produced for the Michaelmas parliament of 1259.[113] This provides that when land held in socage is in the wardship of the next of kin of the heir the guardian is to commit no waste but to take good care of the land on behalf of the heir. It goes on to stipulate that such a guardian is to account for the profits of the land, less his expenses, to the heir when he comes of age. A second sub-clause concerns the socage guardian's wardship of the person of the heir and stipulates that he or she is likewise to be accountable to the heir for the exercise of this right through the giving or selling of the right of marriage over the heir. Clause 12 of the Provisions of Westminster as eventually enacted was no more than a translation of the draft clause into Latin without significant alteration.[114]

REFORMS INTENDED TO IMPROVE THE PROCEDURES OF THE KING'S CENTRAL COURTS

A third set of reforms were intended simply to improve the workings of the king's courts, to make royal justice work better. Although they do not specifically say so, they were primarily concerned with improving the procedures of the main royal court for the hearing of civil cases, the Common Bench at Westminster.

Authorising shorter adjournments in certain types of case

Since the later twelfth century, when the Common Bench had finally achieved its institutional independence from its parent body, the Exchequer, it had normally held sessions for business during four terms each year, though up to 1249 those sessions might be suspended for one or more terms during major eyre visitations. These terms were not of an equal length. Michaelmas term in the autumn was always significantly longer than the other three. While two of the terms (Hilary and Michaelmas) always began on the same day, the beginning of the others

[112] E.g. JUST 1/873, mm. 16, 18d, 22d, 23. [113] Brand, *MCL*, p. 364.

[114] For the text see Appendix I: below, pp. 422–3.

(Easter and Trinity) was determined by movable feast days and thus changed from year to year. Trinity term was also of variable length. The court did not attempt to assign separate business to each individual day within these terms. Instead litigants and others involved in litigation were told or required to appear on specific 'return days',[115] which occurred at roughly weekly intervals within the term.[116] Sheriffs were similarly instructed to return the original or judicial writs which had ordered them to summon or employ mesne process against litigants or others with their report on what they had done on the appropriate 'return day'. If all the requisite parties appeared, a case might be heard on the first day of the actual 'return day', though, given the pressure of business, they might have to wait several days before their case could be heard and (by the 1270s at least) might even have to wait until some time the following week.[117] If not all the parties appeared the party who was present would normally have to make an appearance not just on the return day itself but also on the two succeeding days before he could obtain a judgment of the court on the fourth day, holding that the other party had defaulted and authorising the next stage in mesne process against him.[118] The court's records also reflect this division of its business into return days. The headings on the plea rolls assign cases not to particular days, but to return days within each term, and when writ-files of writs returned into the court begin to survive they too are divided into bundles assigned to particular return days. Well before 1259 even final concords recording formal agreements made in the court begin to be dated by 'return days' rather than individual days within the term.

At each stage in the process of litigation, whether during one of the preliminary stages before the defendant had appeared, when the main concern was with securing his appearance, or during a later stage, when both parties had appeared in court and the case had been adjourned to allow the disputed property to be viewed or to secure the appearance of a vouchee or a coheir of one of the parties or the appearance of a jury, the justices would adjourn the litigation to a subsequent return day. This ceased only when the court had rendered final judgment in the case or had decided that there was nothing further that could be done for the present (as where one of the parties was a minor) where the case would go literally *sine die* ('without a day'). By the middle of the thirteenth

[115] Generally the day after a feast day or a day described as being one, two, three or four weeks after a feast day.

[116] *SCKB*, II, lxxviii–lxxx.

[117] This is clearly implied by the Statute of Westminster I, chapter 46 (*SR*, I, 38).

[118] A similar procedure was also followed when a party sent an essoiner to excuse his absence.

century, a system was in place under which most cases which were heard on one return day and had not been dismissed *sine die* were adjourned to the same return day eight return days later.[119] This system of regular adjournments corresponds closely to that described for the Common Bench in the table of 'Common days in the Bench' ('dies communes in banco') found in the statute books of the later thirteenth and early fourteenth century.[120]

The system was evidently flexible and allowed some discretion to the justices of the Common Bench to make shorter adjournments in particular cases if they thought it desirable. The only absolute limitation as to the minimum interval between stages was that this could never be less than two weeks.[121] This is clearly the assumption, for example, behind clause 23 of the Provisions of Westminster which states that a warrantor living outside the county in which an eyre was being held was to be allowed a 'reasonable summons of at least fifteen days according to the discretion of the justices and the common law'.[122] During the years prior to 1259 the justices had used their discretion in a fairly systematic way to favour litigants who were bringing actions (whether by the assize of darrein presentment or by the writ of *quare impedit*) to assert a right to present their candidate to a vacant ecclesiastical living, though the shorter adjournments given were not uniform.[123] The need for speed in such cases was obvious. If a church remained vacant for longer than six months the bishop was entitled under canon law to collate his own candidate to the

[119] Detailed figures on adjournments in 1249–50 will be found in Brand, 'Contribution', p. 297.

[120] For a printed text see *SR*, I, 208. A slightly different version is to be found in *Fleta*, lib. 2, cap. 35 (II, 137).

[121] Only in the eyre and where both parties lived in the county where the eyre was being held was a shorter adjournment permissible. The two week minimum rule for a summons outside the county is mentioned in the *Leges Henrici Primi*, ed. L.J. Downer (Oxford, 1972), 41, 2a (p. 146). This envisaged a three-week interval where the county was not the neighbouring county but next to a neighbouring county, and a maximum of a month.

[122] Below, pp. 426–7. See also the challenge of a defendant in a 1272 case to the brevity of an adjournment from the octaves of Trinity (27 June) to the quindene of St. John Baptist (9 July) as it contained less than two weeks: KB 26/208A, m. 1.

[123] In Trinity term 1239 intervals of between two and five return days were the norm in *quare impedit* (*CRR*, XV, nos. 743, 748, 1088), a full eight return-day adjournment being found only in a single case adjourned at the request of the parties ('prece parcium') (*CRR*, XV, no. 725). In darrein presentment cases in the same term no adjournment was to a return day more than four return days away (*CRR*, XV, nos. 567, 681, 812). In Michaelmas term 1251 adjournments of three return days were the rule both in darrein presentment (KB 26/145, mm. 12d (by the kings' order), 32d) and in *quare impedit* (KB 26/145, mm. 32d, 49 bis.) In Michaelmas term 1258 and Hilary term 1259, the three adjournments in darrein presentment were all to return days three days away or fewer (KB 26/160, m. 8d; KB 26/162, mm. 4, 41) and of thirteen adjournments in *quare impedit* only three were to return days more than four days away (KB 26/160, mm. 22d, 23d (eight return days), KB 26/162, m. 10 (seven return days)). For the adjournments of four return days or fewer see KB 26/160, mm. 17d, 30d, 40d bis; KB 26/162, mm. 4, 8, 29, 30, 35d.

vacant benefice,[124] and a litigant who was successful after the six months had elapsed would at most recover damages,[125] and the right to re-present the rector who had been collated by the bishop.[126] No other category of case, however, seems to have benefited from a similar regular use of judicial discretion.

Clause 7 of the draft legislation prepared for the Candlemas (February) parliament of 1259 proposed legislative confirmation of the existing practice of giving shorter adjournments in cases about vacant churches and setting a norm of adjournments to a return day three days distant.[127] It also proposed a similar treatment for another whole category of cases. These were where a widow was claiming that she had been assigned none of her dower (the action of dower *unde nichil habet*). There had long existed a strong sentiment in favour of the quick settlement of claims made by widows to their dower. Clause 7 of the first issue of Magna Carta in 1215 had laid down that widows ought to be assigned their dower within forty days of their husband's death,[128] and the same timescale was retained in the later versions of this chapter when it was extensively redrafted for the reissues of 1216 and 1217.[129] This was of course impracticable where the doweress was forced to bring litigation to secure her dower but clearly, if it was felt that she should have been assigned her dower within forty days, it followed that any litigation she had to bring should also be resolved as soon as possible. The strength of her entitlement to an immediate dower share at least of the lands of which her husband had died seised was further recognised by clause 1 of the Provisions of Merton of 1236 which provided that, if the widow had to bring litigation to recover her dower share of these lands, she was to be entitled also to damages in respect of these lands for the whole of the period since her husband's death.[130]

There was no significant alteration to this clause in the published Latin version of this draft legislation, the *Providencia Baronum*,[131] but the clause had been considerably altered by the time the penultimate French text of the Provisions of Westminster was prepared for the Michaelmas parliament of 1259. Clause 7 of this draft made separate provision for the treatment of litigation relating to vacant churches and the widow's action of dower *unde nichil habet*.[132] In the former it was now

[124] For an interesting dispute over the computation of the six months see *Eleanor the Queen Mother (as guardian of Henry de Percy) v. Richard bishop of Lincoln*: CP 40/21, m. 100 (Michaelmas term 1277).

[125] And that only if he brought *quare impedit*, until 1285, when the Statute of Westminster II, chapter 5, authorised the awarding of damages in darrein presentment as well (*SR*, I, 75).

[126] J.W. Gray, 'The Ius Praesentandi in England from the Constitutions of Clarendon to Bracton', *English Historical Review* 67 (1952), 481–509 at 494.

[127] Brand, *MCL*, p. 360.

[128] *SSC*, p. 294.

[129] *SSC*, pp. 337, 341.

[130] *SR*, I, 1.

[131] Jacob, *Studies*, p. 368.

[132] Brand, *MCL*, p. 363.

envisaged that adjournments of as little as two weeks (normally two return days) might be given provided the county concerned was close, but three weeks was retained for more distant counties. Such speed was clearly not thought to be practicable in dower cases. What was now proposed for them was that adjournments be made so as to allow the case to come up for hearing at least four times in a year and never allowing the case to be adjourned beyond the end of the immediately following term. The effect was to lengthen the average interval between hearings in dower cases from the maximum of three return days previously envisaged to a maximum of rather over five return days. As thus amended the legislation passed into law as clauses 6 and 7 of the Provisions of Westminster.[133]

The abbreviation of process and introduction of judgment by default in actions of quare impedit

The same perceived need for a swift disposition in litigation about vacant churches also lay behind two other procedural reforms enacted in 1259. With darrein presentment there was no major problem. If the defendant did not appear in answer to the initial summons, he was resummoned. If he did not appear in answer to the second summons the assize simply proceeded in his absence. The difficulty was with the parallel action of *quare impedit*. This action had to be used if the plaintiff was claiming the right of presentation on the basis of any title other than his own previous presentation to the church or that of one of his ancestors. Mesne process in this action (as in other personal actions) had come by 1259 to consist of no fewer than six different stages (initial summons, first attachment, second attachment, simple distraint, distraint *ita etc., donec etc.* and the grand distress) which represented a gradual escalation of pressure on the defendant to put in an appearance.[134] Assuming the case was not subject to additional delays as a result of the failure of the sheriff or the bailiffs of a liberty to execute one of the stages or by essoins, it would take the plaintiff about two years to reach the final and most compelling stage of mesne process (the grand distress), much longer than the six months which were all that needed to elapse before the bishop gained his right of collation. Some defendants did not appear even then and there was no provision in this or in other personal actions for the case to proceed in

[133] For the text see Appendix I: below, pp. 418–19. The legislation as enacted lacked the explanatory clause indicating that the four adjournments a year were intended to ensure that dower cases came up for a hearing once every term.

[134] Brand, 'Contribution', pp. 309–13.

the absence of the defendant, however contumacious, or for judgment to be given against them on the basis of their default.[135]

Some curtailment of the normal mesne process had once been customary in *quare impedit* cases. It can be seen in such cases during the 1230s,[136] and is also mentioned as customary in *Bracton*.[137] However, the practice had subsequently ceased even though the court had continued to shorten the length of the adjournments between the stages.[138] It was therefore a restoration of previous practice and a placing of that practice on a statutory basis that was being proposed when clause 7 of the penultimate French text of the Provisions of Westminster, prepared for the Michaelmas parliament of 1259, suggested the reduction of mesne process to just three stages (summons, attachment and grand distress).[139] This was evidently an improvement which had suggested itself to the drafters only during the course of drafting, for the sub-clause proposing this change is one attached to the proposed legislation giving briefer adjournments in litigation about vacant churches and actions of dower *unde nichil habet*. It had not formed part of the earlier version of that same clause discussed in the Candlemas parliament of 1259. Evidently the proposal was approved as the reduced mesne process in *quare impedit* formed part of clause 7 of the Provisions of Westminster as promulgated at the end of October 1259.[140] At a still later stage in the drafting process, however (between the drafting of the penultimate version of the Provisions and the drafting of the final published text), a further significant amendment was made to the text. This allowed judgment to be given by default against the defendant in *quare impedit* if he failed to appear after the grand distress had been used against him. As with the analogous employment of judgment by default in the new tenant's action against his lord when distrained for suit of court, such a judgment was to be without prejudice to any subsequent proceedings between the parties.[141] It was thus very different from the kind of judgment by default given in the related assize of darrein presentment which (as with similar judgments in other kinds of petty assize) merely allowed the assize jury to give its verdict in the defendant's absence and was not simply an automatic judgment in the plaintiff's favour. It is also easy to see why the reformers decided to authorise such judgments. The requirement of a speedy disposition of litigation involving vacant churches logically dictated such a move. There may also have been some

[135] The author of *Bracton* had proposed allowing judgment to be given by default in personal actions but the procedures he suggested were very different from those adopted in 1259 and seem unlikely to have influenced them: *Bracton*, fol. 440b (IV, 368).

[136] For examples see *CRR*, XV, nos. 8, 198, 236.

[137] *Bracton*, fols. 247–247b (III, 231).

[138] Above, p. 71.

[139] Brand, *MCL*, p. 363.

[140] For the text see Appendix I: below, pp. 418–19.

[141] Above, p. 52.

limited past precedent for judgment by default in *quare impedit*. In 1236 the court *coram rege* had reviewed the judgment given by the Common Bench in a *quare impedit* case. The lower court had given judgment by default after a defendant had made a single default after an initial essoin. The court *coram rege* had reversed the judgment of the lower court on the grounds that the decision had been 'against the law and customs of the realm'. The stated reason for this was not that judgment by default was unavailable in the action but rather 'because many distraints should have followed before Thomas had recovered by default, that is attachment by plevin and then by better pledges and then attachment by the body'.[142] No example of such a judgment by default has, however, been traced on the plea rolls.

Authorising the overriding of charters of exemption from jury service

Legislation was also needed in 1259 to deal with the problem created by Henry III's charters granting exemption from jury service. The Patent Rolls suggest that such exemptions only came to be granted on a large scale during the 1250s. They were not a particular problem when the recipient was an ordinary free man, for however lavish they may have been, there were always enough free men to serve on juries. They were a problem when the recipient was a knight since twelve knights who were not subject to challenge for being related or otherwise connected to either of the litigants were normally required for the grand assize whether it was concerned with title to land or an advowson or about disputed services,[143] or for making a perambulation of disputed boundaries between two villages.[144] In theory at least, twenty-four such knights were required for attaints, to reverse the verdict of one of the petty assizes.[145] They were a particular problem in those counties, generally the smaller ones, which only possessed a small number of knights in the first place.

Ad hoc solutions to this problem had certainly been used prior to 1259. In a Rutland case heard in the 1247 Buckinghamshire eyre the parties agreed in advance to the election of a panel of eight knights and eight free

[142] *BNB*, pl. 1166. [143] *Early Registers*, p. 321 (J 52).

[144] *Early Registers*, pp. 74–5 (CC 138). For evidence that it was still normal procedure to require the use of twelve proper belted knights in such cases in 1278, but that alternative arrangements could be made if a county did not have that many see CP 40/24, m. 19.

[145] *Early Registers*, pp. 9, 31, 86, 90 (Hib. 22; CA 50; CC 175, 182). But for acceptance of attaint juries of which only some members were 'belted' knights in 1279 and 1288 see CP 40/31, m. 66d and CP 40/75, m. 8. Ingram of Oldcotes served on a Nottinghamshire attaint jury in 1257, some fifteen years before his ill-fated attempt to secure knighthood at the hands of Roger d'Arcy: see Paul Brand, 'Oldcotes v. d'Arcy' in *Medieval Legal Records edited in Memory of C.A.F. Meekings*, ed. R.F. Hunnisett and J.B. Post (London, 1978), pp. 63–118 at p. 67.

men to serve on a jury 'in the manner of the grand assize' ('ad modum magne assise').[146] Rutland was, however, so small that it is not clear that its problem necessarily had anything to do with the king's granting of exemptions from jury service. Two entries on the Close Rolls on 13 January 1253 do specifically link the difficulties in producing sufficient knights to act on grand assizes concerning land in Middlesex and in Staffordshire with the king's granting of exemptions from jury service.[147] The solution adopted in these two cases was to allow knights from neighbouring counties to be added to make up the numbers. Lancashire seems also to have had problems with the number of knights, though again it is unclear whether they were specifically connected with the king's granting of acquittances. In 1255 its sheriff was ordered to make up the numbers for a perambulation in his county from free tenants belonging to the county.[148]

The effect of the king's exemptions from jury service on the ability of certain counties to provide a sufficient number of suitable knights to serve on grand assizes was the subject of complaint in clause 28 of the Petition of the Barons in 1258.[149] A proposal to allow the overriding of such charters in the case of grand assize juries was one of the clauses (clause 8) included in the first draft legislation produced for the Candlemas parliament of 1259.[150] In the course of discussion at the parliament the proposal was amended to extend the possibility of overriding such charters to 'other' (unspecified) 'assizes' where justice could not be done without their participation.[151] By the time the penultimate version of the Provisions was produced for the Michaelmas parliament of 1259 the categories of situation where such charters could be overridden had been considerably extended. They now covered perambulations, attaints and juries where the jury was required to pass a verdict on charters or deeds to which they had been witnesses, where it was normal practice to include all the surviving witnesses with the normal twelve men on the jury, plus other (unspecified) cases where knights were needed for verdict.[152] It was as thus amended that the provision became law as clause 8 of the Provisions of Westminster.[153] The reformers seem also to have been able to secure the almost total discontinuation of the practice of the granting of such charters by the king.[154]

[146] JUST 1/56, m. 34d. [147] *CR 1251–1253*, pp. 442–3. [148] *CR 1254–1256*, p. 162.

[149] *DBM*, pp. 88–9. This clause is not included in the Darley text of the Petition: Brand, *MCL*, pp. 328, 355.

[150] Brand, *MCL*, p. 360. [151] Jacob, *Studies*, p. 368. [152] Brand, *MCL*, p. 364.

[153] For the text see Appendix I: below, pp. 420–1.

[154] Treharne, *Baronial Plan*, p. 174, note 2. Since such grants were made only for life or shorter periods if the discontinuation had continued this would by itself have eventually solved the problem.

Chapter 3

THE MAKING OF THE PROVISIONS OF WESTMINSTER: THE SOCIAL AND LEGAL CONTEXT AND THE EVOLUTION OF THE INDIVIDUAL CLAUSES: II

REFORMS INTENDED TO REDRESS GRIEVANCES ABOUT THE WORKINGS OF THE CRIMINAL JUSTICE SYSTEM

Several clauses of the Provisions were concerned with the workings of the English criminal justice system. These were not intended to produce major changes either in the general principles of the criminal law or in the overall framework of the administration of criminal justice. Their purpose was a much more limited one: to redress a number of grievances about the details of its operation. They were primarily concerned with financial penalties imposed by the justices in eyre during their visitations of counties or by sheriffs and their subordinates when they visited individual hundreds for the biennial sheriff's tourn. Both types of penalty benefited the king and the reforms were therefore ones which potentially at least reduced the king's profits from criminal justice.

The murdrum *fine*

The *murdrum* fine was a collective fine payable whenever the body of a murdered person was discovered, unless the murderer was identified and produced for justice or it could be shown that the victim was of English origin. These characteristics make it plain that its original purpose was to safeguard the lives of a non-English minority facing a hostile native population. It may go back to the period of Danish rule under Cnut and have been originally intended to ensure the safety of Cnut's Danish followers. The alternative possibility is that it was invented shortly after the Norman Conquest and was aimed at preserving the lives of the Conqueror's French followers.[1] Although twelfth-century traditions

[1] The classic discussion of the *murdrum* fine is that of F.C. Hamil, 'The Presentment of Englishry and the Murder Fine', *Speculum* 12 (1937), 285–98. Bruce O'Brien argues that the fine had originated under Cnut but had been revived by the Conqueror: 'From *Mordor* to *Murdrum*: the Preconquest Origin and Norman Revival of the Murder Fine', *Speculum* 71 (1996), 321–57.

asserted that initially the fine had been paid by the village where the body had been found or by the lord of the victim, the normal practice from an early date seems to have been for it to be paid by the hundred within which the body was found. During the twelfth century it was the practice for any liberties within such a hundred to be exempted from paying their share of the fine assessed against the hundred as a whole. At the end of the twelfth century liberties ceased to share even nominal responsibility for any fine paid by the hundred within which they were situated but became liable for a separate fine if a victim's body was found in their own area.[2] The fine seems originally to have been fixed at the substantial sum of forty-six marks, of which forty marks went to the king and six to the relatives of the victim. By 1130 it had ceased to be levied at a fixed rate and was being assessed at amounts that varied between a low of seven marks and a high of twenty.[3] By the end of the twelfth century the amount of the fine assessed against any particular hundred was evidently related not to the number of bodies found within that hundred since the last eyre for which the fine was payable, but solely to the hundred's ability to pay.[4] Nor, by this date, did anyone other than the king receive any share of it. By the middle of the thirteenth century, many of the clerks writing crown pleas rolls recorded no more than a single judgment of *murdrum* against any one hundred or liberty during each visitation. There was no point to them doing more since the number of such judgments made no difference to the amount of the fine.[5]

Certain counties in the north and the west of England seem never to have paid *murdrum* fines.[6] Some towns seem also to have escaped liability for its payment.[7] In those counties and places where it was paid there were two ways of avoiding it. One is well attested by the legal treatises but much less evident in the plea rolls. This was by the capture and conviction of the murderer, or, since the fine was primarily aimed at his detection, by his confession and abjuration of the realm.[8] The other was by proving that the dead man had been English. By the thirteenth century this seems to have involved proving not that he was English by racial origin, but simply that he was of servile birth.[9] This was proved

[2] Meekings, *Crown Pleas*, p. 62.

[3] *Dialogus de Scaccario*, ed. A. Hughes, C.G. Crump and C. Johnson (Oxford, 1902), p. 194.

[4] Hamil, 'Murder Fine', 290.

[5] Meekings, *Crown Pleas*, p. 63.

[6] The counties of Cheshire, Shropshire, Lancashire, Yorkshire, Northumberland, Cumberland, Westmorland and Durham: Hamil, 'Murder Fine', 290.

[7] E.g. London: see *Year Book of the Eyre of London, 14 Edward II (AD 1321)*, ed. H.M. Cam (2 vols., Selden Society vols. 85–6, 1968–9), I, 31, 33, 38; Cambridge: JUST 1/82 m. 3d (Cambridgeshire eyre 1261); King's Lynn and Norwich: JUST 1/565 mm. 35, 35d (Norfolk eyre 1250).

[8] Hamil, 'Murder Fine', 295.

[9] *Dialogus de Scaccario*, pp. 52–3; *Select Cases of Procedure Without Writ under Henry III*, ed. H.G. Richardson and G.O. Sayles (Selden Society vol. 60, 1941), p. ccii: 'Anglecheria, ut dicunt quidam,

by a 'presentment of Englishry' made by a number of the dead man's relations. The precise number of relatives and the ways in which they had to be related to the deceased varied from county to county. The presentment had normally to be made first at the coroner's inquest on the body of the dead man, then at the next session of the county court, and finally yet again at the eyre.[10] There were variations from county to county not only in the number or relatives who had to present Englishry and their relationship with the deceased but also as to whether or not Englishry had to be presented or, in its default, *murdrum* paid, for women as well as for men,[11] and for children as well as adults.[12] With all these possible variations in custom, it was, as *Bracton* noted, one of the first tasks of the justices on opening the crown pleas session of an eyre to enquire about the county's customs in such matters.[13]

Despite the original purpose of the fine, by 1259 it was regularly being adjudged and levied not just for intentional homicides but also for deaths caused by accident in every single county where the *murdrum* fine was paid for which adequate plea roll evidence survives.[14] In at least two counties it can be shown that this practice was of recent origin.[15] *Bracton* held that the fine was properly payable only in respect of felonious homicides and that its imposition in other cases was an abuse. The author, however, suggests that as yet (at the time he was writing) the abuse was one confined to certain parts of the country.[16] Just how the *murdrum* fine came to be adjudged and levied for accidental deaths is unclear. It is possible that the onus of proof that a death was accidental originally rested on

proprie dicitur de vilano, murdrum de libero homine'; JUST 2/258 (Pershore coroner's roll of the late 1260s): 'Nulla Engl' quia liber'.

10 R.F. Hunnisett, *The Medieval Coroner* (Cambridge, 1961), p. 27, note 5. Suggestive evidence of the practice followed before the invention of the coroner is provided by the Gloucestershire custom, attested in the eyre of 1248, that the initial presentment had to be made within three days of the finding of the body at the gate of Gloucester castle (JUST 1/274, m. 1).

11 Counties where later evidence shows that Englishry had to be presented for women include Gloucestershire: JUST 1/280, m. 1 (1287); Herefordshire: JUST 1/302, m. 53 (1292); Norfolk: JUST 1/569A, m. 1 (1268); and Suffolk: JUST 1/827, m. 1 (1286).

12 Later evidence indicates that there was no lower age limit in either Herefordshire or Norfolk: JUST 1/302, m. 53 (1292); JUST 1/596A, m. 1 (1268).

13 *Bracton*, fol. 135b (II, 382).

14 For the relevant evidence from twenty-five counties see Brand,'Contribution', p. 250, note 1.

15 No *murdrum* fines were paid for accidental deaths in the Worcestershire eyre of 1221 although several *murdrum* judgments are recorded against each hundred, but they were being paid for such deaths by 1255: *Rolls of the Justices in Eyre for Lincolnshire (1218–1219) and Worcestershire (1221)*, ed. D.M. Stenton (Selden Society vol. 53, 1934), pp. 534–611 *passim*; JUST 1/1022, m. 31. No *murdrum* fines were paid for accidental deaths in the Kent eyres of 1227 and 1241 but they were said to be owed in respect of such deaths by the time of the eyre of 1255: JUST 1/358, m. 16 *et seq.*; JUST 1/359, m. 27 *et seq.*; JUST 1/361, m. 35. There is no surviving roll for the 1248 eyre.

16 *Bracton*, fols. 134b–135 (II, 379–80).

those attempting to escape the fine, in much the same way as there was an onus of proof on those attempting to escape the fine to show that the deceased had been English. It may perhaps have been the case that such a burden could only be discharged by producing the 'bane' of the dead man (the physical object which had caused his death) in court, as was still the practice in Dorset during the first half of the thirteenth century.[17] This would have meant that the fine had always been paid in respect of some accidental deaths and could have opened the way to a more general liability for such deaths. Whatever the precise mechanism it seems clear that it was the justices in eyre who were responsible for its extension. Their motive was presumably to add to the king's profits from the eyre by increasing the number of *murdrum* fines payable, even if later evidence suggests that the actual impact of such a change was relatively small.[18]

The Petition of the Barons did not complain in any general way about the imposition of *murdrum* fines in the case of accidental deaths. Clause 21 of the Petition did, however, focus on some very specific circumstances in which the fine was payable but in which it was considered wholly inappropriate.[19] During the recent famine many paupers, travelling round the country in search of food, had died of hunger outside their own home districts and had thus rendered the areas where they happened to have died liable to the *murdrum* fine.[20] As the clause pointed out, it was almost impossible in such cases for the area to escape the fine since travelling strangers were unknown to local inhabitants and thus no 'presentment of Englishry' could be made in respect of them.

Although the *murdrum* fine had long lost its original purpose, the reformers were not led by their discussion of this clause to any proposal to abolish the fine itself. What they did propose (in clause 22 of the penultimate French draft of the Provisions) was a conservative reform. This would restrict the incidence of the *murdrum* fine in future to those deaths which the fine had originally purported to punish and deter, felonious homicides, and specifically excluded its imposition in the case of accidental homicides.[21] It was also only this relatively restricted change that was enacted into law through clause 22 of the Provisions of Westminster.[22]

[17] JUST 1/201, m. 1 (1244 Dorset eyre). There was also here an exemption for bodies found in saltwater.

[18] Below, pp. 284–5. [19] *DBM*, pp. 84–5.

[20] On the famine see *Matthaei Parisiensis Chronica Majora*, v, 693–4, 701–2 and *CR 1256–1259*, p. 212 (writ of April 1258 to the sheriffs of the eastern counties allowing the burial of paupers dying of starvation as a result of the famine without waiting for a coroner).

[21] Brand, *MCL*, p. 366. [22] For the text see Appendix I: below, pp. 426–7.

Penalisation of villages for failure to attend inquests 'fully'

Two other clauses of the Provisions dealt with abuses whose origins were much more recent. One was the practice of the justices in eyre amercing villages which had attended coroner's inquests for not having attended them 'fully'. The financial penalisation of villages for failure to attend coroner's inquests had been a regular feature of crown pleas business in the eyres since the late twelfth century, but, as Meekings noted, it was 'in the visitation of 1246–9, and especially in the later eyres of this visitation, that it was imposed more extensively than ever before'.[23] It was moreover, as he also noted, only from the late 1240s that the rolls of the justices began to record amercements not just for failure to attend inquests but also for failure to attend them 'fully'.[24] What seems to have been meant by 'full' attendance was the appearance at the inquest of all those who were in tithing in the villages concerned.[25] Earlier custom, in some areas at least, had allowed the representation of villages at such inquests by four men and the reeve of that village.[26] This recent practice was the object of a specific complaint in clause 14 of the Petition of the Barons.[27]

By the time of the Michaelmas parliament of 1259 the initial complaint had led to the drafting of not one, but two, related clauses.[28] Clause 21 proposed legislation that would have prohibited the justices in eyre amercing villages for failing to attend 'fully' inquests not just into homicides but also into any other crown business heard before the coroner.[29] All that was to be required in future was for enough of the villagers to attend

[23] Meekings, *Crown Pleas*, pp. 103–4.

[24] But for evidence that as early as 1237 the sheriff of Surrey had attempted to amerce two villages for precisely this reason see *CR 1237–1242*, p. 78.

[25] Hence the reference to all aged twelve, the age of entering the tithing, in the legislation (below, pp. 424–5). In an entry in the Essex eyre of 1254 the coroners of Colchester are recorded as attesting 'that inquests into homicides ought to be made in this borough by all who are in tithing' ('quod inquisicio de morte hominis debet fieri in burgo isto per omnes qui fuerunt in decenna'): JUST 1/233, m. 58.

[26] For evidence suggesting this see an entry in the Westmorland eyre of 1256 where three villages were amerced because 'they did not come fully to an inquest but only four men and the reeve' ('quia non venerunt plene ad inquisicionem nisi quatuor homines et prepositus') (JUST 1/979, m. 10d) and the presentment made in the 1272 Essex eyre against the the abbot of Stratford for withdrawing one of the four men who used to represent the village of 'Ginge' before the justices and before the coroners at inquests into homicides: 'villata de Ginge solebat venire coram justiciariis et coronatoribus ad inquisiciones de morte hominis faciendum per quatuor homines et prepositum: et abbas de Stratford unum de quatuor hominibus subtraxit jam (blank) annis elapsis': JUST 1/238, m. 60d.

[27] *DBM*, pp. 82–3. For a variant text of the same complaint see Brand, *MCL*, pp. 82–3. The same clause also complained about the beaupleder fine for which see below, pp. 87–90.

[28] Brand, *MCL*, p. 366.

[29] Other inquisitions are rarely mentioned on the plea rolls but when this legislation was re-enacted in 1267 a specific reference was inserted to inquests into robberies and arson: see below, p. 191. For a reference on the plea roll of the 1249 Hampshire eyre to an inquest into treasure-trove

the inquest to allow the inquest to proceed. Villages were to be liable to amercement only if they failed to ensure this. Clause 22 proposed legislation making it clear that only the justices in eyre had power to impose amercements in connexion with attendance at such inquests and spelling out that neither coroners, sheriffs nor other bailiffs had any power to do this. This was intended to reaffirm the existing position at common law.[30] As eventually enacted, the legislation omitted the second of these two clauses, perhaps precisely because it came to be seen as an unnecessary restatement of an existing rule. It did, however, give legislative force, in clause 21 of the Provisions, and with only one minor amendment, to the first clause.[31]

Penalisation of the sureties of clerics claiming benefit of clergy

A second recent 'abuse' was the practice of amercing the sureties or mainpernors of a cleric who had been arrested on a criminal charge and then bailed on condition that he appear at the eyre if he subsequently refused to answer the charges against him by claiming benefit of clergy. The purported rationale for imposing this amercement was that the sureties had stood surety that the cleric would 'stand to right' at the eyre but that, by pleading his clergy, the clerk was now refusing to do so. The amercement of sureties on this pretext seems to have been unknown before 1249 but it is recorded on the plea rolls of most eyres from the Devon eyre of 1249 onwards.[32] It is just possible that the intention was to bring pressure on clerks to answer for criminal offences in lay courts. It seems more likely, however, that the amercements were no more than an excuse for penalising those who had entered into the obligation of standing surety in the understanding (as the penultimate French version of the Provisions puts it) that they were sureties only for the clerk's appearance and not that he would answer in the lay court.[33] This abuse is not one specifically mentioned in the Petition of the Barons, though it may well have been one of the abuses of which the authors of clause 14 were thinking when

which led to three of the villages attending the inquest being amerced 'because they did not attend fully' see JUST 1/776, m. 25d.

30 For evidence that this had been the previous practice see the 1238 mandate to the sheriff of Surrey: *CR 1237–1242*, p. 78.

31 For the text see Appendix I: below, pp. 424–5. The amendment was to insert a reference to the possibility of an inquest on a plea of the crown taking place before the sheriff as well before the coroners.

32 For examples see JUST 1/176, m. 27d (1249 Devon eyre); JUST 1/564, m. 22 (1250 Norfolk eyre); JUST 1/615, mm. 6d, 11d (1253 Northamptonshire eyre); JUST 1/233, m. 4d (1254 Essex eyre); JUST 1/778, mm. 45d, 48d, 61 (1256 Hampshire. eyre); JUST 1/568, mm. 1, 4 (1257 Norfolk eyre).

33 Brand, *MCL*, p. 367.

they complained 'of several other abuses in connexion with pleas of the crown' ('de aliis pluribus occasionibus de placitis corone').[34] The earliest draft version of the clause to survive is that contained in the penultimate French version of the Provisions of Westminster. Clause 25 of that version carefully explains the context of the amercement. It had arisen where a cleric who was accused of homicide, robbery, theft or some other offence and was bailed, whether by the king's order or otherwise, appeared at the eyre on the opening day of the session but refused to answer there. The proposed legislation was simply intended to prohibit such amercements for the future. It also supplied the justification for doing this. The sureties were only sureties for the cleric's appearance in court and had not undertaken to ensure that he would answer when he did appear. Clause 24 of the Provisions as enacted turned the proposed clause into actual legislation. The main difference was that it omitted any justification for the change.[35]

Attendance at the sheriff's tourn

The sheriff's tourn was a twice-yearly plenary session of the hundred court, generally held once after Easter and once after Michaelmas.[36] To it were summoned not only the regular suitors of the hundred court but also all other free men resident within the hundred and the heads of the tithings, and possibly also (at least in theory) the individual members of each tithing as well. The purpose of these sessions was for the sheriff or his deputy to check on the working of the frankpledge system and to enquire into breaches of the king's peace within the hundred through the articles of the tourn. Thus the sheriff's tourn formed the lowest and most localised part of the criminal justice system. Evidence from a slightly later period indicates the employment of a system of double presentment at these sessions. The chief pledges at the head of each tithing gave their answers to the articles of the tourn. These were then supplemented, confirmed or contradicted by a second jury of twelve free men.[37]

The Petition of the Barons of 1258 included two clauses relating to demands made by sheriffs for attendance at the tourn. Clause 17 alleged that sheriffs were demanding the personal attendance of earls and barons at the tourn even though they held lands in many different places and counties and so could not appear at all of them. It also complained that

[34] *DBM*, pp. 82–3.

[35] For the text see Appendix I: below, pp. 426–7. It was only the final text, however, that explained the cleric's failure to answer as being the result of the invocation of clerical privilege.

[36] On the tourn generally see *Select Pleas*, I, pp. xxvii–xxxviii; *P&M*, I, 558–60.

[37] *Fleta*, lib. 2, cap. 52 (II, 176–7); Statute of Westminster II, chapter 13 (*SR*, 81).

when they failed to appear they were amerced 'without judgment' (without the amount of the amercement being fixed by a jury) on the basis that the sheriff was acting as a royal 'justice' at his tourn. Clause 18 recounted the grievances of a wider group of tenants. Sheriffs, it was claimed, were now demanding attendance at the tourn from those who held nothing more than small parcels of land within a hundred and even when that holding contained no dwelling place. Here too sheriffs were allegedly amercing 'at will' any such tenant who failed to appear at the tourn.[38]

There is other evidence to suggest that sheriffs (and others) had indeed been attempting to extend the obligation of attendance at the tourn and the private equivalent, the view of frankpledge, during the years prior to 1259, probably for purely financial reasons and in order to increase their revenue from amercements for non-attendance. During Hugh Bigod's visitation of Kent early in 1259 one of the complaints made against John of Cobham senior, who had held the hundred of Shamley at fee-farm from the Templars, was that he had distrained 'men holding tenements without dwellings on them within the hundred and not resident there to come to the two lawdays each year as well as those who resided within the hundred',[39] and that the practice was still being continued by John of Cobham junior. The 'lawday' was the equivalent of the sheriff's tourn within such a private hundred.[40] In another case from Bigod's Essex eyre of early 1260 held after the enactment of the Provisions, the plaintiff answered an avowry for a distraint made for default of attendance at a tourn by claiming that he had not been obliged to attend the tourn since he had possessed no residence (*domicilium*) within the hundred concerned. Since the distraint had been made in 1255 the assumption seems to be that the customary rules applicable prior to the enactment of the Provisions had also exempted such men from attendance.[41] In 1257 the sheriff of Essex had also distrained Parnel de St Martin for an amercement for her failure to attend the tourn, evidently in defiance of a traditional exemption of women from attendance.[42] Either in or shortly before Easter term 1258 a judgment was given in the Exchequer that the heads of religious houses were not obliged to attend the tourn. During that term and in Trinity term 1258 and Hilary term 1259 a succession of heads of such houses obtained Exchequer writs citing the judgment and ordering sheriffs to stop distraining them on the basis of their supposed obligation to attend. These indicate that at least eight sheriffs had been attempting to enforce

[38] *DBM*, pp. 84–5.

[39] '... adeo bene ... homines habentes tenementa sine manso in predicto hundredo nec manentes in eodem veniendi ad duos lawdayes per annum quam ipsos qui manentes fuerunt in predicto hundredo'.

[40] JUST 1/873, m. 19d. [41] JUST 1/1189, m. 4. [42] E 159/31, m. 6d.

attendance from such religious office-holders.[43] The most likely basis of the judgment is that the religious had previously been exempt from attendance by custom and that here too sheriffs had been attempting to extend the obligation of attendance. It is less clear what the previous position was in relation to the attendance of earls and barons. A judgment in a case of 1234/5 seems to assume that archbishops and barons as well as other freeholders do have a duty to attend.[44] It is possible, however, that what was new in the years prior to 1259 was a concerted attempt on the part of sheriffs to demand attendance from earls and barons in respect of lands they held outside the areas where they were actually resident and that it was this which gave rise to the complaint in the Petition of the Barons.

A first draft of legislation on attendance at the sheriff's tourn was prepared in time for discussion at the Candlemas parliament of 1259. The first part of clause 5 of this draft proposed a general exemption from attendance at the tourn not just of all abbots and priors (as already provided under the earlier Exchequer judgment) and of all earls and barons (as suggested by the Petition of the Barons) but also of all others who possessed large holdings.[45] Members of these groups were only to be required to attend the tourn if their presence was needed for some special reason. The drafters evidently felt the need to justify the proposed exemption. They did so on the grounds that had traditionally been given for exempting such men from membership of tithings: that their holdings were in themselves sufficient to ensure that they kept the peace and obeyed the law. The second part of the draft clause went far beyond the relatively modest complaint (and implied suggestion for legislation) contained in clause 18 of the Petition. What was now proposed was a general exemption from attendance at the tourn of all those who were outside the jurisdiction at the time the tourn was held and not just of those who were non-resident and had no possible place of residence within the jurisdiction. It was also proposed to exempt all those who were sick or had some other good reason for their absence. Some safeguards were built into the proposal. Excuses for non-attendance were not to be taken on trust, as was the case with essoins in the case of civil litigation. They were only to be accepted if confirmed by the testimony of 'free and lawful men', perhaps

43 E 159/31, mm. 11, 14, 14d; E 159/32, m. 7d. The sheriffs were those of Nottinghamshire and Derbyshire, Lancashire, Northamptonshire, Cambridgeshire and Huntingdonshire, Bedfordshire and Buckinghamshire, Norfolk and Suffolk, Essex and Hertfordshire, Warwickshire and Leicestershire. The writs were obtained by the priors of Sempringham, Chicksands, Marsey, Stanfield, Vaudey and St Andrew's, Northampton. The judgment cannot have been given earlier than Michaelmas term 1257 when such a demand was respited but the judgment not cited: E 159/31, m. 6d.

44 *BNB*, pl. 1110. 45 Brand, *MCL*, p. 360.

the presenting jury itself. They were also only to be accepted if there were enough free men present to allow the presenting jury to perform its functions.

This first draft of clause 5 was radically amended and reshaped at the Candlemas parliament. As published in the *Providencia Baronum* of March 1259 the draft clause 5 included two entirely new sub-clauses. One took up a point made in the two related clauses of the Petition of the Barons but neglected in the original draft. It stipulated that even at the tourn amercements for absence were to be imposed in accordance with Magna Carta: that is, that amercements were to be fixed by a jury rather than the sheriff or other presiding official. The second stipulated that no more men were to be required to attend the tourn from among the unfree of each village than were necessary for the holding of inquisitions into the articles of the tourn. This was not something mentioned in the Petition but it did take up and extend the general principle of requiring attendance only from those whose presence was actually required for the running of the tourn and only amercing for non-attendance on similar grounds. There were also significant changes to those portions of clause 5 that were inherited from the earlier draft. There was a small addition to the number of status categories whose members were to be wholly exempt from attendance: bishops now joined abbots and priors, earls and barons. There had, however, clearly also been an inconclusive further discussion about another group to whom the earlier draft had given automatic exemption: those who possessed large holdings but did not belong to one of the exempted status categories. Some thought, with the framers of the earlier draft, that they should gain automatic exemption from attendance unless their presence was specially needed. Others, however, considered that they should only be exempt if absent from the area where the tourn was being held or prevented by illness or other good cause from attending. The draft version as published placed these two incompatible proposals beside each other with no attempt at resolving the contradiction. The revised draft also omitted one of the other proposals which the earlier draft had contained. There was no longer any proposal to allow a general exemption for others prevented from attendance by absence from the area at the time the tourn was held or sickness or other reasonable excuse.

By the time a penultimate draft of clause 5 was produced for the Michaelmas parliament of 1259 there had been further significant amendment of the proposed legislation. There was some apparent extension of the categories exempt from attendance, which were now specified as including archbishops as well as bishops and 'men of religion' generally as well as abbots and priors and also women. It seems probable, however, that none of these apparent extensions did anything more than codify the existing exemptions already possessed by members of these categories. The main effect of the other changes was to water down the proposed legislation and reduce its potentially adverse effect on the revenue which sheriffs collected through amercements for absence from the tourn. The general exemption of those with extensive lands but who did not belong to one of the groups exempted from attendance at the tourn (a matter of debate at the Candlemas parliament) was withdrawn. It was now to apply only where attendance at the tourn was demanded from them on the basis of a holding that had no dwelling on it. This was significantly less generous than either of the proposals made in March 1259 though a return to the original demand made in clause 18 of the Petition and probably also to the previous customary rule.[46] The sub-clauses which had specifically referred to amercements being made in accordance with Magna Carta and exempting from attendance at the tourn those of the unfree whose presence was not needed for the presentment jury were now represented only by a much less specific (and therefore much weaker) sub-clause referring in general terms to the tourn being held in accordance with Magna Carta and in the way tourns had been held under kings Richard and John.

Discussion and amendment, however, probably continued right up to the last moment. The first part of clause 4 of the Provisions of Westminster as eventually enacted (containing the exemptions of the various status groups) was substantially identical with the penultimate draft.[47] So too was its final part enjoining only that the tourn be held in accordance with Magna Carta and as it had been held in the reigns of kings Richard and John rather than imposing any more specific requirements. However, that part of the clause which dealt with those holding lands in several hundreds now simply exempted them from attendance at tourns other than in the hundred where they resided, rather than just in those hundreds where they did not possess houses.

The beaupleder fine

One other clause also related specifically to the working of the criminal justice system and to financial payments associated with it. Most historians who have written on the subject, seeing the term 'beaupleder' and drawing what seemed to them to be the obvious conclusion, have identified the beaupleder fine with the older fine paid for *miskenning*, a payment made by a litigant to avoid the consequences of purely verbal

[46] Above, p. 84. [47] For the text see Appendix I: below, pp. 418–19.

mistakes in pleading in civil litigation.[48] An initial reason to doubt the accuracy of this identification is that although *miskenning* is one of the Anglo-Saxon words which appear regularly in the lists that give French or Latin equivalents for these older technical legal terms, beaupleder or its Latin equivalent *finis pro pulcre placitando* are never used in these lists to translate it.[49] A second, and even stronger, reason for resisting the identification is that contemporary evidence about the fine indicates that it was normally paid not by individual litigants but by whole counties or by tithings and presenting juries and also that it was paid not during the course of civil litigation but most commonly at the sheriff's tourn or view of frankpledge and thus in connexion with the hearing of criminal pleas.[50]

It was Maitland who long ago suggested that when a beaupleder fine or a fine *ne occasionaretur* was paid by a county in the eyre its intended purpose was to ensure 'that the judges will not be extreme to mark what they say or do amiss'.[51] The purpose seems to have been to avoid the consequences of a judgment being made against the suitors of the county court for a wrongful judgment in connexion with outlawry and similar matters, or for incorrect statements of county custom. The beaupleder fine was identical in its incidence with other types of common fine and amercements for false judgment or wrongful outlawry and the payment of any one of these common fines or amercements precluded the payment of any other during any particular eyre session.[52] None the less, the

48 Treharne, *Baronial Plan*, p. 42; F. Nichols in his edition of *Britton*, I, 80, note r; M. Bateson in *Borough Customs* (Selden Society vol. 18, 1904), I, cii–ciii; Coke, *Second Institutes*, pp. 122–3; F. Liebermann in *Die Gesetze der Angelsachsen*, ed. Felix Liebermann (3 vols., Halle, 1898–1916), II, 585 s.v. 'Missesprechen'; Plucknett, *Statutes*, pp. 155–6.

49 For texts of the *Exposiciones Verborum Antiquorum Anglicorum* see *Red Book of the Exchequer*, ed. H. Hall (3 vols., Rolls Series, London, 1897), III, 1033.

50 See for example the complaint made in the Norfolk eyre of 1257 by the hundred of Walsham against the sheriff 'that the same sheriff takes at his tourn amercements for the defaults of those not coming to his tourn and for not harming those who do appear' ('quod idem vicecomes capit ad turnum suum misericordias pro defaltis non veniencium ad turnum suum et pro venientibus ne occasionarentur'): JUST 1/568 m. 35d; the complaints in the Hundred Rolls enquiry of 1274–5 connecting the payment with the sheriff's tourn in Lincolnshire, *RH*, I, 259; Berkshire, *RH*, I, 17; Essex, *RH*, I, 136; and Norfolk, *RH*, II, 485. A list in *The Mirror of Justices*, ed. W.J. Whittaker and F.W. Maitland (Selden Society vol. 7, 1893), p. 181, of the ways in which the clause on the sheriff's tourn was being ignored starts with the payment of beaupleder fines (and see also p. 26). The hundred of Hoo likewise complained in Bigod's Kent eyre of 1259 that when each hundred came to the county court to present homicides and misadventures the sheriff had started the custom 'that no presentment could be heard out before him before a fine had been made with him for not being harmed' ('quod nulla presentacio potuit exaudiri coram eo antequam fecisset finem cum eo ne occasionarentur'): JUST 1/873 m. 19 (1259) (and cf. ibid., m. 22d).

51 *Pleas of the Crown for the County of Gloucester before the Justices Itinerant, 1221*, ed. F.W. Maitland (London, 1884), p. 154.

52 Meekings, *Crown Pleas*, pp. 113–14.

distinction between a fine paid in advance for an unspecified offence, which may or may not have occurred, and one paid in respect of a judgment already made, is an important one. In effect it was a kind of institutionalised bribe to the king through the justices to overlook their faults, not a punishment for those faults.

A similar kind of purpose seems also to lie behind the payment of such fines when paid at the sheriff's tourn or at franchisal views of frankpledge where they seem to be connected specifically with the verdicts of presenting juries. The clause on the sheriff's tourn added to the 1217 reissue of Magna Carta (clause 42) included an admonition to each sheriff 'that he do not look out for pretexts to amerce' ('quod ... non quaerat occasiones').[53] This is not by itself very revealing. More so is a final concord of 1219 which mentions the *occasiones* which sheriffs might look for and describes them as arising out of the 'forgetfulness' of jurors or as a result of a 'foolish presentment' made by them.[54] The jurors of the hundred of Wolphy complained to the justices of the 1255 Herefordshire eyre about the sheriff's practice of handing over various chapters (articles) to the suitors of the hundred at his tourn and amercing the hundred at will if they did not respond 'word for word' to all the articles delivered to them.[55] It was evidently to avoid just these kinds of amercement that jurors might agree to pay beaupleder fines. A complaint against the bailiffs of the countess of Devon in the Wiltshire eyre of 1268 speaks of beaupleder fines paid by tithings at the 'lawday', the view of frankpledge, 'that they be not challenged in respect of the chapters or on other pleas'.[56] This, they claimed, ought (and used) to free them from the threat of amercement 'if they did not respond adequately to all and each of the chapters delivered to them' but no longer did so.[57] In the Essex eyre of 1285, the jurors of Dengie hundred complained on behalf of the village of Fambridge that although it was paying a beaupleder fine of four shillings at the view of frankpledge, yet it was now being amerced 'for concealment and other trespasses', evidently again in breach of the understood bargain.[58] When much of the apparatus of English local government, including the sheriff's tourn, was imported into Wales by the Statute of Wales in 1284, the new sheriffs were admonished 'not to look for pretexts to impose

[53] *SSC*, p. 342.

[54] *The Cartulary of Cirencester Abbey*, ed. C. Ross (vols. I–II) and M. Devine (vol. III) (3 vols., Oxford, 1974–7), I, 184.

[55] '... ad magnum turnum suum liberavit diversa capitula sectatoribus hundredi, et nisi respondeant de verba ad verbum omnibus capitulis eis liberatis, amerciat dictum hundredum ad voluntatem suam': JUST 1/300C, m. 22.

[56] '... ne calumpniarentur de capitulis vel aliis placitis'. [57] JUST 1/998A, m. 32.

[58] JUST 1/242, m. 69d. There was a similar complaint made in the Sussex eyre of 1279: JUST 1/915, m. 14d.

amercements on those making presentments when receiving their verdicts and not to take from them fines that they be not amerced in this way'.[59]

Clause 14 of the Petition of the Barons complained about only one of the two main types of beaupleder fine, that extorted from individual counties by the justices in eyre.[60] It is curious that it was this beaupleder fine that was singled out for special mention. As we have seen, the county did get something for its money, exemption from the imposition of other common fines. Nor is there any evidence to suggest that beaupleder fines of this kind were turning into a regular imposition, unlike the other main type of beaupleder fine. These tended to become a regular fixed payment due at each session of the sheriff's tourn. It was, however, only the other type of beaupleder fine, that paid in local courts, that was covered by the first draft of legislation on this subject. Clause 6 of the draft text produced for the Candlemas parliament of 1259 prohibited only the payment of fines to 'bailiffs' for beaupleder.[61] This initial draft was then amended at the parliament by omitting the specific reference to 'bailiffs', so as to cover all such fines. It was in this amended and more general form that the draft clause was published as part of the *Providencia Baronum* in March 1259.[62] By the time the penultimate French draft of the legislation was produced for the Michaelmas parliament of 1259, the clause had been amended yet again. It now spelled out all the various courts where the fine might have been paid and where its use was to be prohibited. These included the eyre, the county court and the courts of barons and free men and franchise courts. It was probably only a drafting error that led to the omission of any specific mention of the main court where the fine was regularly levied, the hundred court and its special session, the sheriff's tourn.[63] That same error is reproduced in the Close Roll text of clause 5 of the Provisions of Westminster,[64] but not in the superior text sent to the Exchequer and copied into the Red Book of the Exchequer.[65]

OTHER GRIEVANCES RELATED TO THE FUNCTIONING OF ROYAL JUSTICE IN THE COUNTIES

As has been seen, one of the reasons why lords had been putting pressure on their tenants to perform suit of court during the years prior to 1259 was that they had wanted to secure the financial benefits of the fines and amercements they could collect from suitors for not attending the lord's

[59] *SR*, I, 58. [60] *DBM*, pp. 82–3. [61] Brand, *MCL*, p. 360. [62] Jacob, *Studies*, p. 368.

[63] Such courts would have been covered since the clause also covers all other possible courts by a general 'and elsewhere' ('ne ailurs').

[64] *CR 1259–1261*, p. 148. [65] For this text see Appendix I: below, pp. 418–19.

court.[66] When sheriffs attempted to extend the obligation of attendance at the sheriff's tourn to groups hitherto apparently exempt during the 1250s, their main concern was also evidently with the financial penalties which could be collected when those newly obliged to attend failed to do so.[67] The new obligation enforced against villages by the king's justices to attend inquests 'fully' was even more obviously intended not to secure regular compliance with the new requirement but primarily to secure a new source of income for the king when the new obligation was not met.[68] Thus one common theme running through several of the clauses of the Provisions of Westminster already discussed is the attempt to provide redress against unjustified attempts to extend existing obligations to attend different sorts of court, where the real underlying motive, or at least one of the main underlying motives, was purely financial. A similar concern can also be traced in two other clauses of the Provisions.

When the justices of the general eyre visited a county a writ of summons was issued requiring the attendance at the eyre not just of four men and a reeve from each village and twelve burgesses from each town but also of all the free tenants who held lands in the county including any archbishops, bishops, abbots, earls, barons, knights and others. The earliest surviving writ of summons from 1219 contains such a clause,[69] but the practice of summoning all free tenants in the county to the general eyre is probably much older. It seems likely to go back to the creation of a system of countrywide general eyres during the reign of Henry II. This remained a standard feature of the eyre summons through to the end of the system of general eyres in the final years of the thirteenth century, indeed till the last general eyres were held in the fourth decade of the fourteenth century. The clear implication of the summons was that those summoned were required to appear before the justices at the opening of the eyre. What it did not make plain was how long they had then to stay. In theory, probably all those summoned were supposed to stay until the eyre was over. They might be required to act as jurors not just of the presentment jury for their hundred but also of the petty criminal juries which had replaced the ordeal as the normal way of determining the guilt or innocence of those accused of felonies as well as of civil juries for cases from their area. But the obligation of attendance for the whole of the eyre had certainly become much more of a burden during the course of the first half of the thirteenth century as eyres had begun to last significantly longer. It seems likely that by the late 1240s the eyre

[66] Above, pp. 45–6. [67] Above, pp. 83–4. [68] Above, p. 81.

[69] *Rotuli Litterarum Clausarum in Turri Londinensi asservati*, ed. T.D. Hardy (2 vols., London, 1833–44), I, 403.

justices had come to accept that those freeholders who were not on the presenting jury for their area might go home after the beginning of the eyre, provided they appeared when summoned to act on a petty criminal jury or a jury in a civil case. This 'understanding' had been upset from the late 1240s onwards when the justices in eyre began the practice of imposing an amercement on such freeholders if they were vouched to warranty in the course of ordinary civil proceedings at the eyre and proved not to be present in court and had therefore to be summoned. Such amercements were first imposed during the Essex eyre of 1248, and were subsequently levied in most other eyres down to 1258.[70] They were not, however, consistently imposed,[71] and the analogous amercement of defendants who lived or possessed lands in a county but failed to appear in answer to a summons in personal actions is found only in three eyres during 1248 and 1249 but not in any later eyre.[72]

The amercement of tenants living within a county for absence when vouched to warranty during the course of an eyre is not one of the grievances mentioned in the Petition of the Barons. Nor is there any early version of the relevant legislation. Clause 24 of the penultimate French version of the Provisions drafted for the Michaelmas parliament of 1259 does, however, preserve at least the final stage of the drafting of this part of the legislation. It shows that by this stage the proposed legislation was already intended to prohibit amercements imposed on this particular pretext and also to make it clear that such vouchees were to be entitled to a summons of three or four days if currently resident in the county and at least two weeks if not.[73] The draft clause also, however, preserves at least one feature which did not survive into the final draft. This is a statement of the general principle lying behind the proposed reform: that no free man ought to be amerced for his absence other than at the first day of the eyre. The omission of any such statement from the eventual legislation (clause 23 of the Provisions of Westminster) may have

70 For the only known example from the 1248 Essex eyre see JUST 1/231, m. 20d. For other later examples see JUST 1/560, mm. 9, 14, 21d (1250 Norfolk eyre); JUST 1/233, mm. 13d, 14, 23d, 25d (1255 Essex eyre); JUST 1/361, mm. 6, 18 (1255 Kent eyre); JUST 1/320, m. 7 (1255 Hertfordshire eyre); JUST 1/872, mm. 10d, 14 (1255 Surrey eyre); JUST 1/778, mm. 12, 18 (1256 Hampshire eyre); JUST 1/567, mm. 4, 7, 11d, 16d, 18, 21 (1257 Norfolk eyre); JUST 1/820, mm. 3, 11d (1257 Suffolk eyre).

71 For examples of other cases from the 1255 Kent eyre where an absent warrantor living within the county was vouched but no amercement was imposed see JUST 1/361, mm. 2, 7, 8, 11d, 25, 28, 28d. Possibly these tenants had received permission to go home before the eyre was over once their local crown pleas had been dealt with.

72 JUST 1/231, m. 27d bis (1248 Essex eyre); JUST 1/318, m. 9d (1248 Hertfordshire eyre); JUST 1/777, m. 31 and JUST 1/996, m. 17 (1249 Wiltshire eyre).

73 Brand, *MCL*, p. 366.

been deliberate.[74] It is rather more likely, however, that it is an indication of the carelessness with which the final text was prepared for the eventual text looks like a straight translation of the draft clause as it is found in two of our four MSS. of the text where lack of care in the copying has led to the dropping of the crucial words between two occurrences of the word *amercie* which contain the relevant statement of principle.[75]

Almost three-quarters of a century of tradition sanctioned the summoning of all the freeholders resident within a county to attend the general eyre and there were clearly good reasons of public policy and utility for requiring their attendance at the sessions of these justices. It was much less clear that it was reasonable to expect all the county's freeholders to attend sessions of royal justices with less extensive powers and probably no well-established tradition of them doing so. It was, however, again in the financial interest of the king's government that they should be, for the king could then profit from amercements imposed on those who failed to appear. There had been a complaint at the meeting of the clergy of the province of Canterbury in London in August 1257 about general summonses issued by justices conducting enquiries on the king's behalf (evidently a reference to the justices of the special enquiry of 1255)[76] requiring the attendance of all free men and all villages and their imposition of amercements on absentees, which seems to assume that general summonses should only be issued in connexion with sessions of the general eyre.[77] In clause 19 of the Petition of the Barons the focus was on a different type of royal justice, the assize justices who were commissioned to hear assizes of novel disseisin and mort d'ancestor. Again, however, the grievance was the issuing of general summonses for all the knights and free tenants of the county to attend their sessions and the amercement of those who did not appear.[78]

The earliest draft legislation on this subject is clause 12 of the penultimate French draft of the Provisions of Westminster produced for the Michaelmas parliament of 1259.[79] This specifies all the different kinds of royal official and royal justice who are to lose the power to amerce for default of the common summons, that is, for absence when a general summons is issued. Those mentioned include escheators, enquirers, assize justices and justices of oyer and terminer determining allegations of wrongdoing. Almost all other officials or justices are covered by a blanket 'all other kinds of bailiff' ('ne nule autre manere de bailif'). The power

[74] For the text see Appendix I: below, pp. 426–7. [75] Brand, *MCL*, p. 366 and note 118.

[76] The articles of this enquiry as preserved in the Burton Annals specifically ask whether all free tenants (as well as four men and the reeve of each village) have appeared as the king's writ had ordered: *Annales Monastici*, I, 339.

[77] *Councils and Synods*, II, i, 535. [78] *DBM*, pp. 84–5. [79] Brand, *MCL*, p. 365.

to impose such amercements was to be limited in future to the justices of the general eyre and holders of the newly re-established post of chief justiciar. As eventually enacted as clause 13 of the Provisions of Westminster, the same specific officials and justices were again prohibited from imposing such amercements though the unspecific reference to 'other kinds of bailiff' was eliminated. The clause went on again to give the power to impose such amercements to the chief justiciar and also generally to the 'justices itinerant'.[80] This may be intended as a reference solely to the justices of the general eyre but was probably intended to cover the justices of the forest eyre as well.[81]

RESTRICTIONS ON THE RIGHT OF DISTRAINT

Distraint by chattels, the seizure and impounding of movable property (most commonly animals) belonging to a particular individual, was in common use in the thirteenth century as a way of bringing pressure on that individual to fulfil some particular obligation. It was part of the mesne process not just of the king's courts but also of local courts as a way of securing a defendant's appearance in court. It could also be used by any landowner who found animals belonging to others grazing his arable or pasture if they had no commoning rights there, as a way of securing compensation for the damage done by the animals. It was regularly used by lords against their tenants to enforce the performance of services to which the lord thought himself entitled. The lord could take any animals found on the land his tenant held of him, whether or not they belonged to the tenant himself.[82]

There were a number of rules about the ways in which lords and others could exercise this right. Landowners exercising the right to distrain animals they had found grazing their arable or common had normally to seize the animals on the land itself while they were still 'doing damage' (*damage feasant*), though there may already have existed a right to take animals elsewhere provided they were taken in hot pursuit. Lords distraining their tenants could generally do this only within the boundaries of their own lordship or 'fee' and more specifically on the land which the tenant held of the lord, whether or not that land had subsequently been subinfeudated. The existence of such a rule can be demonstrated from at least 1225 onwards,[83] and it was probably much older than this.

80 For the text see Appendix I: below, pp. 422–3.

81 For evidence that summons for the forest eyre required the attendance of all free tenants who held lands within the area of the forest see *Select Pleas of the Forest*, ed. G.J. Turner (Selden Society vol. 13, 1901), p. li.

82 Brand, *MCL*, pp. 301–24.

83 *CRR*, XII, no. 192. See also *BNB*, pl. 1049, 1059, 1703 and JUST 1/560, m. 4 (1250 Norfolk eyre).

A related rule, specifically prohibiting lords and all others apart from the king and his servants making distraints in the highway, was probably of independent origin and may be connected with notions of the king's special peace as being attached to the public highway. This rule too can be found specifically formulated and applied some years before 1259.[84]

Although there were no complaints about the breaching of either of these two related rules in the Petition of the Barons nor any other indications that transgression of the customary rules on these matters was a major problem in the years prior to 1259, the codification of existing customary restraints on the exercise of seignorial power in the Provisions of Westminster also extended to these two customary rules. Clause 9 of the penultimate version of the Provisions of Westminster prepared for the Michaelmas parliament of 1259 specifically prohibited distraints made outside the fee and in the highway other than by the king or under his authority.[85] The same two restraints became enshrined in legislation with the enactment of clause 11 of the Provisions of Westminster in 1259.[86]

A second clause which also formed part of the Provisions and was also concerned with the exercise of the right of distraint seems, by contrast, not to have been aimed specifically at lords exercising their right of distraint. The probable target was a different, and much more limited, group of lords: those who possessed franchises which gave them the right to exclude the sheriff from their lands and who failed to act to secure the release of distresses when ordered to do so by the sheriff. While such lords might also be the lords who had originally taken the distresses this was not always, and certainly not necessarily, the case.

Once animals or other movables had been taken in distraint, the person who had been distrained had a choice of options. He might simply decide to do what the other party who had distrained him was asking: perform the services owed or pay for the damage caused by his animals or the amercement imposed on him. He would then get his distresses back. He might offer appropriate sureties that he would do what was required of him at some future date. Only if this was acceptable to the distrainor would he get his distresses back. He might simply offer sureties to the distrainor to appear at an appropriate court to contest the justice of the distraint. If he did this he was also entitled as a matter of law to have the distresses released.[87] A fourth possibility, from the later twelfth century onwards, was for the person distrained to bring a legal action (the action

[84] The earliest case in which a defendant was attached to answer in the court *coram rege* for making a distraint on the highway was being brought in Michaelmas term 1253: *Master Godfrey of Tofts v. Roger de Mustreoyl* (KB 26/151, m. 21).

[85] Brand, *MCL*, p. 364. [86] For the text see Appendix I: below, pp. 420–1.

[87] Brand, *MCL*, p. 307 and note 23.

of replevin) contesting the justice of the distraint in the county court. In theory, this was only possible if the distrainor had already refused an offer of sureties to appear in an appropriate court to contest the justice of the distraint. In practice, however, it was not necessary for any such offer to have been made or refused.[88] Such an action could be initiated in one of two ways. The person distrained might go or send to the king's Chancery for a writ of replevin.[89] He might also start proceedings by simply making an oral complaint to the local sheriff.[90] In either case the very first step in the proceedings was for the sheriff or one of his subordinates to secure the release of the distresses which had been taken. They would remain released until the case was determined, with the distrainor only recovering the distresses if his distraint was found to have been justified.

Special procedures were employed and special difficulties might arise if distresses had been impounded within a franchise which enjoyed 'return of writs'.[91] Within such an area it was the bailiffs of the franchise, and not the sheriff and his subordinates, who were responsible for taking measures to ensure the release of distresses when a plaintiff initiated a plea of replevin.[92] When the plea had been initiated by writ, the proper procedure seems to have been for the sheriff to make a 'return' of the writ he had received, a mandate reciting the writ in full and ordering the bailiffs to execute it by securing the release of the distresses and attaching the defendant to appear in the county court. Only if the franchise-holder also possessed the special and higher franchise of hearing pleas of replevin would the case be heard in the franchise-holder's own court. When a plea had been initiated by plaint, the proper procedure seems to have been for the

88 Ibid., pp. 308–10.

89 A specialised writ of replevin available only where the distraint was for services which the person distrained did not acknowledge that he owed is found in *Glanvill*, XII, 12 (p. 142). A general writ of replevin seems to have been in existence by 1204: *PKJ*, III, no. 972 (and see also *CRR*, IV, pp. 57–8 (1205)). The writ of replevin does not appear in the 'Irish' register of writs but it is to be found in another pre-Mertonian register: *Early Registers*, p. 24 (CA 21).

90 The earliest specific reference to initiating proceedings in this way comes from 1208 (*CRR*, V, pp. 252–3). For other early references to this procedure see *Royal Letters, Henry III*, ed. W.W. Shirley (2 vols., London, Rolls Series, 1862–6), I, 101–4 at 102 (1220); *CRR*, XII, no. 361. This form of initiating proceedings is mentioned twice in *Bracton*: fols. 156 (II, 439) and 157 (II, 442). For later cases where the detailed accounts given of the procedure followed in initiating proceedings point to the use of plaint see KB 26/127, m. 9 and KB 26/130, m. 19 (1242); JUST 1/997, m. 9 (1249); KB 26/143, m. 15d (1250); KB 26/158, m. 6 (1257).

91 On this franchise see M.T. Clanchy, 'The Franchise of Return of Writs', *Transactions of the Royal Historical Society* 5th series 17 (1967), 59–82.

92 For later evidence which confirms that the franchise of 'return of writs' also included the right to execute process on cases initiated by plaint see *Abbot of Thame v. Simon of Hertford et al.*: CP 40/136, m. 127 (Hilary term 1301).

sheriff to transmit his own order to the bailiff of the franchise for the release of the distresses.[93] Again, only if the franchise-holder possessed the additional franchise of hearing pleas of replevin would he be entitled to have the resulting case heard in his own court.[94]

The difficulties arose when franchise bailiffs failed to carry out orders they had been given to secure the release of distresses. In 1254 it seems to have taken a judgment of the court *coram rege* to authorise the disregarding of the franchise of the abbey of Peterborough when the abbot's bailiffs had failed to execute a previous order (by writ) to secure the release of distresses taken by the abbot of Thorney and John of Glatton.[95] The following year the king's council seems to have become involved in the drafting of a Chancery writ which was probably intended to become a standard form to deal with much the same kind of situation. This authorised a sheriff who had reported back to the king that the bailiffs of a liberty had failed to act to disregard the liberty and take the requisite action himself. Two different versions of the writ are enrolled on the Close Rolls. The second of these is said to have been authorised by Henry of Bath (a leading royal justice) and others of the king's council. Both were intended to deal with a case where the bailiffs of the abbot of Westminster's Oxfordshire franchise of Islip were refusing to secure the release of distresses taken in the abbot's name.[96] A different approach to the same problem is to be found in the 1258 agreement between the bishop of Worcester and William de Beauchamp, the hereditary sheriff of Worcestershire. This envisaged that when the bishop and his bailiffs failed to act the sheriff would be authorised to disregard the liberty by a judgment of his county court.[97]

It is less clear whether any regular procedure had developed prior to 1259 to deal with the analogous problem that might occur if the litigation had been initiated by plaint. The 1254 agreement between William de Beauchamp and the abbot of Evesham seems to envisage some sort of suspension of the abbot's bailiff if he failed to execute such orders and his payment of a financial penalty to the sheriff at the next county court.

93 See the 1254 agreement between the abbot of Evesham and William de Beauchamp, the hereditary sheriff of Worcestershire in *The Beauchamp Cartulary: Charters 1100–1268*, ed. Emma Mason (Pipe Roll Society new series vol. 43: 1980), no. 60, p. 37, though the abbot seems to have had less than the full complement of rights associated with 'return of writs'.

94 See the 1258 agreement between William de Beauchamp and the bishop of Worcester: *The Beauchamp Cartulary*, no. 50, p. 28.

95 KB 26/151, m. 22.

96 *CR 1254–1256*, pp. 195, 198. For yet another early version of the same writ see *Early Registers*, pp. 59–60 (CC 88).

97 *The Beauchamp Cartulary*, p. 29.

It is much less clear whether or not the agreement envisages the sheriff himself taking action in default of appropriate action by the bailiff.[98] Only the 1258 agreement between the same hereditary sheriff and the bishop of Worcester makes it plain that if the bishop's bailiffs failed to secure a release the county court might authorise the sheriff to take action himself to ensure this.[99] It is uncertain whether or not there were standard procedures for dealing with this problem in other counties and the fact that it was only in the mid-1250s that procedures were developing for dealing with this problem when litigation was initiated by writ may well suggest that there were not.

It is against this background that clause 16 of the penultimate draft text of the Provisions of Westminster needs to be read.[100] This starts by confirming the existing position. Sheriffs are entitled to secure the release of the animals of anyone who has been distrained once the person who has been distrained has made a complaint to them.[101] This seems to be intended to provide the general normative context and justification for the real heart of the legislation. This is a second sentence which spells out that when animals have been taken in distraint within a franchise and the bailiff has failed to secure their release the sheriff is to act instead. It was probably intended to provide a general statutory authority for sheriffs to disregard franchises when this was necessary to secure the release of animals taken in distraint. Where an action of replevin was begun by writ a special writ could provide the necessary authorisation. The proposed legislation was intended to provide a standing authorisation when the action was begun by plaint instead. Clause 17 of the final Provisions of Westminster retained the main substance of this clause but reformulated it as well as translating it into Latin.[102]

STRENGTHENING ROYAL JUSTICE AGAINST SEIGNORIAL ENCROACHMENTS

The reformers were also responsible for drafting a number of clauses which were specifically intended to strengthen and safeguard the system of royal justice against possible encroachments by seignorial courts.

[98] Ibid., p. 37. [99] Ibid., p. 28. [100] Brand, *MCL*, p. 365.

[101] That this was indeed seen simply as a confirmation of the existing legal position can be seen from the phrasing of the clause which talks of the sheriff making the release 'according to the law of the land' ('solum ley de la terre'). For two presentments of the 1250s suggesting some doubt about whether sheriffs were entitled to hold pleas of replevin without writ see Brand, *MCL*, p. 318. It is noticeable, however, that the legislation focuses on the sheriff's power to secure release of distresses rather than on his power to hear the resulting litigation.

[102] For the text see Appendix I: below, pp. 424–5.

The royal monopoly over false judgment cases

The jurisdictional rule reserving all cases in which litigants alleged that a court had given them a 'false judgment', a wrongful judgment, to the crown was an old one. It is already described as being a royal monopoly in the early twelfth century *Leges Henrici Primi*.[103] There is very little sign of any significant challenge to this monopoly during the years immediately prior to 1259. No trace has been found of any complaints made about this matter to the justiciar, Bigod, during 1258 and 1259. Nor is it the subject of any complaint in the Petition of the Barons. Clause 29 of the Petition did complain about what was alleged to have become the custom in several county courts of allowing superior lords to claim for the jurisdiction of their courts actions brought by writ of right once plaintiffs had removed cases into the county court on proving the failure of the immediate lord to whom the writ was addressed to do justice (by the procedure known as *tolt*).[104] This was, however, conceptually quite distinct. What the plaintiff was alleging and proving through the process of *tolt* was a failure to provide justice rather than a false judgment and the allegation secured the removal of the case into the county court and not into a royal court proper, as any allegation of 'false judgment' would have done. It is therefore unclear why such legislation was thought to be needed in 1259. All that is clear from the terms of the legislation is that the concern was specifically with the possibility that superior lords might claim to exercise the right to review 'false' judgments given in the courts of their tenants. However much real need there was for the legislation, a draft clause confirming the crown monopoly of such cases was included in the penultimate draft version of the Provisions of Westminster prepared for the Michaelmas parliament of 1259.[105] This then passed into law in virtually identical form (though in Latin) as clause 16 of the Provisions of Westminster.[106]

Royal authorisation required for compelling free men to answer for their free tenement or its appurtenances

There is slightly more evidence for the prior breaching of a second existing rule which also enhanced the authority of the crown and was likewise reaffirmed by the Provisions of Westminster. The rule that no free man

[103] *Leges Henrici Primi*, 10, 1 (p. 108). For the later history of the rule see Brand, *MCL*, p. 99 and note 100.

[104] *DBM*, pp. 88–91. For an instance of the city court of Exeter wrongly hearing litigation removed by *tolt* out of the court of the Dean and Chapter of Exeter in or before 1245 see *CRR*, XVIII, no. 1716.

[105] Brand, *MCL*, p. 365.

[106] For the text see Appendix I: below, pp. 422–3.

could be made to answer for his free tenement or for anything appurtenant to it without the king's writ probably originated in the reign of Henry II, though how it originated remains controversial.[107] One of its effects was to ensure that the only kind of land litigation which seignorial courts could hear was the action of right since the writ of right was the only royal writ which initiated litigation in the lord's court.[108] The rule was an important weapon for the royal courts in gaining an increasing share in jurisdiction of land cases since they were able to offer a variety of other and more attractive remedies to litigants and seignorial courts were unable to compete with them in doing this. It may also have been viewed as an important safeguard by tenants and would-be tenants since it limited the ability of seignorial courts (which seem often to have been distrusted by tenants) to exercise jurisdiction over land cases. When seignorial courts were authorised to hear such cases by the writ of right the litigants were provided with important safeguards against the lord's failure to provide justice by the *tolt* procedure and by the possibility of bringing an action of false judgment if the case was wrongly decided. By 1230 interpretation of the rule had also extended it to cover tenants against being made to answer for the services which they owed for their tenements without a royal writ. This effectively stopped lords initiating such litigation in their own courts.[109]

There had long existed a writ obtainable from Chancery by a tenant ordering the sheriff to see that the rule was observed.[110] Tenants did not, however, always know of the existence of the writ and lords certainly did not always obey the rule. In the 1255 Surrey eyre there is an incidental mention of a case concerning land being held in the court of the abbot of Chertsey at Epsom without the king's writ and despite the tenant's objection.[111] During Bigod's 1258 visitation it was alleged in an assize of novel disseisin that the earl of Gloucester's court at Thrapston, Northamptonshire, had given a verdict as to who had the greater right in some land despite the objection of the tenants 'that they would not put themselves on any inquest jury nor would they answer anyone for their free tenement without the order of the lord king'.[112] East hundred made a presentment in the Rutland eyre of 1263 alleging that the sheriffs of the county had held 'pleas of disseisin concerning tenements without the

[107] Brand, *MCL*, p. 97 and note 92.

[108] The writ of right of dower also initiated litigation in the lord's court but for most purposes this can be ignored.

[109] Brand, *MCL*, pp. 314–15.

[110] The writ was already available prior to 1236: *Early Registers*, p. 21 (CA 9a).

[111] JUST 1/872, m. 14d.

[112] '. . . quod ipsi in nullam inquisicionem de predicto tenemento capiendam se ponerent nec alicui de libero tenemento suo sine precepto domini regis responderent': JUST 1/1187, m. 27.

writ of the lord king'.[113] The names of the sheriffs mentioned show that this had been happening before 1259 as well as afterwards. There had not, however, been any complaint of breaches of this rule in the Petition of the Barons and the earliest evidence of a perceived need for legislation to reaffirm the existing customary rule is the existence of a draft sub-clause enacting such a rule contained in the penultimate draft of the Provisions of Westminster which was produced for the Michaelmas parliament of 1259.[114] This suggests that the problem normally arose from breaches of the rule by lords rather than by sheriffs. It also suggests more specifically that the problem was with breaches of the rule by magnates for the prohibition is so drafted as to refer specifically to them ('nul haut hom'). The legislation as eventually enacted (as part of clause 18 of the Provisions of Westminster) eliminated the specific reference to magnates but retained the reference to lords, for the prohibition was against anyone distraining his 'tenants' for such a purpose.[115]

The royal monopoly of the right to compel free men to take oaths

A third royal monopoly which also appears to have been of a respectable antiquity was the right to compel free men to take oaths in connexion with legal proceedings or to authorise the use of compulsion by others for this purpose. Its effect was to make it very difficult for anyone other than the king or those to whom he had specifically delegated this power to use any kind of jury trial in their courts. King John had probably been trying to reproduce the effect of the English rule in 1200 when he ordered that no jury trial (*recognicio*) was to take place in his lordship of Ireland other than in his court.[116] *Bracton* also appears to refer to the rule, though without describing it as such.[117]

There had been skirmishes with individual bishops during the 1240s and early 1250s about the application of this customary rule to proceedings in church courts. A 1247 mandate to the sheriffs of the various counties within the bishopric of Lincoln had ordered them not to allow the bishop, his archdeacons, their officials or rural deans to compel the lay men of their counties to serve on juries or give testimony on oath other than in matrimonial and testamentary cases.[118] A 1249 writ enrolled on the Close Rolls had ordered the same bishop to be summoned *coram rege*

[113] '... placita de disseisina de tenementis sine brevi domini regis': JUST 1/721, m. 11.

[114] Brand, *MCL*, p. 365.

[115] For the text see Appendix I: below, pp. 424–5.

[116] *Rotuli Chartarum in Turri Londinensi asservati, 1199–1216*, ed. T.D. Hardy (London, 1837), p. 99.

[117] *Bracton*, fol. 106 (II, 302): but note that he seems to restrict this to proceedings relating to title to free tenement.

[118] *CR 1242–1247*, p. 543.

to answer for compelling lay men and women to appear and take oaths before him against their will 'to the grave prejudice of our crown and the royal dignity and the great harm of our realm' or (in an alternative formulation) 'to the grave prejudice of our crown and dignity and contrary to the custom of our realm'.[119] In 1251 the sheriffs of Gloucestershire and Worcestershire were ordered to stop the bishop of Worcester, whether in person or through his clerks, compelling free men as well as villeins to take oaths in inquests without the king's authorisation 'contrary to custom and the excellence of the royal dignity'.[120]

There had also been prior to 1259 presentments against sheriffs who had compelled free men to take oaths in order to offer jury trial in particular pleas without royal authorisation. In the 1236 Hampshire eyre there was a presentment against Roger Wascelin, recently under-sheriff of Hampshire, for using distraint against the men of Andover when they refused to give a verdict on the entitlement of an unnamed individual to land in Andover without the king's writ and compelling them to redeem the distresses taken for one hundred shillings.[121] From 1246 onwards one of the articles of the eyre specifically asked for information about sheriffs and other bailiffs 'who determine plea of the crown and pleas of replevin and other pleas in the county court or hundred court or elsewhere by the oath of twelve men, since they have no power to do this without the authorisation of the lord king and this by his writ'.[122] Some of the presentments made in response to this article simply presented lords and sheriffs for hearing pleas of replevin without warrant.[123] But others, more properly, responded to the real thrust of the article, the unauthorised use of jury trial, or to both. In the 1250 Norfolk eyre, for example, the hundred of South Greenhoe presented that the sheriff had 'required twelve free men to take oaths against their will' and also that he had held pleas of replevin without warrant.[124] In the 1255 Herefordshire eyre the hundred of Broxash had made a similar complaint against their

[119] *CR 1242–1247*, p. 221. [120] *CR 1247–1251*, p. 554. [121] JUST 1/775, m. 17d.

[122] *SR*, I, 234. For the date see Meekings, *Crown Pleas*, p. 31.

[123] For lords and sheriffs see JUST 1/238, m. 50 (1254 Essex eyre: hundred of Barstable): 'Juratores presentant quod Willelmus Giffard, abbas Westm' et omnes vicecomites Essex qui pro tempore fuerunt tenent placita de namio vetito set nesciunt quo waranto'. For lords alone see, for example, JUST 1/176, m. 32 (1249 Devon eyre): 'Juratores presentant quod ballivi comitisse de Insula tenent placita de namio vetito apud Plinton'. Ideo loquendum. Et super hoc venit ballivus predicte comitisse et dicit quod antecessores ipsius comitisse semper consueverunt tenere talia placita' (and note a similar presentment was made in the previous eyre of 1238: JUST 1/174, m. 38d).

[124] 'Juratores presentant quod Hamo Passelewe ponit xij liberos homines ad sacramentum contra voluntatem suam et tenuit placita namii vetiti sine waranto. Ideo in misericordia': JUST 1/564, m. 8.

local sheriff.[125] A few complaints also refer to magnates doing the same thing. In the 1254 Essex eyre the hundred of Hinckford complained that the bailiffs of the earl of Cornwall and of Peter of Savoy 'distrain free men to put them on oath without the king's order',[126] and in the 1255 Kent eyre a complaint was made against the stewards of the earl of Gloucester, alleging that they 'had made inquests by the oaths of twelve free men without the order of the lord king'.[127]

Again, however, there are no specific complaints about breaches of the customary rule in the Petition of the Barons and none is known to have been made to Bigod during his 1258–9 visitations. Part of the draft clause 18 in the penultimate draft of the Provisions of Westminster prepared for the Michaelmas parliament of 1259 none the less prohibited lords (and more specifically magnates) from breaching the rule, while restating the rule in a form that also covered other possible transgressors.[128] In its final form (as clause 18 of the Provisions) the clause was directed against all lords, not just magnates, and it also preserved the more general reference to the rule being of general application.[129] Thus here again the reformers went out of their way to reaffirm an existing customary rule of benefit to the king and in such a way as to suggest that they were intending primarily to prevent magnates or lords breaching the rule.

BRINGING THE PRACTICE OF LOCAL COURTS INTO LINE WITH THAT OF THE ROYAL COURTS

The remaining clause of the Provisions related to the warranting of essoins in local courts. Here the problem was not that there was any kind of usurpation of royal rights or wrong being committed by the holders of local courts, but simply that procedure in local courts had not changed in line with relatively recent changes in essoining procedure in the king's courts.

In the later twelfth century it had apparently been the practice in the king's courts that, when a litigant had an essoiner present an essoin (or formal excuse for absence) to the court, he had himself on appearance to take a formal oath to confirm that the excuse given had really been genuine and that he had indeed been prevented from appearing in court for the reason given. The pressure of business seems to have led to a subsequent relaxation of the requirement and by the middle of the thirteenth

[125] JUST 1/300C, m. 35.

[126] '. . . distringunt liberos homines ad ponendum eosdem ad sacramentum sine precepto domini regis': JUST 1/233, m. 45.

[127] '. . . fecerunt inquisiciones per sacramentum xij liberorum hominum sine precepto domini regis': JUST 1/361, m. 59.

[128] Brand, *MCL*, p. 365.

[129] For the text see Appendix I: below, pp. 424–5.

century the king's courts had apparently abandoned any attempt to make litigants 'warrant' their essoins on oath. The effect was to allow essoins to be used routinely by defendants, particularly in land actions, simply as a delaying tactic.[130] No such relaxation seems to have taken place in local public or private courts.[131] Indeed, in at least one county (Warwickshire) a sheriff tightened rather than loosened procedure by forcing litigants to bring their own bibles when they took the oath warranting their essoins.[132] By 1259 this was evidently felt to be a grievance. It does not appear as such in the Petition of the Barons but in the draft legislation produced for the Candlemas parliament of 1259 there appears a proposal (in clause 10) to abandon the requirement for warranting essoins on oath together with the outlines of a justification for doing so. When attorneys were appointed to act in litigation and essoined themselves they were excused from swearing to warrant their essoins. Litigants who essoined themselves of bed-sickness (*malo lecti*) were also excused from warranting their essoin on oath.[133] The implication is that the same logic should also apply in other cases. The proposed legislation was then discussed at parliament and the draft prepared for publication.[134] This contained an even more elaborate justification of the proposed relaxation. It also pointed out that essoins were not a necessity since a litigant who was sick could perfectly well be represented by an attorney. Since they were a concession to the defendant, allowing him some additional delay, it was unreasonable that the defendant should be made to take an oath in order to enjoy the possibility of an essoin. The implication seems to be that it was wrong to force men to perjure themselves for this purpose. By the time the penultimate draft version of the Provisions of Westminster was produced for the Michaelmas parliament of 1259, the draft clause 14 had lost all material attempting to justify the change. It now simply prohibited

130 Brand, *OELP*, p. 35.

131 The only piece of evidence pointing in the other direction is a presentment made by the jurors of the hundred of Twyford in the 1255 Kent eyre complaining of a former bailiff of Tonbridge that 'he had levied a new custom, that if anyone had himself essoined in the court of his lord, the essoin was held null unless he took an oath that on the day he had himself essoined he was sick or in such a condition that he could in no wise appear on that day to win or lose' ('levavit quandam novam consuetudinem, scilicet quod si aliquis fecisset se essoniare in curia domini sui, essonium suum pro nullo haberetur nisi faceret sacramentum quod die quo se essoniavit, fuit infirmus vel in tali statu quod nullo modo conparere potuit ad diem illum ad lucrandum vel perdendum'): JUST 1/361, m. 42. Perhaps this was simply a stricter standard than had previously been imposed.

132 JUST 1/951A, m. 2d (1232 Warwickshire eyre): '. . . talem levavit consuetudinem, quod quilibet se essoniavit, cum venerit ad warantizandum essonium suum debet secum deferre librum super quem jurare debet'. But note also that some time before 1212 the attorney of the prior of Ware allegedly brought his own bible when warranting an essoin in the county court of Gloucestershire: *CRR*, VI, 229.

133 Brand, *MCL*, p. 361.

134 Jacob, *Studies*, p. 369 (and see Brand, *MCL*, p. 357).

any attempt to make litigants warrant their essoins on oath. The clause did, however, now specify the main local court of which the reformers were thinking (the county court) and covered other types of local courts by a general 'and elsewhere' (*ne aylurs*).[135] It was in much this form that the clause became law at the end of October 1259 as clause 15 of the Provisions of Westminster, albeit with an even more explicit listing of county courts, hundred courts and courts baron as well as any other courts (*vel alibi*).[136]

[135] Brand, *MCL*, p. 367. [136] For the text see Appendix I: below, pp. 422–3.

Chapter 4

THE ENFORCEMENT OF THE PROVISIONS OF WESTMINSTER DURING THE INITIAL STAGE OF THEIR EXISTENCE, 1259–63

The Michaelmas parliament of 1259 was the highwater mark of the reform movement. The following year saw the gradual abandonment of a number of key elements in the reformers' programme: the prorogation (in June) and subsequently (in the autumn) the abandonment of the special eyre for the remedying of grievances and the substitution of an ordinary general eyre with no special additional powers; the transfer to the magnates themselves of the primary responsibility for investigating and remedying the wrongdoing of their bailiffs; and the abandonment (also in the autumn) of the principle of retaining sheriffs in office only for a single year. In the final months of 1260 the baronial council itself effectively ceased to function.[1] It was not, however, until June 1261 that Henry III published, and then only to a restricted audience, the papal bull granting him absolution from his oath of May 1258 to observe the ordinances of the reformers and also moved more publicly to appoint his own candidates to the posts of justiciar (Philip Basset) and chancellor (Walter of Merton). It was only in July 1261 that he went on to remove the sheriffs appointed by the baronial council and appoint his own candidates to local shrievalties.[2] This last move met with considerable local resistance. Rival 'keepers of counties' also attempted to exercise the functions of local sheriff in many counties. Simon de Montfort, earl of Leicester, and others attempted to build on this resistance by summoning three knights from each county to a general meeting at St Albans in September to consider 'the common business' of the kingdom. Henry III was, however, successful in preventing this meeting and was able to manoeuvre his opponents into accepting arbitration on the major issues at stake between them at Kingston upon Thames in November 1261. The king allowed the 'rebel' counties to choose four candidates for the office of sheriff for the year beginning the previous Michaelmas but the question of the procedures to be applied to future shrieval appointments was referred to a group of six arbitrators (half chosen by the king, half

[1] Maddicott, *Simon de Montfort*, pp. 193–204. [2] Ibid., pp. 209–12.

by his baronial opponents) with the provision that, if they were unable to agree, a decision was to be made by the king's brother Richard, the king of Germany.[3] The wider issues at stake between the king and his opponents were referred to a different group of six arbitrators similarly chosen but with provision in their case that, if they were unable to reach agreement, King Richard was to be added to their number and (in case of continuing disagreement) Louis IX, king of France, as well.[4] When the first group of arbitrators failed to agree, Richard decided in favour of the restoration of the king's traditional right of free appointment of sheriffs.[5] Nothing seems to be known of any discussions held or decisions taken by the second group of arbitrators but in late February 1262 Henry obtained from pope Urban IV a renewal of the papal absolution of the oath he had taken in May 1258,[6] and in a letter sent to each county early in May 1262 announced for the first time to his subjects at large his absolution from the 1258 oath. He justified this move by reference not just to the two papal absolutions but also to the promises and conditions which had been attached to the original oath but which the baronial council had not observed and to other actions taken by the council which had been damaging not just to the king but also to his other subjects.[7] Henry reiterated his willingness to observe both Magna Carta and the Charter of the Forest. He also emphasised his willingness (in implied contrast to the baronial council and its members) to provide lesser men with justice when they had grievances against the magnates. Nothing specific, however, was said about the Provisions of Westminster, whether to confirm their continuing validity or to make it clear that they were no longer in force. Absolution from his oath and denunciation of the damaging measures taken by the baronial council might be thought to imply the latter; but the fact that the council had done many things that were damaging did not necessarily mean that this was true of everything they had done. Henry certainly continued the post of chief justiciar, whose revival had been among the first measures undertaken by the reformers in 1258. The Provisions of Westminster might also be considered among the relatively harmless or even positively beneficial measures promoted and secured by the council. The May pronouncement in effect left the Provisions of Westminster in a kind of limbo, from which they were to be rescued only by their reissue, in an amended form, in January 1263.

This chapter looks at the evidence for the enforcement of the Provisions during this rather confused period of political change and upheaval

[3] *Royal Letters, Henry III*, II, 197–8; *Foedera, Conventiones, Litterae etc.; or Rymer's Foedera, 1066–1383*, ed. Adam Clarke and others (4 vols., vols. I–III in two parts each, London, 1816–69), I, i, 415.

[4] *Annales Monastici*, IV, 128–9; *CR 1261–1264*, p. 126.

[5] *Foedera*, I, i, 415. [6] *DBM*, pp. 248–50. [7] *CR 1261–1264*, p. 123.

between the original enactment of the Provisions in October 1259 and their re-enactment in January 1263. It is unfortunate that a significant proportion of the plea rolls of the main royal courts potentially involved in the enforcement of the Provisions during this period either does not survive at all or survives only in very damaged form. For the Common Bench complete or almost complete rolls survive for only five terms;[8] damaged rolls for a further three (or four) terms;[9] no rolls at all for four terms.[10] Plea rolls survive for sessions in only four of the counties visited by the justices of the special eyre of 1260, though there is other evidence to suggest that sessions were actually held by these justices in at least nine other counties.[11] Of the four general eyre circuits at work in 1261 and 1262, no rolls at all survive from the circuit led by Robert de Briwes which visited Devon and Cornwall in the autumn and winter of 1262–3. From the three counties visited by the circuit led by Gilbert of Preston in 1261 there survive a complete and undamaged roll only from the Oxfordshire eyre and a damaged roll from the Berkshire eyre. No roll at all survives from the Gloucestershire eyre of this circuit. The rolls of the circuit led by Martin of Littlebury fared rather better. Complete or reasonably complete rolls survive from three counties (Warwickshire, Surrey and Sussex) and no roll at all only from the eyre of Leicestershire. The most active of all the circuits was that led by Nicholas de la Tour. Complete or almost complete rolls survive for six of the counties they visited during 1261–2 (Cambridgeshire, Huntingdonshire, Northamptonshire, Buckinghamshire, Bedfordshire and Kent) but only a damaged roll from the eyre of Essex and none at all from the eyre of Hertfordshire.[12] For the court of King's Bench rolls survive for each term in 1260 but only for one term (Trinity) in 1261 and for none at all in 1262.[13]

However, even if the loss of many of the relevant plea rolls means that our knowledge of the enforcement of the legislation during this period must remain incomplete, enough survives of these rolls and enough can be ascertained from other sources of information to show something of the steps that were taken to provide new remedies to give effect to the various clauses of the Provisions and to provide some evidence as to how long these new remedies remained available to those who might wish to take advantage of them. It is also possible to see something of how

8 For Hilary, Easter and Michaelmas terms in 1260; Michaelmas term only in 1261; Easter term only in 1262: KB 26/164, 165, 169, 171 and 166.

9 For Trinity term 1260, Trinity term 1261 and Hilary term 1262: KB 26/225, 221 and 222. The Provisions were enacted during the course of Michaelmas term 1259 for which again only a fragmentary roll (KB 26/219) survives.

10 For Hilary and Easter terms in 1261; Trinity and Michaelmas terms in 1262.

11 David Crook, *Records of the General Eyre* (Public Record Office Handbooks 20, 1982), pp. 189–91.

12 Ibid., pp. 128–32.

13 KB 26/161, 167, 168 and 156.

far, and during which periods, the courts allowed the enforcement of individual clauses of the Provisions through plaints or cited and enforced them in other forms of litigation and how far, and during which periods, the courts acted in accordance with the rules laid down in other clauses of the Provisions in both civil and criminal pleas and in their own process.

THE CREATION OF THE NEW REMEDIES AUTHORISED BY THE LEGISLATION

One of the matters which had been specifically noted for action by the council in October 1259 was the making of arrangements 'coment les brefs de purveances et des establissemenz hors de la chancelerie iscerunt sanz delay'.[14] This may simply refer to the need to ensure Chancery acted quickly in issuing the mandates sent to the counties containing copies of the texts of the Provisions of Westminster. It seems more likely, however, that it refers to the drafting of new Chancery writs which were to be made available to litigants for the enforcement of the Provisions. This was in any case a matter apparently given some priority by the reformers.

Contra formam feoffamenti

The first of the new remedies to be made available by Chancery was the writ for tenants wishing to allege unjust distraint for suit of court by their lords that had been specifically authorised by clause 3 of the Provisions.[15] The first writ of *contra formam feoffamenti* was issued within three months of the enactment of the Provisions, on 18 January 1260.[16] It ordered the sheriff of Hampshire to attach Richard of Westcote to appear in the Common Bench two weeks after Easter to answer for distraining Hilary Porter and his villeins of Holybourne to perform suit to Richard's court in Westcote 'in breach of the terms of the Provision'. The writ summarised the main contents of clause 1 of the Provisions, making it clear which specific 'provision' had allegedly been broken by the distraint. It also ordered the sheriff (in accordance with the Provisions) to secure the interim release of the distresses which Richard had taken. As was common with newly drafted writs, the writ was copied on to the Close Rolls with a marginal note drawing attention to the fact that it was the 'new writ about suits' ('novum breve de sectis'). This first writ was soon followed by others. A second writ was acquired sufficiently soon after the first for the first stage of mesne process in the case also to have been

[14] *DBM*, p. 152. [15] Below, pp. 416–17. [16] *CR 1259–1261*, p. 25.

reported back to the court in time for that same Easter term;[17] and by the following Michaelmas term another four writs had been purchased and mesne process commenced against four further defendants.[18] It is less clear when the five *contra formam feoffamenti* writs which gave rise to litigation heard in the eyres of 1261 were acquired.[19] All five writs were probably in the form of writs returnable before the justices in eyre 'at their first session in the county'. These writs might, in theory, have been acquired at any time during 1260 in expectation of future eyres in the counties concerned but in two of the cases the distraint of which the plaintiff complained had not taken place until September and October 1260.[20] So it seems unlikely that either these or the other writs were in fact acquired much before the end of 1260 when the plans for a normal eyre visitation were first made and announced.[21] It is perhaps more likely still that they were acquired during 1261 and perhaps only shortly before the eyres were held, during the spring and early summer. The six new actions of *contra formam feoffamenti* to be found in progress on the Common Bench plea roll for Michaelmas term 1261 (the only term for which a reasonably complete roll survives) are also likely to have been commenced by original writs purchased very late in 1260 or during 1261 since they do not appear as actions in progress during Michaelmas term 1260.[22]

Before the end of 1261, however, the issuing of *contra formam feoffamenti* writs seems to have been suspended. There are no new cases on the surviving Common Bench plea roll for Easter 1262 nor on the surviving plea rolls of the eyres held in Bedfordshire, Buckinghamshire, Essex, Kent and Sussex during 1262. The two *contra formam feoffamenti* cases which do appear on the plea rolls in 1262 both seem to be continuations of

17 *Nicholas of Docking v. John Lovel*: KB 26/165, m. 2.

18 *Walter de la Berghe v. Geoffrey de la Berghe*: KB 26/169, m. 6; *William of Berwick v. William bishop of Bath and Wells*: KB 26/169, m. 6; *Master William of Broxbourne v. Basilia widow of Richard of Box*: KB 26/169, m. 46; *Prior of Holy Trinity, London v. Nicholas of Lewknor*: KB 26/169, m. 70d.

19 Three of these cases were heard in the Cambridgeshire eyre held in January and February. These are: *Ralph son of Alexander of Melbourne v. prior of Ware*: JUST 1/82, m. 11d; *John Fynnor v. Alexander de Aundeville*: JUST 1/82, m. 2; and *John son of Miles of Babraham v. John des Eschalers*: JUST 1/82, m. 16d. One was heard in the Northamptonshire eyre held in June and July. This is *John Mayn v. William Marshal*: JUST 1/616, m. 11. The other case was an Oxfordshire case heard in the Berkshire eyre in February: *Robert de Brok v. Robert de Leuches*: JUST 1/40, m. 15.

20 In *Melbourne v. prior of Ware* the distraint took place on 22 September; in *Babraham v. Eschalers* the distraint took place on 23 October. The defendant's defence in *Fynnor v. Aundeville* suggests only that the distraint must have taken place after Whitsun 1260. No date at all is given or can be supplied in *Mayn v. Marshal* or in *Brok v. Leuches*.

21 Crook, *Records of the General Eyre*, p. 126.

22 *William de Ponte v. Richard de Graveney*: KB 26/171, m. 4; *Adam of Everingham v. Adam of Jesmond*: KB 26/171, m. 14; *Abbot of Thame v. John de Braybroke*: KB 26/171, m. 20d; *Ralph de Lascelles v. William son of Thomas of Graystoke et al*: KB 26/171, m. 39d; *Alice daughter of William of Langthwayt v. Wiliam de Ros*: KB 26/171, m. 43; *Thomas of Leigh v. Hugh de Loghes*: KB 26/171, m. 78.

actions commenced earlier.[23] It is possible that the demand for such writs simply dried up after an initial rush of enthusiasm. It seems more likely, however, that no more actions were initiated after 1261 because Chancery had ceased making such writs available. The change is probably to be associated with the king's appointment of Walter de Merton as chancellor in July 1261. Either on his appointment or shortly afterwards Merton must simply have ordered that no more writs of *contra formam feoffamenti* be issued. Merton's action may simply reflect the king's dislike for the legislation which the baronial council had enacted and thus for the new remedies which it had authorised. The alternative possibility is that the real dislike was simply for the wording of the writs which had been issued to give effect to the legislation and that it was this alone which led to their suspension.

Although it is possible only to be reasonably certain of the wording of the whole of the original writ in the very first of the cases, where the writ itself was enrolled on the Close Rolls (and even this is a copy of the writ, not the writ itself) it is likely that the enrolments in the other cases give us in fairly accurate form the main part of the writs which had initiated these cases. There is not much variation in the way in which the writs summarised the contents of clause 1 of the legislation and there is little in this to which the king or Merton could have taken exception. The writs simply stated that the legislation had provided 'that no one be distrained by reason of their tenements to perform suit to the courts of their lords unless they are obliged to perform that suit by form of the feoffment or they or their ancestors holding those tenements had customarily performed it before the king's first crossing into Brittany'.[24] What was much more contentious was that sub-clause of the writ which rehearsed the

[23] One is recorded on the Common Bench plea roll for Hilary term 1262. This is *Berewyck v. bishop of Bath and Wells*: KB 26/222, m. 4. This appears to be a later stage of a case first recorded in Michaelmas 1260 (KB 26/169, m. 6) though there are some puzzling differences between the formulation of the writ as recorded in the two enrolments which may indicate that the first writ had at some stage been quashed and a second similar writ been obtained. The other is a case heard in the 1262 Warwickshire eyre. This is *Leigh v. Loghes*: JUST 1/954, m. 10. An earlier procedural stage of this same case is recorded on the Common Bench plea roll for Michaelmas term 1261: KB 26/171, m. 78.

[24] '. . . ne qui occasione tenementorum suorum distringantur ad sectam faciendam ad curiam dominorum suorum nisi per formam feofamenti sui ad sectam illam teneantur vel ipsi aut eorum antecessores illa tenementa tenentes eam facere consueverunt ante primam transfretacionem regis in Britanniam.' Clerks did however have some problems in deciding whether or not the 'courts' or 'of their lords' should be plural in both parts or singular in both parts or mixed as here. There was a similar problem in deciding whether or not the tenant referred to should be in the plural (as here) or in the singular, so one sometimes finds the formulation 'ne quis . . . distringatur' instead. In one case, where the plaintiff was a prior whose predecessors in title were his predecessors, rather than his ancestors, the writ seems to have been emended and amplified to take account of that: KB26/169, m. 70d.

authority which lay behind this legislation. This was almost invariably ascribed to the 'common counsel' ('de communi consilio'),[25] which was then characterised as being either of 'the realm' or of 'the whole realm'.[26] That 'realm' or that 'whole realm' was then qualified still further. It might be described as belonging to 'the king' or 'the lord king' or 'us'.[27] It might also, and rather more neutrally, be described as the 'realm of England'.[28] Alternatively, and even more pointedly, the 'common counsel' might be described as that of 'the king's (or our) magnates' or of 'the magnates of England' or just of 'the magnates of the realm'.[29] Only quite exceptionally was the common counsel described as being just the common counsel 'of the lord king'.[30] The choice of words must have been quite deliberate. Both the main types of formulation were intended to ensure that the plaintiffs who acquired these writs and all others involved in the litigation were reminded of the political process which had produced the Provisions of Westminster. They were being reminded that they had been the product of a process which had responded to requests for legal reform and seen that legal reform enacted as part of English law. They were also being reminded that this had been part of a wider process of reform in which it was the king's subjects, and more especially his magnates, who had taken the initiative rather than the king or his officials.

[25] For a reference merely to 'counsel' see KB 26/165, m. 7d (*Porter v. Westcote*), though the writ as enrolled on the Close Rolls had spoken of 'common counsel' (*CR 1259–1261*, p. 25). For one writ which as enrolled referred to 'common council' (de communi concilio) see JUST 1/82, m. 16d (*Babraham v. des Eschalers*). The latter may, however, just be a variant spelling.

[26] For 'of the realm' ('regni') see KB 26/169, m. 46 (Michaelmas term 1260) and KB 26/171, mm. 29, 39d (Michaelmas term 1261). For 'of the whole realm' ('tocius regni') see KB 26/165, mm. 2, 7d (Easter term 1260) (and *CR 1259–1261*, p. 25); KB 26/169, m. 6 (2x), 70d (Michaelmas term 1260); JUST 1/82, m. 2 (1261 Cambridgeshire eyre); JUST 1/701, m. 6 (1261 Oxfordshire eyre); KB 26/171, mm. 4, 20d (Michaelmas term 1261).

[27] For 'of the king's realm' ('regni regis') see KB 26/165, m. 2 (Easter term 1260) and KB 26/169, m. 70d (Michaelmas term 1260). For 'of the realm of the lord king' ('regni domini regis') see JUST 1/82, m. 2 (1261 Cambridgeshire eyre). For 'of our realm' ('regni nostri') see JUST 1/701, m. 6 (1261 Oxfordshire eyre) and KB 26/171, m. 4 (Michaelmas term 1261).

[28] For 'of the realm of England' ('regni Anglie') see KB 26/165, m. 7d (Easter term 1260) (but note that the version of this writ enrolled on the Close Rolls spoke of 'regni nostri' (*CR 1259–1261*, p. 25); KB 26/169, mm. 6 (2x), 46 (Michaelmas term 1260); KB 26/171, m. 20d (Michaelmas term 1261).

[29] For 'of our magnates' ('magnatum nostrorum') see KB 26/171, m. 78 (Michaelmas term 1261) and KB 26/222, m. 4 (Hilary term 1262). For 'of the magnates of the lord king' ('magnatum domini regis') see JUST 1/82, m. 11d (1261 Cambridgeshire eyre). For 'of the magnates of England' ('magnatum Anglie') see KB 26/171, m. 4 (Michaelmas term 1261) and JUST 1/954, m. 10 (1262 Warwickshire eyre) [this had previously been enrolled as 'magnatum nostrorum' when mesne process in the case was enrolled at Michaelmas term 1261: KB 26/171, m. 78]. For 'of the magnates of the realm' ('magnatum regni') see KB 26/171, m. 43 (Michaelmas term 1261).

[30] JUST 1/82, m. 16d (1261 Cambridgeshire eyre); JUST 1/616, m. 11 (1261 Northamptonshire eyre).

They were thus both recitals of the legislation and subtle propaganda for the regime which had produced it.

Of the seventeen actions commenced during this period it is possible to trace pleadings in only seven. In three cases, all heard in eyres during 1261 (two in the Cambridgeshire eyre, one in the Berkshire eyre), defendants admitted having distrained plaintiffs for suit of court but claimed that their distraint had been justified under the terms of the legislation because their ancestors had been seised of the suit at the hands of the plaintiff's ancestors prior to 1230.[31] In each case, however, the jury found that their ancestors had not been seised before 1230 and damages were awarded to the plaintiffs for the unjust distraint. In two of the cases the losing defendants were also taken into custody pending payment of a fine to the king. An interesting additional sidelight on the legislation and its effectiveness is, however, also cast by these verdicts. In two cases it appears from the jury verdict or the pleadings that the attempted usurpation of suit of court was not something of any long standing but had happened *only after* the enactment of the legislation itself. In the third the attempted usurpation was said by the jury to have taken place only two years previously and while the legislation was under active consideration.[32] One case also suggests the kind of factual situation that might lead to 'misunderstandings' between lord and tenant about suit of court, to a lord being able to try to represent that he was owed suit when the tenant knew that he did not owe it. In *Fynnor v. Aundeville* the jury conceded that the plaintiff's father had indeed sometimes appeared at the defendant's court but insisted that this was only at the defendant's request and only to hold that court (as steward) and not in order to perform suit of court.

These were, however, the only successful plaintiffs. In one *contra formam feoffamenti* case heard in the 1262 Warwickshire eyre the defendant similarly justified his distraint on the grounds that he had been seised of the suit prior to 1230 at the hands of the previous (and unrelated) tenant of the land and issue was joined on this point. The plaintiff was nonsuited before the jury could give its verdict, probably because he knew its verdict was going to be against him.[33] In a second case the defendant successfully claimed that his distraint had been made not in order to compel the performance of suit of court but for another reason entirely.

[31] Two were heard in the 1261 Cambridgeshire eyre (*Fynnor v. Aundeville* and *Babraham v. des Eschalers*); the third (*Brok v. Leuches*) in the 1261 Berkshire eyre: for references see above, note 19. In all three cases the defendant also claimed seisin of the suit from 1230 until a recent withdrawal.

[32] In *Fynnor v. Aundeville* and *Babraham v. des Eschalers* the jury found that the suit had been usurped after the enactment of the legislation. In *Brok v. Leuches* it was said that the usurpation had taken place two years prior to the jury verdict (around Ascensiontide 1259).

[33] *Leigh v. Loghes*: above, note 23.

This was in *Porter v. Westcote*, the case which had led to the issuing of the first writ of *contra formam feoffamenti*.[34] A jury confirmed the defendant's assertion that his distraint had been made in order to compel the plaintiff to appear in court to answer a claim brought against him by a fellow tenant. The plaintiff may, even so, have benefited from having brought his action. A lord who wished to assert his right to claim suit of court from his tenant, even where he had not in fact been distraining him to do so, would probably have waived his right to take issue on the purpose of this particular distraint and taken issue on the question of entitlement; arguably, he needed to do so if he was not in future to be estopped from claiming the suit. Thus, even if not successful in this particular action, the plaintiff may still have succeeded in establishing his freedom from suit by bringing the action. A third plaintiff bringing a case in the 1261 Cambridgeshire eyre was also less fortunate.[35] The defendant justified his distraint as made against a third party and only for arrears of rent, not for arrears of suit. It was the fact that the plaintiff was only a sub-tenant of the lord who was distraining for suit of court that proved decisive. The legislation on suit of court had probably deliberately given a remedy only to tenants and not to their sub-tenants for the latter were not normally considered appropriate parties to litigate about the lord's entitlement to suit or other services owed by his own immediate tenant. Once the defendant had pleaded that the distraint had been made for arrears of service owed by the mesne the case was dismissed and the plaintiff advised to bring his action of mesne against the mesne lord instead. In the remaining case (from the 1261 Northamptonshire eyre) a plaintiff tried to use the new statutory action to attack a claim for suit of court not to a private seignorial court but to a hundred court that was in private hands. He did not even claim to be a tenant of the lord of this hundred.[36] Even on the most liberal reading of the Provisions this was not something covered by the legislation, although the plaintiff did his best to bring his complaint within it by asserting in his count that he held land within the hundred for fixed services and that he was not obliged to perform the suit by the form of his feoffment nor had his ancestors performed it prior to 1230. The defendant at once objected that the writ was inappropriate in this case, as 'this kind of writ was provided for use between lord and tenant for suits claimed to (private) courts and not to hundred courts'.[37] The court agreed with him and dismissed the case.

[34] Above, note 25. [35] *Melbourne v. prior of Ware*: above, note 19.

[36] *Mayn v. Marshal*: above, note 19.

[37] '. . . hujusmodi breve provisum fuit inter dominum et tenentem suum de sectis petitis ad curiam et non ad hundredum'.

Although clause 3 of the Provisions had also apparently envisaged the creation of a new action for lords wanting to claim suit of court which their tenants had withdrawn to match the new tenant's action, there is no evidence that any such action was created during this period.[38] Clause 2 of the Provisions had also created various rights and obligations on the division of a tenement which owed suit of court but said nothing about new actions to allow litigants to enforce them. As will be seen, there is evidence from a slightly later period for the framing of new writs and the creation of new actions to give effect to the various provisions of this clause.[39] None of this evidence, however, suggests any real possibility that the initial attempts at drafting such writs go back to this period.

Writs to secure exemption from attendance at the tourn

Chapter 4 of the legislation had exempted various groups from attendance at the sheriff's tourn.[40] The remedy initially provided was not, as might perhaps have been expected, in the form of a new action against sheriffs who had distrained those whom the legislation exempted from the duty of attendance in order to levy amercements imposed on them for absence from the tourn. Instead, it took the form of a prohibition which simply reminded a particular sheriff of the legislation and required him to observe it in a particular instance. Here, too, a new writ specifically citing the legislation had been drafted within four months of the enactment of the legislation, before the end of February 1260. It was issued for specific complainants (James of Creake and his wife, Sara) and was directed to, and against, the sheriff of Essex. The new writ form was enrolled on the Close Rolls as a model for future writs of a similar sort.[41] Again it specifically cited the legislation, mentioning most, but not all, of the groups which the legislation had exempted from attendance at the tourn, and referred to the authority behind the legislation in terms similar to those found in the *contra formam feoffamenti* enrolments.[42] It went on to prohibit the sheriff from making any distraint contrary to its terms but

[38] As will be seen, there is in fact no evidence to suggest that such an action was ever created: below, pp. 251–2.

[39] Below, pp. 178–9.

[40] Below, pp. 418–19.

[41] *CR 1259–1261*, pp. 153–4: the marginal heading describes it as being the 'new writ on tourns' (*novum breve de turnis*).

[42] 'Quia de communi consilio regni regis provisum est quod abbates, priores, comites, barones aut viri religiosi seu mulieres non habeant necesse venire ad turnos vicecomitum nisi eorum presencia specialiter exigatur, et si qui in hundredis diversis habeant tenementa similiter necesse non habeant venire ad hujusmodi turnum nisi in ballivis ubi fuerint conversantes . . .'

without spelling out to which of the exempt categories James and Sara claimed to belong.[43]

The legislation was also enforced by at least one writ issued by the Exchequer during 1261. Unlike the Chancery writ, this recited only that part of clause 4 which exempted non-residents from attendance at the sheriff's tourn. It also used a rather different formula when referring to the authority behind that clause. The writ ordered the sheriff of Essex to release distraints he had made in connexion with a demand for attendance at his tourn if an individual claiming not to have been resident in the hundred at the time the tourn was held really had not been. The writ is enrolled on the Lord Treasurer's Memoranda Roll for Michaelmas term 1261.[44] It is just possible that Chancery may also have created a modified form of writ covering only the exemption of non-residents at around the same time. The only evidence of this is a writ form found in a register of writs dating from the early years of the reign of Edward I.[45] This rehearses the legislation with a verbal formula found only during the brief period after the original enactment of the Provisions ('Quia de communi consilio magnatum regni nostri provisum est') and then goes on to recite the non-resident exemption. Curiously, however, it qualifies the non-resident exemption by allowing an exception 'if their presence is specially required for another reason', a qualification imposed by the legislation in the case of members of the exempt status groups only.[46] This must be the result of incompetent modification of the fuller writ as drafted in 1260 which covered both the exempt groups and non-residents. This could well have been Chancery itself, but it may point to the wholly unofficial nature of the drafting process which lay behind this particular modified form.

Both Chancery and Exchequer evidently went on issuing prohibitions to local sheriffs in favour of those whom the legislation had exempted from attendance at the tourn. However, by the end of 1261 both had begun to suppress references to the Provisions in those prohibitions. An order in favour of a woman and ordering the release of distresses taken

43 '... mandatum est vicecomiti Essex' quod Jacobum de Crek' et Sarram uxorem ejus occasione tenementi sui quod habent in balliva sua non distringat vel distringi permittat pro predocto turno suo contra formam provisionis predicte. Teste etc.'

44 '*Essex: provisio de turno vicecomitis.* Quia provisum est communiter per consilium regni regis quod illi qui habent tenementa in diversis hundredis non habeant necessitatem venire ad turnum vicecomitis nisi in balliva ubi fuerunt conversantes tempore quo vicecomites tenent turnum suum in eisdem hundredis mandatum est vicecomiti quod demandam quam faciat Luce de Poninges pro turno suo de terra [e]<predicta>[e] sua de Wremundeford si non fuit ibi conversans tempore quo tenuit turnum suum relaxet et averia etc.': E 368/36, m. 1d.

45 BL MS. Harley 409, fol. 38v.

46 'Si quis in diversis hundredis habeat tenementa necesse non habeat venire ad turnum vicecomitis nisi presencia earum ob aliam causam specialiter exigatur nisi in ballivis ubi fuerit conversans ...'

to enforce her attendance at the tourn also enrolled in Michaelmas term 1261 makes no mention of the legislation.[47] A second writ merely respiting a distraint made against another woman (Lucy de Montgomery) for attendance at the tourn enrolled in Hilary term 1262 similarly made no mention of the legislation and suggested that Lucy was entitled to exemption not because she was a woman (in itself grounds for exemption under the Provisions) but because the only land she held in the county was held in dower. This had not been a relevant consideration under the rules laid down in chapter 4 of the Provisions.[48] Nor does there seem to have been any mention of the legislation in a writ issued in favour of the prior of Holy Trinity Aldgate and exempting him from personal attendance at the tourn in Essex that was enrolled on the Memoranda Roll in Easter term 1262.[49] The Close Rolls also contain two writs issued in April 1262 ordering the relaxation by local sheriffs until further order of the distraints they had made on the abbot of Faversham and on Maurice de Berkeley, who was a baron, for amercements for absence from the tourn. Again, neither of them cites the Provisions.[50] It may, however, be wrong to see these writs as enforcing the rules established by the Provisions but deliberately avoiding all reference to them, for the exemption of certain of the groups to which these individuals belonged had also been a feature of custom (and in the case of the exemption of the heads of religious houses, a custom specifically affirmed by Exchequer judgment) prior to the enactment of the Provisions.[51]

Monstravit de compoto

A third new type of writ giving effect to the legislation that was drafted during the first half of 1260 was one based on clause 19 of the Provisions of Westminster. This clause had authorised the use of the process of attachment by the body against bailiffs who had failed to render their accounts when those bailiffs possessed no lands or tenements.[52] Again the writ was drafted for use by a particular plaintiff (Master Michael, the rector of Ockendon) and against a particular defendant (Godfrey of Fornham) although it envisaged litigation not in one of the king's courts but in a London city court. It started with the allegations said to have been made to the king (or rather his Chancery) by the complainant: that Godfrey had recently acted as Master Michael's bailiff at Ockendon (in Essex) with the care and administration of all his property and goods; that he had not

[47] E 368/36, m. 1. [48] E 159/36, m. 6d. [49] E 159/36, m. 8.

[50] *CR 1261–1264*, pp. 38, 44. Maurice had earlier the same year received a temporary respite from the demand for attendance at the tourn on the same grounds: E 159/36, m. 6d (Hilary memoranda).

[51] Above, pp. 84–5. [52] Below, pp. 424–5.

rendered his account; and that he had gone into hiding in London to avoid being found or distrained to render his account.[53] As will be seen, a preliminary allegation of much the same form became a standard feature of writs issued under the authority of the legislation.[54] Indeed, it was the very first word of this standard allegation ('*monstravit*') that subsequently gave its name to this particular type of writ, *monstravit de compoto*.[55] The writ then went on to cite the provisions of legislation, referring to the authority behind the legislation in a similar way to that used in the other 'statutory' writs,[56] before specifically authorising the mayor and sheriffs to have the alleged bailiff attached 'so that you have his body' ('ita quod habeas corpus') for appearance before themselves.[57] The writ was issued early in May 1260 and was also enrolled on the Close Rolls as a specimen writ.[58] Although in its recital of the legislation the writ mentioned the process which the legislation had envisaged (arrest and imprisonment of the defendant pending his appearance in court) it is less clear that the writ itself then required or authorised the use of that statutory process. All it seems to require is his 'attachment', rather than 'attachment by his body'. Such an order could be met simply by requiring the defendant to find sureties for his appearance, rather than by arresting him.

It seems likely that this period also saw the creation of a variant on that initial specimen writ, one which authorised the use of the new process to secure the appearance of a bailiff as defendant to render his account at the Common Bench at Westminster. The evidence comes from the enrolment of a Cornish account case on the plea rolls of the Common Bench for Trinity term 1261.[59] This summarises the original writ in the case as requiring the defendant to answer as to why 'whereas the same Henry had been his bailiff in "Westwevelshyre", having the care

53 'Monstravit nobis magister Michaelis persona de Wokindon' quod cum Godefridus de Fornham nuper extiterit ballivus suus in Wokindon' omnium rerum et bonorum suorum curam habens et administracionem, idem Godefridus compoto suo non soluto subterfugia querens latitat in balliva vestra ne possit inveniri vel distringi ad reddendum compotum predictum'.

54 It is a curious feature of this, as well as of the later writs, that the preliminary set of allegations says nothing about the defendant not possessing lands or tenements which would allow him to be distrained to render his account.

55 Below, p. 313.

56 'Et quia de communi consilio tocius regni nostri provisum est quod, si ballivi qui dominis suis compotum reddere tenentur se substraxerint et terras et tenementa non habeant per que distringi valeant per eorum corpora attachientur, ita quod vicecomites in quorum ballivis invenientur eos venire faciant ad compotum suum reddendum . . .'

57 '. . . vobis precipimus quod . . . predictum Godefridum attachiari faciatis, ita quod habeatis corpus ejus coram vobis in curia vestra civitatis nostre London' ad reddendum predicto Michaeli compotum suum predictum . . .'

58 *CR 1259–1261*, p. 162. A marginal note again records that this is the 'new writ of account' (*novum breve de compoto*).

59 *Geoffrey de Sully v. Henry le Waleys*: KB 26/221, m. 4d.

and administration of all of his property and goods, the same Henry, without having rendered his account, had sought out hiding places and was lurking within the sheriff's bailiwick so that he could not be found or distrained to render his account'.[60] It does not, however, as enrolled, go on specifically to cite the Provisions. Although the enrolment does not reproduce the initial *monstravit nobis* phrase found in the Close Roll writ or its reference to the legislation its other core phrases are identical to those in the specimen writ and those used in later actions of *monstravit de compoto*, and these are very different and much more elaborate than those used in the standard action of account. It seems probable, therefore, that the writ used in this action was a writ of *monstravit de compoto* and did contain a reference to the legislation but that the court clerk simply omitted this reference when he came to make the enrolment. The process, apparently the initial process, used in this case and ordered in the writ now being returned into the court also suggests that the writ was one specifically designed to give effect to the Statute. It was not the usual initial writ of summons but an order to the sheriff of Cornwall to 'have the defendant's body' in court on this return day.[61] Again, this was not quite what had been envisaged in the Provisions but could easily have resulted from an order to the sheriff of Cornwall similar in form to that contained in the specimen writ to the mayor and sheriffs of London. The next stage in the case appears the following Michaelmas term when a very similar summary of the writ initiating the action is given.[62]

The prohibition of beaupleder fines

There is also some evidence to suggest the drafting during this same period of a writ giving effect to the prohibition against demands for the payment of beaupleder fines. This comes from two different Edwardian registers of writs, of which at least one seems to belong to the earliest period of the king's reign. These reproduce just such a prohibition addressed to a sheriff, reciting the terms of the legislation and alleging that his bailiffs within a particular hundred have been demanding such a fine and ordering him to have them desist from demanding such fines in future and to release the distresses they have taken.[63] This is provided in one

[60] '. . . de placito quod cum idem Henricus extiterit ballivus suus in Westwevelshyre omnium rerum et bonorum suorum curam habens et administracionem, idem Henricus compoto suo non soluto subterfugia querens, latitat in balliva ejusdem vicecomitis ne possit inveniri vel distringi ad reddendum compotum predictum . . .'

[61] 'Et preceptum fuit vicecomiti quod haberet corpus ejus ad hunc diem'.

[62] KB 26/171, m. 68; see also below, p. 135.

[63] BL MSS. Additional 38821, fols. 15r–v; BL MS. Lansdowne 564, fol. 35v (omitting by mistake most of the specific allegation of a current distraint).

of the manuscripts with the suggestive rubric 'breve de nova provisione de pulcre placitando' ('writ on the new provision on beaupleder') which looks as though it should have applied to a writ drafted shortly after the enactment of the relevant legislation.[64] Also suggestive is the way these writs refer to the political authority behind the legislation which is being recited: 'Cum de consilio magnatum nostrorum provisum sit *or* Cum de consilio magnatum nostrorum per nos provisum sit...'[65] The former is close to the form adopted in other recitals of legislative authority during this period and its emphasis on the role of the magnates in the making of legislation seems (as will be seen) to be typical only of a relatively short period in and after 1259. The latter seems to be a minor (and perhaps unauthorised) modification of the same formula by a scribe who found the original formulation no longer in accordance with current views of the political proprieties.

ENFORCEMENT BY MEANS OF PLAINTS

Although, as far as can be seen from the surviving evidence, these four types of writ were the only new writs based on the Provisions to be created during the initial stage of the enforcement of the Provisions of Westminster in their original and unamended form, litigants who wanted remedies based on the legislation were not wholly reliant on the king's Chancery and its willingness to frame appropriate remedies. It was also possible to seek the enforcement of individual clauses of the Provisions through plaints made before chief justiciars on their visits to individual counties or before the justices of the special eyre of 1260. There are at least two examples (and possibly a third) of attempts to secure the enforcement of one of the clauses of the legislation by means of a plaint in one of these sessions.

One clear example of an individual plaint invoking the Provisions is that made by William Marmiun during the visit of the second justiciar, Hugh Despenser, to Sussex in 1260–1.[66] It was directed against John de la Rede, the bailiff of Peter of Savoy in charge of his hundred of Longbridge. It alleged that despite the 'legislation recently made in the general parliament of the lord king by the counsel of the princes and magnates of the kingdom of England'[67] which had 'prohibited that any money be

[64] BL MS. Lansdowne 564, fol. 35v.

[65] The legislation itself is recited in the following form: 'quod nec in itinere justiciariorum nostrorum nec in comitatibus nec in hundredis nec in curiis baronum decetero ab aliquibus recipantur fines pro pulcre placitando neque per sic quod non occasionentur'. There are only minor verbal differences between the two forms.

[66] Jacob, *Studies*, pp. 354–5. The plaint was made at the session held at Lewes in December 1260.

[67] '... cum per provisionem in generali parleamento domini regis nuper factam per consilium procerum et magnatum regni Anglie ...'.

given for beaupleder either in the king's court or in any other court'[68] (a reference to clause 5 of the Provisions) John had distrained William and his men of Barwick to pay forty shillings for beaupleder in the hundred. John had allegedly taken their animals on the Wednesday after Hokeday 1260 'contrary to the provision and after the making of the provision'.[69] William evidently had an additional grievance about the fine. It had previously been levied at the rate of twenty shillings. John had now increased it to forty shillings. John did not deny levying the fine. He was, however, able to plead in his defence that the money had been levied for his lord, and not for his own profit. He also added that by exacting the fine he was merely preserving his lord's seisin of the fine. This was confirmed by the jury. The complaint was dismissed and William told to sue Peter instead.

There is also a second example of a plaint, but this time a collective plaint, made during this same period to secure enforcement of the Provisions. This was made by the hundred of Bloxham during the special Oxfordshire eyre of 1260.[70] Their complaint was that the sheriff had at the two sessions of the view of frankpledge which had been held since the enactment of the legislation demanded from the hundred two kinds of payment that the legislation had prohibited.[71] They had paid them only because 'they did not then know of the legislation made by the barons'.[72] One was a fine 'pro occasionibus relaxandis', presumably a beaupleder fine, of the kind prohibited by clause 14 of the Provisions. The other was a fine '(pro) essoniis relaxandis'. It is not wholly clear to which of the Provisions this refers. It is just possible that it is a reference to clause 15 on the warranting of essoins, though this clause was not concerned with essoins at the view of frankpledge. It is, however, unclear what, if any, action was taken as a result of the presentment.

A third plaint is represented only by a brief enrolment of the resulting judgment made in the Cambridgeshire eyre of 1261.[73] Richard of Tollesland was amerced for distraining Nicholas son of Michael of Burwell for half a mark he was levying for John des Eschalers, the sheriff of Cambridgeshire, on the basis of a default made by Nicholas at the sheriff's tourn. Richard's distraint was found to be unjust because Nicholas

[68] '. . . prohibitum sit ne aliqui denarii dentur pro pulcre placitando in curia regis vel in alia quacumque curia . . .'.

[69] '. . . contra predictam provisionem et post eandem provisionem predictam'

[70] *Select Cases of Procedure Without Writ*, pp. 105–6.

[71] The reference to two sessions of the view of frankpledge is puzzling since the eyre session was held in January 1260. There could not have been more than one session of the view of frankpledge held since the enactment of the legislation in October 1259. The reference to the 'providenciam factam' and the 'providenciis factis per barones' suggests that they may mistakenly have supposed the *Providencia Baronum* to be actual, and not draft, legislation.

[72] '. . . tunc nescierunt de providenciis factis per barones'.

[73] *Select Cases of Procedure without Writ*, p. 121.

held only three acres of land without a messuage. Nothing is said in this enrolment about the distraint having been in breach of clause 4 of the Provisions which had exempted non-residents from attendance at the tourn. However, the distraint is likely to have been made after the enactment of the legislation since it was only at Michaelmas 1259 that John des Eschalers became sheriff of Cambridgeshire and it may well be that the plaint itself (if not the resulting enrolment) did specifically refer to the legislation.

There are also two other plaints about matters touched on by the Provisions made during this period but which, perhaps surprisingly, do not specifically invoke the legislation. When Hugh Bigod, the justiciar, visited Essex in December 1259 William son of William Oyn made a plaint against Roger Duntesheye and his wife, Gundreda, probably his mother and step-father, alleging that they had committed and were committing waste in the seven acres and one messuage in Matching they held in wardship of his inheritance as socage guardians.[74] Although this was something specifically prohibited by the newly enacted Provisions (in clause 12), the statutory prohibition is nowhere mentioned in the entry. This may be because the plaint was one which had been formulated before the Provisions were enacted and thus the plaint was based not on the legislation but rather on existing local, or even national, custom. The case seems to have been abandoned or settled out of court before any judgment was rendered.

A second plaint which might have been based on one of the clauses of the legislation but which makes no specific reference to it was one made by Thomas Clinton in the special Warwickshire eyre of early 1260. Thomas complained that the preceptor of Temple Balsall had acquired land held of him by two of his free tenants 'to the deceit and disinheritance of Thomas . . . by which he will lose wardship and reliefs'.[75] He did not specifically allege that the acquisitions had been made without his consent. He claimed damages of sixty marks for this. This was clearly an example of an acquisition in mortmain made without the immediate lord's consent as forbidden by clause 14 of the Provisions.[76] It seems probable, however, that these acquisitions had taken place before the enactment of the Provisions and so did not contravene the legislation. They were merely in breach of the much looser customary rules which had protected lords against such alienations prior to enactment of the Provisions.[77] The defendant did not, in any case, make any kind of substantive response to the complaint. His answer was that as the head of a Templar preceptory he was simply an official removable at the will of the

[74] Ibid., p. 98.
[75] '. . . in fraudem et exheredacionem ipsius Thome . . . per quod amissurus est wardas et relevia.'
[76] Below, pp. 422–3. [77] Above, pp. 60–1.

master of the Templars and so could not answer this or any other litigation without him. As the master was currently abroad with the king and enjoyed the king's protection during his absence, the case was adjourned without day.[78]

THE CITATION, ENFORCEMENT AND OBSERVANCE OF THE PROVISIONS IN OTHER FORMS OF LITIGATION

The courts also cited and enforced the legislation during this period in other forms of litigation in which the legislation was a relevant consideration or to which the legislation was considered applicable, even when they were not brought directly in order to secure its enforcement.

Clause 4 of the legislation on attendance at the sheriff's tourn, for example, was cited by the justices, though not apparently by either of the parties, in an action of mesne heard in the Cambridgeshire eyre of 1261.[79] Simon of Mattishall sued Henry of Childerley to acquit him of service being demanded on behalf of the king in respect of a tenement consisting of twelve acres which he held of Henry in Wimpole. The service claimed was attendance at the sheriff's tourn and Simon alleged he had been distrained to pay two shillings for a default at the tourn. The justices intervened even before the defendant had a chance to answer the complaint to ask whether Simon had any domicile in Wimpole or lived or was in frankpledge there.[80] When he answered in the negative the sheriff of Cambridgeshire was asked why he had distrained him 'since it had been provided by the lord king and his barons that no one was to be distrained for [attendance at] the sheriff's tourn other than in the hundred where he was living'.[81] The sheriff attempted to justify his distraint on the grounds that the money was part of his farm, apparently suggesting that it was part of a common fine paid by the village at the tourn rather than something specifically levied for absence from the tourn. The justices held that even this could not be justified. It was wrong to make someone pay a share of a fine owed by a village when they were not resident in that village. The sheriff was therefore amerced for his distraint. Only then did the defendant have a chance to make his defence. This was to plead that attendance at the tourn was a personal, rather than a tenurial, service, and so he was not obliged to acquit the plaintiff of it. The court agreed and dismissed the claim.

[78] JUST 1/953, m. 6d. [79] JUST 1/82, m. 11.

[80] '. . . et Symon requisitus si habeat domicilium vel sit manens in villa de Wynepol vel ibidem fuerit in liberum plegium . . .'

[81] '. . . desicut provisum est per dominum regem et barones suos quod nullus distringatur ad turnum vicecomitis nisi in hundredo ubi fuerat manens.'

Clause 9 of the Provisions had authorised the courts to award damages where heirs had been in wardship to their lords but the lords held on to their lands after they had come of age and the heir was forced to bring his assize of mort d'ancestor or action of aiel or cosinage for the recovery of the land.[82] There are at least three assizes heard in eyres during 1261–2 in which the provisions of the legislation were applied and the awarding of damages specifically justified by reference to a period of prior wardship. None specifically cites the Provisions as the authority for the award of damages,[83] and in one the damages awarded covered a period going back as far as 1257 and thus prior to the legislation. However, damages had not been awarded in such actions prior to 1259 and it was thus the Provisions which (however tacitly) authorised this.[84]

The clause was evidently intended to cover only the situation where the lord had rightfully been in possession of the heir's tenement because he held that tenement of the lord by military service. It came, however, during this period to be extended by analogy to authorise the awarding of damages in a quite different, if equally meritorious, situation: where the lord had usurped the wardship of land which was held in socage. Damages were awarded to heirs recovering against such lords in a single assize in the 1262 Buckinghamshire eyre,[85] and in two assizes in the Bedfordshire eyre of the same year.[86] In the second of these cases damages were awarded only as a result of the plaintiff securing a certification of an earlier assize, apparently one heard in the special eyre of 1260, with the specific object of seeking damages 'in accordance with the new provision recently made by the council of the lord king at Oxford'.[87] The legislation was taken as authorising the awarding of damages even where the plaintiff was still a minor,[88] and in at least one case damages were awarded for each of the six years the lord had held the land rather than just for the three years since the enactment of the legislation.[89]

[82] Below, pp. 420–1.

[83] They are *Richard Danvers v. William of Leatherhead and his wife Sara* heard in the 1261 Oxfordshire eyre (JUST 1/701, m. 3d); *Margery wife of Hugh Madus v. Simon le Parmeter* from the 1261 Huntingdonshire eyre (JUST 1/343, m. 2); and *Lucy sister of Peter de la More v. William Malerbe* from the 1262 Bedfordshire eyre (JUST 1/5, m. 2).

[84] *De La More v. Malerbe.*

[85] *Anastasia daughter of John of Burton v. abbot of Missenden*: JUST 1/57, m. 5 (=/58, m. 2).

[86] *Alice fitzSimon v. William fitzSimon*: JUST 1/5, m. 13 (=/58, m. 14d)); *Thomas son of Hamon Arkeng v. Hugh le Hare*: JUST 1/5, m. 19d.

[87] '... per novam provisionem nuper factam per consilium domini regis apud Oxon'.

[88] *Burton v. abbot of Missenden*: above, note 85; *FitzSimon v. FitzSimon*: above, note 86. In *Walter de Caen v. Walter of Merton* (JUST 1/82, m. 10d), an assize heard in the 1261 Cambridgeshire eyre, the plaintiff is noted as being of the age of twenty but as waiving such damages.

[89] *FitzSimon v. FitzSimon*: above, note 86.

Clause 10 of the Provisions had authorised the awarding of damages in the same range of actions but in a rather different situation: where the heir was already of age at the death of his ancestor and his lord had entered the tenement first and had then refused to surrender it to him.[90] Several cases provide evidence for the enforcement of this clause in the courts, though only during 1260 and 1261.[91] Two of these cases, both from 1260, specifically cite the legislation as authority for the awarding of damages;[92] and one of them draws an even closer connexion between damages and legislation by its specification that the damages were being awarded only in respect of the period since the promulgation of the statute.[93]

Clause 11 of the Provisions, prohibiting distraints made outside the fee or in the highway,[94] is known to have been cited, but only once, in litigation during this same period. The case had been brought in a session held before the justiciar Hugh le Despenser in 1261, and the reference is little more than an embellishment of a request for judgment against a defendant which would have been perfectly valid if based on existing common law rules, as the very wording of the plea itself reveals. The plaintiff asked in this case for judgment 'of his acknowledgement that he had made the distraint outside the fee of his lord, because this is against the law of the land and specifically against the new provision etc.'.[95]

In the case of clause 12 of the Provisions (on the accountability of socage guardians)[96] the evidence is only of the invocation of the general principle of accountability, not of any direct citation of the legislation. This comes in two connected cases heard in the 1262 Buckinghamshire eyre. Thomas of Sandford and his wife, Isabel, claiming as guardians in

[90] Below, pp. 420–1.

[91] *Andrew Busse v. Nicholas Treddel*: JUST 1/911, m. 6 (Despenser's Sussex eyre of 1260); *Nicholas FitzRalph [of Merton] v. John of Blaby*: JUST 1/953, m. 2d *Simon son of Simon of Sowe v. Hugh de Loges*: JUST 1/953, m. 3 (both Warwickshire special eyre of 1260); *Maud wife of Phillip of Gloucester v. Phillip Culling and his wife Alice*: KB 26/168, m. 5 (court *coram rege* for Michaelmas term 1260); *Alice wife of Robert of Kentwood v. Roger Gifford et al.*: JUST 1/701, m. 5 (1261 Oxfordshire eyre); *Abel son of William of Rissenden v. Reginald le Marchand*: JUST 1/616, m. 16 (1261 Northamptonshire eyre).

[92] *Busse v. Treddel*: 'because the defendant is lord of the fee he is therefore to answer for damages according to the new provision' ('ideo respondeat de dampnis secundum novam provisionem'); *Gloucester v. Culling*: 'it is adjudged in accordance with the statutes made in the parliament of the lord king that they recover the damages which they sustained by reason of the detention of the said land' ('consideratum est . . . secundum statuta facta in generali colloquio domini regis recuperent dampna sua que habuerunt occasionis detencionis predicte terre').

[93] *Gloucester v. Culling*: 'their damages which they sustained by reason of the retention of the said land since the promulgation of the said statutes' ('dampna sua que habuerunt occasione detencionis predicte terre post promulgacionem predictorum statutorum').

[94] Below, pp. 420–1.

[95] 'De hoc quod cognoscit quod fecit districcionem extra feodum domini sui quia hoc est contra legem terre et precise contra novam provisionem etc.': *Select Cases of Procedure without Writ*, p. 133.

[96] Below, pp. 422–3.

socage of Isabel's daughter Anastasia, recovered the wardship of some land in a writ of right of wardship case against the abbot of Missenden.[97] When the court gave judgment in their favour it was careful to add as condition of the recovery the rider 'provided that when Anastasia comes of age they answer to her for all the issues and profits coming from the said tenements with due allowance for the costs of her upbringing and their interim costs and expenses'.[98] A similar proviso was added when damages were awarded in a parallel assize of mort d'ancestor brought by Thomas and Isabel in the heiress's name in the same eyre.[99] Although there is no direct citation of the Provisions in either case the substantive requirement is exactly the same as that laid down by the Provisions and such riders are not to be found in similar judgments given earlier.

We have already noted what may be one attempt to ensure the enforcement of clause 14 of the Provisions by means of a plaint in the special Warwickshire eyre of 1260.[100] The same clause was also invoked, but this time by the justices, in an assize of novel disseisin heard in the special Leicestershire eyre of the same year before the same panel of justices. The defendant had claimed in pleading that the plaintiff, a prior, had entered the land only through a death-bed feoffment made by a curtesy tenant, and that on the curtesy tenant's death he had asserted his rights as reversioner by ejecting the plaintiff. The assize found this story untrue but nevertheless asked the aid of the justices in deciding whether or not the plaintiff's seisin had been of sufficient duration for him to have been disseised by the defendant. Judgment was eventually given for the defendant both on the grounds that the seisin had been too short for the protection of the assize and with a specific citation of the legislation. The prior's entry had been, it was said, 'without the permission and against the will of the said Ralph the chief lord of that fee contrary to the constitution made by the magnates and common counsel of the kingdom of England'.[101]

97 JUST 1/57, m. 11d (=/58, m. 16).

98 'Ita quod cum eadem Anastasia ad plenam etatem pervenerit, respondeant ei de exitibus et omnibus proficuis provenientibus de predictis tenementis salva rationabili sustentatione ejusdem Anastasie et salvis eisdem Thome et Isabella custis suis et expensis interim apponendis.'

99 '... et dampna sua que taxantur per predictos juratores ad c solidos ... et de consilio curie provisum est quod predicti c solidi liberentur predicto Thome de Sanford custodienda ad opus predicte Anastasie et similiter predictum mesuagium et terra tenenda usque ad legitimam etatem ipsius Anastasie, ita quod cum eadem Anastasia ad plenam etatem pervenerit respondeat de exitibus et omnibus proficuis provenientibus de predicto mesuagio et terra, salvo racionabili sustentacione ejusdem Anastasie': JUST 1/57, m. 5 (=/58, m. 2).

100 Above, p. 122.

101 '... sine licencia et voluntate predicti Radulfi capitalis domini feodi illius contra constitucionem factam per magnates et commune consilium regni Anglie': *Prior of Alvecote v. Ralph Basset*: JUST 1/456, m. 3.

Much more dubious evidence for the enforcement of the Provisions at a local level is provided by an enrolment on the court roll of the manor of Redgrave in Suffolk in 1260.[102] One of the tenants of the manor was suing one of his fellows for cutting down and carrying away the trees around his messuage. The defendant objected that he himself was in seisin of the tenement where the plaintiff alleged the trees had been cut down and so by answering the charge he would in effect be answering for his free tenement and refused to do this without the king's writ.[103] The plaintiff said his complaint related only to the wrongful removal of his chattels and was not tantamount to a complaint relating to title to the free tenement. The case was then adjourned for judgment. Although the case invoked the rule recently confirmed by clause 18 of the Provisions,[104] the pleadings as enrolled do not specifically invoke the recent legislation and are probably better seen as simply invoking the existing common law rule rather than its recent statutory confirmation.

Observance of the legislation produces positive evidence in the case of all of these clauses. It is more difficult to find clear evidence for the enforcement and observance of legislation where the evidence is merely negative. Clause 23 of the Provisions had provided that no vouchee who was vouched to warranty in an eyre should be amerced for his absence from court when vouched even if he was resident in the county where the eyre was being held.[105] Here the only possible evidence for compliance with the legislation is the absence of amercements against vouchees. That is indeed what the surviving evidence shows.[106]

Clause 8 of the Provisions allowed the overriding of charters of exemption from jury service where this was necessary in the interests of justice.[107] Evidence for this is particularly difficult to find for, if the disregarding of an exemption took place successfully, there would be nothing on the face of the record to show that it had occurred. Fortunately, in at least one instance, resistance to the overriding of an exemption by its holder leaves positive evidence in the record. Herbert Pecche had been granted such a charter in November 1250.[108] During the course of the Berkshire eyre of 1261 Gilbert of Preston and his colleagues authorised the overriding of his charter and attempted to compel Herbert to serve

102 University of Chicago, Bacon MS. 1, m. 1.

103 '. . . dicens quod non vult respondere de libero tenemento suo sine precepto domini regis eo quod nominat certum locum et tenementum super quod dicte arbores steterunt de quo tenemento idem Adam est in seisina . . .'

104 Below, pp. 426–7.

105 Below, pp. 426–7.

106 For examples of warrantors resident in the counties concerned being vouched and then summoned for a later day but not being amerced for their absence see JUST 1/82, m. 5 (1261 Cambridgeshire eyre); JUST 1/616, mm. 3d, 5d, 17d, 29d, 33 (1261–2 Northamptonshire eyre).

107 Below, pp. 420–1.

108 *CPR 1247–58*, p. 82.

on a jury. When he refused to serve on it they amerced him for contempt and the amercement was subsequently assessed at half a mark.[109] This was not, however, the end of the story. The Berkshire eyre ended at the very beginning of March 1261 and the justices then sent estreats of the fines and amercements of the eyre into the Exchequer. Before the barons of the Exchequer could make any attempt to have the amercement levied Herbert approached the king to have the amercement cancelled. The resulting writ was issued on 20 May 1261 and enrolled on both the Chancery fine rolls and the Exchequer memoranda rolls.[110] It says nothing at all about the legislation but revealingly treats Hubert's exemption from jury service as unqualified and absolute:

> As the king has conceded to Herbert Pecche an exemption from assizes, juries and recognitions in perpetuity he has pardoned him the half mark at which he was recently amerced before the king's justices lately itinerant in the county of Berkshire because he refused to be placed on a certain assize before the said justices contrary to the said acquittance. And the barons of the Exchequer are ordered to acquit the same Herbert of the said half mark.[111]

The justices of the Berkshire eyre were merely following the Provisions. This is likely to have been known to whoever drafted this writ for Herbert Pecche. It is clear that in their eyes, and as early as May 1261, the Provisions were a nullity and of no effect, particularly perhaps in a case like this where they purported to invalidate or at least suspend the effect of a royal grant of privileges.

OBSERVANCE OF THE PROVISIONS IN JUDGMENTS RELATING TO CROWN PLEAS FINES AND AMERCEMENTS

Murdrum fines

Clause 22 of the Provisions of Westminster had stipulated that in future the *murdrum* fine was only to be adjudged in cases of felonious homicide and not for accidental deaths.[112] Here the surviving plea rolls certainly show how far this legislation was observed by the justices in eyre. But they also seem to show rather more. They seem to show just how well aware individual county communities were of the legislation and its relevance

[109] JUST 1/40, m. 4d. [110] C 60/58, m. 9; E 159/34, m. 15.

[111] 'Quia Rex concessit Herberto Pecche quietanciam de assisis, juratis et recognicionibus suo perpetuo perdonavit ei dimidiam marcam ad quam nuper amerciatus fuit coram justiciariis regis ultimo itinerantibus in comitatu Berkes' eo quod contempsit poni in quadam assisa coram prefatis justiciariis contra quietanciam predictam. Et mandatum est baronibus de scaccario quod eundem Herbertum de predicta dimida marca quietum esse faciant.'

[112] Below, pp. 426–7.

and how much care they took to draw the legislation to the attention of the justices. Their opportunity to do this came when they were asked early on in the eyre what the county's custom was with regard to the 'presentment of Englishry'.

At least two counties on the eyre circuit led by Nicholas de la Tour in 1261–2 seem specifically to have cited the legislation to the justices when asked about the county's custom. Cambridgeshire was visited in January and February 1261. When asked about Englishry the county confirmed that its custom was that it be presented by one relative from each side of the family.[113] The county then seems to have gone on to cite the recent legislation to the justices to limit their obligation to present Englishry, and also by implication their liability to pay the *murdrum* fine if they failed to do so, to cases where death was the result of a felonious killing rather than an accident: 'And since it has recently been provided by the king's council that *murdrum* is not to be adjudged in the kingdom where only accidental death has been presented but is to apply only for those killed by felony and not otherwise Englishry is only to be presented in future for those killed by felony in the said form'.[114] The other county on this circuit to cite the legislation was the county of Buckinghamshire, visited in the eyre of January–February and April 1262. Here again the county started by stating the county's custom in the presentment of Englishry, requiring one male to present from each side of the family and for them to be the cousins of the deceased (the son of an uncle on the father's side and of an aunt on the mother's side) and to be aged at least twelve. An initial stated limitation of this obligation to felonies ('et hoc de feloniis tantum') was then expanded by a specific reference to the legislation that is virtually identical to that made by the county of Cambridgeshire.[115] In both counties the legislation was also observed by the justices when it came to adjudging *murdrum* fines.

The way in which the reference to the recent legislation and its effects was tacked on to the initial statement of county custom makes it possible (but as we will see, unlikely) that both entries are not just a straight record of the county's statement of its custom but a compound

[113] JUST 1/82, m. 23.

[114] 'Et quia de novo provisum est per consilium domini regis quod murdrum non adjudicetur in regno ubi infortunium tantummodo presentatur set locum teneat de interfectis per feloniam et non aliter, ideo Englescheria de cetero non presentetur nisi de interfectis per feloniam in forma predicta etc.'

[115] 'Et quia de novo provisum est per consilium domini regis quod murdrum decetero non judicetur in regno ubi infortunium tantumodo presentatur sed locum teneat de interfectis per feloniam et non aliter, ideo murdrum decetero non presentetur in comitatu isto nisi tantum de masculis et hoc etatis xij annorum et amplius': JUST 1/58, m. 20. The last sub-clause is clearly the result of clerical error.

enrolment which makes a silent transition in the middle from a statement of county custom to a declaration on the part of the justices, rather than the counties concerned, of the existence of the new legislation and how it was going to affect the county community. What renders this the less likely of the two possible interpretations is the fact that there was no similar statement regarding the new legislation and its effect in two other counties on the same circuit for which there survive similar statements of custom. In the county of Huntingdonshire, which was visited in between the two sessions of the Cambridgeshire eyre during February 1261, all the county did when it presented its custom was to state that Englishry could be presented by one relative from either side of the family and also specifically to state that it only applied in cases of felonious homicide.[116] The latter restriction was not in keeping with the previous custom of the county but neither county nor justices evidently felt any need to justify this departure from prior custom by specific reference to the legislation. The new restriction was similarly observed by the justices in adjudging *murdrum* fines. No plea roll now survives for the Hertfordshire eyre of October–November 1262 but a reference on the plea roll of the 1287 eyre indicates that a similar statement of custom was made by this county, also contrary to previous custom. Again there seems to have been no specific reference to the legislation as providing justification for the change.[117]

There is also evidence from a second circuit, that led by Gilbert of Preston, of a third county citing the legislation when asked for its custom with regard to the presentment of Englishry. When this circuit of justices visited Oxfordshire in January and February 1261 the county stated its prior custom as that of making the presentment by one relative on each side of the family of the deceased victim and that it needed to be made for both accidental deaths and felonious homicides ('et tam de fortuniis quam de feloniis'). It then went on, however, to specifically cite the legislation (which they misascribed to the parliament of Oxford) as providing that in future the *murdrum* fine should only be adjudged in respect of felonious homicides: 'but by the council of the lord king in the parliament of Oxford it was provided that the *murdrum* fine be not adjudged except for

[116] 'Englescheria presentatum est in comitatu per unum ex parte patris vel unum ex parte matris et de feloniis tantum': JUST 1/343, m. 11.

[117] 'Totus comitatus recordatur quod Englechria non presentatur in comitatu isto, et compertum est per rotulos N. de Turry et sociorum suorum quondam justiciariorum itinerancium in comitatu isto quod Eng' presentatur in comitatu isto per unum masculum ex parte patris et alium masculum ex parte matris. Et hoc de eis qui sunt septem annorum et amplius in feloniis et non in infortuniis. Et totus comitatus prius recordatur quod nulla Engl' presentatum fuit in comitatu isto. Ideo totus comitatus in misericordia. Et similiter compertum est per rotulos ultimi itineris quod murdrum adjudicatum fuit in comitatu isto': JUST 1/327, m. 1. The plea rolls of the intervening eyre of 1278 include no statement of Englishry custom.

felonies'.[118] No *murdrum* fines were adjudged for accidental deaths in this eyre.

In at least four of these five counties (and probably in all five) the legislation was observed in practice by the justices in making their judgments imposing the *murdrum* fine. This also seems to have been the case in at least two other counties. Essex was visited by de la Tour and his colleagues in June and July 1262. Its recorded statement of custom in regard to the presentment of Englishry specifically admitted liability for accidental deaths as well as felonious homicides,[119] but what survives of the damaged crown pleas section of the plea roll contains no judgments of *murdrum* in respect of accidental deaths and suggests, even if it does not conclusively prove, that in practice the justices observed the legislation. The legislation was also observed during the visitation of Warwickshire by Martin of Littlebury and his colleagues in June and July of 1262. Here the county's statement of Englishry custom apparently denied that Englishry was presented in the county at all and the justices seem to have taken this as conceding that *murdrum* would be adjudged in all cases.[120] Previous custom (as shown by the 1247 eyre in the county) had allowed the justices to impose *murdrum* fines in respect of accidental deaths and, had this precedent been followed, *murdrum* fines would have been levied for such deaths in this eyre as well. It was not. In most hundreds the clerks recorded only a single judgment of *murdrum* and it could easily have been chance that in all these cases the first death for which a *murdrum* fine was adjudged happened to be a felonious killing. However, in one hundred (Barlichway) the first judgment of *murdrum* is recorded only after two cases of accidental death for which no such judgment is recorded and this makes it clear that the legislation really was being observed by the justices.[121]

There are, however, at least two counties visited by two different groups of justices during the same period where it is clear that the legislation was deliberately disregarded by the justices. The county of Berkshire was visited by Gilbert of Preston and his colleagues in February and March 1261 just after they had visited Oxfordshire and had been reminded of the legislation on the *murdrum* fine. The surviving plea roll does not contain any statement of the county's custom on *murdrum* or the presentment of

[118] '. . . set de consilio domini regis in parliamento Oxon' provisum fuit quod murdum non adjudicaretur nisi de feloniis tantum': JUST 1/701, m. 19.

[119] 'Et presentatur Englescheria tam de infortuniis quam de feloniis': JUST 1/236B, m. CR1.

[120] 'Et sciendum quod in comitatu isto non presentatur Englescheria, ideo murdrum': JUST 1/954, m. 48.

[121] JUST 1/954, m. 48d: a pauper who had died from cold and a man found dead but without any wounds and of whose death no one was suspected. Even had Englishry been presented in the county none could have been presented in these cases as both men were unknown.

Englishry. What it does contain, however, are at least two judgments of *murdrum* in cases where a death was clearly accidental and not felonious.[122] The county of Sussex was visited by Martin of Littlebury and his colleagues in November and December 1262. Here the county's statement of its custom with regard to the presentment of Englishry is recorded and we therefore know that it was the county which had initially stated its liability to present Englishry (and, in default, its liability to pay the *murdrum* fine) both in respect of felonious homicides and for accidental deaths.[123] What is also clear, however, is that despite their earlier compliance with the legislation in the Warwickshire eyre of the summer of the same year Littlebury and his colleagues chose to disregard the legislation and adjudged *murdrum* in several cases of accidental death.[124]

Other amercements imposed in connexion with crown pleas

Clause 21 of the Provisions had provided that villages should not be amerced in future at the eyre for failure to attend inquests before sheriffs or coroners into crown pleas 'fully', provided enough of the residents attended to allow the holding of the inquest.[125] Here too in the 1261 Oxfordshire eyre there was what seems to be a deliberate attempt by the county to remind the justices of the existence of the legislation (again apparently ascribing it incorrectly to the parliament of Oxford),[126] and the justices in practice observed the legislation. No other county is recorded as having reminded the justices of the legislation in the same way and in at least two counties Martin of Littlebury and his colleagues can be found deliberately disregarding it. One such amercement is recorded without any comment or any attempted justification on the rolls of the Sussex eyre held in November and early December 1262.[127] A second such amercement is recorded on the rolls of the Surrey eyre whose first session took place in October 1262 and whose second session began in

[122] JUST 1/40, mm. 24d, 25d (in both cases deodands were forfeited). For other possible examples see JUST 1/40, mm. 23, 23d, 24, 26d, 27.

[123] 'Totus comitatus presentat quod Englescheria presentatur in isto comitatu per unum ex parte patris et alium ex parte matris de masculis tantum cujuscumque etatis fuerunt tam de infortuniis quam de feloniis': JUST 1/912A, m. 35.

[124] For examples see JUST 1/912A, m. 35 (*murdrum* adjudged in the case of a man who died who had had the falling-sickness); m. 35d (a leper with the falling-sickness); m. 36d (a man accidentally crushed in a marl-pit).

[125] Below, pp. 424–5.

[126] 'Set de consilio domini regis in parliamento Oxon' provisum fuit . . . similiter quod villate non amerciarentur pro infortuniis quamvis plenarie non venerunt ad inquisicionem: JUST 1/701, m. 19. The 'pro infortuniis' has clearly been incorrectly inserted here and belongs to the intervening clause about the *murdrum* fine.

[127] JUST 1/912A, m. 35.

mid-January 1263, more than a week before the justices received the text of the first reissue of the Provisions which was issued very much under the king's aegis and with his approval.[128] In this case the amercement of the four vills of Clapham, Tooting Bec, Battersea and Wandsworth was specifically justified by the justices as being in accordance with county and hundredal custom as attested by both the county and the hundred jurors. This was said to require the attendance at inquests into homicides of all those aged twelve and over who were resident (and in frankpledge) in the villages concerned.[129] The amercement was probably imposed before the justices were notified of the reissued Provisions, for it is difficult to believe that they would have disregarded the reissued legislation or tried to argue that local custom alone was sufficient to authorise deviation from its provisions. The attempted appeal to local custom makes most sense in the context of judicial awareness of legislation no longer considered binding by the court but of which a courtroom audience might itself be aware.

Of the other form of crown pleas amercement prohibited by the Provisions (in clause 24), the amercement of the sureties of clerics released on bail who then pleaded their clerical status,[130] the plea rolls have much less to say. There are no enrolments recording the specific invocation of the legislation but equally no enrolments which show the justices disregarding it.

ENFORCEMENT THROUGH PRESENTMENTS

Another way in which the Provisions may have been enforced is through action taken in response to presentments made at sessions of the general eyre. The evidence for this is, however, ambiguous. There was, for example, a presentment made against the steward of the abbot of St Albans at the 1262 Hertfordshire eyre for putting 'free men of the town of St Albans on oath without the special order of the lord king or warrant'.[131] However, the presentment as enrolled makes no specific mention of clause 18 of the Provisions,[132] nor does it make plain whether the steward had

[128] See below, p. 144. The second session began on 13 January and the copy of the text of the Provisions sent to these justices was dated 20 January and must have taken at least a day to reach them.

[129] '. . . et quia testatum est per comitatus et per xij quod quilibet xij annorum per sommonicionem vicecomitis vel ballivorum suorum venire debent ad inquisicionem de morte hominis, et villate de Clopham, Totinge le Bek, Baudrichesegh' et Wendlesurth non venerunt sicut summoniti fuerunt. Ideo in misericordia': JUST 1/874A, m. 25.

[130] Below, pp. 426–7.

[131] '. . . ponit liberos homines de villa sancti Albani ad sacramentum prestandum sine speciali precepto domini regis vel waranto': JUST 1/321, m. 1.

[132] Below, pp. 424–5.

been doing this before or after 1259 or both. Since there had been a customary rule prohibiting the practice prior to 1259,[133] it is not clear whether or not the presentment should be seen as presenting a breach of this customary rule or of the Provisions. Much the same applies to the presentment made in the 1262 Sussex eyre by the jurors of the hundred of Grinstead against the bailiffs of Peter of Savoy for 'making free tenants take oaths without the order of the lord king for the inquests they make into the cutting down of trees in the forest'.[134]

OBSERVANCE OF THE PROVISIONS ON INITIAL AND MESNE PROCESS

One further way of tracking the compliance of Chancery and the courts with the legislation of 1259 is through observing the processes used in the new statutory actions to secure the attendance of defendants in court, to see how far they match those laid down by the legislation, and by measuring how far the courts observed the provisions about changes in mesne process in the existing action of *quare impedit* that were laid down by clause 7 of the Provisions.

Clause 3 of the Provisions of Westminster had established a streamlined mesne process for the new tenant's action (*contra formam feoffamenti*) against a lord distraining for suit of court.[135] Initial attachment was to be followed by *facias venire* and then the grand distress and, on continued contumacy, the awarding of judgment by default. All the actions recorded on surviving plea rolls do seem to have begun, as the legislation required, with an order to the appropriate sheriff to attach, rather than summon, the defendant. It also seems probable that all the original writs in these actions also authorised the sheriff to secure the interim release of the distresses taken by the defendant, as provided by clause 3 of the Provisions.[136] Such a clause is certainly included in the specimen writ enrolled on the Close Rolls.[137] It is also included, though probably only as a result of scribal error (since it has no real part to play in the functioning of the action as enrolled), in the two enrolments of a single case heard in the 1261 Oxfordshire and Berkshire eyres.[138] Normal enrolment practice would have led to its omission. Thus the silence of other entries should not be taken to imply its omission from the writs by which they had been

[133] Above, pp. 101–3.

[134] '. . . faciendo libere tenentes jurare sine precepto domini regis ad inquisiciones quas faciunt de arboribus abscisis in foresta': JUST 1/912A, m. 39d.

[135] Below, pp. 416–17. [136] Below, pp. 416–17. [137] Above, p. 109.

[138] JUST 1/701, m. 6: 'Et averia ipsius. . . . si que ea occasione capta fuerunt . . .'; JUST 1/40, m. 15: '. . . si que ea occasione capta fuerunt sine dilacione replegiari facias . . .'

commenced. In two early cases (from Easter and Michaelmas terms in 1260) an initial attachment was followed, as the legislation required, by *facias venire*,[139] but in another two cases from the same Michaelmas term and in three cases from Michaelmas term 1261 an initial attachment was followed (as in ordinary mesne process) by a second attachment by better pledges.[140] Michaelmas term 1261 also supplies the one clear example of *facias venire* being followed by the grand distress as stipulated in the legislation;[141] but in another case heard the same term it was ordinary (and not a grand) distress that was ordered after an unspecified earlier stage, in clear contravention of the Provisions.[142] There are no examples during this period of plaintiffs recovering by default but equally no cases which had obviously reached the stage at which judgment by default would have been appropriate under the legislation.

Clause 19 of the legislation laid down rules only about the new initial process that was to become available against landless bailiffs in what was to become the new action of *monstravit de compoto*.[143] As we have already seen, there is some doubt as to whether the new non-returnable and returnable writs (even though they correctly recited the legislation) also properly ordered the correct action to be taken to secure the attendance of such defendants.[144] Confirmation that the courts too may have been confused about what the legislation required is provided by the Common Bench at Trinity term 1261 accepting a sheriff's return that he had accepted two mainpernors for appearance provided by the defendant, rather than arresting him, as the legislation required, and then ordering that the grand distress be used against the defendant to secure his appearance at the quindene of Martinmas.[145] Even more confusion on the part of both court and plaintiff seems to be shown by the enrolment made at that return day. This records the sheriff as having been ordered to summon (rather than distrain) the defendant and that he had failed to do this, giving as his excuse that the defendant possessed no property within his bailiwick, something apparently presupposed in the original writ. Even more curiously, the entry goes on to record the plaintiff or his agent attesting 'that he does have lands and tenements at Combe in sufficiency where he can be summoned',[146] thereby apparently contradicting

139 KB 26/165, m. 2 (Easter term 1260); KB 26/169, m. 6 (Michaelmas term 1260).

140 KB 26/169 mm. 46, 70d (Michaelmas term 1260); KB 26/171 mm. 14, 39d, 78 (Michaelmas term 1261).

141 KB 26/171, m. 4 (Michaelmas term 1261).

142 KB 26/171, m. 43: an order that the defendant 'be distrained by his lands etc., so that the sheriff have his body' follows an unspecified earlier stage, the defendant being said simply to have made several defaults.

143 Below, pp. 424–5. 144 Above, pp. 118–19. 145 KB 26/221, m. 4d.

146 '... quod habet terras et tenementa apud Cumb' ad sufficientiam ubi potest summoneri'.

the presupposition of his original writ. And more curiously still, this then led to the issuing of an order for a further summons of the defendant.[147] Whatever the court thought it was doing in this case it clearly did not have the provisions of clause 19 in mind.

Clause 7 of the Provisions had reduced the mesne process in *quare impedit* to just three stages: summons, attachment and grand distress, followed by judgment by default.[148] Here, too, the record of the courts in observing the legislation is (as with *contra formam feoffamenti*) a patchy one and seems to reflect a considerable confusion in the minds of the justices about the actual provisions of the legislation. In two cases in Hilary term 1260 an attachment was indeed followed, as the legislation required, by a grand distress,[149] but in Michaelmas term 1260 an attachment was followed by a second attachment,[150] and in two other cases that term an essoin was followed by a *facias venire*, not a type of process previously used in the action.[151] A note appended to one of these enrolments even claims the authority of the Provisions for this process.[152] This must reflect a confusion either in the minds of the justices or in their text of the Provisions between the abbreviated process authorised by the legislation for *quare impedit* and the abbreviated process authorised in *contra formam feoffamenti* of which *facias venire* was indeed a stage. The confusion seems to have persisted. A similar *facias venire* stage was authorised in Michaelmas term in 1261 in another *quare impedit* case in which the king was the plaintiff.[153] In another case from the same term in which the king was also the plaintiff, however, the grand distress was correctly awarded after the first attachment.[154] Nor is there any evidence for the courts awarding judgment by default in an action of *quare impedit* during this period although there is at least one case in which it would have been appropriate.[155]

ADJOURNMENTS

One last measure of the effectiveness and enforcement of the legislation by the courts between 1259 and the end of 1262 is how well they observed the requirements of clauses 6 and 7 about the minimum numbers of days

[147] KB 26/171, m. 68. [148] Below, pp. 418–19. [149] KB 26/164, mm. 5, 31.
[150] KB 26/169, m. 20. [151] KB 26/169, mm. 45d, 59.
[152] '. . . per autenticum nove provisionis': KB 26/169, m. 45d.
[153] KB 26/171, m. 71. [154] KB 26/171, m. 9.
[155] *Abbot of Hales v. Baldwin de Lisle*: KB 26/164, m. ld (Hilary term 1260): the defendant had been distrained and had found two mainpernors, grand distress was awarded for the month of Easter; KB 26/165, m. 18 (Month Easter 1260): unfinished entry; KB 26/225, m. 11 (quindene of Trinity 1260): grand distress, mainpernors found, repeated order for grand distress; KB 26/169, m. 5 (Michaelmas term 1260): pleadings in the case.

Table 1 *The length of adjournments in actions of dower in the Common Bench, 1260–2*

	Length of adjournments (by return days)				
Term	7	6	5 (% affected)	4	3
Hilary 1260		10	50	25	10
Easter 1260		30	20	20	
Michaelmas 1260	13	40	15	20	
Michaelmas 1261	10	13	20	33	
Easter 1262			22	60	

Sources: Based on the length of adjournments (in terms of how many return days distant the day to which the case is adjourned lies) in cases of dower *unde nichil habet* recorded in KB 26/164, 165, 169, 171 and 166, expressed as a percentage of the total number of dower cases for which there are recorded adjournments that term and omitting those where the evidence is ambiguous.

to be given in actions of dower *unde nichil habet*, darrein presentment and *quare impedit*.[156]

Actions of dower unde nichil habet

There are only five terms during this period for which substantially complete Common Bench plea rolls survive.[157] It is therefore not possible to trace individual dower cases all the way through to see how many days a year were actually given in each case and whether this was in accordance with the legislation. Nor is it possible to see whether the number of days actually given in such cases in the course of a year changed materially over the course of the period. What the surviving plea rolls do allow, however, is an analysis of the length of the adjournments made in such cases during those terms, and this provides at least an approximation to the evidence we are seeking, since it was the length of individual adjournments which ultimately governed the number of days that were given in each case each year. The results of an analysis of the adjournments recorded on the faces of each of these plea rolls are summarised in Table 1. A majority of adjournments in each of these terms other than Michaelmas term 1260 clearly met the 'target' figure of adjourning the case for a further hearing at a day no more than five return days away and (given the length of Michaelmas term) somewhat longer adjournments than this would still

[156] Below, pp. 418–19. [157] Above, p. 108.

have been compatible with the stated purpose of the legislation of giving at least one day in each term in such cases. The 'normal' interval between stages in dower cases had in any case been reduced by two, three or four return days from that generally obtaining in dower cases previously.

Darrein presentment and quare impedit

The story with regard to the courts' compliance with clause 7 of the Provisions and adjournments in actions on vacant churches is both more complicated and more difficult to interpret. During Hilary and Easter terms 1260 most adjournments do indeed seem to span just two or three return days.[158] There are a number of longer adjournments as well, however.[159] Some of these may be in cases where the living was known to be no longer vacant. Other longer adjournments may have been at the plaintiff's own request though, if so, this should have been noted. However, some, and in particular the shorter adjournments which still fall short of the statutory requirement, are perhaps best interpreted as indicating an intention not to be bound by the letter of the legislation but to honour its spirit, that of ensuring the relatively rapid hearing of such cases. Compliance with the legislation is much less evident in Michaelmas term 1260 where only two (or possibly three cases) have the two or three return day adjournments fixed by the legislation,[160] and five cases all have longer adjournments. A majority are still shorter than the normal adjournment.[161] In Michaelmas term 1261 there are again two cases in which the adjournment was of the two or three return day kind stipulated by the legislation,[162] but in another four cases the adjournment ranged from four return days to seven return days away. Again all are shorter than the standard adjournment.[163] The fragmentary roll for Hilary term 1262 has one adjournment that is in accordance with the statutory norm and one that is not,[164] while the fuller roll for Easter term 1262 has only one in accordance with the statute,[165] and four that are not, though of

[158] KB 26/164, mm. 1, 5, 7, 22d, 23 ter., 25, 27d, 31; KB 26/165, mm. 1, 2d bis, 4 ter, 5d, 16d.

[159] There is one to a return day nine return days away (KB 26/165, m. 3d), one to a return day six return days away (KB 26/164, m. 1d), two to return days five return days away (KB 26/165, m. 6d bis) and one to a return day four return days away (KB 26/165, m. 11).

[160] KB 26/169, mm. 57d, 59 and possibly m. 45d.

[161] KB 26/169, m. 9d (four return days away), mm. 1d, 5 (five return days away) and mm. 13, 20 (as many as eight return days away: but note that in the second case the adjournment was at the request of the parties).

[162] KB 26/171, mm. 61d, 71.

[163] KB 26/171, m. 8 (four return days away), m. 28 (four or five return days away), m. 9 (six return days away) and m. 63 (seven return days away).

[164] KB 26/222, m. 2d (three return days away) and m. 6 (six return days away).

[165] KB 26/166, m. 7 (three return days away).

these three are still shorter than the standard adjournment.[166] The overall conclusion seems to be that compliance with the legislation was never perfect but that this came closest to being achieved immediately after the passage of the legislation in Hilary and Easter terms 1260. Thereafter the statutory target was only ever met in a minority of cases. Even in those in which it was not it is not necessarily the case that the statute was ineffective. It may still have been the legislation that helped to ensure that in most cases, and perhaps in all cases where the church was indeed still vacant, a shorter adjournment was made than the normal process of the court would have provided.

[166] KB 26/166, m. 4 (four return days away), m. 31 (six return days away) and m. 3 (eight return days away).

Chapter 5

THE REVISION AND REISSUING OF THE PROVISIONS, 1263–4

THE POLITICAL BACKGROUND TO THE REISSUES OF 1263

Henry III returned to England from a long visit to France in December 1262 to face a general Welsh rising, discontent on the part of those members of the Lord Edward's retinue who had been dismissed in the summer of 1262, and widespread local disaffection.[1] One easy way for him to make a conciliatory gesture towards some of the more moderate of his opponents was for him to end the uncertainty which had hung over the Provisions of Westminster ever since his ambiguous repudiation of the work of the reforming council in May 1262.[2] This he did by reissuing the Provisions in a revised text in January 1263. This marked his own personal acceptance and approval of the legislation but at the same time put his own distinctive stamp on it. A second reissue followed in June of the same year. The reasons for this reissue are much less obvious. Henry's opponents had already renewed their commitment to the Provisions of Oxford and begun attacks on aliens, royalists and courtiers. It is difficult to see what Henry may have thought he would gain by such a reissue, particularly as no significant changes were made in it at this time.

THE TEXTS OF THE 1263 REISSUES

Three texts of these reissues are known to exist. All are in Latin. Two are now to be found in the Bodleian Library at Oxford. MS. Douce 139 is one of a number of MSS. which once belonged to the Elizabethan antiquary Henry Ferrers that were bequeathed to the Bodleian in 1834 by Francis Douce.[3] This volume seems originally to have been put together at Coventry cathedral priory, though not all of it was necessarily written there. Twenty of its folios, containing material relating exclusively to

[1] Maddicott, *Simon de Montfort*, pp. 220–1. [2] Above, p. 107.

[3] For a description of this manuscript see *A Summary Catalogue of Western Manuscripts in the Bodleian Library Oxford* (7 vols., (in 8), Oxford, 1897–1953), IV, 534–5 (where it is described as MS. Additional 21713).

the priory, were removed by Douce from the MS. and given by him to Thomas Sharpe of Coventry. Sharpe also himself copied ten further pages of Coventry material, mainly about homages performed to the prior of Coventry, from those other leaves of the MS. 'which could not be separated from the rest without injury to the main contents of the volume'.[4] This composite Coventry volume was seen and noted by the editors of the revised *Monasticon.*[5] It subsequently passed to the Birmingham Reference Library where it was destroyed by fire in 1879.[6] MS. Douce 139 is a legal reference work containing a register of writs belonging to the 1270s but with an appendix of later writs, a collection of statutory texts, a collection of short legal treatises and law reports mainly from 'northern' circuit eyres of the 1280s and other legal materials, including a text of Ralph de Hengham's 1285 consultation on 'quo waranto' law.[7] The volume seems to have been put together over a considerable period of time. The section to which this text of the Provisions belongs runs from fol. 62 to fol. 115 of the MS. It starts with three legal treatises (a *summa* about charters derived from *Bracton*, a Latin version of *Cadit Assisa* and a text of *Hengham Magna*) but then turns to statutory texts. These include the *Sententia Lata* of 1253, Magna Carta and the Charter of the Forest as reissued in 1225, the Provisions of Merton, this text of the Provisions (at fols. 103v–105r), the Statute of Westminster I (1275), an erased beginning of the Statute *de Moneta* of 1284, the Statute of Marlborough of 1267 and the Statute of Jewry of 1275. The section must have been copied after 1275 but may well have been copied not long after that date for there are no texts of the Statute of Gloucester of 1278 or of the Statute of Mortmain of 1279 in it and the erased text of the Statute

4 For material the volume still contains connecting it with Coventry see the initial miscellaneous section (at fols. 1–5) which contains (on fol. 1v) a list of the Easter days of the years of the deaths of the kings of England down to King John and the bishops of Coventry down to Bishop Walter Durdent (ob. 1159) and also of the days of those deaths; (on fol. 2r) a list of bishops of the see of Lichfield, Chester and Coventry from its foundation to Bishop Roger Meuland (1258–95); (on fol. 2v) an undated note relating to a case in which the prior of Coventry was a judge and in which a consultation was obtained; (on fol. 3r) an undated copy of an enrolment of an assize of novel disseisin about land at Smithfield in London that was held of the priory (which belongs to 1297); (on fol. 3v) a copy of a writ of Henry III commissioning Gilbert of Preston to enquire into a proposed assart to be made by the prior of Coventry. On fol. 141v has been added a copy of royal letters patent of 6 Edward III authorising the imparking of waste land and woodland by the priory plus a mandate of 1332 of the bishop of Lincoln in favour of the priory; on fol. 171r a long and detailed memorandum about the performance of homage to the prior by Simon Basset of Sapcote on 3 July 1286 and on fols. 171v, 177r, 177v, 178r notes relating to similar homages performed in 1286, 1288, 1291 and 1293; on fol. 187v copies of charters of Ranulph, earl of Chester in favour of the priory.

5 William Dugdale, *Monasticon Anglicanum*, revised by J. Caley and others (6 vols., (in 8), London, 1817–30), III, 185, note a.

6 G.R.C. Davis, *Medieval Cartularies of Great Britain: a Short Catalogue* (London, 1958), no. 277.

7 Brand, *MCL*, pp. 393–443.

de Moneta looks to be a slightly later addition. The section was almost certainly copied prior to 1285 for a contemporary hand has annotated the Statute of Westminster I as '*Magna Statuta Westmonasterii*', an unlikely description to be applied to the Statute after the enactment of a second 'great' Statute of Westminster in 1285. It is only chance that has given us this copy of the reissued Provisions. The scribe was evidently working from an older collection of statutes which had contained the Provisions and to which they may have been added shortly after their enactment. He seems not to have known that the Provisions had effectively been superseded by the Statute of Marlborough. The older collection had probably also contained a copy of a text of the second reissue of the Provisions by the Monfortian regime in December 1264 for the text of this version ends with a clause about the enforcement of the Provisions which is not found in either of the other MSS. of this version but is found in the various versions of that reissue and was almost certainly, but mistakenly, borrowed from such a text.[8] Just how lucky we are to have even this text is unwittingly revealed by a contemporary annotator who has noted in the margin of this text, 'These statutes are to be disregarded for they are included in the Statute of Marlborough'.[9] Any later copyist seeing this note would have omitted the text and looked instead for a copy of the Statute of Marlborough.

The second text of the same reissue is to be found on fols. 133r–135r of MS. Bodley 91. This is a composite volume consisting of four manuscripts of different dates and possibly different provenance bound up together.[10] These folios form part of a manuscript which comes from Hyde abbey at Winchester. The main item in it is a copy of a set of Winchester Annals running down to the year 1280.[11] The reissued Provisions form the first item in an appendix of original documents found at the end of the chronicle. Ten of them come from 1263–4 and are connected

[8] The text, which is rather corrupt, runs 'Et quia nolumus quod aliquis super observacionem premissorum decetero possit se per ignoranciam excusare seu quod dicta provisiones et consuetudines a verbosis reputentur set quod singuli et universi predicto opere complenitur de consilio prelatorum precipimus firmiter injungentes quod eedem provisiones et consuetudines per vicecomites de mense in mensem in comitatibus, hundredis, wappentaciis suis necnon in curiis baronum pupplicentur et ad utilitatem tocius communitatis Anglie ab omnibus firmiter abserventur. Et si aliquis dictis provisionibus et consuetudinibus contraire presumperint volumus quod ipsi per vicecomites nostros tanquam preceptis nostris contemptores et earum provisionum et consuetudinum transgressores puniantur. Quod si vicecomites ad hoc non sufficiant tunc nomina eorumdem nobis scire faciat ut ipsos [et] predictos vicecomites qui super premissis negligentes vel remissi fuerunt punire faciemus prout de jure fuerit faciendum. In cujus rei etc.'. Compare the text of the concluding clause of the 1264 reissue in Appendix II: below, p. 450.

[9] 'Ista statuta vacant quia continentur in statuto de Marleberg'.

[10] *Summary Catalogue of Western MSS. in the Bodleian Library*, II, i, 101.

[11] Noel Denholm-Young, *Collected Papers* (Cardiff, 1969), pp. 86–95.

with the political events of those years; three more come from 1271 and are connected with Jewish legislation enacted that year.[12] Although this manuscript cannot have been copied earlier than 1280 it seems likely that the lost Winchester Annals from which this set of annals and its appendix were derived were written more or less contemporaneously with the years to which they refer and the documents copied into it at the same time.

The third text of the Provisions is a contemporary official text. It is the only document contained in a schedule attached to m. 14 of the Patent Roll for 47 Henry III (1262–3).[13] Membrane 14 itself contains documents of various dates between 24 March and 22 April 1263 but the attachment of this schedule to that membrane does not necessarily imply that the schedule belongs to that same period. Indeed, as will be seen, the preamble to this text places the making of the legislation as belonging to some date after 28 October 1262 but before 24 March 1263.[14] There is also, however, a memorandum at the end of the text in what seems to be a different hand noting that this legislation had been sent to the sheriff of Norfolk and Suffolk and to the sheriff of every other county by letters close of 12 June 1263, that letters patent enclosing the Provisions were also sent to each county on the same date, and that other copies were sent to the justices of the Common Bench and to the justices of the Lincolnshire eyre.

THE DATING OF THESE REISSUES AND THEIR PUBLICATION

The proem of all three texts of this reissue of the Provisions begins, like the preamble to the original Provisions of Westminster of October 1259, by giving the date of their enactment in terms both of the year of grace and of the relevant regnal year.[15] This places the reissue as belonging to some date between 28 October 1262, when Henry III's forty-seventh regnal year began, and 24 March 1263, when the old-style year of grace 1262 ended. Only the text in MS. Douce 139 then goes on, like the original Provisions, to give a more specific date and place for the reissue: the feast of St Hilary (13 January) at Westminster.[16] This is a date when the king is known to have been at Westminster. Its plausibility is also confirmed by the evidence of enrolments relating to the receipt of what were evidently texts of this reissue by the justices in eyre in Kent and Surrey and by the barons of the Exchequer. The enrolment on the plea roll of the Kent eyre

[12] Ibid., pp. 94–5.
[13] C 66/79, m. 14 schedule. For the text see Appendix II: below, pp. 430–51.
[14] See below, pp. 187–8. [15] For the text see Appendix II: below, pp. 430–1.
[16] See Appendix II: below, p. 430, note 1.

of Nicholas de la Tour and his colleagues records their receipt of an undated writ couched in similar terms to the preamble to these three texts and enclosing 'statuta et consuetudines'.[17] It is to be found on that section of the plea roll which records pleas heard in the eyre's second session held at Canterbury between 14 January and 3 February 1263.[18] The enrolment on a plea roll of the Surrey eyre of Martin of Littlebury and his colleagues records their receipt of a very similar covering writ specifically dated 20 January 1263 and this time enclosing what are more correctly characterised as 'statuta et constituciones'.[19] It is to be found on that section of the plea roll which records pleas heard at Guildford between 14 January and 3 February 1263.[20] A third writ enrolled on the Memoranda Roll of the Lord Treasurer's Remembrancer among the Hilary *communia* similarly records the receipt by the Exchequer of a third writ in much the same terms but dated 23 January 1263 which also encloses 'statuta et constituciones'.[21] The Osney chronicler also notes a reissue of the Provisions about the feast of the conversion of St Paul the Apostle (25 January) and says that the king sent them to each county under his seal. The date is perhaps the date that Oxfordshire received its copy.[22] That copies of the reissued Provisions were sent to each county is confirmed by other chronicle evidence.[23] It was also the normal practice with legislation. It seems likely that both the Winchester and the Coventry texts of the Provisions were ultimately derived from county texts of this kind.

The note appended to the Patent Roll text is the only evidence that there was a second reissue of the Provisions in June 1263. It has been suggested that the date 12 June in this memorandum is simply a scribal error for 12 January,[24] but the reference to the Lincolnshire eyre shows that this cannot be the case. The Lincolnshire eyre did not begin its sessions before 9 April and it was still in session in mid-June.[25] It is therefore plain that there must indeed have been a second reissue of the Provisions in June 1263 but that this was done without making any further changes to the text, not even apparently those made necessary by the lapse of time, such as altering the year of grace given in the preamble

[17] JUST 1/363, m. 27: '*consuetudines*' must be a clerical error for '*constituciones*'.

[18] Crook, *Records of the General Eyre*, p. 131.

[19] JUST 1/874, m. 12d.

[20] Crook, *Records of the General Eyre*, p. 132.

[21] E 368/37, m.11: The marginal heading is 'Breve missum baronibus de constitucionibus Oxon' observandis'. For the use here and elsewhere of the term 'Provisions' or 'Constitutions' of 'Oxford' for the Provisions of Westminster see Jacob, *Studies*, pp. 123–4.

[22] *Annales Monastici*, IV, 130–1.

[23] *Flores Historiarum, per Matthaeum Westmonasteriensem collecti*, ed. H.R. Luard (3 vols., Rolls Series, London, 1890), III, 477; *Chronicles, Edward I and Edward II*, ed. W. Stubbs (2 vols., Rolls Series, London, 1882–3), I, 58–9; *De Antiquis Legibus Liber*, pp. 52–3.

[24] Treharne, *Baronial Plan*, p. 295, note 6; *DBM*, p. 138, note b.

[25] Crook, *Records of the General Eyre*, p. 132.

for the making of the Provisions or the figure in clause 1 of the number of years which had elapsed since the king's crossing into Brittany.

CHANGES MADE FOR THE 1263 REISSUE

The basis for the text of this reissue was an official Latin text of the Provisions as issued in October 1259. The reissued text incorporated a new preamble, some of whose phrasing is also taken up in the covering writs sent to the justices in eyre and to the barons of the Exchequer. Only one clause was omitted from the reissue but a number of clauses were amended and some new clauses added. There may also have been some rearrangement of the order of the individual clauses.

Changes to the preamble

Both the new preamble and the covering writs sent with copies of the reissued Provisions emphasized the king's role in both their making and publication. In the original Provisions the legislation was said to have been 'made by king and magnates by the common counsel and consent of the king and the magnates'.[26] The magnates were thus portrayed not just as advisers to the king in the making of the legislation but also as consenting to it along with him, indeed even as jointly making it with him. The corresponding clause of the 1263 reissue is very different. Even now the king is not shown as acting without taking advice but the advice which the preamble mentions is that not of his magnates but of his 'lieges',[27] men deliberately described in a way that ascribes to them no independent importance in their own right but whose right to give advice arises purely out of their position as loyal subjects to the king. No one in this preamble 'consents' to the legislation other than the king himself and the preamble places particular emphasis on the free will he is exercising in doing so.[28] It may also be the king's wish to distance himself from the original Provisions which explains why he or his clerks chose now to describe the legislation as 'constitutions' (*constituciones*) rather than 'provisions' (*provisiones*).[29] Less significance is perhaps to be attached to

[26] For the text see Appendix I: below, pp. 414–15.

[27] '. . . interveniente consilio fidelium . . .' in the legislation; 'interveniente consilio fidelium suorum/regis' in the writs.

[28] '. . . de mera et libera voluntate ipsius domini regis in plena et libera potestate ipsius . . .' in the legislation; 'de mera et libera voluntate sua et in plena postestate sua/ipsius regis' in the writs.

[29] The original Provisions of 1259 do, however, also refer to themselves as being a 'constitucio' in clauses 1 and 3 and there was no real difference in substance between the two terms. The writs sent to the justices in eyre and the barons of the Exchequer also describe this same legislation as 'statuta et constituciones'.

the fact that only the revised version of the preamble (echoed in the covering writs) justified the issuing of the legislation in terms of 'the reform and improvement of his realm' ('ad reformationem et melioracionem regni sui/Anglie') for such a view of the legislation had also clearly been implicit in the whole relationship between the legislation and the reform process. A further point was, however, clearly being made in the revised text when it referred to the publication and enforcement of the legislation. The 1259 Provisions had implied, though not with absolute clarity, that publication was also a joint matter undertaken by both king and magnates and had not found it necessary to say anything specific about enforcement, the clear implication being that as properly made legislation it was of course intended for enforcement. The 1263 reissue emphasised that publication had been by the king alone;[30] it also went on to spell out that it was also the king alone who on his own authority had ordered the enforcement of the legislation.[31] One other point about the text of the preamble illuminates the king's view of the Provisions as originally enacted and published in 1259. There is almost nothing in the preamble to give even a hint that the legislation which follows is a revised version of legislation which had first been issued a little over three years earlier. Someone who knew the previous legislation well would see just how carefully the revised preamble had been drafted to spell out the king's view of the legislative process as contrasted with that of the reforming council enunciated in the earlier text. Apart from this, there is no reference to the earlier text and it seems clear from this that, as far as the king was concerned, the earlier legislation was indeed a nullity, something to which he had only consented under duress. It was only now that the legislation (in its new, revised form) had properly come into effect.[32]

The omitted clause on mortmain alienations

Only one clause of the original Provisions was omitted. This was clause 14 which had required that alienations in mortmain receive the consent of the lord of whom the tenement being alienated was held. It is conceivable that it was only omitted by error and the omission not noticed in time for, as will be seen, there is some reason to suppose that the rearrangement

30 '. . . per ipsum' in the Patent Roll text and in MS. Bodley 91; 'per ipsum regem' in MS. Douce 139. But note that the justices in eyre and the barons of the Exchequer were also instructed to have the legislation read and published on the king's behalf.

31 '. . . ac observacioni auctoritate sua generaliter demandate'; the 'fideliter' of MS. Douce 139 which replaces 'generaliter' in that text is almost certainly a scribal error. Again the justices in eyre and the barons of the Exchequer were also ordered to have the legislation observed.

32 Contrast the view of Treharne and Sanders (*DBM*, p. 42) that what Henry III 'announced' in January 1263 was that 'he had reissued the Provisions of Westminster with some added clauses'.

in the order of the clauses was the product of unintended omissions that were only noticed and corrected late in the copying process.[33] There is little indication that the legislation had posed or caused any major problems for religious houses acquiring property. Indeed, as has been seen, there is relatively little evidence for the enforcement of this clause between 1259 and 1263.[34] It is, therefore, difficult to believe that there can have been much of a demand for the omission of this clause from the reissue. Yet the balance of probabilities seems to favour deliberate omission. Other unintended omissions were noticed and corrected. It also seems unlikely to be simply coincidence that one of the four clauses added to the legislation for this reissue was also one whose sole beneficiaries were the heads of religious houses.[35] Some kind of lobbying by religious houses, though perhaps only by some major religious houses, must lie behind both changes to the legislation.

Amendments to the Provisions

Some of the amendments were comparatively minor. The reissue removed the reference in clause 1 to the legislation as having been 'provided and jointly decided' ('provisum est et concorditer statutum'). This was no longer in keeping with the preamble's emphasis on the king's pre-eminent role in the legislative process. It was replaced with the much more abrupt 'in future the following is to be observed' ('decetero sic observandum est'). A second alteration to the same clause was necessitated simply by the lapse of time since the enactment of the original legislation. Clause 1 as originally enacted had spelled out the number of years which had elapsed since the king's crossing to Brittany as twenty-nine. This clearly needed to be altered. The Patent Roll text and that in MS. Bodley 91 both agree in giving the incorrect revised figure of thirty-two years. Only MS. Douce 139 gives the correct figure, which was thirty-two and a half years.[36]

The first substantive alteration to the legislation came in clause 5 relating to beaupleder fines. This was given an additional sub-clause which substantially qualified what had been in the original a total prohibition of beaupleder fines. This allowed the survival and continued exaction both by the king's bailiffs and by others of any beaupleder fine which had been levied as a fixed payment continuously since the king's first crossing into Brittany (in 1230).[37] The practical effect was probably to

33 Below, pp. 160–1. 34 Above, pp. 122–3, 126. 35 Below, pp. 149–50.

36 See Appendix II, below, pp. 432–3. But MS. Douce 139 is not always the better text. In clause 3 it omits, probably as the result of homoteleuton, the whole of a passage between the two occurrences of 'mandetur vicecomiti'.

37 For the text of this addition see Appendix II: below, pp. 436–7.

make it rather more difficult to avoid payment of the fine on the basis of the legislation. There was also a substantive alteration to clause 6 on the length of adjournments in pleas of dower *unde nichil habet*. The original Provisions had set a minimum target of at least four days in court in such pleas each year. The target was now increased to a minimum of five days with six specified as the desirable goal. But the clause was amended in a very clumsy way. The wording of the original clause was retained and the new sub-clause with the alternative target simply tacked on at the end, as though there was no contradiction between them.[38]

The additional clauses on process

Two new clauses were added between what had been clauses 7 and 8 of the original Provisions. One (clause 8 in this reissue) continued and extended the process begun in the original Provisions (but there applied only in the new action of *contra formam feoffamenti* and in the existing action of *quare impedit*) of reducing the number of stages of mesne process which needed to be gone through in personal actions before the grand distress was reached. This may well have taken up the proposals of the committee established to look into mesne process in personal actions at the Michaelmas parliament of 1259.[39] It abolished all stages in the mesne process in personal actions generally between the second attachment and the grand distress.[40] The second additional clause inserted at this point (clause 9 in this resissue) was rather longer. It also dealt with mesne process in personal actions but its concern was with the process used after the joinder of issue for jury trial. Here the change being introduced was even more drastic and innovative. There had been no problem, even prior to 1263, in securing the attendance of the plaintiff after joinder of issue. Any default by the plaintiff (whether before or after joinder of issue) would lead to the case being dismissed *sine die* and his pledges for prosecution being amerced. No such rule applied to defendants. Since both litigants needed to be present before the jury could give its verdict the court might find itself forced to employ its mesne process all over again after the defendant's first appearance when the parties pleaded in order to secure the defendant's attendance at the jury stage. The normal practice of the court even before 1263 was, however, to employ a much abbreviated mesne process for this purpose. The court's first order was for *habeas corpus*[41] or *venire facias*[42] and they were then immediately followed

[38] For the text of this addition see Appendix II: below, pp. 436–7. [39] Above, p. 41.

[40] For the text of this new clause (clause 8 of this reissue) see Appendix II: below, pp. 438–9.

[41] E.g. *CRR*, XIV, no. 731. [42] E.g. KB 26/171, m. 70.

by the grand distress.[43] This last stage might, however, have to be repeated indefinitely till the defendant appeared. The additional clause solved the problem of the defaulting defendant. In future no defendant was to be allowed more than a single essoin or a single default. At the next day appointed for hearing the jury's verdict was to be taken, whether or not the defendant appeared. Judgment was then to be given in accordance with its verdict. This in effect introduced the procedure typical of the petty assizes into all personal actions. The defendant's absence was to be punished not by giving judgment by default against him (as was typical of the real actions) but by allowing the jury to deliver its verdict in his absence. If the jury verdict was given in the Westminster Bench or before the justices in eyre judgment could then be given immediately for either party in accordance with that verdict. An additional problem might arise if the jury verdict was taken locally in the county court or before a specially commissioned royal justice. Judgment in such cases could only be given in the Common Bench after the verdict had been returned into the court. Hitherto it had been necessary to secure the attendance of both parties in court before any judgment could be given. The new procedure allowed the defendant a single default or essoin after the verdict had been returned to the court. At the following court day judgment was to be given in accordance with the verdict, whether he was present or not.[44]

The additional clauses giving new remedies to ecclesiastics

The other new clauses were added at the very end of the Provisions. Clause 24 authorised the creation of two new types of action for the heads of religious houses. Such heads were regarded in law as owners of all the movable property belonging to their houses and they alone could bring suit for any goods wrongfully taken out of the possession of the house. The main drawback to this was that when that head died any right of action he possessed in respect of the house's movable property died with him. Thus, if he had been bringing such an action but had not yet secured a judgment, his successor was not allowed to revive that action. If he had not yet started an action, his successor was equally barred from any kind of remedy. The first part of the new clause specifically gave the successor a remedy in both kinds of situation, though it required the seizure of the property to have been a recent one.[45] The clause is less clear about the kind of remedy being contemplated. Some of the

[43] E.g. KB 26/169, m. 34. [44] For the text of this clause see Appendix II: below, pp. 438–9.
[45] For the text of this part of the clause see Appendix II: below, pp. 446–7.

language used (*depredaciones* and *rapine*) sounds criminal and it is tempting to read it as intended to allow the successor the right to bring a criminal appeal against the takers. Yet other parts of the language (its reference to *transgressores*) and the fact that the clause talks only of securing the return of the property rather than of securing the conviction and capital punishment of the offender point to some kind of action of trespass. It remains puzzling, however, that the legislation talks in terms of the recovery of the property itself for trespass actions normally only secured the payment of damages. If those damages were equivalent to the value of the property taken this came, of course, to much the same thing.

The second part of clause 24 dealt with another and quite distinct problem connected with the current legal rules relating to religious houses and the remedies available to the heads of those houses. Lay tenants were relatively well protected by legal actions against persons (whether third parties or their lords) who entered without title some or all of the lands held by their immediate predecessors in title at the time of their death or who tried to hold on to land they held in wardship or of which they had first seisin. If the deceased ancestor was a close kinsman there was the assize of mort d'ancestor; in the case of more remote kinsmen there were the actions of aiel and cosinage. The Provisions of Westminster had additionally given them the right to recover damages against such intruders or unjust withholders.[46] There was no similar simple remedy for the heads of religious houses against those who intruded into land belonging to the house during a vacancy, whether that intrusion was (like the lord's) made possible by the intruder having temporary custody of the house's lands during a vacancy or took place as the result of what purported to have been a grant made by such a temporary custodian or was simply an intrusion made without any colour of entitlement. Novel disseisin was not available since the new head of the religious house could not properly claim ever to have been in possession of the lands concerned. Mort d'ancestor and its congeners were not available since they were appropriate only to lay inheritance and not to ecclesiastical succession. There was no writ of entry available to cover the situation.[47] The new clause authorised the creation of a new action to cover precisely this situation and also allowed the head of the religious house to recover damages in the new action.[48]

[46] Above, p. 57.

[47] But for evidence of a writ of entry being used in 1220 to reclaim land said to have been alienated by such a custodian see *CRR*, IX, 279 in which the abbot of Ramsey claimed land against Robert Blundel 'ut ius ecclesie sue et ut illam in quam idem Robertus non habet ingressum nisi per Rogerum de Neovill' qui eam ei dimisit dum habuit custodiam ejusdem abbatie'.

[48] For the text of this part of the clause see Appendix II: below, pp. 446–7.

The additional clause authorising writs of entry in the post

The second new clause added at the end of the Provisions was by far the most important of the additions made to the legislation in this reissue. Clause 25 authorised for the first time the extension of the availability of writs of entry 'outside the degrees'. Writs of entry were a special sub-group of the general type of writ *precipe quod reddat* for land, which initiated litigation directly in one of the king's courts by means of a mandate addressed to the appropriate local sheriff, requiring him to convey to the tenant of specific land an order requiring him 'justly and without delay' to surrender that land to a particular claimant but giving him the alternative of appearance in the king's court to show why he had not done this. In writs of entry the claimant also alleged in his writ the existence of a single flaw in the tenant's title to the land being claimed. It was, so the demandant was implicitly asserting, as a consequence of this basic flaw that he had a better right to the land than its present tenant. They were called writs of entry because most, though not all, of them used the characteristic phrase 'into which he has no entry except through...' ('in quam/quod non habet ingressum nisi per') to introduce the explanation of the alleged fatal flaw in the tenant's title.[49] They took a variety of forms which covered a variety of different factual situations. The simplest case was that supposed in the writ of entry *sur disseisin*. Here the claimant simply alleged that he or an ancestor of his had lost the land through an unjust disseisin. In a related form, the writ of intrusion, the claimant alleged that the tenant or a predecessor in title had entered the land not through a disseisin but by entering the land after the death of a tenant for life (a doweress or curtesy tenant or life tenant by special grant) when the land should have reverted to the claimant or his ancestor or predecessor. In a second sub-category of writ of entry the alleged flaw was in a transaction by which the claimant or his ancestor had purported to alienate the land but which, as the claimant asserted, was, and always had been, voidable. This might be because when he or his ancestor had purported to alienate the land he had not been mentally competent to do so (*dum non compos mentis sue*) or because at that time he had still been below the age at which he was capable of making a valid permanent grant (*dum infra etatem*). In a third sub-category the writs alleged that the tenant's title to the land derived from a grant which had been made by someone with only a temporary control over the land which had subsequently ended or by someone who possessed only an apparent title or *de facto* control over

[49] The phrase was not used in the writ of entry *ad terminum qui preteriit* when the action was brought against the original lessee or mortgagee or in the writs of entry *dum infra etatem* and *dum non compos* when these were brought against the original alienee.

the land. A widow might allege that her late husband had alienated her inheritance, her marriage-portion or her dower from a previous husband during the period of their marriage while he had control over her and her lands (*cui in vita sua contradicere non potuit*); an heir who had since come of age might allege that a guardian whose period of wardship over his ward's lands had now ended had alienated that land during the wardship; the successor of the head of a religious house or a bishop might allege that his predecessor had alienated property belonging to the house or to the see during his period of office without the consent of his convent or chapter (*sine assensu conventus/capituli sui*); the freehold owner of property might assert that the person who had purported to alienate land had controlled that land only as a bailiff or as one of his villein tenants. In a fourth subcategory the claimant conceded that property had validly passed out of the control of himself, his ancestor or predecessor by a mortgage, vifgage or lease (either for a fixed term or from year to year at will or for the grantee's lifetime) but asserted that the flaw in the tenant's title was that the lessee or mortgagee had held on to the land after the lease was over or the debt repaid or had purported to grant it away to some third party during the period of the lease or the mortgage (*ad terminum qui preteriit*). In a related group of writs of entry the claimant conceded that land had been validly held by a doweress or by a curtesy tenant but asserted that the flaw in the tenant's title was that he or she had subsequently attempted to grant the land in perpetuity or for a period exceeding their own lives.

The isolation of a single basic flaw in the tenant's title was not the only common characteristic of writs of entry. Their second common trait prior to 1263 had been that each writ also showed how the land had passed after that original single alleged act of disseisin or intrusion or invalid or voidable grant to its current tenant. That tenant might, of course, still be the original beneficiary of that wrongful act. If he was not, the writ would trace the path by which it had passed to him, whether by inheritance (or by succession in office) or by grant or by assignment in dower.

The other two shared, and indeed connected, characteristics of the actions based on these writs were that in each of them the normal mode of proof for proving or disproving the assertions contained in the writ was ordinary jury trial, and not trial by battle or the grand assize; and that any judgment given in such litigation did not bar subsequent proceedings between the same parties and about the same land by an action of right in which battle or the grand assize would be the normal mode or proof.

At least four different types of writ of entry had made their appearance before the promulgation of the first issue of Magna Carta in 1215. The earliest known example is the early form of writ of entry *ad terminum qui preteriit* that is found in *Glanvill*. It is for a debtor who had handed over land as security for a loan but who was trying to recover the land from his creditor.[50] It does not actually use the term 'entry' at all but this is of no great significance since it was also characteristic of the later 'classic' form of the writ as between lessor and lessee that the term 'entry' formed no part of this variant of the writ. 'Entry' language is found in two of the three versions of this same writ found in the collection of surviving original and judicial writs of 1199 printed by D.M. Stenton.[51] The earliest action against the alienee of a guardian, whose enrolment seems to reflect the actual wording of the writ used (and which uses 'entry' terminology) is to be found in 1200.[52] The writ of entry *sur disseisin* was drafted and made a writ of course in 1204 but for long remained comparatively uncommon because of the restrictions on the circumstances under which it could be used.[53] The writ of entry *cui in vita* appears in the register of writs prepared for use in Ireland shortly after John's visit in 1210,[54] and a clear example of its use in the English courts is to be found in 1212.[55] But the early history of writs of entry is complicated by the relatively close relationship that evidently existed during this period between writs of entry and writs of right. It was possible for claimants who had initiated litigation by the general *precipe* writ which existed prior to 1215 (and perhaps even by an ordinary writ of right once they had removed the case into a royal court) to add to their initial count an additional assertion as to some specific flaw in the tenant's title which (they asserted) gave them a better title to the land than the tenant, using language which closely resembled that used in writs of entry.[56] It can sometimes be difficult to distinguish the enrolments of cases where this has occurred from enrolments of cases where the litigation has been initiated by writ of entry.[57]

Clause 34 of the 1215 issue of Magna Carta sought to protect the jurisdiction of feudal courts by prohibiting the issuing of writs *precipe* in cases where this might lead to a free man losing the right to hear a case in his court. This did not lead to any suspension in the issuing of writs of entry, though it is unclear whether Professor Milsom's assertion that the kinds of claim that were made through writs of entry were in fact unsuited to trial through an action of right outside the king's court is the correct explanation for this. Milsom has also argued that the same clause

[50] *Glanvill*, x, 9 (p. 125).

[51] *PKJ*, I, nos. 3487 and 3506 (but contrast no. 3538 where entry language is not used).

[52] *CRR*, I, 182 (and 249–50).

[53] G.D.G. Hall, 'The Early History of Entry Sur Disseisin', *Tulane Law Review* 42 (1968), 584–602.

[54] *Early Registers*, p. 10 (Hib. 26). On the dating of this register see Brand, *MCL*, pp. 450–6.

[55] *CRR*, VI, 218.

[56] S.F.C. Milsom, *The Legal Framework of English Feudalism* (Cambridge, 1976), pp. 95–7.

[57] Ibid., pp. 97–101.

may have led to a proliferation of writs of entry after 1215 as the old writ *precipe* disappeared and claimants who wanted to ensure that their cases were heard in the king's court began to need to include in their writ some sort of justification of the kind that entry clause provided for the case being heard there.[58] There seems, however, to be little real evidence to support this. Only two new forms of writ of entry appear shortly after the enactment of Magna Carta: the writ of entry *sine assensu capituli* and the writ of entry on an alienation by a doweress, which are both first found in 1220.[59] Other additional forms of writ of entry appear only much later. The earliest clear example of *dum non compos mentis* I have found comes from 1244;[60] the earliest example of *dum infra etatem* only in 1249.[61] In any case, it is the writs of entry which had appeared already prior to 1215 that remained the most commonly used types of writ.

Not every claimant who could point to a single flaw in a tenant's title, even when that flaw was one specifically covered by one of the generally available forms of writ of entry, could bring a writ of entry to recover the land. For most forms of writ of entry it was necessary that the demandant (or the last ancestor or predecessor of his to have had possession of the land being claimed prior to the event or transaction which constituted the basis of the demandant's claim) should have been in seisin of it at some time within the limitation period set for the assize of mort d'ancestor. This was clearly already the rule when limitation dates were changed in 1237 and a single limitation date was set for both mort d'ancestor and writs of entry.[62] It also seems to be assumed in a case of 1222 where the tenant's plea was that he and his father had held the land concerned since before the reign of King Richard and before the limitation date for mort d'ancestor.[63] A different limitation date, however, applied in the writ of entry *sur disseisin*. This was the limitation date which applied in the assize of novel disseisin and it fits the origins of the action as little more than a limited extension of the assize. If the disseisin or other event had taken place before these limitation dates the claimant could make his claim to the land only through an action of right. This would normally mean that instead of being able to initiate litigation directly in the king's courts, the demandant would be forced to bring his action initially in the court of the lord of whom the land was held. From that court he would have to remove the case to the county court by tolt and then get a writ *pone* to

[58] Ibid., pp. 101–2. [59] *CRR*, VIII, 212; *CRR*, IX, 252.

[60] *CRR*, XVIII, no. 1629; but there is also a writ form in *Bracton* at fol. 323b (IV, 36).

[61] KB 26/135, m. 29. For another early example see KB 26/137, m. 10.

[62] *CR 1234–1237*, pp. 520–1. This is summarised in the *textus receptus* of the Statute of Merton as chapter 8 of the Statute (*SR*, I, 3).

[63] *CRR*, X, 286. It is also the limitation date mentioned by *Bracton* at fol. 317b (IV, 23).

remove the case into the Common Bench or the eyre. Additional delay might be caused by the fact that it was also possible in the action of right (unlike the writ of entry) for the tenant to essoin himself for a year and a day by the essoin of bed-sickness. Trial in the writ of right was normally either by battle or by the grand assize and it was the tenant who had the choice of defending his title by either of these means, so that opting for battle and hiring the better champion might win the day for a tenant whose title was weak.

By the early fourteenth century there was also a second related limitation to the use of writs of entry. If the claimant based his claim on the possession of the land by an ancestor and then some subsequent event which had led to the land wrongfully passing out of his possession that ancestor could not be more remote from the claimant than his great-grandfather.[64] This was the same degree of relationship within which it was possible to bring an action of cosinage based on the seisin of that ancestor at the time of their death. It is not clear whether any such rule applied in the first half of the thirteenth century. In what seems to be a writ of entry *ad terminum qui preteriit* of 1200 a claimant alleged that land had been gaged by his great-grandmother.[65] At this time there was no action of cosinage and she was much too distantly related for the claimant to have been able to use the assize of mort d'ancestor to claim on the basis of her possession at the time of her death. It may also be significant that the writ forms given by *Bracton* for the writ of entry for an alienation made by a guardian include variants to cover the demandant's father, mother, brother, sister, grandfather, grandmother, uncle, aunt, kinsman, kinswoman, as well as a generic *antecessor* as the ward whose property had been alienated, as though it did not matter how remote the relationship between demandant and ancestor might be.[66]

The most important restriction on the use of writs of entry prior to 1263, however, was that imposed by the 'degrees', the requirement that the land should only have changed hands (whether by alienation or inheritance or succession) a limited number of times since the event which constituted the basis of the claimant's claim. Once that number was exceeded the land had passed 'outside the degrees' and the claimant would be forced to bring a writ of right if he wished to assert his right to it. *Bracton* talks of writs of entry not exceeding the 'third degree' (*tercium gradum*) but does not explain exactly how the number of degrees in any given writ was calculated.[67] In practice, the degrees seem not to have been calculated with reference to any particular numerical formula but

[64] *YB 33–35 EI*, p. 125. [65] *CRR*, I, 359–60. [66] *Bracton*, fol. 324 (IV, 38).

[67] *Bracton*, fol. 318 (IV, 21). For later and mutually inconsistent methods of calculating the number of degrees in writs of entry see Milsom's account in *NN* at pp. cxxxv–cxxxvii.

to have observed a formal verbal restriction. This allowed as many, and no more, alienations or devolutions of the land as could be described in any given writ with the aid of the two prepositions '*per*' and '*cui*', each of which could only be used once. This restriction, however, worked out differently for the different kinds of writ. In the case of writs of entry *ad terminum qui preteriit* the use of *per* and *cui* allowed the lessor or his heir to reach no further than the lessee himself, his heir (though never specifically described as such), his widow and his grantee.[68] The writs of entry *cui in vita, dum non compos mentis, dum infra etatem, sine assensu capituli/conventus* and alleging entry through a doweress worked in a similar way. In the case of entry *sur disseisin*, however, the use of '*per*' and '*cui*' allowed the demandant to reach not just the disseisor and his heir, widow or grantee but also the grantee or heir or widow of that grantee.[69] The writ of entry alleging entry through a guardian worked the same way. As Milsom notes, in the first type of writ (like *ad terminum qui preteriit*) the basis of the claim was a 'voluntary grant of some sort', something which granted an interest which had since expired or constituted a voidable, but not a void, grant. His characterisation of the basis of the second type of writ is that it was used where land 'was simply taken from the tenant or his predecessor'.[70] This works well for entry *sur disseisin* but does not seem to be applicable to entry through a guardian.

Legal historians have advanced a variety of conjectures as to the reasons why only writs of entry within the degrees were allowed or issued prior to 1263. Maitland suggested that it might have been connected with the desire to ensure that 'the new procedure' did not 'encroach on the proper sphere of the old and sacral procedure', or with old rules about warranty.[71] Milsom once suggested that it was analogous to the rule which removed the special character of gifts in frank marriage after the third heir had inherited, the feeling that 'after so many devolutions the demandant could no longer go back to impugn some initial transaction: he must put in issue the right between himself and the tenant'.[72] Robert Palmer has advanced an ingenious argument attempting to relate the reach of writs of entry to a policy decision to provide a remedy only against the disruption to what had been the normal internal economy of the lordship caused

[68] '... in quam idem [tenant] non habet ingressum nisi per [the original lessee] cui [the original lessor] illam dimisit ad terminum qui preteriit'.

[69] '... in quam idem [tenant] non habet ingressum nisi per [the first alienee] cui [the disseisor granted the land] qui disseisivit predictum [demandant or his ancestor] post primam etc.'

[70] *NN*, pp. cxxxv–cxxxvii.

[71] *P&M*, II, 65.

[72] S.F.C. Milsom, *Historical Foundations of the Common Law*, 1st edition (London, 1969), p. 122. The passage no longer appears in the second edition of this work published in 1981.

by the assizes of novel disseisin and mort d'ancestor.[73] It seems probable, however, that the 'rule' owed its origins to nothing more substantial than a belief that it was proper for any writ of entry to mention all the links in the chain of title that connected the current tenant with the original event that constituted the basis of the tenant's claim (as only in this way was it possible to show with a sufficient degree of clarity and particularity how the current tenant was supposed to have gained his title or his 'entry' into the land) interacting with a desire on the part of the draftsmen of Chancery writs to avoid clumsy writs. The more links mentioned in a writ the clumsier the writ became: and so the decision was taken only to issue writs 'within' the degrees. That there may have been no great objection in principle is suggested by the appearance in 1228 of at least three examples of writs of entry *ad terminum qui preteriit* and of writs of entry *cui in vita* which reached at least one transfer or transmission of title further than was normally possible in writs of this kind but to which there is no recorded objection on the rolls.[74] It is possible, none the less, that the barrier erected by normal Chancery practice against the issuing writs of entry 'outside' the degrees was subsequently reinforced by political pressures from the magnates. Any extension of writs of entry would inevitably lead to fewer actions of right being brought in feudal courts, diminishing their jurisdiction and reducing their profits. The magnates are certainly known to have objected in the 1230s to the creation of the new remedies of aiel and cosinage on much these grounds, and they were able to use clause 34 of Magna Carta to support their ultimately unsuccessful stand on this issue.[75] But there is no positive evidence that there were substantial magnate objections to the extension of writs of entry outside the degrees and the fact that proposals for making such an extension were advanced at an early stage in the reform process may well suggest this not to have been the case.

There was no demand for an extension of writs of entry outside the degrees in the Petition of the Barons. However, a general extension was proposed in the first French draft of the *Providencia Baronum*.[76] This suggested legislation to make writs of entry available outside the degrees although still subject to the same prescription period as other writs of entry.[77] It also suggested a form of words which might be used in such

[73] Robert C. Palmer, 'The Origins of Property in England', *Law and History Review* 3 (1985), 24–50 at 43–6.

[74] *CRR*, XIII, nos. 405, 730; *CRR*, XIV, no. 905. There is also a cautious suggestion for the extension of the writ of entry *sur disseisin* outside the degrees in *Bracton* at fol. 319b (III, 160).

[75] *SCKB*, II, cxxxviii and clvi. [76] Above, p. 28.

[77] 'Derichef il est purveu qe la action le bref qe est apele de entree ne seit desoremes restreint a degres cum estre sout mes mesmes la prescription seit en cest accioun qe est en cele mort de auncestre': Brand, *MCL*, pp. 360–1.

cases, though only one to cover one particular form of the writ of entry (*ad terminum qui preteriit*).[78] This marks the first stage in the evolution of the form eventually adopted for such writs and it is worth noting that at this stage the formula proposed included neither the word *post* (*dimissionem* or *disseisinam*) which was later to give the writ outside the degrees its common generic name nor even the word 'entry' (*ingressum*). The published Latin version of this same draft clause is phrased much more elegantly but is to much the same effect.[79] This draft also gives a possible writ form which is little more than a translation of the French draft writ without any significant change in its content. Again there is no attempt to show how the writ might be phrased for other kinds of situation.[80] The only real difference is in the use of three real personal names in place of the *cely*, B. and *celuy* of the earlier draft. It can be no coincidence that Roger de Mortimer and Peter de Montfort (two of the names used) were the names of men who were themselves members of the king's council and who had presumably been involved in the discussion of the draft legislation.

The only evidence that this same clause went through a further revision is to be found in BL MS. Cotton Nero D i, the *Liber Additamentorum* of Matthew Paris. At the end of a French draft text of the 1259 Provisions of Westminster which the *Liber Additamentorum* contains are two further draft clauses both in Latin.[81] Both are drafts of clauses that were dropped from the final text of the Provisions. This version drops the reference in the earlier drafts to the counsel and consent of the magnates but does include some sort of justification for the extension of writs of entry, in terms of the need to avoid the defrauding of claimants. Otherwise the substance, and even much of the vocabulary, is substantially the same as in the previous Latin draft even if the actual wording of the whole text has been subjected to a thorough revision.[82] The phrase introducing the

78 'La fourme del bref est ceste: "Ly rey salue le visconte. Comandez a cely qe il adreit e sanz delay rende a B. ^{i}<de>^{i} cel lieu le maner de Stok' ove les apurtenance qe celuy B. lessa a celuy a terme qe ja passe est e qe a luy deit torner sicom il est dit. Ee si il ne face etc." '

79 'Provisum est eciam de consilio et consensu magnatum et procerum ut accio sive breve de ingressu ad gradus de cetero non artetur sed locum habeat ad quantumcumque gradum res perveniat deforciata dumtamen hujus accionis prescriptio viam non precludat petenti. Fit autem hujus accionis prescripcio sicut et mortis antecessoris.'

80 'Forma autem brevis talis in hujusmodi causis competenter esse potest: "Rex vicecomiti salutem. Precipe Rogero de Mortuo Mari quod juste et sine dilacione reddat Petro de Monte Forti manerium de Stoke cum pertinenciis quod idem dimisit Roger de Sancto Johanne ad terminum qui preteriit et quod ad ipsum Petrum reverti debet ut dicitur. Et nisi fecerit etc." '

81 Brand, *MCL*, p. 350.

82 'Item propter fraudem que passim fieri consuevit provisum est ne breve quod dicitur de ingressu artari debeat de cetero ad gradus set locum habeat contra omnes ad quos res deforciata pervenerit, ita tamen quod accio illa tempus debitum et consuetum non excedat.'

proposed draft writ is exactly the same as in the previous Latin draft. The draft writ itself, however, though still a draft specifically of a form to fit the writ of entry *ad terminum qui preteriit*, has lost the specific names associated with the members of the baronial council but gained an additional phrase showing that it could be used either by the lessor or by his heir and another clause explaining why the land ought now to revert. At the end is what seems to be a proposal or a note for the addition of a further sub-clause to spell out that it was the defendant who was now withholding the land from the claimant.[83] What this draft writ still does not include is any reference to the tenant's or defendant's 'entry' into the land of the kind standard in writs of entry within the degrees and later also found in writs of entry in the *post*. Nor does it have the particular '*post dimissionem/disseisinam*' formula which was to be characteristic of the eventual class of writs of entry in the *post* and gave them their classic name.

It is uncertain to what stage of the drafting process this last clause belongs. It is unlikely that it comes from as late as October 1259 or even from the preparations for the parliament held then since no such clause appears in any of the other French texts of the draft legislation prepared for that parliament. Yet it looks as though it must be later than the published Latin draft text of March 1259. Might it perhaps come from the otherwise unrecorded drafting stage associated with the June parliament of 1259?[84] What is quite clear, however, is that the proposal to extend writs of entry outside the degrees had been dropped by the time the final French draft of the legislation was prepared in or before October 1259. This does not necessarily mean there was significant opposition to the proposal although the magnates who were then dominant members of the king's council are, as has been seen, the one group with an obvious interest that might be damaged by the proposal. All it may signify is that it was felt that more work still needed to be done on the drafting of the writs before the proposal could go ahead. The continuing revision of the proposed forms and the fact that even in the third draft of the clause the drafters had only got round to tackling a single form of writ of entry, and were still talking in very hesitant terms about the forms to be adopted even for that, certainly lends some support for the latter view.

If further work had been done on the drafting of such writs between 1259 and 1263 it is certainly not reflected in the legislation itself. Indeed,

83 '"Rex vicecomiti salutem. Precipe tali quod juste et sine dilacione reddat tali N. manerium de Stok' cum pertinenciis quod idem talis vel pater ejus N., cujus heres ipse est, dimisit tali ad terminum qui preteriit et quod per formam dicte dimissionis ad ipsum talem post terminum predictum reverti debet ut dicit." Addi[cio?] post hec clausula: "Et quod idem talis ei defecit [?rectius: deforciat] ut dicit"'.

84 Above, pp. 33–4.

the legislation also lends some additional credence to the suggestion that the major obstacle to the enactment of the legislation prior to 1263 had not been any kind of objection in principle or even out of self-interest but rather a problem in coming up with a satisfactory form for the new writs. The legislation effectively finessed this problem. What it did was to authorise the extension of writs of entry outside the degrees as a point of general principle, but then left the specific details as to the form of the writs to be issued to be settled by the king's council.[85] The wording owed little or nothing to the previous drafts;[86] and the reference to the drafting of appropriate writs by the king's council provides interesting confirmation that, whatever the king's talk in the preamble about his sole legislative power, this legislation must in fact have been enacted in a legislative context where a larger legislative body of some sort was effectively making the legislation but then delegating detailed power to draft appropriate writ forms to the king's council.

Changes in the order of the clauses

There seems also to have been some rearrangement of the order of the text of the Provisions. No significance is to be attached to the fact that all three versions of the 1263 reissue place what had been clause 11 of the 1259 Provisions before what had been clauses 9 and 10 in that text since that is also the position of that clause in the best (Red Book of the Exchequer) version of the Provisions. The Winchester and Patent Roll texts likewise place what had been clause 18 of the 1259 Provisions after clause 24 of that text and before the two new final clauses while the Coventry text (MS. Douce 139) omits that clause entirely. The Patent Roll text, but only that text, places what had been clause 8 of the 1259 Provisions after the two additional clauses at the end. It is difficult to see any particular reason for these changes. There does not seem to be any particular legal or indeed any other logic behind them. The most likely explanation for them is error in copying the 1259 text for this reissue. Relatively short clauses were easily omitted in copying, particularly when scribes were not working from texts of the legislation which numbered the individual clauses.[87] Clause 18 may have been omitted and space found for it only

[85] Plucknett noticed long ago (*Statutes*, p. 80) that there are no grounds for the view that the legislation authorised only writs *sur disseisin* in the *post*, but was taken as an authority for writs in the *post* generally. Such a view is, none the less, to be found in P&M, II, 71, note 1, and was repeated in the first edition of Milsom, *Historical Foundations*, pp. 122, 123 but was omitted from the second edition.

[86] For the text of this clause see Appendix II: below, pp. 448–9.

[87] The enumeration of the clauses of the Provisions of Westminster is not original but the work of modern scholars. Nor is there any reason to think that the official text of the Statute of

at the very end of the original text and Douce 139's exemplar copied before this omission was even noted. The strange position of clause 8 in the Patent Roll text presumably indicates that this too was omitted at a later copying stage and possibly only in this very text and the omission noted too late to copy it into anywhere except the very end.

THE TEXTS OF THE 1264 REISSUE

The following year brought the armed clash between the king and the baronial reformers at the battle of Lewes. What was at stake between the two sides was control of the government of England, and the Provisions of Westminster (to which both sides had now proclaimed their adherence, if not quite to identical texts) played little, if any, part in the quarrel between them. Montfort's success at Lewes led to a search for a new political settlement which would ensure his continued control of the royal administration. Even before that settlement was reached, Montfort's wish to secure the better observance of the Provisions led to their reissue in December 1264.[88] Three texts of this reissue are known to exist, all of them in Latin. None is in any sense an 'official' text.

One is to be found on fols. 33v–37r of Public Record Office, E 164/24, a cartulary of Malmesbury abbey.[89] This cartulary was written in the late thirteenth century. It contains copies of several other statutes, starting with copies of the 1225 reissue of Magna Carta and the Forest Charter, the Provisions of Merton of 1236, the Statute of Westminster I of 1275 and the Statute of Jewry and the Distresses of the Exchequer of the same year (plus the form for levying the aid granted to the king in 1275), the Statute of Gloucester of 1278 and the first Quo Waranto statute of the same year, the Statute of Mortmain of 1279 (though this is a later addition) and the Statutes of Westminster II and Winchester of 1285. It also includes a text of the assizes of bread and ale. It looks as if these various statutes were copied into the volume not much after 1285, since no statute of a later date is included in the volume. It is difficult to be certain why the copyist included a text of the 1264 reissue of the Provisions among the major statutory texts in his volume. It may well be significant that these other texts did not include a text of the Statute of Marlborough which is

Marlborough had any kind of official numbering of its clauses. The enumeration of the clauses found in later books of statutes (and used by later lawyers) has no kind of contemporary official warrant or status.

88 This reissue is also noticed by the Osney chronicler: *Annales Monastici*, IV, 158–9. That the Statute of Marlborough was largely a re-enactment of legislation originally enacted during the time of Simon de Montfort is noted in *De Antiquis Legibus Liber*, p. 226.

89 *Registrum Malmesburiense: the Register of Malmesbury Abbey*, ed. J.S. Brewer and C.T. Martin (2 vols., Rolls Series, London, 1879–80), I, 42–50.

normally included in other similar collections of major statutory texts. It is possible that he simply had no text of that Statute readily to hand but did possess a copy of this text and just possible that he thought this text an adequate substitute for the Statute of Marlborough, since so much of the later Statute merely re-enacted what was in this text. The text which he copied took the form of letters patent addressed to the men of Devonshire issued at Worcester on 14 December 1264 and is evidently derived from the text of the reissued Provisions sent to the county of Devon. Malmesbury had a daughter house at Pilton in Devon which may explain how the abbey had access to this Devonshire copy.[90] There is, however, also a second copy of the same Devonshire text (though here the letters patent are dated 13 December 1264) on fols. 173v–175v of MS. LC 14.3 in the Hampton L. Carson Collection of the Philadelphia Free Library. This is a mainly legal manuscript compiled at the end of the thirteenth or beginning of the fourteenth century, containing treatises on estate management, minor legal treatises, a copy of *Britton* and texts of a number of statutes. It also contains the unique French draft of the *Providencia Baronum*.[91] The third text is on fols. 128–131 of British Library MS. Cotton Claudius D. ii in a section of the manuscript which contains other documents relating to the same period. Neil Ker has shown that this part of the MS. once formed part of an early fourteenth-century London legal manuscript known as the *Liber Legum Antiquorum Regum*.[92] It is in the form of letters patent addressed to the men of Middlesex, also dated 13 December 1264. It was evidently copied (though probably at one or more removes) from the copy sent to the county of Middlesex.

Apart from the differences in addressees and in the dates of the covering letters patent these texts are virtually identical. The main text of the Provisions is, in its turn, identical with that of the 1263 reissues. It contains exactly the same additional clauses and in exactly the same places. It omits the same clause (clause 14 on mortmain alienations). It also has exactly the same amendments to clause 5 (on beaupleder fines) and to clause 1. The latter not only retains the curt 'decetero sic observandum est' of the 1263 reissue but also repeats what had then been the correct calculation of the number of years which had elapsed since the king's crossing into Brittany in 1230 (thirty-two and a half years). The latter had been correct in January 1263. It was obviously erroneous when repeated without any

[90] D. Knowles and R.N. Hadcock, *Medieval Religious Houses: England and Wales* (London, 1972), p. 74.

[91] Baker, *English Legal MSS. in the United States of America, part 1*, no. 162, pp. 57–8; Brand, *MCL*, p. 337.

[92] N.R. Ker, '*Liber Custumarum* and Other Manuscripts Formerly at the Guildhall', *Guildhall Miscellany* 3 (1954), 37–45.

attempt at alteration almost two years later. It is plain, then, that no thought was given to any revision of the substance of this text of the Provisions. It may even be the case that those who reissued the text were unaware that the text they were reissuing differed in material respects from the original text of the 1259 Provisions.

Such thought and care as did go into the 1264 reissue of the Provisions went into the drafting of yet another new preamble plus a new concluding clause for the Provisions. This preamble marked a radical departure from the model followed by the preambles included in both prior versions of the Provisions in that it said nothing about the circumstances which had given rise to the Provisions which were now being published. Nothing was said about who had made or who consented to the legislation; nothing about whose authority lay behind their publication and enforcement. It also departed radically from the model established by the previous reissue in openly avowing that it was a reissue of an existing legislative text.[93] Indeed, by calling the legislation 'provisions and constitutions' (*provisiones et constitutiones*) it may have been alluding, albeit only indirectly, to the fact that it was in effect republishing the 1259 Provisions (which for the most part call themselves *provisiones*) as well as the 1263 Provisions (which for the most part call themselves *constituciones*).[94] The reissue was specifically linked to the recent civil war. It was the latter that was blamed for the fact that the Provisions had not been properly observed hitherto. Part of the answer to the problem of non-observance, it was suggested, was for the Provisions to be republished.[95]

The non-observance of the legislation and the need to publicise it in order to secure its observance were both themes also taken up and expanded in a new concluding clause. The Montfortian regime (speaking through the king, in whose name the reissue was made) expressed the king's wish that no one 'in future can excuse himself from observance of the foregoing by ignorance'; that 'the said provisions and constitutions' be not 'reputed by anyone hereafter as mere words'; but 'that all and each be put into force'.[96] To ensure that in future there should be no ignorance of the Provisions not only was there to be this formal reissue of the Provisions which would naturally be proclaimed in the county court and perhaps in other courts as well but the decision was taken (here, at least, specifically on the advice of the king's prelates and magnates) that the sheriffs be ordered to have the legislation published each month in

93 For the text of the preamble see Appendix II: below, pp. 430–1.

94 There may also be an indirect reference to that 1263 reissue in its backward reference to the prior legislation as having been made 'for the reform and improvement of our realm' ('ad reformacionem et melioracionem regni nostri'), the same terms as are used in the preamble to the 1263 reissue.

95 See Appendix II: below, pp. 430–1.

96 See Appendix II: below, pp. 450–1.

their county courts and in hundreds and wapentake courts as well as in courts baron.[97] This was a perfectly practical scheme so far as the county courts were concerned since they did indeed meet every month and the sheriff was their presiding officer and so could easily ensure the Provisions were proclaimed there. It made much less sense in the case of other courts which typically met every three weeks and which (in the case of the courts baron and privately held hundreds and wapentakes) were not under the control or regular oversight of the sheriff. A new theme was then sounded: practical measures to ensure that the Provisions were observed and those who breached them were punished. Firm observance of the Provisions was said to be enjoined by the king (again implicitly on the advice of the prelates and magnates) 'for the benefit of the whole community of England'.[98] Nothing was said about enforcement of the legislation through the royal courts or by remedies obtainable from Chancery. Local enforcement was evidently thought to be the key to making the legislation effective and it was the county sheriffs who were made responsible for punishing anyone who breached the legislation: 'if anyone presumes to go against the said provisions and constitutions, we wish that they be heavily punished by our said sheriffs as being in contempt of our order and as offenders against the said provisions and constitutions'.[99] Only if sheriffs were unable to impose punishment themselves (the obvious contingency the legislators had in mind was a local magnate too powerful for the sheriff to act against) was the sheriff to notify the king for him to take appropriate action, and even then the sheriff himself was threatened with punishment as well if it turned out that he had been negligent in failing to take appropriate action.[100] It may indeed be no coincidence that all three copies of the legislation are copies of texts sent to individual counties. Legislative texts were normally sent not only to counties but to all the main royal courts. This may also have been true in December 1264. But the emphasis in this final clause on enforcement through purely local mechanisms suggests that the legislation may on this occasion have been published only locally and not in the usual way. Since the legislation was merely a reissue of the 1263 legislation there was perhaps no need to notify the central courts of what the legislation contained anyway.

97 See Appendix II: below, pp. 450–1.
98 See Appendix II: below, pp. 450–1.
99 See Appendix II: below, pp. 450–1.
100 See Appendix II: below, pp. 450–1.

Chapter 6

THE REVISED PROVISIONS IN ACTION, 1263–7

THE POLITICAL SETTING AND THE SURVIVING EVIDENCE

Although Henry III faced mounting opposition from January 1263 onwards it was only in July of that year that he was forced to agree to the reinstatement of the regime of conciliar control of governmental machinery that had been created at Oxford in the summer of 1258, to the dismissal of the current royal appointees to the posts of chancellor, justiciar and treasurer and their replacement by new baronial appointees, and to a new measure for the expulsion from England of all aliens except for those whose continued residence was acceptable to the king's subjects.[1] The new regime's hold on power was, however, no more than tenuous. By November the king had once more taken control of his administration and appointed his own candidates to the posts of chancellor, treasurer and chief justiciar.[2] In January 1264 King Louis IX of France, to whom the differences between the king and his opponents had earlier been referred, provided a secular counterpart to the two prior papal condemnations of the Provisions of Oxford and all that followed from them in his pronouncement in the Mise of Amiens.[3] The Mise, like the papal pronouncements, was not acceptable to Simon de Montfort or to other radical opponents of the king and civil war began in April 1264, culminating with baronial victory at the battle of Lewes in May 1264. The unexpected victory at Lewes brought to power a regime that was dominated and largely controlled by Simon de Montfort with the king 'ruling' only as a virtual captive of the earl. It lasted for little more than a year until Montfort's defeat and death at the battle of Evesham in August 1265. The defeat of the Montfortians at Evesham did not bring peace. The resistance of the 'disinherited', those whose lands had been forfeited by their adherence to the Montfortian cause, continued even beyond the Dictum of Kenilworth of October 1266 and until after the earl of Gloucester's march on, and occupation of, London in 1267. It was only

[1] Maddicott, *Simon de Montfort*, pp. 229–33. [2] Ibid., pp. 239–47. [3] Ibid., pp. 256–64.

with the publication of yet another revised reissue of the Provisions of Westminster as the Statute of Marlborough in November 1267 that this period of political upheaval can be said finally to have come to an end.

The Provisions of Westminster were hardly a major issue between the two sides during this period for, despite their origins as part of the baronial reform programme, they had, as has already been seen, been accepted twice by the king during 1263. Nor, in truth, was there much for the king to object to in them. It is therefore hardly surprising to find evidence that they were enforced both during periods when the king was in control and in periods when royal government was controlled by his opponents. The main thing that changed from period to period was the formulas used by Chancery and the Exchequer in the writs they provided for those wishing to secure enforcement of individual Provisions, the different phrases they used to refer to the authority which lay behind their enactment. Even tracing this in detail is difficult, however, because of gaps in the surviving court records of this period.

If there had been no disruptions, the Common Bench would have held sessions during a total of twenty terms between the first reissue of the Provisions of Westminster in January 1263 and their final reissue as the Statute of Marlborough in November 1267. Political disturbances prevented the court holding sessions for most of Michaelmas term in 1263 (and for a small period at the very end of the previous Trinity term);[4] for the whole of Easter and Trinity terms in 1264;[5] for part of Trinity term 1265;[6] and while the earl of Gloucester and his allies occupied London during Easter term 1267.[7] The absence of surviving final concords suggests that the court may also not have sat in Hilary term 1264.[8] Substantially complete plea rolls survive for only four of the remaining terms: for two consecutive terms (Easter and Trinity) in 1263 and again for two consecutive terms at the end of 1266 and beginning of 1267 (Michaelmas 1266 and Hilary 1267).[9] A fifth term (Easter 1265) is represented only by a damaged and incomplete roll.[10] There are no surviving rolls for the remaining ten terms during which the court is known to have

[4] From the octaves of St John the Baptist to the octaves of Martinmas: *CR 1261–1264*, p. 372. This evidence is also confirmed in part by E 368/39, m. 16d and E 159/38, m. 2.

[5] KB 26/210, m. 10; CP 52/1/1A, part I, no. 14.

[6] The Exchequer Memoranda Roll notes the appearance of a Common Bench litigant at the quindene of St John the Baptist in the Exchequer. He had come on the day appointed to him and, finding no justices sitting there as they had already left Westminster by order of the king ('qui prius recesserunt per preceptum domini regis'), wanted to ensure his appearance was recorded by the barons: E 159/39, m. 31.

[7] The fact that there are no surviving fines for this term helps confirm this: *BNB*, I, 144.

[8] Ibid. [9] KB 26/172, 173, 176 and 180.

[10] KB 26/210. There are also damaged duplicate rolls for Trinity 1263 and Hilary 1267: KB 26/211 and 179.

conducted business. Sessions of the general eyre were held in seven counties during 1263.[11] No rolls at all survive from three of these session,[12] and only a foreign pleas roll from a fourth.[13] Good rolls, however, survive for the remaining three eyres.[14] It is more difficult to be certain for how many terms the court of King's Bench held sessions although it seems likely that it was for roughly the same number as the Common Bench. Only a similarly small proportion of its rolls survive, covering five terms in all.[15] Fortunately, the evidence to be derived from the rather disappointing number of surviving plea rolls of the main royal courts can be supplemented by evidence derived from a number of surviving assize rolls from the period, from the evidence of surviving Chancery rolls and also, and most importantly, from the complete surviving set of Exchequer memoranda rolls for this period.

ENFORCEMENT OF THE PROVISIONS: THE CONTINUING USE OF THE NEW REMEDIES INVENTED BETWEEN 1259 AND 1263

As has been seen, at least three and possibly four different types of remedy had been created prior to 1263 to give effect to different clauses of the Provisions: *contra formam feoffamenti*, the new remedy authorised by clause 3 of the Provisions but which gave effect to clause 1; a prohibition to give effect to clause 4 of the Provisions on demands for attendance at the sheriff's tourn; *monstravit de compoto*, the writ for the attachment of the bodies of landless bailiffs authorised by clause 19 of the Provisions; and perhaps a prohibition against the exaction of beaupleder fines based on clause 5.[16] This section examines the evidence for the continuing availability of these new writs and actions during the period between the first reissue of the Provisions in January 1263 and their final reissue as the Statute of Marlborough in November 1267.

[11] Crook, *Records of the General Eyre*, pp. 131–3.

[12] The sessions held by Briwes and his colleagues in Devon (in January and February) and Somerset (between April and June); the sessions held by Littlebury and his colleagues in Lincolnshire (between April and June and in September).

[13] The Hampshire eyre held by de la Tour and his colleagues between April and June: JUST 1/1195, mm. 9–16, 18d-19.

[14] Those held by de la Tour in Kent in January and February (though there is only a fragmentary crown pleas roll for this eyre); by Littlebury in Surrey during the same period and by Preston in Rutland in April and May: JUST 1/363 (and JUST 1/1195 (part) and JUST 1/1582); JUST 1/874 (and JUST 1/912B, mm. 5–7); JUST 1/721.

[15] For Michaelmas term 1265, Hilary and Michaelmas terms in 1266, and Hilary and Michaelmas terms in 1267: KB 26/174, 175, 177, 178, 181.

[16] Above, pp. 109–20.

Contra formam feoffamenti

As has been seen, the evidence suggests that writs of *contra formam feoffamenti* ceased to be available from Chancery by the middle of 1261 and that this suspension of their issue was associated with Walter of Merton's appointment to the chancellorship and is possibly to be explained in terms of his and the king's dislike of the verbal formulas used in those writs to refer to the authority that lay behind the enactment of the Provisions.[17] One effect of the royalist reissue of the Provisions in January 1263 was evidently to cause a resumption of the issuing of writs for the enforcement of clause 1. The first such writ was issued in time for it to initiate litigation in the first session of the Rutland eyre held in April 1263. It was, however, of an entirely different form to that used for earlier writs of *contra formam feoffamenti*.[18] It took the form not of a returnable writ but of mandate from the king to the justices reciting the statutory rules about suit of court in a form that reflected the wording of the 1263 reissue.[19] The writ went on to set out the main alleged facts of the case: that Ebles de Mountz and his predecessors as tenants of the manor of Ketton and their men had performed no suit to the court of Richard, the king's brother and the king of the Germans, in Oakham until the king's thirty-fifth year (1249–50) when the defendant, Richard of Seaton, Richard's bailiff, had unjustly distrained his predecessor and his tenants for suit which they neither owed nor acknowledged owing contrary to the 'provision and constitution'.[20] The writ concluded by ordering the justices of the eyre to see justice done.[21] This was no ordinary writ and no ordinary plaintiff. Ebles was a Savoyard who had been one of the stewards of the king's household since 1256 and Ketton had been granted to him by the king's son Edward in 1257.[22] This was one of two similar writs which were issued for him for use in this eyre.[23] Richard of Seaton was the target of both and in the

[17] Above, pp. 110–11. [18] JUST 1/721, m. 6d.

[19] '. . . cum de consilio fidelium suorum provideri fecerit et statui necnon per totum regnum suum publicari ne aliqui ad sectas faciendas compellantur nisi per formam feoffamenti sui ad hoc teneantur aut ipsi vel eorum predecessores eam facere consueverunt ante primam transfretacionem domini regis in Britanniam . . .'

[20] 'Et Ebulo de Montibus et predecessores sui manerium de Keten' et homines sui ejusdem manerii de secta facienda ad curiam regis Alemannie fratris sui de Okham, quam nec sibi recognoscunt nec facere sibi debent, ut dicunt, immunes extiterint usque ad annum tricesimum quintum, Ricardus de Seyton ballivus dicti domini regis Almanie dictum Ebulonem et homines suos predictos de Keten' injuste distringit ad sectam faciendam ad curiam predictam contra provisionem et constitucionem supradictam.'

[21] 'Dominus Rex mandavit justiciariis hic quod cum . . . [et] quod in itinere suo plenam et celerem justiciam eidem Ebuloni et hominibus suis predictis super hoc exhibeant etc.'

[22] *VCH Rutland*, II, 254.

[23] The other writ is on JUST 1/721, m. 5. It alleged that Richard had wrongly refused to allow Ebles exemption from vicecomital authority within the manor and had extorted amercements from his tenants.

second he is specifically identified as the sheriff of Rutland. Behind him, perhaps as the unidentified target, was Richard, king of the Germans, whose agent he was. Although the writ looks as though it is intended to be a full and complete complaint in itself, Ebles or his lawyer then seems to have made a further count in court complaining of a particular distraint made earlier in 1263 on the basis of an alleged default at the court of Oakham. What he did not allege, and could not have alleged, was that the manor was held of Richard, king of Germany and thus, despite the initial recitation of the Provisions, the situation was not one to which the Provisions as enacted actually applied for this was not a case of tenurial suit of court owed to the lord's court. If this objection was made by the defendant or his serjeant, however, the objection was not enrolled. All Richard is recorded as pleading is that he had never demanded any suit from him to the court of Oakham or made any distraint against him to enforce such a demand. No judgment is recorded on this defence.

The new writ form used in this case did not, however, replace the one previously in use except for this one case. The Common Bench plea rolls for Trinity term 1263 record what are evidently the initial procedural stages of two new cases initiated by a version of the previous writ of *contra formam feoffamenti*.[24] The writs used to initiate these cases used a different, and much more royalist, way of referring to the authority which lay behind the enactment of the legislation,[25] but in almost all other respects the writs seem to have resembled the writs issued in 1260 and 1261.[26] These are, however, the only new cases of *contra formam feoffamenti* recorded on the surviving plea rolls prior to 1267. This suggests that their issue may once more have been suspended some time after 1263 for, had writs been available, it might have been expected that there would have been at least mesne process in cases initiated by them on the surviving plea rolls for Michaelmas 1266 and Hilary 1267.

24 *Walter fitzHumphrey v. Hugh de Neville* and *Aunger de Tatlington v. John fitzAlan*: KB 26/173, mm. 17, 17d (=KB 26/211, mm. 9, 11d). There is also a non-suit recorded in what seems to have been a third such case in the same term (*Richard of Creeting and his wife Hawise v. Master of the Templars and brother Simon of Bovington*) but the enrolment does not give the full terms of the writ ('de placito quare . . . distringant ipsos ad faciendam sectam ad curiam suam de Parva Sutton' contra provisionem et constitucionem regni . . .'): KB 26/173, m. 5d (=KB 26/211, m. 2).

25 '. . . cum de communi consilio fidelium nostrorum provideri fecimus et statui necnon per totum regnum pupplicari . . .' A similar form of words was used in the writ summarised in an enrolment of a case heard in the 1268 Yorkshire eyre (*Stephen of Hatfield v. Master of the Templars*: JUST 1/1050, m. 26). This may suggest that the writ used in the case had been issued originally during this period as well.

26 In the first but not the second of these actions the writ is enrolled as describing the distraint as having been made 'contrary to the said provision and constitution' ('contra provisionem et constitucionem predictam'), a slightly more elaborate form of words than previously used. See also above, note 24 for a still more elaborate formula used in a third action non-suited that same term.

Writs to secure exemption from attendance at the tourn

There is also plentiful evidence from this period of the continued availability from the Exchequer, if not from Chancery, of prohibitions directed against local sheriffs and intended to secure for those entitled under clause 4 of the Provisions to exemption from the sheriff's tourn freedom from distraint for attendance or the payment of amercements for their absence. The much better survival of the memoranda rolls for this period allows us to trace this and the succession of changes in the phraseology of the writs issued on a term by term basis for the whole of this period.

The earliest of the enrolled writs, coming from Hilary term 1263 but apparently issued after the reissued Provisions of Westminster had been received in the Exchequer, continues the practice already noted in 1262 of issuing such prohibitions without citing any specific authority for the exemption. It is a mandate to the sheriff of Warwickshire ordering that the prior of Warmington be allowed freedom from being compelled to attend the sheriff's tourn in person.[27] A similar writ was issued later that same term to the sheriff of Cambridgeshire and Huntingdonshire in favour of the abbot of St Albans and to relieve him from distraints intended to ensure that he attended the tourn either in person or by attorney in those two counties. Again this made no mention of the legislation and cited as its justification only the fact that the abbey's only holding in Huntingdonshire was a parish church and appurtenant lands.[28] Still later that same term, however, an order was issued to the sheriff of Norfolk requiring him to cease distraining Ralph of Worcester for attendance at the tourn. Ralph was a tenant in chief in Ireland and lived there and the writ specifically cited as its justification the legislation exempting non-residents from attendance at the tourn. The citation of the legislation in this writ differs from the Exchequer prohibitions of an earlier period in the way that it describes the authority behind the legislation. This was considerably more royalist in tone ('because it had been provided by our council and conceded by us') but much less royalist than the formulation used by Chancery in the *contra formam feoffamenti* writs it issued during this period.[29] A second writ of similar form was enrolled in Michaelmas term 1263. This again cited the legislation in similar terms and ordered the sheriff of Essex to cease troubling Bartholomew Parker for attendance at the tourn on the basis of the land he held in the county as he had no house

[27] E 159/37, m. 10. [28] E 159/37, m. 12.

[29] 'Quia provisum est per consilium nostrum et a nobis concessum quod illi qui habeant terras et tenementa in diversis hundredis non habeant necesse venire ad turnos vicecomitis nisi in ballivis ubi fuerunt conversantes . . .': E 159/37, m. 10d.

there and did not live in the county.[30] However, a further writ enrolled still later that same term and again addressed to the sheriff of Essex which was intended to secure the freedom of another non-resident (Robert de Ginges) from demands for attendance at the tourn conspicuously did not cite the legislation but based itself instead on an alleged rule of unspecified authority or origin.[31]

There are then no further enrolled writs of this sort until after the Montfortian victory at the battle of Lewes. From the period after the battle but prior to the Montfortian reissue of the Provisions comes a curiously worded writ apparently citing the legislation on the exemption of the religious from attendance at the tourn and addressed to the sheriff of Bedfordshire and Buckinghamshire in favour of the prior of St Mary's Southwark.[32] From the period after the reissue comes a writ dated 21 February 1265 in favour of an alleged non-resident (J. de Gynges) who held property in Essex but lived in Middlesex. This cited the legislation in a way ('because it has been provided by the magnates of the king's council . . .') that made it sound as though it was solely the work of the magnates belonging to the king's council and that the king had played no part at all in its making.[33]

Such prohibitions also continued to be issued after the royalist victory at the battle of Evesham. The memoranda roll for Michaelmas term 1265 has a mandate to the sheriff of Cambridgeshire and Huntingdonshire expressly based on legislation but with a curiously non-royalist, even Montfortian, formulation for the authority behind the legislation ('Because it has been provided by the counsel of the magnates who are of the king's council . . .'). It is in favour of a woman (Margery la Noreyse) and describes her as belonging to a category which the legislation had exempted. It also goes on to cite the second part of clause 4 in a way that suggests that the exemption of women from attendance at the tourn was also in accordance with previous custom. The margination suggests a similar writ was also issued at the same time for a member of a different

[30] 'Quia provisum est per commune consilium nostrum et a nobis concessum quod illi qui habent terras in diversis hundredis non debent facere sectam ad turnum vicecomitis nisi in hundredis ubi fuerunt conversantes . . .': E 159/38, m. 2d.

[31] 'Quia turnus vicecomitis consuevit teneri in comitatibus nostris racione personarum tenencium terras in eisdem comitatibus qui debent venire ad eundem turnum et non racione earundem terrarum . . .': E 159/38, m. 4.

[32] 'Quia per commune consilium regis coram baronibus quod omnes viri religiosi quieti sint de turnis vicecomitis in propriis personis suis . . .': E 159/39, m. 7d.

[33] '. . . quia per magnates de consilio regis provisum est quod illi qui habent terras et tenementa in diversis hundredis non habeant necesse venire ad turnum vicecomitis nisi in ballivis ubi fuerunt conversantes . . .': E 159/39, m. 12d.

exempt group, the prior of Huntingdon.[34] There is also a second similar writ from the same period to the sheriff of Nottinghamshire in favour of the prior of Swineshead. This again specifically cites the legislation as exempting the religious from attendance at the tourn and also goes on to cite the second half of clause 4 on the tourn being held in accordance with Magna Carta and as it had been held in the reigns of the king's predecessors.[35] The formulation adopted for the authority behind the legislation is equally, if not more, Montfortian sounding in its emphasis on the magnate role in making the legislation ('because it has been provided by the counsel of the magnates . . .'). The roll indicates that similar writs were subsequently issued for the heads of nine other religious houses.[36]

Monstravit de compoto

There is no evidence from this period to indicate any further use by litigants in the common law courts of the writ of *monstravit de compoto*. Clause 19 of the Provisions was, however, cited in a writ directed to the sheriff of Suffolk that was enrolled on the memoranda roll of the Exchequer in Hilary term 1263.[37] It ordered him to 'attach' Roger Heyward of Stowe 'by his body' to appear in the Exchequer on the morrow of the close of Easter to render an account to Master J. of Essex, a clerk of the Exchequer, for the period he had acted as his bailiff at South Elmham. It is thus in effect a *monstravit de compoto* but one brought under the privilege jurisdiction of the Exchequer by an Exchequer official. Its citation of the legislation uses, but glosses, the words of the Provisions and bears almost no resemblance to the earlier (or later) *monstravit de compoto* writs issued by Chancery. Its formulation for the authority behind the legislation bears a close resemblance to that used in the tourn exemption writs issued by the

[34] 'Quia provisum est per consilium magnatum qui sunt de consilio regis quod mulieres quiete sint in propriis personis suis de turno vicecomitis nisi earum presencia specialiter exigatur et quod turnus predictus teneatur sicut temporibus predecessorum regis regum Anglie teneri consuevit . . .': E 159/40, m. 2d.

[35] 'Quia provisum est per consilium magnatum qui sunt de consilio nostro quod viri religiosi non habeant necesse venire in propriis personis suis ad turnum vicecomitis nisi eorum presencia specialiter exigatur et quod turni vicecomitis teneantur secundum tenorem magne carte nostre et sicut temporibus predecessorum nostrorum regum Anglie teneri consueverunt . . .': E 159/40, m. 4d.

[36] For the abbot of Revesby to the sheriff of Lincolnshire, for the prioress of Clerkenwell to the sheriff of Essex, for the abbot of Waltham to the sheriff(s) of Essex and Hertfordshire, for the abbot of Stratford and the abbot of Newstead to the sheriff of Essex, for the prior of Dunmow to the sheriff of Norfolk, for the abbot of Old Warden to the sheriff of Essex, for the abbot of Bruerne to the sheriff of Oxfordshire and for the abbot of Sawtry to the sheriff of Cambridgeshire.

[37] E 159/37, m. 12.

Exchequer during this same period.[38] It also adopts a radically different interpretation of the legislation and its intended effects. Chancery, as we have seen, took the legislation to authorise 'attachment by the body' as the initial process against landless bailiffs. The Exchequer writ, by contrast, took the Provisions as authorising the use of 'attachment by the body' only at a later stage in the process, when the local sheriff had made a return to the court to the effect that the bailiff/defendant had no lands by which he was to be attached. The writ as issued specifically cited that prior return as well as the legislation as the authorisation for the writ as issued.

The prohibition of beaupleder fines

There is also evidence from this period of the drafting of a second version of the writ for the use of plaintiffs wishing to complain about being compelled to pay beaupleder fines. It does not seem to have been drafted for a real case since it does not use actual names and somewhat puzzlingly it cites Magna Carta (as recently confirmed) rather than the Provisions as the basis for the action.[39] The writ was enrolled on the Close Roll early in 1265.[40] Powicke noted this writ and suggested that 'the terms of the writ suggest a desire to make the Great Charter a joint and several guardian even of recent reforms in the law'. He connected the writ with the clause forbidding unreasonable amercement for minor offences.[41] It seems more likely, however, that it refers either to the clause added in 1217 on the sheriff's tourn or, as the relevant clause in the Petition of the Barons might suggest, to the clause about 'selling or denying' justice. There is also other evidence for the enforcement of the prohibition on beaupleder fines. This is an order which is enrolled on the Memoranda Roll in Easter term 1265 but which cites neither the Provisions nor Magna Carta. All it does is to order the sheriff of Norfolk to respite a demand on the men of Humbleyard hundred for forty shillings for a beaupleder fine, without providing any justification for doing so.[42]

[38] 'Quia provisum est per commune consilium regni et a rege concessum quod ballivi qui compotum dominis suis reddere tenentur si se subtrahant et terras et tenementa non habeant per que distringi possint attachientur per corpora eorum quod veniant coram eisdem dominis suis ad compotum suum reddendum . . .'

[39] 'Ostensurus quare, cum de consilio nostro et magnatum regni nostri communiter provisum sit quod libertates in magna carta nostra contente in singulis articulis earundem tam pro parte nostra quam aliorum de regno nostro plenius observentur, talis distringit talem ad finem dandum pro pulchre placitando in curia sua de N. contra provisionem et libertates predictas ut dicit . . .'

[40] *CR 1264–1268*, p. 100.

[41] Powicke, *Henry III and the Lord Edward*, p. 489, note 2.

[42] E 159/39, m. 14d. At the same time the hundred also obtained a respite of a demand for an amercement of sixty shillings imposed on the twelve jurors of the hundred for concealment at the sheriff's tourn.

ENFORCEMENT THROUGH PRE-EXISTING FORMS OF ACTION

Awarding of damages in the assize of mort d'ancestor

Clauses 9 and 10 authorised the awarding of damages in assizes of mort d'ancestor when the defendant was a lord refusing to deliver a tenement to the heir when he came of age, or when the lord had managed to enter land before an heir who was of age.[43] Both continued to be enforced during this period. Damages of three shillings were awarded to an heir already of age refused admission by his lord in a Cambridgeshire assize of mort d'ancestor heard in the Common Bench in Trinity term 1263. The judgment awarding the damages did not cite the legislation directly as its authority for doing so but was careful to note that the defendant (John le Rus) was a chief lord who had maliciously kept the claimant out of seisin of his tenement, thereby indirectly quoting the legislation as authority for its award.[44] Clause 9 of the legislation authorising the awarding of damages where a lord held on to land after an heir came of age was applied in an assize of mort d'ancestor heard in King's Bench at Winchester on the morrow of Martinmas 1267, just one week before the final royal confirmation of the Provisions of Westminster through the enactment of the Statute of Marlborough. Again there was no direct citation of the Provisions but the awarding of damages (of fifty shillings) was specifically justified by reference to the fact that the claimant had been in the wardship of the defendant and he had retained the land for five years after he had come of age, an unmistakeable indirect reference to the legislation.[45]

Application of clause 1 in an action of customs and services

As has been seen, clause 1 of the Provisions of Westminster was enforced both before and after the reissue of 1263 through the action of *contra formam feoffamenti*.[46] This was an action for tenants when their claim was that they had been distrained for suit when they did not owe it. The legislation had also envisaged the creation of a second form of action for lords whose tenants had withdrawn suit which they owed under the rules

[43] Below, pp. 420–1. For previous enforcement of these clauses see above, pp. 124–5.

[44] 'Et quia predictus Johannes le Rus capitalis dominus feodi illius tenuit ipsum Johannem maliciose extra seisinam ideo predictus Johannes de Castro Bernardo recuperet dampna sua . . .': *John of Barnard Castle v. John le Rus*: KB 26/173, m. 19d.

[45] 'Et quia predictus Nicholaus dum fuit infra etatem fuit in custodia predicti Walteri et postquam idem Nicholaus pervenerit ad plenam etatem detinuit ei predictam terram per quinque annos consideratum est quod predictus Nicholaus recuperet damna sua . . .': *Nicholas Bernard v. Walter parson of Kingsclere*: KB 26/181, m. 22.

[46] Above, pp. 109–15, 168–9.

laid down by the legislation. It did not, however, say that they could not go on using their existing common law remedy of the action of customs and services nor make it wholly clear whether, if they did so, it was the rules established by the legislation which were henceforward to be applicable in it. The period between the first reissue of the Provisions in January 1263 and their final reissue in the Statute of Marlborough in November 1267 provides the only known example of a court taking what seems to be the logical view: that the legislation was indeed applicable in the lord's common law action. The case was one heard in the 1263 Kent eyre probably shortly after the justices had been notified of the reissuing of the Provisions.[47] Robert le Blund of Newington was suing Roger Beselet and his brother Stephen for the services he claimed they owed him for the messuage and half an acre they held of him in Newington. These were a rent of sixteen pence, two hens and five eggs a year and three-weekly suit to his court of Newington. His claim was that he had been seised of both rent and suit at their hands until two years ago when they had ceased to pay or perform them. The tenants admitted owing the rent but denied that it was in arrears; they denied owing the suit on the grounds that they had been enfeoffed of the holding by Robert's ancestor(s) by a charter which had made no mention of suit of court.[48] The justices then intervened to ask Robert about his title to claim suit contrary to the tenor of their charter. His reply cited only his own seisin for a period of years that did not take him back to before 1230.[49] The court held that as his claim was based on his own seisin after 1230 and acquired in contravention of the terms of their feoffment this claim should, in accordance with the legislation (here again referred to as the 'Provisions of Oxford'), be dismissed.[50]

OBSERVANCE OF THE PROVISIONS ON CROWN PLEAS FINES AND AMERCEMENTS

There was effectively only one eyre which took place wholly after the reissue of the Provisions for which a crown pleas roll survives, the Rutland eyre of 1263. Its recorded statement of Englishry custom on what seems

47 JUST 1/363, m. 28.

48 'Quia dicunt quod ipsi feofati fuerunt de antecessoribus predicti Roberti per cartam, ita quod nulla mencio facta est in eadem carta quod tenantur ad aliquam sectam faciendam . . .'

49 The precise number of years can no longer be read because of damage to the plea roll.

50 'Et quia idem Robertus nichil aliud ostendit per quod ei tenetur in predicta secta nisi de seisina sua post primam transfretacionem domini [regis in Britanniam et] contra formam feofamenti sui consideratum est secundum provisionem Oxon' quod predictus Rogerus et Stephanus quo ad predictam sectam sine die et Robertus nichil capiat per breve istud set sit in misericordia pro falso clamore etc.'

to be the plea roll made for the chief justice neither admitted nor denied liability for accidental deaths,[51] but in the event no *murdrum* fine was adjudged or paid in respect of non-felonious homicides. Curiously, in the next eyre in the county held in 1286 it was said that the statement of custom made in this eyre had been that Englishry only needed to be presented for 'known males killed *by felony*' although this had clearly not been the case.[52]

OBSERVANCE OF THE PROVISIONS ON INITIAL AND MESNE PROCESS

Both the ordinary actions of *contra formam feoffamenti* initiated in the Common Bench seem to have followed the prescriptions of clause 3 of the Provisions by requiring attachment as the initial stage in mesne process against the defendant.[53] This compliance was not, however, matched by any similar compliance on the part of the court in ordering the next stage in the process. In the one case where the sheriff had in fact made an attachment the court incorrectly ordered this to be followed by a second attachment, rather than *facias venire*.[54]

There is a single case of *quare impedit* recorded in Easter term 1263 where a first attachment in the action was wrongly followed by a second attachment,[55] but the correct procedure of following a first attachment with the grand distress was followed in a case brought by the king and queen in Hilary term 1267.[56] The same case also supplies the only known example from before 1267 of the application of that provision of the legislation allowing the recovery of a presentment by default in the event of a further default after the grand distress.[57] The more general abbreviation of mesne process in personal actions, omitting all stages of process between the second attachment and the grand distress, introduced by one of the clauses added for the January 1263 reissue,[58] was generally followed in the Common Bench in all except a single case in Easter term 1263.[59] It was universally observed in Trinity term 1263 and in Michaelmas term 1266 and Hilary term 1267. Other stages of mesne process are, however, also to be found in cases in the court of King's Bench in Hilary term 1267.[60]

[51] 'Englescheria presentatur in comitatu isto per unum ex parte patris et unum ex parte matris et tantummodo de masculo dummodo excesserit xij annos': JUST 1/721, m. 9.

[52] '. . . notis masculis occisis per feloniam': JUST 1/722, m. 10.

[53] Above, pp. 434–5. For earlier observance of this clause see above, pp. 134–5.

[54] KB 26/173, m. 11 (= KB 26/211, m. 11d).

[55] KB 26/172, m. 3d.

[56] KB 26/180, m. 1.

[57] *King and queen as guardians of lands and heir of Edmund de Lacy v. Earl Warenne*: KB 26/180, m. 27.

[58] Below, pp. 438–9.

[59] The one case in which it was not followed is recorded on KB 26/172, m. 1.

[60] KB 26/181, mm. 12, 25 and see KB 136/1/4/2.

Table 2 *The length of adjournments in actions of dower in the Common Bench, 1263–7*

Term	Length of adjournments (by return days) 5	4 (% affected)	3
Easter 1263	25	33	10
Trinity 1263	20	66	
Michaelmas 1266		80	
Hilary 1267		87	

Sources: Based on the length of adjournments (in terms of how many return days distant the day to which the case is adjourned lies) in cases of dower *unde nichil habet* recorded on the rectos of KB 26/172, 173, 176 and 180, expressed as a percentage of the total number of dower cases for which there are recorded adjournments that term and omitting those where the evidence is ambiguous.

ADJOURNMENTS

Dower 'unde nichil habet'

The reissued Provisions of 1263 had increased the target number of days per year in dower *unde nichil habet* from four to five with six days a year stated as a desirable goal.[61] The surviving rolls do not allow us to observe the process of individual cases over particular years but they do allow us to see the intervals between individual stages of such cases as recorded in adjournments. Table 2 is based on an analysis of the adjournments recorded in dower cases on the dorse of each of the surviving plea rolls for this period and shows the percentage of cases with adjournments of the stated length. This indicates that the best terms for relatively short adjournments in such cases are Michaelmas term 1266 and Hilary term 1267 but that a majority of adjournments met the target length of being no more than four return days away in Trinity term 1263 as well.

Quare impedit *and darrein presentment*

The lengths of adjournments in cases of *quare impedit* and assizes of darrein presentment remained highly variable after 1263 as they had been prior to the 1263 reissue of the Provisions.[62] In Easter term 1263 there was one adjournment to a day as many as seven return days away but also another to a day only two return days away.[63] In Trinity term 1263 there was one

[61] Below, pp. 418–19. [62] Above, pp. 138–9. [63] KB 26/172, mm. 3d, 21.

adjournment to a day five return days away and another to a day four return days away. Neither meets the requirements of the Provisions.[64] The damaged plea roll for Easter term 1265 provides another example of an adjournment to a day seven return days away but also another to a day three or four return days away.[65] Michaelmas term 1266 marks a distinct improvement. In all three cases the adjournment was to a day only four return days away.[66] However, this was still one return day longer than the maximum required by the Provisions. The record for Hilary term 1267 is markedly better. The days appointed for next hearings are four, three, two and just one return day away.[67]

THE CREATION OF NEW REMEDIES

Writs for the enforcement of clause 2

Although there is nothing on the surviving plea rolls of the period to show it later evidence suggests that this period may have seen the drafting of two different writs to give effect to that part of clause 2 of the Provisions of Westminster which said that on the division of a tenement the lord from whom it was held was not in future to demand more than a single suit from the coheirs or other tenants of a divided tenement. There is a writ for use in just such a situation in a register of writs now in the Bodleian Library, MS. Rawlinson C331 which belongs to the final years of the reign of Henry III.[68] The writ takes the form of a writ of attachment brought by Master Walter of Stainsby against Joce de Stepping, the steward of M., the earl or countess of Lincoln. It requires Joce to answer for having distrained Master Walter to perform suit to the court of Lusby contrary to the terms of the legislation. These are real people and there is every reason to suppose that the writ was used in a real case. Joce of Stepping is mentioned as having been the bailiff of Margaret, countess of Lincoln in the Hundred Rolls enquiry;[69] Master Walter was sued for a dower share of a bovate of land at Winceby by the widow of William son of Thomas of Lusby in Michaelmas term 1266.[70] The writ must date from before the death of Countess Margaret in March 1266,[71] but is likely to date from

[64] KB 26/173, mm. 5d, 40d.
[65] KB 26/210, mm. 4d, 73d.
[66] KB 26/176, mm. 5, 9, 24.
[67] KB 26/180, mm. 18, 1, 23d and 23 respectively.
[68] On fol. 16v. A second copy of the same writ is to be found (with the names reduced to initials) in Trinity College, Oxford, MS. 27, fol. 67r.
[69] *RH*, I, 369. For an action of recaption being brought against Margaret, countess of Lincoln, Joce of Stepping and John of Lusby in Easter term 1262 see KB 26/166, m. 10.
[70] KB 26/176, m. 7.
[71] G.E. C[okayne], *The Complete Peerage*, edited by V. Gibbs, H.A. Doubleday and others, new edition (13 vols., 1910–59), VII, 680.

after the 1263 reissue of the Provisions for the words it uses to rehearse the relevant part of the legislation resemble those used in the preamble to the 1263 reissue.[72]

A second but rather different writ form for much the same circumstances also bears marks of having been drafted during this period. This is found in the legal treatise *Fleta*, a compendium of earlier material (mainly taken from *Bracton*), apparently compiled in the early 1290s. It takes the form of a writ of prohibition beginning with the words 'A. and B. have shown us' (*Monstraverunt nobis A. et B.*). It goes on to recite the legislation but introduces it with a different phrase, again particularly reminiscent of the 1263 reissue of legislation (and close to that used in two Common Bench *contra formam feoffamenti* cases of 1263).[73] Its recital of the legislation is even more elaborate than that used in the register's writ as it covers not just the lord not being entitled to more than one suit but also those parts of clause 2 which stipulated that the tenant who held the share of the eldest was obliged to perform the suit and that the others were to contribute to the cost of doing so. It ends with a phrase about the distraint being 'contrary to the said provision and constitution', again a phrase used in one of the *contra formam feoffamenti* cases.[74] It seems likely that the writ was drafted in 1263 or shortly thereafter and copied into a register of writs from whence it found its way into *Fleta*.

Writs of entry in the post

The additional clause in the reissued Provisions had specifically left the business of drafting the new writs of entry 'outside the degrees' to the king's council. A tradition recorded in the lectures of an anonymous law teacher of the second half of the 1270s ascribed the work of drafting these writs not implausibly to Walter de Merton, who was indeed chancellor at the time the legislation was enacted. The story is somewhat spoilt, however, by the teacher also ascribing a whole group of other writs to Merton, many of which are most unlikely to have been his work.[75] In

[72] 'Cum ad melioracionem et reformacionem status regni nostri sit provisum quod si hereditas aliqua de qua unica tantum secta debeatur ad plures heredes participes vel ad alios per vendicionem vel alio modo devolvatur quod unica fiat secta pro hereditate illa sicut prius fieri consuevit . . .'

[73] 'Cum de communi consilio fidelium nostrorum provideri fecimus necnon per totum regnum pupplicari . . .': *Fleta*, lib. 2, *c.* 66 (II, 222).

[74] '. . . contra provisionem et constitucionem predictam . . .'

[75] 'Si la terre seyt descendue outre le terz degre si ne poet nul autre bref sourdre en cel cas fors qe le bref de dreyt ne en autres plusurs cas. Dount syre Wauter de Merton akun tenz chaunceler qui mult saveyt de droyt pur peril, defaute, desheritesouns qe chekun povre homme e femme en checkun petite demaunde ne poet pas aver championn prest si purveust les ix bref qe par commun assentement del roy e del realme furent conferme e establiez en le regal: des queus les uns sunt

the revised version of the same lectures the invention of the writ of entry *ad terminum qui preteriit* in the *post* is ascribed jointly to Walter of Merton and Richard of Middleton, his successor as chancellor, but who had only been a junior royal justice in 1262–3.[76] This elaboration is unlikely to be correct. It suggests that the teacher did not know that the first writs of entry in the *post* dated back to 1263 rather than 1267 and therefore only guessed at the identity of the drafters of these writs. Whoever may have been responsible for the drafting of the new writs the process itself has left some trace. This is in the form of an undated schedule containing a number of draft writ forms attached to the dorse of one of the membranes of the Close Roll for 47 Henry III (1262–3).[77] This particular membrane contains material from early March 1263. One writ seems to be a draft version of a writ of entry *cui in vita* within the degrees for the case where a *maritagium* has been given to a husband and wife and been alienated by the husband. As such writs seem already to have been in use in 1263 it is perhaps a botched attempt at a writ of *cui in vita* in the *post*. The other two writs are more certainly drafts of writs of entry outside the degrees. The first is a draft writ of entry *cui in vita* in the *post*:

> Precipe A. quod juste etc. reddat B. que fuit uxor C. de N. novem acras terre cum pertinenciis in N., quas clamat esse jus et maritagium suum et in quas idem A. non habet ingressum nisi post dimissionem quam predictus C. quondam vir ipsius B. cui in vita sua contradicere non potuit inde fecit D.[78] et quas idem A. ei injuste deforciat etc. Et nisi etc.

This differs from writs of entry *cui in vita* in the *post* of the form later current only in the use of the phrase 'et quas idem A. ei injuste deforciat etc.' instead of the later 'et unde queritur quod idem A. ei injuste deforciat'.

The second writ seems to be a draft writ of entry *ad terminum qui preteriit* in the *post*, though the initials used for the parties make it appear as though the tenant and the original lessee are one and the same person, and the relationship between demandant and original lessor is left unexplained:

de possessioun, com de bref de ael, bref de cosinage, meyn, bref de mortdancestre, bref de nuper obiit de renable partye, bref de post disseisiam, bref de quare ejecit, bref de post dimissionem, bref de intrusion, bref de causa matrimonii': BL MS. Lansdowne 467, fol. 151r.

[76] 'Et si devez saver qe outre le tierz degre de entree sur terme si gist un bref de mesme la nature qe est apele post dimissionem et furent fet ces e autres par les sages gens sire Richard de Mideltone e sire W. de Mertone la ou onqe bref ne soleit aver fors le bref de dreyt; e ceo pur eschure le delay e le peril en le bref de dreyt': Harvard Law School MS. 33, (unfoliated); *Brevia Placitata*, p. 201; BL MS. Harley 1208, fol. 204v.

[77] C 54/80, m. 10d schedule. Printed (but not entirely accurately) in *CR 1261–1264*, p. 293.

[78] This initial is omitted in the printed text.

Precipe A. quod juste et sine dilacione reddat B. quinque acras terre cum pertinenciis in N. quas H. dimisit A. ad terminum qui preteriit et que ad ipsum B. post terminum predictum reverti debent ut dicit, et unde queritur quod predictus A. ei injuste deforciat. Et nisi etc.

The only other possibility is that it was intended as a draft of a writ *ad terminum qui preteriit* for the situation where the reversioner had assigned his reversion to a stranger. This seems unlikely as nothing is said of any such transaction. If it is indeed a draft writ of entry *ad terminum qui preteriit* in the *post*, it is interesting to note that although, unlike the draft *cui in vita* in the *post*, it uses the concluding formula of later writs in the *post*, it does not use the 'non habet ingressum nisi post dimissionem' formula found in later writs and in the specimen writ of *cui in vita* in the *post*.

The first actual evidence of litigation brought by a writ of entry in the *post* is recorded on that part of the plea roll of the Rutland eyre of 1263 which contains cases heard in the session held in the second week of April. It is a writ of entry *cui in vita* brought by Hawise, widow of Geoffrey le Waleys against Beatrice Trille to claim a toft and its appurtenances in North Luffenham.[79] Hawise claimed the toft as her right (*jus*) without further qualification and as that to which Beatrice had gained title only after the grant (*post dimissionem*) made by her late husband, Geoffrey, whom she had been unable to gainsay during his lifetime, to William son of Hugh. The enrolment does not reproduce enough of the writ to show whether or not it used the 'et quas ... ei injuste deforciat etc.' of the March 1263 draft or the 'et unde queritur quod ... ei injuste deforciat' of the later standard form. There is no recorded challenge to this writ. The tenant simply vouched her own father to warranty and he in turn vouched Robert son of Hugh of North Luffenham. Robert alleged that Hawise's husband was not dead and this was the issue put to the jury.

There is then no further surviving evidence of the use of a writ of entry in the *post* until Hilary term 1267. In that term Agnes de la Hide brought a writ of entry *sur disseisin* in the *post* against John Flavel of Chichester claiming half a virgate at Frilsham in Berkshire as her right (*jus suum etc.*) 'and to which he had only gained title after the disseisin of Agnes by Walter Wylard'.[80] The tenant objected to the writ on the grounds that 'it was outside the common form of the writ of entry and no one is

[79] JUST 1/721, m. 4d (and see also the cancelled entry on m. 7 and the suit between the same parties by an unspecified writ on m. 8d).

[80] 'Et in quam non habet ingresssum nisi post disseisinam quam Walterus Wylard eidem Agneti inde fecit post primam etc.': KB 26/180, m. 24. The enrolment of an earlier procedural stage in the same case during Michaelmas term 1266 gives no indication that the case is being brought by a writ of entry in the *post*: KB 26/176, m. 33d.

obliged to answer for his free tenement to any newly drafted writ unless it has been drafted by the common council of the whole kingdom'.[81] At first sight the tenant seems to be denying the validity of the Provisions as reissued in 1263 and 1264. This is puzzling since, as has been seen, the first and second reissues did indeed have royal approval and there is no obvious reason why the litigant would think that the courts would be sympathetic to any such attack. A more careful reading of the objection suggests, however, that he may not have been doing this. All he may have been doing is denying that this particular writ was properly issued under the authority of the Provisions. He may just have been saying that this writ had not received the full approval of the king's council required under the clause on writs of entry in the *post* before being issued. Or, even more interestingly, he could have been saying that the 'common counsel of the realm' which had approved the 1263 legislation could not delegate its authority to approve all newly drafted 'writs of course' (as it had appeared to have purported to do under that clause) and thus that the new writs provided by the king's council still needed wider approval before they could be issued or even that this was what the legislation itself had envisaged all along. Unfortunately there is no recorded discussion or judgment on this objection.

New remedies for the heads of ecclesiastical corporations

Part of the clause added to the Provisions in 1263 in favour of the heads of ecclesiastical corporations had allowed them to recover lands of which their predecessor had died seised.[82] This also gave rise to at least one new form of writ during this period. In Easter term 1263 the rolls record the first stage of an action brought by the abbot of Combermere against Roger son of John Lestrange claiming a moiety of the manor of Little Ercall on the basis that his predecessor, William of Waresley, had been seised of that moiety at the time of his death.[83] The writ as enrolled does not specifically mention the legislation but was unmistakably drafted in response to it and specifically warranted by it. No pleading occurred on this writ as all that happened was that Roger vouched his father, John Lestrange, to warranty. The case was continued (but without the writ

[81] 'Et dicit quod non debet ei ad hoc breve respondere quia dicit quod breve istud formatum est extra communam formam brevis de ingressu nec aliquis debet respondere de libero tenemento suo ad aliquod breve de novo formatum nisi formatum fuerit per commune consilium tocius regni . . .'

[82] Below, pp. 446–7.

[83] '. . . de qua Willelmus de Waresley quondam abbas de Cumbremer predecessor ipsius abbatis fuit seisitus in dominico suo ut de feodo [et] jure ecclesie sue de Cumbremer die quo obiit': KB 26/172, m. 19d.

form itself being reproduced) in Easter term 1265.[84] As will be seen, it was later revived, using a writ of a rather different form but one also authorised by the legislation, in 1272.[85]

A second writ which may also have been drafted in response to (and with the implicit authority of) the legislation but which again does not mention that legislation is that brought in the Common Bench in Easter term 1265 by James Fresel, the parson of Bledlow, against the prior of Ogbourne claiming two-thirds of the crop of every tenth acre of the prior's demesne in Bledlow on the basis that his predecessor, Master Gilbert of Norton, had been seised of this profit as an appurtenance of his church on the day of his death. Again there is no recorded pleading; the plea roll simply records an order for attachment after the failure of an initial summons to secure the appearance of the defendant.[86]

CITATION OF THE REPEALED CLAUSE ON MORTMAIN ALIENATIONS

The December 1264 reissue of the Provisions eventually committed the Montfortian regime to the view that it was the revised version of the Provisions as reissued in 1263 that had been in force prior to that reissue. Thus the 'official' view from then onwards was certainly that the clause requiring mortmain alienations to have the consent of the lord of whom the land alienated was held was no longer in force. There is, however, evidence from a case heard in November 1264 to suggest that this had not necessarily been the general understanding prior to that date. This indicates that at that time there were at least some lawyers, and perhaps even some justices, who thought that it was the original Provisions which had included the clause that should properly be considered as the legislation in force. The case is an assize of novel disseisin brought by the prior of Barnwell against the master of the Templars and others heard at Royston before Nicholas de la Tour and an associate (probably Saer de Freville), most likely in November 1264. The prior claimed to have been disseised of a messuage, eight acres of meadow and four shillings of rent in Waterbeach in Cambridgeshire.[87] The master initially attempted to plead his privilege of not answering any pleas except before the king or his

[84] KB 26/210, m. 8d. [85] Below, pp. 343. [86] KB 26/210, m. 21d.

[87] JUST 1/1191, m. 15. This face of the membrane bears no heading other than one saying that it is a continuation of the assizes at Royston ('adhuc de assisis captis apud Crucem Roysie'). Membrane 14d also has an assize there on an undated day in the forty-ninth regnal year (after 28 October 1264). Judgment in our assize was adjourned to Monday the morrow of St Andrew Apostle (1 December) which would fit 1264 and indicate that the main assize was heard some time before 1 December, most probably in November.

chief justiciar. He then waived this in order to justify the alleged disseisin as no more than an attempt to prevent their tenant, John des Eschalers, from enfeoffing the prior and transferring seisin to him. He might have relied on his generally accepted common law right to do this but chose instead to plead justification under the Provisions of Westminster (here misdescribed as the 'constitucionem Oxon') which had laid down that no religious house was allowed to 'enter the fee' of another lord without his permission.[88] The prior (now joined by John) did not deny that the legislation was valid or in force but did show how the land had passed by a series of subinfeudations from Robert de Hastinges to John des Eschalers, so that there were many mesne lords between the Templars and the holding. They also claimed that the prior had taken seisin and retained it until he had been ejected by a group who had set fire to the buildings on the tenement. The master of the Templars in effect conceded the point about not being the immediate lord of the tenement (the only lord whose interests were protected by the legislation) but showed how Robert de Hastinges had been granted the tenement by his kinsman, Richard de Hastinges, who had been master of the Templars and how the Templars had continued to receive a rent from the tenement, in effect claiming that this alone gave them a sufficient interest to impede the alienation, even if they were not the immediate lords.[89] The jurors refused to give a verdict as to whether or not this was part of the Templars' fee or whether or not they were in receipt of a rent from this tenement but concentrated on the transfer of seisin, showing how the prior had been in seisin from after dinner one Thursday till prime on Friday and had been ejected by force, by the burning of the buildings and by the wounding of the prior's men and killing of one of them. They left it up to the justices to say whether or not the seisin enjoyed by the prior had been sufficiently good and long to merit the protection of the assize. The justices adjourned the case first to the beginning of December and then to January at Westminster and the case was eventually settled by an agreement which divided the property between Barnwell and the Templars.

[88] '... et per constitucionem Oxon' ordinatum est quod non licet domui religiose intrare in feodum alicujus sine licencia capitalis domini feodi illius ...'

[89] '... bene licet eis impedire quominus alia domus religiosa sine licencia sua intret in feodum eorum ...'

Chapter 7

THE FINAL REVISION AND REISSUE OF THE PROVISIONS OF WESTMINSTER: THE STATUTE OF MARLBOROUGH OF 1267

THE POLITICAL CONTEXT

The defeat of the Montfortians and the death of Simon de Montfort and many of his leading supporters at the battle of Evesham in August 1265 allowed Henry III to regain control of the machinery of government. It was followed, however, by sustained military resistance in many parts of the country from those whose support for the Montfortian regime meant, as legislation enacted at the parliament of Winchester in mid-September 1265 made plain, that they were to be deprived of all their lands and other possessions.[1] The strength and persistence of this resistence as well as pressure from the papal legate Ottobuono for some measure of conciliation of the former rebels led to the appointment of a committee of four prelates and eight laymen at the parliament summoned to Kenilworth in late August 1266. This was to suggest changes to the policy of total disinheritance of the Montfortians which would conciliate the rebels and help re-establish domestic peace.[2] When this committee submitted its report at the end of October it made a series of detailed recommendations about the substitution of fines related both to the value of the rebels' lands and to their degree of involvement on the Montfortian side in place of the policy of blanket disinheritance and redistribution to others of the rebels' lands.[3] In the fuller texts of the so-called 'Dictum' of Kenilworth there are also a number of other, unrelated clauses at the start. These make a number of suggestions about other measures needed for the re-establishment of royal authority and the conciliation of the former Montfortians. They restate the general rules of English political society underpinning the king's authority and emphasise the desirability of the appointment of suitable royal justices to provide justice for his subjects; remind the king of the need to uphold the liberties of the Church and observe Magna Carta and the Charter of the Forest; and also recommend

[1] C.H. Knowles, 'The Resettlement of England after the Barons' War, 1264–67', *Transactions of the Royal Historical Society* 5th series 32 (1982), 25–41.

[2] *CPR 1258–66*, pp. 671–2. [3] *SR*, I, 12–17; *DBM*, pp. 320–6.

that the king continue to observe those 'concessions which he has made spontaneously and without coercion' and that he should 'confirm on a permanent basis other necessary measures devised by his men with his agreement'.[4] The latter phrase sounds like a reference to the Provisions of Westminster as reissued in 1263. What the committee seems to have been recommending was a further reissue and confirmation of the Provisions.[5]

It was probably this recommendation which led to the final reissue of the Provisions of Westminster in November 1267 as the Statute of Marlborough.[6] This reissue included both a new preamble and eight new clauses. It also saw some further modification of a number of the clauses included in the previous versions of the Provisions. The new clauses were all placed at the very beginning of the text between the new preamble and the reissued clauses taken over from earlier versions of the Provisions. No documents survive to shed light on the process of revision or who participated in it. Nor can we be certain how long the process took, though it seems not unlikely that it began shortly after the publication of the Dictum in October 1266.

THE TEXTS OF THE STATUTE OF MARLBOROUGH

No contemporary official copy of the text of this Statute survives among the records of Chancery. There is no evidence to suggest that it was ever copied on to either the Patent or the Close Roll, unlike earlier versions of the legislation. Perhaps Chancery kept it in the form of a separate roll which has not survived. There is, however, what seems to be a contemporary copy of the official text of the Statute as sent to the Exchequer in the Red Book of the Exchequer.[7] There is also a second, apparently also almost contemporary, but in this case unofficial, text of the Statute. This is in the London *De Antiquis Legibus Liber* which is probably derived from the copy sent to London.[8] At least thirty pairs of

[4] *SR*, I, 13; *DBM*, p. 320.

[5] Treharne and Sanders read the first of the two phrases in the same way: *DBM*, p. 321, note 7.

[6] For a full text and translation of the Statute see Appendix III below: pp. 453–83.

[7] E 164/2, fols. 243r–244v. The heading of this text reads: 'Provisiones facte apud Marleberg' presentibus domino rege Henrico et R. rege Alem' et domino Edward filio ejusdem H. regis primogenito et domino Octobuono tunc legato in Anglia'. The 'ejusdem H.' seems to be a later insertion, indicating that the original text was written before 1272. It seems likely that it was copied into the Red Book in 1267. The Red Book was rightly used as the main source of the *Statutes of the Realm* text of the Statute: *SR*, I, 19–25. I have re-checked the MS. for the edition of the Statute in Appendix III below: at pp. 453–83.

[8] *De Antiquis Legibus Liber*, pp. 227–34. The text is simply headed 'Incipiunt Nove Provisiones'. It is preceded by a list of 'Capitula Provisionum factarum anno Domini M CC sexagesimo septimo, quorum major pars ordinata fuit tempore comitis Leycestrie, anno M CC lxiiij'. The *De Antiquis*

official copies of the Statute are known to have been made, presumably mainly for local distribution.[9] A text of the Statute is also to be found in almost all later books of statutes.

A NEW PREAMBLE

The Statute of Marlborough started with yet another new preamble.[10] This resembles the preambles drafted both for the original Provisions of Westminster of 1259 and for the first reissue of the Provisions of January 1263 in assigning a particular date to the issuing of the legislation both in terms of the year of grace (1267) and in terms of the king's regnal year (his fifty-second). It also follows the former and the best text of the latter in assigning a specific date (the octave of St Martin) to the legislation.[11] It departs from the earlier model only in omitting all mention of the place (Marlborough) where the legislation was enacted. In the Red Book of the Exchequer Marlborough is mentioned in the rubric to the text which also records the presence there not just of the king but also of Richard, king of Germany, the Lord Edward and the legate Ottobuono; in most other texts it is only the name assigned to the legislation which perpetuates the existence of any connexion between the legislation and the place of its enactment.

The 1267 preamble, like that of the 1263 reissue, emphasises the king's role in the making of the legislation, though without the almost neurotic emphasis of the 1263 reissue on the king's free will in the performance of that role. The 1267 preamble also resembles that of 1263 in conceding a limited role in the making of the legislation not to the magnates, but to a more heterogeneous group of the king's 'lieges'.[12] It mentions that the making of the legislation had been preceded by a meeting between the king and the 'wiser men of the same kingdom, both the great men and the lesser men', talks of the legislation as a 'salutary remedy' ('remedium salubre') needing to be applied 'by the king and his faithful subjects', and speaks of the legislation as having been 'provided and decreed and

Legibus Liber is thought to have been written about 1270: N.R. Ker, *Medieval Manuscripts in British Libraries, I: London* (Oxford, 1969), pp. 22–7.

9 *Calendar of Liberate Rolls, 1267–1272* (London, 1961), no. 228.

10 For the text of this preamble see Appendix III: below, pp. 454–5.

11 Above, pp. 15, 143. The octave of Martinmas (18 November) should probably not be taken too literally but was approximately the date of the beginning of the session of the king and his council where the Statute was enacted. For a case said to have been 'recorded' before the king and council at Marlborough also at the octave of Martinmas see JUST 1/1198, m. 7.

12 But note that when the court of King's Bench referred to the legislation only a year later it referred to clause 6 as having been 'provided by agreement by the lord king and the magnates of England' ('per dominum regem et magnates Anglie concorditer provisum est . . .'): below, p. 199, note 60.

ordained by general agreement'. Although later known as the 'Statute' of Marlborough the legislation describes itself as the 'provisions, ordinances and statutes written below', and although 'provisions' was the term used in 1259, 'ordinances and statutes' are new terms being used for the first time in this final reissue of 1267. Curiously, and unlike the 1259 and 1263 Provisions, it says nothing about the 'publication' of the legislation. But it does contain a clause about its enforcement, requiring that all the inhabitants of the realm, both great men and lesser, should observe the legislation firmly and inviolably for all time. However, the fuller clause about enforcement added at the end of the Statute in a number of manuscripts seems unlikely to be genuine and looks as if it has been wrongly borrowed from the enforcement clause found at the end of the 1264 reissue of the Provisions.[13]

The 1267 preamble also resembles its 1263 precursor in the care it takes to justify and explain the making of the legislation. It does this, however, at much greater length. It starts by mentioning the amelioration of the kingdom and the king's duty to secure the better administration of justice. It then goes on to sketch in the background of recent troubles and disturbances in the realm which now necessitated a reform of the laws by which the peace and tranquillity of the inhabitants of England might be preserved. It gives not the slightest hint that only eight of the twenty-nine chapters which follow are entirely new.[14] A reader might easily reach the mistaken conclusion that the whole of the legislation had been framed with the disorders of the recent past (and particularly of the period 1264–7) in mind.

THE FINAL VERSION OF THE PROVISIONS OF WESTMINSTER

Chapters 9 to 29 are a third and final recension of the text of the Provisions of Westminster as originally issued in 1259. The starting-point for work on these chapters was evidently a text of the Provisions as already revised for the reissues of 1263 and 1264. It therefore already included all the amendments and additions to the original Provisions made in 1263. The revision seems to have retained all the clauses included in the 1263 reissue but made some further amendments to their text.

[13] *SR*, I, 25, note a. Above, pp. 163–4 and Appendix II: below, pp. 450–1.

[14] Another way in which it resembles the 1263 Provisions, which likewise make no mention of the 1259 Provisions on which they are based: above, p. 146.

A possibly omitted clause

There is only one clause about whose inclusion there is any real room for doubt. This is the clause corresponding to clause 11 of the Provisions of 1259, prohibiting the making of distraints outside the fee and in the king's highway. The clause was, as will be seen, partially superseded or at least re-enacted by the new chapter 2 added to the Statute in 1267.[15] It is not to be found in the two earliest texts of the Statute. It is also omitted from a number of other copies of the Statute which seem to belong to the period prior to 1300.[16] It is, however, found in a number of other early manuscript copies of the Statute apparently also dating from before 1300.[17] Moreover, as will be seen, writs whose wording makes it clear that they were based not on chapter 2 but on the earlier clause were being regularly issued by Chancery within a few years of 1267.[18] That also suggests that the clause was included. As the clause is a short one, easily omitted by mistake by a careless copyist and not wholly superseded by the new chapter 2, it seems likely that any omission from the final official text was not intentional. It is even possible that it was mistakenly omitted from some official copies but included in others.

The amended clauses

The most important of the amendments was the addition to that part of chapter 9 which corresponded to clause 1 of the original Provisions (establishing the basic rules relating to the obligation to perform suit of court) of a wholly new sentence in favour of those tenants who held their land by virtue of charters specifying the performance of any fixed service, such as a certain annual rent, 'for all service'.[19] It provided that they were not in future to be obliged to perform either suit of court or any other service in addition to that specified in their charter of feoffment. In effect, this resurrected the suggested rule originally included in the *Providencia Baronum* of 1259 but which had been dropped from clause 1 by the time of the penultimate French draft version of the Provisions. This would have made a tenant's charter binding not just where it stipulated the performance of suit but also where it excluded any demand for its performance

[15] Below, p. 193.

[16] Bodleian MSS. Additional A 228, Douce 139; BL. MSS. Additional 38821, Harley 79, 409, 489, 746, 1033, 1259, 4975, Lansdowne 467.

[17] Bodleian MSS. Additional C 188, Rawlinson C 668A, C 820; BL. MSS. Additional 32085, Harley 395, 529, 673, 748, 1120, 1690, Lansdowne 472.

[18] Below, pp. 369–70.

[19] The text of the additional sentence is printed below in Appendix III at pp. 466–7.

by stipulating the performance of a fixed service 'for all service'.[20] But it also dramatically extended it, for it made the rule applicable not just to claims for suit of court but also to claims for any other kind of service. A second amendment to the same chapter of the Statute was of much less significance. Clause 1 of the Provisions had included a reference to the king's voyage to Brittany in May 1230 and spelled out the number of years which had elapsed since then. The true total by November 1267 was thirty-seven and a half years. The two earliest manuscripts and what seems to be a majority of other pre-1300 manuscripts give the inaccurate figure of thirty-nine and a half years.[21] Other MSS. give figures of thirty and a half years,[22] thirty-one and a half years[23] and thirty-nine years.[24] Presumably there was an error in the revised text itself.

Only a single addition was made to chapter 17 of the Statute, which corresponded to clause 12 of the Provisions, the clause establishing or confirming the accountability of socage guardians. Although this additional sentence is not very clearly worded what it seems to mean is that such guardians were to be held accountable for the whole of the period they had held such wardships, not just the period since the enactment of this (or perhaps also the earlier) legislation.[25] The contortions of the language are a little difficult to understand but may reflect a positive wish to avoid specific references here to the original Provisions of Westminster of October 1259.

Two of the amendments safeguarded the rights of the king or clawed back concessions previously made that had damaged his financial interests. When clauses 9 and 10 of the Provision were re-enacted as chapter 16 of the Statute, a new sentence was added specifically exempting the king from full compliance with the provisions of the chapter and preserving his prerogative right of 'primer seisin' in the case of tenants-in-chief who died leaving heirs who were already of age. The king was to continue to be entitled to take full possession of the land held by a dead tenant-in-chief, whether or not the heir was on the land at the time of the ancestor's death.[26] There seems to be no evidence that this prerogative right had been adversely affected by the previous legislation in

[20] Above, p. 36 and note 81.

[21] E 164/2 (Red Book of the Exchequer), *De Antiquis Legibus Liber*, Bodleian MSS. Additional A 228, C 188, Douce 139, Rawlinson C 668A, C 820; BL. MSS. Additional 32085, 38821, Harley 79, 395, 409, 489, 493A, 746, 748, 1120, 1259, Lansdowne 467.

[22] BL. MSS. Harley 748, 4975.

[23] Bodleian MS. Rawlinson C 668A.

[24] BL MS Harley 1033.

[25] The text of the additional sentence is printed below in Appendix III at pp. 476–7.

[26] The text of the two additional sentences is printed below in Appendix III at pp. 474–5.

its unamended form,[27] and the addition seems to reflect no more than an abundance of caution on the part of the king and his advisers and their care to ensure that the king's prerogatives were preserved intact. The amendments made to clause 21 of the Provisions when it became chapter 24 of the Statute were much more significant. The original clause had prohibited the justices in eyre from amercing villages for failure to attend local crown inquests if a sufficient number of men had attended the inquests to carry out the business at hand. A new sentence at the end of the clause excluded the coroner's inquest into unnatural death from the scope of the concession. The main part of the clause was also modified at the same time to specify only inquests into robberies, arsons and other matters belonging to the crown in place of the 'inquests into homicides and other matters belonging to the crown' mentioned in the original legislation.[28] There is little evidence of villages being amerced by the justices in eyre for failing to attend inquests into any type of crown plea other than unnatural deaths. The effect of the modification was, for most practical purposes, to repeal the clause.

Possible reintroduction of the mortmain clause

There is also some evidence to suggest that the revisers may have reintroduced the one clause deliberately omitted from the 1263 reissue. This was clause 14 of the original Provisions, which had required the consent of the lord of whom land was held for its alienation into mortmain. At least two relatively early texts of the Statute include this clause,[29] and it was officially stated to have formed part of the Statute during the late 1270s.[30] However, neither of the two earliest texts of the Statute includes it and it is also omitted from other thirteenth-century texts of the Statute. It also seems unlikely that it would have been deliberately reintroduced into the revised Provisions at a conciliar session at which the papal legate, Ottobuono, was a prominent attender.[31] The balance of probabilities seems therefore to favour the view that the clause did not form part of the Statute as enacted in 1267, whatever the later belief or assertions made during the later 1270s.

[27] There seem, unfortunately, to be no examples of cases brought in the king's name against heirs interrupting his primer seisin during this period, but for a case in which the right was asserted against a third party see *Rex v. William le Waleys et al.* (KB 26/171 m. 70, Michaelmas term 1261).

[28] For the text of the chapter as amended see Appendix III: below, pp. 480–1.

[29] BL MSS. Harley 673, 1259. [30] Below, pp. 277–8.

[31] Maitland (*P&M*, I, 334) and Bean (*Decline of English Feudalism*, p. 64) both attribute the omission solely to ecclesiastical pressure in 1267. Neither seems to have been aware of its omission from the revised text of the Provisions issued in 1263 and the use of the revised text as the basis for the text of the Statute of Marlborough.

THE EIGHT NEW CLAUSES ADDED

Chapters 1–4: the reassertion of royal jurisdictional power

The first four new chapters of the Statute of Marlborough are in effect an expanded version of the opening clause of the Dictum of Kenilworth, intended to restate and reaffirm some of the basic rules of the English thirteenth-century legal system relating to the exercise of royal and private jurisdiction and the need to follow due process in seeking compensation for alleged wrongs. There is little, if anything, that is new about the norms they state. Any novelty they possess lies purely in the increased punishment which the Statute authorised for those who infringed these pre-existing norms. The restatement and the imposition of new penalties seems to have been intended to provide ideological as well as practical support for the reassertion of royal power in the very special circumstances of the aftermath of civil war and civil disorder.

Chapter 1 makes this plain by sketching in as the background to all four chapters the refusal of many magnates and others both during the civil war itself and afterwards to seek justice from the king and his court as had been customary earlier in the king's reign and in the reigns of his predecessors and their opting instead to seek redress for wrongs by taking revenge against their neighbours or by making distraints against them to recover whatever compensation the distrainor considered appropriate. It also cites the current (and related) refusal of many magnates and others to allow themselves to be subject to the process of the king's courts as enforced by royal officials and more especially to allow the release of the distresses they had taken.[32] Chapter 1 goes on to restate what had come to be, or at least was coming to be, a general norm of the English legal system. Everyone, whether great or small, ought to seek a remedy in the king's court for any wrongs or losses he had suffered and not to take his own revenge for them or to seek compensation for them by making his own unauthorised distraints against those who had done him wrong. Its failure even to mention the possibility of seeking redress in other courts (county, hundred or seignorial) may not be deliberate but simply the result of attempting to keep the clause as simple and short as possible. As will be seen, chapter 2 certainly recognised the possibility, if only indirectly, that it might be perfectly proper in the right circumstances to seek redress for wrongs in other courts. Chapter 1 then went on further to give additional teeth to these norms. Taking revenge or making a distraint against a neighbour was in future to be punished on conviction by 'ransom', that is by the imposition of a fine by the king's court of an amount fixed by

[32] For the text of this chapter see Appendix III: below, pp. 456–7.

that court in accordance with the seriousness of the offence and enforced by the sanction of imprisonment.

Chapter 2 was similarly concerned with preserving the jurisdiction of the king's courts and preventing the wrongful use of distraint. The norms which it restated were that no one was to distrain anyone to come to his court who did not belong to his fee (in the case of a private seignorial court) or over whom he did not possess jurisdiction (in the case of a hundred or other court) and that (more generally) no one was to make distraints outside his fee or outside the area of his jurisdiction.[33] Any breach of these norms was in future to lead to a similar punishment by a 'ransom' whose amount was to correspond to the seriousness of the offence. It looks as though this clause may have been something of an afterthought. It is not prefigured in the preamble to these clauses (in the opening section of clause 1) but is sandwiched in between two clauses which are. Perhaps discussion of the wholly extra-legal type of distraint of neighbour against neighbour without any colour of authorisation mentioned in chapter 1 suggested the need to consider also other forms of distraint which had some colour of justification but were equally in breach of the norms relating to distraint: distraints which in effect usurped the jurisdiction that rightfully belonged to the king or others (distraints made by the lords of private or franchisal courts on those not subject to their jurisdiction) and distraints which disregarded the restraints which played a significant role in hobbling the effectiveness of private jurisdictions to the benefit of the king's courts (distraints made outside a lord's fee or outside the area subject to the jurisdiction of a franchisal court).

Chapter 3 consists of two distinct sections.[34] The first resumed the restatement of the norms which the preamble to the section included in chapter 1 had mentioned as the subject of recent breaches and the imposition of additional punishments for their infraction. Here, however, the two are melded into a single statement of the punishment to be imposed for the infraction of the norms. Refusal to allow the release of distresses by the king's officials or to allow the king's officials to execute the judgments of the king's courts or to make summonses and attachments was to be punished in future by a 'ransom' whose amount was to reflect the seriousness of the offence.[35] The second half of chapter 3 was essentially a saving proviso to chapter 1, spelling out that nothing it contained was to lead to the imposition of any additional punishment by way of ransom

33 For the text of this chapter see Appendix III: below, pp. 458–9.

34 For the text of this chapter see Appendix III: below, pp. 458–9.

35 From the way it is phrased it seems possible that, as originally drafted, this section of the chapter dealt only with resistence to the releases of distresses and that resistence to the execution of judgments and of the court's process was an afterthought, only added late in the drafting process.

on a lord who had distrained one of his tenants for a service or customary due or other obligation if it was subsequently found that the tenant did not owe the service or other obligation for which the distraint had been made, provided the lord had allowed the release of the distress when the tenant brought his action challenging the distraint.

Chapter 4 concludes this sub-section of the Statute by restating two further traditional common law norms with regard to the making of distraints and the distrainor's conduct after doing this.[36] Distraints were to be 'reasonable' and not too harsh. No distrainor was to drive the distresses he had taken out of the county where he had taken them. Infraction of these norms was generally again to incur the punishment of a 'ransom' proportionate to the gravity of the offence, but an exception was made for the lord distraining his tenant who then drove the distresses out of the county, who was only to be heavily amerced. The general principle that the value of the chattels taken in distraint should not be disproportionately high, in comparison to the reason for the making of the distraint is one expressed in *Bracton*.[37] It was also a principle enforced in a number of cases found on the plea rolls before 1267.[38] That driving animals taken in distraint out of one county into another was *prima facie* in itself a trespass is also shown by a series of cases on the plea rolls of the king's courts from the beginning of John's reign onwards.[39]

Chapter 5: the confirmation of Magna Carta

Chapter 5 of the Statute can also be seen as a permanent legislative response to part of one of the clauses included in the opening section

[36] For the text of this chapter see Appendix III: below, pp. 460–1.

[37] '. . . poterit esse (districcio) iniuriosa si fuerit nimia et districcio modum excedat in qualibet specie. Non enim fieri debet magna districcio pro minimo delicto vel pro minimo servicio, cum sit modus in rebus, sunt certi denique fines ultraque citraque nequit consistere rectum': *Bracton*, fol. 217b (III, 154).

[38] *CRR*, XIV, no. 936 (1230); CRR, XVIII, no. 235 (1243) where the abbot was amerced one hundred shillings for his trespass in taking five oxen for ten shillings owed when two would have been sufficient 'because he made an inappropriate distraint'; *John Buvemore v. John, serjeant of Mouland et al.*: JUST 1/176, m. 37d (Devon eyre 1249) where John was amerced for his trespass 'because he made so great a distraint for so small an offence' ('quia fecit tam magnam districcionem pro tam parvo delicto'); *Felicia prioress of Catesby v. Walter of Aylesbury et al.*, JUST 1/616, m. 32 (Northamptonshire eyre 1261), in which the plaintiff sought judgment 'of so heavy a distraint for so small an offence' ('de tam gravi districcione pro tam modico delicto').

[39] *CRR*, II, 10; *CRR*, VIII, 319; *CRR*, XIII, no. 2113. For possible defences see *CRR*, XVII, no. 1956 (1243): the defendant claimed his ancestors had customarily made distraints in Lincolnshire and driven the distresses into Rutland; *Giles of Stepney v. Ralph Champneys*, JUST 1/872, m. 11d (Surrey eyre 1255): the defendant had been distrained in Surrey to release the distress he had taken from the plaintiff in London and had therefore driven the distresses from London to Surrey. See also *Bracton*, fols. 157–157b (II, 443).

of the Dictum of Kenilworth, in this case to the clause which had asked the king to keep and observe Magna Carta and the Forest Charter, as he had previously promised to do.[40] It ordered that Magna Carta be kept in all its clauses, both those relating to the king himself and those relating to others.[41] It was to be enforced both by the justices in eyre on their circuits and by individual sheriffs within their counties whenever necessary. Writs were also to be made freely available to implead those who had breached the charter either in King's Bench, the Common Bench or before the justices in eyre. Later manuscripts of the Statute add at the end of this chapter a sentence confirming the Forest Charter. Although this was also something requested in the Dictum of Kenilworth, the manuscript evidence suggests that it formed no part of the Statute as originally enacted.[42]

Chapter 8 on redisseisin

One other chapter belonging to these eight apparently 'new' chapters added to the Provisions in 1267 seems in effect to be no more than a confirmation or reaffirmation of the existing law. This is chapter 8. This stated that those arrested and imprisoned for redisseisin were not to be released save on the special order of the king and after making a fine for their offence. Sheriffs who released them without such an order were to be heavily amerced and any persons thus released were still to be punished for their offence.[43] A special procedure to deal with cases of redisseisin locally had been established in 1236 by what later became known as chapter 3 of the Provisions of Merton.[44] Before then such cases seem to have been dealt with through actions of *quare intrusit* in the Common Bench.[45] The punishment specified in the legislation was imprisonment till release by the king in return for a ransom 'vel alio modo': the same as that specified in this chapter. The weakness of the procedure seems to have been that no adequate check was kept upon the issue of writs of redisseisin and no attempt made to discover

40 Above, p. 185.

41 For the text of this chapter see Appendix III: below, pp. 460–1.

42 The sentence mentioning the Forest Charter is found in none of the thirteenth-century texts I have examined. See also *SR*, I, 20, note 9.

43 For the text of this chapter see Appendix III: below, pp. 464–5.

44 *CR 1234–1237*, p. 338. For the garbled summary version of this legislation in the accepted text of chapter 3 of the Provisions see *SR*, I, 2. Such a text was clearly the only one generally known as early as 1285 for chapter 26 of the Statute of Westminster II (*SR*, I, 85) found it necessary to expressly authorise actions of post-disseisin, although the authentic text of the original legislation had also authorised such actions.

45 Sutherland, *The Assize of Novel Disseisin*, p. 64 and note 1.

whether or not the defendant had been convicted of redisseisin. The hearing of the case was delegated to the sheriff and coroners who made no return of the outcome to Chancery or the Exchequer. There must have been a temptation for sheriffs to reach an agreement with convicted redisseisors for their release which would ensure that the fine was received by the sheriff rather than the crown.[46] Just how common this was is neither known nor knowable. This chapter was an initial attempt to deal with the problem by threatening specific penalties against sheriffs so acting.

Chapter 6 on the evasion of wardship

The most obviously innovative of these eight chapters are the two chapters (6 and 7) dealing with the law of wardship and the procedures applicable in the action of writ of right of wardship. In his commentary on chapter 6 Coke suggested that the first section of the chapter was drafted by Robert Walerand.[47] Maitland was able to show that Coke's suggestion was based on a misreading of a passage in *Britton* and that there is no reason to think Robert Walerand played any special part in the drafting or approval of this chapter.[48] However, as will be seen, there is some reason to think that this first section may have been the product of discussion of a case then pending in the courts and that the second part of chapter 6 really was associated with a particular individual. The individual concerned was Walter of Merton, the former chancellor.

Chapter 6 was an attempt to deal with two particular kinds of device which were being used, according to the legislators, in a deliberate attempt to deprive lords with a right to the wardship of the lands and persons of their tenants who succeeded under the age of majority of those wardship rights. That means mainly, but not exclusively, the lords of whom land was held by knight service.[49] The first of these devices, as described by the Statute, was deceptively simple: enfeoffment by the sitting tenant of his eldest son and heir apparent while the latter was still under age, so that at his father's death the son was already in the land he would have inherited, but by acquisition rather than inheritance.[50] If

46 But for examples of specific mandates for the release of those convicted of redisseisin issued prior to 1267 see *CR 1237–42*, pp. 285–6; *CR 1251–1253*, pp. 4, 416.

47 'Robert Walerand penned and preferred this act and by aid and common assent of the great lords of the realme, obtained to passe it for a statute': Coke, *Second Institutes*, p. 110.

48 Maitland, *Collected Papers*, II, 182–9 at 185–6.

49 For previous discussions of this chapter see Plucknett, *Legislation*, pp. 79–80 and Bean, *Decline of English Feudalism*, pp. 23–4.

50 For the text see Appendix III: below, pp. 462–3.

the father had granted all his lands to his eldest son in this way, the lord would lose the wardship not just of the lands but also of his person. If he had granted only some of them, the lord would lose wardship of those lands but not of his person. The working of this device is, however, a little more complicated than the Statute suggests or than Plucknett seems to have believed.[51] It does not seem to have been the normal practice for the heir or any other underage feoffee to be given possession of the land granted. What happened was that the grantor or feoffor (here the father) appointed a quasi-guardian to take possession in their name,[52] and to answer to the heir when he came of age for the profits of the land.[53] This removed any possible difficulty about the feoffee's capacity to take seisin of the land he had been granted. It also effectively sidestepped the possible difficulties about establishing an effective livery of seisin from father to son when (as would commonly be the case) father and son continued to live together in the same household.[54] Nor is it necessarily the case that such underage enfeoffments were aimed, as the Statute suggests, solely, or even principally, at defrauding lords of their wardships. Such an enfeoffment of an underage heir might perhaps also be a necessary preliminary to a marriage between the heir and a woman whose relatives insisted that he be given part of his father's lands in advance of his father's death in order to safeguard the woman's right to dower and the rights of inheritance of any children of the new couple against the possibility of the

[51] 'One principle lay at the root of the law of wardship, namely, that it attached to one who entered as heir of the deceased tenant. The evasory devices therefore consisted principally of attempts to enable the heir to succeed to the land by some other means than inheritance. The easiest and earliest of these devices was of classical simplicity: the tenant in possession merely enfeoffed his eldest son during his own lifetime': Plucknett, *Legislation*, p. 79.

[52] For evidence of such appointments see *Bracton*, fol. 86 (II, 250); *CRR*, XIV, no. 1941; *BNB*, pl. 954, 999; KB 26/123, m. 18 (Easter term 1242); JUST 1/454, m. 9 (Leicestershire eyre 1247); *CR 1242–47*, p. 405; KB 26/142, mm. 14d, 21d (Trinity term 1250). For an actual deed of appointment of such a guardian from the end of the thirteen century see PRO E 210/9578. This is in the form of letters patent by Sir Richard de la Vache and his wife, Mabel, announcing 'nos fecisse et constituisse Willelmum filium Rogeri le Clerke de Shenle custodem Ricardi de la Vache filii nostri qui infra etatem est et omnium terrarum et tenementorum suorum quas et que ei dedimus in Berton', Caldecote et Brunne in comitatu Cantebr' et omnium bonorum et catallorum ipsius Ricardi ad disponendum et inde ordinare ad commodum ipsius Ricardi et ad negocia ipsius Ricardi in omnibus prosequenda, defendenda, protegenda et manutenenda usque ad plenam et legitimam etatem ipsius Ricardi filii nostri vel quamdiu nobis placuerit . . .'

[53] For actions of account against such quasi-guardians see JUST 1/365, m. 60d (Kent eyre 1271); JUST 1/985, m. 6 (Westmorland eyre 1292); CP 40/59, m. 45d (Trinity term 1285) and revived in CP 40/92, m. 20 (Hilary term 1292); CP 40/83, m. 100 (Trinity term 1290); CP 40/106, m. 27d (Michaelmas term 1294).

[54] Bean was wrong in thinking that 'when a landowner enfeoffed his heir who was under age we must assume that he remained in occupation of the land' (*Decline of English Feudalism*, p. 24). If he had remained in occupation no transfer of seisin would have been effected and the lord could have asserted his right of wardship.

father alienating his lands to strangers or the son predeceasing his father.[55] It was perhaps only from the perspective of lords that such enfeoffments were seen as intended primarily to defraud them of their rights of wardship.

Such enfeoffments were hardly a new development in 1267. The courts seem previously to have accepted their validity and held that they were an effective bar to any wardship claim by the lord. Almost twenty years before, in Trinity term 1250, the Common Bench had heard a wardship case from Cornwall in which Richard Cokus had sought the wardship of the land and heir of Roger of Morton against Robert de Cadleg' on the basis that Roger's father, Walter of Morton, had held land of him by knight service and that Roger had predeceased his father. Robert's defence had been that five years before his death Walter had enfeoffed the heir (his grandson) of all the lands he held of Richard and handed over the wardship of the land and of the heir to the defendant as his quasi-guardian. Walter had therefore not died in seisin of these lands. This was not quite the situation envisaged by the Statute, for it involved a feoffment by a grandfather rather than a father. However, much the same principles were involved and exactly the same device was used. The court did not rule as to whether or not the enfeoffment had been valid but the fact that the case went to jury trial on whether a feoffment had indeed taken place as was alleged suggests that it saw no difficulty in principle with the effectiveness of such enfeoffments. The parties subsequently reached an agreement. This left the quasi-guardian in possession of the wardship of the land and with the right of marriage over the heir in exchange for the relatively small payment of ten marks.[56]

It is possible, even likely, that it was a particular case pending in the courts in 1267 that raised once more the question of the validity of such enfeoffments and suggested the need for legislation on this matter. The case was an assize of novel disseisin brought by William of Witcombe against Richard de Boulogne and others relating to a tenement in Witcombe in Martock in Somerset. The facts of the case, as far as they can be reconstructed from the enrolment of a later hearing in King's Bench in Trinity term 1268, were that William's father, Walter, had enfeoffed William, his eldest son, on the Wednesday before his death

[55] See for example the 1249 deed of Osbert Selvein granting Anketin Malore the marriage of his son and heir Ralph for marriage to his daughter Margery and acknowledging that he had given his son Ralph all his land of Wylteby with its appurtenances to endow Margery and conceding that he would not alienate, sell or gage his other lands to the disinheritance of his son Ralph: KB 26/136, m. 16. Here it was the father-in-law who was given custody of the heir's body but it may well have been a quasi-guardian who was given custody of the lands.

[56] KB 26/142, m. 14d.

and appointed Robert Trice (who was suing the assize in William's name) as his guardian. He had then had himself carried off to his brother's house outside the village.[57] Robert Trice had taken the fealties of the tenants but Walter had gone on receiving the profits of the land. Walter had also left his goods on the land and his servants had remained on the land until his death on the following Monday. Richard de Boulogne was the lord of whom the land was held. He had taken seisin of the holding immediately after Walter's death but during the period of Montfortian rule Richard had been ejected by Brian de Gouiz and his followers. Richard had recovered possession only after the battle of Evesham. William and his guardian seem then to have brought their assize of novel disseisin before Martin of Littlebury at Westford Bridge in Somerset. This gave a verdict in favour of Richard. William and his guardian then set about reversing this verdict. During 1266 they obtained a commission addressed to Robert de Briwes and William of Stanton authorising them to hear a certification of the assize.[58] This presumably did not give them what they wanted for by August 1267 they were also bringing an action of attaint before Littlebury to reverse the previous verdict.[59] In late August or early September this last action was apparently adjourned to the Common Bench. It was still pending there at the time of the enactment of the Statute of Marlborough. It may have been the justices of the Common Bench who raised the problem of fraudulent feoffments of the kind revealed by the assize for discussion by the king's council at Marlborough, which led to the legislation enacting that 'no lord was to lose his wardship by virtue of such a feoffment'. More likely this was done by Martin of Littlebury himself. The sequel is also suggestive. The facts found by the jury verdict were quite enough in themselves to hold that the purported enfeoffment of William by his father was ineffective and thus that his father had died in seisin of the lands and Richard had properly taken possession of them. The judgment, however, went out of its way to mention the provisions of chapter 6 as well. This may have been because the judgment also purported to award wardship of William's person to Richard and this was not something at stake in the assize. It may also have been because the justices well knew that it had been this very case that had raised the problem which this part of chapter 6 addressed and was therefore intended to solve and so thought it appropriate to cite the legislation in their judgment.[60]

[57] KB 26/185, m. 3. [58] C 66/84, m. 11d. [59] JUST 1/1200, m. 19d.

[60] '. . . quia per dominum regem et magnates Anglie concorditer provisum est quod occasione feoffamentorum factorum in fraudem et prejudicium capitalium dominorum et pro custodiis et maritagiis suis sibi spectantibus maliciose auferendis nichil decetero eis depereat': KB 26/185, m. 3. Note, however, that as late as 1278 Richard de Boulogne was bringing a suit in the Common

The second of the devices, as the second part of chapter 6 itself acknowledged, was intended not just to deprive lords of their rights of wardship but also to allow the creation of secure leases, which were normally interrupted by a wardship.[61] The device used here was rather more complicated and more obviously collusive and fraudulent in nature. As the Statute explains it, the tenant wanting to lease his lands for a fixed and secure period of time made what was in form a feoffment of the lands being leased, reserving services for the period of the lease but stating in the feoffment that these had been performed or paid in full for the period of the lease. The feoffment reserved services greatly in excess of the value of the land from the end of this period in order to ensure that the lessee really did surrender the land at the end of his lease.[62] Such a conveyance was on its face a feoffment. Thus the lessee during his term had all the rights of a feoffee, including the right to secure tenure of the land during any wardship of his lessor's lands as well as the protection of the freeholder's remedies against other kinds of dispossession. However, at the end of the term the land would revert to the lessor/feoffor just as if the conveyance had been a lease.

There is little evidence to suggest that collusive feoffments of this kind had become common prior to 1267. The only evidence I have found of their existence and use prior to 1267 comes from a dower case heard in the Common Bench a little over five years before the enactment of the Statute, in Hilary term 1262. It was a case brought by Isabel, widow of William of Milding against Urian de St Peter. She brought it to claim her dower third of sixteen virgates, one windmill and six shillings rent at Dadlington in Leicestershire. By Hilary term 1262 Urian had already reached the point of having vouched Peter, the son and heir of William of Milding, to warranty.[63] Peter was still under age and in the wardship of Walter of Merton, the king's chancellor, who held this wardship by the king's grant.[64] Walter had sought the king's aid in contesting the supposed obligation of warranty. It was the king's serjeant, Laurence del Brok, who asked Urian for the deed attesting the heir's obligation to provide warranty. Urian (or his serjeant) then produced the deed by virtue of which he held the land and under which William had promised him warranty on behalf of himself and his heirs. The deed is reproduced

Bench against Robert Trice, ostensibly to claim wardship of the lands and person of the heir of Walter of Witcombe: CP 40/27, m. 131.

61 *Bracton*, fol. 30 (II, 100).

62 For the text of this second section of the chapter see Appendix III: below, pp. 462–3.

63 KB 26/222, m. 7d.

64 *Excerpta e Rotulis Finium in Turri Londinensi asservati, Henry III, 1216–72*, ed. C. Roberts (2 vols., London, 1835–6), II, 326.

virtually in full in the enrolment, omitting only the witnesses and dating clause. It corresponds in almost all respects with the form of 'feoffment' mentioned in chapter 6.[65] William had purported to grant his manor of Dadlington to Urian for life (whereas the legislation's use of *feoffati* suggests a grant in fee) for a rent of forty pounds a year but had stated in the grant that he had already been paid the whole of the rent for the first fifteen years, reserving only a half mark a year still to be paid, and that the forty pounds was only to be payable after fifteen years or, in case of unforeseen interruptions, after Urian had received fifteen crops. William had also built in a specific condition for the reversion of the tenement if Urian failed to pay the additional rent after the receipt of the fifteen crops. Since the lands were clearly not worth forty pounds a year this was evidently in essence a fifteen-year lease but in the form of a life grant.[66] Laurence objected to the contradictory nature of the deed. It was in form both a life grant and a lease for fifteen years plus a right to extend the lease for the lessee's life. He argued that its inconsistencies meant that it

[65] The deed as reproduced in the enrolment reads: 'Anno regni regis Henrici filii Johannis quadagesimo tercio in festo Omnium Sanctorum facta est convencio inter Willelmum de Meaulinges ex una parte et Urianum de Sancto Petro ex altera, scilicet quod predictus Willelmus dimisit et tradidit dicto Uriano totum manerium suum de Dodelington' cum capitali mesuagio et omnibus pertinenciis ut in molendinis, wardis, releviis, escheatis et omnibus aliis que idem Willelmus habuit in eodem manerio exceptis homagiis liberorum hominum tenendum et habendum dicto Uriano tota vita sua libere et quiete, reddendo inde annuatim dicto Willelmo et heredibus suis quadraginta libras sterlingorum ad duos anni terminos, scilicet ad festum sancti Michaelis viginti libras et ad Pascha viginti libras, pro omnibus. Et quia dictus Urianus firmam quindecim annorum predicto Willelmo pacavit pre manibus dictus Willelmus concessit pro se et heredibus suis eidem Uriano quod ipse Urianus et heredes sui vel assignati sui predictum manerium cum pertinenciis, sicut predictum est, habeant et teneant usque ad terminum quindecim annorum plenarie completorum et donec inde quindecim croppos perceperint ita quiete et libere quod nec dictus Willelmus nec heredes sui ab eis aliquid infra predictum terminum causa predicti manerii poterunt exigere vel habere nisi dimidiam marcam per annum, scilicet ad Pascha quadraginta denarios et ad festum sancti Michaelis xl denarios. Finitis vero quindecim annis et quindecim croppis plenarie receptis dictus Urianus et heredes sui vel assignati dicto Willelmo et heredibus suis quadraginta libras annuatim quamdiu predictum manerium tenere voluerint ad terminos prenominatos persolverint. Convenit eciam inter predictos Willelmum et Urianum quod si predictus Urianus vel heredes sui vel assignati per defectum dicti Willelmi vel heredum suorum dampnum, molestiam aut gravamen incurrerint dictus Willelmus vel heredes sui dampna sua per visum legalium virorum restituerint antequam dictus Willelmus vel heredes suis seisinam de predicto manerio habeant vel aliquam firmam inde percipiant. Dictus eciam Willelmus et heredes sui dictum manerium cum pertinenciis suis dicto Uriano et heredibus suis vel assignatis ut predictum est contra omnes homines warantizabunt, aquietabunt et defendent salvo forinseco. Si vero dictus Urianus vel heredes sui vel assignati post lapsum quindecim annorum et postquam quindecim croppos asportaverunt quadraginta libros annuatim solvere noluerint et dampna sua si qua ut predictum est incurrerint eis per dictum Willelmum vel heredes suos restituantur dictum manerium cum omnibus pertinenciis dicto Willelmo et heredibus suis quietum et solutum revertetur una cum dominicis warectandis rebinandis et feno et foragio sicut Urianus recepit sine omni contradiccione vel impedimento dicti Uriani vel heredum suorum vel assignatorum etc.'

[66] In 1274 after Peter's death the manor was valued at just over fifteen pounds a year: C 133/4, no. 13.

was not sufficient in law to oblige the heir to warranty and therefore also insufficient to oblige the king as the warrantor of his guardian to warranty. The case was then adjourned for judgment. Before judgment could be given the case was discussed by the king and the whole of his council. They evidently had a record of the case before them and appreciated the potential implications of the deed produced by Urian. Deeds of this kind posed a real threat to the rights of wardship enjoyed by lords. Their decision, as communicated to the justices of Common Bench by a royal writ issued on 24 February 1262 at Windsor that was authorised by the king and the whole of the council, was that Isabel should be given her dower from the lands held by Urian, though only on a temporary basis (*in tenenciam*). They adjourned for further consideration of a definitive judgment on whether or not Urian was entitled to his warranty.[67]

This case involved a 'fictitious feoffment' of almost exactly the form mentioned in the legislation; the case was one involving not just the king but also one of his leading counsellors and servants, Walter of Merton; and the case evidently led to consiliar discussion about the validity of such feoffments and whether they should be allowed to deprive lords of their rights of wardship. It did not lead to legislation in 1262, perhaps because there was then some continuing doubt and discussion about whether such deeds should be treated as wholly void (as Laurence del Brok had argued) or as voidable in so far as they attempted to deprive the lord of his wardship though valid as against the grantor and his heirs once they had come of age. For much of the intervening period the council was perhaps too busy with other matters anyway to discuss it further. But it was probably this case which then led to the drafting of the second part of chapter 6 of the Statute of Marlborough. The Statute laid down as a general principle that such fraudulent feoffments were not to be

[67] 'H. dei gracia etc. Sciatis quod cum Isabella que fuit uxor Willelmi de Meaulinges in curia nostra coram vobis apud Westm' peteret versus Urianum de Sancto Petro terciam partem duorum mesuagiorum et septemdecim virgatarum terre, sex solidatarum redditus, unius molendini ad ventum cum pertinenciis in Dadelington' in comitatu Leyc' ut dotem suam et idem Urianus venisset in eadem curia nostra coram vobis et Petrum filium et heredem predicti Willelmi, qui est infra etatem et in custodia nostra, vocasset inde ad warantum versus eam per quoddam scriptum eidem Uriano ab eodem Willelmo inde factum, quod scriptum valde scrupulosum nobis et consilio nostro videbatur, de consilio curie nostre coram nobis propter inconvenienciam ejusdem scripti confecti in talem collusionem per quam nos et alii de regno nostro capitales domini custodiis nostris fraudulenter possemus defraudari si hujusmodi scriptum a curia nostra approbaretur, provisum est quod predicta Isabella terciam partem predictorum mesuagiorum, septemdecim virgatarum terre, sex solidatarum redditus et predicti molendini cum pertinenciis in predicta villa nomine dotis habeat in tenenciam donec in curia nostra per consideracionem curie nostre diffinitum fuerit utrum per scriptum predictum eidem Uriano warantiam debeatur necne. Et ideo vobis mandamus quod in loquela illa inter eamdem Isabellam petentem et predictum Urianum coram vobis agitata sine dilacione in forma predicta procedentes ita fieri faciatis. Teste me ipso apud Windesores xxiiij die Februarii anno xlvj. Per dominum regem et totum consilium.'

allowed to deprive lords of their wardships. Lords were not, however, to be allowed to treat them as void *ab initio*. They were not to be allowed simply to disseise such 'feoffees'. They were to be required instead to prove the fraudulent nature of these conveyances in order to void them for the purposes of wardship rights. The Statute lays down a detailed procedure for this. The lord was to bring his action of wardship. When the defendant pleaded his 'feoffment', the lord was to be allowed to object that it was a 'feigned' feoffment. He would then have to prove this through a jury consisting of the witnesses to the charter plus a local jury who were to weigh the value of the tenement against the sum payable after the end of the term. If the lord failed to prove his case he was to be heavily amerced and to pay the defendant his damages and expenses. And even if the deed was voidable *vis-à-vis* the lord it remained valid as against the grantor's heir, thereby allowing the lessee to recover the remainder of his term once the heir had come of age, just as in the case of a lease interrupted by wardship. The opposite decision might have deterred lessees from accepting such feoffments in future, but it would clearly have been inequitable that the lessor's heir should be allowed to profit in such a case from the wrongdoing of his ancestor and at the expense of the lessee. It was in keeping with the spirit of this last provision that we find Urian de St Peter in Michaelmas term 1268 suing Peter of Milding (evidently now of age) to warrant the dower third that Isabel had been claiming.[68]

Chapter 7: allowing judgment by default in wardship cases

Chapter 7 was a further measure of procedural reform and, like other such reforms, was probably suggested to the king's council by the judiciary as technical experts. It brought a further, relatively modest extension of the procedural changes introduced by the original Provisions of 1259 and extended by the first reissue of 1263. The change introduced was to allow the giving of judgment by default in favour of the plaintiff in the writ of right of wardship in the case of continued non-appearance by the defendant. Judgment by default had been introduced in 1259 in the action of *quare impedit* and, perhaps in view of the special need for speed in this

[68] KB 26/195, m. 12. If Peter was now of age this suggests that his father's 'feigned feoffment' of 1258 was probably not made purely with the intention of avoiding wardship, since a feigned feoffment with a concealed lease of ten years or less would evidently have sufficed for this purpose, unless Peter had died before reaching his majority. Peter's lands, however, apparently remained in Merton's wardship as late as 1276 while Merton recovered the value of Peter's marriage. Merton had lost the chance to arrange this while Peter was out of his control during the period of disturbances in Henry III's reign: CP 40/17, m. 86d.

action to avoid the bishop enjoying his right of collation, the legislation allowed such a judgment to be given immediately after a defendant failed to appear in response to the grand distress.[69] Although there was some need for speed in the action of wardship (which was of little use once the heir had come of age) that need was not nearly as pressing and so rather more complicated procedures could be instituted by way of safeguards to ensure that the defendant knew of the litigation pending against him before judgment was given by default. Judgment was not to be given at once after the defendant failed to respond to the grand distress but the latter was to be repeated two or three times during the following half year, with the appropriate sheriff on each occasion having the writ read out in the county court, publicly warning the defendant to appear, as well as seeking him out in the normal way.[70] Only if he still failed to appear was he to lose seisin of the wardship in question. Other provisos and safeguards were also built into the new process. The defendant's right to bring an action himself against the successful plaintiff for the recovery of his wardship was expressly safeguarded. Nor was the new process to prejudice heirs where the defendant's title to the wardship was not his own but derived from the wardship of another heir ('wardship by reason of wardship'). The Statute does not, however, really explain how this was supposed to work.

[69] Above, p. 74.
[70] For the text of this chapter see Appendix III: below, pp. 464–5.

PART II

Beyond politics: the enforcement and interpretation of the Statute of Marlborough in the courts, 1267–1307

Chapter 8

CONTRA FORMAM FEOFFAMENTI: THE STATUTORY ACTION FOR TENANTS CONTESTING LIABILITY TO SUIT OF COURT AFTER 1267

Earlier chapters looked at the early history of the use of the writ of *contra formam feoffamenti* from the time of its initial drafting in 1260, shortly after the publication of the first issue of the Provisions of Westminster, up to the time of the enactment of a final revised version of the Provisions of Westminster as the Statute of Marlborough in 1267.[1] This chapter looks at the use made by litigants of the action during the four decades after that final reaffirmation of the legislation in 1267 and at the ways in which the courts interpreted the legislation during that period.

THE WORDING OF THE ORIGINAL WRIT OF *CONTRA FORMAM FEOFFAMENTI*

The authority behind the Statute

One of the major themes of the earlier discussion of the writ of *contra formam feoffamenti* was just how closely the different formulas used in the writ to refer to the legislative authority behind the enactment of the legislation reflected the changing political climate during that period.[2] When Chancery resumed the issuing of such writs in 1267 it seems initially, and rather surprisingly, to have reverted to one of the more radically 'baronial' formulations for many, if not all, of the writs it issued.[3]

[1] Above, pp. 109–15, 168–9. [2] Above, pp. 111–13, 169.

[3] The earliest example is *Prior of Hertford v. John de Montgomery and Hugh de Ruton* of which there is a procedural stage in Michaelmas term 1268. Here the enacting words used are 'whereas it has been provided by the common counsel of the magnates of the king's realm' ('cum de communi consilio magnatum regni regis provisum sit'): KB 26/195, m. 42d. An almost identical form of words but substituting 'of our realm' for 'the king's realm' ('quare cum de communi consilio magnatum regni nostri') is found in the procedural stage of *Roger Bydulf v. the bailiffs of John de Verdun of Alton* enrolled in Michaelmas term 1269: KB 26/194, m. 36 but cf. the related enrolment of the same case in Easter term 1271 where 'magnates of our realm' ('magnatum regni nostri') has become 'magnates of the king's realm' ('magnatum regni regis'): KB 26/202, m. 5. For a variant, referring to the 'magnates of the lord king' ('magnatum domini regis'), see *Prior of Worksop v. Nicholas Wake* of Trinity term 1270 (KB 26/199, m. 7d) though by the Easter term 1271 enrolment of the same case the enacting formula has become the standard one: KB 26/202, m. 2. For a further variant,

It was not until two or three years later that it adopted a relatively neutral formula ('since by the common council of the king's realm it has been provided') to refer to that legislative authority.[4]

The limitation date

The Provisions of Westminster and the Statute of Marlborough had both specified King Henry III's first voyage to Brittany (1230) as the date *before* which a lord had to show seisin of suit if he was to prove that he was justified in distraining for it on the basis of his seisin rather than a specific written obligation to perform suit contained in the tenant's feoffment. This requirement was also recited in that part of the writ of *contra formam feoffamenti* which summarised the main provisions of the legislation. In 1267, as in 1259, Henry III's first voyage to Brittany also happened to be the limitation date used in the assize of novel disseisin, though this was not the reason for the use of the same date in the legislation on suit of court.[5] For disseisins to be 'novel' and thus remediable by the assize they had to have taken place *after* 1230. In 1275, the limitation date for the assize was moved forward by chapter 39 of the Statute of Westminster I, to the date of the same king's first crossing into Gascony which had taken place in 1242. The change was not to take immediate effect but only to apply to writs acquired from Chancery after St John's Day (24 June) 1276.[6] Although the legislation said nothing about *contra formam feoffamenti* Chancery evidently assumed that the change in the limitation date was intended to apply not just to novel disseisin but also to *contra formam feoffamenti*. Between Michaelmas term 1277 and Trinity term 1303 the limitation date mentioned in such writs was invariably that of Henry III's first voyage to Gascony, not that of his first voyage to Brittany.[7]

referring to 'our magnates' ('magnatum nostrorum') see the enrolled pleading in Case 70A (and in the process stage of the same case in Trinity term: KB 26/199, m. 18d), and a reference to 'magnates' but without any further characterisation of them ('quare cum de communi consilio magnatum provisum sit') is to be found in Easter 1273 in the mesne process stage of *Walter de Tybey v. Emelina countess of Ulster*: CP 40/2A, m. 19d. For a case apparently brought by a writ of the form in use after the re-enactment of 1263 see Case 68A. As already suggested, the writ used in this case may have been acquired prior to the enactment of the Statute of Marlborough.

[4] There may have been a transitional phase when the formula of authority referred to the 'council of the lord king' ('quare cum de consilio domini regis'). This is used in Case 70B. Another early variant (issued in Case 72B) refers to the 'council of the lord king's kingdom' ('quare cum de consilio regni domini regis'). The classic formula is first found in the enrolment of the procedural stage of *Miles de Hastings v. Godfrey bishop of Worcester* in Michaelmas term 1269: KB 26/194, m. 17.

[5] Above, pp. 52–3. [6] *SR*, I, 36.

[7] For the earliest examples of writs citing the new limitation date see CP 40/21 mm. 9, 52, 83, (Michaelmas term 1277). In Hilary term 1277 the limitation date mentioned was still Henry III's

From Trinity term 1303, however, Chancery reverted, and on a permanent basis, to issuing writs using the limitation date specified in the Statute of Marlborough. It looks as though it was the judgment given in the Common Bench in one particular case which led to this change, though it is possible that it was an unrecorded conciliar discussion of the point raised in pleading in this and a number of other contemporary cases that in fact determined both the specific judgment and the change in Chancery practice. In Michaelmas term 1301 John son of Peter de Seyville brought an action of *contra formam feoffamenti* in the Common Bench against the prior of Pontefract, complaining that the prior had been distraining him to perform three-weekly suit to his court of Barnsley. A report of the case shows the prior's counsel (Ashby) trying various arguments against the count and against the writ before finally coming up with the objection that the writ was defective because it purported to be based on the Statute of Marlborough. This had mentioned only Henry III's voyage to Brittany but the writ itself specified the same king's voyage to Gascony.[8] Mutford, for the plaintiff, responded (inaccurately) that the writ had been in this form ever since the enactment of the Statute. Neither of the two justices mentioned in the report as being present in court seems to have been sympathetic to the challenge. Chief Justice Hengham pointed out that the voyage to Gascony had been more recent. The change had made things easier for the defendant, because it made it easier for him to show title to the suit. The implication was that it was foolish of the defendant to object to the writ on these grounds. Justice Bereford spoke as though the objection had been to the words of the count rather than those of the writ and pointed out that, if the plaintiff's count had mentioned the date specified in the Statute, the count would have diverged from the writ. This would have been foolish behaviour on the plaintiff's part since it would have led to the quashing of the writ.[9] What the report does not reveal, however, is the sequel. It is only the plea roll enrolment of the case which shows that the case was adjourned

crossing into Brittany: CP 40/18 mm. 53, 61d. In one case (*Master of Templars v. earl of Cornwall*) the limitation as enrolled in Hilary term 1277 was the crossing into Brittany (CP 40/18 m. 53) but this had changed to Gascony for later stages of the mesne process in the same case in Michaelmas 1277 and in Hilary 1278 (CP 40/21 m. 59; CP 40/23 m. 53d).

[8] BL MS. Additional 31826, fol. 119r: '*Esse*. Uncore ne entendums point qe a cest bref deivent estre respondu qe cest bref prent sa nessance de le avantdit statut de Marl' que doune remedie en tel cas si nun pus [le passage] le rey etc. en Breteyne e vostre bref veut pus [le passage] meme celi rey en Gascon'. E demandom jugement de la variance.'

[9] BL MS. Additional 31826, fol. 119r: '*Mutf'*. Tut tens pus la confeccioun de cel statut si ad cel bref este de cele forme. *Hengh'*. Le passage en Gascon' si suppose plus tardif tens dunt de tant vus doune il le plus de avantage. *Ber'*. Si vous ussez acorde a la limitacion del statut si ussez vus varie de vostre bref, e si ceo ussez fet si vus ust il tenu pur fol.'

for judgment and that judgment was not given for over a year.[10] When it was eventually given, in Hilary term 1303, the case was dismissed on the grounds that the original writ was not warranted by the Statute. As this was not the plaintiff's fault (since he could not have obtained a writ of any other form) his amercement was pardoned.[11] There is also a report apparently belonging to Hilary term 1303 which may be a report of a rehearing of this case prior to judgment but with different counsel now speaking for the two parties.[12] If so, the best that Middleton could do by way of answer to the objection was to suggest that Henry III had gone to Brittany and Gascony at one and the same time, so that there was really no difference between the two limitation dates.[13] This report shows Chief Justice Hengham dismissing the case for variation between the wording of the writ and the wording of the Statute and on the grounds that the court did not wish to change the limitation dates contained in the legislation.[14] One sequel, though it was one which unfolded only early in Edward II's reign, was for the plaintiff to bring a new writ, now in the proper form, against the prior's successor.[15] The other was for Chancery to revert to the statutory limitation date in the writs which it issued henceforward.

During the interval between pleadings and final judgment in this case, the same point had also been raised in at least two other cases. In a case brought by John son of William of Carthorpe against Thomas, archbishop of York in Hilary term 1302 the archbishop also objected to the wording of the writ on the grounds that it was not warranted by the Statute.[16] Here the plaintiff seems to have made a spirited defence of his writ, arguing that his writ was of the form normally taken by such writs and that conformity to the 'common form' of Chancery, rather than the

10 CP 40/135, m. 179d.

11 'Et quia in predicto statuto etc. super quo predictum breve fundatum est etc. nulla fit mencio de transfretacione domini Henrici regis in Vasconiam immo de transfretacione ejusdem in Britanniam et sic predictum breve variatur eidem statuto, consideratum est quod predictus prior et alii inde sine die et Johannes nichil capiat per breve suum set sit in misericordia pro falso clamore etc. set perdonatur per justiciarios etc.'

12 LI MS. Miscellaneous 738, fol. 17v. The names of the parties are given as just 'John' and 'Roger' which provides no help for securely identifying the case reported.

13 '*Middleton.* Mesme ceu tens qil passa en Gascoygne si passa yl en Brittaygne.' It is true that Henry III had gone on from Brittany to Gascony in 1230 but his 'first crossing' to Gascony certainly refers to 1242 rather than 1230.

14 '*Hengham.* Cesti bref est lymite par statut e nous ne volome mye changer les paroles de la limitacioun conteneuz en meyme le statut. E pur coe qe vostre bref dyt "post primam transfretacionem domini Henrici regis patris etc. in Vasconiam" par la ou yl duyt dyre "post primam etc. in Britanniam" e issi acordant al statut, si agarde la court qe rien ne prengez par vostre bref, mes seez en la merci pur vostre fause pleynte'.

15 *YB 2 & 3 Edward II (1308–10)*, pp. 93–5.

16 CP 40/141, m. 57: 'Et dicit quod non debet ei inde ad hoc breve respondere. Dicit enim quod hujusmodi breve formatum de communi consilio etc. habet limitacionem suam ante primam transfretacionem etc. in Bretanniam et non in Vasconiam, unde petit judicium de brevi etc.'

wording of the Statute, should rule in such cases. The defendant ought therefore to be made to answer his writ. The case was adjourned for judgment. It was still pending in Hilary term 1303. No judgment has been traced.[17] In a third case, brought by Thomas son of Henry of Cayton against John fitzReginald of Londesborough, the plaintiff asked for judgment by default on the basis of the defendant's continued non-appearance during Easter term 1302.[18] The court refused to give judgment on the grounds that the limitation date contained in the writ was not the same as that specified in the Statute but adjourned the plaintiff to the following Michaelmas term.[19] This suggests that even prior to Hilary term 1303 there were at least some justices in the Common Bench who held that the writ ought to have mentioned Henry III's voyage to Brittany in conformity with the Statute. When the plaintiff appeared in court that term he asked for, and received, permission to withdraw from his writ.

The point was, moreover, evidently not a new one even in 1301. The report, though not the enrolment, of a case heard in Trinity term 1300 shows that exactly the same point had been raised in that case by Serjeant Friskney.[20] Counsel for his opponent (Tilton) had responded that no other form of writ was available in Chancery and the pleading passed on to other matters.[21] The same point is also made in two other reports, probably of a second case brought against the same lord during that same term.[22] In this case it was Harle who objected to the limitation date included in the writ as not being warranted by the Statute.[23] One of the reports ascribes to a second serjeant, Ashby, the response that they were all a single voyage (Middleton's argument in 1303) and that no other writ was available from Chancery;[24] the other simply mentions a judgment by

[17] CP 40/146, m. 155d. [18] CP 40/142, m. 196d.

[19] 'Et quia terminus in brevi insertus discordat termino hujusmodi brevis in predicto statuto contento datus est ei dies de audiendo judicio suo hic a die sancti Michaelis in unum mensem'.

[20] '*Frisk'*. Le bref est fundu sur statut e prent sa limitacioun del premer passage etc. en Bretagne; le bref dit "premer passage en Gascoyne". Jugement du bref.': LI MS. Hale 188, fol. 44v. The enrolment is CP 40/134, m. 153d. The case is *William Stormy v. John fitzReginald [of Londesborough]*.

[21] '*Tilton*. Cest a doner altre forme etc. mes en la chancelrie naverez autre forme': LI MS. Hale 188, fol. 44v.

[22] The case is *William Matheu of Langtoft v. John son of Reginald [of Londesborough]*. The reports are in Harvard Law School MS. 206, fol. 90v and CUL MS. Ee.6.18. fols. 41v–42r. The plea roll enrolment is CP 40/134, m. 115. What seems to be a report of the same case in BL MS. Additional 37657, fol. 27v does not mention this argument.

[23] '*Harle*. La ou vus ditez qe statut veut "quod non distringatur etc." si ly ne ses auncestres leient fet peus le passage le roi H. en Gascoine, sire, il ni ad nul tiel statut car statut dit "in Britanniam", issint cest bref saunz garaunte. Jugement etc.': Harvard Law School MS. 206, fol. 90v; '*Harl'*. Sire, nus demandum jugement desicom cesti bref est fundu sur statut e le bref prent limitacioun de tens del passage le rey en Gasscon e le statut veut limitacioun du tens del passage le roy H. en Bretayngne. E demandom jugement': CUL MS. Ee.6.18, fols. 41v–42r.

[24] '*Ass'*. Tut est un passage e vus naverez autre bref en la chauncerie': Harvard Law School MS. 206, fol. 90v.

Chief Justice Mettingham forcing the defendant to answer over on the grounds that the plaintiff was unable to get a writ of any other form.[25] If this is indeed a correct statement of Mettingham's views, it may only have been the change in the court's personnel (Mettingham's death and his replacement by Hengham) late in 1301 that made possible the later reversal to the date stipulated by the statute.

Variant forms of the writ

We have already noted one pleaded case from 1261 where Chancery seems to have been willing to issue a writ of *contra formam feoffamenti* in respect of a distraint made to secure the performance of suit to a hundred court but in which the court rejected this attempt to extend the ambit of the statutory remedy.[26] Although the period after 1267 saw the extension of the legislation on exemptions from attendance at the sheriff's tourn to apply to the analogous private institution, the view of frankpledge,[27] there is no clear evidence of the courts accepting a parallel (albeit reverse) extension of ambit of the legislation on suit from private courts to public, communal ones, whether in private or in royal hands. Chancery seems to have been willing on at least two occasions during the 1270s to issue writs purporting to be based on the legislation on suit of court but applying that legislation to communal courts. The cartulary of Byland abbey contains a copy of a prohibition issued in the name of Henry III on 8 February 1272 and addressed to the bailiffs of Edmund of Lancaster at Pickering, citing the legislation as prohibiting distraint for the performance of suit to wapentake courts as well as seignorial courts unless the distrainee was obliged by the form of his feoffment to perform it or had performed the suit prior to 1230 and ordering them not to distrain the abbot for suit to Edmund's wapentake of Pickering since he was not so obliged.[28] There is also a case of which only a preliminary procedural stage has been found on the Common Bench plea roll for Hilary term 1275 brought by

25 '*Metingham*. Il ne pusce aver auter bref en ceu cas en la chauncelrie. E pur ceo responez outre': CUL MS. Ee.6.18, fols. 41v–42r.

26 Above, p. 114. And for another pre-1267 case attempting to extend the ambit of the legislation in a similar way see above, pp. 168–9.

27 Below, pp. 288–93.

28 'Henricus dei gracia rex Anglie, dominus Hibernie et dux Aquitanie ballivis Edmundi filii sui de Pykering' salutem. Cum de consilio nostro provisum sit ne qui occasione tenementorum suorum distringantur ad sectam faciendam wapentachii et ad curiam dominorum suorum nisi per formam feoffamenti sui ad sectam illam teneantur vel ipsi aut eorum antecessores tenementa illa tenentes eam facere consueverunt ante primam transfretacionem nostram in Britanniam vobis precipimus quod non distringatis abbatem de Bell' ad sectam faciendam ad wapentachium predicti domini vestri. Teste me ipso apud Turrim London' viij die Februarii anno regni nostri lvi°': BL MS. Egerton 2823, fol. 92r.

Walter Tyway of Chenford. This alleged that Emelina, countess of Ulster had distrained him contrary to the terms of the legislation for suit to her hundred of Sutton in Northamptonshire.[29] No pleading has been traced in either case and there are no later cases where it is assumed that this part of chapter 9 is applicable to courts other than private seignorial ones.

One writ purportedly based on the legislation but very different in form from the standard writ of *contra formam feoffamenti* had already been used prior to 1267 in litigation brought in the 1263 Rutland eyre.[30] Another non-standard tenant's writ, also purportedly based on the legislation, was used in a case pleaded in Hilary term 1288. In addition to the normal recital of the statutory provisions this apparently went on to recite the specific facts which allegedly supported the plaintiff's claim to exemption from suit of court.[31] The writ seems to have ended with an allegation that the plaintiff had none the less been distrained to perform suit to the defendant's court contrary to the terms of the original feoffment and the legislation.[32] This writ also seems to have been a singleton without any further writs of the same form subsequently being made available to litigants by Chancery. The reasons for its issue in this particular case remain a puzzle.

MESNE PROCESS IN ACTIONS OF *CONTRA FORMAM FEOFFAMENTI*

Chapter 9 of the Statute of Marlborough (like the original clause 3 of the Provisions of Westminster) appears to make it clear that the legislation

[29] CP 40/7, m. 23d. Earlier litigation against the same defendant of which only a procedural stage has been found and which was brought by multiple plaintiffs simply describes the court as her 'court' of Sutton: CP 40/2A, m. 24.

[30] Above, pp. 168–9.

[31] These were that Cassandra, the widow of Geoffrey Baynard, the defendant's great-grandmother, had enfeoffed Nicholas of Holme, the plaintiff's father, of seven acres and half a perch in Holme to be held for two shillings a year for all service and that subsequently Geoffrey, the son of Geoffrey Baynard, the defendant's father, had confirmed the tenement to Nicholas for the same service.

[32] '. . . de placito quare cum de communi consilio regni regis provisum sit ne qui occasione tenementorum suorum distringantur ad sectam faciendam ad curias dominorum suorum nisi per formam feoffamenti sui ad sectam illam teneantur vel ipsi aut eorum antecessores tenementa illa tenentes eam facere consueverunt ante primam transfretacionem etc., ac quedam Cassandra que fuit uxor Galfridi Baynard proavia predicti Jacobi feoffasset Nicholaum de Hulmo patrem predicti Godefridi, cujus heres ipse est, de septem acris terre et dimidia perticata cum pertinenciis in Hulmo tenendum sibi et heredibus suis pro duobus solidis per annum pro omni servicio, et postea predictus Galfridus filius Galfridi Baynard pater predicti Jacobi, cujus heres ipse est, per cartam suam concessisset et confirmasset predicto Nicholao de Hulmo patri predicti Godefridi predicta tenementa tenenda per predictum servicium duorum solidorum tantum, predictus Jacobus distringit predictum Galfridum ad faciendum sectam ad curiam suam de Hulmo de tribus septimanis in tres septimanas contra formam feoffamenti predicti et contra provisionem predictam . . .': Case 88A.

is in itself a standing prohibition of any distraint for suit where the lord was not entitled to the suit under the terms of the legislation. If a tenant alleged that he had been distrained contrary to its terms, the legislation provided that he was to be entitled at once, and without any further preliminaries, to obtain a writ from Chancery for the attachment of the lord, requiring him to find two sureties for appearance in the king's court to answer for having done so. It seems none the less to have become the practice from the early 1270s onwards to require such a tenant, as a necessary preliminary stage to initiating any such litigation, to obtain from Chancery an initial prohibition addressed to his lord or that lord's bailiffs reciting the legislation and prohibiting the distraint of his tenant to perform suit of court in contravention of it and ordering the release of the tenant's animals or other chattels taken in distraint.[33] It was only if, and when, the lord made a further distraint that the tenant could obtain from Chancery a second writ, a writ of attachment, to secure the appearance of the lord in the king's court to answer not just for breach of the provisions but also for breach of this prior prohibition.[34] The earliest term in which such a prohibition is mentioned in the enrolment of mesne process is Michaelmas 1269, and the clumsiness of the reference to the prohibition in the enrolment of one of the two cases in which prohibition is mentioned tends to confirm that it was still then a novel procedure.[35] The two forms of procedure seem to have coexisted between 1270 and 1273 but the latest term in which the old type of procedure is mentioned is Easter term 1273.[36] That the prohibition was taken seriously is shown not only by the fact that allegations of service of the prohibition and of distraint after its service seem to have become a standard part of the plaintiff's count in the action,[37] but also by the fact that in at least one action the defendant took issue on the assertion that he had not distrained for suit after the service of the prohibition and was allowed to wage law on his denial.[38] In a second action the defendant took issue (for jury trial) on his denial that he had ever distrained the plaintiff abbot to perform suit after his election as abbot or after the prohibition had been purchased on 16 June that year.[39] Around the same time there seems also to have developed an alternative, but never common, form of initial process for *contra formam feoffamenti* cases. This allowed the tenant to dispense with

[33] For the form of the prohibition, see *Early Registers*, pp. 105–6 (CC 234).

[34] But for a case where prohibition was followed by a summons before attachment see *Robert Payn of Newport Pagnel v. Roger Somery* in Trinity term 1281: CP 40/41, m. 6.

[35] KB 26/194, m. 36. The other case in the same term in which such a prohibition is mentioned is KB 26/194, m. 17. Note, however, that no prohibition is mentioned in two later stages of mesne process in the same case: KB 26/196, m. 18d (Hilary term 1270) and KB 26/202, m. 35d (Easter term 1271).

[36] CP 40/2A, mm. 20d, 24. [37] Below, pp. 226–8. [38] Case 76A. [39] Case 84B.

this initial prohibition but made him begin with an initial summons before going on as a second stage to the more stringent procedure of an attachment.[40] Given the care which had gone into the drafting of clause 3 of the Provisions, and how recently it had been reaffirmed in the Statute of Marlborough, these are rather surprising developments.

It comes as less of a surprise, in view of the cavalier attitude adopted by the courts towards the express provisions of the legislation about mesne process prior to 1267,[41] to discover that there are no cases after 1267 in which *facias venire* was employed as part of the mesne process and that, despite the legislation's explicit provision that there be only one attachment stage in this action, it was usual to order a second attachment, if the first failed, between 1267 and 1275. It was only when the second attachment was finally abolished in personal actions generally by chapter 45 of the Statute of Westminster I that it also disappeared from cases of *contra formam feoffamenti*.[42]

JUDGMENT BY DEFAULT IN *CONTRA FORMAM FEOFFAMENTI*

The legislation had also provided that plaintiffs might recover by default in the statutory action if the defendant failed to appear in court after the grand distress had been ordered. The plaintiff would thereby secure the permanent release of the distresses which had been taken and released on a purely interim basis at the start of the litigation and was also to secure at least an interim freedom from being distrained to perform suit of court.[43] There are no examples of the application of the provisions of this section prior to 1267,[44] and only three cases in which they were applied during the succeeding four decades. In the earliest of these, in Trinity 1270, judgment was given by default after a single application of the grand distress and without any specific mention of the Statute of Marlborough.[45] There was then a gap of thirty years till the next such

40 For examples see KB 26/206, m. 32d (Hilary term 1272); CP 40/31, m. 106 (Michaelmas term 1279); CP 40/61, m. 23d (Hilary term 1286); CP 40/87, m. 100 (Hilary term 1291); CP 40/106, m. 151d (Michaelmas term 1294). For other cases where no prohibition is mentioned see CP 40/86, m. 95d (Michaelmas term 1290) and CP 40/93, m. 68d (Easter term 1292); CP 40/96, m. 16 (Michaelmas term 1292) [but one is mentioned in the report of the same case at *YB 21 & 22 Edward I*, pp. 147–51]; JUST 1/375, m. 51 (Kent eyre 1293).

41 Above, pp. 134–5, 176.

42 *SR*, I, 37–8. For examples of the use of second attachment between 1267 and 1275 see KB 26/199, mm. 5, 7d (Trinity term 1270); KB 26/208A, m. 19 (Trinity term 1272); CP 40/5, m. 100 (Michaelmas term 1274); CP 40/9, m. 39 (Easter term 1275).

43 Above, p. 52. 44 Above, pp. 135, 176.

45 KB 26/199, m. 15d (*Humphrey de Grauncourt v. Robert de Stuteville*). The judgment as enrolled was that Humphrey was to go without day and that the animals and distresses taken were to remain released 'saving to Robert his right whenever on another occasion he might wish to raise it'

judgment. This was in the case of *Nicholas de Oglethorpe v. John fitzReginald of Londesborough* in Trinity term 1300. This time judgment by default was given only after a second use of the grand distress and the Statute of Marlborough was specifically cited as authorising the judgment.[46] The third judgment by default was given in a case brought by a different plaintiff but against the same defendant (*John Randolph of Butterwick v. John fitzReginald of Londesborough*) some four years later, this time only after a single distraint. Again the enrolment makes specific reference to there being statutory authority behind the judgment, though (as enrolled) there is no specific mention of the Statute of Marlborough itself.[47]

Rather more revealing are the three cases in which plaintiffs are known to have attempted unsuccessfully to secure judgment by default. All are cases brought against the John fitzReginald of Londesborough against whom judgment was successfully obtained in the cases of 1300 and 1304. In the first of these, also heard in Trinity term 1300, the plea roll reveals nothing of any unsuccessful attempt to secure judgment by default. It is revealed only by the chance survival of a report of the same case.[48] This shows Serjeant Ashby asking for judgment on grounds of the defendant's default at the previous day assigned for his appearance when the writ of grand distress was returned, citing the provisions of the Statute and asking for the 'benefit of the Statute'.[49] The report shows the senior clerk, Hervey of Stanton, telling him that he had waived the benefit of the statute by failing to seek judgment when the first writ of grand distress was returned and suing the next stage of process (a grand distress *sicut alias*). It was too late to ask for judgment now that his opponent was in court.[50] The plaintiff was then driven to making a formal count. There are three other reports and a note which may also be of this case.[51] However, each of these reports and the note assign a similar judgment

('salvo ipsi Roberto jure suo cum alias inde loqui voluerit etc.'). For previous stages of process in the same case see KB 26/194, m. 8 and KB 26/196, m. 14d.

46 CP 40/134, m. 96d: 'Et per statutum Marleberg' consideratum est quod averia predicti Nicholai remaneant deliberata et quod idem Nicholaus sit quietus de predicta secta quousque predictus Johannes sectam illam per consideracionem curie domini regis recuperaverit.'

47 CP 40/149, m. 345d: 'Ideo consideratum est quod predictus Johannes Randolf eat inde sine die et habeat suos equos deliberatos etc. per quos predictus Johannes filius Reginaldi ipsum distrixit per formam statuti domini regis inde provisi quousque predictus Johannes filius Reginaldi sectam illam in curia regis versus predictum Johannem Randolf etc. disracionaverit etc. Et Johannes filius Reginaldi in misericordia etc.'

48 Case 00B.

49 'Vous est venu par la grante distresse en curt e statut veut qe si le seygnur ne viegne a jor qe done ly est par la destresse ayle la partie pleyntif sanz jor e ces avers ou autre destresse remeygnent deliverez si la qil se purchace ver son tenant par veye de ley. E priom benefice del statut.'

50 'Vous avez veyve cel avantage qe a la primere distresse returne dussez aver prie benefice de statut. Mes adonke suystes sicut alias e par tant veyvastes vous etc. et ly acceptastes etc.'

51 See reports listed under Case 00A.

rejecting the attempt to claim judgment by default not to Stanton but to Justice Bereford,[52] and, although there are similarities in much (but not all) of the reported pleadings between the first reports and the others, it seems more likely that they are reports not of this case but of a third case brought against the same defendant this same term.[53] For the other case heard in Easter term 1302 (*Thomas son of Henry of Cayton v. John fitzReginald of Londesborough)* no report has yet been found but the enrolment itself reveals a plaintiff attempting to secure judgment by default in accordance with the Statute of Marlborough on the defendant's continuing absence after the return of the grand distress, but the court adjourning judgment because the limitation date contained in the writ was not that warranted by the Statute.[54] The plaintiff was ultimately granted permission to withdraw from his writ.[55] It is only these unsuccessful cases that clearly indicate that judgment by default was not a matter in which the court itself took the initiative, but one where the initiative had to be taken by the plaintiff or his legal representatives. They also indicate that there was a clear understanding on the court's part that judgment by default could only be claimed at the time the default was made and that it was not something that could be obtained later when the defendant was actually present in court. It is probably the first of these that helps to explain the relatively small number of successful judgments by default obtained in actions of *contra formam feoffamenti*.[56] Not all plaintiffs or their lawyers

[52] '*Ber*'. Quey feystes vus lendmeyn de la Chaundeleur quant il fit defaute? Vous gerpistis cele avauntage par non chalenge en tens e ore par novel proces estes venuz en court par quey il covent qe vous responez outre': BL MS. Additional 37657; '*Ber*'. Quant la destresse fut primes returne e vostre adversarie ne vynt pas vus deusez aver demande ceo qe vous demandez ore e cel avauntage avez perdu par vostre defaute demene, par qei ditez ceo qe vus volez vers la partie': Harvard Law School MS. 206; '*Berford, Justice*. Moultes des excepcions perdent lour vertue e lour force pur ceo ke il ne sunt pas alleggez en sesoun e ausi vus dy jeo en ceo cas ke [si] cest excepcion uste este allegge a len demain de la Purificacion kant la grant destresse fu return le tenant par aventure ust este quites de cele seute solum la form de statust. Mes hor sembel il ke la seyson est mult passe pur ceo ke le seygnur est hor venu en courte e est prest a pleder e pur co vous seyngnur responez a ceo bref': CUL MS. Ee.6.18; '*Ber*'. Ne est la partie ore a vostre suite venuz en court par la grant destresce e prest a pleder etc.? Vous avez sursis vostre avantage quar ceo que ws priez ore ws dusset aver dit au procheyn jour passe. E pur ceo ke adonk ne deystes ore fauderez cena vigilantibus etc. E pur ceo countez ver ly': BL MS. Stowe 386.

[53] Case OOA. [54] Above, p. 211. [55] CP 40/142, m. 196d.

[56] For examples of cases where judgment by default could in theory have been obtained but where the case was pleaded only after renewed orders for distraint had been issued see the mesne process stages of *Ralph fitz Ralph fitz Fulk v. Gerard de Furnivall* in 1280 (CP 40/32, m., 42d and /34, m. 33d) which was not pleaded till 1284 (CP 40/52, m. 29); the mesne process stage of *Edmund Maunsayl v. Richard Malebysse* in 1288 (CP 40/73, m. 40d) which was pleaded later that year (CP 40/75, m. 143); the mesne process stage of *William Batekyng v. Nicholas Lowys* in 1288 (CP 40/75, m. 123) which was pleaded in 1289 (CP 40/78, m. 13d). For examples of cases where judgment by default could in theory have been obtained but where no pleading at all has been traced see *Gregory of Gatwick v. John son of Robert of Horbury* in 1284 (CP 40/53, m. 61d); *Abbot of Fountains v. Roger de Lascelles* in 1285 (CP 40/57, m. 10d).

may have known of the provisions of the statute. If they did not, the court evidently did not feel it necessary to point them out. Even where plaintiffs did know of them they may often have preferred to persevere with their actions and further mesne process against their opponents in the hope of obtaining damages against their lords (not obtainable where judgment was given by default) and a more definitive judgment after a jury verdict against those lords.

PLEADED CASES OF *CONTRA FORMAM FEOFFAMENTI*, 1267–1307

The action of *contra formam feoffamenti* was in regular, but not common, use during the forty-year period between the enactment of the statute of Marlborough and the end of the reign of Edward I. During this period ninety-five cases reached the stage of being pleaded, an average of fewer than three cases a year.[57] This should be compared with the annual totals for actions of replevin, the more general non-statutory action for challenging the use of distraint, pleaded in the Common Bench during the same period. In at least seven individual years between 1290 and 1307 the annual total of pleaded replevin cases for a single year exceeded this forty-year total of *contra formam feoffamenti* cases.[58] There was, moreover, a considerable yearly variation in the number of pleaded cases during the period. In nine of the forty years there were no pleaded *contra formam feoffamenti* cases at all.[59] In 1291, however, there were as many as eight and in 1289 as many as nine. The vast majority of cases that were pleaded (seventy-eight of the ninety-five) were pleaded in the Common Bench. Only seventeen were pleaded in sessions of the general eyre. Two cases were also brought in the court of King's Bench during the final years of the reign of Henry III but for neither are there any recorded pleadings.[60] The King's Remembrancer's Memoranda Roll for Michaelmas term 1268 also contains a prohibition based on the legislation and issued in favour of a constable of the Exchequer but again there is no record of any subsequent litigation in the Exchequer on the breach of that prohibition.[61] There is also evidence from the escheator's roll of Richard of Holbrook

[57] See appendix to this chapter (List of pleaded cases of *contra formam feoffamenti* heard between 1267 and 1307), below pp. 242–9.

[58] Brand, *MCL*, p. 299.

[59] In 1269, 1271, 1273, 1295, 1297, 1303, 1304, 1305 and 1307.

[60] *Gilbert Pecche v. Maud countess of Gloucester* (in 1271–2): KB 26/204, m. 1d; /205, m. 2; /207, m. 9d; *Henry Lovel v. abbess of Burnham* (in 1272): KB 26/207, m. 7.

[61] 'Quia de consilio magnatum anno regni regis lij° in octabis sancti Martini provisum fuit et statutum ac concorditer ordinatum quod nullus feoffatus sine carta a tempore conquestus vel alio

of a mandate dated 10 July 1281 for the holding of an inquisition by the escheator and the sheriff of Essex into the demands and distraints made by the bailiff of the escheated honours of Boulogne and Peverel to compel the performance of suit of court by Robert de Valoignes junior and his wife, Eve, as tenants of Tolleshunt and Bluntshall in Essex. The suit demanded for Bluntshall was to the court of the honour of Boulogne and for Tolleshunt to the court of the honour of Peverel. Robert and Eve were asserting that no suit was owed to either court according to the law and custom of the realm since neither they nor her ancestors had performed the suit before Henry III's first crossing to Gascony.[62] The inquest was to be returned to the king three weeks after Michaelmas. The mandate does not specifically cite the statute but is evidently based on it. It shows the existence of an administrative remedy for breaches of the statute when these were committed in the king's name by his own bailiffs; and the inquisition was probably being returned to the king at three weeks after Michaelmas so that its findings could be considered and appropriate redress given at the meeting of parliament scheduled for then.

The comparative infrequency of pleaded cases of *contra formam feoffamenti* may have more than one explanation. In part, it was probably because the focus of the action (on challenging distraints made for suit of court) was so narrow. If a lord and his tenant were in dispute, as they often were, about the lord's entitlement to a range of services including suit of court the tenant could use replevin to secure the return of the distresses the lord had taken for all the services in dispute (including suit of court) and litigate about all of them through that action; whereas if he brought *contra formam feoffamenti* to challenge the lord's entitlement to suit he would still need to bring replevin to challenge the lord's title to the other services. Tenants would, for obvious reasons, therefore normally prefer to bring just the one action rather than two. Using replevin was also much simpler. It did not require a Chancery writ to initiate, though one might be used. It did not, initially at least, require the plaintiff to travel to Westminster or hire a lawyer to pursue his case for him. There came, moreover, to be significant restrictions on the circumstances under

antiquo feoffamento distringeretur de cetero ad sectam faciendam ad curiam domini sui nisi ipse et antecessores sui eam consueti essent facere ante primam transfretacionem regis in Britanniam mandatum est vicecomiti quod de demanda quam frater Robertus de Tureville preceptor domus Templi de Kersing' facit Johanni Peverel constabulario scaccarii de secta facienda ad curiam suam apud Waham pro terra de Hanningefeld quam idem Johannes tenet de magistro milicie Templi in Anglia de antiquo feoffamento ut dicitur ei pacem habere in forma predicta et averia sua seu catalla ea occasione capta ei deliberari faciat. Teste etc.': E 159/43, m. 5.

62 E 152/1, m. 5d.

which *contra formam feoffamenti* could be used. These limited its availability even where it was only liability for suit of court that was at stake. One situation where it came to be settled that *contra formam feoffamenti* could not be used was where the person whose chattels had been taken in distraint was a sub-tenant of the person from whom suit was being demanded. Both the legislation and the writ of *contra formam feoffamenti* apparently assumed that the person distrained and the person from whom suit was being demanded would always be one and the same. This was quite often not the case. A case heard in the 1268 Yorkshire eyre seems to have settled that *contra formam feoffamenti* could not be used under these circumstances by the sub-tenant whose chattels had been taken in distraint.[63] In this case a plaintiff complained of having been distrained for three-weekly suit to the defendant's court, and asserted that neither he nor his ancestors had performed such suit before 1230 and that by the form of his feoffment he did not owe such suit. In reply the defendant denied distraining the plaintiff for suit, claiming that his distraint had been on his immediate tenant, Thomas of Gunby.[64] The court dismissed the case because the plaintiff could not show that he held the land concerned of the defendant and 'this writ was specially provided for use between lord and tenant' ('breve istud specialiter fuit provisum inter dominum et tenentem'). A very similar judgment dismissed a second case brought by a sub-tenant in the Easter 1284 session of the 1281–4 Lincolnshire eyre.[65] In a further case heard in the Common Bench in 1292 a tenant who had not himself been distrained, but whose sub-tenant had been, brought an action of *contra formam feoffamenti* against his lord.[66] The defendant argued that the only person entitled to bring *contra formam feoffamenti* was the tenant in demesne, the person whose chattels had been taken in distraint.[67] The plaintiff responded that he was the tenant in demesne as far as the defendant was concerned,[68] presumably on the grounds that it was no concern of his lord whether or not he had made a subinfeudation of the land. He also pointed out that the sub-tenant, the only person, according to the defendant's argument, who could use the action, would be left without a

[63] Case 68A.

[64] It seems virtually certain, although it is nowhere stated, that the plaintiff was a sub-tenant of Gunby. He does not allege that the defendant had distrained out of his fee nor is there any dispute about where the distresses were taken, and his count had carefully avoided alleging that he held the land concerned of the defendant and merely claimed that the distraint had been made on Stephen's land.

[65] Case 84C. [66] Case 92A.

[67] '. . . dicit quod istud breve habet locum inter tenentem dominicum et liberum tenementum et dominum distringentem . . .'

[68] '. . . ipse sit tenens dominici et liberi tenementi etc. respectu ipsius Willelmi.'

remedy for freeing himself from the burden of the suit for which the lord had distrained.[69] The defendant denied that this was true. The sub-tenant could bring either the action of replevin against the person distraining him, or the action of mesne against his warrantor, who in the present case would be the plaintiff.[70] The plaintiff pointed out that in either case the burden of suit would come to rest on him. Any avowry in replevin would be made on him, and if the tenant in demesne brought the action of mesne, he would be held liable to acquit his tenant of the suit that was being claimed since he owed his tenant the duty of acquitting him of any additional services claimed by the chief lords. If he could not use *contra formam feoffamenti* he would have no way of discharging the burden of suit. Although in form directed only at quashing the writ (stopping him using this particular remedy), the defendant's exception would, in effect, extinguish his right of action.[71] No judgment is recorded in this case, but it seems probable that the defendant's plea was successful. Certainly there is no subsequent evidence to indicate mesne lords bringing *contra formam feoffamenti* in such circumstances. Thus the end effect of these two cases appears to have been to ensure that when the lord distrained a sub-tenant for suit of court the action of *contra formam feoffamenti* was not available to either mesne lord or sub-tenant to challenge that distraint.

The legislation on suit of court had also apparently envisaged that the present tenant who held the tenement would also be the direct *descendant* of the person originally enfeoffed of that tenement. The clause talks of individuals who have themselves been enfeoffed or whose *ancestors* have performed suit before the first crossing into Brittany. It says nothing about the position of those who have acquired their title to the tenement concerned through an enfeoffment by substitution, the form of enfeoffment already in use before 1290 that became virtually universal after 1290 with the enactment of the Statute of *Quia Emptores*. It was not that the legislators were living in a world where enfeoffment of this kind was rare. They had themselves dealt (or attempted to deal) in clause 2 with the problems which arose when several feoffees were enfeoffed of portions of a single inheritance. The first case to raise the position of the feoffee had occurred as early as 1262. In the Warwickshire eyre of

69 Thinking presumably of the fact that he was not entitled in the circumstances to use *contra formam feoffamenti*.

70 In fact only the action of mesne would have discharged him from the burden of suit as he could not have taken issue in replevin with the lord paramount on whether suit was owed or not.

71 If he was barred from the use of *contra formam feoffamenti* on these facts and his tenant could only use mesne or replevin he would not be able to discharge himself from suit presumably because of the rule that the new rules about suit only applied in the new suit actions: see below, pp. 252–4.

that year Thomas of Leigh brought an action of *contra formam feoffamenti* against Hugh de Loghes in which he tried to take advantage of a charter of feoffment granting a tenement to be held for the service for twelve pence *pro omni servicio* which Hugh had granted to one Nicholas Clerk and which conferred exemption from suit.[72] He then traced the subsequent devolution of the tenement through enfeoffments by substitution made by Master Simon of Walton and Robert of Walton to himself. He added that none of them had performed suit until two years previously when he had been distrained to perform suit. Hugh does not seem to have objected to Thomas bringing the action as a strange purchaser of the land but did allege that the initial purchaser of the land had performed suit of court and that suit had been done until Master Simon of Walton had acquired the land after 1230. Objections were, however, raised in the report of a case heard in the 1272 Cambridgeshire eyre.[73] The plaintiff's count in this case did not attempt to disguise the fact that he had himself acquired the tenement. It specifically spoke of him having been enfeoffed by Isabel, daughter of Robert le Ber to hold of the chief lords by the services due and of the fact that neither Isabel nor her ancestors had performed suit prior to 1230. The defendant's counsel raised the objection, based on the wording of the legislation, that the action was only available to those who held their tenements by hereditary descent. This was met by the objection that, given the form of his feoffment, the plaintiff would have no remedy to challenge an unjust distraint if he was not allowed this action, as he had no action of mesne against his feoffor. That this was thought to be a good answer which supported the plaintiff's use of the action seems to be indicated by the fact that the defendant then attempted to switch to a rather different argument. This accepted the validity of the plaintiff using the action but set against the principles laid down by the legislation the equally strong principle that no purchaser of a tenement could or ought be in a better position than the tenant from whom he acquired it. The defendant therefore pleaded as his title the fact that the feoffor had herself performed suit and the plaintiff also. The report (together with the Barnwell *Liber Memorandorum*) tells us that judgment was eventually given for the defendant after the case had been adjourned into the Common Bench. This judgment has not, however, been traced and neither source tells us the grounds for the judgment. The same problem came up again in a case brought in the 1285 Northamptonshire eyre, of which there is also a report.[74] Here there is nothing in

[72] Above, p. 113.

[73] Case 72D. For the eventual outcome see *Liber Memorandorum Ecclesie de Bernewell,* ed. J. Willis Clark (Cambridge, 1907), p. 131.

[74] Case 85D.

the plaintiff's count (either as enrolled or as reported) to indicate that he had recently acquired the land. His count talks quite unashamedly of 'his' feoffment and of the fact that neither he nor his 'ancestors' holding his tenements had performed the suit prior to 1230. It is the defendant who, knowing the recent history of the tenement, raised the objection to the count, and to his use of the writ, that he could not properly claim, as the writ required, to have had 'ancestors' holding the tenement before 1242. It was only recently that he had acquired the tenement by enfeoffment. The enrolment adds that this had occurred within the previous three years. The plaintiff, however, according to the enrolment, argued that the use of the writ was not limited to heirs. The report also tells us that Mettingham J. argued that the 'antecessores' of the legislation was in fact ambiguous. It could refer either to 'ancestors' or just to the previous tenants of the land and the failure to include in the writ the phrase 'cujus heredes ipsi sunt etc.' or to alter the wording of the writ when the plaintiff was an abbot or prior pointed to the second of these two meanings. The court did not actually give a ruling on the point but these arguments seem to have persuaded the defendant's counsel to waive their objections. Further problems then arose similar in nature to those raised by the 1272 Cambridgeshire case. The defendant attempted to argue that his seisin of suit at the hands of the plaintiff's feoffor as well as those of the plaintiff should suffice as title. The plaintiff admitted that the defendant had been so seised but wished to be allowed to show that the original feoffment had not required the performance of suit and that no suit had been done for the tenement prior to 1242. The same objection to the use of the writ by a feoffee seems to have been made (but waived) in a case heard in 1292, though this is mentioned only in the report of the case.[75] That *contra formam feoffamenti* was still being used by strange purchasers after this is suggested by a number of cases in which defendants took special care to lay seisin at the hands of those who had held the tenement before the limitation date, rather than at the hands of the plaintiff's ancestors.[76] Thus it seems only to have been after this period that the action came to be available only to those who could claim to be the direct descendants of those who had held the tenement from which the suit was claimed prior to the limitation date.[77] None the less the doubts which had been raised so persistently may have deterred some purchasers from bringing this action and may have suggested to them that there were few benefits to doing so.

[75] Case 92E. [76] For examples see the counts in Cases 93C, 98A, 06A.

[77] *Reg. Omn. Brev.*, fol. 176r: 'Cest briefe voet estre port per la ou le pleintife claime per auncester et nemy come purchaceour.'

THE FORM OF PLEADING IN THESE CASES

The plaintiff's count

The standard form of count in the action of *contra formam feoffamenti* consisted of three main elements. An initial section set out the terms on which the plaintiff claimed to hold his tenement of the defendant in order to establish that these did not render him liable to suit of court or, in a limited number of cases, to the specific variety of suit of court that was being claimed. A second section established that the plaintiff had served the defendant with a royal prohibition forbidding him from distraining for suit of court contrary to the terms of the plaintiff's feoffment and contrary to the terms of the legislation.[78] A third section asserted that the defendant had breached the terms of this prohibition by a subsequent distraint intended to ensure the performance of suit and claimed specific damages for this breach.[79] By no means all enrolled counts in actions of *contra formam feoffamenti* contain all these three elements. However, the existence of at least one reported case of *contra formam feoffamenti* which contains an element omitted from the enrolled count of the same case suggests that the enrolments may not always accurately represent the counts actually given in court.[80] It also seems likely that the variation in the amount of detail given for each of these sections in the enrolled reports is more likely to represent the vagaries of the recording process than significant variations in the actual amount of detail given in the counts themselves.

The most complex and the most variable of these three elements in the standard count was the first one, establishing the basis of the plaintiff's claim to be exempt from the obligation to perform suit of court or (in a very few cases) the particular form of suit of court that the defendant was allegedly claiming.[81] There were as many as five different ways of doing this. The first (found in seven counts) drew a direct connexion between the exemption claimed and the terms of the tenant's original feoffment.[82] More common were counts (found in twenty-nine cases) in which the

[78] But for the cases where no prohibition was stated to have been served see above, p. 215.

[79] In those cases where no prohibition had been served the plaintiff simply claimed damages for having been distrained contrary to the terms of the prohibition.

[80] Contrast the enrolment and report of Case 92E. But for instances where the enrolled count is much fuller than that given by the report see Cases 92A, 01A.

[81] For the three cases in which the plaintiff admitted that he owed some suit of court but denied owing the suit for which he was being distrained see Cases 00A, 00B, 02A.

[82] In four cases the plaintiff set out the services (in each case, a specific rent 'for all service') by which he claimed to hold his tenement and also produced his charter of feoffment in court to provide evidentiary support: Cases 76C, 89D, 89F, 91C. In three cases the plaintiff went back to the original grant that had created the tenurial relationship in order to establish the terms on which he held and to show that they excluded liability for performing suit of court, but the enrolment

plaintiff asserted that he currently held the tenement for a specific service (that did not include suit) but did not refer to the transaction creating the tenure.[83] In a third type of count (found in nine cases) the plaintiff asserted that he held by a specific service but also joined with this an assertion that his feoffment excluded liability to perform suit.[84] Two counts (both made and enrolled in the same term) are the sole representatives of a fourth type. This seems simply to have specified the tenement the tenant held without specifying the services owed for it and then to have added to this the assertion that his tenure of it was 'without performing suit'.[85] The fifth and final type (found in twenty-six cases) attempted in this first section of the count to exclude in advance the possibility that the plaintiff might be liable to the obligation to perform suit of court not just under the terms of their feoffment but also on the basis that their ancestors had customarily performed suit of court prior to the limitation date.[86] Twenty of the enrolled *contra formam feoffamenti* counts omit this part of

says nothing of him producing the relevant charter of feoffment in court: Cases 89C, 93A, 93B. A similar assertion is made in the special writ used in Case 88A.

83 For the twenty-four cases in which the claim was to hold by a specific service 'for all services' see Cases 74A, 75A, 77A, 78D, 79A, 80A, 81C, 85B, 85C, 86A, 88C, 88D, 89B, 89H, 90E, 90F, 91A, 91B, 91F, 93C, 96A, 98B, 99A, 00A. In Case 83B the plaintiff claimed to hold by free and pure alms and in Case 80B for a specific service 'without doing any suit'. In Cases 89I, 93D, 00B the plaintiff simply said he held by a specific service and only implicitly repudiated any liability for suit.

84 For counts where the plaintiff claimed that his feoffment mentioned no obligation to perform suit see Cases 81A, 92F, 99B. For counts where he claimed his feoffment excluded any additional services of any kind see Cases 90A, 98A, 01A. For counts where the plaintiff simply alleged that he owed only the services specified 'under the terms of his feoffment' see Cases 92B, 92E, 02E (but here the plaintiff admitted owing suit twice a year).

85 Cases 91D, 91E.

86 In eight counts plaintiffs asserted that they held their tenement by a specific service 'for all service' without being obliged to perform suit by the terms of their feoffment or they or their ancestors ever having performed suit prior to the limitation date (or ever having performed suit): Cases 70A, 72E, 76B, 81D, 85A, 90D, 91G, 92A. In another eight counts plaintiffs asserted that they held a particular tenement for a particular service 'for all services and suits of court' or 'for all service' or in free and perpetual alms without them or their ancestors (or predecessors) having performed suit of court prior to the limitation date but without specific reference to the terms of their feoffment: Cases 74A, 79C, 81B, 89G, 90C, 91H, 92D, 94A. In four counts plaintiffs asserted that they held a particular tenement (but with no mention of the services which they owed for it) without either they or their ancestors ever having performed suit (or having performed suit before the limitation date) or being obliged to perform suit by the terms of their feoffment: Cases 68A (before the limitation date), 70B, 72B (before the limitation date), 72C (before the limitation date). For a variant form of count where not even the tenure of a particular tenement is mentioned but in which the same two assertions are made see Cases 82A, 85D (but note that the reports of this case mention a specification of particular tenement and a specified service 'for all services'), 87A. In another three counts plaintiffs said just that they held a particular tenement (without mention of the services owed for it) without themselves or their ancestors having performed suit before the limitation date but without any mention of the terms of their feoffment: Cases 88B, 89E, 72D (but here it was the plaintiff's feoffor and his ancestors who had not performed the suit and the plaintiff had been enfeoffed to hold by the customary (but unspecified) services due).

the count, though we cannot be sure (other than in a single case) that the count that was made in court did not include it.[87]

The service of a prohibition by the plaintiff on the defendant is mentioned or implied in the counts enrolled or reported in as many as seventy-one of the ninety-five cases. However, in thirteen of these cases the prohibition is only mentioned in passing at the end of the initial recital of the writ without any further details being given in the section recording the count proper.[88] In a further five cases the only mention of a prohibition comes in the complaint made in the count of a distraint made in breach of a prohibition, but again without any further details of the actual prohibition.[89] In six cases the enrolment (or a report) specifically mentions the service of prohibition as a separate and distinct element but provides no further details of it.[90] All the other counts provide a little more detail. The date of the service of the prohibition alone is given in twelve counts;[91] the names of the witnesses to the service of the prohibition alone in a single count;[92] the date and the place of the service alone in nineteen counts;[93] the date and the names of some of the witnesses in a single count;[94] the date and place of the service and the names of some of the witnesses in fourteen counts.[95] Analysis of the dates mentioned in these counts sheds some useful light on the period of time which might normally elapse between the initial service of prohibition in such actions and the case coming to court. In eighteen instances this was less than a year;[96] in a further fifteen between one and two years;[97] in ten between two and five years.[98] Only in two quite exceptional cases was it longer than five years.[99] The location most commonly given for the service of the prohibition was the village or town where the court was held where the suit was being claimed. In some, but perhaps not all, cases the prohibition may have been served at the place the court itself was

[87] Cases 72A, 76A, 78A, 78B, 78C, 79B, 80C, 80D, 80E, 83A, 83C, 84A, 84B, 85E, 87B, 89A, 90B, 92C, 93E, 06A. Of these cases, no other elements of the count are recorded either for Case 85E and 93E and in 92C the enrolment tells us that the plaintiff failed to make any count.

[88] Cases 81A, 81B, 81C, 83C, 84A, 85B, 85C, 86A, 89B, 90D, 90F, 91A, 91B.

[89] Cases 88B, 88D, 89C, 89E, 89I.

[90] Cases 74A, 74B, 80D, 92E (only mentioned in report), 93A, 93B.

[91] Cases 72B, 72E, 76A, 80A, 87B, 88C, 90E, 91D, 91E, 92B (regnal year only), 92F, 06A.

[92] Case 89H.

[93] Cases 76B, 76C, 77A, 78D, 80B, 80C, 80E, 82A, 83A, 83B, 85D, 87A, 89D, 89F, 89G, 90A, 90C, 91F, 99A.

[94] Case 85A.

[95] Cases 81D, 91C, 91H, 92A, 92B, 93D, 96A, 98A, 98B, 99B, 00A, 00B, 01A, 02A.

[96] Cases 72B, 76A, 80A, 80E, 81D, 83A, 85D, 87B, 89F, 90A, 91D, 91F, 92B, 93D, 96A, 99A, 99B, 02A.

[97] Cases 72E, 76C, 77A, 80B, 80C, 82A, 83B, 89D, 90E, 91C, 92A, 98A, 98B, 00B, 01A.

[98] Cases 76B, 78D, 85A, 87A, 89G, 90C, 91E, 91H, 92F, 06A.

[99] Over seven years in Case 88C; six years in Case 00A.

held within that village or town.[100] Two of the prohibitions were said to have been served in a session of the relevant county court.[101] One was served in the hall of the abbey of St Mary, York on Shrove Tuesday;[102] one in the minster church of St John of Beverley on Easter Saturday.[103] The remainder were served at a variety of places away from the villages or towns where the court was held.[104] Most of the witnesses named appear to be men with local connexions with the area where the prohibition was being served. They also, however, include (for the above-mentioned prohibition served in the hall of the abbey of St Mary, York in respect of suit demanded to the Yorkshire court of Ousefleet) the royal justice John of Mettingham and his clerk, Anger of Ripon, who were also both present at the Lincolnshire eyre where the case was heard;[105] a local professional lawyer (Robert of Stoke) for the delivery on Robert fitzJohn at Coventry of a prohibition on the Friday before All Saints' Day 1295;[106] and the Common Bench serjeant William of Roston and two different relatives of his in prohibitions served on John fitzReginald of Londesborough in 1298 at York (before William became a serjeant)[107] and on Thomas, archbishop of York at Bishop Burton near Beverley in 1301.[108]

The third and final element in the count was the allegation of a distraint in breach of the prohibition (or, where there had been no prohibition, in breach of the legislation) and the associated claim for damages on grounds of this breach. Since little depended on the specific details of the distraint or distraints made it was only a small minority of enrolments that bothered to record what had been taken in distraint,[109] or what had been taken

[100] For prohibitions specifically said to have been delivered at a session of the defendant's court see Cases 80B and 83A. For prohibitions said to have been delivered in the defendant's house or manor, which may also have been the location of their court, see Cases 76B, 76C, 91F, 92A. For a prohibition said to have been delivered in a village church see Case 82A. The other counts which, as recorded, specify only the relevant village, town or city in general terms are Cases 80C, 80E, 85D, 89D, 89F, 90A, 90C, 91C, 91H, 92B, 98A, 99A, 00A, 01A, 02A.

[101] Of Yorkshire in Case 83B; of Nottinghamshire in Case 87A (but only as initially enrolled in Michaelmas term 1286 in CP 40/64, m. 16d).

[102] Case 81D. [103] Case 93D.

[104] Two were served on the archbishop of York at Beverley in respect of suit being demanded to his nearby court of Bishop's Burton: see Cases 77A, 78D. Other locations specified include: Coventry for service on Robert fitzJohn in respect of suit being demanded to his nearby court of Barnacle: Case 96A; Poppleton outside York for service on the abbot of St Mary, York in respect of suit to his court in York: Case 99B; York for service on John fitzReginald of Londesborough in respect of suit to his court at Londesborough: Case 00B; Harringworth, apparently her main place of residence in Northamptonshire, for service on Milisent de Montalt in respect of suit to her Bedfordshire court of Eaton Bray: Case 89G; Hickleton for service on Peter de Rocheford in respect of suit being demanded to his court of Morley: Case 98B.

[105] Case 81D.

[106] Case 96A. On Robert of Stoke see Robert C. Palmer, *The County Courts of Medieval England, 1150–1350* (Princeton, 1982), pp. 109–10.

[107] Case 00B (with his brother Geoffrey). [108] Case 02A (with Alan of Roston).

[109] Cases 75A, 84A, 85D, 91H, 92E (report only).

and when it had been taken,[110] or (at its fullest) what had been taken and where and when it had been taken.[111] The vast majority of recorded counts as enrolled did, however, end with a claim for damages in the common form of rounded (and often heavily inflated) figures, for which no justification was needed and which seem only to have functioned as an upper limit on what could in practice be recovered.[112] The amounts claimed varied between a low of two pounds (forty shillings) (in four cases) and a high of one hundred pounds (in five cases) with the largest individual group of plaintiffs (twenty-three) claiming five pounds and substantial groups claiming ten pounds (fifteen plaintiffs), twenty pounds (fifteen plaintiffs) and forty pounds (ten plaintiffs). A smaller group claimed forty marks and single plaintiffs claimed other amounts (three pounds or sixty shillings, ten marks, twenty marks, thirty pounds, fifty pounds and sixty pounds).

Defences

It was normally only the lord in whose name the distraint had been made who was sued as a defendant. There are, however, a small number of cases in which that lord's bailiffs, the men who had actually made the distraint, were sued either as sole,[113] or as joint,[114] defendants. In the latter case at least, the normal procedure seems to have been similar to that used in replevin, the lord avowing the action of his bailiffs and taking upon himself the sole burden of the defence. A report of a case heard in Michaelmas term 1301 shows an objection being made for the defendant (by Serjeant Ashby) that the writ was a writ of right like the action of *ne vexes* to which the proper parties were the lord and the tenant only and that the bailiff who was the co-defendant had no interest in the seignory and should not have been joined as a defendant. Mutford (for the plaintiff), however, insisted that the plea was of a mixed nature since it alleged a wrongful distraint, but also sought to discharge the tenant's liability. The justices of the court agreed he was properly named as a defendant as he

110 Cases 83C, 87A, 87B, 90C, 90D, 06A. 111 Cases 68A, 76C, 82A.

112 But there are at least thirteen pleaded cases in which there is no estimate of damages in the enrolled count or no enrolled count or damage to the roll at the relevant point.

113 For examples (none of which came to being pleaded) see *Roger Bydolf v. John de Wheathampstead, Henry de Bray and Alan Thes, the bailiffs of John de Verdun of Alton*: mesne process in Michaelmas term 1269 and Easter term 1271: KB 26/202, m. 5, KB 26/194, m. 36; *Adam son of William of Belton v. Richard of Walsingham and three other (named) bailiffs of John de Bernak:* mesne process in Easter and Michaelmas terms of 1276 and Hilary term 1277: CP 40/14, m. 67d, CP 40/17, m. 131, CP 40/18, m. 68d; *Robert son of Hugh de Genge v. John de Pomeroy and John Carter, the bailiffs of Fulk fitz Warin of Wantage*: mesne process in Michaelmas term 1277 and Hilary term 1278: CP 40/21, m. 52, CP 40/23, m. 37d.

114 For pleaded examples see Cases 72A, 76C.

had made the distraint and because the writ was (as Bereford said) a writ of trespass, not of right.[115]

There were different complications if the lord who had distrained for suit had only a limited interest in his or her lordship. Two defendants had cases dismissed on the grounds that the courts which they held were held only in right of their wives and their wives had not been joined as defendants in the action.[116] In two cases, the husband held a court in curtesy in right of a wife who was now dead. In one he sought the aid of his two daughters, who were the heirs of his wife, but the aid-prayer was counterpleaded. This was on the grounds that neither the wife nor any of her ancestors had been seised of the suit. Issue was then taken on the widower's claim that his wife's father had been seised of suit and he himself seised of distraint for suit.[117] In the other the defendant is simply recorded as justifying his distraint on the grounds that he had been seised of the suit during his wife's lifetime, without any attempt at aid-prayer, and issue was joined as to whether the defendant had ever been peacefully seised in his wife's lifetime or since.[118] In six cases the defendant was a widow who held the court as part of her dower. In four of these she appears simply to have been allowed to seek the aid of the reversioner of her dower.[119] In two the aid-prayer was counterpleaded by the plaintiff and issue then taken on whether or not the defendant had usurped the suit after the court was assigned to her in dower.[120] In two of the four cases where aid was allowed the reversioner is known to have joined with the doweress and pleaded to issue on entitlement to suit.[121] In a single case, aid-prayer was allowed when the defendant lord pleaded that his interest in the lordship was one enjoyable only until he was provided with an annual rent of ten marks a year elsewhere;[122] in another a prebendary was allowed the aid of the dean and chapter of his cathedral in answering the suit brought against him.[123] No pleading has been found in the one case where a defendant was sued who was the guardian of a minor (in 1272–3), but the absence of later cases of a similar kind suggests that either then or later it was decided that the guardian's interest in the lordship was too limited to allow him to be a proper party to such proceedings.[124] Aid-prayer was also allowed in three cases (involving only two sets of litigants) where the defendant was the coheir of a divided inheritance (in both instances an inheritance divided since 1230).[125] In none of the

[115] Case 01A. [116] Cases 72A, 89A. [117] Case 86A. [118] Case 74B.
[119] Cases 89C, 89E, 91E, 91H. [120] Cases 75A, 81B. [121] Cases 89E, 91H.
[122] Case 80C. [123] Case 72A.
[124] *Andrew Trenecglose v. Walter de Tremur, guardian of the land and heir of William de Tresagu*: KB 26/208A, m. 19 (Trinity term 1272); CP 40/3, m. 28d (Trinity term 1273).
[125] *Richard Peres v. Milisent de Montalt*: CP 40/75, m. 109 (Michaelmas term 1288) and CP 40/91, m. 125 (Michaelmas term 1291); Case 90B.

three cases is any attempt recorded to counterplead the aid-prayer, but in only one instance is the parcener known to have appeared and joined the defendant in taking issue on title to the suit.[126]

It was comparatively rare, though not wholly unknown, for plaintiff and defendant to disagree about whether or not the plaintiff had been distrained,[127] or about the reasons for the making of the distraint.[128] Generally, however, both parties agreed that the plaintiff had been distrained and as to the reasons for the distraint and the main focus of the litigation was on whether or not the lord was entitled to the suit for which he had distrained. In the overwhelming majority of cases the tenant (as has been seen) was claiming to be wholly free of any obligation to perform suit of court;[129] in the vast majority of cases the lord seems to have been claiming that the tenant owed three-weekly suit to his court.[130]

The legislation had talked of lords possessing two kinds of title to suit, either under the terms of the tenant's feoffment, or by them showing seisin of the suit prior to 1230, and plaintiffs in their counts, as has been seen, might allude to both kinds of possible title.[131] In practice, however, it was unknown for lords in their defences to rely on the wording of the tenant's charter of feoffment as their title to demand suit. This is less surprising than it might seem. When a feoffment was made it was normally only the

[126] Case 89G.

[127] But for cases where the defendant denied having made any distraint after the service of the prohibition see above, p. 214.

[128] As has been seen, the reasons for the making of the distraint were disputed in the very first pleaded action of *contra formam feoffamenti*: above, p. 114. In a case of 1283 (Case 83B) the defendant admitted he had been distraining for suit but denied he was claiming it in respect of the tenement specified by the plaintiff in his count and claimed he was demanding it in respect of another tenement for which it was owed. For cases where the parties agreed that the distraint had been for suit of court but disagreed on the quantum of suit being demanded by the lord see Cases 72C (tenant asserts lord is demanding regular three-weekly suit; lord says he is only claiming three-weekly suit when there is a writ of right in the court or one tenant makes a complaint against another in the court or his presence is needed for the afforcement of the court), 91D (tenant asserts lord is demanding three-weekly suit; lord says he is only claiming suit for afforcement of the court when a thief is to be judged or the king's writ of right is in the court), 92E (tenant asserts lord is demanding three-weekly suit and two attendances at court each year; lord says he is only demanding two attendances a year).

[129] For the exceptions see above, note 81. In 00A counsel (Harle) tried the argument (based on a literal reading of the text of the statutory provision) that *contra formam feoffamenti* could only be used by tenants who denied owing any suit, not by those who admitted owing some but denied liability for the specific form of suit claimed by the lord. This argument was overruled by Bereford.

[130] For exceptions see Cases 92E (lord claims both three-weekly suit and twice-yearly attendances at his court), 88B (lord claims only three appearances a year), 72C (lord claims three-weekly suit only when a writ of right was being heard in the court, when a tenant was bringing a plaint against another tenant and where the tenant was required for the afforcement of the court). In almost a third of the pleaded cases the nature of the suit the lord is claiming is not further specified but it is reasonable to assume that it is three-weekly suit.

[131] Above, pp. 224–5.

tenant who retained a copy of it and there was no mechanism to allow lords to compel tenants to produce their charters of feoffment in court. Not that lords did not try. In what seem to be reports of two cases brought against the same lord (John fitzReginald of Londesborough) in Trinity term 1300, Friskney (in one case) and Herle or Hartlepoole (in the other case) attempted to compel the tenant to show the charter of feoffment by which he claimed to be quit of suit of court and asked for judgment against the tenant when he failed to do so. Both were forced to answer over. The reports suggest that it was Justice Bereford who argued that the feoffment could well have been without charter and that the tenant could not therefore be made to produce his charter if he asserted that he and his ancestors had held without performing suit prior to 1242.[132] The nearest lords came to relying on written feoffments was in two cases of the early 1290s. In both they attempted to use what appear in both cases to have been not the original charters of feoffment but subsequent deeds in which plaintiffs or their ancestors had made acknowledgments of the obligation to perform suit of court. In a case of Michaelmas term 1290 the defendant lord produced a deed in the name of the plaintiff by which he had acknowledged that he owed suit of court to the court of the plaintiff's father and his heirs. The plaintiff asserted that he was not bound by the deed as he had then been under age. The parties then took issue on this.[133] In the second case, heard two years later, the defendant lord pleaded an agreement made between himself and William Constantine and his wife, Alice, the father and mother of the plaintiff, after litigation he had brought against them claiming the tenement itself. Under it he had quitclaimed all right to the tenement and they had agreed to make two annual appearances at his court, the suit he was now claiming. He argued that this showed that he had been in seisin at their hands and later at her hands by virtue of the agreement and not by distraint.[134] This agreement too was challenged on the grounds that the land had belonged to Alice and any agreement her husband had made was not binding on her or her heirs. The defendant was then forced to establish a different title to the suit he claimed.

The defence normally pleaded in *contra formam feoffamenti* cases was that the plaintiff or his ancestors or predecessors had customarily performed suit before the limitation date. The seisin relied on as title by the defendant might be his own seisin,[135] or (in the case of an ageing widow) the seisin of her first and her second husbands.[136] Alternatively, and more

[132] See reports of Cases 00A and 00B. [133] Case 90F. [134] Case 92E.

[135] For the only two known examples, both claiming seisin at the hands of the plaintiff's father prior to the limitation date, see Cases 78A and 83A.

[136] For the sole example see Case 76B.

commonly, it would be both his or her own seisin and that of one or more of their ancestors.[137] More commonly still, it was just the seisin of the defendant's ancestors before the limitation date. The ancestors were often not specified except in generic form (in the enrolment at least),[138] but sometimes the seisin alleged was that of a specified ancestor. He is sometimes, but not always, named.[139] When the defendant was an ecclesiastic, the seisin might be that of the defendant and his predecessors.[140] Much more commonly it was that of the predecessors alone, named either generically[141] or specifically.[142] The earliest case in which a defendant specifically pleaded the seisin of suit before the limitation date by a predecessor in title comes from Michaelmas term 1285.[143] It was followed by at least six other cases in which such a title was pleaded between 1285 and 1296.[144] There are no recorded objections to lords using such a title in claiming suit.

Defendants sometimes went further than strictly required in making their title to the suit they claimed. It was not uncommon for a defendant to claim that both he and his ancestors (or she and her ancestors) or just his or her ancestors had been seised *after* as well as before the limitation date.[145] There are also a small number of cases in which the defendant alleged that his ancestors or predecessors had been seised of the suit not just before the limitation date but (more generously) since time out of mind,[146] or even in one case ever since the Conquest.[147]

In the majority of cases, as enrolled, the parties seem simply to have joined issue on the title to suit alleged by the defendant and that issue gone to jury trial. There are, however, a few exceptions to this general pattern. These are of particular interest. In two cases plaintiffs were allowed through replications to the defendant's defence to get on to the formal record their confession that the defendant had indeed been seised of the suit claimed but their avoidance that this had only been since the limitation date and as a result of the heavy use of distraint by the defendant in the recent past, precisely the kind of illicit pressure whose effects the legislation was intended to reverse. This was a form of replication that was not strictly necessary, since it amounted in effect to no more than

[137] For examples see Cases 72C, 80A, 89E, 89F, 89G, 89H.

[138] This is the case in nine enrolments. For an example see Case 74A.

[139] For an example of reliance on the seisin of a named and specified ancestor see Case 78C (seisin of the lord's father, Hugh Wake). Other examples will be found in Cases 78B, 89B. For reliance on the seisin of a specified, but unnamed ancestor, see Cases 80B, 81C, 84A. In Case 85B the lord relied on the seisin of his father and his own name supplies us with the name.

[140] The sole example of this is Case 70B.

[141] For examples see Cases 92F, 93C, 99A, 06A.

[142] For examples see Cases 77A, 78D.

[143] Case 85C.

[144] Cases 87A, 87B, 90C, 91B, 94A, 96A.

[145] For examples see Cases 79C, 88A, 90D, 92B.

[146] There are four examples: Cases 72B, 79A, 83C, 85A.

[147] Case 72E.

a denial of the defendant's title based on seisin prior to the limitation date. Its effect, however, was to ensure that the jury focused its attention on when the defendant had become seised of the suit and how this had been achieved.[148] In a third case a plaintiff was allowed a different kind of replication, which again was probably not strictly necessary, but which was also evidently intended to ensure that the jury was not misled by an appearance of entitlement on the defendant's part. Here the plaintiff acknowledged that the defendant and his ancestors had indeed made distraints for suit of court but denied that they had ever gained seisin of the suit for which they had distrained.[149] Another unnecessary replication, again probably aimed primarily at the potentially misleadable jury, is to be found in a fourth case where a plaintiff (in response to the defendant's assertion that he had himself been seised of the suit he claimed at the hands of the plaintiff's father prior to the limitation date) was allowed to get on record the claim that the tenements had not been granted to his father until after the limitation date and had then been granted to hold for rent only *pro omni servicio* and thus the defendant had not been seised of suit before the limitation date.[150] In two further cases the plaintiffs were allowed a rather different form of what amounted to a confession and avoidance, one that tacitly admitted that the defendant's ancestor or predecessor in title had been seised of suit before the limitation date but pleaded a subsequent transaction under which the title to the suit had been renounced. In one, the plaintiff claimed that the tenement had been in the hands of a predecessor of the abbess since the limitation date and had then been regranted to him on terms that freed him from any liability to suit and that he had performed no suit since the grant. The defendant responded by admitting this recent feoffment but asserting that the terms of the feoffment had required the plaintiff not merely to pay rent but also to perform the services owed for the tenement of old and customarily performed for it (*faciendo servicia antiquitus inde debita et consueta*) and offering to prove that suit had been customarily performed for it. The issue that went to the jury was on the terms of this feoffment.[151] In the other the plaintiff pleaded a remission of part of the rent owed for the tenement on the marriage of the plaintiff's father to the lord's daughter after the limitation date and an acknowledgement that only that rent and forinsec service was owed for the tenement (thereby tacitly renouncing any

[148] These are Cases 72B (forced to perform suit through heavy distraints often made during the previous twenty years), 81D (forced to perform suit fifteen years ago by heavy distraints).

[149] Case 83C. [150] Case 83A.

[151] Case 93C. For another case whose enrolment has been badly damaged but in which the plaintiff's replication may refer to two enfeoffments made after the limitation date without reserving suit and the defendant's response may assert post-limitation date seisin as his title see Case 70A.

entitlement to suit). He subsequently added that his father had indeed ceased performing suit thereafter. The defendant responded that the lord who had made the remission had been continuously seised of the suit before and after the limitation date. The parties then joined issue on whether or not the lord had been in continuous seisin before and after the limitation date.[152]

THE USE OF CHARTERS OF FEOFFMENT GRANTING LAND TO BE HELD BY A FIXED SERVICE '*PRO OMNI SERVICIO*'

When the legislation on suit of court was re-enacted in 1267 a clause was added apparently exempting those who held charters enfeoffing them for a certain service *pro omni servicio* from the performance either of suit or of any other service in addition to that mentioned in the charter.[153] The clause was not entirely clear on what it meant by a 'certain' service. It cited as an example the rent of so many shillings a year but gave no other instances. There were potentially two ways in which the clause could be invoked in the action of *contra formam feoffamenti* as a way of rebutting a lord's claim to suit. One was by a specific mention of it in the plaintiff's opening count; the other was in the plaintiff's response to the defendant's avowry (justification) of a distraint for suit of court.

The earliest case of *contra formam feoffamenti* in which such a charter is known to have been pleaded and produced in court is one of 1276. In it the plaintiff seems to have mentioned the charter in his opening count.[154] The charter was one from the defendant's predecessor granting the tenement from which suit was being demanded to be held for the service of twelve pence *pro omni servicio*. This was clearly a charter which fell within the scope of the clause and ought to have ensured the plaintiff's freedom from suit. The defendant was, however, allowed to respond to the charter (which seems to have been granted before 1230) as though it was an ordinary charter made before that date and allowed to offer to prove title through his house's seisin of the suit at the hands of the wife's father before the limitation date. An equal lack of respect was shown for such a charter in a case pleaded in Trinity term 1283.[155] Here the lord responded to a general allegation of unjust distraint to compel the performance of three-weekly suit by claiming that he had been seised of such suit prior to 1242 at the hands of the father of the tenant. The tenant in response produced the charter of enfeoffment made after 1242 by which the lord had enfeoffed his father to hold for a rent of thirty-one shillings and eight pence *pro omni servicio*. He did not use it as a

[152] Case 96A. [153] Above, p. 189. [154] Case 76C. [155] Case 83A.

bar to the claim, simply as evidence that the lord could not have been seised before 1242, and it was this question of fact which then went to a jury. More readily understandable perhaps is what happened in the 1285 Northamptonshire eyre case in which the defendant (but only towards the end of pleading) produced an original feoffment of his predecessor in title by the lord's predecessor in title to hold the tenement (with other tenements) for twelve shillings *pro omni servicio*.[156] As neither party was privy (as either one of the parties or one of their heirs) to the parties in the original deed the tenant could not use it as an absolute bar but used it merely to demonstrate that suit had not originally been owed for the tenement.

The next case in which such a charter is mentioned is the action apparently brought by a special writ in Hilary term 1288 (*Hulme v. Baynard*). Here the plaintiff's writ (and probably also his count) specifically mentioned the original charter by which the defendant's great-grandmother had enfeoffed the plaintiff's father for two shillings a year for all service and the defendant's father had confirmed the tenement for the same service.[157] The lord again tried to justify the distraint on the grounds that his ancestors had been seised of the suit before 1242 and he had also been seised during his own time as lord; but the plaintiff said that it required some later specialty to overcome the evidence of the two deeds showing that no suit was owed for the tenement. This time the court agreed that mere seisin of the suit was not enough to create an obligation to perform the suit. There is nothing to explain the court's change of mind for the case is not reported. Nor, as we shall see, was the precedent it appeared to have set followed thereafter.

The first subsequent case in which a *pro omni servicio* charter was pleaded was another Norfolk case heard in Trinity term 1289.[158] This was brought by an ordinary writ but the plaintiff's count (as enrolled) began by mentioning a grant made by the lord's father to the tenant's mother, conceding the tenement concerned to be held for twelve pence a year *pro omni servicio*, and ended with a proffer of the charter. This charter was probably made after 1242 for the lord's response was not to offer to prove seisin before 1242 but to offer to prove the seisin of his father and his grandmother before the making of the charter, at the time it was made, and subsequently. Issue was then joined on this. In the following Michaelmas term another plaintiff brought an ordinary writ but in his count claimed to hold for homage and five shillings *pro omni servicio* and produced a deed in the name of Roger de Cramaville and of Henry de Cramaville (of whom the defendant was the heir) attesting that the tenement had been granted

[156] Discussed above, pp. 222–3. [157] Case 88A. [158] Case 89D.

to Robert de Feypo (whose assign the tenant claimed to be) for the said rent *pro omni servicio*.[159] In response the lord simply offered to prove that he and his ancestors had been seised of suit before 1242. The tenant then produced a further deed in the name of William de Feypo (the heir of Robert de Feypo) granting the tenant the tenements for the services due to the chief lords. The tenant asked for judgment as to whether seisin could create a title in the particular case of an enfeoffment to hold for a certain service of so much rent for all service when the Statute (whose wording he cited) specifically said that a tenant enfeoffed in this way was not to be obliged to anything in addition to what was in his charter. The case was adjourned for judgment, an indication that the argument was felt to be a strong one but that the court needed more time to think about it.

Another litigant that same term seems to have been even less lucky, though we know this only by chance. The plea roll records that Richard Peres had brought a case of *contra formam feoffamenti* against Milisent de Montalt (who sought and obtained the aid of her parcener, John de Hastings) alleging that he held two virgates in Whipsnade for six shillings *pro omni servicio* and that neither he nor his ancestors holding the tenement had performed suit customarily before 1242 but that he had been distrained by Milisent to perform three-weekly suit.[160] The defendants in reply claimed that they and their ancestors had been seised of the suit before 1242 and ever since, and issue was joined on this. There is nothing here to indicate that Richard had produced a charter or had attempted to rely on it. But a complaint made to the king and his council against one of the justices of the Bench, William of Brunton, shortly afterwards tells a quite different story.[161] What had really happened, Richard asserted, when the defendant had made her defence, was that his attorney had proffered a charter of feoffment and a confirmation of that feoffment by the defendant's grandfather to his grandfather which had discharged the tenement of all services other than the six shillings annual rent. The plaintiff (or his lawyers) had then specifically appealed to the doctrine laid down in *Hulme v. Baynard*,[162] and asked for judgment as to whether the defendant could avow for suit against the deeds of her ancestors, since she had no specialty of later date which obliged the tenement to the performance of suit. Brunton had, however, allegedly out of favour for the defendant, refused to allow this exception or its enrolment and had

[159] Case 89F. [160] Case 89G.

[161] SC 8/107, no. 5338. Brunton was dismissed from the Common Bench at the beginning of 1290, shortly after hearing the case.

[162] Peres even enclosed with his petition a copy of the plea roll record of *Hulme v. Baynard* which he had been trying to use as a precedent.

threatened to give judgment against the plaintiff if his attorney would not deny the seisin which the defendant was offering to aver. Eventually he had told the clerk to enter on the plea roll that the plaintiff's attorney had traversed the issue tendered by the defendant. But it seems not just to have been favour for Milisent and John that decided the day in 1289 for the sequel indicates that the court had in effect decided to abandon the doctrine of *Hulme*'s case and return to the earlier doctrine which had allowed lords to use subsequent seisin as a response even to a charter for service certain *pro omni servicio*. Richard Peres was told to go to Chancery and to purchase a writ to bring the record and process of the case before King's Bench. He does not, however, seem to have done so,[163] nor does he seem to have been one of those who made further complaints against Brunton during 1290.[164] Instead, after proceedings in the original action had been allowed to lapse, probably after Hilary term 1290,[165] he seems to have commenced his action anew in Easter term 1291.[166] When issue was joined in Hilary term 1292, even though the tenant's count specifically referred to the form of his feoffment as being for homage, six shillings and a pound of cumin the defendant was again allowed to offer to aver seisin before the limitation date and ever since as her title.[167]

This was in accordance with the rules followed in a number of other cases of the early 1290s. In Hilary term 1290 William of Layer sued Luke of Little Broxstead, claiming to hold his tenement of him by homage and six pence rent *pro omni servicio* but alleging that he had been distrained for three-weekly suit.[168] The lord attempted to justify the distraint on the basis that the tenant's ancestors had done suit before 1242. It was only in response to this that the tenant tried to make use of a charter granted by the lord's ancestor to his ancestor granting the land for six pence *pro omni servicio* and again cited the Statute of Marlborough (this time by name) as barring any claim for additional services when the tenant had such a charter.[169] The defendant was, however, successful in arguing that, even where tenants were not obliged by their charters to perform suit, they were obliged to its performance if they or their ancestors had done it before 1242 and successfully offered to prove such seisin. Something similar may have happened in a second case of Hilary term 1291 in which

[163] There is no record of the case in the King's Bench plea rolls between Michaelmas 1289 and Michaelmas 1291.

[164] See JUST 1/541B *passim* for charges made against Brunton at this time.

[165] CP 40/81, m. 101d seems to be the last entry.

[166] In that term an order was given to the sheriff of Bedfordshire for the attachment of the defendant, the plaintiff having failed previously to find pledges to prosecute: CP 40/89, m. 36.

[167] Case 92B. [168] Case 90A.

[169] The enrolment misses the essential point that this rule applied only to *pro omni servicio* charters but it seems likely that the defendant's counsel got it right.

the plaintiff claimed to hold for ten shillings 'for all service' and offering a charter of one Maynard of Newbold granting him the tenement for ten shillings *pro omnibus serviciis* but in which the lord was able to plead seisin before and after 1242 as his title.[170] In two cases heard in the Staffordshire eyre of 1293,[171] plaintiffs proffered *pro omni servicio* charters and claimed that they were not held to suit but the defendant claimed that his ancestors had been seised of suit before 1242 and sought judgment whether he was not entitled to avow such seisin. Clearly the court was again unfavourable to the view that such charters could be used to bar claims for suit, and the defendants were driven to traversing the seisin. Both plaintiffs, obviously disappointed in their hopes, were non-suited before a verdict was given. There is no subsequent evidence of plaintiffs in *contra formam feoffamenti* suits even attempting to use such charters.[172]

SOCIAL AND GEOGRAPHICAL ANALYSIS OF THE PLEADED CASES

Thus far we have been concerned mainly with the legal dynamics and workings of the action of *contra formam feoffamenti*. The details provided by the pleaded cases, however, allow us to do rather more than this. It is also possible to say something about the identity and the holdings of the plaintiffs in these actions and the identity of the defendants and the nature and location of the courts to which suit was being claimed.

The standard form of count for plaintiffs developed in and after 1267 generally (but by no means invariably) specified the plaintiff's holding as part of the first element of the count. Of those counts which do mention the nature of the plaintiff's holding five mention holdings consisting of one knight's fee or larger,[173] and a further four describe that holding as consisting of a whole manor.[174] At the other extreme, eleven holdings mentioned are of less than twenty acres of arable, though some of these may have been rendered more valuable by the appurtenances that went with them.[175] The other holdings seem all to fall somewhere between these: either fractions of anything between one-twentieth and one-half

[170] Case 91C (but this case was complicated by devolutions of both the tenancy and the lordship).

[171] Cases 93A, 93B.

[172] But see below, pp. 257–62, for the use of such charters in actions of replevin.

[173] For land in seven villages held by homage and two and one-eighth knight's fees see Case 91A; for land in six villages held for two knight's fees see Case 72B; for land held for one knight's fee see Case 80A; for a manor held for homage and one knight's fee see Case 88D; for one messuage and two carucates then held in frankmarriage but which will subsequently owe one knight's fee see Case 89C.

[174] Cases 88B, 89E, 91E, 92D.

[175] The smallest of these seems to be the five acres and one-third of a messuage mentioned in Case 89B and the one messuage mentioned in Case 93C.

of a knight's fee; holdings denominated in ferlings, carucates, bovates or virgates; or holdings of twenty acres or larger. Despite the origins of this form of action in legislation sparked off by ecclesiastical complaints, ecclesiastics were not particularly common as plaintiffs in the pleaded cases. They included just one rector of a parish church (himself suing a prior), four abbots and one prior.[176]

It is more difficult to say much about the lords mentioned in these cases for their holdings or seignories are not specified in the course of pleading. It is none the less interesting, in view of the probable origins of the legislation authorising the action in a complaint of an ecclesiastical council, to note that no fewer than twelve of the defendants (in fourteen different cases) were the heads of religious houses;[177] that a further four cases were brought against three successive archbishops of York;[178] and that one other case was brought against the master of a chapel.[179] Of the lay defendants, at least seventeen men and women seem to have been of baronial status or above,[180] and twenty-three (involved in a total of thirty cases) seem to have been members of the substantial gentry.[181] Only twenty-four (involved in twenty-six cases) were apparently lesser men and women.[182] This may simply reflect the pattern of the distribution of the possession of private courts among the members of these groups. The line between plaintiffs and defendants does not seem to have been a very significant one, for there is at least one example of a man who was a plaintiff in a 1278 case himself in turn being sued in a case only five years later.[183] We also find the reverse phenomenon, of a man being sued by

176 The rector is in Case 79A, the abbots in Cases 83B, 84B, 85E, 90C, and the prior in Case 90B.

177 Cases 70B, 72D, 72E, 76C, 79A, 85C, 91B, 91F, 92C, 93C, 99A, 99B, 01A, 06A.

178 Cases 77A, 78D, 92F, 02A. 179 Case 94A.

180 The men include Norman d'Arcy, Roger la Zouche, Baldwin Wake, Robert de Ros, Hugh de Oddingesells, Roger de Somery, Gerard de Furnivall, William son of Thomas of Greystoke, John son of William of Greystoke, John de Bellew and Gilbert de Gaunt. The women include Isabel d'Aubigny, Milisent de Montalt, Parnel, the wife of William of Narford and Isabel de Forz, countess of Aumale.

181 These include William Constable of Halsham, Geoffrey Gacelyn, Lucy of Kyme, Denise de Mountchesney, Robert de Grey and his wife, Lucy, William Belet and his wife, Margery, William de Saham, Andrew de Neville, Franco le Tyeys, Nicholas de Meynill, Master William and Peter de Montfort, Ranulph de Neville, Richard Malebysse, Walter of Rothbury and his wife, Isabel, Peter Rocelyn, William and Isabel de Ros, Roger de Lasceles, Henry de Cramaville, Alan fitzRoald, Peter de Rocheford, Marmaduke of Thweng, Robert fitzJohn and Mauger le Vavasur.

182 These include Maud de Estur of Gatcombe, Nicholaa, the widow of Jordan of Askeby, Adam Gerdeling, Simon of North Leverton, John of Sharstead, Walter of Ousefleet, William de Barneville and his wife, Christine, Richard Foliot, William of Felton, William of Goldingham, Robert of Tudham, James son of Geoffrey Baynard, Nicholas Lowys, Luke of Little Broxtead, Grimbald le Fraunceys, Richard of Dalby and his wife, Alice, Ralph de Glyn, William Ryvel of Fenny Neubold, Walter son of Nicholas of Grendale, Alice de Boseville, William of Atton, Richard de Friville, and John fitzReginald of Londesborough.

183 See Cases 78A, 83B.

four different plaintiffs between 1280 and 1285 and then himself suing two other defendants in litigation pleaded in 1289 and 1292.[184]

It is still more difficult to classify with any degree of certainty the nature of the courts to which the suit was said to be owed. Thirty-three of them were located in the same village as the tenement from which the suit was said to be owed and are probably for the most part manorial courts. Thirty-six of the courts were in other villages. Some of these were clearly honorial courts, others less certainly of this kind. In the remainder, the enrolment records where the court is located but not the location of the tenement from which the suit was said to be due. What does seem rather more remarkable is the geographical distribution of these courts. They were located in twenty-two different counties. Most counties account for between one and four cases each, but three provide significantly more. Lincolnshire and Norfolk account for eight pleaded cases each; Yorkshire for a massive thirty-six cases, well in excess of one-third of all pleaded cases. It is less clear what the explanation for this is. Maybe suit of court was particularly contentious in Yorkshire; it may also be that the bringing of cases was sufficiently frequent in this county to draw the attention of other litigants and lawyers to the possibility of doing so.

THE OUTCOME OF THE PLEADED CASES

By far the most common outcome for pleaded cases of *contra formam feoffamenti* was for them simply to disappear from the rolls after issue had been joined for jury trial (or in one case, wager of law)[185] without any recorded verdict. This was what happened in forty-seven of the ninety-five pleaded cases. In most of these it seems likely that the plaintiff simply ceased at some stage to sue out further process in the case or died, and that neither of these facts was formally recorded on the plea roll at the end of the relevant enrolment. A non-suit may reflect an out-of-court settlement, exhaustion of the plaintiff's resources or a belief that the jury was likely to give its verdict against him. The plaintiff's non-suit after joinder of issue for jury trial is specifically mentioned in a further six cases,[186] and the non-suit or death of the plaintiff can be deduced from other evidence in two more.[187] Four cases disappear from the rolls after

[184] For the suits against Andrew de Neville see Cases 80D, 83C, 84B, 85A. For the suits brought by Andrew see Cases 89C, 92D.

[185] Case 76A.

[186] Cases 89E, 91A (but only recorded in CP 40/101, m. 46 at Trinity term 1293), 91H, 93A, 93B, 93C.

[187] Case 89G, where the plaintiff's non-suit can be deduced from the subsequent revival of the same suit in case 92B; Case 92D, where the plaintiff's non-suit or death can be deduced from the revival of the suit by his heir in 1298 in Case 98B.

the granting of aid-prayer;[188] another four after inconclusive pleading.[189] In all these cases the most probable explanation is that the plaintiff ceased to prosecute but the defendant did not take care to have his non-suit recorded by the court.

Of the cases where a final outcome is recorded, eleven were decided by the judgment of the court without any kind of preliminary jury verdict. In three of these, the plaintiff secured the permanent release of his distresses and an interim freedom from distraint for suit of court simply on grounds of the defendant's repeated failure to appear, through a default judgment.[190] In one other case the defendant lost on the basis of the pleading in the case, without the need for jury trial.[191] In the other seven cases so decided judgment was given in favour of the defendant. In one this was because the plaintiff simply failed to make any count against him;[192] in the other six because of defects in the plaintiff's writ.[193] Fifteen were decided by the verdict of a jury. The recorded jury verdicts are disproportionately in favour of plaintiffs. There are eleven of these as against only four in favour of defendants. In two of these eleven (where the defendants were a doweress and a tenant in curtesy and the reversioner had not been prayed in aid) the judgment given was not one that made any longer-term determination that suit was not due, deciding merely that the defendant was not entitled to claim it, but the plaintiffs did also win damages of one hundred shillings and half a mark respectively.[194] In the other nine, the judgment based on the verdict really does seem to have settled the matter of entitlement on a more permanent basis. In one case no damages were awarded but the defendant was remanded to gaol pending payment of a fine for having distrained after receipt of a prohibition.[195] Damages were awarded in all other cases but the amounts varied from sums as small as ten,[196] twenty[197] or forty shillings[198] up to as much as one hundred shillings.[199] The four jury verdicts in favour of defendants all found their distraints to have been justified. The earliest judgment (in a case of 1278) awarded damages of one mark to the defendant.[200] No such award was made in the other three cases but they did award the return of the distresses taken to the defendant.[201]

188 Cases 80C, 89C, 90B, 91E. 189 Cases 85D, 89F, 92A, 02A.

190 Above, pp. 215–16. 191 Above, p. 235. 192 Case 92C.

193 For its failure to name the defendant's wife, whose right the court was, in Cases 72A, 89A; for omission of the word *predicte* after *provisionis* in Case 93E; for mentioning the wrong limitation period in Case 01A (and see above, pp. 209–10); for not being an appropriate party to bring the action (above, p. 220). The reasons for judgment in the other case are unknown (above, p. 222).

194 Cases 74B, 75A. 195 Case 80E. 196 Case 91C. 197 In Cases 80D, 81C, 87B.

198 In Case 85A. 199 In Cases 70B, 83C, 00A. 200 In Case 78C.

201 In Cases 84A, 91F, 99B.

Eight other disputes about liability to perform suit of court were settled by some kind of agreement. Only four of the eight seem to have been reached at the same time as the case was pleaded. In all four the lord remitted some or all of the suit he had been claiming.[202] In the remaining four several years seem to have elapsed between the pleading of the case and the eventual settlement. In three the settlement led to the lord remitting some or all of the suit he had been claiming,[203] but in one the terms of the settlement confirmed the lord's entitlement to the suit she had been claiming.[204] One other case adjourned at the request of the parties after the defendant had made only a formal defence and which then disappears was also presumably settled, but out of court.[205]

Appendix: List of pleaded cases of contra formam feoffamenti *heard between 1267 and 1307*

The following is a list of all the cases of *contra formam feoffamenti* for which pleading is recorded that were heard after the enactment of the Statute of Marlborough in 1267. It is arranged chronologically, with a note of where the enrolment of the case is to be found and any identified reports of the case. Unless otherwise stated the cases were heard in the Common Bench and only the term when they were heard is noted. The list excludes cases where judgment was given by default in the absence of the defendant, even though it seems likely that some pleading took place in these cases.

To save space in the footnotes to this chapter, each of the cases has also been allocated a brief case reference number. The number is the final two digits of the year in which the case was heard; the letter provides a unique reference for each case heard that year.

[202] There is no recorded pleading in *Godwin Beche v. Gilbert Pecche* which was settled by a final concord in Hilary term 1271 under which the lord waived all suit except a twice-yearly attendance at his court (CP 25(1)/25/32, no. 17), but for earlier process in this case see KB 26/200A, m. 7d; Case 72B was settled by a final concord under which the lord remitted all claim to suit for twenty marks: *Final Concords of the County of Lincoln, 1244–1272,* ed. C.W. Foster (Lincoln Record Society vol. 17, 1920), p. 241, no. 3; Case 79A was settled by a concord (enrolled with the pleading) quitclaiming the suit; Case 85E was settled by a concord there remitting the suit as we learn from the 1290 fin fet suit between the same parties enrolled on CP 40/82, m. 33d.

[203] Case 76B was in effect settled through a final concord in 1281, though this was based on a separate action of customs and services: *Feet of Fines for Essex*, vol. II, ed. R.E.G. Kirk and E.F. Kirk (Essex Archaeological Society, 1913–28), p. 32; Cases 77A and 78D were both settled by releases of all except special suit by the archbishop's successor in 1290: *The Register of John le Romeyn, lord archbishop of York, 1286–1296*, ed. W. Brown (2 vols., Surtees Society vols. 123 and 128: 1913 and 1917), II, 67–8.

[204] Case 80A settled by final concord in the 1285 Essex eyre: *Feet of Fines for Essex, vol. II*, p. 46, no. 288.

[205] Case 93D.

1268

Case 68A: *Stephen of Hatfield v. Master of the Templars*: JUST 1/1050, m. 26 (Yorkshire eyre)
Total: 1

1270

Case 70A: *Robert of Gloucester v. William Constable of Halsham*: KB 26/200C, m. 14d (Michaelmas)
Case 70B: *Stephen of Englebourne v. prior of Totnes*: JUST 1/178, m. 5d (Devon eyre)
Total: 2

1271

[No pleaded cases: but see 72B below]
Total: Nil

1272

Case 72A: *John la Ware v. Geoffrey Gacelyn and Richard of Horne*: KB 26/206, m. 2 (Hilary)
Case 72B: *Ralph fitzSimon v. Norman d'Arcy*: JUST 1/483, m. 46d (Lincolnshire eyre of 1271–2)
Case 72C: *John de la Brygge v. Maud de Estur of Gatcombe*: JUST 1/779A, m. 25 (Hampshire eyre)
Case 72D: *Reginald Cherewind v. prior of Barnwell*: JUST 1/84, m. 19 (Cambridgeshire eyre); reports: Merton College, Oxford MS. 321, ff. 43r–v; BL MS. Additional 31826, ff. 43r–v
Case 72E: *Guy de Waterville v. abbot of Peterborough*: JUST 1/344B, m. 9 (Huntingdonshire eyre)
Total: 5

1273

[No pleaded cases]
Total: Nil

1274

Case 74A: *William of Normanton v. Nicholaa widow of Jordan of Askeby*: CP 40/5, m. 4d (Michaelmas)
Case 74B: *John of Gaddesden v. Roger la Zouche*: CP 40/5, m. 8d (Michaelmas)
Total: 2

1275

Case 75A: *Ralph de Normanville v. Lucy de Kyme*: CP 40/9, m. 10 (Easter); report: *EELR*, vol. 1, 31–2
Total: 1

1276

Case 76A: *Henry le Parmenter v. Adam Gerdeling*: CP 40/13, m. 18d (Hilary)
Case 76B: *Thomas son of Lambert of Moulton v. Denise de Munchesney*: CP 40/14, m. 33d (Easter)
Case 76C: *Ralph son of Richard of Danby and wife v. abbot of Chester et al.*: CP 40/15, m. 59 (Trinity)
Total: 3

1277

Case 77A: *John son of Stephen Passemer v. Walter archbishop of York*: CP 40/19, m. 26 (Easter)
Total: 1

1278

Case 78A: *Nicholas Meynill v. Robert de Ros*: CP 40/26, m. 9d (Michaelmas)
Case 78B: *John Brennand of South Leverton v. Simon of North Leverton*: CP 40/26, m. 76 (Michaelmas)
Case 78C: *Hugh of Boothby v. Baldwin Wake*: CP 40/26, m. 77 (Michaelmas)
Case 78D: *John Hauteyn v. Walter archbishop of York*: CP 40/26, m. 102 (Michaelmas)
Total: 4

1279

Case 79A: *Thomas of Sharstead rector of Purley v. Thomas prior of Christ Church Canterbury*: CP 40/29, m. 3 (Easter)
Case 79B: *Robert of Gedding v. Hugh de Oddingesells*: CP 40/29, m. 60 (Easter)
Case 79C: *Thomas of Rampeston v. Robert de Grey and his wife Lucy*: CP 40/31, m. 106 (Michaelmas)
Total: 3

1280

Case 80A: *Gilbert Bakun and his wife Sabina v. Denise de Munchesney*: CP 40/32, m. 39d (Hilary)
Case 80B: *Ralph of Marham v. William Belet and his wife Margery*: CP 40/32, m. 69 (Hilary)
Case 80C: *Maud de Somery v. William de Saham*: CP 40/36, m. 46 (Michaelmas)
Case 80D: *William fitz Ellis v. Andrew de Neville*: JUST 1/1065, m. 30d (Yorkshire eyre 1279–81: Hilary 1280 session)
Case 80E: *John Sibri and his wife Sibyl v. Franco le Tyeys*: JUST 1/1067, m. 38 (Yorkshire eyre 1279–81: Michaelmas 1280 session)
Total: 5

1281

Case 81A: *Robert Payn of Newport Pagnel v. Roger de Somery*: CP 40/42, m. 71 (Michaelmas)

Case 81B: *Andrew de Scharneburg v. Isabel d'Aubigny*: CP 40/42, m. 85d (Michaelmas)
Case 81C: *Sara of Linstead v. John of Sharstead*: CP 40/42, m. 134d (Michaelmas)
Case 81D: *John son of Eve of Ousefleet v. Walter of Ousefleet*: JUST 1/501, m. 26d (Lincolnshire eyre 1281–4: Trinity 1281 session)
Total: 4

1282

82A: *Roger Warner of Tonworth v. William de Barneville and his wife Christine*: CP 40/47, m. 67d (Michaelmas)
Total: 1

1283

Case 83A: *John Deuyas (?or Denyas) v. Richard Foliot*: CP 40/50, m. 16 (Trinity)
Case 83B: *Abbot of Rievaulx v. Nicholas de Meynil*: CP 40/50, m. 28 (Trinity)
Case 83C: *Geoffrey of Pikehale v. Andrew de Neville*: CP 40/51, m. 63d (Michaelmas)
Total: 3

1284

Case 84A: *Ralph fitzRalph fitzFulk v. Gerard de Furnivall*: CP 40/52, m. 29 (Hilary)
Case 84B: *Abbot of Fountains v. Andrew de Neville*: CP 40/55, m. 62d (Michaelmas)
Case 84C: *William son of William de Murers v. prior of Sixhills*: JUST 1/496, m. 4d (Lincolnshire eyre 1281–4: Easter 1284 session)
Total: 3

1285

Case 85A: *Agnes of Morton v. Andrew de Neville*: CP 40/59, m. 12 (Trinity)
Case 85B: *Ralph de Lasceles v. William son of Thomas of Greystoke*: CP 40/59, m. 55 (Trinity)
Case 85C: *John Sewale and his wife Alice, Robert of Eliland and his wife Margery, John of Swaffham and his wife Alice and Reginald le Shireve v. prior of Westacre*: CP 40/60, m. 73d (Michaelmas)
Case 85D: *William Aylmer of Boddington v. William of Felton*: JUST 1/622, m. 21d (Northamptonshire eyre); report: in a single report found in five different manuscripts: BL MSS. Stowe 386, ff. 199r–v, Additional 5925, f. 94r, Additional 37657, ff. 62v–63r, Harley 493A, ff. 246v–247r and in LI MS. Hale 188, f. 44r.
Case 85E: *Abbot of Pipewell v. William of Goldingham*: Northants eyre: JUST 1/622, m. 48d (Northamptonshire eyre)
Total: 5

1286

Case 86A: *Richard Malebys v. John de Bellewe*: CP 40/61, m. 30 (Hilary)
Total: 1

1287

Case 87A: *Hugh de Oddingesells v. Master William de Montfort and Peter de Montfort*: CP 40/66, m. 15d (Hilary)
Case 87B: *Roger of Abington v. Robert of Tudham*: CP 40/68, m. 25d (Trinity)
Total: 2

1288

Case 88A: *Godfrey son of Nicholas of Hulme v. James son of Geoffrey Baynard* (special writ): CP 40/70, m. 50d (Hilary)
Case 88B: *John of Bulmer v. Rannulph de Neville*: CP 40/73, m. 76d (Trinity)
Case 88C: *Peter de la Stane v. Gilbert de Gaunt*: CP 40/75, m. 15 (Michaelmas)
Case 88D: *Edmund Maunsayl v. Richard Malebysse*: CP 40/75, m. 143 (Michaelmas)
Total: 4

1289

Case 89A: *William Batekyng v. Nicholas Lowys*: CP 40/78, m. 13d (Easter)
Case 89B: *Paulinus Toke and his wife Sarra v. William Belet and his wife Margery*: CP 40/78, m. 47 (Easter)
Case 89C: *Andrew de Neville v. Walter of Rothbury and his wife Isabel*: CP 40/78, m. 68d (Easter)
Case 89D: *John of Yarmouth v. Peter Rocelyn*: CP 40/79, m. 87d (Trinity)
Case 89E: *Gilbert de Neville v. William and Isabel de Ros*: CP 40/80, m. 16 (Michaelmas)
Case 89F: *Henry de Clerbek v. Henry de Cramaville*: CP 40/80, m. 45d (Michaelmas)
Case 89G: *Richard Peres v. Milisent de Montalt*: CP 40/80, m. 58 (Michaelmas)
Case 89H: *Picot of Staverton v. Roger de Lasceles*: CP 40/80, m. 77d (Michaelmas)
Case 89I: *Ralph de Lascelles v. John son of William of Graystoke*: CP 40/80, m. 156 (Michaelmas)
Total: 9

1290

Case 90A: *William de Leyre v. Luke of Little Broxtead*: CP 40/81, m. 13d (Hilary)
Case 90B: *Prior of Rumburgh v. William of Narford and his wife Parnel*: CP 40/86, m. 94d (Michaelmas)
Case 90C: *Abbot of St Agatha v. Grimbald le Fraunceys*: CP 40/86, m. 175 (Michaelmas)
Case 90D: *Joce le Scrope of Coleby v. Richard of Dalby and his wife Alice*: CP 40/86, m. 192 (Michaelmas)
Case 90E: *Richard Mile of Waleton v. Alan fitzRoald*: CP 40/86, m. 226d (Michaelmas)
Case 90F: *William de Valeys v. Ralph de Glyn*: CP 40/86, m. 254 (Michaelmas)
Total: 6

1291

Case 91A: *Thomas of Lincoln v. Isabel de Ros*: CP 40/87, m. 33d (Hilary)
Case 91B: *Ace of Yarborough v. William prior of Alvingham*: CP 40/87, m. 69 (Hilary)

Case 91C: *William Boydyn of Stratton v. William Ryvel of Fenny Newbold*: CP 40/87, m. 89 (Hilary)
Case 91D: *William of Besingby v. Walter son of Nicholas of Grendale*: CP 40/89, m. 90 (Easter)
Case 91E: *William de Boyvill v. Isabel de Forz, countess of Aumale*: CP 40/89, m. 93 (Easter)
Case 91F: *Robert Smith of Yarborough and his wife Mabel v. William prior of Alvingham*: CP 40/89, m. 19d (Trinity)
Case 91G: *Adam Breertewysil, William Bynethegate and John de Skyres v. Alice de Boseville*: CP 40/90, m. 87 (Trinity)
Case 91H: *John de Kent of Coleby v. Isabel de Ros*: CP 40/91, m. 199 (Michaelmas)
Total: 8

1292

Case 92A: *Hugh de la Warde v. William of Atton*: CP 40/92, m. 153 (Hilary); report: *YB 20 & 21 Edward I*, pp. 356, 367–8.
Case 92B: *Richard Peres v. Milisent de Montalt*: CP 40/92, m. 193d (Hilary)
Case 92C: *John le Bere v. abbot of Ramsey*: CP 40/93, m. 48 (Easter)
Case 92D: *Andrew de Neville v. Peter of Rotherfield*: CP 40/93, m. 68d (Easter)
Case 92E: *Mabel widow of John de Coudre v. Richard de Friville*: CP 40/96, m. 16 (Michaelmas); report: *YB 21 & 22 Edward I*, pp. 147–51
Case 92F: *William son of William of Carthorpe v. John archbishop of York*: CP 40/96, m. 256 (Michaelmas)
Total: 6

1293

Case 93A: *John Brown v. Robert son of Robert of Meleburn*: JUST 1/804, m. 18 (Staffordshire eyre)
Case 93B: *Richard Merus v. Robert son of Robert of Meleburn*: JUST 1/804, m. 18 (Staffordshire eyre)
Case 93C: *Adam Savage v. Sarra abbess of Malling*: JUST 1/375, m. 51 (Kent eyre)
Case 93D: *William of Easington of Lund v. Marmaduke of Thweng*: JUST 1/1084, m. 23 (1293–4 Yorkshire eyre: Michaelmas 1293 session)
Case 93E: *Richard son of Alan of Trehampton v. Roger de Lascelles*: JUST 1/1085, m. 36 (1293–4 Yorkshire eyre: Michaelmas 1293 session)
Total: 5

1294

Case 94A: *Alexander Wymer of Skerning v. Thomas de St Quintin master of chapel of St Nicholas of Rugholme of Gressenhall*: CP 40/106, m. 151d (Michaelmas)
Total: 1

1295

[No pleaded cases]
Total: None

1296

Case 96A: *William son of Godfrey of Shulton v. Robert fitzJohn*: CP 40/115, m. 185 (Michaelmas)
Total: 1

1297

[No pleaded cases]
Total: None

1298

Case 98A: *Robert of Middleton v. Mauger le Vavasur*: CP 40/125, m. 11 (Michaelmas)
Case 98B: *Jollan de Neville v. Peter de Rocheford*: M: CP 40/125, m. 108d (Michaelmas)
Total: 2

1299

Case 99A: *William de Bozhale v. Benedict abbot of St Mary, York*: CP 40/126, m. 159d (Hilary)
Case 99B: *Simon de Fribois of Ruddeston v. Benedict abbot of St Mary, York*: CP 40/129, m. 133d (Trinity)
Total: 2

1300

Case 00A: *William Mattheu of Langtoft v. John fitzReginald [of Londesborough]*: CP 40/134, m. 115 (Trinity); reports: Harvard MS. 206, f. 90v; CUL Ee.6.18. ff. 41v–42r; BL MS. Additional 37657, f. 27v; BL MS. Stowe 386, f. 120v (tentative identifications)
Case 00B: *William Sturmy v. John fitzReginald [of Londesborough]*: CP 40/134, m. 153d (Trinity); report: LI MS. Hale 188, f. 44v.
Total: 2

1301

Case 01A: *John son of Peter de Seyville v. William prior of Pontefract and his bailiff Walter of Sutton*: CP 40/135, m. 179d (Michaelmas); report: BL MS. Additional 31826, f. 119r and (of a later stage) LI MS. Miscellaneous 738, f. 17v (but this identification is a tentative one)
Total: 1

1302

Case 02A: *John son of William of Carthorpe v. Thomas archbishop of York*: CP 40/141, m. 57 (Hilary)
Total: 1

1303

[No pleaded cases]
Total: None

1304

[No pleaded cases]
Total: None

1305

[No pleaded cases]
Total: None

1306

Case 06A: *William Salter v. Robert abbot of Tavistock*: CP 40/158, m. 188d (Hilary)

1307

[No pleaded cases]
Total: None

Chapter 9

OTHER MECHANISMS FOR THE ENFORCEMENT OF CHAPTER 9; OTHER REFORMS AFFECTING THE LORD–TENANT RELATIONSHIP

The previous chapter told what constitutes the largest part of the story of the enforcement of chapter 9 of the Statute of Marlborough after 1267, that of the development and use of the action of *contra formam feoffamenti* during the following four decades. This chapter looks at a number of other aspects of that history: the continued failure to create the statutory action for lords envisaged by the legislation; the early fourteenth-century developments which saw the rules about entitlement to suit of court laid down by the legislation applied in the non-statutory action of replevin and a significant reinterpretation of the statutory provisions barring any claims for additional services from those enfeoffed to hold for a fixed, specific service; and the creation and application of actions to give effect to that part of chapter 9 which governed liability for the performance of suit in the event of the division of a tenement obliged to perform suit of court. It also looks briefly at the post-1267 history of a second reform that was intended to provide protection to tenants against the abuse of their rights by lords. What became chapter 16 of the Statute of Marlborough allowed tenants to recover damages in the assize of mort d'ancestor and its congeners, if they had to bring these actions to secure the return of lands which had been held in wardship or by right of primer seisin. Already prior to 1267 this had been extended to allow tenants to recover damages against lords who usurped the wardship of lands held of them by services that did not entitle them to wardship. The chapter also looks at the use and interpretation of another chapter of the Statute likewise connected with lord–tenant relations, but unequivocally intended for the protection of lords. This is chapter 6 which protected lords against the use of conveyancing devices by their tenants that resulted in the lord losing his rights of wardship and marriage over the heirs of those tenants. The chapter concludes by looking at the curious history of one of the clauses which had been included in the original Provisions of Westminster of 1259 but had been dropped from the reissues of 1263 and 1264 and was also excluded from the Statute of Marlborough: the provision requiring alienations in mortmain to have the consent of the lord of whom the land to be alienated was held. Within twenty years of the enactment of the Statute of Marlborough it was wrongly supposed to have formed part of the statute and it was a discussion of the status of this legislation, as will be seen, that formed a significant part of the background to the enactment of the Statute of Mortmain in 1279. As will also be seen, even the enactment of that statute did not end attempts to enforce this earlier, repealed legislation.

THE LORD'S ACTION AUTHORISED BY CHAPTER 9

There is plentiful evidence for the existence and working of the tenant's action created by clause 3 of the Provisions of Westminster and continued by chapter 9 of the Statute of Marlborough, the action of *contra formam feoffamenti*. Care had also been taken in the same clause to authorise the creation of a matching lord's action for asserting the lord's right to suit withdrawn by his tenant after the enactment of the legislation.[1] Chapter 9 of the Statute of Marlborough had renewed that authorisation. T.F.T. Plucknett assumed that the lord's action must have come into existence and even went so far as to give it a name (*de secto subtracto*).[2] But there is no evidence for the creation or use of this lord's action, whether before or after 1267. There are no entries on the plea rolls of cases brought using it. Nor is there any evidence from registers of writs or the Chancery rolls of the drafting of an appropriate form of original writ for initiating such a case. That it was never created or used is hardly surprising. By the last quarter of the thirteenth century most lords seem to have preferred the use of extra-judicial distraint to any form of litigation as a means of securing the performance of services, including suit of court, which they thought were in arrears and they were normally in a position to do this.[3] All they lost by using distraint rather than the lord's action authorised by the Statute was the right to recover damages in respect of the withdrawal and against these would have had to be set the costs and inconvenience of bringing the litigation. The lord who was unable or unwilling to use distraint could still use the existing common law action of customs and services, which had the added advantage of allowing the lord to claim any other services that were in arrears at the same time. The minor procedural advantages which the statutory lord's action would have had over the action of customs and services were removed by the legislation of 1263 and 1275, which speeded up mesne process in the action of customs and

[1] Above, p. 52.

[2] Plucknett, *Statutes*, p. 92; Plucknett, *Legislation*, p. 67. This ought to have been *de secta subtracta*.

[3] Brand, *MCL*, pp. 321–4.

services as in other personal actions.[4] If lords had been able (as originally proposed) to recover suit by default in the action some might have been attracted into using it; once this possibility was removed in the course of drafting it is hardly surprising that the lord's action authorised and envisaged by the statute was still-born.[5]

THE APPLICATION OF THE STATUTORY RULES ABOUT SUIT IN COMMON LAW ACTIONS

If it was the intention of the legislators to ensure that all litigation about the use of distraint to enforce the performance of suit of court was conducted through the new statutory action of *contra formam feoffamenti*, as seems likely, the legislation manifestly failed in its objective. As has already been seen, there were, or came to be, a number of different reasons why a tenant might prefer, or might be compelled, to use the action of replevin rather than the action of *contra formam feoffamenti* to challenge his lord's distraint for suit of court.[6] Just how often actions of replevin that were brought and finally determined in county courts revolved in part or in whole about the use of distraint to enforce the performance of suit of court is unknowable since the records of county courts do not survive. It is, none the less, a reasonable assumption that there were a fairly large number of such cases, for the legislation had not actually prohibited continuation of the existing, and increasingly popular, practice of determining whether or not a particular distraint, even a distraint for suit, had been justified through the action of replevin, and almost all replevin litigation was initiated in the county courts. All that is known for certain is the number of actions of replevin removed out of the county courts into the Common Bench which included avowries in which the lord justified his distraint as being (though usually only in part) for suit of court. There are around 367 such replevin cases during the reign of Edward I. The question of whether or not distraint for suit of court was justified was therefore, in practice, much more likely to be determined, even in the Common Bench, by replevin than by *contra formam feoffamenti*, for even in the Common Bench replevin cases which raised the question of entitlement to suit of court were around four times as common as pleaded cases of *contra formam feoffamenti*.

That most litigation about the justification of distraint to perform suit of court took the form of actions of replevin rather than actions of *contra formam feoffamenti* was of considerable significance, because quite different rules about that entitlement applied in the two actions. Under

[4] Above, p. 148; below, pp. 306–7. [5] Above, pp. 52, 53. [6] Above, pp. 219–20.

the rules which applied in the action of replevin prior to 1285, a lord was only entitled to distrain for arrears of any service (including suit) if he had himself been in seisin of that service or his immediate ancestor or predecessor had died in seisin of it. Legislation enacted in 1285 made it a somewhat less possessory action. The lord was now entitled to distrain for a service if he could show his own seisin of that service or that of an ancestor or predecessor at any time since 1242.[7] In the action of *contra formam feoffamenti*, by contrast, a lord would only succeed in justifying his distraint for suit if he could show seisin on the part of himself, his ancestor or predecessor prior to 1242 or, after the reversion in 1303 to the limitation date authorised by the statute, prior to 1230.[8]

The first suggestion that the new statutory rules about suit of court might still be applicable even if the form of action being used was not that created by the statute occurs quite soon after the enactment of the original legislation and in an action of customs and services, rather than an action of replevin. The case was one heard in the 1263 Kent eyre, probably shortly after its justices had been notified of the reissuing of the Provisions.[9] Robert le Blund of Newington was suing Roger Beselet and his brother Stephen through an action of customs and services for the services he claimed they owed him for the messuage and half an acre they held of him in Newington. These were a rent of sixteen pence, two hens and five eggs a year and three-weekly suit to his court of Newington. His claim was that he had been seised of both rent and suit at the hands of the defendants until two years previously when they had ceased to pay or perform them. The tenants admitted owing the rent but denied that it was in arrears. They also denied owing the suit on the grounds that they had been enfeoffed of the holding by Robert's ancestor(s) by a charter which had made no mention of suit of court.[10] The justices then intervened to ask Robert about his title to claim suit contrary to the tenor of their charter. His reply cited only his own seisin for a period of years that did not take him back before 1230.[11] The court held that as his claim was based on his own seisin after 1230 and this had been acquired in contravention of the terms of their feoffment this claim should, in accordance with the legislation (referred to as the 'Provisions of Oxford'), be dismissed.[12]

[7] Brand, *MCL*, pp. 292–4. [8] Above, pp. 208–12. [9] JUST 1/363, m. 28.

[10] 'Quia dicunt quod ipsi feofati fuerunt de antecessoribus predicti Roberti per cartam, ita quod nulla mencio facta est in eadem carta quod teneantur ad aliquam sectam faciendam.'

[11] The precise number of years can no longer be read because of damage to the plea roll.

[12] 'Et quia idem Robertus nichil aliud ostendit per quod ei tenetur in predicta secta nisi de seisina sua post primam transfretacionem domini [regis in Britanniam et] contra formam feofamenti sui consideratum est secundum provisionem Oxon' quod predictus Rogerus et Stephanus quo ad predictam sectam sine die et Robertus nichil capiat per breve istud set sit in misericordia pro falso clamore etc.'

But this doctrine, which would have made the rules about suit of court contained in the legislation of general validity rather than rules which could only be invoked in the statutory action, was not followed in any subsequent case prior to the early fourteenth century. The occasional litigant evidently attempted to argue that it should be. This is what seems to have happened in a case of 1277. The plea roll enrolment of the case records an avowry by the bishop of Salisbury on Theobald de Verdun as tenant of the Wiltshire manor of Wilsford for the services of homage, fealty, three-weekly suit of court and the provision of a candle for the great altar of Salisbury cathedral. The bishop justified the distraint as having been made for arrears of the homage and the suit. The roll then records an adjournment of the case at the request of the parties. A report, however, tells us rather more of the ultimately inconclusive argument in the case.[13] This suggests that the bishop cited as his title for making the distraint the seisin of these services enjoyed by his predecessor, Bishop Walter (who had died in 1271), at the hands of Theobald's father, John, and his claim that he had acted with the requisite expedition after his succession to the see to continue his predecessor's seisin. Theobald's counsel, in response, is reported as claiming that it was necessary for a lord claiming suit (or, the report suggests, other services)[14] to ground his claim either on the terms of the tenant's feoffment or on a long-continued seisin of them 'before the time limited by statute', but that the original feoffment in this case required only the provision of the candle. If Theobald's father had performed additional services this was only as a result of wrongful distraints made against him. The statute cited must be the Statute of Marlborough and counsel seems to be arguing for the application of the statutory rules in this common law action of replevin. The bishop's counsel responded that an action of replevin was not the correct way of deciding questions of entitlement to services. The action was trespassory in nature and all the defendant needed to make a successful defence was to show his predecessor's seisin of the services for which he had distrained. The report ends with a rather confused version of a speech by the chief justice, Master Roger of Seaton, that appears to accept the plaintiff's argument for the application of the statutory rules. However, no final judgment is recorded in the case. The case certainly did not lead to any kind of more general breakthrough in the application of the Statute outside the statutory action.

[13] *EELR*, I, 71–4 (1277.1).

[14] It is unclear whether counsel really did make a claim quite as extensive as this, or whether the reporter misheard what was said.

That came only in 1305, in a replevin action brought by Nicholas del Auney against the abbot of Tavistock.[15] Nicholas was the tenant of three Cornish manors which were held of the abbot by homage and fealty and the service of four knights' fees. The abbot claimed that Nicholas also owed suit of court every three weeks to the abbot's Devonshire court of Hardwick and avowed a distraint made to ensure performance of that suit on the basis of his own seisin at the hands of William, his father. The enrolment records that Nicholas responded by citing the Statute of Marlborough (chapter 9) for the proposition that no one was to be distrained for suit unless he was obliged to perform it by the terms of his feoffment or because he or his ancestors had performed suit before Henry III's voyage to Brittany (in 1230) and his offer to prove that neither the abbot nor any of his predecessors had ever been seised of the suit prior to 1230. The enrolment then records an initial response by the abbot citing the subsequent statute of Edward I (Westminster II, ch. 2) for the proposition that a justifiable distraint could be avowed by a lord for services of which the lord had been seised at the hands of his tenant since the first voyage of Henry III to Gascony (1242) and offering to prove that he and his predecessors had indeed been seised of the suit since 1242. He asked for judgment whether this did not mean that his distraint was justified. A *postea* then adds, but without explanation, a subsequent tacit waiver of this line of argument by the abbot and his offer to prove that his predecessors had been seised of suit at the hands of the ancestors of Nicholas prior to 1230. This issue then went to a jury drawn from both counties, with no recorded verdict or final outcome.

This case is also reported in five apparently independent reports.[16] These indicate that counsel for the tenant did indeed respond immediately and directly to the initial avowry by invoking the provisions of the Statute of Marlborough to show that any tenant holding by ancient enfeoffment without charter was not liable to distraint to make him perform suit, if he could show that neither he nor his predecessors had performed that suit prior to 1230. They also indicate that counsel for the abbot initially objected simply that replevin was not the appropriate action for attempting to invoke the provisions of the statute. This should be done, he argued, through the statutory action of *contra formam feoffamenti*. That action would be rendered valueless if such a plea was to be allowed in the more possessory common law action. Chief Justice Hengham was

[15] CP 40/153, m. 372.

[16] *YB 33–35 Edward I*, 79–83; BL MS. Additional 31826, fol. 333v (and in a shorter form in BL MS. Hargrave 375, fols. 133r–v); LI MS. Misc. 738, fol. 40r; Bodleian MS. Holkham Misc. 30, fols. 87v–88r; BL MS. Harley 25, fols. 125v–126r [=BL MS. Additional 35116, fol. 181v].

unsympathetic to this argument, citing the very specific words of the statute as prohibiting the use of distraint unless the lord could show the kind of title the statute required. He subsequently compelled the lord to answer over. It was only then that counsel for the lord went on to make the second response, the one recorded on the plea roll, arguing that the provisions of the later statute (Westminster II, ch. 2) allowed the lord to distrain if he could show that he or an ancestor or predecessor had been seised of a service since 1242. The reporters seem to have had some difficulty in understanding the response made by the plaintiff's counsel to this argument, since all seem to give a more or less garbled version of it. He seems to have argued that the later statute did not, even tacitly, repeal the earlier one. For suit of court, at least, there was a higher standard which could be invoked by the tenant. The lord could only distrain if he could show title to the suit as well as a possessory right. The former could only be shown by proving a pre-1230 seisin. But Hengham seems not, at this stage at least, to have been very convinced by this argument. He reproved counsel for 'glossing' the Statute and suggested that it was common for one statute to repeal the provisions of another. The case seems then to have been adjourned for judgment to a later day the same term.[17] It was only then, and probably after consulting with his colleagues, that Hengham seems to have determined that the lord would have to show seisin prior to 1230. One report specifically comments that Kinsham joined issued on this point as he feared that judgment would go against him if he demurred.

The case marks less of a dramatic turning-point than might at first sight appear. It did apparently establish that if a plaintiff in a replevin case specifically invoked the statutory rules about suit of court he could make the lord justify his distraint by reference to the statutory criterion of pre-1230 seisin. What it did not mean was that henceforward the courts would automatically apply the statutory rules in every replevin case where the lord avowed a distraint as having been made to compel the performance of suit. There certainly continued to be cases where lord and tenant joined issue, apparently without any difficulty, on the question of whether or not the lord or his predecessor in title had been seised of the suit for which he had distrained since 1242.[18]

[17] An adjournment for judgment as to the kind of seisin to be proved by the lord is mentioned in BL MS. Harley 25, fols. 125v–126r [=BL MS. Additional 35116, fol. 181v]; a final stage of argument on a subsequent day is mentioned in Bodleian MS. Holkham Misc. 30, fols. 87v–88r.

[18] For subsequent cases in which defendants were allowed to justify distraints by reference to post-1242 seisin see *John son of Hugh of Ancaster v. prior of Wilsford*: CP 40/158, m. 176d (Hilary term 1306); *Michael atteRye v. John de Benefield and others*: CP 40/164, m. 181 (Trinity term 1307).

THE PLEADING OF '*PRO OMNI SERVICIO*' CHARTERS IN REPLEVIN CASES

There are a succession of replevin cases from the middle years of the reign of Edward I onwards in which a tenant's claim to hold for lesser services than those specified by the lord in his avowry was explicitly based on a charter from the lord or a predecessor in title, granting him the tenement for these lesser services 'for all service', or quitclaiming or renouncing additional services hitherto performed for the tenement. This is precisely the kind of situation in which the additional sentence added to the legislation on suit of court when it was re-enacted as chapter 9 of the Statute of Marlborough in 1267 appeared to provide that the tenant was to be protected from such claims.[19] In practice, however, as will be seen, the courts down to the early years of the fourteenth century adopted a very restrictive interpretation of the statutory provisions that robbed them of all, or almost all, practical effect; and it was only a major change in the interpretation of the Statute during the years just after 1300 that began for the first time to give real protection to tenants who possessed such charters.

The question is first recorded as arising in a replevin case of 1288. A lord avowed on his tenant as owing him the services of homage, three-weekly suit and a rent of twelve shillings and six pence and claimed that his distraint had been made because the rent was two years in arrears.[20] In response the tenant produced a charter from the lord's great-great-grandfather, granting the tenements to his father to be held for the service of just three shillings a year 'for all service' (*pro omni servicio*). The tenant asked for the court's judgment as to whether the lord was entitled to avow for any additional services contrary to the deed of his ancestor. The lord did not deny the charter but simply pleaded his own seisin of the rent for which he had distrained at the hands of the tenant for twenty years prior to the distraint. He asked for judgment as to whether or not such a long and peaceful seisin was a good title to make a distraint. The court gave judgment in favour of the lord. The clear implication is that a charter of feoffment for lesser services, even if technically within the provisions of the Statute of Marlborough, could not be pleaded in this action to avoid a subsequent seisin of greater services. In 1290 Hugh de Courtenay avowed a distraint made against the abbot of Ford as tenant both of the site of his abbey and of various other (unspecified) manors in return for the rather unusual services of providing him with an iron-wheeled

[19] Above, pp. 189–90. But for the restrictive interpretation of the same sub-clause adopted in most actions of *contra formam feoffamenti* during the same period see above, pp. 234–8.

[20] *Theobald de Brochole v. John Butler and others*: CP 40/75, m. 48.

cart and cart-horse in wartime, of looking after two destriers or palfreys plus their two grooms at the abbey and of providing the horses with saddlecloths, and of looking after a female greyhound or brachet and its pups until they were one year old. Hugh claimed that his father had been seised of all these services at the hands of the abbot's predecessor.[21] In response the abbot produced a charter from the abbey's founder, Alice, the daughter of Baldwin (de Redvers), granting the abbey all the tenements now part of Hugh's fee to hold in frankalmoin quit of all secular service plus a second charter from Hugh's grandfather confirming the manor of Thorcombe (where the distraint had been made) to be held by the same service. Despite the charters, Hugh was allowed to plead in avoidance seisin of the services claimed both by his father and by himself. Eventually the abbot, unable to deny that these services had been performed, was driven to pleading that this was not by way of fulfilment of a tenurial obligation but merely as a curtesy, a fitting gesture for an abbot to perform in respect of the patron of his abbey. A report of the same case indicates that Chief Justice Mettingham thought it relevant that the charter of feoffment had been made prior to 1242 (the date after which the lord had to show seisin of services if he was to succeed in an action of replevin under the provisions of Westminster II, ch. 2) and that the lord had shown seisin after that date. Mettingham also later distinguished between services owed *de jure* under the terms of a feoffment and services performed *de facto* and insisted that all that a lord needed to succeed in making an avowry in replevin was to prove possession of the latter. The report does not, however, mention any specific attempt by the abbot to rely on this particular sentence in chapter 9 of the Statute of Marlborough.[22]

Tenants were no more successful in pleading confirmations, whether these had been made by the lords who were making the distraints for additional services or by their predecessors in title. In a replevin case of 1288 a lord avowed for arrears of suit of court, of which he had been seised at the tenant's hands, together with other (unspecified) services.[23] In response the tenant produced the lord's own charter, apparently granting him the land to hold for a rose 'for all services, suits of court and all other demands'.[24] The lord claimed that a former tenant of the same tenement, one Philip Clerk, had owed suit for the tenement as well as other services

[21] CP 40/86, m. 163d.

[22] Versions of a single report of this case survive in four different MSS.: LI MS. Hale 188, fols. 33r–v, BL MSS. Harley 25, fols. 135v–136r [=BL MS. Additional 35116, fols. 163v–164r] and Harley 2183, fols. 102r–103r.

[23] *John de Esthale v. Richard de Cornewaile and William Hayward*: CP 40/70, m. 78.

[24] '. . . pro omnibus serviciis, sectis curie et omnibus aliis demandis.'

and that it had been Philip who had enfeoffed the tenant of the land, presumably by substitution and to hold for the same services. He was allowed to plead in avoidance of his own charter, effectively a charter of confirmation, that he had been seised of the suit before the making of the tenant's charter and after it as well. Evidence of seisin of additional services (here suit of court) was allowed to trump the evidence of the lord's own charter, but the lord did have to show seisin both before and after the making of the charter of confirmation. In a 1290 case the lord avowed on the tenant as holding a messuage and a bovate for the service of homage and half a mark rent, claiming that the distraint had been made because the rent was sixteen years in arrears.[25] The tenant's response was to proffer a charter from the lord's father to his father, showing he had granted him the tenement for the rent of only one penny a year. That this was again a charter of confirmation rather than an original charter of feoffment is shown by the lord then being allowed to plead in answer to the charter that his father had been in seisin of the higher rent before the making of the charter, at the time of its making and since, and that he too had been seised of it until sixteen years previously.

The change to a more literal, indeed more faithful, interpretation of the provisions of chapter 9 of the Statute of Marlborough arguably began with the case of the *Prior of St Andrew's, York v. Alice, widow of Peter de la Lunde*, heard in Michaelmas term 1303.[26] In this case the lord asserted that the prior held five bovates of her in Bugthorpe by homage, fealty, an annual wapentake fine of four pence and the service of one-tenth of a knight's fee. She avowed her distraint as having been made for homage and sixteen years arrears of the wapentake fine and claimed that she had been seised of these services at the hands of the prior's predecessor, John de Morers. In reply, the prior traced the previous history of the tenement from which the services were being demanded. He started with the tenure of the tenement by Jordan son of Geoffrey Breton of Bugthorpe, who had held of Robert son of Roger de Chauncy. Jordan had granted the tenement to the plaintiff's predecessor to hold in frankalmoin, a grant confirmed by his lord, Robert. Subsequently Alice had acquired the seignory of this tenement from Thomas, the son of Robert de Chauncy. The prior asked whether Alice was allowed to avow for additional services contrary to the deed of Robert, confirming the gift in frankalmoin, since she now had the estate of Thomas and Thomas would have been bound by his father's deed. Alice claimed that the prior had formerly held

[25] *William de la Sale of Wyardestone v. Henry de Skone*: CP 40/82, m. 110.
[26] Enrolled on CP 40/145, m. 196d; reported in *YB 30 & 31 Edward I*, pp. 379–83.

the tenements by the services she was now claiming of Walter de Gray, who had been mesne lord between the prior and Thomas de Chauncy; that on Walter's death without issue his mesne lordship had escheated to Thomas, as Walter had been a bastard, and Thomas had subsequently been seised of the services by way of escheat. Alice too had been seised of them after the grant of the lordship. These were, she argued, sufficient grounds for her to be able to claim additional services without contravening the original confirmation issued by Robert de Chauncy.[27] The prior continued to assert that he held in frankalmoin and that his tenure had been confirmed in writing by Robert de Chauncy. He called in aid the provisions of chapter 9 of the Statute of Marlborough which stipulated that no one who had been enfeoffed by charter was to be obliged to perform other services than those contained in that charter.[28] But the heart of the prior's plea was really an argument about proof. He argued that Alice should not be permitted by the court to attempt to undo the effect of Robert's charter on the basis of her own unsupported assertion (*simplicem vocem*) of a subsequent, and legitimate, acquisition of entitlement to the services, even if that was to be tried by a jury. After an adjournment made at the request of the parties, Alice defaulted and the case then disappears from the rolls without leaving any further trace.[29] It is in this case that for the first time, as far as we can see, a tenant used chapter 9 of the Statute of Marlborough in an attempt to bar a claim for additional services based on a later seisin of those services.[30] The lord appears to have accepted that the charter would indeed bar such a claim unless she could show a subsequent and legitimate acquisition of title to those services.

The new understanding of the relevant part of ch. 9 of the Statute of Marlborough emerges even more clearly in the case of *Simon of Holcombe v. William de Pyn* heard in Michaelmas term 1304.[31] William asserted that Simon held a messuage and one and a half ferlings for homage, fealty,

[27] For evidence indicating that Walter de Gray, a canon of York, and namesake and probable relative of Archbishop Walter Gray, had acquired his property in Bugthorpe of Jordan of Bugthorpe and to be held of Jordan and his heirs, for 200 marks in 1253 see E 326/575 and E 210/149 (*Catalogue of Ancient Deeds*, I, 268 and III, 422). In an action of escheat brought in 1278 Jordan's son Geoffrey claimed this property had been held of his father and ought to have escheated to him, but that it was currently held by Peter del Lund and his wife, Agnes, the lord in the 1303 case: CP 40/27, m. 83.

[28] '. . . ac in statuto Marleberge contineatur quod nullus feoffatus per cartam ad alia servitia teneatur nisi ad ea que in ipsa carta contineantur.'

[29] Alice had in fact died in the interim: see *CIPM*, IV, no. 212.

[30] Though note that the report suggests that it may have been Chief Justice Hengham who first raised the question of the applicability of ch. 9 of Marlborough to the facts of this case.

[31] The case is enrolled on CP 40/149, m. 352. It is reported in BL MS. Harley 25, fols. 123v–124r [=BL MS. Additional 35116, fols. 179v–180r] and (less fully) in CUL MS. Ee.6.18, fols. 93v–94r.

a rent of six shillings, scutage at the rate of twenty-two shillings and six pence to a forty-shilling scutage and three-weekly suit to his court; that he had been seised of all these services at the hands of Simon's father; and that he had distrained for arrears of the rent and suit. In response Simon produced the original enfeoffment of Baldwin son of Ailward by William's grandfather, Hugh, to hold by six shillings only 'for all service, exaction etc.'; traced how the tenement had then passed by way of substitution from Baldwin to Simon's father, Richard, to hold for the same service; and showed that William's father, Peter, had confirmed Richard's tenure of the tenement in accordance with the terms of Baldwin's original charter. He then invoked ch. 9 of the Statute of Marlborough and its provision that when a tenant was enfeoffed to hold for a certain service he was not to be distrained for other services contrary to the terms of his feoffment. He asked for judgment as to whether William was allowed to avow a distraint for suit contrary to the terms of the deeds of his ancestors. No judgment was given on this point, but Simon withdrew in contempt of court and William recovered his damages and secured the permanent release of the distresses taken from him. The reports of this case show that pleading in the case was rather more complex than the enrolment would suggest. They show that counsel for the lord (Tilton) tried the classic argument found in the older cases, that the subsequent seisin he had shown of the suit in effect voided the charters, but that this was rejected by the court. They also show that the same counsel then tried to invoke the authority of ch. 9 of the Statute of Marlborough as allowing the lord to distrain for suit of court if he could show seisin of the suit prior to 1230 and offering to prove such seisin. Counsel for the tenant (Harle) in response distinguished between the two different parts of the chapter. There was indeed a general provision about distraint for suit which allowed lords who could show such seisin to distrain; but there was also the specific provision about tenants who could show they had been enfeoffed for certain services that barred them from being distrained for suit, irrespective of whether or not the lord could show pre-1230 seisin. This interpretation was confirmed by the justices when they looked at the Statute. The final argument, which went wholly unrecorded in the enrolment, adopted a similar stategy to that adopted by the lord in the previous case. Counsel for the lord argued finally that, after the deeds had been made, the lord's ancestor had recovered the tenement by a judgment of the king's court and subsequently regranted the land to the tenant to hold by the services now claimed. He thus had an entitlement to the services that was unaffected by the terms of the previous deeds. There was a further parallel with the previous case, however. It was because he had no evidence to support this claim that he then withdrew, an acknowledgement that such a claim could only be made with written evidence to back it up.

Although a remark of Howard, J. in a case of 1306, if it is reported correctly, suggests that he was of the opinion that it was a good answer to a plea using a charter for fixed services to bar a claim to additional services to plead seisin of the additional services prior to 1230, there is no other evidence to suggest any acceptance of this viewpoint by the courts.[32] Two other pleaded cases of the final years of the reign of Edward I do indeed show lords apparently accepting the new doctrine but finding other possible answers to such charters when produced against them. In a case of 1305 the lord avowed on the tenant as holding a toft by homage, fealty, suit every three weeks and a rent of twelve pence and on the basis of his own seisin of these services at the hands of the plaintiff's brother. He avowed the distraint as made for homage.[33] The tenant in response produced a charter from the lord's grandfather to his own grandfather granting him the toft for the service of twelve pence 'for all service', asserting (under the terms of ch. 9 of the Statute) that this barred the lord from claiming additional services. The lord did not deny this claim or this view of the law but did assert that the toft mentioned in the charter was a different one. Issue was then taken on this point. In a case of 1307, the lord avowed on the tenant as holding a messuage and an acre by the service of fealty, two shillings, two attendances at his court and providing him with twelve gallons of ale each time he brewed, and asserted that he had been seised of these services at the tenant's own hands. He avowed his distraint as made for forty-eight gallons of ale owed him in respect of four brewings.[34] In response the tenant produced what he claimed to be a charter from the lord's father, granting the tenement to the tenant and his wife for a rent of two shillings 'for all services except the service of the king'. He asked for judgment whether the lord could properly avow for services other than those contained in the charter. Instead of arguing that, even on its own terms, the charter was not covered by the 'service certain' clause because of the uncertainty of the king's service, the lord simply denied that it was his father's deed and the parties joined issue on this point.

32 *YB 33–35 Edward I*, pp. 339–49 at p. 343. But there is no mention of this in a second report of the same case found in BL MSS. Hargrave 375, fols. 171v–172v and Harley 2183, fols. 97v, 98r and 99r–v. It does, however, also correspond with the view expressed in passing by the Common Bench serjeant Mablethorpe in a report of the 1305 case of *Del Auney v. abbot of Tavistock* in BL MS. Additional 31826, fol. 333v.

33 *Richard of Applegarth v. David of Flitwick*: CP 40/156, m. 201.

34 *Henry son of William of Mitcheldean v. John of Abinghall*: CP 40/164, m. 182d.

THE CREATION AND USE OF ACTIONS RELATING TO LIABILITY FOR THE PERFORMANCE OF SUIT ON THE DIVISION OF A TENEMENT

Clause 2 of the Provisions of Westminster of 1259 and the corresponding section of chapter 9 of the Statute of Marlborough had created a set of rules about what was to happen when a tenement which owed suit of court was divided. Neither said anything about creating corresponding statutory actions for their enforcement.[35] This was none the less what happened, though only relatively gradually, over the period of just under half a century between the initial enactment of the legislation and the end of the reign of Edward I.

Actions against lords claiming multiple suits

The earliest of these actions for which there is any evidence is that for the tenants of a divided inheritance to use against a lord who was distraining them to perform more than one suit for a holding which had previously owed only one. Although there is nothing on the surviving plea rolls of the period between 1263 and 1267 to show it, there is some later evidence to suggest that this period may have seen the drafting of two different writ forms for this purpose.[36] The earliest action of this type found on surviving plea rolls comes from after 1267. It is a case of which a procedural stage only is enrolled on the Common Bench roll for Easter term 1271.[37] The alleged circumstances of the case, as revealed by the terms of the writ recited in the enrolment, were that the plaintiff wife's father had acquired a parcel of land at Hannington in Northamptonshire from Ralph atteChurch of Hannington and that the plaintiffs were now being distrained for suit in respect of that land, despite the fact that Ralph's heir was continuing to perform suit for Ralph's other land. The writ was a writ of summons to answer for making the distraint and cited the legislation, with appropriate modifications to fit the circumstances of the case.[38] Enough can be read of a second, but damaged, enrolment of

[35] Above, pp. 51–3. [36] Above, pp. 178–9.

[37] *Henry Grauntvic and his wife Maud v. Henry Wardedeu*: KB 26/202, m. 6d.

[38] '. . . de placito quare, cum de consilio regis provisum sit quod si hereditas aliqua de qua unica secta debebatur ad plures heredes vel alio modo per vendicionem vel donacionem devolvatur, unica fiat secta sicut prius inde fieri consuevit, et Radulphus Attechirche de Hanyton quandam partem hereditatis sue in Hanyton de qua unica secta prefato Henrico Wardedeu et antecessoribus suis debebatur Waltero Prikemere patri predicte Matillidis, cujus heres ipsa est, per cartam suam dederat, ut dicitur, idem Henricus Wardedeu, quamvis heres prefati Radulphi sectam illam pro dicta hereditate ei adhuc faciat, sicut prius fieri consuevit, predictos Henricum Grantvic et Matillidem distringit ad sectam faciendam ad curiam suam predictam occasione partis sue predicte ad grave dampnum eorundem Henrici Grauntvic et Matillidis et contra formam provisionis predicte etc.'

litigation in King's Bench in Michaelmas term 1274 to deduce that the John de la Fenne who was bringing the litigation against the sheriff of Wiltshire for distraining him to perform suit to a Wiltshire hundred court was claiming to be the purchaser of part of the inheritance of Alexander Ewyas and that the tenant of another part of the same inheritance (Geoffrey Huse) was performing the suit which Alexander and his ancestors had previously owed for the inheritance. This suggests that in this case the whole of the inheritance had passed to third parties.[39] Here, however, the litigation seems to have come to the court only after a first, disregarded prohibition and as the result of a second prohibition that gave the sheriff the alternatives of compliance or appearance to justify his distraint. The sheriff appeared but not the plaintiff. This led to the sheriff being authorised to renew his previous distraint. It is unclear whether or not this is a case of the whole of an inheritance passing by sale to third parties or of purchasers acquiring shares of a divided inheritance from the coheirs. In another case brought the same term in the Common Bench John Muscegros, Joan of Willington and Roger of Burghill were suing John Giffard of Brimpsfield for distraining them to perform separate suits for their shares of the inheritance of Henry de Miners in Down Hatherley to his court of Badgeworth. The writ as summarised in the enrolment recited the relevant part of the legislation and explained some, but not all, of the circumstances of the case: the devolution of Henry's inheritance to the plaintiffs; and the single suit which had been performed for it in Henry's time. It required John Giffard to answer for distraining them to perform separate suits to his court against the form of the provision and a prior prohibition.[40] What the writ does not make clear is quite how Henry's inheritance had come to the plaintiffs. It is only other evidence that allows us to see that only one of the three (Roger of Burghill) was an heir in blood of one of the three daughters between whom the inheritance had been divided and the other two had evidently acquired their shares of these tenements.[41] By Trinity term 1276 that litigation had evidently been dropped but the litigation had been revived in the name

[39] KB 27/11, m. 22.

[40] '. . . de placito quare cum de communi consilio regni nostri provisum sit quod si hereditas aliqua de qua unica secta tantum debeatur ad plures heredes participes ejusdem hereditatis seu ad alios per vendicionem vel alio modo devolvatur unica tantum fiat secta pro hereditate illa sicut prius fieri consuevit, ac quedam terre et tenementa que fuerunt Henrici de Miners in Dunhatherleye pro quibus unica tantum secta ad curiam predicti Johannis Gyffard de Beggeworth temporibus ipsius Henrici fieri consuevit ad prefatos . . . sit devoluta ut dicitur, idem Johannes Gyffard prefatos . . . distringit ad diversas sectas pro porcionibus ipsos inde contingentibus separatim faciendas ad curiam suam predictam contra formam provisionis predicte et prohibicionem etc.'

[41] *VCH Gloucestershire*, x, 85–6; *Placita de Quo Warranto*, ed. W. Illingworth and J. Caley (London, 1818), p. 264.

of John Muscegros' widow, Cecilia, plus the same two co-plaintiffs.[42] There were probably one or more purchasers of shares of the inheritance of Adam de la Graunge among the five plaintiffs (two accompanied by their husbands) who were suing Isabel de Forz, countess of Aumale in Trinity term 1285 for distraining them to perform separate suits to her court of Topsham in Devon contrary to the terms of the provision and in breach of a prior prohibition. Again the writ summarises the relevant part of the legislation and then goes on to give some of the circumstances of the case (the devolution of the inheritance to the plaintiffs and the single suit previously owed for the inheritance) before requiring the countess to answer for the distraint, but again it does not explain how the inheritance had passed to the plaintiffs or characterise them as parceners.[43] In Trinity term 1292 John Basset of North Luffenham and Ralph Trille and his wife, Maud, were suing named bailiffs of William de Beauchamp for distraining them to perform separate suits to William's Rutland hundred of Wrongdike in respect of an inheritance for which a single suit had previously been owed. The enrolment indicates that the legislation was recited in the writ and that the devolution of the inheritance to them was as parceners by sale, and the continuing distraint was said to be in breach of a prior prohibition.[44] Although the defendant bailiffs appeared in court no substantive pleading took place because Ralph and Maud did not appear. The case was adjourned to allow them to be summoned to sue with John.[45] The whole of an inheritance seems to have passed by sale to third parties (though perhaps again only by the sale of the parceners who had inherited it) in a further case heard in Hilary term 1307 in which William Waryn of Itteringham and three other plaintiffs sued Simon Crepping and his wife, Maud, for distraining them for

[42] CP 40/15, m. 59d.

[43] '. . . de placito quare cum de communi consilio regni regis provisum sit quod si hereditas aliqua de qua unica secta tantum debebatur ad plures heredes participes ejusdem hereditatis vel alios per vendicionem aut alio modo devolvatur unica tantum fiat secta pro hereditate illa sicut prius fieri consuevit, ac quedam hereditas que fuit Ade de la Graunge in villa de Sancto Leonardo de qua unica secta tantum debetur ad curiam ipsius comitisse de Toppesham ad predictos . . . sit devoluta, predicta comitissa distringit ipsos . . . ad diversas sectas pro porcionibus suis hereditatis illius separatim faciendas ad curiam suam predictam contra formam provisionis predicte et contra prohibicionem etc.': CP 40/59, m. 81.

[44] '. . . de placito quare cum de communi consilio regni regis provisum sit quod si hereditas aliqua de qua unica secta tantum debebatur ad plures heredes participes ejusdem hereditatis seu ad alios per vendicionem seu alio modo devolvatur unicta tantum fiat secta pro hereditate illa sicut prius fieri consuevit ac quedam hereditas in North Luffenham que fuit Estrilde filie Gilberti pro qua unica secta tantum ad hundredum predicti Willelmi de Wrongdik ad predictos Johannem Basset, Radulphum et Matillidem participes ejusdem hereditatis per vendicionem sit devoluta ut accepimus, iidem Johannes de Neville et Johannes Waryn distrinxerunt prefatos Johannem Basset, Radulphum et Matillidem ad diversas sectas ad curiam predicti domini sui de Wrongham contra formam statuti predicti et contra mandatum regis prius sibi inde directum etc.'

[45] CP 40/95, m. 69.

separate suits to their court of Saxthorpe in Norfolk, in respect of the inheritance of Ketel Strut in Itteringham, which had passed to them and a fourth party by sale. The writ again summarised the legislation and the particular circumstances of the case and spoke of a previous disregarded prohibition.[46]

There are only two cases to be found on the plea rolls in which it is quite clear that the plaintiffs bringing the action are themselves the coheirs of a divided tenement. The first of these is a case brought in Michaelmas term 1278 by John son of Bartholomew and his coheirs, John son of Thomas, Richard son of Henry and Thomas son of Michael, against James of Creake.[47] The writ initiating the litigation seems (from the enrolment) merely to have recited the legislation and the devolution of an inheritance to the plaintiffs for which only a single suit was owed to the defendant's court as parceners and their allegation that the defendant was distraining them for separate suits for their shares of the inheritance contrary to the legislation and to a prior prohibition.[48] The count, however, added flesh to the information contained in the writ by naming the deceased tenant whose inheritance had been divided and the quantity of the tenements inherited from him and the date of delivery of the prohibition. It also added the assertion, not that the eldest coheir was already performing the suit owed for the inheritance, but that he was ready to perform it. However, again no substantive pleading is recorded as taking place. All that is recorded is the defendant's plea that he held his lordship by curtesy and seeking the aid of his wife's son and heir. The second case is one of which only a procedural stage has been traced but in which Thomas of Wiggenden and his two brothers sued the abbot of Ghent and two of his brethren, who were bailiffs of the abbot at Lewisham in Kent, in Hilary term 1283 by a writ reciting the legislation and the circumstances of their case and requiring the defendants to answer for distraining them to perform separate suits to the abbot's court of Lewisham for their portions of the inheritance of William of Wiggenden in Cowden against the form of the provision and in breach of a prior prohibition.[49] In a third

[46] CP 40/162, m. 307d.

[47] CP 40/31, m. 97d. There are earlier stages at CP 40/ 26, m. 152; /29, m. 62d; /30, m. 80d.

[48] '. . . de placito quod cum de communi consilio regni regis provisum sit quod si hereditas aliqua de qua unica secta tantum debebatur ad plures heredes participes ejusdem hereditatis seu ad alios per vendicionem vel alio modo devolvatur unica tantum fiat secta pro hereditate illa sicut prius fieri consuevit, ac quedam hereditas in Antingham ad predictos . . . participes ejusdem hereditatis de qua unica secta tantum debebatur ad curiam predicti Jacobi de Mecton debetur sit devoluta idem Jacobus prefatos . . . distringit ad diversas sectas pro porcionibus ipsos . . . inde contingentibus separatim faciendas ad curiam predicti Jacobi de Mecton contra formam provisionis predicte et contra prohibicionem etc.'

[49] CP 40/48, m. 46d.

case brought in Trinity term 1288 by Denise, widow of Fulk Constable, and five other women and their husbands against John, archbishop of York for distraining them for separate suits to his court of Patrington for their shares of the inheritance of John of Frismarsk in Frismarsk and Colswainsthorpe, the writ of the plaintiffs again recited the legislation and the circumstances of their case (the devolution of John's inheritance to them and the fact that only one suit was owed for it) and required the archbishop to answer for a distraint contrary to the terms of the legislation and in breach of a prohibition. The recital of the circumstances of the case does not make it entirely clear whether or not the plaintiffs were all coheirs of a single inheritance.[50] However, the fact that the litigation was brought in the names of all six but that only one husband and wife were suing and that the case was adjourned to allow the summons of the other nominal co-plaintiffs to join the suit may suggest that they were indeed coheirs.

The relative paucity of cases shows that this never became a common form of action. There is an even greater paucity of cases with pleading on matters of substance. One thing does seem, however, to emerge relatively clearly. Counsel was to allege in a Year Book case from Edward III's reign that the provisions of this part of the Statute of Marlborough did not apply to suit real (suit owed to county and hundred courts), and that on the division of a tenement owing such suit, suit was owed by each parcel, as had been the case with suit service before the passage of the legislation.[51] The evidence from this period suggests, however, that Chancery thought that the legislation did extend to suit real as well as suit service, with the sheriff of Wiltshire being sued in respect of suit to a hundred court still in royal hands and the action brought in the Common Bench in 1292 against the bailiffs of William de Beauchamp for demanding separate suits from two tenants of a single inheritance to William's hundred court of Wrongdike in Rutland.[52] The early fourteenth-century register of writs printed by de Haas and Hall also includes a note also stating that writs prohibiting the demand for several suits from one inheritance can be made for suits due to wapentakes, hundreds, etc.[53] There was also a clear assumption that the legislation applied to suit owed to hundred courts in the complaints made against the lord of one Norfolk hundred (John de

50 CP 40/73, m. 80d.

51 *Year Books 11–12 Edward III: Year Books of the Reign of King Edward the Third: Years XI and XII*, ed A.J. Horwood and L.O. Pike (Rolls Series, London, 1883), pp. 152–8 (as noted by Plucknett, *Legislation*, p. 66, note 1).

52 Above, p. 264, 265.

53 *Early Registers*, p. 256 (R 637). The printed register also includes precedents for the use of such writs in connexion with the demand for suit to either county or hundred courts: *Reg. Omn. Brev.*, fols. 176–176b.

Warenne, earl of Surrey, lord of Gallow) and against the bailiffs of another Norfolk hundred (North Erpingham) for claiming more than one suit from the tenants of divided tenements that owed suit of court in the Hundred Rolls enquiry of 1274–5.[54] Less clear is the complaint made by a petition possibly, but not certainly, belonging to 1278, by which five of the coheirs of Helewise of Leavington (who died in 1278) complained about being distrained for individual suits to the county court of Cumberland when only one suit was owed by the eldest coheir, who was under age and in the king's wardship. They did not, however, specifically appeal to the rule laid down by the legislation and simply asked for an enquiry as to whether the suit was owed by each of them and if it had been customarily performed by each of them.[55]

Actions claiming contributions to the cost of performing suit

The earliest example of an action brought by the eldest coheir against his or her fellow heirs for a contribution towards the costs of performing suit is to be found in 1279–80.[56] The writ summarised the relevant part of the Statute and then set out the particular circumstances of the case in question (the devolution of the inheritance of Master William Oxe in Horton by Farningham in Kent to the plaintiff and the defendant and John of Twytton, the performance of suit to the king's hundred of 'Axton' by the plaintiff as holder of the share of the eldest coheir on behalf of himself and the defendants) and then the refusal of the defendant to contribute to the costs of the plaintiff in performing the suit.[57] In contrast to the action brought against the lord, and for obvious reasons, nothing was said of any prior prohibition. Only the procedural stages of this particular action have been found and it was perhaps settled out of court. A similar form of writ was used in two closely connected cases in the 1287 Gloucestershire eyre in which Adam Spilman and his wife, Margery, sued Margery's younger sister, Lucy, and her husband, John of Wick, for a contribution to the suit

54 *RH*, 1, 455, 498.

55 *Rotuli Parliamentorum* (6 vols., London, 1783), 1, 12, no. 55.

56 *John de St Denis v. Felice of Halstead*: CP 40/31, m. 40d; CP 40/32, m. 85.

57 '. . . de placito quare cum de communi consilio regni regis provisum sit quod si hereditas aliqua de qua unica secta tantum debebatur ad plures participes ejusdem hereditatis seu ad alios per vendicionem vel alio modo devolvatur unica tantum fiat secta pro hereditate illa sicut prius fieri consuevit et quod ille qui habet eyneciam hereditatis illius sectam illam pro se et participibus suis ejusdem hereditatis faciat et participes sui ad sectam illam faciendam contribuant ac quedam hereditas que fuit magistri Willelmi Oxe in Horton prope Frenigham ad predictum Johannem, Johannam de Twytton et predictam Feliciam sit devoluta et predictus Johannes qui habet eyneciam ejusdem hereditatis sectam ad hundredum domini regis de Acstan inde debitam pro se et participibus suis predictis faciat, predicta Felicia ad hoc contribuere contradicit ad grave dampnum ipsius Johannis et contra formam provisionis predicte etc.'

which the plaintiffs were performing on behalf of the lands inherited by the wives from Walter de Bayuse at Randwick to two different courts, the court of the hundred of Wyston and the court of the abbot of Gloucester at Gloucester.[58] Both writs were quashed for drafting defects that had implied the inheritance had descended to the husbands as well as the wives. When the cases were renewed with amended writs later in the same eyre the parties reached a settlement.[59] Similar writs seem also to have been used in three other later cases from Edward I's reign. For none of these has any pleading been traced.[60]

A similar writ was also used in a single pleaded case from the 1288 Sussex eyre, even though the plaintiff's count revealed that the defendants were not his coheirs but had acquired the share of what had been originally a single coheir.[61] This case raised a major problem of interpretation. Did the legislation apply in the case of tenements which had been divided before its enactment? The original division of the tenement from which the suit was owed had taken place in the reign of King John. The defendants claimed that neither the younger sister, immediately after this division, nor any of those who had since held her lands had ever contributed to the cost of the suit. They asked for judgment as to whether a contribution could now be claimed, if the plaintiff could show no seisin of such a contribution 'after the making of the legislation on such contributions'.[62] The plaintiff did not directly traverse this last point but claimed that both the younger sister and her son had contributed to the cost of the suit. This was the issue put to the jury. The parties agreed out of court, however, before the jury gave its verdict, the defendants agreeing to pay a fixed sum each year as a contribution. The same problem arose in a Year Book case from the reign of Edward II although in this case both parties were privy to the two sisters between whom the tenement owing the suit had been divided, again in John's reign.[63] After some argument the issue taken was that to which the defendant's argument had pointed in the previous case, and from which they were probably driven only because of their status as feoffees, that of whether

[58] JUST 1/283, mm. 9, 10.

[59] JUST 1/283, m. 24d. For the terms of the settlement see CP 25(1)/75/33, no. 99.

[60] A writ was issued for the case of *Isabel widow of Richard of Haresfield v. Richard de Crupes* on 22 March 1287. This is now to be found in a writ file associated with the 1292 Herefordshire eyre: JUST 4/2/12. A procedural stage of *William de la Hale v. Margery de Akrugge and Richard son of Richard Ingayn* is enrolled on the Common Bench plea roll for Easter term 1299: CP 40/127, m. 121. Procedural stages of *John of Atton v. Matthew of Clivedon* are enrolled on the Common Bench plea rolls in Michaelmas term 1299 and Michaelmas term 1305: CP 40/130, m. 301 and CP 40/153, m. 386.

[61] *Robert de Houtot v. William of Warmington and his wife Annora and others*: JUST 1/929, m. 33d.

[62] '. . . post statutum de hujusmodi contribucionibus faciendis provisum'.

[63] *Year Books 4 Edward II (1310–11)*, ed. G.J. Turner (Selden Society vol. 26, 1911), p. 143.

or not the plaintiff's ancestor had been seised of a contribution after the making of the Statute.

A writ of a rather different form was required when an inheritance was divided up by alienation and one of the alienees was performing suit on behalf of himself and the other alienees and was suing them for a contribution. The earliest evidence that a writ to cover this situation had been drafted and was already in use comes from a procedural stage of an action brought by Adam of Walpole against William Halleplay and fifteen others in Hilary term 1280 and related to suit owed to the royal hundred of Wangford in Suffolk for a tenement in Shipmeadow and Mettingham formerly held by Walter of Shipmeadow.[64] The procedural stages of two other such actions have been found, but no pleaded cases. One was brought by Master John of Battlebridge in Trinity term 1300 against Robert de Gernardeby and five others for contributions to the performance of suit to Walter of Langton's Yorkshire court of Buttercrambe for lands once held by Henry son of Odo at Ougate Sutton;[65] the other by Ralph of Shipdham against John son of William de la Rede and twenty-seven others for contributions to the performance of suit to Thomas Bardulf's Norfolk court at Wormgay for lands once held by William de la Rede in Shipdham and three other villages.[66] Nothing was said in any of these cases of the other feoffees having agreed to the plaintiff performing suit for them. The variants in the contribution writ to be found in an early fourteenth-century register of writs to adapt it for the use of purchasers, although reflecting some confusion on the part of the scribe or compiler, seem to envisage the use of a similar writ.[67] This form was, however, later replaced by another which in reciting the legislation specifically recited the provisions of the legislation as to the liability of all the feoffees to contribute *pro rata*,[68] and in the recital of the particular circumstances of the case also included the additional assertion that the plaintiff was performing the suit with the assent of the other feoffees. The contribution writ for feoffees in the printed register

[64] The writ as given in the enrolment summoned the defendants to answer 'de placito quod quare cum de communi consilio regni regis provisum sit quod si hereditas aliqua de qua unica secta tantum debebatur ad plures heredes participes ejusdem hereditatis seu ad alios per vendicionem vel alio modo devolvatur unica tantum fiat secta pro hereditate illa sicut prius fieri consuevit et ad sectam illam faciendam singuli participes contribuant, ac quedam hereditas que fuit Walteri de Schipmedwe in Schipmede et Metinham ad predictos . . . per vendicionem sit devoluta de qua unica secta tantum ad hundredum regis de Wayneford debetur et predictus Adam sectam illam ad idem hundredum pro se et participibus suis predictis faciat iidem . . . ad hoc contribuere contradicunt ad grave dampnum ipsius Ade et contra formam provisionis predicte etc.'

[65] CP 40/134, m. 196d. [66] CP 40/162, m. 164d. [67] *Early Registers*, p. 257 (R 641).

[68] '. . . et si feoffati illi warantum vel medium non habeant qui eos aquietare debeat, tunc omnes feoffati illi contribuant pro porcione ad sectam illam faciendam.'

is of this form.[69] Although it is stated in the register that the writ was ordained in 17 Edward III (1343/4) it was in fact evidently already in use by Michaelmas term 1325.[70]

Actions for the junior parceners against the lord

There was one other type of situation for which a separate enforcement action came eventually to be invented. This was where the junior parceners of a divided inheritance were being distrained by the lord for the suit which the eldest parcener ought to have been performing on behalf of them all but was not. A special writ for this situation is found in the printed register of writs and is noted by Fitzherbert.[71] There is, however, no trace of such an action on the plea rolls or in the printed or unprinted law reports or in the registers of writs of the period. It seems likely that it was created only at a later date.

DAMAGES AWARDED AGAINST LORDS IN THE ASSIZE OF MORT D'ANCESTOR AND ITS CONGENERS

Clause 9 of the original Provisions of Westminster of 1259 had authorised the courts to award damages where an heir had been in his lord's wardship but the lord had held on to his land after he had come of age and the heir was forced to bring his assize of mort d'ancestor or action of aiel or cosinage for the recovery of his land.[72] This clause was evidently intended only to cover the situation where the lord had rightfully been in possession of the heir's tenement because he held that tenement of the lord by military service. It had came, however, even prior to 1267 to be extended to authorise the awarding of damages in a quite different, if equally meritorious, situation. This was where the lord had wrongfully assumed the wardship of land which was held of him in socage or by some other form of tenure which did not entitle the lord to its wardship.[73] Clause 10 of the Provisions of Westminster had similarly authorised the awarding of damages in the same range of actions where the heir was already of age at the death of his ancestor and his lord had entered the tenement first and had then refused to surrender it to him.[74] These two clauses were combined into a single chapter in the final reissue of the Provisions as the Statute of Marlborough, of which they formed

69 *Reg. Omn. Brev.*, fol. 176v.
70 See *Del Bayl de Thwancastre v. atte Bothe et al.*, CP 40/258 m. 464 and CP 40/264 m. 206d.
71 *Reg. Omn. Brev.*, fol. 177r; A. Fitzherbert, *The New Natura Brevium*, 9th edition (London, 1794), fol. 162c.
72 Below, pp. 420–1. 73 Above, p. 124. 74 Below, pp. 420–1.

chapter 16. The new chapter also included a new section at the end which made it clear that the legislation was not to prejudice the king's prerogative right of primer seisin.[75]

This chapter was one of the shortest-lived chapters of the Statute. In 1278 it was effectively superseded by the enactment of chapter 1 of the Statute of Gloucester. This authorised the awarding of damages in mort d'ancestor and its congeners against any defendant, not just against the lord of whom the land was held.[76] It is none the less possible to demonstrate its operation during the intervening eleven years along the lines which had developed prior to 1267. Wards who had to sue their lords by mort d'ancestor or one of its congeners to recover lands the lord had held in wardship and which he had retained after they had come of age, without due excuse, can be shown to have continued recovering damages under the provisions of the legislation down to 1267.[77] The legislation also continued to be used to authorise the awarding of damages where a lord had usurped the wardship of land held in socage or by some other tenure that did not entitle the lord to wardship.[78] Heirs who were above age when they succeeded also continued to benefit from its provisions down to 1278 when they had to sue to recover their lands since they also recovered damages when they did so.[79]

THE ENFORCEMENT AND INTERPRETATION OF CHAPTER 6 OF THE STATUTE SAFEGUARDING THE LORD'S RIGHTS OF WARDSHIP

Chapter 6 of the Statute of Marlborough was one of the chapters that was new in 1267. It was intended to provide some protection for lords against the use of certain conveyancing devices by their tenants which resulted in the loss by lords of rights of wardship and marriage over the heirs of those tenants and their lands.[80] During the four decades between the enactment of the Statute of Marlborough and the end of the reign of Edward I there are at least seven cases in which the provisions of the first part of chapter 6 of the Statute (relating to the enfeoffment of heirs apparent) were invoked, but only three have been found in which the provisions of the second part (relating to fictitious feoffments) were invoked or applied.

[75] Below, pp. 474–5. [76] *SR*, I, 47.

[77] For examples see JUST 1/238, m. 4d (1272 Essex eyre); JUST 1/483, m. 39d (1271–2 Lincolnshire eyre).

[78] For an example see JUST 1/8, m. 26d (1276–7 Bedfordshire eyre).

[79] For examples see JUST 1/365, m. 30 (1271 Kent eyre); JUST 1/802, mm. 3, 4, 5, 5d (1272 Staffordshire eyre); JUST 1/8, mm. 3, 7d (1276–7 Bedfordshire eyre).

[80] Above, pp. 196–203.

The cases in which the provisions of the first part of the chapter were either expressly invoked or mentioned in passing or which raise similar problems occur both ways round. Two were assizes of novel disseisin in which the heir (or in one case both that heir and his wife) was suing a lord who had already successfully seized the land, claiming wardship, and where the assize was brought to challenge that seizure.[81] A third case is slightly more complicated. This is an assize of novel disseisin in which the widow of an heir who had been enfeoffed jointly with her late husband sued for the return of her jointure.[82] Four cases were the other way round. These are actions of wardship brought by lords to assert their rights. In two the lord sued a woman, probably a future wife of the underage heir who had been enfeoffed with the heir, for wardship of his lands and person.[83] In the other two the defendant seems to have been the quasi-guardian appointed by the father who had made the enfeoffment to take custody of the heir's lands until he came of age.[84]

As the reported discussion in the latter of these two cases (a case of 1301) indicates, and as the diversity of the defendants sued in the wardship cases might suggest, the failure of this part of the Statute to make any specific provision for its enforcement created a real problem for lords in knowing whom to sue. Serjeant Scrope argued that the proper defendant in such a case was the ward himself but that he should be given a different name as defendant from the name he bore as ward for the purposes of the litigation. This was roundly denied by Chief Justice Hengham and his colleague Bereford. As has been seen, in two cases it was the joint feoffee, probably the future wife, of the heir who was sued. This was perhaps only possible if she was herself above age, and therefore plausibly to be described as being in possession of the land. The couple also probably had not yet to be married because once she was married she could probably refuse to answer without her husband. This device was also obviously not

[81] *William of Handsacre and his wife Maud v. William son of Ralph Butler and Thomas of Chalfont*: JUST 1/1029, m. 8d (1284 Worcestershire assize session before Fulks and Berkeley); *John son of Adam of Neufmarche v. Master Robert of Barnby*: CP 40/98, m. 119d (1292 Yorkshire assize session before Hartforth and his colleagues adjourned into the Common Bench for Hilary term 1293).

[82] *Cecily widow of Richard son of Simon of Lamport v. John of Bridgwater and Fina widow of John Fauvel*: JUST 1/625, m. 5d (1293 Northamptonshire assizes before Crokedayk and Roger of Burton).

[83] *Thomas of Doynton v. Joan daughter of Thomas fitzEllis*: CP 40/10, m. 65d (Trinity term 1275); *John Fiton v. Maud widow of Simon of Moulton*: CP 40/147, m. 176 (Easter term 1303), of which there are also reports in BL MSS. Additional 31826, fol. 278v and Additional 5925, fols. 73r–v and LI MS. Miscellaneous 738, fol. 21r. In the second of these two cases the widow claimed to be jointly enfeoffed with the heir of only half the land at stake and said that the heir had been enfeoffed without her of the other half.

[84] *Thomas Weyland v. John of Brampton*: CP 40/70, m. 55 (Hilary term 1288); *William Trussell of 'Cubelisdon' v. Roger of Aston*: CP 40/135, m. 9d (Michaelmas term 1301). There are reports of this second case in BL MSS. Additional 37657, fol. 141r and Hargrave 375, fol. 141r; LI MS. Miscellaneous 87, fols. 47r–v and in CUL MS. Ee.6.18, fols. 63r–v.

possible if the heir was the sole feoffee. The arguments against making the quasi-guardian appointed by the feoffor, but answerable to the heir, the main defendant were rehearsed at length in the 1301 case. Their core element was that his estate was simply too 'feeble' to make him a proper party. The court none the less ultimately drove the quasi-guardian defendant to answer, as such a defendant had (albeit without recorded objection) in 1288.

The pleaded cases reveal that the context of most, if not all, of the feoffments was either a marriage or the property arrangements preceding a marriage of the heir. They suggest that the enfeoffments in question may not have been intended primarily to defraud the lord of his wardship but rather to put in place the jointure or other settlement of the father's (or other ancestor's) land required by the arrangements agreed between the two families of the marriage partners. In only one of the seven cases (a 1292 assize case) is nothing at all said about marriage arrangements involving the heir in question.[85] This matrimonial context, under which most of the enfeoffments were enfeoffments not just of the heir but also of his current or future wife, created obvious problems in relation to the Statute, for that had considered only the much simpler case, where it was only the heir who was being enfeoffed. Only one lord was powerful enough simply to disregard the separate interest that the wife enjoyed and to seize the land into his own hands by way of wardship for an alienation in breach of the Statute of Marlborough. That was the king.[86] But it was certainly not entirely clear that a joint feoffment with a wife did take a feoffment outside the provisions of the Statute. In a 1303 report Serjeant Harle argued that a joint feoffment with a stranger would have been outside the Statute but that a joint feoffment with a wife was not.[87] That there was felt to be some force to this argument is suggested by the pleading in other cases. In a 1284 assize we find a man and his wife arguing that at the time of the feoffment the wife was not yet married to the husband, and thus effectively a stranger, and that she had given money in return for her interest, again a characteristic of an arms-length relationship.[88] In the 1301 wardship case the quasi-guardian shifted at once from arguing that he was not the proper party to the suit to arguing that the ancestor (here the heir's grandfather) had not held the tenements concerned by knight service of the plaintiff.[89] Only one lord won a straight-out victory in what seems on the face of it to have been the simple case of only the heir being enfeoffed by his ancestor. The successful

85 *Neufmarche v. Barnby*: above, note 81. 86 *Lamport v. Bridgwater and Fauvel*: above, note 82.
87 *Fiton v. Moulton*: above, note 83. 88 *Handsacre v. Butler and Chalfont*: above, note 81.
89 *Trussell of 'Cubelisdon' v. Aston*: above, note 84.

plaintiff was Thomas Weyland. He is almost certainly to be identified as the man who was the chief justice of the Common Bench at the time the case was being heard (in 1288).[90]

There are only three cases from the same period in which there seems to have been any attempt to invoke the provisions of the second part of chapter 6 or to apply those provisions. They are a wardship case heard in the 1285 Northamptonshire eyre,[91] a dower case heard in the Trinity 1293 session of the 1293–4 Yorkshire eyre[92] and a wardship case pleaded in Michaelmas term 1300.[93] In all three cases it looks as though the feoffments were indeed intended to secure genuine leases and not simply to deprive the lord of the profits of wardship.[94] In the 1285 case this was a seven-year lease beginning at Michaelmas 1271 to one (or possibly two) named individuals (Philip de Burne and perhaps also to Solomon de Burne) of a substantial holding at Thenford in Northamptonshire, which was being leased for a yearly payment of thirteen shillings and four pence. There was also probably some capital consideration paid or received at the beginning of the lease. In the 1293 Yorkshire case it was a seventeen-year lease to two named individuals (William Skinner and William Forester) for the nominal rent of one rose each year, again presumably with some other prior consideration. Here the enfeoffment even included a clause of a kind more appropriate to a lease, prohibiting the commission of waste within the seventeen-year period. The jury subsequently confirmed that the arrangement had indeed been made to provide greater security for the lessees. In the 1300 case it was a thirty-nine year lease of fifteen acres at Bradford in Wiltshire for which the plaintiffs had even been able to find a parallel indenture of lease, presumably among the deeds of their deceased tenant.

The form of the 'feoffment' in at least two of these cases differed significantly from that mentioned in the 1262 case behind the legislation and probably, therefore, also from that envisaged in that legislation.[95] Instead of stipulating a constant but excessive rent which the deed of feoffment also recorded had been paid in advance for the period of the lease, these two 'feoffments' adopted a rather different strategy. This was

[90] *Weyland v. Brampton*: above, note 84.

[91] *John de Boys v. Philip (and Solomon) of Burne*. The enrolment of this case is JUST 1/622, m. 15d. The reports are (i) BL MS. Royal 10.A.V, fols. 100v–101r; (ii) LI MS. Miscellaneous 87, fol. 44v, CUL MS. Dd.7.14, fols. 372r–v, BL MS. Additional 35116, fols. 256r–v (and BL MS. Harley 25, fols. 158r–v); (iii) LI MS. Miscellaneous 87, fol. 45r; BL MS. Additional 31826, fols. 221v–222r.

[92] *Emma widow of Ingram de Monceaux v. John de Monceaux et al.*: JUST 1/1090, m. 29 (and see m. 8).

[93] *John of Bradford and his wife Isabel v. William de la Sale of Bradford and his wife Katherine*. The enrolment is CP 40/131, m. 99d. The reports are (i) BL MS. Additional 37657, fol. 37r; LI MS. Miscellaneous 87, fol. 45v; (ii) BL MS. Additional 31826, fol. 317v.

[94] Above, p. 200. [95] Above, pp. 200–1.

of a low or even nominal initial rent for the period of the lease which was then to rise, but only at the expiry of the period of the intended lease, to a rent in excess of the yearly value. Thus in the 1285 Northamptonshire case the initial rent for the period of the seven-year lease was fixed at one mark (thirteen shillings and four pence) a year but at the end of the period was to rise to twenty pounds a year, well in excess of the value of the tenement. In the 1293 Yorkshire case the rent for the initial seventeen years of the lease was fixed at a nominal rose each year but was then to rise to thirty pounds a year, although (as the jury confirmed) the land was worth only twelve pounds a year. In the 1300 case no details are given of the alleged feoffment and the plaintiffs merely produced the lease in their possession as presumptive evidence that it had been collusive.

In one of these three cases the provisions of the second part of chapter 6 of the Statute of Marlborough were invoked in the context of a dower case. Roger of Higham (the king's serjeant) intervened to say that the lands at stake in the case ought to have been in the king's hands along with the other lands belonging to John, the son and heir of Ingram de Monceaux, not by way of wardship, but because of proceedings on the crown pleas side of the eyre, because the indented writing that William Forester had produced to demonstrate that he held the land jointly with William Skinner revealed that the intention had been to create a lease rather than an enfeoffment. He did not specifically invoke the Statute but it is clearly what lies behind his argument. Interestingly, the jury verdict in the case reveals that the king was not the only lord to take 'executive' action to enforce his rights against fraudulent feoffments. The immediate lord of the holding, John de Faucunberge, had apparently seized the land into his hands by way of wardship at Ingram's death in early 1292 and had only restored the land to the lessees after being 'satisfied' for his rights.[96]

The other two cases were both brought by actions of wardship and in both the Statute was directly involved and cited. The 1300 case brought by the chirographer of the Common Bench and his wife was the simpler of the two. The plaintiffs had only to produce an actual indenture of lease to the defendants to create the presumption that any supposed 'enfeoffment' had been a fraudulent one. This was denied by the defendants. The issue as to whether or not it had been went to a jury. The 1285 case is the most complicated and also the one about which we are best informed. The defendant in this case tried to argue that his possession of

[96] But for another case (an assize of novel disseisin heard before assize justices in 1301) in which one of the defendants alleged that he had been granted the wardship of the land by the earl of Lincoln after the earl had seized the land into his hands on his tenant's death despite a prior 'fictitious' feoffment in favour of the plaintiff see *Robert Ivon of Winfrith v. Roger son of Roger of Calston and others*: JUST 1/1318, m. 17.

a freehold interest in the land (despite the evidence of the deed showing a 'feigned' feoffment) was a matter of record and thus incontrovertible. After the feoffment had taken place, he had been disseised of the land by Osbert Giffard and had recovered the free tenement by the verdict of an assize of novel disseisin. He thus had a 'free tenement', a freehold interest in the land, by virtue of the judgment. It was one of the presiding justices, Saham, who provided the counter-argument. The verdict was not binding in the current proceedings since the assize had been against a third party and not the plaintiff, and could have been collusive. The defendant then shifted tack by attempting to vouch John Lovel to warranty. This was on the basis that this same land had been seized after the death of the heir's ancestor by the plaintiff's father (Ernald de Boys) by way of wardship. Again we note that the lord concerned had disregarded the supposed enfeoffment by making the seizure, suggesting that perhaps other lords also took 'executive' action rather than bringing litigation, whatever the Statute may have said.[97] Ernald had then sold its wardship to John Lovel senior who in turn had sold it to the defendant, Philip de Burne. This was in fact a perfectly good title to the wardship of the land and, if the defendant had been allowed by the court to claim two simultaneous interests in the same land, he would have succeeded. But he lost on pleading grounds. His initial defence claiming hereditary right in the land had been a peremptory exception and under the pleading rules he was not allowed, after such an exception was overruled, to proceed to make a voucher to warranty, a 'lower' answer in the scale of answers. The court therefore gave judgment for the plaintiff and awarded him both the wardship and damages assessed at a hundred marks, of which half was to go to the clerks of the court.

ENFORCEMENT OF THE REPEALED LEGISLATION ON MORTMAIN ALIENATIONS

The Statute of Marlborough did not include a clause corresponding to clause 14 of the Provisions of Westminster of 1259, requiring the consent of the lord of whom land was held before it was alienated into mortmain. The clause had already been dropped from the reissues of 1263 and 1264 and was not reinstated.[98] Only ten years after the passage of the Statute of Marlborough, however, it had apparently come to be believed that a clause along the lines of the original clause 14 had in fact been included in the Statute. In Michaelmas term 1277 the abbot of Croxton was summoned to answer Robert Luterell in the Common Bench as to why 'whereas it

[97] Above, p. 203. [98] Above, p. 191.

is contained in the Provision of Marlborough that the religious are not allowed to enter the fee of anyone without the permission and agreement of the chief lord of that fee, namely the lord of whom the property is immediately held',[99] he had nevertheless entered land held of the plaintiff 'without the permission and agreement of the same Robert and against the terms of the said provision'.[100] No pleadings have been found in this case and it was probably settled out of court.[101]

In another case from the Yorkshire eyre of 1279–81, which was almost certainly heard in Trinity term 1279, the defendants (the master of the Templars and others) were summoned to answer why 'whereas it has been provided by the common council of the realm that the religious are not allowed to enter the fee of anyone without the permission and agreement of the chief lord of that fee, namely the lord of whom that property is immediately held'[102] they had entered land held of the plaintiff without his permission and agreement.[103] The plaintiff claimed damages of a hundred pounds in respect of the entry, which was said to have taken place on 7 May 1276. No particular statute was mentioned in this case. The defendants objected to the writ on the grounds that no such legislation had ever been published by the present king or his ancestors. The justices, however, advised the defendants to answer over. Writs of a similar form had, they said, been previously issued by Chancery and this indicated that they had already received royal approval.[104] The defendants, however, continued to object to the writ, arguing that the princes and

[99] '. . . cum in provisione de Marleberge contineatur quod viris religiosis non liceat feodum alicuius ingredi sine licencia et voluntate capitalis domini feodi illius, scilicet de quo res ipsa immediate teneatur . . .'

[100] '. . . sine licencia et voluntate ipsius Roberti et contra formam provisionis predicte . . .': CP 40/21, m. 58d. An almost identical writ to that behind this enrolment, differing from it only slightly as to the amounts of land involved, is to be found on the Close Rolls in 1278, the defendant being summoned apparently for appearance in Michaelmas term 1278 rather than Michaelmas term 1277 (*CCR 1272–9*, pp. 500–1). The Close Roll writ alone is noted and discussed by Bean (*Decline of English Feudalism*, p. 51).

[101] A charter confirming all the gifts made by the plaintiff's tenants to the defendant was confirmed by the king in 1291: *Calendar of Charter Rolls* (6 vols., London, 1903–27), II. 377. The original charter must be dated between 1275 and 1278 since it mentions William Hamelyn as being sheriff of Leicestershire.

[102] '. . . cum de communi consilio regni provisum sit quod viris religiosis non liceat feodum alicuius (ingredi) sine licencia et voluntate capitalis domini feodi illius, scilicet de quo res ipsa immediate teneatur.'

[103] *Roger d'Eyville v. Brother Robert de Turville, master of the Templars and Brother Robert of Faxfleet*: JUST 1/1074, m. 19d. Because of the length of the eyre the civil pleas were divided into separate terms. This roll contains only cases heard in Trinity term 1279. For another identical record of the same case see JUST 1/1055, m. 30d.

[104] This may be a reference to earlier writs issued relating to the same case. The register of writs in BL MS. Harley 1033 contains (at fol. 170r) a writ of *sicut alias* addressed to an unspecified sheriff reciting an unspecified statute against the entry of the religious into anyone's fee without the lord's permission and asserting that a brother of the Templar order had secretly entered a lord's

magnates of England had never agreed to such legislation or assented to its publication. They refused to answer the writ until the king's wishes in the matter were known. The plaintiff in return sought judgment of the defendants as undefended. Before judgment could be given, however, the parties reached a settlement, at the octaves of Hilary 1280, under which the defendants were allowed to retain the land. They had, however, to pay sixty marks for this permission and also to agree to hold the land directly of the plaintiffs.[105]

In a second case from the same eyre the defendants were simply summoned to answer for having entered certain lands held of the plaintiff against his will and without his permission 'whereas the religious are not allowed to enter the fee of anyone without the permission and agreement of the chief lord of that fee of whom the property is directly held'.[106] The chief defendant, however, had no need to demur to the alleged statement of the law contained in the writ. He was able instead to make the much more straightforward objection, that he had found his church seised of the land concerned on becoming abbot. Judgment was given for him, presumably on the grounds that if anyone had entered the land it was not him.

The first of these cases not only cast doubt upon the existence of any general statutory restraint on mortmain alienations in favour of lords, but also raised a constitutional point of some importance. These were matters which required discussion in parliament. Despite the fact that no adjournment of the case to parliament is recorded on the roll it seems quite probable that the case or the points which it raised were discussed at the next meeting of parliament at Michaelmas 1279.[107] It seems quite

fee by initially taking the land at champarty and then just before harvest asserting a feoffment, and ordered the sheriff to assist the lord in resisting the entry by enjoining the Templars to seek permission and providing assistance to the lord. The initials fit those of the parties in this case as do the quantities of the land. The same register also has a follow-up writ of attachment for appearance before unspecified royal justices. The register of writs in Bodleian MS. Douce 139 has (at fol. 57r) a variant form of the second writ with less helpful initials but specifically addressed to the sheriff of Yorkshire and ordering the summons of the defendant before itinerant justices.

105 *Feet of Fines for the County of York 1272–1300*, ed. F.H. Slingsby (Yorkshire Archaeological Society Records Series vol. 112, 1956), p. 38. The money may also have been in part payment for d'Eyville's withdrawal from a suit against the conservator of the Templars' privileges for breach of a royal prohibition: JUST 1/1074, m. 17d.

106 '. . . cum non liceat viris religiosis ingredi feodum alicujus sine licencia et voluntate capitalis domini feodi illius de quo res ipsa in mediate tenetur . . .': *Adam of Leaventhorpe v. abbot of Whitby and Brother Robert of Buckton*: JUST 1/1055, m. 83, cf. JUST 1/1062, m. 17. This may have been the writ for which the plaintiff paid twenty shillings in 1277: C 60/74, m. 8.

107 Some at least of the justices of the Yorkshire eyre are known to have been present at this parliament (*SCKB*, I, 50–1) and could have reported on their difficulties in person. The omission from the plea roll of any mention of an adjournment to parliament can be parallelled by the King's Bench

possible that it was these discussions rather than Edward I's disagreements with Pecham which led to the enactment of the Statute of Mortmain during the course of the parliament.[108] This would, among other things, explain why the Statute goes out of its way, in its opening passage, to contain support for the view that earlier legislation prohibiting alienations in mortmain made without the consent of the lord of whom the land was held was still in force, an assertion hardly necessary in the context of the legislation being enacted but understandable if that legislation had arisen out of discussions about that very point.[109]

The earlier, but apparently repealed, legislation remained of some significance even after 1279. In at least two cases brought after 1279 the immediate lords of tenements alienated in mortmain sued for damages against the alienees in mortmain instead of entering the lands alienated, as they were entitled to do under the Statute of Mortmain and as if the legislation of 1259, cited in its preamble by the Statute of Mortmain, had not effectively been repealed (a second time) by that Statute.[110] The first case was one for which only a procedural stage has been found, in Michaelmas term 1285. In it the prior of Torksey was attached to answer 'why whereas it has been provided by the common council of the realm that the religious are not allowed to enter the fee of anyone without the permission and agreement of the chief lord of that fee, namely the lord of whom that property is immediately held' the said prior had acquired five shillings of rent with appurtenances in Hardwick and Torksey which William, vicar of the church of St Mary Torksey, held of the fee of Ralph of Ketelthorp and entered the fee of the said Ralph without his permission and agreement to the disinheritance of the same Ralph and against the terms of the said provision.[111] In a second case heard in Easter term 1291, the abbot of Rievaulx was summoned to answer a writ which cited the legislation in similar terms but talked of the defendant failing to obtain not only the lord's licence but also that of the king, 'to the manifest

plea record of *William Butler v. Walter of Hopton* (KB 27/128, m. 8d) in 1291/2 which contains no record of such an adjournment although the judgment given in the case was made only after a detailed discussion in parliament of the case and of the issues which it raised (*Rotuli Parliamentorum*, I, 79). Moreover the reaching of a final concord in the case at the beginning of Hilary term 1280 also fits this hypothesis, as this would have been at the beginning of the first session after the conclusion of the Michaelmas parliament.

108 The explanation of the timing of the Statute favoured by Bean, *Decline of English Feudalism*, pp. 52–3 and D.L. Douie, *Archbishop Pecham* (Oxford, 1952), p. 119.

109 *SR*, I, 51.

110 It is true to say that the Statute of Mortmain did not *expressis verbis* repeal the earlier legislation, whose existence it expressly confirmed, though it would seem to be a natural assumption to make from the Statute.

111 '. . . quare cum de communi consilio regni regis provisum sit quod non liceat viris religiosis ingredi feodum alicuius sine licencia et voluntate capitalis domini feodi illius, scilicet de quo res ipsa immediate teneatur . . .': CP 40/60, m. 145.

contempt of the lord king and no small damage and grievance of the said William'.[112] The allegedly unlicensed entry had taken place in 1286 and the plaintiff specifically counted for damages. In reply the defendant at once objected to the form of the writ: 'He says that writs of the form of this writ are hitherto unheard of and since new original writs ought to be provided by the common council of the realm, he asks for judgment whether he is obliged to answer this new writ . . .'[113] No judgment is recorded but it may be significant that no writs of a similar form are to be found later.[114]

In a third case heard in the court *coram rege* in Easter term 1286, the prior of Bullington was summoned to answer the king for contravention of legislation that had provided that 'the religious or others are not allowed to enter the fee of anyone in such a way that it comes into mortmain, without the permission and agreement of the king and the chief lord of whom that property is immediately held'.[115] This is a significantly different formula, and one that is much closer in its terms to the legislation of 1279, at least as it was being applied through the licensing system by this date. The king's attorney, one Edmund of St Clement's, based the king's case not only on his rights as king, but also on his rights as guardian of the temporalities of the vacant see of York. His count does not, however, seem to have claimed either damages or the forfeiture. In any case the action was dismissed, the prior being able to show that he had already been acquitted by a jury on the same charge elsewhere. It is not wholly clear therefore whether this case should or should not be counted with the other two cases as evidence of the survival of the 1259 legislation in the period after 1279.

112 *William de Mowbray v. abbot of Rievaulx*: CP 40/89, m. 71d. For an earlier stage in the mesne process see CP 40/86, m. 206 (Michaelmas term 1290).

113 '. . . dicit quod hucusque inaudita sunt brevia forme hujus brevis, unde cum nova brevia originalia per commune consilium regni provideri debeant, petit judicium si ad istud novum breve debeat respondere . . .'

114 The count given in *NN* at pp. 136–7 (B 276) may well derive from a similar case heard between 1279 and 1292, or possibly from the period before 1279. It seems to reflect the circumstances of an actual case involving one William Francoberge (or? Fauconberg) and the prior of St Bartholomew Gloucester (see *NN*, p. 136, note). The count given is for damages, and not (pace Milsom, *Novae Narrationes*, p. lx) for a lord 'seeking to enforce the forfeiture'.

115 '. . . non liceat viris religiosis seu aliis ingredi feodum alicujus, ita quod ad mortuam manum deveniat, sine licencia et voluntate regis et capitalis domini de quo res illa immediate tenetur . . .': KB 27/98, m. 7.

Chapter 10

REFORMS IN THE CRIMINAL JUSTICE SYSTEM

This chapter looks at the ways in which the various different chapters of the Statute of Marlborough concerned with reforms in the system of criminal justice, at both a national and a local level, were enforced and interpreted during the four decades after 1267.[1]

MURDRUM FINES

Clause 22 of the Provisions of Westminster of 1259 had restricted the incidence of the *murdrum* fine to felonious homicides and prohibited its imposition in the case of accidental deaths. This clause was re-enacted in 1267 without alteration as chapter 25 of the Statute of Marlborough.[2] The re-enactment was immediately reflected in statements made during eyres in 1268 by three counties as to the local custom regarding the presentment of Englishry. In each of them the limitation on the duty to present Englishry to felonious deaths was ascribed variously to the 'king's concession to the county' or to the operation of the 'king's grace'.[3] Both are clearly references to the statutory provisions. In a further eleven counties the first recorded statement of the county about its customs in the presentment of Englishry made after 1267 specifically excluded presentment for accidental deaths and, by implication, thereby also excluded the payment of *murdrum* in such cases.[4] In another five counties, although the justices rejected the statement of custom about Englishry made by

[1] For the earlier story of the enforcement of the corresponding clauses of the Provisions of Westminster see pp. 128–33, 175–6.

[2] Below, pp. 480–1.

[3] JUST 1/202, m. 20 (Dorset); JUST 1/569A, m. 1 (Norfolk); JUST 1/703, m. 1 (Oxfordshire).

[4] Berkshire (1284): 'et hoc de feloniis tantum': JUST 1/44, m. 1; Cambridgeshire (1272): 'et hoc intelligendum est de feloniis tantum': JUST 1/85, m. 1; Herefordshire (1292): 'et hoc de feloniis tantum': JUST 1/302, m. 53; Huntingdonshire (1286): 'et hoc intelligendum est de feloniis tantum': JUST 1/351A, m. 1; Kent (1279): 'de feloniis tantum': JUST 1/369, m. 1; Somerset (1280): 'de omnibus feloniis': JUST 1/759, m. 1; Hampshire (1272): 'et hoc tantum de masculis occisis per feloniam': JUST 1/780, m. 1; Surrey (1279): 'de feloniis tantum': JUST 1/876, m. 42; Warwickshire (1285): 'quocienscunque aliquis inventus fuerit occisus et non fuerit notus': JUST 1/956, m. 34; Wiltshire (1268): 'et hoc tam de masculis occisis per feloniam quam de feminis': JUST

the county as contrary to that given in previous eyres, the custom of the county, as stated by the justices themselves, specifically excluded accidental deaths.[5] In six counties no definite statement is forthcoming from the period after 1267 as to whether the *murdrum* fine or the presentment of Englishry was due in cases of accidental death. An examination of the plea roll of eyres in the counties concerned suggests, however, that *murdrum* was not paid for accidental death in any of them.[6]

There remains, however, a group of five counties in which a statement of custom made in an eyre after 1267 specifically admitted the liability of the county to present Englishry for both felonious and accidental deaths. Two of the counties concerned were Buckinghamshire and Bedfordshire. Beside being neighbours, these counties also shared the same sheriff.[7] In neither county was *murdrum* in practice adjudged for an accidental death despite the county's admission of liability. The same is also true of the counties of Essex[8] and Suffolk.[9] Only in one county does such a statement seem to have led to an actual judgment of *murdrum* for an accidental death. This was Sussex, where the admission was made at the eyre of 1279,[10] and judgment was given in the case of a man who had been found dead but who was known to have had the falling-sickness, presumably epilepsy.[11] There are, however, another three instances from the

1/998A, m. 24; Worcestershire (1275): 'et hoc de feloniis et de masculo tantummodo et non de infortuniis': JUST 1/1025, m. 1.

5 Gloucestershire (1287): 'de feloniis tantum': JUST 1/280, m. 1; Hertfordshire (1287): 'in feloniis et non in infortuniis': JUST 1/325, m. 23; Lincolnshire (1281–4): 'aliquis ignotus inventus fuerit occisus': JUST 1/486, m. 1; Northamptonshire (1285): 'masculis occisis': JUST 1/621, m. 2; Rutland (1286): 'de notis masculis occisis per feloniam': JUST 1/722, m. 10.

6 Derbyshire (1281): JUST 1/152; Devon (1281): JUST 1/181; Leicestershire (1284): JUST 1/457; Middlesex (1274): JUST 1/640; Nottinghamshire (1280): JUST 1/669; Staffordshire (1272): JUST 1/802.

7 Buckinghamshire (1272): JUST 1/60, m. 22 (1272) and cf. JUST 1/63, m. 36 (1286) for a similar statement from the next eyre; Bedfordshire 1276: JUST 1/7, m. 27 (1276). The same presentment had been made in 1272 at the opening of the eyre which was then prorogued owing to the death of Henry III: JUST 1/7, m. 39.

8 JUST 1/238, m. 46 (1272). But note that in 1285 the county stated that it presented Englishry only for felonious deaths: JUST 1/242, m. 65.

9 JUST 1/827 m. 1 (1286). Note, moreover, that as late as 1362, after the *murdrum* fine itself had been abolished, Englishry was still being presented at a Suffolk coroner's inquest for an accidental death: *Select Cases from the Coroners' Rolls (1265–1413)*, ed. Carles Gross (Selden Society vol. 9, 1895), pp. xliii–xliv. Clearly by this date the presentment of Englishry and the *murdrum* fine had become quite disassociated.

10 For the county's statement of custom see JUST 1/921, m. 1 (the chief justice's roll); cf. JUST 1/917, m. 3 (Boyland's roll). In the Rex roll and that of Solomon of Rochester the statement of custom is unfinished, reading no more than 'totus comitatus recordatur quod Engl' ': JUST 1/915, m. 3; JUST 1/923, m. 1. cf. Hunnisett, *Medieval Coroner*, p. 29, note 1.

11 JUST 1/921, m. 7d (hundred of Totnore); cf. JUST 1/915, m. 14; JUST 1/917, m. 13, and JUST 1/923, m. 11d where there are marginal notes of both '*infortunium*' and '*murdrum*' besides this case. It was the only judgment of *murdrum* noted against the hundred, and cost the hundred twenty shillings: JUST 1/917, m. 38.

same eyre in which a judgment of *murdrum* might have been expected for an accidental death but none was recorded. In two of these cases relations who had previously presented Englishry were absent, so no successful presentment can have been made.[12] In the third, in the hundred of East Grinstead, an unknown stranger was found dead. No Englishry can have been presented for him and no other *murdrum* fine was adjudged against the hundred but no such judgment was awarded.[13] In the following eyre, that of 1288, the county claimed that it only presented Englishry for felonies. Although the justices examined the records of the previous eyre and discovered that the county had mis-stated its custom with regard to the relations who had to present Englishry, they accepted the limitation to felonious deaths, even, apparently, claiming that this limitation was included in the statement of custom made in the previous eyre.[14]

With this one exception, therefore, the legislation seems to have been effective in bringing an end to the practice of adjudging *murdrum* fines for accidental deaths. It is, however, reasonably clear that it made very little difference in practice to the number of such fines paid. Most hundreds continued to pay a fine as the result of a judgment made against them in respect of a felonious death. This is true not only of counties with comparatively large hundreds such as Leicestershire[15] and Staffordshire,[16] but also of counties with very small hundreds such as Berkshire[17] and Kent.[18] The only *murdrum*-paying units which seem to have benefited financially from the reform were the very smallest liberties which did not

[12] JUST 1/923, mm. 4d, 6. [13] JUST 1/923, m. 12d.

[14] JUST 1/924, m. 44, cf. JUST 1/926, m. 1, JUST 1/928, m. 1, JUST 1/930, m. 1.

[15] Both in the eyre of 1247 when *murdrum* was adjudged for accidental deaths and in the eyre of 1284 when *murdrum* was adjudged only for felonious deaths, all four hundreds were liable for *murdrum:* JUST 1/455, mm. 1, 1d, 2, 6 (Goscote), mm. 7, 7d (Framland), m. 9 (Guthlaxton) and m. 12 (Gartree); JUST 1/463, mm. 7, 7d, 8, 9d (Goscote), mm. 4d, 5 (Framland), m. 12d (Guthlaxton) and m. 1 (Gartree).

[16] All five hundreds paid *murdrum* both in the eyre of 1228 when *murdrum* was adjudged for accidents as well as felonious deaths and in the eyres of 1272 and 1293 where *murdrum* was adjudged only for felonious deaths: JUST 1/801, m. 10 (Seisdon), mm. 11, 11d (Offlow), mm. 12, 12d (Cuttlestone), mm. 13, 13d (Pirehill) and m. 14 (Totmonslow) (1228); JUST 1/802, mm. 42d, 43 (Seisdon), 54 (Offlow), 44 (Cuttlestone), 49 (Pirehill) and 45d (Totmonslow) (1272); JUST 1/804, mm. 53d (Seisdon), 61d (Offlow), 65 (Cuttlestone), 67 (Pirehill) and 57 (Totmonslow) (1293).

[17] Of some twenty-six areas described as hundreds by 1284, some of which had earlier been described as vills, twenty-one paid *murdrum* in 1241 when *murdrum* was paid for accidents as well as felonious deaths, eighteen in 1248 when the same was true, nineteen in 1261 when again the same was true, and no fewer than twenty-five in 1284 when *murdrum* was paid only for felonious killings: JUST 1/37 (1241), JUST 1/38 (1248), JUST 1/40 (1261), and JUST 1/48 (1284).

[18] Of about seventy-three units, including some vills and half hundreds which answered separately in the eyre, fifty-three paid *murdrum* in 1255 when *murdrum* was paid also for accidental deaths: JUST 1/361. The number was reduced only to forty-eight in 1279 when the legislation was being observed: JUST 1/369.

answer separately at the eyre. Even for them it is difficult to prove this conclusively.[19]

PENALISATION OF VILLAGES FOR NOT ATTENDING INQUESTS FULLY

Clause 21 of the Provisions of Westminster had been reissued without alteration in 1263 and 1264. It was, however, subject to drastic modification when reissued in 1267 as chapter 24 of the Statute of Marlborough.[20] A new clause at the end excluded the coroner's inquest into unnatural death from the scope of the concession, and in keeping with this alteration, the wording of the main part of the clause was also modified to read 'inquisitions into robberies and arsons or other matters belonging to the crown' in place of the 'inquisitions into homicide or other matters belonging to the crown' of the original legislation.

As has been seen, there is little evidence of vills being amerced by the justices in eyre for failing to attend inquests into any type of crown plea other than unnatural deaths.[21] The effect of the modification made in 1267 was, therefore, for most practical purposes, to repeal it. As might be expected, references to vills being amerced for failure to attend coroners' inquests are common again after 1267.[22] Vills seem to have escaped the duty of attending such inquests fully and their liability to pay an amercement if they failed to do so only in the fourteenth century with the ending of the general eyre.[23]

AMERCEMENT OF THE SURETIES OF CLERKS PLEADING BENEFIT OF CLERGY

Amercement of the sureties of clerks pleading their clergy had been forbidden in 1259 by clause 24 of the Provisions of Westminster. This was re-enacted without alteration in 1267 as chapter 27 of the Statute of Marlborough.[24] Nothing has been found on the plea rolls to suggest that it was disregarded after 1267.

[19] At first sight the Leicestershire evidence from the eyres of 1247 and 1284 proves the point, only seven *murdrum* fines being paid by such liberties from 1284 compared with twenty-six in 1247. However, of the twenty-six only eight are attributable to judgments for accidental deaths. In Berkshire the number actually rose from two in 1241, one in 1248 and two in 1261, to eight in 1284.

[20] Below, pp. 480–1. [21] Above, p. 191.

[22] E.g. JUST 1/998A, m. 24 et seq. (Wiltshire eyre 1268); JUST 1/1051, mm. 7d, 10 (Yorkshire eyre 1268); JUST 1/780, m. 1 (Hampshire eyre 1272); JUST 1/737, m. 23 (Shropshire eyre 1272); JUST 1/1026, mm. 38, 40, 46, 47 (Worcestershire eyre 1275).

[23] Hunnisett, *Medieval Coroner*, p. 14. [24] Below, pp. 480–1.

EXEMPTION FROM ATTENDANCE AT THE SHERIFF'S TOURN

Clause 4 of the Provisions of Westminster of 1259 which had exempted members of various groups from attendance at the sheriff's tourn was re-enacted without alteration in 1267 as chapter 10 of the Statute of Marlborough.[25] The earliest post-1267 evidence for the enforcement of this legislation is a writ enrolled on the King's Remembrancer's Memoranda Roll in Trinity term 1268. It is a writ of prohibition addressed to the sheriff of Essex on behalf of John of Weston, the steward of Eleanor, the wife of the Lord Edward. It begins with a phrase reciting the legislation that is reminiscent of those used in the Statute of Marlborough itself,[26] and recites the exemption mandated by the legislation from the requirement of attendance at the tourn of those who were not resident in the area for which the tourn had been held. It goes on to order the sheriff to respect its provisions in relation to John of Weston since he was constantly in the company (*conversans*) of Eleanor.[27] Although of a redrafted form, the prohibition is clearly in a direct line of descent from the series of such prohibitions issued in favour of non-resident landholders by the Exchequer from 1261 onwards.[28]

This prohibition is followed on the roll by what seems to be a related writ, also addressed to the sheriff of Essex, in favour of the 'men' (probably here meaning the unfree tenants) of the same John of Weston and of the prominent Exchequer clerk, Robert of Fulham, in the Essex villages of 'Gingelaundry' and 'Gingejoyberd', both now part of Buttsbury. This ordered a respite of the amercement being levied against them by the sheriff for their failure to present John of Weston and John de Ginges for being in default at the sheriff's last tourn held in the hundred of Chelmsford.[29] The unstated grounds for this respite are presumably that both men were exempt from the duty of attendance by virtue of their non-residence in the hundred at the time the tourn was held. There seems to be no pre-1267 precedent for this kind of mandate, following

[25] Below, pp. 468–9.

[26] 'Quia convocatis discretioribus regni provisum est et statutum ac concorditer ordinatum . . .'

[27] *'Essex pro Johanne de Weston' de turno vicecomitis.* Quia convocatis discrecioribus regni provisum est et statutum ac concorditer ordinatum quod si qui in hundredis diversis habeant tenementa non habeant necesse venire ad turnum vicecomitis nisi in ballivis in quibus fuerunt conversantes et idem Johannes senescallus Alienore consortis Edwardi filii regis sit conversans cum ea mandatum est vicecomiti quod de demanda quam ei facit veniendi ad turnum suum ei pacem etc. Et averia etc.': E 159/42, m. 18 (communia of Trinity term 1268).

[28] Above, pp. 116–17, 170–1.

[29] *'Pro hominibus Johannis de Weston' et Roberti de Foleham'.* Mandatum est vicecomiti quod ponat in respectum usque super compotum suum proximum ad scaccarium demandam quam facit hominibus eorundem Johannis et Roberti in villis de Gingelaundry et Gingejoyberd eo quod non presentaverunt predictum Johannem et Johannem de Ginges esse in defaltam ad ultimum turnum suum in hundredo de Chelmeresford'. Et averia etc.': E 159/42, m. 18.

through on the exemption of non-residents from attendance at the tourn in order to ensure the presenting jurors were not amerced for failing to present them for absence from the tourn. John de Ginges had secured a personal prohibition addressed to the sheriff of Essex against demands for attendance at the tourn on grounds of non-residence prior to 1267.[30]

There is also some evidence to suggest that a new form of general prohibition to give effect to chapter 10 of the Statute of Marlborough may have been drafted not long after the enactment of the Statute for issue by Chancery. At least four registers, of which two seem to belong mainly to the earliest years of the reign of Edward I, contain a specimen writ of prohibition which recites not just the legislative exemption of members of most, but not quite all, of the various specified groups from attendance at the tourn but also the provision allowing others exemption from attendance at the tourn outside the jurisdiction where they were resident.[31] Perhaps significantly, the two omitted groups (archbishops and bishops) are exactly the same as those omitted from the specimen sheriff's tourn prohibition writ which had been enrolled on the Close Roll in 1260. This also shares with this writ the peculiarity of also reciting the non-residential exemption.[32] But there is at least one significant difference from that earlier form which suggests that, even if the 1260 prohibition does in some sense lie behind the writ found in these registers, it does so at one remove. This is in the introductory formula which three of the four registers (including one early one) use to refer to the authority behind the legislation. The formulation used ('Cum ad melioracionem status regni nostri provideri fecimus') is quite unlike that used in 1260 and is also unlike the form later used in similar writs. It is, however, reminiscent of some of the wording of the Statute of Marlborough.[33] This suggests that not long after 1267 Chancery may have made available a form of prohibition for the enforcement of the Statute that was based on the 1260 form but had been revised to reflect the changed political climate and which emphasized the royal, rather than magnate, authority that lay behind the legislation.

[30] Above, p. 171.

[31] BL MS. Lansdowne 564, fol. 35v: 'quod abbates, priores, comites, barones, viri religiosi seu mulieres non teneantur venire ad tornos vicecomitis nisi eorum presencia exigatur et si [qui] in hundredis diversis habeant tenementa [similiter] necesse non habeant venire ad hujusmodi turnos nisi in ballivis ubi fuerunt conversantes . . .' A similar form of words appears in BL MS. Additional 38821, fol. 15r, a second register dating from the early years of Edward I and in BL MS. Additional 34194, fol. 19r, a register with material from this period but also some much later material, and BL MS. Additional 5762, fol. 27v, a register dating from *c.* 1300. Both of these substitute 'compellantur' for 'non teneantur'.

[32] Above, pp. 454–5.

[33] BL MS. Additional 38821, fol. 15r, the other register dating from early in the reign of Edward I, uses instead the more conventional form: 'Quia de communi consilio regni provisum sit.'

This form of prohibition seems later to have been replaced by two separate forms which recited the authority behind the legislation in more conventional form,[34] and then recited the provisions of the legislation as they applied solely to non-residents or to members of the other exempt groups respectively. The non-resident prohibition form appears in a register of writs whose forms appear to belong in the main to no later than the second half of the 1270s;[35] a prohibition in favour of members of some (but not all) of the exempt groups, covering archbishops, bishops, abbots, priors and other religious men and women (but neither earls nor barons), is found in two registers of the same period.[36] No greater precision than this is possible because such writs were never enrolled on the rolls of Chancery and did not give rise to litigation. Their existence and potential availability can only be traced at some distance through the chance survival of specimen writs in surviving registers of writs.

EXEMPTION FROM ATTENDANCE AT VIEW OF FRANKPLEDGE

The legislation of 1259, reissued and confirmed in 1263/4 and 1267, governed only demands for attendance at the sheriff's tourn. It said nothing about attendance at the private, franchisal equivalent of the sheriff's tourn, the view of frankpledge. Nor is there any evidence prior to 1267 of any extension of the legislation to cover attendance at the view. From Michaelmas term 1270, however, comes the first evidence for just such an extension, although the first writ issued related to a view of frankpledge for a privately held hundred and the writ even apparently described the privately held view as being a 'sheriff's tourn'. This was in litigation in the Common Bench of which only a preliminary procedural stage has been found and which was brought by the abbot of Eynsham against John Ashewy. This cited only that part of the legislation exempting various kinds of religious from attendance at the tourn and alleged that John was breaching the legislation by distraining the abbot for attendance at

34 The form used is 'Cum de communi consilio regni nostri provisum sit . . .'

35 'Si qui in hundredis diversis habeant tenementa necesse non habeant venire ad turnum vicecomitis nisi in ballivis ubi fuerunt conversantes . . .': BL MS. Lansdowne 564, fol. 65r. The writ seems to be taken from a real example issued in favour of Humphrey de Barent' (? = Barenton). For later examples see e.g. BL MSS. Egerton 656, fols. 63v–64r and Harley 323, fol. 85v.

36 '. . . archiepiscopi, episcopi, abbates, priores seu aliqui viri religiosi seu mulieres non habeant necesse venire ad turnum vicecomitis nisi eorum presencia ob aliam causam specialiter requiratur': BL MS. Lansdowne 564, fol. 65r. A similar form of words (but reading 'alii viri religiosi') is found in BL MS. Harley 409, fol. 38v and, albeit heavily abbreviated, in BL MS. Egerton 656, fol. 51r, a register dating from the very end of the thirteenth century. All three writ forms continue at the end, after ordering the release of any distresses taken by the sheriff, to warn him that further measures will be taken if he does not comply with the order: 'ne iteratus clamor ad nos inde perveniat per quod manum/manus ad hoc aliter apponere debeamus'.

the sheriff's tourn in the Gloucestershire hundred of Slaughter which was held by the abbot of Bec.[37]

Nothing was said in the enrolment of this case about any preliminary prohibition. Such prohibitions are, however, regularly mentioned as having been breached in later enrolments of cases alleging wrongful distraint to enforce attendance at the view of frankpledge. The earliest such enrolment comes from Michaelmas term 1274 and cites only that part of the legislation which exempted non-residents from the duty of attendance at sessions outside the jurisdiction within which they resided. The case was brought against two named bailiffs of Edmund, earl of Lancaster for allegedly distraining the plaintiff to attend the view of frankpledge held for the earl's honour of Leicester in Northamptonshire. Only a procedural stage of this case has been found.[38] The following year the same part of the legislation was again cited in an action brought against Richard of Gravesend, the bishop of Lincoln, relating to a distraint for attendance at view of frankpledge in his court of Leicester. Again, only the preliminary procedural stages of the case have been found.[39] Similar enrolments show the same specific part of the legislation being invoked in litigation under way in 1276,[40] 1277,[41] 1278[42] and 1291.[43] None of these cases seems ever to have reached the pleading stage.

[37] '. . . de placito quare cum de communi consilio regni nostri provisum sit quod abbates, priores et alii viri religiosi non habeant necesse venire ad turnum vicecomitis nisi eorum presencia ob aliquam causam exigatur, idem Johannes distringit predictum abbatem occasione tenementi sui quod habet in Wal . . . ad hujusmodi turnos in hundredo de Sloghtre contra formam provisionis predicte': KB 26/200C, m. 20.

[38] '. . . de placito quare cum de communi consilio regni domini regis provisum sit quod si qui in diversis hundredis habeant tenementa necesse non habeant venire ad visum franci plegii nisi in ballivis ubi fuerint conversantes iidem Ricardus et Johannes distringunt predictum Johannem de Roseles ad veniendum ad visum franciplegii in curia predicti domini sui honoris Leyc' in comitatu predicto contra formam provisionis predicte et contra prohibitionem nostram': *John de Roseles v. Richard de Shelton and John of Hodingg', the bailiffs of Edmund earl of Cornwall (recte Lancaster)*: CP 40/5, m. 51d.

[39] '. . . de placito quare cum de communi consilio [regni] regis provisum sit quod si qui habeant tenementa in diversis hundredis non habeant necesse venire ad visum franci plegii nisi in ballivis ubi fuerint conversantes predictus episcopus prefatum Willelmum distringit ad veniendum ad visum franciplegii in curia sua de Leyc' contra formam provisionis predicte et contra prohibitionem etc.': *William Touk v. Richard of Gravesend bishop of Lincoln*: CP 40/9, m. 53d (Easter term 1275); a later stage is enrolled in Hilary term 1276: CP 40/13, m. 72.

[40] *William Mowyn v. Alice daughter of Hugh le Brun*: CP 40/14, m. 12d (the enrolment here makes no specific mention of any prior prohibition); *Michael of Northampton v. Robert of Babraham chaplain*: CP 40/14, m. 45d (a hundredal view of frankpledge).

[41] *William of Upton v. Walter de Evereus and Richard of Marham and his wife Margery*: CP 40/21, m. 92. A later stage is enrolled in 1278: CP 40/24, m. 32.

[42] *Michael of Northampton v. Robert Chaplain of Babraham and William of Foxcroft, the king's bailiffs of the honour of Brittany of Babraham*: CP 40/23, m. 25 (apparently a revival in amended form of the second of the two 1276 cases, though the view is now said to be for the honour of Brittany and held at Babraham).

[43] *Hugh of Bereford v. Thomas de Blacheston, the king's bailiff of the honour of Peverel*: CP 40/91, m. 140.

There were, however, at least two pleaded cases which were brought by writs which cited this specific part of the legislation. In Trinity term 1293 Richard Franceys of Wimpole sued William Latimer for attempting to compel him to attend his view of frankpledge contrary to a prior prohibition.[44] Richard claimed that although he was living in Cambridgeshire on lands he held at Wimpole and Wetherley he had been distrained at Wrestlingworth in Bedfordshire in 1292 to attend William's view of frankpledge at Sutton. Despite having served a prohibition on William's steward on the Tuesday next after the Ascension, the distraint for attendance at the view had later been renewed. William did not deny having made or ordered a distraint but he claimed that it was not for attendance at the tourn. He said it had been for arrears of the homage, scutage and fealty owed by his immediate tenant at Wrestlingworth, Roger of Hertford. Richard attempted to plead that this was no proper answer to his count. William, however, insisted that this action was in effect no different from an action of replevin. It was up to the defendant to assign reasons for his distraint and thereafter to maintain them. The case was adjourned for judgment on this point of pleading, which was also a tussle about who was to be assigned the burden of proof in the case. The second case was heard less than two years afterwards, in Hilary term 1295. In it Ralph Bomound sued Simon of Stevington and William de la Contesse, the bailiffs of John of Brittany at Babraham in Cambridgeshire, for distraining him at Wimpole on the Monday before Michaelmas 1293 to attend the view of frankpledge at John's court at Babraham, although he was not resident in the county, contrary to a prior prohibition, and for then driving the horse taken out of the county into Bedfordshire.[45] Simon avowed the distraint as made to secure Ralph's attendance not at a view of frankpledge but at a private sheriff's tourn held at Kneesworth on the grounds that the lands Ralph held at Wimpole were within the earl's manor of Babraham and the earl enjoyed the right to hold the sheriff's tourn with jurisdiction over all lands held by his tenants in Cambridgeshire. The distraint was said to have been for a default Ralph had made at a tourn held at Kneesworth on the Monday after Martinmas 1293 although this took place only after the date of the alleged distraint. Ralph's lawyers evidently noted the discrepancy and secured judgment against Simon.

All these cases were brought by the non-residents who were claiming exemption. One register of writs also has a prohibition (apparently based on a writ actually issued) brought by Walter de Langton on behalf of his villeins in the village of Weston on Avon in Gloucestershire who were

[44] CP 40/101, m. 39d. [45] CP 40/107, m. 81.

attending the sheriff's tourn in the hundred of Kiftsgate in Gloucestershire but being distrained to attend the view of frankpledge of the honour of Leicester at Ilmington in Warwickshire by the bailiffs of Edmund of Lancaster.[46] There is no evidence for a similar variant being used in any other cases.

The earliest cases brought by writs citing that part of the legislation which had exempted members of various ecclesiastical categories from attendance at the tourn, but as now extended to view of frankpledge, also seem to be represented only by enrolments of procedural stages and the cases to have been dropped before being pleaded. The earliest of these from 1277 cites the exemption not just of the various ecclesiastical categories mentioned by the legislation but also that of women;[47] the next (of 1279) recites the exemption only of the much more limited categories of abbots, priors and other religious.[48] The first pleaded case of this type comes from Trinity term 1284 and, although brought by the abbot of Malmesbury against Milisent de Montalt, it seems (from the related enrolments) to have been brought by a writ citing only the exemption of 'religious men' and not (as might have been expected) the specific exemption of abbots.[49] Interestingly, the case seems to have been pleaded and enrolled but then to have been repleaded within the same term and the initial enrolment marked for cancellation. Since the pleading took quite a different form on the second occasion it looks as

46 BL MS. Lansdowne 564, fol. 49v.

47 '. . . de placito quare cum de communi consilio regni regis provisum sit quod archiepiscopi, episcopi, abbates, priores aut alii viri religiosi seu mulieres non habeant necesse venire ad visum franciplegii nisi eorum presencia ob aliam causam specialiter exigatur idem Eudo distringit predictum abbatem ad veniendum ad visum franciplegii in hundredo suo de Calne contra formam provisionis predicte et contra prohibicionem etc.': *Abbot of Malmesbury v. Eudo la Zouche:* CP 40/21, m. 97. For a revival of this suit against Eudo's widow but using a different writ see below, note 49. A prohibition of a similar form but addressed to the bailiffs of Edmund of Lancaster and in favour of the master of the Templars and his brethren is to be found in the register of writs in BL MS. Additional 34194 at fol. 19r and again in favour of the Templars, but without the specific address, in a register of the 1270s in BL MS. Landowne 564 at fols. 35r–v.

48 '. . . de placito quare cum de communi consilio regni regis provisum sit quod abbates aut priores aut ceteri viri religiosi non habeant necesse venire ad visum franciplegii, nisi eorum presencia ob aliam causam specialiter exigatur, iidem Henricus et Reginaldus distringunt predictum abbatem ad veniendum ad visum franciplegii in curia Edmundi fratris regis nunc de honore de Lancastre in comitatu Noting' contra formam provisionis predicte et contra prohibicionem etc.': *Abbot of Rufford v. Henry of Nottingham and Reginald of Alfreton:* CP 40/31, m. 49. For later stages see CP 40/32, mm. 47d and 58 and CP 40/34, m. 68d.

49 '. . . de placito quare cum de communi consilio regni regis provisum sit quod viri religiosi non habeant necesse venire ad visum franciplegii nisi eorum presencia ob aliam causam ad hoc specialiter exigatur predicta Milisenta distrinxit predictum abbatem ad veniendum ad visum franciplegii in hundredo suo de Calne contra formam provisionis predicte et contra prohibicionem': CP 40/54, m. 44d and CP 40/54, m. 46d (cancelled entry). This was a revival, using a different writ, of a case the abbot had brought against Milisent's late husband, Eudo la Zouche: see above, note 47.

though there must have been some kind of internal appeal process within the Common Bench which led to the quashing of the first judgment. As initially pleaded, the abbot alleged the serving of a prohibition on the morrow of Michaelmas 1282 and Milisent's subsequent disregard of that prohibition by a distraint made on the Thursday before St Dunstan (15 October 1282) to compel the abbot to attend her view of frankpledge in the hundred of Calne. As originally pleaded, Milisent's claim was that the abbot owed suit twice a year for a manor that he held within the hundred and the distraint had been made because he had failed to appear to perform it. The abbot insisted that the legislation had exempted abbots and clerks and the religious from attendance at the view of frankpledge and that these twice-yearly sessions for which she was claiming suit were sessions of the view of frankpledge because it was only view of frankpledge business that was done there. Attendance at such sessions could only be claimed on the basis of a personal duty to attend and not on the basis of a tenurial obligation of attendance. Milisent attempted to salvage her case by claiming that other business was done as well and that he owed suit for the reinforcement of the court and had been summoned for that purpose. But the court had found this unconvincing and awarded judgment in favour of the abbot. When the case was repleaded, the abbot alleged service of the prohibition less plausibly on the morrow of Martinmas 1282 (after the date of the allegedly subsequent distraint) and again avowed the distraint as made for one of the two suits he owed each year to her hundred of Calne. This time the enrolment records that Milisent alleged seisin of the suit by the king during the minority of her elder brother, George de Cantilupe, as well as by herself. The abbot (presumably under pressure from the court) this time took issue on this alleged seisin rather than denying the validity of the claim to suit at what were evidently sessions of the view of frankpledge. No jury verdict is recorded.

In a case heard in Michaelmas term 1285 the abbot of Osney sued Roger de Somery for breaching the legislation by attempting to make him attend the view of frankpledge at his court of Oving in Buckinghamshire.[50] Again the case seems (from the related enrolment) to have been brought by a writ citing only the exemption of 'religious men' and not, as might have been expected, the specific exemption of abbots.[51] Here everything had taken place in a matter of days. Roger had

[50] CP 40/60, m. 22.

[51] '. . . de placito quare cum de communi consilio regni regis provisum sit quod viri religiosi non habeant necesse venire ad visum franci plegii nisi eorum presencia ob aliam causam ad hoc specialiter exigatur idem Rogerus distrinxit ipsum abbatem ad veniendum ad visum franciplegii in curia predicti Rogeri de Ovyng' contra formam provisionis predicte et contra prohibicionem etc.'

ensured that the abbot was summoned to a view of frankpledge held at Oving on the Monday after Hockday (16 April) 1285 and had adjudged him in default when he had not appeared. He had brought a prohibition on the following day (17 April) and Roger had disregarded the prohibition by making a distraint on the Wednesday (18 April). Roger did not attempt to justify the distraint but simply denied ever having had him summoned to the view or that he had adjudged him in default or had him distrained. This went to a jury whose verdict is not recorded. Something rather similar took place in a third case heard in Hilary term 1303 when it was the abbot of Croxton who was suing five named royal bailiffs of the honour of Eye in the county of Lincolnshire for a distraint made in 1302 to compel him to attend the view of frankpledge held for the honour at Ancaster or, more precisely, to pay the amercement owed for his failure to attend the view.[52] Again the defendants denied ever having made any such distraint. On this occasion, however, there is a recorded jury verdict from a *nisi prius* session returned to the court at the octaves of Martinmas 1304. This found that one of the defendants (John of Norton of Wellesbourne) had indeed taken a horse in distraint because the abbot had not attended a view of frankpledge and was still keeping it but that the others had not been involved. Judgment was given that the abbot recover his horse and damages taxed at four pounds.[53]

No examples have been found from the reign of Edward I of litigation being brought to enforce the exemption from attendance at the tourn or view of frankpledge of women[54] or of archbishops or bishops.[55]

ENFORCEMENT THROUGH COMMON LAW ACTIONS

The legislation on attendance at the sheriff's tourn (and by extension at the view of frankpledge) was also cited in a number of non-statutory

[52] CP 40/146, m. 129d.

[53] For two other cases of the 1290s of which only preliminary procedural stages have been found see *Abbot of St James outside Northampton v. Richard of Watford rector of Ashridge:* CP 40/89, m. 102 (Easter term 1291); *Prior of Farley v. Stephen de la More (with David le Blund):* CP 40/130, m. 12 (Michaelmas term 1299). Both cite the legislation as merely exempting the religious in general. For a form from a register of writs which looks like one issued in a real case in the final years of the thirteenth century, but which may never have led to litigation, see BL MS. Egerton 656, fols. 50v–51v (prohibition to the bailiffs of Gilbert of Clare of the honour of Clare in favour of the prior of Barnwell).

[54] But for an action from early in the reign of Edward II against a sheriff to enforce exemption from attendance at the tourn for a woman see *Maud La Marechale (of Kent) v. John of Harpsfield late sheriff of Hertfordshire:* CP 40/169 m. 145d (1308).

[55] For a form in a register of writs that looks as though it may have been issued in a real case in favour of the dean of St Paul's and which seems to date from the final decade of the thirteenth century see BL MS. Harley 748, fol. 47r.

actions, as it had been between 1259 and 1267.[56] Two of them were about demands for attendance at the sheriff's tourn made by third parties. In an action of mesne heard in the Common Bench in Michaelmas term 1274 the prior of St Bartholomew's Smithfield in London sued Hubert de Ruylly to acquit him of three-weekly suit to the hundred court of Tendring in Essex, castle guard at Colchester, twice-yearly attendance at the tourn in the hundred and a contribution to the common amercement of the county at the last Essex eyre.[57] He was being distrained for all of these by the royal bailiffs of the hundred of Tendring in respect of the one hundred and twenty acres he held in frankalmoin at Bradfield. Hubert was obliged to acquittance by a deed. Hubert asserted that attendance at the tourn was a personal rather than a tenurial obligation which all free tenants owed and denied any duty to acquit the prior of this demand. The court agreed, citing Magna Carta (by which Marlborough must have been meant) for the general proposition that the religious were not required to attend the tourn or perform suit to it and so dismissed this part of the claim. Something rather similar occurred in another case in the 1278 Hertfordshire eyre of which there is a report as well as a plea roll enrolment. In this case the prior of Anglesea was seeking acquittance of various demands made by the sheriff of Hertfordshire. These included attendance at the sheriff's tourn twice yearly.[58] The prior's action against Ralph fitz Ralph fitz Simon was, however, initiated by writ of fin fet rather than mesne because the claim to acquittance was based on a promise of acquittance contained in a final concord of 1275 rather than just on a charter. Again the claim for acquittance of attendance at the sheriff's tourn was rejected both because this was a personal, rather than a tenurial obligation, and because legislation of Henry III's reign (which the report of the case spells out to be a reference to the Statute of Marlborough) had exempted the religious from attendance at the tourn unless their presence was required for some special reason.

In a replevin case heard in 1295, of which there is not just an official plea roll enrolment but also a number of separate reports, John Malemeyns challenged the distraint made against him by Hugh de Poynz and Henry de Grey as joint lords of the manor and hundred of Hoo in Kent for the amercements imposed on him for absence from two sessions of their leet (in effect their view of frankpledge).[59] The claim was that the obligation to attend the leet arose from John's tenure of the manor of Stoke within

[56] Above, p. 123. [57] CP 40/5, m. 38d.

[58] JUST 1/323, m. 4d (reported in BL MS. Lansdowne 564, fols. 99v–100v: printed in *Casus Placitorum* as Collection II, no. 11 at pp. 111–13).

[59] CP 40/110, m. 98d: reported in BL MSS. Stowe 386, fol. 158v; Additional 37657, fols. 8r (note) and 9v; LI MS. Hale 188, fols. 27r and 34r.

their hundred. This was at once challenged by counsel for the plaintiff on the grounds that attendance at the leet was an obligation that arose from personal residence within the leet's jurisdiction and was indeed incumbent as much on the landless as those who held land. It could not, therefore, be said to be owed by reason of tenure of any particular holding. The implication, later spelled out, is that John had not been resident within the jurisdiction of the leet when the leet was held and so should have been exempt from attendance at it. Counsel for the defendants attempted to respond that attendance at the tourn had been owed on that basis since time out of mind (or perhaps more plausibly, as the plea roll suggests, ever since the initial acquisition of the hundred by the ancestors of the defendants in the reign of King Richard) by the tenants of the plaintiff's manor. Chief Justice Mettingham's eventual judgment in the case held that, even if they had been so seised, this seisin would have been defeated by the Statute of Marlborough. This had laid down the general rule that no attendance at the view could be claimed from persons not resident within the jurisdiction of the leet when the leet was held. Since the defendants had tacitly conceded that the plaintiff was not resident within the leet jurisdiction when the leet was held the distraint had been unjustified.

Rather more puzzling is a reference to the Statute in the enrolled defence of the archbishop of York to a *quo waranto* suit in the 1287 Gloucestershire eyre which challenged the exemption of the archbishop (and of his men) from suit to the county court.[60] The archbishop seems to have said that the most that he could be said to owe to the county court was two attendances each year but that he was quit of them both as the king's baron and because statute (evidently the Statute of Marlborough) said that no one needed to attend the sheriff's tourn except where they were resident and that the religious and women did not need to attend unless their attendance was specially required. There seems here to be a confusion between the sheriff's tourn in each hundred and the two more fully attended sessions of the county court.

BEAUPLEDER FINES

Clause 5 of the original Provisions of Westminster prohibiting demands for beaupleder fines had, as has been seen, been substantially modified in 1263 to allow the survival and continued exaction, both by the king's bailiffs and by others, of any beaupleder fine which had been levied as a fixed payment continuously since the king's first crossing into Brittany

[60] *Placita de Quo Warranto*, pp. 253–4.

(in 1230). It had been in this amended and watered-down form that clause 5 was re-enacted as chapter 11 of the Statute of Marlborough in 1267.[61]

The earliest evidence for the enforcement of the re-enacted beaupleder legislation after 1267 comes from the Memoranda Rolls of the Exchequer. In Michaelmas term 1268 and Michaelmas term 1272 there are writs enrolled on these rolls addressed to the sheriff of Essex and Hertfordshire which order him to desist from exacting such fines from a named village and from the men of three hundreds respectively.[62] The earliest action brought by a Chancery writ citing the legislation, though in a form which does not mention the exception made by the Statute in favour of fines fixed before 1230,[63] is to be found in Michaelmas term 1277. This is only a procedural stage and without any pleadings.[64] A previous disregarded prohibition is mentioned in this and later cases.[65] There may well also have been another early prohibition writ issued by Chancery which did not lead to litigation or which did not lead to litigation enrolled on any surviving plea roll. The evidence for this is a writ form found in four Edwardian registers of writs (of which two seem to belong to the later 1270s) that is evidently based on an actual prohibition issued by or in the name of Edward I and addressed to the bailiffs of his mother in the Sussex rape of Pevensey. This recited the legislation and a complaint from the community of the hundred of Shiplake within that rape about a demand for a beaupleder fine. It ordered the end of such demands and the release of distresses taken to enforce its payment.[66]

A number of other later cases, of which again only procedural stages have been found, show the legislation being invoked by the whole communities of other rapes. In 1298 it was invoked by the community of the rape of Hastings against Harsculph de Cleseby, John of Brittany's bailiff for the rape,[67] and in 1301 against John of Brittany himself.[68] In 1298 it was invoked by the community of the rape of Pevensey against the royal bailiff of that rape.[69] Litigation was also brought in 1301 by the communities of fourteen Bedfordshire villages against two named royal bailiffs of the

[61] Below, pp. 436–7, 470–1.

[62] E 159/43 m. 5; E 159/47 m. ld. Both writs specifically cite that part of the legislation which excepted fines fixed before 1230.

[63] Unlike the Memoranda Roll writs which do.

[64] *John le Brokere and Walter Miller of Stodham v. Robert Idwyn et al.*: CP 40/21 m. 30. The court to which the fine demanded was payable is not mentioned.

[65] There is no evidence, despite Fitzherbert (*New Natura Brevium*, fol. 170c), for the use of attachment without prior prohibition.

[66] BL MS. Harley 409, fol. 41v; Trinity College Cambridge MS. O.3.45, fol. 8r; BL MS. Lansdowne 564, fols. 79v–80r; CUL MS. Ll.4.17, fol. 305v.

[67] CP 40/125, m. 68d. [68] CP 40/139, m. 57d. [69] CP 40/125, m. 42d.

hundred of Willey for demanding a beaupleder fine. The plaintiffs were later non-suited.[70] At a still more local level there is evidence of a case being brought in 1300 against the prior of Southwick by the community of the village of Prior's Dean alleging a demand for a beaupleder fine in the prior's court in the village.[71] The early fourteenth-century register of writs printed by de Haas and Hall suggests that there also existed a variant of the writ to cover the exaction of such a fine by a sheriff from the community of his county, but no such action has been found on the plea rolls.[72]

The only case brought by such a writ for which pleadings have been found on the rolls was one heard in Michaelmas 1285.[73] Here the defendant, Roger de Somery, admitted having made a distraint against the plaintiff, the abbot of Osney, for a fine but claimed that this had been not a beaupleder fine but a fine levied for the plaintiff's default at the view of frankpledge, as the plaintiff had himself admitted by bringing another action against him in the same term in respect of the same distraint.[74] There is, however, also an as yet unidentified copy of an enrolment in a Cambridge University Library MS. of what seems to be a suit brought by writ by the men of an unidentified village of 'Hanebunte' against the prior of St Swithin's Winchester. They were seeking that he answer them on a plea as to why 'whereas it has been provided by the common council of our realm that fines be not taken for beaupleder'[75] he was distraining them unjustly against the provision to make a fine for beaupleder *(pulcre placitando)*.[76] The case seems, however, then to have revolved around the status of these men: whether they were free and thus able to challenge the exaction or the prior's villeins and so incapable of doing so. Since their claim to ancient demesne status had recently been rejected in prior litigation the men's attempt to claim free status failed.

The legislation was also enforced by means of plaints and presentments. In the Hampshire eyre of 1280 a presentment was made against Maud, countess of Gloucester and her bailiff by the town of Petersfield. It was alleged that the bailiff was demanding two marks a year for a beaupleder fine in the town.[77] Maud's defence was that the king had assigned her the two marks out of the inheritance of her son Gilbert as part of her

[70] CP 40/135, m. 129.

[71] The writ initiating this litigation and issued on 28 March 1300 is on the writ file for one month after Easter 1300 in CP 52. It mentions a prior prohibition and orders the interim release of the distresses taken.

[72] *Early Registers*, p. 255 (R 634 variant).

[73] *Abbot of Oseney v. Roger de Somery*: CP 40/60 m. 22d.

[74] For the other action see CP 40/60, m. 22 and above, pp. 292–3.

[75] '. . . cum de communi consilio regni nostri provisum sit ne fines capiantur pro pulcre placitando . . .'

[76] CUL MS. Ll.4.18, fol. 228r. [77] JUST 1/784, m. 18.

dower while he was in wardship to the king. She vouched her son to warranty.[78] The case was then adjourned to the Wiltshire eyre of 1281 where it appears as a plaint in the foreign pleas section of the eyre.[79] The enrolment shows Richard de la Putte suing on behalf of the community of the town against the countess and specifically citing the legislation.[80] He alleged that she had breached it by distraining the community for two marks a year for a beaupleder fine. On their behalf he claimed damages of one hundred shillings. The earl of Gloucester now warranted the countess and claimed the fine was his 'free tenement' appurtenant to his manor of Mapledurham and that he was not obliged to answer for it without the king's writ, merely in response to a plaint. The response to this was that it could not be his 'free tenement' since it had only originated in the extortion of his late father in 39 Henry III (1254–5). The response to this maintained the original objection and argued that, as the town had conceded that his father had died seised, he could not be made to answer without a writ. Judgment was adjourned to later in the same circuit at Exeter at the quindene of Martinmas, but none has been traced.

A number of complaints about the exaction of beaupleder fines were also made during the course of the Hundred Rolls enquiry. Several of these refer specifically to the recent origins of the fine being levied.[81] The evidence provided by the enquiry that the legislation was being ignored on a grand scale seems to have been the reason for the re-enactment of the legislation against beaupleder fines in 1275 as chapter 8 of the Statute of Westminster I.[82] Although Britton suggests that an article specifically enquiring into such fines was included in the articles of the eyre,[83] there is no other evidence for the existence of such an article, and the articles

[78] For a similar voucher made in the course of the 1281 Wiltshire eyre see JUST 1/1005, m. 147 (hundred of Alderbury). This was a presentment stating that while Ralph de Aungers had been the steward of William Lungespeye in the reign of Henry III he had levied a fine twice yearly within the hundred for beaupleder and that the bailiffs and stewards of John Giffard and his wife, Maud, from then until the present had received it, both before and after it had been provided by the lord king Henry and his council at Marlborough that such moneys should not be taken ('provisum fuit per dominum H. regem et consilium suum apud Marleberge quod hujusmodi denarii non caperentur'.) John and Maud appeared and said they held in dower and that Maud had been endowed by the king and the fine included in the extent. They vouched Henry de Lacy, earl of Lincoln and his wife, Margaret, to warrant for the fine.

[79] JUST 1/1000, m. 90; also in JUST 1/1005, m. 94d.

[80] '. . . whereas by the common council of the realm of England it had been provided that neither in eyres nor county courts nor in hundred courts nor in courts baron were fines for beaupleder, or so as not be harmed, to be received . . .'

[81] For examples see *RH*, I, 58 (fine first exacted by the steward of the queen mother during her wardship of the Ferrars lands, i.e. between 1257 and 1260); *RH*, II, 12 (fine first levied eighteen years before); *RH*, I, 5, 6, 38, 45 (fine first levied in Bedfordshire and Buckinghamshire by Alexander de Hamden, sheriff 1249–52 and 1259–63); *RH*, II, 203 (fine levied only since 1267–9).

[82] *SR*, I, 28.

[83] *Britton*, I, xxi, 4 (I, 80).

asking generally about new customs or the oppression of bailiffs seem to have provided sufficient scope for those wishing to complain about such matters. Those presented for levying beaupleder fines often had some defence to offer for doing so: the king's authorisation and command for levying it;[84] that the fine had been included in the revenues assigned to the recipient by the king;[85] that the fine had been fixed ever since 1230.[86] Sometimes, however, the roll records no appearance and no defence being offered and simply records the sheriff being ordered to ensure that the fine was not levied in future.[87] A presentment relating to the exaction of such fines was also made in the course of Kirkby's Quest by the hundred of Wyleton in Somerset against William de Welles, the bailiff of the hundred. It was alleged that he received fines from each tithing of two, three or four shillings and more or less as they were able to make fine with him for beaupleder as other bailiffs were accustomed to do at the lawday even though this had not been customary of old.[88]

[84] JUST 1/915, m. 5 (1279 Sussex eyre: the hundred of Colspure, follow-up to inquisitions taken before Briaunzoun). The hundred used to give two marks at the tourn in the time of Peter of Savoy and Ralph the clerk, his bailiff, raised seven marks instead and then John de la Rede, John of Wangford and Adam de la Ryge had levied seven marks. When the hundred had come to the hands of John of Brittany (in 1274) he had sent Simon de St Leodegar to keep the hundred and rape of Lewes. Under the provisions of the king's Statute he had given up the additional five marks newly levied and took the original two marks only. Subsequently, in response to the king's letter, he had levied both the new five marks and the old two marks as his lord had received the rape of Lewes in exchange by extent and the seven marks had been included in that; Simon produced the king's writ of 25 May 1276 to the bailiff of the rape authorising him to levy £32 10s arrears.

[85] JUST 1/930, m. 2 (1288 Sussex eyre: the hundred of Hawksborough): a jury presentment against John of Brittany alleging that he had taken five marks and eleven shillings each year for beaupleder. The presentment was adjourned to a fortnight after Trinity when John appeared and said that the rape of Hastings had once belonged to Henry III and he had given it to Peter of Savoy in exchange for lands Peter held of honour of Richmond and the sum had been included with other fines in the extent. The presentment was then adjourned for judgment. See also JUST 1/930, m. 4 (the hundred of Stapley): like presentment against bailiffs of John of Brittany alleging they were taking £4 2s 8d for beaupleder.

[86] JUST 1/915, m. 10d (the hundred of Buttinghill): jury presentment that John, earl of Surrey received forty shillings through his bailiffs (Richard de la Vache, Walter Dragun, Oliver son of Ernest) of a common fine for beaupleder; also forty shillings from the hundred of Street, twenty-four shillings from the hundred of Barcomb and the half hundred of Woodham. The earl said the fines were arrented in the time of his father, William, and he had died seised during the reign of Henry III and that the king had received the fines while he had been in his wardship. The court dismissed the presentment on the grounds that the Statute of Marlborough had exempted such fines.

[87] JUST 1/493, m. 4 (1281–4 Lincolnshire eyre: the wapentake of Aveland): presentment that John Marshal of Aslackby and the master of Templars had levied 'new customs' in the village of Aslackby by taking from the free tenants at each court next after Michaelmas fines for beaupleder contrary to statute. They were simply amerced and the sheriff instructed to prevent them from receiving these fines on penalty of ten pounds.

[88] E 198/3/1A, m. 2.

The legislation was also cited and enforced in a number of actions of replevin brought to challenge distraints made to enforce beaupleder fines. Three separate actions of replevin heard in Michaelmas term 1285 challenged distraints made by the lord of the Somerset hundred of Wellow (Nicholas de Montfort) to enforce payments allegedly owed by tithingmen twice yearly on behalf of their tithings to the hundred court. Nicholas claimed that these were fixed payments of which his brother had died seised, though not specifically that they had been fixed ever since 1230. The plaintiffs claimed that they were variable beaupleder fines and thus implicitly barred by the legislation. The question of the nature of the fines was sent to a jury for its verdict.[89] In a replevin case heard in Michaelmas term 1289, the avowry made by the warden of Merton College, Oxford was for a fixed sum of money (half a mark) owed to the defendant as a contribution to the rent of twenty shillings paid by that defendant to a third party (Richard de Harecurt) in return for being allowed his own view of frankpledge at Kibworth Harcourt in Leicestershire. The plaintiff responded that the payment was a variable one paid to excuse the plaintiff (Lawrence of Aptoft) and his tenants from attendance at the third party's view. When the jury found it a variable payment the court categorised it as a beaupleder fine and so held the distraint unjustified.[90]

The legislation was also used by Gilbert de Clare, earl of Gloucester in his own defence when impleaded by the king by *quo waranto* in the 1280 Dorset eyre for withdrawing the thirty-four shillings his tenants had customarily paid at the tourn in the Dorset hundred of Rowborough and the eight shillings they had used to pay at the hundred of Hasilor. Gilbert said that King Henry III at Marlborough had granted to the community of the realm and provided by the assent and will of the community for himself and his heirs that nothing be paid for beaupleder and that this should be observed. But he also made no claim to the sums himself and the court awarded seisin to the king.[91] The presentment of the Hasilor subtraction is particularly interesting as it suggests that the money had been withdrawn at the time of the 'Provisions of Oxford' and been unpaid since then, suggesting that here at least the original Provisions of Westminster with their absolute prohibition on beaupleder fines had been effective and the local shrieval administration had not been able to

89 CP 40/60, mm. 94 (*Ralph le Messer and Robert Mody v. Nicholas de Montfort et al.*), 98d (Hugh le Jovene against same) and 95d (John Dunnyng against same).

90 CP 40/80, m. 221d. For a 1305 avowry for a fixed payment owed by a Wiltshire tithing which Bereford J. specifically noted as escaping the statutory prohibition of beaupleder fines for that very reason see *YB 33–35 EI*, pp. 97–101 (identifiable as a report of CP 40/153, m. 235d: *John prior of Maiden Bradley v. Adam de la Forde and others*).

91 *Placita de Quo Warranto*, p. 183.

claw back the fine even after the 1263 legislation had confirmed fines fixed since before 1230.[92]

There is very little positive evidence for the enforcement of the legislation on beaupleder fines in the eyre. Beaupleder fines under that name seem to have disappeared after 1259,[93] but the other common fines continued to be exacted. These include the fines paid 'before judgment for false judgment and other offences' (*ante judicium pro falso judicio et aliis transgressionibus*) in the Dorset eyre of 1288[94] and another fine paid 'before judgment' by the county in the Cornish eyre of 1302.[95]

92 JUST 1/204, m. 45.

93 Unless the orders issued in Hilary 1262 to the sheriffs of Gloucestershire and Oxfordshire for a relaxation of demands on the abbot of Winchcombe for a share 'de fine comitatus pro pulcre placitando' refer to fines made in the eyres of 1261 in those counties: E 159/36, m. 5d.

94 JUST 1/210, m. 24.

95 *YB 30 & 31 EI*, p. 241.

Chapter 11

REFORMS IN THE PROCEDURES OF THE ROYAL COURTS

Various changes had been made by the Provisions of Westminster and by the Statute of Marlborough in the procedures, and especially in the mesne process, used in the royal courts.[1] These had mainly been made in an effort to make the central royal courts more efficient and to afford absent defendants less opportunity for delay. Shorter adjournments than normal were authorised in certain types of litigation; mesne process was abbreviated in certain types of case; the initial process was made harsher under certain circumstances in the action of account. There were also a number of other minor changes which were intended to eliminate what had been perceived as abuses in the operation of royal courts. This chapter will examine how these various changes worked in practice during the four decades between the enactment of the Statute of Marlborough and the end of the reign of Edward I.

ADJOURNMENTS IN ACTIONS OF DOWER

As has been seen, clause 6 of the Provisions of Westminster was among the clauses significantly amended when the Provision were reissued in 1263 and it was in this amended form that it was further reissued in 1267 as part of chapter 12 of the Statute of Marlborough.[2] The original Provisions had set a minimum target of at least four days in court each year for pleas of dower *unde nichil habet*, but the 1263 reissue (followed by chapter 12 of the Statute of Marlborough) increased the target to a minimum of five days in court each year with six specified as the desirable goal.

Once the plea rolls begin to survive in an almost continuous and well-preserved series from the mid-1270s onwards it becomes possible to trace individual cases on the plea rolls from adjournment to adjournment, though cases disappear from the plea rolls when the parties are essoined. This is not possible for an earlier period, when there are significant gaps in

[1] Above, pp. 65–6, 69–75, 148–9, 203–4. [2] Above, p. 148; below, pp. 470–1.

Table 3 *The length of adjournments in actions of dower in selected terms, 1268–90*

	Length of adjournments (by return days)							
Term	8	7	6	5	4 (% affected)	3	2	1
Michaelmas 1268	0	0	10	10	60	10	0	0
Michaelmas 1269	0	0	0	10	70	0	0	0
Trinity 1270	0	0	0	0	70	10	0	0
Easter 1271	0	0	0	10	55	16	0	0
Hilary 1280	0	0	0	14	55	16	0	0
Easter 1280	0	0	0	0	58	20	0	0
Trinity 1280	0	0	0	0	21	47	17	0
Michaelmas 1280	0	0	14	18	45	0	0	0
Hilary 1290	0	0	0	12	48	22	12	0
Easter 1290	0	0	0	7	44	20	0	0
Trinity 1290	0	10	53	18	10	0	0	0
Michaelmas 1290	16[a]	10	14	13	30	0	0	0

Sources: All adjournments on the rectos of KB 26/195, 194, 200A, 202; CP 40/32, 33, 34, 36; CP 40/81, 82, 83, 86.
Note: [a] Almost half of these are adjournments made at the request of the demandant from the quindene of Michaelmas to the quindene of Hilary.

the surviving rolls and more of the rolls are damaged. For this period the only alternative is to look at the length of the adjournments recorded at individual stages of the dower cases recorded on these rolls. The number of return days in a year varied from year to year, but in an 'average' year was around twenty. This meant that in order to ensure that a case would come up at least five times in a year, the case needed to be adjourned to a return day no more than four return days later. To make it possible to compare the rate of compliance with the provisions of the legislation over time a similar methodology has also to be adopted for analysing the dower cases on the later rolls. Table 3 is based on an analysis of the adjournments in dower cases on all the recto membranes of the plea rolls for Michaelmas term 1268, Michaelmas term 1269, Trinity term 1270, Easter term 1271 and for all four terms in 1280 and 1290. Excluded from the table (though not from the overall percentages) are those dower cases which are recorded on membranes that ascribe the cases they contain to more than one return day or to none.

It will be seen from Table 3 that with the exception of Trinity and Michaelmas terms in 1290, the evidence suggests substantial compliance with the requirements of the legislation. Even in those two terms the amount of deviation from the norm was not very great. The system clearly retained some degree of flexibility, but dower cases were regularly given significantly shorter adjournments than most other litigation. This meant that they passed through the system at twice the speed of other litigation,[3] which was indeed broadly speaking in accordance with the expectations established by the legislation. The court's practice is also roughly in accordance with the schemes of adjournments found in the various (and varying) different texts of *Dies Communes de Dote*, which show dower cases being regularly adjourned to a return day four return days later.[4] The precise status and role of these texts is unclear. They cannot have been used on a continuing basis as a practical guide by the clerks and justices of the Common Bench since they make inadequate allowance for the variations from year to year in the length of Hilary and Trinity terms. Perhaps they were derived from a working list of standard adjournments used in one particular year which subsequently reached wider circulation within the profession.

ADJOURNMENTS IN *QUARE IMPEDIT* AND DARREIN PRESENTMENT

Clause 7 of the Provisions of Westminster of 1259 had provided that, in litigation initiated by the writ of *quare impedit* and in the assize of darrein presentment relating to disputes about the right to present to vacant ecclesiastical livings, adjournments of as little as two weeks (normally two return days) might be given provided the county concerned was close to the court. Three-week adjournments (normally three return days) were to be given where the living was located in one of the more distant counties. This clause was unchanged in the 1263 reissue and in 1267 became part of chapter 12 of the Statute of Marlborough, also without amendment.[5]

Table 4 presents an analysis of the length of adjournments in all cases of *quare impedit* and darrein presentment recorded on the plea rolls for selected terms between 1267 and 1290. The fractions reflect cases recorded on membranes ascribing the business to more than one return day. At first sight Table 4 suggests that the courts were much less compliant with legislation on adjournments in darrein presentment and *quare impedit* than

[3] Hence the note in CUL MS. Additional 3129, fol. 57r: 'Sciendum quod in brevi de dote semper dantur duo dies ubi in aliis brevibus non datur nisi unus.'

[4] Printed from a single text with a note of variants from one other MS. in *SR*, I, 208.

[5] Above, pp. 72–3.

Table 4 *The length of adjournments in actions of* quare impedit *and in assizes of darrein presentment in selected terms, 1267–90*

	Length of adjournments (by return days)								
	9	8	7	6	5	4	3	2	1[a]
Term	(number of cases)								
Easter 1268	0	0	0	0	0	0.5	1.5	0	1
Michaelmas 1268	0	0	0	1	1	2	1	0	0
Michaelmas 1269	0	2	0	1	0	1	2	2	1
Trinity 1270	0	0	0	0	0	3	0	1	5
Easter 1271	1	0	0	0	0	0	5	0	0
Hilary 1272	0	0	0	0	0	0	2	0	0
Trinity 1272	0	0	0	0	0	0	3	0	0
Hilary 1280	0	1[b]	0	0	0	4	1	3	2
Easter 1280	0	0	0	0	0	1	3	0	0
Trinity 1280	0	1[c]	0	0	0	0	2	0	1
Michaelmas 1280	1[c]	3[d]	0.333	0.333	1.333	1.5	0	0	3
Hilary 1290	0	0	0	0	0	0.5	1.5	1	0
Easter 1290	0	0	0	0	0	3	4.5	2.5	0
Trinity 1290	0	0	0	0.5	1.5	3.5	1	1.5	1
Michaelmas 1290	0	0	1.5	1	4	8	1	0.5	1

Notes: [a] All these adjournments are from the last day of one term to the first day of the next term.

[b] The same stage of this same case also appears on the plea roll for Easter term with the same day appointed for its next stage: compare CP 40/32, m. 16 and CP 40/33, m. 23.

[c] A day given at the request of the parties.

[d] One adjournment was made at the request of the parties and one at the request of the claimant.

with that on adjournments in the action of dower *unde nichil habet*. This may, however, be erroneous. The legislation only applied in the case of actions that concerned 'vacant churches'. On occasion, litigation which had commenced while a church was vacant seems to have continued after the bishop had collated to the living on the lapse of the initial six months.[6] Once this had happened, there was no further need for any extraordinary speed in the mesne process; the cases with relatively long adjournments may all be of this kind.

[6] E.g. the *quare impedit* case of the *Prior of Kirkham v. Nicholas of Seagrave* in 1280 where the original summons was for the octave of Purification (CP 40/32, m. 85) but in which the case was still dragging on in Michaelmas term, a jury being respited for lack of recognitors from the octaves of Michaelmas to the octaves of St Martin (CP 40/36 m. 1). The case had thus lasted for well over six months.

Awareness of the specific terms of the legislation is also manifest in the action of at least one litigant (the dean and chapter of Lichfield) in obtaining a privy seal writ from the king at Caernarvon in June 1284. This reproved the justices of the Common Bench for making too brief an adjournment when adjourning an essoiner in an assize of darrein presentment brought by Henry of Edgbaston against the dean and chapter the previous Easter term on the grounds that the church (at Edgbaston) was in a remote part of Warwickshire. The Statute of Marlborough had said that days were to be assigned fortnightly or three-weekly 'according to whether the place was close or remote'. They had only adjourned him to a day two weeks later. The writ ordered them to suspend hearing the case until later in the term when they would be assisted by someone the king would send to join them.[7]

THE ABBREVIATION OF MESNE PROCESS

Clause 7 of the Provisions of Westminster of 1259 had also eliminated all stages in mesne process in the action of *quare impedit* between the first attachment and the grand distress. This provision was left unamended when the legislation was reissued in 1263 and again when it became part of chapter 12 of the Statute of Marlborough in 1267.[8] There are no known instances of additional stages of distraint being ordered between the second attachment and the grand distress, probably because these stages had been eliminated in other actions as well in 1263. Shortly after the final re-enactment of the legislation in 1267, in Easter term 1268, however, there are two actions of *quare impedit* in which a first attachment was followed by orders for a second attachment.[9] The correct practice seems to have been followed henceforward.[10] After 1275, the second attachment was eliminated from process in other personal actions as well, by Westminster I, ch. 45, and mesne process in *quare impedit* became once more identical with that followed in other actions.[11]

One of the clauses added to the Provisions in 1263 had eliminated all stages in mesne process in personal actions generally between the second attachment and the grand distress.[12] This was re-enacted without

[7] CP 40/54, m. 30. [8] Below, pp. 470–1. [9] KB 26/184B, mm. 1d, 2d.

[10] E.g. KB 26/194, mm. 24, 36 (Michaelmas term 1269); JUST 1/365, m. 94 (Kent eyre 1271); KB 26/208A, m. 2 (Trinity term 1272); CP 40/2A, m. 27 (Easter term 1273); CP 40/9, mm. 35, 44d (Easter term 1275); CP 40/10, mm. 15, 29, 72d (Trinity term 1275).

[11] *SR*, I, 37–8. [12] Above, p. 148.

alteration in 1267 as part of chapter 12 of the Statute of Marlborough.[13] The courts seem to have complied fully with this provision.[14]

JUDGMENT BY DEFAULT

Quare impedit

The Provisions of Westminster of 1259 had provided (also in clause 7) for the courts to award judgment by default in favour of the plaintiff in the action of *quare impedit* if the defendant failed to appear after the grand distress had been awarded against him.[15] The clause was re-enacted without alteration in 1263 and in 1267 became without alteration part of chapter 12 of the Statute of Marlborough.[16] The first post-1267 example of a judgment being awarded under this provision of the legislation seems to have been in 1271.[17] Other examples of such judgments can be found in Trinity term 1272,[18] and also later.[19]

There were difficulties with the application of the legislation in cases where the defendant held no lands in the county where the church lay, since that meant he could not be distrained by the grand distress, and the legislation had said that judgment could be given by default only after the defendant had been distrained to appear by the grand distress and had failed to appear. In Hilary term 1272 a default judgment was awarded in a *quare impedit* case brought by Edmund, the king's son, against Robert de Ferrers, the erstwhile earl of Derby, when the sheriff returned to a writ of attachment that the defendant had not been found and had nothing by which he could be attached, 'nor is it known where he may be attached in any other county' ('nec scitur ubi potest attachiari in aliquo alio comitatu'), without any attempt being made to proceed to the grand distress.[20] The sheriff's return is hardly believable and it looks as though the court was deliberately bending the law in favour of the king's younger son. In another *quare impedit* case of 1276 in King's Bench, judgment by default was given in favour of the king after the court had ordered the attachment of the defendant and then the grand distress

[13] Below, pp. 470–1.

[14] For examples of cases where the second attachment was followed by the grand distress from plea rolls of the period immediately after the passage of the Statute see e.g. KB 26/184B, m. 26 (Easter term 1268); KB 26/195, mm. 5, 10, 30, 32 (Michaelmas term 1268).

[15] Below, pp. 418–19. [16] Below, pp. 470–1. [17] KB 26/202, m. 31.

[18] KB 26/208A, m. 29d.

[19] E.g. CP 40/5, m. 47d (Michaelmas term 1274); CP 40/9, m. 18 (Easter term 1275); CP 40/10, mm. 64d, 72d (Trinity term 1275); CP 40/12 m. 26 (Michaelmas term 1275) and, for the king, KB 27/31 m. 5 (*coram rege* Easter term 1277). There do not, however, seem to have been any examples in either 1280 or 1290.

[20] KB 26/206, m. 35.

against him, even though it had been attested that the defendant had no lands or tenements where he could be attached.[21] The same procedure was followed in a case heard in Michaelmas term 1297 where the court was careful to award the grand distress after the failure to attach a defendant who possessed no property within the relevant jurisdiction, citing 'the Statute' as its authority (or reason) for doing this, presumably because only if this process was followed was the court justified in giving judgment by default.[22] But the justices of the Common Bench could also prove more inventive in such procedural matters. In Michaelmas term 1290 the court borrowed from the procedure used in the action of wardship in the case of another landless defendant.[23] The sheriff had returned to a writ of grand distress that the defendant had neither lands nor tenements by which he could be distrained. He was ordered to distrain the defendant a second time, 'and to make formal proclamation in full county court and also at the said church on some feast day and have Peter warned in all the ways by which this can best be done that he be here on the said day if this seems expedient to him . . .'[24] This seems to be a preliminary to awarding judgment by default. Unfortunately the judgment itself has not been found. No such procedure has been noted in later cases, which seem to have reverted to the older practice of giving judgment by default after an order for the grand distress, even when it was then attested that the defendant had no lands or tenements where he could be distrained.[25] There was also an analogous difficulty where the suit was brought against a husband and wife and the wife alone defaulted, for all her movable goods in law belonged to her husband. In Trinity term 1288 judgment was only given by default against the wife after the wife had been distrained by goods of her husband and she had failed to appear.[26] Another potential difficulty occurred if the successful plaintiff gaining judgment by default was an ecclesiastic, for the recovery (if only of the right of presentation on

[21] *Rex v. Ralph of Winterflood*: KB 27/21, m. 2d.

[22] *William de Beauchamp earl of Warwick v. Nicholas Burdon*: CP 40/121, m. 258.

[23] See below, pp. 309–10.

[24] '. . . et . . . solempniter proclamari faciat in pleno comitatu et similiter ad predictam ecclesiam aliquo die solempni et omnibus modis quibus melius poterit predictum Petrum premunire faciat quod sit hic ad prefatum terminum si sibi viderit expedire . . .': *Michael of Barnwell v. Peter Whippe*: CP 40/86, m. 234. For another reported case of Michaelmas term 1302 (*John of Hastings v. Anthony bishop of Durham*) where an attestation that a defendant had no property seems to have led to an order for his summons at the church in dispute see LI MS. Miscellaneous 738, fol. 29r.

[25] For an example see the Hilary 1294 default judgment in *Richard of Kenn and others v. Lawrence son of Simon of Ludgate*: CP 40/103, m. 8. But for an Easter 1301 case where judgment by default was only awarded after two such attestations see *Elizabeth de Gamage v. David bishop of St David's*: CP 40/138, m. 150d.

[26] *Mabel of Kennington v. Ellis de Hauville and his wife Amice*: CP 40/73, m. 75d.

this one occasion) might still be considered (after 1279) to be in breach of the Statute of Mortmain. Judgment was awarded by default in a case brought by a prior in Hilary term 1307 but its execution suspended until an enquiry *quale jus* had been held as to possible collusion between the parties, under the provisions of ch. 32 of the Statute of Westminster II.[27] The Statute only authorised judgment by default on continued defaults prior to appearance. However, in a case of Michaelmas 1292 the justices of the Common Bench in effect extended the Statute by analogy to justify awarding judgment by default when a defendant defaulted after appearance and putting himself on a jury, holding that a defendant should be no less punished for this than if he had defaulted after the grand distress.[28]

The Statute of Westminster II (1285), ch. 5 authorised (among other things) the awarding of damages when plaintiffs made successful recoveries in this action. These were to be to the value of half the annual value of the church, if the six months had not yet elapsed, and to double the annual value if they had.[29] It is not wholly clear from the wording of the Statute whether or not the legislators intended this also to apply in the case of recoveries by default. Within ten years of the Statute, however, damages began to be awarded in such cases as well.[30]

Writ of right of wardship

In 1267 judgment by default was extended by chapter 7 of the Statute of Marlborough to the action of wardship. As with *quare impedit* there was no provision for an enquiry into the plaintiff's title before judgment was given. The procedures to be applied before judgment was given were, however, much lengthier and more complicated.[31] If the defendant failed to appear after the grand distress, it was to be reissued twice or three times

27 *Prior of Ormsby v. Henry of Laughton*: CP 40/162, m. 218; *SR*, I, 87. Cf. Coke, *Second Institutes*, pp. 429–30.

28 *Simon of Kyme and his wife Maud v. Thomas of Rigsby and others*: CP 40/96, m. 103d. For another case where the same rule seems also to have been applied see *Rex v. Master Robert de Lacy*: CP 40/152, m. 54d (Trinity term 1304).

29 *SR*, I, 75–7.

30 For the earliest example noted of such an award (of damages to half the value of the church) see the Michaelmas 1295 case of *Walter of Benham v. Peter son of Goscelin*: CP 40/110, m. 71. For later examples see the similar award in the Trinity 1304 case of *Edmund Hoese v. William of Dummer and his wife Maud*: CP 40/152, m. 188; and the award of damages to double the annual value (but with execution of the judgment suspended until process had been returned against a third defendant) in the Michaelmas 1305 case of *Margaret, widow of Edmund of Cornwall v. William de Boville and others*: CP 40/153, m. 285d.

31 Below, pp. 464–5.

during the following half year, the sheriff on each occasion reading out the writ in the county court, publicly warning the defendant to appear, as well as seeking him out in the normal way. If the defendant still failed to appear he was to lose seisin of the wardship in question, though his right to bring an action for its recovery on another occasion was expressly safeguarded. The legislation did not, however, apply in those cases where the defendant's title was not his own but derived from the wardship of another.[32]

The earliest case in which the new procedure was followed seems to have been one brought in the Gloucestershire eyre of Michaelmas 1268. In *Fromund v. Tantefer* the sheriff was ordered to distrain the defendant and produce his body at Northampton at the quindene of St John Baptist, 1269, that is six months later, 'and that he was to have this writ read etc.' ('et quod legi faciat breve istud etc.').[33] Unfortunately, the Northamptonshire eyre roll does not survive, so it is not possible to see whether or not a default judgment for recovery was awarded. The first case in which such a judgment has been traced is one brought in the Common Bench in 1274–5. At the morrow of All Souls' 1274, the sheriff of Yorkshire returned to the writ of grand distress that the defendant had found two mainpernors. The sheriff had also already been ordered that 'he was to have the king's writ which had come to him on this read in his full county court and was to publicly warn that the same Gregory should appear on this day to defend his right if it seemed expedient to him, and that he was to report on this day on the execution of the king's writ'.[34] He returned that he had read out and publicly proclaimed the writ, as he had been ordered. He was then ordered to repeat the whole process for Hilary term 1275.[35] He then returned that the defendant had been distrained by all of his goods which could be found and had found two mainpernors and that he had again read the writ as ordered. As the defendant again failed to appear, the plaintiff now recovered seisin of the wardship by default.[36] The only other successful recovery by default I have found on the rolls of the Common Bench for this period is one awarded in Easter term 1301.[37] A further judgment by default was awarded in Trinity term

[32] The legislation does not explain how the justices were to discover whether a particular case fell within this category, the plaintiff only, and not the defendant, disclosing his alleged title in advance. Possibly some kind of receipt of the infant or his relations was envisaged.

[33] JUST 1/275, m. 48d.

[34] '. . . quod breve regis quod sibi inde venit in pleno comitatu suo legi et puplice denunciari faceret ut idem Gregorius veniret ad hunc diem jus suum defensurus, si viderit expedire, et qualiter preceptum regis fuerat executus scire faceret hic ad hunc diem . . .'

[35] CP 40/5, m. 60d: *Maud widow of Robert of Ravensthorpe v. Gregory of London.*

[36] CP 40/7, m. 36d.

[37] CP 40/138, m. 177: *William son of Robert of Somercotes v. Philip le Boneyre of Saltfleetby.*

1307 but suspended, because the plaintiff was an ecclesiastic, until a jury *quale jus* had discovered whether the default was a collusive evasion of the Statute of Mortmain.[38] Rather more common are judgments ordering the preliminary proclamations authorised by the Statute as a preliminary to the giving of such judgments.[39]

There was, however, a much larger number of writ of right of wardship cases in which the statutory procedures were not used but the writ of grand distress simply issued and reissued. One good example is the Sussex case of *Audham v. Paynel* in which repeated use of the grand distress between Easter 1268 and Hilary 1270 failed altogether to secure the appearance of the defendant.[40] Renewed distraint, rather than renewed distraint plus proclamation, seems indeed to have remained the normal procedure in wardship cases despite the Statute.[41] The reasons for this general disregarding of the legislation are probably similar to those that made judgment by default in *contra formam feoffamenti* so uncommon.[42] The provisions of the legislation were perhaps not generally known. The justices of the court knew of the king's interest in the forfeited issues of the grand distress and may have been reluctant to allow judgments by default, which might secure the interests of plaintiffs but prejudiced those of the king.[43]

[38] CP 40/164, m. 169d.

[39] For examples see *Ralph de Beauchamp v. William de Mountchesney*: CP 40/11, m. 5 (Michaelmas term 1275); the 1276 case of *John de Hertwayton v. Robert de Lisle*: CP 40/15, m. 82; *Master Thomas of Byrlaund v. Richard of Seaton*: JUST 1/668, m. 30d (1280 Nottinghamshire eyre); *Ela countess of Warwick v. Godfrey bishop of Worcester*: CP 40/51, m. 77d and CP 40/52, m. 2d (Michaelmas term 1283 and Hilary term 1284); *John Lovel v. John of Newland and his wife Anna* and *Robert de Brus v. John Bek*: CP 40/53, mm. 16d, 28 (Easter term 1284); *Ralph de Beauchamp v. William de Mountchesney*: CP 40/60, m. 54d and CP 40/61, m. 47d (Michaelmas term 1285 and Hilary term 1286); *Thomas de Neville v. Ellis of Byrton and his wife Cecilia*: CP 40/102, m. 182 (Michaelmas term 1293).

[40] The initial grand distress was returnable at Sherbourn at the quindene of Easter 1268; on the sheriff's failure to act the order was repeated for the morrow of Ascension at the same venue (JUST 1/202, m. 15) at which (ibid., m. 11d) the order was renewed for the morrow of Trinity 1268 at Reading. At Oxford on the morrow of SS Peter and Paul 1268 (JUST 1/702B, m. 1) the order was again repeated. The case was still proceeding in the Common Bench in Michaelmas term 1269 (KB 26/194, m. 8d) when four mainpernors were amerced for failing to produce the defendant, and the sheriff was amerced for not producing any issues, the grand distress being renewed for the quindene of Hilary 1270.

[41] For examples see JUST 1/643, m. 9 (Northumberland eyre 1269); JUST 1/483, m. 40 (Lincolnshire eyre 1271–2); KB 26/184B, m. 3 (Easter term 1268); KB 26/195, mm. 7, 8, 36 (Michaelmas term 1268); KB 26/194, mm. 15d, 16d, 20d (Michaelmas term 1269); KB 26/208A, mm. 20, 45 (Trinity term 1272); CP 40/32, mm. 36, 75 (Hilary term 1280); CP 40/34, mm. 51, 52 (Trinity term 1272); CP 40/36, mm. 14, 27, 78, 134 (Michaelmas term 1280).

[42] Above, pp. 216–18.

[43] Cf. *YB 3 Edward II (1309–1310)*, ed. F.W. Maitland (Selden Society vol. 20, 1905), pp. 91–3: 'It will be to the King's prejudice to maintain this writ of account. For as long as he has lands and tenements, the sheriff shall answer for the issues, and that is to the King's advantage' (per Scrope).

MESNE PROCESS IN PERSONAL ACTIONS AFTER THE JOINDER OF ISSUE

One of the clauses added to the Provisions of Westminster on their reissue in 1263 had authorised a significant change in the mesne process against defendants applicable in personal actions after the joinder of issue for jury trial. No defendant was in future to be allowed more than a single essoin or a single default. After just one essoin or one default the jury's verdict was to be taken, whether or not the defendant appeared. Judgment was then to be given in accordance with its verdict. If the jury verdict was taken in the Westminster Bench or before the justices in eyre judgment could then be given immediately for either party in accordance with that verdict. If the jury verdict was taken locally in the county court or before a specially commissioned royal justice, judgment could only be given in the Common Bench after the verdict had been returned into the court. This clause was re-enacted in 1267 without change as chapter 13 of the Statute of Marlborough.[44] The workings of this procedure can be shown in a number of cases after 1267.[45] Chapter 13 of the Statute of Marlborough was further amended in 1285 by chapter 27 of the Statute of Westminster II.[46] This established that after the parties had put themselves on the verdict of a jury, the defendant would be allowed to essoin himself only at the immediately following return day. Thereafter the inquest would be taken despite the defendant's absence if the jury appeared but he essoined himself, even if this was the first time he had done so.

MONSTRAVIT DE COMPOTO

Clause 19 of the original Provisions of Westminster had authorised the use of 'attachment by the body' to secure the appearance in court of bailiffs who had not rendered an account to their lords for their period in charge of their lord's property, if the bailiffs concerned did not possess lands or tenements by which they could be distrained for this purpose.[47] Chancery had then created a special writ of *monstravit de compoto* to authorise sheriffs to take this drastic step as the initial stage in process against such bailiffs.[48] This clause had not been amended in 1263 and was re-enacted in 1267 without alteration as part of chapter 23 of the Statute of Marlborough.[49]

44 Below, pp. 472–3.

45 See for example JUST 1/275, m. 21 (1268 Gloucestershire eyre); JUST 1/323, m. 24 (1278 Hertfordshire eyre); CP 40/32, m. 17d (Hilary term 1280); CP 40/34, m. 7 (Trinity term 1280); CP 40/36, m. 46d (Michaelmas term 1280).

46 *SR*, I, 85. 47 Below, pp. 424–5. 48 Above, pp. 117–19. 49 Below, pp. 479–80.

The different forms of the writ and the procedure for obtaining them

The earliest form of *monstravit de compoto* to be drafted was, as has been seen, of a non-returnable form, authorising the initiation of litigation in the London husting court.[50] Later registers of writs indicate that writs of a similar form remained in use throughout the period down to 1307 and beyond.[51] There is, however, no evidence to suggest that Chancery ever created or made available any other type of non-returnable writ of *monstravit de compoto* for use in other cities or in county courts. A returnable form of *monstravit de compoto* had probably also been drafted by 1261.[52] It too was certainly in regular use after 1267. There is a surviving example on the Common Bench writ file for Michaelmas term 1272.[53]

Most types of original writ could apparently be obtained simply by appearing at Chancery and asking (and paying) for them. The procedure for obtaining *monstravit de compoto* was rather more complicated. This is shown by two related writs included in an early fourteenth-century register of writs printed by de Haas and Hall. A writ authorising mainprise of the defendant where it was alleged that the writ of *monstravit de compoto* had been obtained by deceit states simply that the writ of *monstravit de compoto* had been obtained by a 'suggestion' in Chancery that the defendant did not possess lands and tenements by which he could be distrained and that he was hiding away within the sheriff's jurisdiction so that he could not be found and compelled to render account.[54] The following writ of deceit spells out (but in a slightly different and more explicit way) what is meant by 'suggestion'.[55] This indicates that before the plaintiff could obtain the writ of *monstravit de compoto* it was necessary for him to make an oral affirmation in Chancery,[56] to affirm both that the defendant really had been his bailiff (or receiver) and that he did not

[50] Above, pp. 117–18.

[51] *Early Registers*, pp. 209–10 (R 425); *Reg. Omn. Brev.*, fol. 137r. [52] Above, pp. 118–19.

[53] CP 52/1/1A, pt. 1, no. 40. This confirms something suggested by the evidence of various surviving registers of writs of the later thirteenth and early fourteenth centuries: that the writ normally included the phrase 'as he can reasonably show . . .' ('sicut . . . rationabiliter monstrare poterit etc.') at its conclusion. This phrase had hitherto served as one of the verbal markers distinguishing non-returnable from returnable writs, so its inclusion in this returnable writ is something of an anomaly. For the forms in registers see *Early Registers*, p. 209 (R 424); CUL MSS Additional 3022, fol. 26r, Ll.4.17, fol. 279v; BL MS. Harley 748, fol. 23r; *Reg. Omn. Brev.*, fol. 136v. It was normally omitted from enrolments; but for cases where it was included see CP 40/15, m. 104 (Trinity term 1276) ('ita quod haberet corpus ejus ad hunc diem ad reddendum eidem Roberto compotum suum predictum sicut racionabiliter monstrare poterit quod ei reddere debet etc.'); CP 40/30, m. 79d (Trinity term 1279) ('et ob hoc preceptum fuit vicecomiti quod attachiaret predictum Philippum, ita quod haberet corpus ejus hic ad hunc diem ad reddendum compotum suum predictum sicut racionabiliter monstrare poterit quod ei reddere debeat').

[54] *Early Registers*, pp. 210–11 (R 429). [55] *Early Registers*, p. 211 (R 430).

[56] '. . . per fidem quam prestitit in cancellaria nostra prout moris est . . .'

possess lands or tenements by which he could be distrained. Perhaps it was necessary in practice to swear to all three of these things. Some form of this procedure apparently goes back to at least the late 1270s, for a register of writs of that date has a note to the effect that anyone wanting to sue out the writ must affirm (*affidare*) that the bailiff against whom he is suing his writ has neither lands nor tenements nor chattels within the kingdom of England by which he could be distrained to render his account.[57]

There also seems some reason for supposing that initially at least, and despite the statutory origins of the writ, it may only have been available to those who enjoyed special royal favour. It is not perhaps surprising that the thirty-six plaintiffs bringing writs of *monstravit de compoto* between 1267 and 1280 should have included some of the greatest men and women of the realm like Gilbert de Clare, earl of Gloucester,[58] Robert de Vere, earl of Oxford,[59] Geoffrey de Lusignan,[60] Agnes de Vescy,[61] Robert de Brus[62] and the prior of Ely.[63] But the list of plaintiffs also includes what seems to be a disproportionate number of men who were merely prominent royal servants. These include the two royal justices, Ralph Hengham[64] and Master Roger of Seaton,[65] the king's chancellor, Robert Burnel,[66] the former steward of the household and royal councillor, Robert Aguillon,[67] the prominent royal clerk and diplomat, Master Bonet de St Quintin,[68] the royal clerk and brother of the more famous Robert Walerand, John Walerand,[69] and the former royal surgeon, Thomas of Weasenham, who sued as steward of the royal forest of Cannock.[70] Less prominent plaintiffs who were also in the king's service include the household knight, Eustace of Hatch,[71] the Exchequer of the Jews and Common Bench clerk, William of Middleton,[72] and the Exchequer clerk, Hugh Oyldeboef.[73]

57 Bodleian Library MS. Douce 139, fol. 25r: 'sciendum est quod quicumque hoc breve habere voluerit affidare debet quod ille ballivus non habet terras nec tenementa neque catalla infra regnum Anglie per que distringi valeat ad prefatum compotum'.

58 CP 40/19, m. 71d (and for later stages see /21, m. 69; /23, m. 41; /26, m. 61d; /28, m. 69; /30, m. 69d).

59 CP 40/15, m. 104 (and for later stages see /17, m. 35; /18, m. 73; /19, m. 61d; /23, m. 36d).

60 CP 40/5, m. 85d.

61 CP 40/3, m. 27 (and for later stages see /5, m. 104d; /9, m. 40).

62 CP 40/17, mm. 22, 24 (and for later stages see /18, mm. 24d, 27d; /19, m. 22d).

63 CP 40/19, m. 69d.

64 CP 40/23, m. 20d (and for later stages see /24, m. 27d; /26, m. 42; /28, m. 7d); CP 40/23, m. 40.

65 CP 40/23, m. 20d

66 CP 40/14, m. 37.

67 CP 40/9, m. 21.

68 CP 40/23, m. 8d (and for later stages see /24, m. 4; /26, m. 55; /28, m. 26d; /29, m. 28d; /30, m. 85d; /31, m. 138d).

69 KB 26/200C, m. 17d.

70 KB 26/196, m. 2d (and for later stages see /199, m. 27d; /202, m. 28d).

71 CP 40/32, m. 12.

72 CP 40/31, mm. 19d, 150 (and for later stages see /32, m. 25; /33, m. 26d).

73 CP 40/17, m. 142 (and for a later stage see /18, m. 60d).

The frequency of the use of monstravit de compoto *after 1267*

Actions of account initiated by the returnable writ of *monstravit de compoto* were never as common as actions initiated by the ordinary action of account, but they do seem to have become relatively common in the Common Bench, especially after *c.* 1290. Early cases are easily identifiable by the enrolment not only of the initial clause of the writ, setting out the basic facts which allegedly justified the issuing of the writ in this particular case,[74] but also of the relevant passage from the legislation authorising this form of writ.[75] From the mid-1290s it becomes more difficult to identify such cases,[76] for the usual form of enrolment of *monstravit de compoto* cases came to be reduced to the form 'on a plea that he render to him a reasonable account for the time when he was his bailiff in G., having the care and administration of all his possessions and goods'.[77] It is only the additional phrase about 'having the care and administration of all his possessions and goods' that distinguished such cases from those initiated by the ordinary writ of account.[78] In some other later cases the only evidence that the writ of account being used is *monstravit de compoto* is the insertion of the phrase 'by writ of statute' (*per breve de statuto*)[79] or a note that the defendant has been attached 'by his body' (*per corpus suum*), sometimes with an additional phrase in the

[74] '. . . de placito quare cum idem [defendant] extiterit ballivus suus in N. omnium rerum et bonorum suorum curam habens et administracionem idem [defendant] compoto suo non soluto subterfugia querens latitat in balliva vicecomitis ne possit inveniri vel distringi ad reddendum compotum suum predictum . . .'

[75] '. . . et quia de communi consilio regni regis provisum est quod si ballivi qui dominis suis compotum reddere tenentur se subtraxerint et terras et tenementa non habeant per que distringi valeant per eorum corpora attachientur, ita quod vicecomites in quorum ballivis invenientur eos venire faciant ad compotum suum reddendum . . .'

[76] But for a much earlier example of what is probably an enrolment of a pleaded case initiated by a *monstravit* where the only evidence of this is the use of the phrase 'omnium rerum et bonorum suorum curam habens et administracionem' in the summary of the writ (and where the count also mentions that 'hucusque subterfugia quesivit et se a predicto compoto reddendo fugit') see CP 40/10, m. 40 (Trinity term 1275). For an enrolment of the process stage of what seems to be an action of *monstravit de compoto* in which the only evidence of this is the fact that the enrolment notes that the sheriff has been ordered to attach the defendant by his body see CP 40/38, m. 15 (Hilary term 1281).

[77] '. . . de placito quod reddat ei rationabilem compotum de tempore quo fuit ballivus suus in G. omnium rerum et bonorum suorum curam habens et administracionem . . .'

[78] See CP 40/106, m. 145 (Michaelmas term 1294) where the sheriff in an action so enrolled, having been ordered to attach the defendant by his body, reported that he had accepted two pledges and was ordered again to attach the defendant by his body (and see also ibid., m. 163). In the same term, however, in another case the older and fuller form of enrolment also appears in CP 40/106, m. 206. Compare also CP 40/143, m. 22 (Trinity term 1302) and the related report in BL MS. Additional 31826, fol. 131r where the enrolment has the short additional phrase and the report reveals the case is brought by a *monstravit*.

[79] E.g. CP 40/153, m. 414d (Michaelmas term 1305).

enrolled count referring to the fact that he was 'hiding away' (*subterfugia querens*).[80]

Actions initiated by this writ seem to have been remarkably rare in the eyre. I have found only one clear example of an action of account initiated by a writ of *monstravit de compoto* in the eyre, a case brought in the 1293 Kent eyre.[81] There is also at least one unmistakable example of a *monstravit de compoto* case brought in the court of King's Bench, enrolled on the plea roll for Michaelmas term 1305 with a full recital of the provisions of the Statute, but without any hint as to why the litigation was being brought there, rather than in the Common Bench.[82]

The first clear evidence of the continued use of the variant of the writ of *monstravit de compoto* after 1267 to initiate an action of account in London comes from a 1288 Common Bench enrolment. This recites a writ issued when the sheriffs of London refused the sureties offered by Dovelin Junge for his appearance in the husting court to answer what was evidently a writ of *monstravit de compoto* brought by James de Beauchamp.[83] Surviving rolls for the London husting of common pleas sessions do not contain many actions of account that can be identified with any certainty as being initiated by the London variant of *monstravit de compoto*. That this may simply be because such actions were normally enrolled as though ordinary actions of account is, however, suggested by one of the two actions which

80 For an example see CP 40/147, m. 94d (Easter term 1303) and compare the reports of this case in BL MS. Additional 31826, fol. 133v and CUL MS. Ee.6.18, fols. 77v–78r.

81 JUST 1/375, m. 30d: *Adam of Lyminge v. Alan Cornmonger of Wingham*.

82 KB 27/182, m. 1: '*Linc*'. Gilbertus Apehele attachiatus fuit ad respondendum Radulpho de Rocheford de placito quare cum idem Gilbertus extiterit ballivus predicti Radulphi in Suth Stoke omnium rerum et bonorum suorum curam habens et administracionem idem Gilbertus compoto suo non soluto subterfugia querens latitat in comitatu predicto ne posset inveniri et distringi ad reddendum predicto Radulpho compotum suum predictum. Et quia de communi consilio regni regis provisum est quod si ballivi qui dominis suis compotum reddere tenentur se subtraxerint et terras et tenementa non habeant per que distringi valeant per eorum corpora attachientur, ita quod vicecomites in quorum ballivis invenientur eos venire faciant ad compotum suum reddendum. Et unde queritur quod . . .'

83 'Cum nuper preceptum fuisset vicecomitibus London' quod Dovelinum Junge dudum ballivum Jacobi de Bello Campo pro arreragiis compoti sui tanquam subterfugia querentem attachiarent, ita quod corpus suum in hustengo regis London' ad certum diem haberent ad reddendum prefato Jacobo compotum suum, non tamen intencionis domini regis fuit quod ipsum Dovelinum carceri de Neugate manciparetur dum tamen sufficientem securitatem invenire posset ad reddendum compotum predictum juxta tenorem brevis domini regis inde vobis directi, quam quidem securitatem idem Dovelinus vicecomitibus optulit et quam capere renuerunt. Et quia [six named] mercatores London' manuceperunt ad habendum ipsum Dovelinum hic ad hunc diem ad reddendum compotum suum predicto Jacobo de arreragiis predictis et vicecomitibus preceptum fuisset quod predictum Dovelinum per manucapcionem predictam a prisona qua detinetur interim deliberari facerent . . .': CP 40/78, m. 58; *CCR 1279–1288*, p. 487. This is discussed further below at p. 319.

can be identified as an action initiated by such a writ on the rolls.[84] In 1301 James de Columbariis brought an action against Peter Maupyn of London for an account of the time he had acted as receiver of his moneys both in London and elsewhere within England and overseas. He had allegedly received money and rents to the value of four hundred marks and fifty shillings between 12 Edward I (1283–4) and 15 Edward I (1286–7).[85] Nothing in the enrolment of the plaintiff's count gives any hint that this is an action initiated by *monstravit de compoto*. This only emerged when the defendant asked for a hearing of the original writ and what was read out was a *monstravit*. The ordinary writ of account used in the city seems to have routinely referred to London custom while the *monstravit de compoto* evidently did not and thus was (as the defendant accepted) 'formed and ordered according to common law'. The defendant argued that as a London citizen he was none the less entitled to the benefit of London custom in the same way as he would have been had the action been an ordinary action of account. Thus his total denial of having acted as the defendant's receiver was to be proved by wager of law, and not, as at common law, by jury trial. The plaintiff accepted that city custom ruled even in this case but asserted that jury trial was the proper mode of proof for such an issue under city custom. Eventually at the next court the court ruled in his favour and the issue went to jury trial. There is also other, incidental, evidence for the continuing use of the London *monstravit* writ. The earliest special action alleging deceit in obtaining the writ of *monstravit* was heard in King's Bench in Easter term 1294.[86] Neither the writ as enrolled nor the count tells us where the original action had been brought though they do indicate a London connexion for the litigation. That the litigation had been brought in the husting court only emerged clearly after the jury verdict had been given in the case at Michaelmas 1294 when the court, prior to giving judgment, decided that it needed to made enquiries as to when the original writ of *monstravit de compoto* had been issued. It sought information from the warden of the city of London. This can only mean that the original litigation had been heard in the husting court, for the keeper of writs and rolls would have had any original writ for litigation brought in the Common Bench. The second writ of deceit issued, for the use of William of Weston, chaplain, against John Long, in 1298 may also have been brought in

[84] For the other action which the terms of the enrolment reveal as having been initiated by *monstravit de compoto* see CLRO Husting of Common Pleas, Roll 18, m. 11d (1290): *Stephen of Cambridge v. William of Bealing*.

[85] CLRO Husting of Common Pleas, Roll 26, m. 1d.

[86] *(Rex and) Poteman v. Fuleham* in *SCKB*, III, 24–5. Discussed further below at pp. 324–5.

connexion with a London husting *monstravit de compoto.*[87] The suit was certainly said to have been brought in London and the plaintiff was said to have been imprisoned in Newgate gaol. Further evidence of use of the non-returnable London variant of the writ comes from two complaints brought in 1303 by Thomas of Wrotham and Stephen of Blakeneye in the London husting against two former sheriffs of London (Luke of Havering and Richard of Campes) who had been sheriffs in 1300–1. The sheriffs had arrested defendants in response to writs of *monstravit de compoto* but had then released them on mainprise. The mainpernors had, however, then failed to produce the defendants at the following husting court.[88] In 1304 Richard le Cunreyur brought an action of trespass in the husting court alleging deception by Adam Apsolon in procuring a writ of *monstravit* in 1303 when the plaintiff possessed lands and tenements in Middlesex by which he could have been distrained to render any account he owed.[89] There is, however, no recorded defence to this action and it seems not improbable that the defendant successfully objected to the court hearing such a plea.[90]

Initial process on the writ of monstravit de compoto

An order for 'attachment by the body', the initial stage in process ordered by the writ of *monstravit de compoto*, was relatively clear. It authorised the sheriff to use arrest and imprisonment to ensure that the defendant appeared in court. Sheriffs who returned that they had attached the defendant in the normal fashion, by simply accepting two sureties for his appearance,[91] or who had distrained the defendant by his chattels and had then accepted a single mainpernor for his appearance,[92] or who returned that the defendant 'has no lands and tenements in his bailiwick by which he can be attached',[93] were all clearly failing to execute the order sent to them.

[87] *(Rex and) Weston v. Long:* in *SCKB*, III, 64–5.

[88] CLRO, Husting of Common Pleas, Roll 28, m. 4d. These cases are further discussed below at pp. 319–20.

[89] CLRO, Husting of Common Pleas, Roll 29, m. 15.

[90] At the same court the same plaintiff also sued the same defendant for an account as the receiver of his moneys. This action went to jury trial when the defendant denied having been such.

[91] For instances see CP 40/5, m. 85d (Michaelmas term 1274) (though here the initial attachment was by four sureties); CP 40/9, mm. 53, 53d (Easter term 1275); CP 40/14, mm. 26d, 37 (Easter term 1276); CP 40/17, mm. 35, 100d (Michaelmas term 1276); CP 40/19, mm. 69d, 71 (Easter term 1277) (here the initial attachment was by four and six sureties respectively); CP 40/38, mm. 11, 24 (Hilary term 1281); CP 40/47, m. 125 (Michaelmas term 1282) (again the initial attachment was by four sureties).

[92] For an instance see CP 40/17, m. 24 (Michaelmas term 1276). He was given a further order to attach the defendant by his body.

[93] For an instance see CP 40/18, m. 27d (Hilary term 1277).

What was rather less clear was whether or not a sheriff had complied with the order if he had made an arrest of the defendant but had then accepted an offer of a mainprise guaranteeing his appearance in court. In at least five early cases where the sheriff returned that the defendant had been mainprised but the defendant then failed to appear the court simply issued a further order for attachment of the defendant by his body.[94] The apparent implication of these cases, that mainprise had not satisfied the requirement of the original order, is directly spelled out in a case of 1278. In it the bailiffs of Worcester were amerced and ordered to renew the attachment 'because they had not attached him by his body'.[95] Something not dissimilar happened in a case of 1287 where a sheriff was amerced one hundred shillings for allowing a release by mainprise when he had accepted two mainpernors for the appearance of a defendant.[96] The following year, however, a writ appeared on the Close Rolls and was enrolled on the Common Bench plea roll which suggested a very different interpretation of the meaning of the same order. An action of *monstravit de compoto* had been brought in the city of London with the sheriffs of London being ordered to 'attach the body' of Dovelin Junge for appearance in the London husting court to render account to James de Beauchamp. Dovelin had offered mainprise for his appearance but the sheriffs had refused it and committed him to Newgate. The follow-up writ stated that it had not been the king's intention in ordering him to be attached by his body that he be imprisoned if he was able to find sufficient mainprise for his appearance and ordered his release on mainprise now that he had found sufficient mainpernors for his appearance in the Common Bench.[97] It is not, however, clear whether this writ made any permanent change in the interpretion of the law. There is a writ of mainprise in the early fourteenth-century register of writs printed by de Haas and Hall for the special situation where it had been attested in Chancery that the defendant did have sufficient lands and chattels to ensure that he rendered account and paid the balance due (if any) on rendering his account.[98] But the existence of such a writ appears to suggest that mainprise was available *only* when specifically authorised and then only in the special circumstances mentioned in the writ. In 1303 Thomas of Wrotham and Stephen of Blakeneye had (as already noted)

[94] KB 26/196, m. 2d (Hilary term 1270); CP 40/7, m. 21 (Hilary term 1275); CP 40/23, m. 22d (Hilary term 1278); CP 40/28, m. 21d (Hilary term 1279); CP 40/31, m. 129 (Michaelmas term 1279).

[95] '. . . quia non attachiaverunt eum per corpus': CP 40/23, m. 22d (Hilary term 1278).

[96] CP 40/68, m. 75.

[97] Above, note 83.

[98] 'Ex parte W. capti et detenti in prisona nostra de S . . . propter quod corpus ipsius W. per te attachiari et imprisonari procuravit . . .': *Early Registers*, pp. 210–11 (R 429).

brought complaints against two former London sheriffs for releasing on mainprise defendants whom they had arrested on writs of *monstravit de compoto* and who then failed to appear.[99] Both actions sought to hold the sheriffs answerable for the money owed on account by the defendants concerned. There was no statutory authority for holding sheriffs responsible in these circumstances nor any specific city regulation for doing so, but the plaintiffs must have believed that they had some chance of success in attempting to hold sheriffs responsible for failing to secure the presence of the defendants in court. The defendants made a similar answer to both plaints. This consisted of three related points. Since the action on which the plaintiffs based their complaint had been taken in response to a writ, they could not now be made to answer in an action by plaint, only in an action by writ. Moreover, the *monstravit* was an action at common law and it was not therefore appropriate that they should be made to answer in an action by plaint where city custom was the applicable set of legal rules. And although there was statutory (and other) authority for holding sheriffs responsible for producing either the body of the defendant or the sum for which he was liable this was limited by statute (and common law) to three kinds of situation: where the defendant had been arrested on a statute merchant debt, where the accounting official or agent had been arrested by the auditors after he had accounted and handed over to the sheriff and where the agent had been found to owe an account by final judgment. The current situation did not belong to any of these three types and so they were not answerable for the money claimed. The cases were adjourned for judgment but none is recorded.

Mesne process on monstravit de compoto

Monstravit de compoto simply authorised a particular, and particularly stringent, initial process to be used to ensure the defendant's appearance in the action of account. The legislation said nothing about what process was to follow if this initial process did not succeed in ensuring the defendant's appearance, perhaps because it did not think that so drastic a process would fail to ensure it. In practice, however, the writ commonly failed to achieve its intended result. Most commonly the sheriff's return to an initial order for the 'attachment by the body' stated that the defendant was not to be found and had nothing by which he could be attached. This then led to the issue of a writ of *capias* which was in effect a repetition, albeit in different words, of the 'attachment by the body'

[99] See note 88.

ordered in the original writ.[100] Only in two cases did the *capias* issue after a return stating simply that the defendant had not been found.[101] There is also at least one case where such a return was followed by an attestation that the defendants were living at a particular location in the county and could be attached by their bodies there and to the renewal of the initial order for 'attachment by the body'.[102] After 1285, when chapter 11 of the Statute of Westminster II authorised the use of outlawry in the action of account, *capias* might in turn be followed by an order for exaction to outlawry.[103] The earliest example noted of an order for the exaction of a *monstravit* defendant comes from Trinity term 1286.[104]

When the sheriff's return to the initial writ of *monstravit* was that the defendant had been mainprised or attached he might simply be ordered to repeat the initial attachment by the body.[105] However, other responses also found include on at least two occasions prior to 1275 a wholly inappropriate order for attachment by better pledges (as if the initial attachment had been an attachment of the normal kind)[106] and orders for the use of the grand distress,[107] as well as orders to proceed to the use of the *capias.*[108] A *capias* might also follow after an unsuccessful order for distraint had produced the return that the defendant had not been found and had nothing by which he could be distrained.[109]

Even in its earliest days *monstravit de compoto* was not particularly effective in securing the defendant's appearance despite the harsher initial process used. In only four cases out of thirty-six initiated by the writ prior to 1280 did the defendant appear and plead. In two of these four, there is no record of earlier mesne process,[110] while in the other two

[100] For examples see CP 40/9, m. 21 (Easter term 1275); CP 40/13, m. 39 (Hilary term 1276); CP 40/23, mm. 8d, 20d (Hilary term 1278); CP 40/24, m. 36d (Easter term 1278); CP 40/31, m. 19d (Michaelmas term 1279); CP 40/32, m. 6d (Hilary term 1280); CP 40/34, m. 24 (Trinity term 1280).

[101] CP 40/23, m. 46 (Hilary term 1278); CP 40/30, m. 96 (Trinity term 1279). But for an earlier *capias* issued after an initial renewal of the order for attachment by the body had produced a return that the defendant had not been found and an attestation that the defendant was 'vagabund in the bailiwick of the sheriff where he could often be found' ('quod est vagabundus in balliva ubi sepius potest inveniri') see KB 26/200A, m. 28d (Trinity term 1270) and for later renewals of the *capias* in the same case see KB 26/202, mm. 28d (to the sheriff of another county), 31.

[102] CP 40/3, m. 41. [103] *SR*, I, 80–1. [104] CP 40/63, m. 5. [105] Above, p. 319.

[106] CP 40/5, m. 85d (Michaelmas term 1274); CP 40/9, m. 53d (Easter term 1275).

[107] CP 40/3, m. 17 (Trinity term 1273); CP 40/5, m. 85d (Michaelmas term 1274); CP 40/14, mm. 26d, 37 (Easter term 1276); CP 40/17, m. 35 (Michaelmas term 1276); CP 40/19, mm. 69d, 71d (Easter term 1277).

[108] E.g. CP 40/30, m. 79d (Trinity term 1279).

[109] KB 26/202, m. 12 (Easter term 1271) (repeated in Hilary term 1272: KB 26/206, m. 1d).

[110] *Thomas of Pontesbury v. William of Frankton*: CP 40/17, m. 38d (Michaelmas term 1276) (but note that the record shows that difficulty was experienced in securing the defendant's appearance after verdict); *Eustace of Hatch v. John de St Mauro*: CP 40/32, m. 12 (Hilary term 1280).

mesne process had been dragging on for a year[111] and a year and a half[112] respectively. The longest unsuccessful use of the mesne process to be traced in an action of *monstravit de compoto* lasted some two and a half years.[113] Since the first of these stages was a default after a day given *prece parcium* process must in fact have been going on even longer. At every stage except the last the sheriff was ordered to distrain the defendant; at the last a *capias* was issued. The case is therefore not really a judgment on the inefficacy of attachment by the body but on that of grand distress.

Types of defendant

In establishing the process of *monstravit de compoto* clause 19 of the Provisions of Westminster and chapter 23 of the Statute of Marlborough both referred to the use of the new initial process only against 'bailiffs'. This is readily explicable because at the time of the enactment of this legislation a defendant in the action of account could only be charged as a bailiff and a separate category of 'receiver', whether mercantile or not, seems to have been unknown. This does not mean that the kind of mercantile agent or employee later sued as a 'receiver' was beyond the reach of the action of account, simply that such defendants were then being sued as 'bailiffs' rather than as 'receivers'.[114] Chancery began to make available a variant of the writ of account for use against a 'receiver' in or shortly

111 *Walter de la Lynde v. John Malet of Irby et al.*: CP 40/14, m. 26d (Easter term 1276); CP 40/17, mm. 14, 28, 31 (Michaelmas term 1276); CP 40/18, m. 28d (Hilary term 1277); CP 40/19, m. 31d (Easter term 1277).

112 *Robert de Vere, earl of Oxford v. Walter Spicer of Dunmow*: CP 40/15, m. 104 (Trinity term 1276); CP 40/17, m. 35 (Michaelmas term 1276); CP 40/18, m. 73 (Hilary term 1277); CP 40/19, m. 61d (Easter term 1277); CP 40/23, m. 36d (Hilary term 1278).

113 *Henry of Stokes v. Richard Marshal*: CP 40/17, m. 128 (Michaelmas term 1276); CP 40/18, m. 68d. (Hilary term 1277); CP 40/19, m. 65 (Easter term 1277); CP 40/26, m. 142 (Michaelmas term 1278); CP 40/28, m. 57d (Hilary term 1279); CP 40/29, m. 52 (Easter term 1279).

114 For a good example see *Martin of Ottringham v. Stephen of Woodgate* heard in Easter term 1262 where the defendant was charged as the plaintiff's 'bailiff' in York and Pontefract and the account demanded was of two hundred marks given him for buying merchandise to the plaintiff's use and of the sale of wood, wax, alum and cloth worth a thousand marks and of the keeping of two shops in the two towns: KB 26/166, m. 26d. Such a defendant would later have been charged as a receiver of the plaintiff's moneys. For the early fourteenth-century distinction between bailiffs and receivers see *Pirton v. Tumby*: *YB 8 Edward II (1314–1315)*, ed. W.C. Bolland (Selden Society vol. 41, 1924), p. 59 and cf. T.F.T. Plucknett, *The Medieval Bailiff* (London, 1953), pp. 16–18. In the report of a 1292 *monstravit* case Goldington argued that the term 'bailiff' was appropriate only for an agent in charge of a manor, not for an agent in charge of merchandise, but Inge argued that a 'receiver' was properly an agent who solely received money. Chief Justice Mettingham thought the relevant criteria were whether or not the agent was part of the employer's household and trading on his behalf: see BL MS. Harley 2183, fols. 111r–v (report of CP 40/93, m. 1: *William Spicer of Oxford v. Simon Baret*).

before 1277.[115] The first *monstravit de compoto* to be brought against a 'receiver' dates from around the same time.[116] In a 1310 case the use of *monstravit de compoto* against a receiver was challenged on the grounds that the Statute of Marlborough did not specifically mention receivers. Bereford claimed that this extension was indirectly authorised by statute because there had been a reference to the Statute of Marlborough in chapter 11 of the Statute of Westminster II, whose subject (understood) was the 'serjeants, bailiffs, chamberlains and receivers of all kinds, who are obliged to render account' of the beginning of the chapter.[117] His ruling was that the writ was therefore warranted by statute or, rather, by a combination of the two statutes, the remedy granted by the one being granted against all those categories mentioned in the other. Coke also asserted that *monstravit de compoto* was available against guardians in socage to make them render account.[118] He cited no evidence for this assertion and there is certainly no evidence from this period to suggest the availability of the writ against them.

Deception and the writ of monstravit de compoto

There is no evidence prior to the mid-1290s for the existence of any remedy for a bailiff or receiver who possessed lands and tenements by which he might have been distrained but who had none the less been attached by his body by a writ of *monstravit de compoto*. Indeed, there are even three cases from before 1280 in which in the course of mesne process on a *monstravit de compoto* a plaintiff himself attested that the defendant had lands and tenements *ad sufficientiam* in a certain place. In two of these the lands were in another county,[119] but in the third, the plaintiff or his attorney attested on no fewer than three occasions to the defendant's possession of sufficient lands in the county where he was bringing his suit.[120]

[115] The earliest cases against 'receivers' are to be found in Michaelmas term 1277: *Alexander Spilesman (of Mursley) v. Richard FitzRobert*: CP 40/21, m. 22d and cf. ibid., m. 8d. For other early examples see CP 40/26, m. 44d (Michaelmas term 1278) and CP 40/32, m. 22d (Hilary term 1280).

[116] E.g. *Roger Champneys of Shrewsbury merchant v. Thomas Mauntel merchant*: CP 40/23, m. 22d (Hilary term 1278). For an earlier case of *monstravit de compoto* in which the defendant was charged both as bailiff of a manor and as a receiver of moneys for the pleas and profits of the court of the honour of Huntingdon see *Robert Brus v. Henry Turner*: CP 40/17, m. 24 (Michaelmas term 1276).

[117] *Year Books 4 Edward II (1310–11)*, ed. G.J. Turner (Selden Society vol. 26, 1911), pp. 3–4 and cf. *Year Book 7 Edward II (1313–1314)*, ed. W.C. Bolland (Selden Society vol. 39, 1922), p. 9.

[118] Coke, *Second Institutes*, p. 144.

[119] *Robert de Vere, earl of Oxford v. Walter Spicer of Dunmow*: CP 40/19, m. 61d (Easter term 1277); *Gervase of Barnack v. Henry Seymour*: CP 40/28, m. 74 (Hilary term 1277).

[120] *Master Bonet de St Quintin v. Richard the chaplain of Calverley*: CP 40/26, m. 55 (Michaelmas term 1278); CP 40/29, m. 28d (Easter term 1279); CP 40/31, m. 138d (Michaelmas term 1279).

Judgment was sought against a writ in an unidentified but reported case, apparently from the southern eyre circuit of the 1280s, on the grounds that the defendant possessed sufficient lands. It is probably significant, however, that it was raised only at once to be waived.[121]

The earliest special action alleging deceit in obtaining the writ of *monstravit* was heard in the King's Bench in Easter term 1294.[122] The writ as enrolled set out the alleged facts of the case. These were that the plaintiff (Henry Poteman), who was suing both on his own behalf and on behalf of the king, had been residing continuously in the city of London and possessed lands, tenements and rents both in London and in Kent by which he could have been distrained to render any account he might owe the defendant (Geoffrey of Fulham); that the defendant had made the false assertion on oath (*fide mediante*) in Chancery that the plaintiff was in hiding in the city, had not rendered his account as the receiver of Geoffrey's moneys and had no lands and tenements by which he could be forced to render his account; and that on the basis of this false claim he had obtained a writ to attach him by his body and had thereby procured his arrest contrary to the law and custom of the realm and contrary to the terms of the Statute. The count then spelled out the details. He had been arrested on All Saints' Day 1293 and had been imprisoned for two days before being released on mainprise. He claimed damages of a thousand pounds for the king for the alleged deception and forty pounds for himself. What neither writ nor count tells us but can be deduced from information that emerges later is that the original action had been brought not in the Common Bench but in the London husting court. The defence was that the 'suggestion' made in Chancery had not been untrue because, as the defendant understood it, Henry did not then possess either lands or other property, whether in London or Kent. The jury verdict, given at Michaelmas 1294, was that two years ago Henry had possessed 'sufficient' lands and rents in London by which he could have been constrained to appear to answer and still had them and that Geoffrey knew where he resided in the city because they were neighbours. The warden of the city of London, as custodian of writs from the husting court, was able to inform the court that it had been issued on 22 November 1293 and it therefore became clear that Henry had held the property before and after the date the writ was issued, the

121 'Et J. petit judicium desicut istud non debet concedi nisi quando ballivus non habet terras per quas distringi possit et iste habet satis; petit judicium de brevi. *War'*. Non potestis dedicere quin fuisti ballivus suus ibidem . . .': CUL MS. Dd.7.14, fol. 268v. The only identifiable justice in the case is Solomon of Rochester, a puisne and then the senior justice of the southern eyre circuit until his disgrace in 1290.

122 *(Rex and) Poteman v. Fulham*: *SCKB*, III, 24–5.

court awarded damage of four pounds as assessed by the jurors and the discretion of the justices. Geoffrey was arrested until he agreed to pay a fine of one mark to the king.

By the time the second writ of deceit was issued for William of Weston against John Long in 1298 there had evidently been some significant modification in the wording of the writ, producing something almost identical to the standard form of writ later current.[123] The main difference was that the plaintiff no longer asserted that he had been continually resident in a particular place though he did still assert that he possessed lands and tenements by which he could have been distrained to render any account that he might owe.[124] This time the count (made jointly by William and the king's attorney, Richard de Bretteville) specified not only when the plaintiff had been attached (the Thursday after the Purification) but also when the relevant writ was issued (the previous Thursday) and alleged that he had been in prison ever since and was still in Newgate gaol. This time the damages were claimed jointly on behalf of William and the king and were put at only one hundred pounds. Since the suit was brought in London it seems probable that this too related to a case brought in the London husting court. The defendant again alleged justification in the fact that William had then possessed no lands. The jury verdict was given at York during Easter term 1299 and, although William's property holdings were comparatively small ones (a messuage worth three shillings at Braybrooke, a messuage worth four shillings at Harringworth, a meadow worth two shillings at Killamarsh), the use of attachment by the body was found malicious and damages of twenty marks were awarded to William. John was arrested until he had agreed to pay a fine of forty shillings.

The first Common Bench deception writ was brought in Michaelmas term 1299 and for it we possess a report as well as an enrolment.[125] Again the action was brought in the name of the king as well as of the plaintiff

[123] *(Rex and) Weston v. Long*: *SCKB*, III, 64–5. The writ was also enrolled on the dorse of the Close Roll in June 1298: *CCR 1296–1302*, p. 214. For the standard form of the writ see *Early Registers*, p. 211 (R 430). The only major difference is that in the 1298 enrolment the defendant is said simply to possess lands and tenements; the standard later writ alleged that he had *sufficient* lands and tenements. For a Common Bench enrolment of mesne process in a deceit action that reproduces almost all the phrasing of the underlying writ and shows that it was in a form that is virtually identical to the writ in *Early Registers* (except for omitting any reference to the 'sufficiency' of the lands and tenements) see CP 40/134, m. 41.

[124] But for a writ of deceit brought in Michaelmas term 1310 by a monk and his prior in which the main element of deceit alleged was that the defendant was resident, as a religious, at his monastery, rather than that he possessed lands and tenements by which he could have been distrained, see *Matthew prior of Weybridge and Brother Thomas of Weybridge v. Walter Brown*: CP 40/183, m. 133d.

[125] *Rex and Richard Hopman of Lynn v. Hugh of Massingham, Henry Hamer and Robert of Marham*: CP 40/130, m. 54 (and for earlier mesne process see CP 40/129, m. 49d). It is reported in BL MS. Additional 31826, fol. 112v.

against three defendants. No count is enrolled but the report shows that the plaintiff had indeed made one. This specified that the plaintiff had been attached by his body to answer one month after Easter, evidently in the Common Bench, for the time he had been the receiver of their moneys. The report indicates that counsel for the defendants (Warwick) challenged the count for failing to specify in which villages the plaintiff held lands and for failing to be sufficiently specific in stating how he had been harmed by the issuing of the writ by showing for how many days he had been imprisoned. Counsel for the plaintiff responded to both these objections. It was not up to the plaintiff to specify where he held lands but up to the counsel for the defendants to offer the averment by a jury that the plaintiff held no lands. The counsel for the defendants seems then to have waived this point. On the second point, counsel for the plaintiff (here Ashby) said that he had by implication made this point quite clearly by stating in the count that he had been attached by his body three weeks after Easter for an appearance one month after Easter. Chief Justice Mettingham, however, was inclined to consider that the count had been insufficiently precise, not in failing to specify the length of imprisonment but in failing to specify where it had taken place, whether at Norwich or Lynn. He then adjourned the case for judgment. The judgment recorded on the plea roll, however, was on quite another point, that there had been a grammatical error in the writ, with *asserens* used where the plural *asserentes* should have been and so the plaintiff was allowed to withdraw from his writ.

The second reported case from the Common Bench was heard in Trinity term 1300 and was brought by the plaintiff in his own name alone.[126] The writ seems to have been virtually identical to that used in the 1299 case but the count, which is this time contained in the enrolment, met one of the objections made in the previous case by specifying the three villages where the plaintiff held lands, lands that were here specified as being 'sufficient' (*ad sufficienciam*). The count, as enrolled, did not give any details of the plaintiff's arrest, although the report suggests that the count made in court did talk of the harm done to the plaintiff as having come from the plaintiff being imprisoned. The plaintiff claimed damages of ten pounds. Both report and enrolment agree in showing that the defendant immediately objected to the plaintiff's writ on the grounds of a variance between its claim that the defendant had previously sought an account from the plaintiff as the receiver of his moneys and the actual allegation made in the prior litigation which was that the defendant had

[126] *Nicholas Profet of Garthorpe v. Richard de Lisle*: CP 40/134, m. 89. It is reported in BL MS. Additional 37657, fol. 25v. For the subsequent revival of this case see n. 131 below.

been his bailiff. According to the report Tothby (counsel for the plaintiff) attempted to salvage the day for his client by claiming that the writ merely acted as a means of getting the party into court and that once he was there he should answer the main gravamen of the count, the deceit in suing the *monstravit*, even if the specifics were wrong, but that his client then decided to take the decision recorded on the plea roll of getting the court's permission to withdraw from this writ in order to bring a better one. There were then further Common Bench deceit actions in Hilary term 1303,[127] Trinity term 1304,[128] Michaelmas term 1304,[129] Hilary term 1305,[130] Trinity term 1305[131] and Michaelmas term 1306.[132]

For a period it was possible for a bailiff or receiver who possessed lands but against whom a *monstravit* was brought either to bring the writ of deceit or to except to the writ of *monstravit* itself. The earliest case in which such an exception was allowed was the Herefordshire case of *William son of Roger of Orleton v. William le Spicer (of Coventry)* heard in Hilary term 1303 in which the defendant claimed that he was not obliged to reply to the writ, 'because he says that such a writ of attachment by the body was provided for the case when those who are obliged to render account have no tenements by which they can be compelled to render account . . .',[133] and he possessed lands and tenements at Coventry. The plaintiff then traversed this issue.[134] The reports of this case indicate that it was Chief Justice Hengham who effectively overruled the argument made by counsel for the plaintiff that the defendant had a separate remedy through the action of deceit if he possessed lands and so should not be allowed this answer to the action of *monstravit*. They also indicate that the defendant tried to argue that to bar the use of the *monstravit* it was necessary to show that the defendant possessed lands in the same county as that in which the account was being claimed and that it was Hengham who overruled this argument as well. However, in a case heard the following Easter term a second defendant who attempted to plead

127 *Henry of Shipmeadow v. Robert of Sefield*: CP 40/146, m. 85d.

128 *William of Stowe v. prioress of Stratford*: CP 40/152, m. 55.

129 *William of Whitfield v. John of Goshale*: CP 40/149, m. 379.

130 *Rex and Roger of Bradwell of Oxford v. William of Holme and wife Maud*: CP 40/154, m. 27. This is reported in BL MSS. Hargrave 375, fols. 29r–v and Stowe 386, fol. 196r and LI MS. Miscellaneous 738, fol. 30v.

131 *Nicholas Profet v. Richard de Lisle*: CP 40/156, m. 148d. This is a revival of the earlier case of 1300: above, note 126.

132 *William of Legbourne of Louth v. Mariota widow of Hugh Spicer of Lincoln*: CP 40/161, m. 232.

133 '. . . quia dicit quod hujusmodi breve de attachiamento per corpus provisum est in casu quando illi qui compotum reddere tenentur nulla habent tenementa per que compelli possunt ad compotum reddendum . . .'

134 CP 40/146, m. 9d. The case is reported in BL MSS. Additional 31826, fol. 147r and Stowe 386, fol. 169v and in LI MS. Miscellaneous 738, fol. 15r.

the same exception in the same court before Hengham and Staunton (while still a clerk) found the exception overruled, largely (it seems) because Staunton ridiculed its use.[135] Defendants can then be found pleading the same exception in a number of cases in Trinity and Michaelmas terms 1303,[136] and again in Trinity term 1304.[137] In the case of *Rednesse v. Plomere (of Northampton)* heard during Michaelmas term 1304 a defendant pleading the same exception was told after discussion to answer over and was driven to a denial that he had ever been the plaintiff's receiver.[138] A year later, in a case brought in Michaelmas term 1305, Hengham enunciated as a general rule the doctrine established by that case, that the court would not allow such exceptions to the *monstravit*.[139]

Despite Hengham's ruling, the argument that the exception of sufficiency ought to be allowed against the use of the *monstravit* evidently remained an attractive one. In a case heard in Trinity term 1307 in which the defendant was charged as the receiver of the plaintiff's moneys, he objected that the plaintiff had, at Michaelmas 1305, brought ordinary writs of account against him which were still pending, by which he had supposed that he possessed lands and tenements 'by which he could be made to answer in court . . .'[140] The plaintiff demurred that the defendant did not possess sufficient lands. Judgment was given on the demurrer for the defendant, quashing the writ, 'because the same Ralph cannot deny that he had brought the said writ against him, supposing him to have tenements by which he could be made to answer in court, and that writ is still pending without an outcome . . .'[141] The more general use of the exception of sufficiency can again be found in pleading early in Edward II's reign in the *monstravit de compoto* case reported in the Year Books as *Box v. Palmer* and in many later cases.[142]

135 BL MS. Additional 31826, fol. 133v and CUL MS. Ee.6.18, fols. 77v–78r. The unsuccessful exception is not mentioned in the plea roll enrolment of the same case in CP 40/147, m. 94d.

136 CP 40/148, mm. 1d, 19d, 69, 71 (Trinity term 1303); CP 40/145, m. 14 (Michaelmas term 1303). The reports show it also being pleaded in a second case heard in Michaelmas term 1303 but being overruled on the grounds that the property concerned was not valuable enough for the purpose: BL MSS. Additional 5925, fols. 152v–153r and Stowe 386, fol. 186r. It is not mentioned in the plea roll enrolment of the same case in CP 40/145, m. 153d.

137 CP 40/152, m. 39d.

138 CP 40/149, m. 264.

139 *YB 33–35 EI*, pp. 4–6.

140 '. . . per que potuit justiciari . . .'

141 '. . . quia idem Radulphus non potest hoc dedicere quin (tulit) predictum breve versus eum supponendo ipsum habere tenementa per que justiciari potest, quod quidem breve ad huc pendet indecisum . . .': *Ralph de Beaufou v. Simon Cook of North Luffenham*: CP 40/164, m. 68d. Apart from the argument and the note at the end that the plaintiff take nothing by his writ '. . . quod dicitur monstravit . . .' there is nothing else to show that this is a *monstravit*.

142 *YB 3 Edward II (1309–10)*, pp. 91–2; *YB 4 Edward II (1310–11)*, p. 37. The defendant admitted that he was also bringing his writ of deceit against the plaintiff in King's Bench. For later examples see CP 40/183, mm. 12d, 268d, 425d (Michaelmas term 1310); CP 40/201, mm. 203, 242d (Michaelmas term 1313); CP 40/212A, m. 310 (Michaelmas term 1315).

One possible consequence of allowing defendants to except on the grounds of sufficiency is shown by two cases which were brought by the same plaintiff (Michael le Bret) against the same defendant (John atte Wyken of Burnham Thorpe), though in one he charged him as his bailiff and in the other as his receiver.[143] When the verdict of the jury as to the value of the defendant's lands was deemed to have shown that the defendant did not have adequate lands, he was still allowed to put himself on the verdict of a second jury on the issue of whether or not he had been the plaintiff's bailiff or receiver.[144] In one report of this case, however, we are told that Bereford J. told the attorney for the plaintiff when he objected to the second jury trial that it was his own fault. He ought to have insisted before agreeing to the jury trial on the first issue that this be to win or lose in the case as a whole.[145]

One continuing difficulty raised both by actions of deceit and by the exceptions pleaded in actions of *monstravit* was in deciding whether the legislators had intended that *monstravit de compoto* might be used only where the bailiff concerned was wholly landless, or whether they had also intended to allow its use where the lands he possessed were 'insufficient', that is, where their value was so small that distraining them was likely to be of little or no value in securing his appearance in court. The wording of the legislation was ambiguous, speaking as it did of those bailiffs who absconded and 'do not have lands or tenements by which they might be distrained'. The second phrase might be taken either as an additional qualification to the 'lands or tenements' or as an explanation of the significance of the requirement that the bailiff possess no lands or tenements. On the first reading, *monstravit de compoto* might legitimately be used if the bailiff did not possess lands and tenements of sufficient value for distraint to be effective against him;[146] on the second it could only be used if the bailiff had no lands at all.

In the report of the first deception case heard in the Common Bench in 1299 when counsel for the defendant objected that the plaintiff had failed to specify in his count the villages where he held lands, the plaintiff's response was to say that it was up to the defendant to offer an averment to the contrary and that he had to offer to aver that the plaintiff had *no*

[143] CP 40/148 m. 69 (Trinity term 1303) (bailiff); CP 40/145, m. 14 (Michaelmas term 1303) (receiver).

[144] *YB 32 & 33 EI*, pp. 114–16 and BL MS. Stowe 386, fols. 199v and 205v (Easter 1304).

[145] Harvard Law School MS. 206, fol. 87v. And see the unidentified pre-1308 case reported in BL MS. Harley 2183, fols. 110v–111r where Bereford warned a defendant against excepting on grounds of his possession of 'sufficient' lands because, if it was found that he did not, he would be required to account and would not be allowed any further answer.

[146] This interpretation is supported by the use in the 1260 specimen writ of the phrase 'per que distringi valeant' for the 'per que distringi possint' of the Provisions.

land in the county. The implication seems to be that the possession of any land would be sufficient to ground an action of deceit.[147] When, however, counsel for the defendant attempted to argue in a reported *monstravit de compoto* case of Michaelmas term 1303 that the Statute only allowed use of the writ where the defendant had no lands, Hengham ruled that it was necessary to show that the tenements were of *sufficient* value for the purposes of distraint. He also went on to rule that the fifteen shillings of rent the defendant claimed to hold in Oxford were not sufficient in the current context, where account was being claimed of the administration of chattels to the value of twenty pounds.[148] A similar view of the meaning of the Statute was taken in a ruling in the Common Bench in Easter term 1304 on a jury verdict at *nisi prius* on a *monstravit*, finding that the defendant's lands were worth only five shillings or less a year. The court held he should now answer the case 'because of the smallness of the tenement' ('pur la petitesse du tenement').[149] The same understanding of the Statute was also adopted in a deceit action heard in Trinity term 1305 where the defendant pleaded in his defence that the lands the plaintiff possessed 'were not sufficient to render this kind of account' ('non sufficiunt ad hujusmodi compotum reddendum') where the account being claimed was for one and a half years of the revenue of a church worth one hundred marks a year and the plaintiff responded that the lands he held were sufficient for this purpose.[150] Although in several early cases the issue put to the jury was the ambiguous one of whether or not the defendant (in *monstravit* cases) or plaintiff (in deceit cases) had lands and tenements 'by which he could be distrained to render his account',[151] it was more common to ask them much less ambiguously whether or not he possessed lands and tenements 'sufficient' for the rendering of the account.[152] Even in cases where sufficiency was specifically mentioned

[147] BL MS. Additional 31826, fol. 112v: '*War*' defendi e chalenga le cunte entant cum le pleyntif naveit pas dit en cuntant en queles viles ses terres furent . . . *Tilton*. Par tel dit ne peut il sun cunte defere sanz ceo qe il ne tendisist laverment qe il nout nule terre en le cunte . . .'

[148] BL MSS. Additional 5925, fols. 152v–153r and Stowe 386, fol. 186r. This is not mentioned in the enrolment in CP 40/145, m. 153d.

[149] BL MS. Stowe 386, fol. 205v (cf. ibid., fol. 199v, Harvard Law School MS. 206, fol. 87v and *YB 32 & 33 EI*, pp. 115–17). The enrolment of the case is CP 40/145, m. 14.

[150] CP 40/156, m. 148d.

[151] E.g. the 1294 and 1298 cases cited above (pp. 324–5) and in CP 40/146, mm. 9d (*monstravit*) and m. 85d (deceit) (Hilary term 1303); CP 40/148, m. 19d (*monstravit*) (Trinity term 1303); CP 40/152, m. 39d (*monstravit*) (Trinity term 1304).

[152] CP 40/148, m. 1d (*monstravit*) (Trinity term 1303); CP 40/145, m. 14 (*monstravit*) (Michaelmas term 1303); CP 40/152, m. 55 (deceit) (Trinity term 1304); CP 40/149, m. 264 (*monstravit*) (Michaelmas term 1304); CP 40/154, m. 27 (deceit) (Hilary term 1305); CP 40/156, m. 148d (deceit) (Trinity term 1305); CP 40/161, m. 232 (deceit) (Michaelmas term 1306).

neither in the pleading nor in the issue put to the jury there is evidence to suggest that it may have been taken into account.[153]

In the *monstravit* case of *Box v. Palmer* heard in Edward II's reign Scrope, for the defendant, argued that use of the writ was authorised by statute only where the bailiff or receiver had no lands or tenements at all.[154] Although the traditional doctrine was argued by Stanton, Chief Justice Bereford supported Scrope with the additional argument that it was in the king's interest that the common law writ of account be used instead of the *monstravit*, since he would thereby receive the profits of the issues of the land, whether or not the forfeiture of the issues was sufficient to secure the attendance of the bailiff. Although the traditional view is still found in a reported case attributed to Trinity term 1311,[155] and apparently in several cases in Michaelmas 1313,[156] the new doctrine was again apparently successful in a deceit action reported as having been heard in that term.[157] Although this is said to have been the settled doctrine of the later law,[158] sufficiency is still mentioned in a deceit case in Hilary Term 1316[159] and in the deceit writ in the printed register.[160]

There was also some doubt about whether or not the bailiff had to be able to show that he possessed lands and tenements specifically in the county where the account was said to be owed or whether his possession of lands and tenements anywhere in the country was enough to bar the use of *monstravit* or to allow the recovery of damages for its use in the action of deceit. There are several cases in which a bailiff was allowed to show possession of lands and tenements in a county other than where the account was being demanded,[161] and the reports of a *monstravit* case heard in Hilary term 1303 show Chief Justice Hengham specifically ruling that

153 For example in the 1294 deceit case of *Rex and Poteman v. Fulham* where the jury found that the plaintiff had houses and rents *ad sufficientiam* in London; in the 1298 deceit case of *Rex and Weston v. Long* where the jurors were careful to give the value of the plaintiff's lands; CP 40/152 m. 39d (Trinity term 1304) where judgment was respited in a *monstravit* after the jury had found that the defendant held lands worth sixty shillings a year.

154 Above, p. 323.

155 *Year Books 4 Edward II (1311)*, ed. G.J. Turner (Selden Society vol. 42, 1925), p. 159.

156 CP 40/201 mm. 203 (*monstravit*), 333 (deceit), 346 (deceit), 315d (*monstravit*).

157 *Pole v. Mount*: *Year Book 7 Edward II (1313–1314)*, pp. 9–12; no plea roll entry of the case was found by the editor. It may be the case of *Thomas de la Pole de Honeton v. John Moriz* at CP 40/201 m. 333 though the plea roll entry of the pleadings has no special features and does not indicate that the doctrine was adopted there.

158 Coke, *Second Institutes*, p. 144. 159 CP 40/213, m. 6. 160 *Reg. Omn. Brev.*, fol. 137r.

161 E.g. *William son of Roger of Oreleton v. William Spicer of Coventry*: CP 40/146, m. 9d (Hilary term 1303): *monstravit* brought in Herefordshire but the defendant claimed to hold land at Coventry in Warwickshire (and see next note for reports of this case); *William of Stowe v. prioress of Stratford*: CP 40/152, m. 55 (Trinity term 1304): *monstravit* brought in Essex but the bailiff claimed to hold land in Norfolk; *Nicholas Profet v. Richard de Lisle*: CP 40/156, m. 148d (Trinity term 1305): *monstravit* brought in Huntingdonshire but the bailiff claimed to hold land in Lincolnshire.

it was not necessary to show that the bailiff or receiver from whom the account was being demanded possessed lands or tenements in the same county as that in which the account was being claimed.[162] However, Hengham ruled the opposite way in a deceit case of Hilary term 1305, where the plaintiff was able to allege only that he had lands in Oxfordshire but where the *monstravit* had claimed an account from him for the period he had acted as a bailiff in Berkshire.[163] This did not, however, change the general rule in the court for there is the case of Trinity term 1305 in which the plaintiff alleged possession of lands and tenements in Lincolnshire in the deceit action brought to challenge a *monstravit de compoto* for the account of the Huntingdonshire church.[164] There were later demurrers on a similar point in cases heard in Michaelmas term 1310 and Michaelmas term 1311.[165]

The mere suing out of a writ of *monstravit* was not in itself sufficient grounds for bringing the writ of deceit. Apparently the writ had to have been prosecuted and process to have been brought against the bailiff or receiver before the action lay.[166] In a King's Bench deceit case of Michaelmas 1303 it was also decided that such an action could not be brought while judgment was still pending in the Common Bench in an action of *monstravit* where the defendant had excepted that he held lands and tenements.[167]

Damages in actions of deceit could be substantial. In the Nottinghamshire case of *Atte Crouche (of London) v. de Wodeburgh*, in which pleadings were heard in Trinity 1307 but in which the verdict was not given until Hilary 1309, the successful plaintiff recovered damages of fifty pounds

162 BL MSS. Additional 31826, fol. 147r and Stowe 386, fol. 169v; LI MS. Miscellaneous 738, fol. 15r. These are reports of *William son of Roger of Oreleton v. William Spicer of Coventry*, enrolled on CP 40/146, m. 9d

163 BL MSS. Hargrave 375, fols. 29r–v and Stowe 386, fol. 196r and LI MS. Miscellaneous 738, fol. 30v. These are reports of *Rex and Roger of Bradwell of Oxford v. William of Holme and his wife Maud*, enrolled on CP 40/154, m. 27. The plaintiff had secured the quashing of the *monstravit de compoto* against him because it had been directed to the sheriff of Oxfordshire where the account was claimed against him in respect of a manor in Berkshire: see above, note 148.

164 *Nicholas Profet v. Richard de Lisle*: CP 40/156, m. 148d.

165 *Richard of Whitace v. William of Walmesford*: CP 40/183, m. 393d; *John Whitbread (Blauncpayn) v. Joce Pikard*: CP 40/189, m. 219d. In the latter case the plaintiff argued strongly 'quod in statuto domini regis continentur quod ballivi et receptores terras vel tenementa non habentes per corpora sua attachientur etc. absque aliqua mencione facienda in quibus comitatibus habeant terras vel tenementa'.

166 See, for example, *William of Whitfield v. John of Gosehale*: CP 40/149, m. 379 (Michaelmas term 1304). The defendant in this case claimed that he had not found pledges to prosecute his *monstravit* and the action had thus lapsed. This was confirmed by checking the writ file.

167 *John of Wyken v. Michael le Bret, rector of Great Snoring*: KB 27/174, m. 67. For the *monstravit* case in the Common Bench see above, note 143.

while in a case heard in Michaelmas term 1313 damages of one hundred pounds were eventually awarded.[168]

OVERRIDING CHARTERS OF EXEMPTION FROM JURY SERVICE

One other reform initially provided in 1259 as part of the Provisions of Westminster was also evidently intended in part to improve the working of the royal courts, to make it easier for them to secure the necessary jurors in certain specific situations where there was a shortage of eligible jurors or a requirement that particular individuals serve on the jury. This was clause 8 of the Provisions of Westminster and it authorised the overriding of royal charters granting particular individuals exemption from jury service under such circumstances.[169] This clause was re-enacted unaltered in 1267 as chapter 14 of the Statute of Marlborough. It seems probable that the courts continued to make use of its provisions though their records rarely demonstrate that fact. There does, however, survive from 1290 a petition submitted to parliament by John de Garston, who had once belonged to the household of Henry III.[170] In it he complained that although by virtue of charters of Henry III and Edward I he enjoyed the privilege of not being compelled to serve on any inquest, jury or assize against his will,[171] and had enjoyed this privilege down to 1280–1 (9 Edward I), he had then been called before Weyland and Brunton, justices of the Common Bench at Westminster, to serve on an inquest jury between Robert of Walton and John Marshal. They had ordered him to take the oath and he had refused and said he was not obliged to do so and shown them his charters of exemption. They had refused to allow them and when he had still refused to swear had amerced him at ten pounds. He had paid two pounds and now asked for pardon of the rest on grounds of poverty. The king pardoned half of the remainder and agreed that the rest be paid by instalments. It is unfortunate that we do not know the precise context of the refusal by Weyland and Brunton to honour the king's charter of exemption. What the petition certainly does make clear is that they were still acting on the assumption that it was possible in the interests of justice to override such charters and the king's refusal to pardon more than part of the amercement indicates that he thought it was quite proper that they should have acted in this way.[172]

[168] CP 40/164, m. 169; CP 40/201, m. 346. [169] Above, pp. 175–6; below, pp. 420–1.

[170] SC 8/201, no. 10010 (summarised in SC 9/2, no. 61).

[171] The earlier of these exemptions was issued in 1251: *CPR 1247–58*, p. 107; the later has not been traced.

[172] But for an amercement imposed in like circumstances prior to his death in 1274 by Gilbert of Preston on Thomas de Valoynes, pardoned possibly after a petition to the Easter parliament of 1275, see *CCR 1272–9*, pp. 178–9.

What the legislation certainly did not completely solve were the problems of those counties in which only very limited numbers of knights were available for service on the grand assize. In two cases in the Westmorland eyre of 1278 the four electors of the grand assize were unable to make an election because, after challenges had been allowed, there were only eight knights eligible.[173] Faced with this difficulty the justices applied for royal instruction. They were told that on this occasion and on any such future occasion they should also make up the numbers required by including knights from the borders of neighbouring counties. This was also the solution followed in a writ of right of advowson case in the Common Bench in Michaelmas term 1302 from Lancashire. The electors of the grand assize said there were only thirteen knights in the county and when five of these had been challenged by the parties this left only eight. The court duly decided in Trinity term 1303 to go for the remaining knights to the border of the neighbouring county of Yorkshire.[174] Flexible procedures may have been as important as the statutory reform in solving this particular problem.

ELIMINATING PERCEIVED ABUSES IN THE OPERATION OF ROYAL COURTS

One of the small pinpricks that were the subject of complaint and then of remedial legislation in 1259 had been the practice of the justices of the eyre of amercing those vouched to warranty, if they lived within the county where the eyre was held and were not present in court to concede or counterplead the warranty. The practice was initially prohibited in 1259 by clause 23 of the Provisions of Westminster and this clause was re-enacted almost word for word in 1267 as chapter 26 of the Statute of Marlborough.[175] The plea rolls indicate that there was no attempt after 1267 to infringe its provisions and that the practice disappeared.

A second pinprick had been the extension of the 'common summons' to allow a general summons to be made for sessions of justices other than the general and forest eyres, and amercements to be imposed when those summoned did not appear. Clause 13 of the Provisions of Westminster of 1259 had deprived escheators, the holders of inquisitions, justices of assize and justices of oyer and terminer of the power to amerce for default of common summons and made it plain that the power was one enjoyed only by the chief justiciar and the justices in eyre on their eyres.[176] This clause was another repeated in identical terms in the Statute of Marlborough, as

[173] JUST 1/981, mm. 8d, 13.
[174] CP 40/144, m. 184d. Cf. *YB 32 & 33 EI*, pp. 387–9.
[175] Below, pp. 426–7, 480–1.
[176] Below, pp. 422–3.

chapter 18 of that Statute, preserving the reference to the chief justiciar even after the disappearance of that office. There is no evidence to suggest that this clause too was not observed. However, in the 1278 Hertfordshire eyre it was presented that John of Balsham had summoned the free tenants of Hatfield to the number of forty and more to Waltham Cross before John of Cobham to act as assize jurors. When they had appeared he had said to them, 'Now you know what the bailiffs of the lord king can do,'[177] but he had done nothing more than this. He was imprisoned briefly as a preliminary to extracting a fine from him for his wrongdoing.[178]

[177] '. . . modo scitis quod ballivi domini regis possunt facere . . .'

[178] JUST 1/323, m. 47.

Chapter 12

THE EXTENSION OF EXISTING REMEDIES

Most of the remedies whose creation was authorised by the Provisions of Westminster or by the Statute of Marlborough bear clear witness to that statutory authorisation in their wording. But not all. One obvious exception is the new writs of entry in the *post* whose creation was authorised in one of the new clauses added to the Provisions of Westminster when they were reissued in 1263 and which was itself reissued in 1267 without amendment as chapter 29 of the Statute of Marlborough.[1] The other obvious exceptions are the various actions for ecclesiastical plaintiffs whose creation was authorised by one of the other new clauses also added to the Provisions in 1263 and which then became chapter 28 of the Statute of Marlborough. These allowed them to bring actions of trespass for goods and chattels taken from the possession of their predecessors and to bring actions to recover possession of lands and other property which their predecessors had held at the time of their death.[2] In both cases, the general remedy was not new. What was new was a significant extension of the reach of that existing remedy. There is also a third possible example: the extension of the writ of waste to cover waste committed by lessees. This may have been implicitly authorised by clause 20 of the Provisions of Westminster of 1259, which was enacted with only minor additions as part of chapter 23 of the Statute of Marlborough in 1267.[3]

WRITS OF ENTRY IN THE *POST*

The first writs of entry in the *post* had been drafted as well as issued for individual litigants prior to 1267: individual examples of a writ of entry *cui in vita* and *sur disseisin* in the *post*.[4] By the end of the reign of Henry III, and thus within no more than five years of the enactment of the Statute of Marlborough, it is possible to find instances of the full range of writs of

[1] Below, pp. 448–9, 482–3. [2] Below, pp. 447–8, 482–3. [3] Below, pp. 424–5, 478–9.
[4] Above, pp. 181–2.

entry in the *post*: entry *ad terminum qui preteriit*,[5] entry *sur disseisin*,[6] entry through a guardian,[7] entry *cui in vita*,[8] entry *dum non compos mentis*,[9] entry *dum infra etatem*,[10] entry through a villein,[11] entry through a prisoner,[12] entry through a wife without her husband's consent,[13] entry *sine assensu conventus*[14] and of intrusion with an entry formulation.[15]

The extension of writs of entry through the approval of the invention of writs of entry in the *post* was evidently intended to make available to a wider range of litigants than had hitherto been the case the advantages of the writ of entry as a form of action allowing claimants to bring a form of action that focused in advance on the particular flaw in the chain of title possessed by the current tenant. This allowed the claimant to avoid bringing the writ of right, hitherto the only action available in the kinds of circumstance where there was such a flaw in the tenant's title but the chain of title since that flawed transaction was too long to be accommodated in a writ of entry 'within the degrees'. The claimant could escape the need to initiate his claim in the court of his lord (from which it could only be removed in two stages into the king's court) and could instead bring it directly, and from the very beginning, in a royal court. He could avoid the other delays associated with the availability of the essoin *de malo lecti* in the action of right. He could also ensure that his claim would be decided by an ordinary jury and escape having to offer his opponent the choice between the relatively slow form of jury trial available through the grand assize and the lottery of trial by battle.

The best gauge of the success of the measure in making available to a wider range of claimants the advantages of the action of entry is by looking at the relative numbers of writs of entry and writs of right on the plea rolls of the king's courts a few years prior to the legislation and then some years after the reform. Tables 5–7 give both the total numbers and the percentages of pleaded actions initiated by writs of entry and by

[5] The earliest examples are to be found in the Wiltshire and Yorkshire eyres of 1268: JUST 1/998A, m. 14; JUST 1/1050, mm. 27d, 82d.

[6] The earliest example is to be found in the Common Bench in Michaelmas term 1269: KB 26/194, m. 32d.

[7] The earliest example is to be found in the 1268 Yorkshire eyre: JUST 1/1050, m. 36.

[8] The earliest examples are to be found in the 1268 Yorkshire eyre: JUST 1/1050, mm. 43d, 44.

[9] The earliest example is to be found in the 1268 Yorkshire eyre: JUST 1/1050, m. 25.

[10] The earliest example is to be found in the Common Bench in Trinity term 1272: KB 26/208A, m. 16d.

[11] The earliest example is to be found in the Common Bench in Easter term 1271: KB 26/202, m. 9.

[12] The earliest example is to be found in the 1272 Cambridgeshire eyre: JUST 1/84, m. 24d.

[13] The earliest example is to be found in the 1271 Kent eyre: JUST 1/365, m. 37.

[14] The earliest example is to be found in the 1271 Kent eyre: JUST 1/365, m. 85.

[15] The earliest example is to be found in the 1272 Shropshire eyre: JUST 1/736, m. 12.

Table 5 *Writs of entry and writs of right, c. 1250*

Session	Record	Writs of entry: Number of cases	Writs of entry: % of total	Writs of right: Number of cases	Writs of right: % of total
Bucks 1247	JUST 1/56	27	82	6	18
Dorset 1244	JUST 1/200	7	70	3	30
Essex 1254	JUST 1/233	36	80	9	20
Gloucs 1248	JUST 1/273	50	62	31	38
Kent 1255	JUST 1/361	54	73	21	27
Oxon 1247	JUST 1/699	28	56	21	44
Sussex 1248	JUST 1/909A	18	88	3	12
Warwicks 1247	JUST 1/952	20	66	10	33
Common Bench Hilary 1250	KB 26/138	4	79	3	21
Total		244	70	107	30

Table 6 *Writs of entry and writs of right, c. 1270*

Session	Record	Entry within degrees	%	Entry in the *post*	%	Writs of right	%
Bucks 1272	JUST 1/60	16	70	3	13	4	17
Dorset 1268	JUST 1/202	4	80	1	20	0	0
Essex 1272	JUST 1/238	32	47	29	43	7	10
Gloucs 1268	JUST 1/275	39	53	12	16	22	31
Kent 1271	JUST 1/365	146	66	61	27	15	7
Oxon 1268	JUST 1/702A	7	58	3	25	2	17
Sussex 1271	JUST 1/913	25	55	16	36	4	9
Warwicks 1272	JUST 1/955	16	40	14	35	10	25
Common Bench Hilary 1272	KB 26/206	5	42	4	33	3	25
Total		290	58	143	29	67	13

writs of right, in eight different counties and in a single Common Bench term *c.* 1250, 1270 and 1290.[16]

These figures suggest that the invention of writs of entry in the *post* had the effect, by 1270, of halving the use of writs of right and, by 1290,

[16] The tables exclude cases where all that happened was that the tenant requested a view. They also exclude cases of formedon, escheat and (in 1290) cessavit.

Table 7 *Writs of entry and writs of right, c. 1290*

Session	Record	Entry within degrees	%	Entry in in the *post*	%	Writs of right	%
Bucks 1286	JUST 1/67	18	60	8	30	3	10
Dorset 1288	JUST 1/213	14	58	10	42	0	0
Essex 1285	JUST 1/246	61	62	30	30	8	8
Gloucs 1287	JUST 1/283	31	65	13	27	4	8
Kent 1293	JUST 1/375	90	65	40	29	8	6
Oxon 1285	JUST 1/710	32	72	10	23	2	5
Sussex 1288	JUST 1/929	35	56	22	36	5	8
Warwicks 1285	JUST 1/960	29	55	22	41	2	4
Common Bench Hilary 1290	CP 40/81	31	78	8	19	1	3
Total		351	64	163	30	33	6

of further halving the 1270 figure. The 1270 figures, furthermore, appear to suggest that the writ of entry in the *post* was also taking business away from the writs of entry within the degrees. This seems unlikely, as the proportion of business done in 1290 by writs of entry in the *post* was the same as that done in 1270, though by 1290 there was no possibility of competition between them, as chapter 40 of the Statute of Westminster I of 1275 had by then established that writs of entry in the *post* could not be used if the devolutions of the land could be described by a writ within the degrees.[17] The more likely explanation is that the writ of entry in the *post* was initially more successful than the writ of entry within the degrees in attracting new business to the king's courts, and that not all the business done by writs of entry in the *post* would formerly have reached the king's court in actions of right.

NEW REMEDIES FOR ECCLESIASTICAL TENANTS

The first section of chapter 28 of the Statute of Marlborough allowed abbots and other heads of religious corporations to bring an action to recover goods belonging to their houses which had been forcibly seized or taken from those houses during the time of their predecessors, provided this had been shortly before their deaths, but whether or not the predecessor had himself begun action for their recovery. In effect this extended the availability of actions of trespass for wrongs done to the head

[17] *SR*, I, 36. For the application of this legislation see, for example, *Alice widow of William Gaugy of Stapleford v. Edmund of Lancaster*: CP 40/15, m. 59 (Trinity term 1276).

of a religious corporation past the lifetime of the abbot or other head of that religious corporation. Only one action has been found which looks as though it may have been authorised by this part of the chapter. This is an action of trespass brought by the abbot of Hyde against Master Gilbert of Popham in Trinity term 1306.[18] As summarised in the enrolment, the writ required Master Gilbert to answer for 'having taken and carried off with force and arms goods and chattels belonging to the house and church of the same abbot of Hyde by Winchester during the time of Robert of Popham, late abbot of Hyde by Winchester, the predecessor of the said abbot, and perpetrated other enormities to the grave damage of the same abbot and against the peace etc.'[19] The alleged seizure had taken place fourteen years before at North Stoneham in Hampshire and the goods taken had included horses, silver vessels, books and jewellery valued at two hundred marks. The defendant pleaded not guilty. The jury which appeared in Michaelmas term the same year found that he had taken goods to that value (and specified them in detail). The court duly awarded damages assessed at a hundred marks. It can be no coincidence that the defendant and the abbot's predecessor had shared the same toponymic surname. It seems likely they were relatives. It is also probably no coincidence that 1292 (the date of the supposed seizure) was also the date of Robert of Popham's death.[20] Some kind of gift of some of the abbot's movables to a kinsman just before his death is one possible scenario to explain the litigation: the kinsman might see this as a valid gift, the abbot's successor as an invalid gift made by an abbot no longer in full possession of his faculties. It is also probably no mere chance that no action had been taken during the period of office of Robert of Popham's immediate successor, Simon Canning, and that it was only after his successor, Geoffrey of Ferrings, had become abbot (in 1304) that Master Gilbert was sued for these movables. The abbot's immediate successor had accepted the validity of the gift; only that abbot's successor thought the gift could and should be challenged.

Another similar action (*Prior of Wallingford v. Raundes parson of Buckland et al.*) was brought in Michaelmas term 1318,[21] and the printed register gives versions of the same writ for the use of an abbot, a warden, a master and the prior of a hospital.[22] The Year Books of Edward II also include reports of cases brought by such writs. In the case of the *Prior of Lenton*

[18] CP 40/160, m. 242.

[19] '. . . de placito quare vi et armis bona et catalla domus et ecclesie ipsius abbatis de Hyde juxta Wynton' tempore Roberti de Poppeham nuper abbatis de Hyde juxta Wynton' predecessoris predicti Abbatis inventa cepit et asportavit et alia enormia ibidem perpetravit ad grave dampnum ipsius Abbatis et contra pacem etc.'

[20] *VCH Hants*, II, 122. [21] CP 40/225, m. 18. [22] *Reg. Omn. Brev.*, fol. 96v.

v. Shaldeford, various possible exceptions to the writ were discussed and rejected. It was argued that the property in a chattel could not belong to a church (rejected on the grounds that this form of writ was given by statute), that the intention of the Statute in speaking of an action '*ad bona repetenda*' was to allow the use of the actions of detinue or replevin in which the goods themselves were recovered, rather than of trespass where only damages were obtained (likewise rejected), and that the abbot's predecessor was not dead but had only been deposed (also rejected).[23] A similar writ was used in the case of the *Abbot of Battle v. Attebregge et al.*,[24] and in a case in 16 Edward III (1342–3) where the action was allowed despite the objection that the trespass complained of had occurred in 14 Edward II (1320–1) and that any right of action should by then have lapsed.[25]

The same section was also cited in argument by serjeants to support the availability of other types of remedy. In an unidentified report of a late thirteenth- or early fourteenth-century case in the Common Bench a prior brought an action of detinue of chattels for the delivery of ten quarters of wheat which his predecessor had lent to the defendant and whose repayment had been due at the following Michaelmas.[26] The prior had only suit to prove the arrangement. Counsel for the defendant asked whether he was bound to answer a claim based on a bailment made by a third party without specialty. The prior's counsel (Sutton) had three answers to this: that the goods handed over had belonged to his house and not his predecessor personally; that the receipt of the wheat and its carrying away had been sufficiently public that a jury could be expected to have a knowledge of it; and that the Statute provided that the successor was to have the same action as his predecessor in respect of goods and chattels.[27] That this was indeed a distorted reference to the provisions of this clause of the Statute of Marlborough is confirmed by the response of counsel for the defendant (Huntingdon) who noted that the Statute spoke only of 'goods and chattels carried off and taken away against the peace'.[28] Eventually the defendant was made to answer the claim but allowed to wage his law to deny owing anything. The same chapter was also cited to support the availability of the action of annual rent to the rector of a parish church for the recovery of a rent in arrears

[23] *YB 4 Edward II (1311)*, p. 134.

[24] *Year Book 5 Edward II (1312)*, ed. W.C. Bolland (Selden Society vol. 33, 1916), p. 14.

[25] *Year Books 16 Edward III–II: Year Books of the Reign of King Edward the Third: Year XVI (Second Part)*, ed. L.O. Pike (Rolls Series, London, 1900), p. 247.

[26] BL MS. Harley 572, fol. 11v.

[27] 'Estre ceo le statut vust qe de bens e chateux eit le successour mesme le accion qe le predecessour.'

[28] 'Statut parle de bens e chateux cariez e enportez encontre la pees . . .'

since the time of one of his predecessors. The action was brought in the 1285 Northamptonshire eyre by one of the justices of that eyre, Master Thomas of Siddington, the rector of the church of Passenham. Master Thomas claimed fourteen years' arrears of annual rents of a quarter of wheat and four pence owed to his church by three defendants (the abbot of Grestein, John le Lou and Robert de Pavely).[29] They challenged his entitlement to claim arrears of an annual rent of which he had never been seised and of which even his immediate predecessor had not been seised. The response of Master Thomas was to assert that he was claiming not on the basis of his own seisin but on the basis of the seisin of his church. His predecessor, William of Cirencester, had been seised of the rent in Henry III's reign and all William's predecessors since time out of mind. Withdrawal of the rent had occurred during the time of William's successor, Hugh de la Penne. Hugh had started litigation against the defendants but had been prevented by the civil war from pursuing it. The immediate predecessor of Master Thomas in the living, Hugh of London, had intruded into the living on his own authority, seizing it from Hugh de la Penne. He should therefore not be regarded as having properly been rector of the church. In essence therefore, the rent had only been withdrawn in the time of his immediate predecessor, who had been taking action to recover it but had died before succeeding in doing so. Master Thomas cited the Statute as allowing successors the same action as their predecessors for things subtracted from their churches, if the latter had failed to obtain justice during their lifetime.[30] A report of the same case, however, suggests that the justice hearing the case, Saham, may originally have cited not this but the following section of the same chapter in support of his colleague's case.[31] Saham asserted that the Statute of Marlborough provided general authority for allowing a successor to recover property belonging to a church of which his predecessor had died seised, together with damages.[32] This was not denied. The subsequent argument was about whether this could in fact be said to be true in the circumstances of the case, where his immediate predecessor had been an intruder and the previous incumbent had not received the rent during a period of civil disturbances. It is unclear whether either the reporter or the clerk misunderstood what was said. Perhaps the argument in the

[29] JUST 1/622, m. 22d.

[30] 'Et dicit quod per statutum de Marleberge debet ei et ecclesie sue subveniri in hoc casu ubi in favorem sancte ecclesie conceditur successoribus accio que competeret predecessoribus quando de subtraccionibus factis ecclesie sue suo tempore non fuerunt justiciam [consecuti] . . .'

[31] BL MS. Additional 37657, fols. 93r–v.

[32] 'E dautre part nous trovom lestatut de Marleberg' tot plein en ceo case qe dit qe si persone murge seisi com del dreit de sa eglise son successour, si [hom] ly deforce eyt sun recoveryr en queu cas damages ly serrunt agardez, par qey nus agardum qe vous responez a cesti bref si vous volez dire.'

case brought up both sections of the Statute and the two different sources each record only part of that argument.

The second part of chapter 28 of the Statute of Marlborough allowed ecclesiastics a remedy against those who intruded into lands belonging to their church during a vacancy and also authorised the awarding of damages in such actions.[33] The effect was to allow ecclesiastical tenants to enjoy a remedy equivalent to the action of intrusion or to the assize of mort d'ancestor (and its congeners) already available to lay tenants.

Two different forms of writ are to be found on the rolls.[34] Each has a reasonable claim to be the form of action authorised by the legislation, since neither form seems to have existed prior to 1263. One took the form of a writ resembling the congeners of mort d'ancestor. In it the claimant asserted that the land being claimed was land of which a specific predecessor had been seised in his demesne as of the fee and right of his church on the day of his death. This form of writ had been drafted by Easter term 1263 when it was being used by the abbot of Combermere in a case being brought against Roger l'Estrange.[35] Walter de Merton was chancellor at the time of its drafting and it is probably not a coincidence that he was the next claimant to use a similar writ in 1274, just after he had become bishop of Rochester. He used it to claim lands held by his predecessor, Lawrence de St Martin, at the time of his death (in June 1274).[36] Pleading in the case took place during Michaelmas 1274, but the writ itself may well have been issued during the final months of Merton's second period of office as chancellor.[37] His opponent in the litigation was Thomas de St Martin, the bishop's heir, and the heart of the dispute was whether land Lawrence had acquired to himself and his heirs or successors should pass to his heir or to his successor. Merton succeeded in the litigation because he was able to show that the land had belonged to the fee of the bishopric. The court held that the land should be deemed to have been quitclaimed to the bishop in his ecclesiastical capacity rather than acquired by him in his secular one. Merton also brought similar litigation against a different tenant in Michaelmas term 1276 for land in

[33] Below, pp. 482–3.

[34] But also note a reference to the same chapter of the Statute made by the abbot of Roche, not in an action brought under the Statute, but in the course of his complaint to the *auditores querelarum* in 1290, when he was attempting to reverse a judgment in a land plea wrongly given against his predecessor, allegedly after his death, see *State Trials of the Reign of Edward the First, 1289–1293*, ed. T.F. Tout and Hilda Johnstone (Camden 3rd Series vol. 9, 1906), pp. 1–5.

[35] Above, p. 183.

[36] The writ claimed a carucate of land in Kent 'de qua Laurencius quondam Roffensis episcopus ultimus predecessor suus fuit seisitus in dominico suo tanquam de iure ecclesie sue Roffensis die quo obiit etc.'

[37] CP 40/5, m. 104. Merton's successor, Robert Burnell, was appointed on 21 September 1274. Merton was elected to Rochester on 20 July.

Cambridgeshire.[38] That writ was quashed because the tenant claimed not to hold all the land concerned but it was renewed with an amended statement of the quantities claimed in Easter 1277. This time the issue was the much simpler one of whether or not Merton's predecessor had been seised of the land.[39] No further instance of the writ has been noted prior to Michaelmas term 1305 when the master of the hospital of St Margaret of West Monkton in Somerset used a writ of the same form to claim a messuage, one acre and three roods in Taunton against the prior of Taunton.[40] The prior denied that the claimant really was the legitimate master of the hospital and issue was joined on this. That other writs of a similar form had been drafted for use by abbots or priors and may even have been issued is suggested by the occurrence in a late thirteenth- or early fourteenth-century register of a writ of similar form to cover their case. This also has a variant to cover the case where the predecessor had surrendered office rather than died.[41]

The first example of a second kind of writ which bore a close resemblance to one of the forms of the writ of intrusion which was available to lay men seems, a little surprisingly, to have first been used in a post-1267 revival of the action brought by the abbot of Combermere against Roger l'Estrange, even though (as has been seen) the pre-1267 action had been initiated by a writ of the first type.[42] The case came up for a hearing in the Common Bench in Hilary term 1272, where the writ was quashed for technical reasons.[43] The writ was reissued in an amended form in time to be pleaded in the Shropshire eyre of 1272.[44] The abbot lost his claim this time because a jury agreed that his predecessor had initially only held the land as a security and then held it in wardship by the grant of Roger's father. A second action brought by a similar, but not identical, form of writ was pleaded in the Common Bench in Hilary 1280.[45] In it Richard, bishop of London claimed a messuage and forty-one acres

[38] CP 40/17, m. 29. [39] CP 40/19, m. 68. [40] CP 40/153, m. 385.

[41] CUL MS. Ll.4.17, f. 304r: '*quando abbas petit terram ut jus ecclesie sue.* Rex vicecomiti salutem. Precipe A. quod juste etc. reddat abbati vel priori de tali loco x acras terre cum pertinenciis in W. de quibus T. quondam abbas vel prior de tali loco predecessor predicti abbatis vel prioris fuit seisitus ut jus ecclesie sue de tali loco die quo obiit ut dicit, vel die quo cessit a prioratu suo ut dicit. Et nisi etc.'

[42] Above, p. 183.

[43] The abbot claimed the land 'ut jus ecclesie sue de Cumbermere et in quam idem Rogerus non habet ingressum hisi per intrusionem quam in eam fecit tempore vacacionis abbacie predicte post mortem Willelmi de Weresleg' quondam abbatis ejusdem abbacie, predecessoris predicti abbatis.': *EELR*, I, pp. 11–12 (1272.1)

[44] JUST 1/736, m. 11d.

[45] The claimant alleged that the land was the right of his church 'et in que iidem . . . non habent ingressum nisi per Philippum Basset qui se in eas intrusit post mortem Fulconis Basset quondam episcopi Londoniensis predecessoris predicti episcopi': CP 40/32, m. 30.

in two Essex villages against Roger Bigod, earl of Norfolk, and his wife, Alina. He claimed that their title was derived from Phillip Basset (Alina's father) but that Phillip had intruded into this land after the death of Fulk Basset, late bishop of London. Again, their defence was that this was land Fulk had held in his own right and Phillip had quite properly entered as his heir. The nature of Fulk Basset's title to the land then went to a jury. A related form of writ (but in the *post*) was used by the same bishop in Michaelmas term 1291 to claim a messuage, eighty-nine acres of arable and one and half acres of meadow in the same two villages against Thomas of Twinstead.[46] Thomas vouched Hugh Despenser to warranty. Hugh denied that Fulk had ever been seised of this land in right of his church. The jury verdict given at Easter 1292 found that Fulk had been seised in right of his church and the bishop recovered the land, though no damages.

WASTE COMMITTED BY LESSEES

Clause 20 of the Provisions of Westminster of 1259 had stated that no lessee was to commit waste, sale or exile during his lease unless he had in writing specific authorisation for doing this. If he did so without this necessary written authority damages could be recovered. This provision was re-enacted without significant alterations, other than the addition at the end of the clause of a phrase indicating that such defendants were also to be heavily amerced, as part of chapter 23 of the Statute of Marlborough of 1267.[47]

Although it looks as though the chapter was intended to authorise an extension of the action of waste so that it might be available against lessees, the only evidence of such an extension during the following decade is an action of which only the preliminary procedural stages have been found. This was being brought in Michaelmas term 1276 and Michaelmas term 1277 by Isabel, the widow of William of Milding, against Master Laurence of Denardeston.[48] The writ used does not seem to have cited any statutory authority for holding the defendant answerable for the waste he had committed.[49] This chapter of the Statute was then effectively superseded in 1278 when chapter 5 of the Statute of Gloucester, as part of a general

46 CP 40/91, m. 35d. 47 Below, pp. 424–5, 478–9.

48 CP 40/17, m. 119; CP 40/21, m. 100d.

49 The defendant was required to answer 'de placito quare cum eadem Isabella quasdam terras et quedam tenementa sua in dicta villa de Malling' prefato Laurenci ad terminum qui nondum pretriit dimisisset una cum boscis, gardinis et villenagiis ad terras et tenementa illa pertinentibus idem Laurencius infra terminum illum fecit vastum et destruccionem de boscis, gardinis et villenagiis ad dampnum ipsius Isabelle decem librarum'.

overall reform of the action of waste, reaffirmed the possibility of using an action of waste against lessees.[50] The avowedly statutory actions found thereafter in use against lessees are best seen as being based on the Statute of Gloucester rather than on the Statute of Marlborough.[51]

Part of the background to the enactment of the Statute of Gloucester may be the actions of waste brought against a tenant for life and against two curtesy tenants found in Trinity term 1276[52] and Easter term 1277 respectively.[53] All three purport to be based on statutes. That legislation is likely to be the Statute of Marlborough, though as extended by analogy from tenants for years to tenants for the term of a life, and thus to the curtesy tenant, a special type of life tenant.[54] It may have been challenges to this very extended interpretation of the Statute that led to a reconsideration of the scope of the action of waste and to the decision to give proper legislative authority for the extension of its scope in the Statute of Gloucester.

The rule confirmed by the Statute (but probably already an older common law rule) could be, and sometimes was, also invoked in other

[50] *SR*, I, 48.

[51] For the writ invoking the provisions of the Statute of Gloucester (and talking of leases either for life or for a term of years) see *Early Registers*, pp. 149–50 (R165). For an early example see JUST 1/783, m. 17 (1280 Hants eyre): *Alan Plukenet v. Simon of Winchester* [but note that the writ here spoke only of a lease for a term of years].

[52] *John Tayllard and his wife Beatrice and her sister Isabel v. Martin des Roches and the prior of Southwick*: CP 40/15, m. 90. For later stages see CP 40/18, m. 32 (Hilary term 1277) and CP 40/19, m. 50 (Easter term 1277). The defendant was summoned to answer in a plea 'quare cum de communi consilio regni regis provisum sit quod non liceat alicui destruccionem, vendicionem seu vastum facere de terris, domibus, gardinis et boscis . . . cuicumque dimissis ad terminum vite, iidem (defendants) de domibus, gardinis et boscis in Ulsefeud quos Ricardus de Boville frater predictarum Beatricis et Isabelle, cujus heredes ipse sunt, predicto (defendant) dimisit ad terminum vite sue, destruccionem fecerunt contra formam provisionis predicte ad exheredacionem ipsarum Beatricis et Isabelle'.

[53] In *Walter de Coleville v. Hugh de Charnley* the defendant had been attached to answer 'de placito quare cum de communi consilio regni provisum sit quod non liceat alicui distruccionem, vendicionem seu vastum facere in terris, domibus, gardinis seu boscis que sibi acciderint tenendum ad terminum vite per legem Anglie, idem Hugo de terris, domibus et gardinis que tenet per legem Anglie ad terminum vite per mortem Beatricis de Coleville quondam uxoris sue consanguinee predicti Walteri, cujus heres ipse est, distruccionem et vendicionem facit contra formam provisionis predicte ad exheredacionem ipsius Walteri et contra pacem etc.': CP 40/19, m. 38; in *Reginald fitzMary v. Roger Goldsmith (le Orfevre)* the defendant had been summoned to answer 'de placito quare cum de communi consilio regni regis provisum sit quod non liceat alicui destreccionem, vendicionem seu vastum facere de terris, domibus, gardinis seu boscis que tenet ad terminum vite per legem Anglie, idem Rogerus de domibus quas tenet per legem Anglie ad terminum vite per mortem Alicie que fuit uxor ipsius Rogeri amite predicti Reginaldi, cujus heres ipse est, vendicionem et destruccionem fecit contra formam provisionis predicte ad exheredacionem ipsius Reginaldi': CP 40/19, m. 66.

[54] Maitland seems to have accepted Coke's view that chapter 23 of the Statute of Marlborough was intended to apply to tenants for life as well as lessees (*P&M*, II, 9). The printed register (*Reg. Omn. Brev.*, fol. 72r), however, supports the view here advanced that the Statute only authorised an action against the lessee for term of years. In any case the curtesy tenant hardly came within either category.

actions. In a covenant action heard in Michaelmas term 1304 the plaintiffs (Robert Turgys and his wife, Willelma) were suing the tenant (John de la Rokele of Wymondham) to whom the wife had leased a wood she had held in dower for the remainder of her life and who had then committed waste in the wood. This had resulted in an action of waste brought by the reversioner who had recovered the place wasted and also damages against the plaintiffs. The reports of the case show that the defendant tried to make the plaintiffs show written evidence of the lease and evidence that under its terms he was not allowed to commit waste. The defendant was driven to abandon this argument when the court agreed with counsel for the plaintiffs that the common law presumption in the case of all leases was that the defendant was not allowed to commit waste and that the presumption could only be rebutted by his showing his lease with a clause specifically permitting him to do this.[55]

[55] See the reports of *Robert Turgys and Willelma v. John de la Rokele of Wymondham* (enrolled on CP 40/149, m. 257d) in BL MSS. Additional 31826, fol. 345v, Harley 25, fol. 196r and Harley 572, fols. 163v–164r.

Chapter 13

ENFORCING THE ACCOUNTABILITY OF SOCAGE GUARDIANS

Clause 12 of the Provisions of Westminster of 1259 had, among other things, provided a clear general statement of the obligation of the guardians of lands held by socage tenure to render an account to the heirs for the issues of those lands and for the value of any marriage they might have arranged for them once the heirs came of age. Its provisions were retained without alteration in the 1263 reissue of the Provisions and further retained with only a minor amendment, probably intended only for clarification, in the final reissue of the Provisions as the Statute of Marlborough in 1267 as chapter 17 of that Statute.[1] The legislation said nothing about the creation of any new form of action for its enforcement and there is no sign of the legislation being taken as authority for the creation of one prior to 1267. Nor is there any evidence of the accountability of the socage guardian being enforced through an adaptation of the ordinary action of account during this period.[2]

THE CREATION OF AN ENFORCEMENT ACTION IN THE KING'S COURT

The king's council and Chancery do not seem to have been in much of a hurry to create a new action or to authorise the adaptation of the existing remedy after 1267 either. Indeed, it is more than a decade after the enactment of the Statute of Marlborough before the first action of account to be brought against a socage guardian by an heir is to be found on the plea rolls of the king's courts. The action was evidently initiated by a writ specifically reciting the legislation.[3] It authorised the sheriff of Sussex to summon Henry Gundewine of Chichester and his wife, Alice,

1 Below, pp. 422–3, 476–7. 2 Above, p. 322.

3 The defendant was summoned to answer 'de placito quare cum de communi consilio regni regis provisum sit quod custodes terrarum et tenementorum que tenentur in socagio heredibus terrarum illarum et tenementorum cum ad plenam etatem pervenerint reddant racionabilem compotum suum de exitibus de terris et tenementis illis provenientibus tempore quo custodiam illam habuerunt racione minoris etatis heredum predictorum . . .'

to answer Peter of Inlands for refusing, despite the legislation, to provide Peter with an account for the issues of the socage lands and tenements of Peter at Inlands in Westbourne during his minority. Alice had held that wardship, probably as the widow of Peter's father. A first stage of mesne process in this case is recorded on the Common Bench plea roll for Hilary term 1278 and subsequent stages on the rolls for Michaelmas term 1278 and Easter term 1279.[4] The case was eventually heard during the course of the Sussex eyre of 1279.[5] The enrolment gives no details of the extent of the lands concerned or of the period for which they had been held by Alice, but it does show that Peter claimed ten marks in damages for the alleged refusal to account. The defendants admitted that they had held the lands in wardship with Peter but claimed that the cost of providing for Peter and his brother John while they lived with them and of the upkeep of the buildings on the land had exceeded their income from the property. The court directed an enquiry to be held into the value of the land and the time for which it had been held and as to the money spent for the various purposes, but no outcome of that enquiry is recorded. It is entirely in keeping with this comparatively late date for the issuing of the first original writ based on the legislation that there is no writ of this kind in the Luffield Register, which mostly belongs to the final years of the reign of Henry III. A writ of similar form to that used in this litigation is, however, found in the early fourteenth-century register of writs printed by de Haas and Hall,[6] and appears earlier in two registers of the mid-1290s.[7]

A number of variants on this basic form were also drafted and issued by Chancery prior to 1307. A special writ was drafted for litigation against a lord who had allegedly usurped the wardship of land held in socage shortly before 1286,[8] though standard writs were later used by plaintiffs

[4] CP 40/23, m. 32; CP 40/26, m. 81; CP 40/29, m. 6d. [5] JUST 1/914, m. 9.

[6] *Early Registers*, p. 210 (R 428): 'Rex vicecomiti salutem. Si A. fecerit te securum etc. tunc summone etc. B quod sit coram justiciariis nostris etc. ostensurus quare, cum de communi consilio regni nostri Anglie provisum sit quod custodes terrarum et tenementorum que tenentur in socagio heredibus terrarum illarum et tenementorum cum ad plenam etatem pervenerint reddant racionabilem compotum suum de exitibus de terris et tenementis illis provenientibus de tempore quo custodiam illam habuerunt racione minoris etatis heredum predictorum, idem A. prefato B. racionabilem compotum suum de exitibus provenientibus de terris et tenementis ipsius B. in N. que tenentur in socagio et quorum custodiam eadem A. habuit dum predictus B. infra etatem fuit reddere contradicit ut dicit.' A similar writ appears in *Reg. Omn. Brev.*, fol. 136r.

[7] CUL MS. Additional 3022, fol. 26r and BL MS. Harley 748, fol. 22v. The former of these writs is addressed to the sheriff of Northamptonshire and ascribes to Edward I the additional title of 'superior lord of Scotland', suggesting a date in the early 1290s.

[8] See *John son of John de Paris v. abbot of St Denis and Brother Robert, the former prior of the abbot's cell of Deerhurst (and brother Stephen the current prior)* as enrolled in CP 40/61, m. 69 (Hilary term 1286) and JUST 1/283, mm. 9, 32d (1287 Gloucestershire eyre): 'de placito quare, cum de communi

under similar circumstances.[9] A modified form of the standard writ which substituted 'gavelkind' for 'socage' throughout was used in a writ relating to Kentish lands issued at Westminster on 1 December 1291 and initiating litigation in the Common Bench in the following Hilary term, and also in another Kentish case for which only a preliminary mesne process stage has been found, enrolled in Michaelmas term 1292.[10] Ordinary writs were, however, apparently used in other Kentish cases, even where they seem to have involved lands held in gavelkind, both before and after this date.[11] Only a mesne process stage has been found (in Hilary term 1300) of a further variant for use by the heir against the executors of a socage guardian.[12]

LOCAL ENFORCEMENT

The 1291 gavelkind variant and the writs in the registers are certainly returnable forms of the writ, initiating litigation in the Common Bench.

consilio regni provisum sit quod illi qui sunt propinquiores heredibus defunctorum qui terram suam tenuerunt in sokagium habeant custodiam hujusmodi heredum et terre sue, ita quod custodes illi heredibus illis cum ad etatem suam pervenerunt racionabilem compotum suum de exitibus inde provenientibus reddere teneantur, predicti abbas et frater Robertus dum fuit prior predicte celle de quibus Johannes de Paris pater predicti Johannis, cujus heres ipse est, terram suam apud La Leye tenuit in sokagium, falso confingentes terram illam de eis teneri per servicium militare et non in sokagium, eundem Johannem et terram suam in manum suam ceperunt et ipsum Johannem infra etatem existentem, nullo compoto de exitibus terre sue sibi adhuc reddito, maritari fecerunt et alia enormia ei intulerunt ad dampnum ipsius Johannis trescentarum librarum et contra legem et consuetudinem regni etc.' Only preliminary procedural stages of this case have been found.

9 Below, pp. 359–60.

10 JUST 4/2/18: *William son of Thomas of Hackington v. Joan widow of Thomas of Hackington*; CP 40/96, m. 296: *Thomas son of Solomon of Whitfield v. Walter of Shofford and his wife Agnes*: 'de placito quare, cum de communi consilio regni regis provisum sit quod custodes terrarum et tenementorum que tenentur in gavylikende heredibus terrarum illarum et tenementorum cum ad plenam etatem pervenerint reddant compotum suum de exitibus de terris et tenementis illis provenientibus tempore quo custodiam illam habuerint racione minoris etatis heredum predictorum, iidem Walterus et Agnes prefato Thome racionabile compotum suum de exitibus de terris et tenementis ipsius Thome in Maydenstan et Stapilhurst que tenentur in gavelykende et quorum custodiam iidem Walterus et Agnes habuerunt dum predictus Thomas infra etatem fuit reddere contradicunt etc.'

11 For an earlier case see *Hugh son of Adam of Gillingham and his brother Geoffrey v. Hugh of Blyth of Rochester*: CP 40/66, m. 1d (Hilary term 1287). For contemporary and later cases see *Thomas son of Simon of Brunsford v. John Holte*: JUST 1/365, m. 25d (1293 Kent eyre); *John of Walton v. Walter of Ripley*: CP 40/112, m. 126 (Easter term 1296); *John of Ditton and wife Elizabeth v. Robert of Hormington*: CP 40/155, m. 96 (Easter term 1305).

12 *Nicholas son of Gilbert of Louth v. executors of Master Henry of Newark*: CP 40/132, m. 23. For a request for the drafting of a writ which could be used against the successor of a prior who had usurped a wardship made in the Lent parliament of 1305 and the agreement in principle that one should be provided see *Memoranda de Parliamento*, ed. F.W. Maitland (Rolls Series, London, 1893), pp. 158–9.

At least one register also has a non-returnable form of the same writ for initiating such litigation in the county court.[13] There is also clear evidence for the existence of such a form in a writ *pone* for the removal of such a case out of the county court of Lincolnshire that is quoted in full in an enrolment in Easter term 1294. This noted a complaint made by the defendants who had brought the writ *pone* about the sheriff's failure to return the writ despite their delivery of the *pone* in good time, as attested by a bill of the sub-sheriff of the county. Their complaint led to an order to the assize justices to enquire into the matter and to discover the damages they had suffered from his failure to execute the mandate.[14] It is fortunate that this particular failure of execution occurred for there is nothing in the case after its removal to suggest that it had originally been initiated in the county court.[15] This may suggest that other cases on the Common Bench rolls may also have been initiated by such writs but subsequently removed into the Common Bench, where only a comprehensive search of the surviving writ files would identify them. It also suggests that there may have been a significant number of other cases brought and determined in county courts, of which nothing is now known.

The accountability of socage guardians was probably also enforced at a local level through plaints and other procedures associated with local courts. The only evidence known to me on this point relates to the special case of Kent gavelkind tenure, where there is some evidence from before 1259 of the enforcement of the accountability of such guardians.[16] In a

[13] BL MS. Harley 748, fol. 22v.

[14] CP 40/104, m. 126 (Easter term 1294): '*Linc*'. Ostensum fuit domino regi ex parte Ricardi filii Willelmi de Spaldyng' et Agnetis uxoris ejus quod cum iidem Ricardus et Agnes detulissent quoddam breve domini regis eidem vicecomiti returnabile hic in Bancum a die Pasche in unum mensem in hec verba: "Edwardus dei gracia rex Anglie, dominus Hibernie et dux Aquitanie vicecomiti Linc' salutem. Pone coram justiciariis nostris apud Westm' a die Pasche in unum mensem loquelam que est in comitatu tuo per breve nostrum inter Nicholaum Baret de Spalding' petentem et Ricardum filium Willelmi de Spaldyng' et Agnetem uxorem ejus de eo quod iidem Ricardus et Agnes reddant prefato Nicholao racionabilem compotum de exitibus provenientibus de terris et tenementis ipsius Nicholai in Spaldyng' que tenentur in socagio et quorum custodiam eadem Agnes habuit dum prefatus Nicholaus infra etatem fuit ut dicitur. Et dic prefato Nicholao quod tunc sit ibi loquelam suam versus prefatos Ricardum et Agnetem uxorem ejus inde prosecuturus si voluerit. Et habeas ibi hoc breve et aliud breve. Teste me ipso apud Dovor' xiiij die Aprilis anno regni nostri xxiij°", quod quidem breve liberatum fuit die sabbati in septimana Pasche anno predicto prout patet per bylettum subvicecomitis sigillo signatum, quod quidem breve idem vicecomes non returnavit in [i]<ipsius>[i] domini regis contemptum et predictorum Ricardi et Agnetis dampnum etc. Mandatum est per statutum justiciariis assignatis in comitatu quo die breve predictum vicecomiti vel subvicecomiti erat liberatum et cujus sigillo bilettum erat signatum etc. et eciam de dampnis quod diligenter inquirant; et quid inquisierint scire faciant hic in octabis sancti Michaelis etc.'

[15] CP 40/110, m. 122d (repleaded at m. 185) (Michaelmas term 1295).

[16] Above, p. 67.

case heard in Easter 1325 it was asserted in pleading as a gavelkind custom used since time out of mind that when the gavelkind heir came of age at fifteen and came to his lord's court to perform fealty, the court would secure the attendance of the heir's guardian for the purpose of rendering account, and would levy any arrears owed by the guardian.[17] Earlier, in 1294, it was claimed to be the custom of gavelkind tenure in Kent that when land was inherited by an underage gavelkind tenant it was taken into the lord's hand until the *prochein amy* (the guardian in socage) went to the lord to provide surety that he would answer for the issues of the land when the heir came of age. Otherwise the lord was himself entitled to retain the land, but subject to a similar duty to account once the heir came of age.[18] The Kent eyre of 1293 also produced three examples of the accountability of those who had been the guardians of gavelkind land being enforced through plaints in the eyre.[19]

The existence of purely local procedures and of a non-returnable form of the writ may well mean that the forty-six cases that are recorded on the plea rolls of the Common Bench and the eyres are only the tip of a much larger iceberg of cases through which the accountability of such guardians was enforced. It is, however, only this tip that is visible and it shows no more than a relatively small trickle of cases. There are no more than one or two cases in most years and in some years none, though the number rose to as many as five cases in 1293.

ANALYSIS OF RECORDED CASES

The plaintiff's count in the pleaded actions as enrolled normally provided a detailed specification of where the lands concerned were located and their quantity but not of their annual value. There are a few cases where the latter is given but not the former,[20] and also a few where both are given.[21] The stated valuations run as high as one hundred

[17] *William of Burstowe and his brother Robert v. Michael Franceys and others*: CP 40/256, m. 135d. This case is Avowry 220 in Anthony Fitzherbert's *La Graunde Abridgement* (London, 1577).

[18] *John son of Ralph of Farningham v. Roger of Tilmanstone and others*: JUST 1/1298, m. 116 (an assize of novel disseisin brought before Kirby and Lisle).

[19] JUST 1/375, mm. 81d (*John de Ovene v. Luke de Vienne*), 82d (*Henry atte Children and his wife Joan v. Edmund de Vienne*), 87 (*John atteDoune v. Alan Richer of Shelving*). But note that in the first two of these cases it appears to have been the lord of whom the land was held who was being required to answer for the issues of the gavelkind land. Doubts about the propriety of using the statutory writ against the lord may explain why these plaintiffs used a plaint.

[20] *John le Baud v. Roger of Bedfont*: CP 40/51, m. 75 (Michaelmas term 1283); *John of Cleeton v. Richard Carbonel of Aliford*: JUST 1/739, m. 17 (1292 Shropshire eyre).

[21] *John de Stretlinges and his wife Maud v. Godfrey bishop of Worcester*: CP 40/102, m. 97 (Michaelmas term 1293) and reported in IT MS. Miscellaneous 1, fol. 14r and BL MSS. Harley 493B,

pounds and as low as just over two pounds a year.[22] The lands concerned are located in twenty different counties. Lincolnshire produces the largest number of cases (eight),[23] and Northumberland,[24] Kent[25] and Leicestershire[26] four cases each. Two counties produce three cases each. These are Nottinghamshire[27] and Shropshire.[28] There are just two cases

fols. 1r–2r and Harley 2183, fols. 109r–v; *Nicholas Baret of Spalding v Richard son of William of Spalding and his wife Agnes*: CP 40/110, m. 122d (Michaelmas term 1295); *Richard de Louches of Wallingford v. Thomas Hycon*: CP 40/145, m. 168d (Michaelmas term 1303).

22 An account for the wardship of land valued at one hundred pounds in Stepney was demanded in *John le Baud v. Roger of Bedfont*: CP 40/51, m. 75; of lands and rents worth only just over two pounds in *Nicholas Baret of Spalding v. Richard son of William of Spalding and his wife Agnes*: CP 40/110, m. 122d.

23 *Geoffrey Mabelot v. William son of Agnes of Stowe*: JUST 1/492, m. 79 (1281–4 Lincolnshire eyre); *Roger of Norfolk v. Simon of Pinchbeck and his wife Alice*: CP 40/61, m. 61d (Hilary term 1286); *Roger of Alford v. Thomas son of John of Rigsby and others*: CP 40/75, m. 109 (Michaelmas term 1288); *William of Blackwell v. Martin son of Simon of Holbeach and his wife Maud*: CP 40/83, m. 65d (Trinity term 1290); *Robert of Gipthorpe and wife Alice v. John of Birthorpe*: CP 40/103, m. 46d (Hilary term 1294); *Nicholas Baret of Spalding v. Richard son of William of Spalding and his wife Agnes*: CP 40/110, mm. 122d and 185 (Michaelmas term 1295); *Gilbert son of Benedict of Hagham v. Richard Rudde of Barton*: CP 40/144, m. 184d (Michaelmas term 1302) and reported in *YB 30 & 31 EI*, pp. 31–5 (with related reports in LI MS. Miscellaneous 738, fols. 31v and 29r and CUL MS. Ee.6.18, fol. 70r) and in BL MS. Stowe 386, fol. 157r, and there is a related note in BL MS. Additional 37657, fol. 177r and *YB 32 & 33 EI*, p. 187; *John Orger of Frieston v. William son of Thomas of Wigtoft*: CP 40/152, m. 75d (Trinity term 1304).

24 *Robert de Lisle of Chipchase v. Robert de Lisle of Woodburn*: *EELR*, II, 201–4 (Trinity term 1285); *Guy de Arreynes v. Robert de Stuteville and his wife Eleanor*: JUST 1/650, m. 14 (1292 Northumberland eyre); *Adam of Otterington and his wife Isabel v. Adam of Cambo and his wife Margery*: JUST 1/650, m. 23 (same); *Robert of Wooton v. Walter of Edlingham*: JUST 1/650, m. 16d (same).

25 *Hugh son of Adam of Gillingham and his brother Geoffrey v. Hugh of Blyth of Rochester*: CP 40/66, m. 1d (Hilary term 1287); *Thomas son of Simon of Brunnesford v. John Holte*: JUST 1/365, m. 25d (1293 Kent eyre) and reported in BL MS. Harley 2183, fols 109v–110r; *John of Walton v. Walter of Ripley*: CP 40/112, m. 126 (Easter term 1296); *John of Ditton and his wife Elizabeth v. Robert of Hormington*: CP 40/155, m. 96 (Easter term 1305) and reported in *YB 32 & 33 EI*, pp. 411–3 (and BL MS. Additional 31826, fols. 338v–339r) and BL MS. Hargrave 375, fol. 32r.

26 *Robert son of Richard of Flixthorpe v. Aubrey of Whittlebury and his wife Margery*: JUST 1/460, m. 10 (1284 Leicestershire eyre); *Thomas Costeyn of Leicester v. Robert son of William of Quenby*: CP 40/87, m. 46d (Hilary term 1291); *John son of William of Checkendon v. Henry of Nottingham*: CP 40/95, m. 134: (Trinity term 1292) [but writ quashed when it was found that the lands concerned were in Oxfordshire]; *Hugh of Houghton v. Walter Daude of Little Stratton and his wife Juliana*: CP 40/146, m. 115d (Hilary term 1303) of which there are reports on BL MS. Additional 31826, fol. 151v and LI MS. Miscellaneous 738, fol. 18r.

27 All three were brought by the same plaintiff. *Richard son of Richard Bugge of Willoughby v. Richard de Grey*: CP 40/80, m. 72 (Michaelmas term 1289); *Richard son of Richard Bugge v. Robert of Strelley and his wife Elizabeth*: CP 40/104, m. 47d (Easter term 1294); *Richard son of Richard Bugge v. John de Heriz*: CP 40/123, m. 84 (Easter term 1298) and reported in BL MS. Additional 31826, fols. 242r–v.

28 *William of Orleton v. Roger de Attleborough*: CP 40/92, m. 148d (Hilary term 1292); *John of Cleeton v. Richard Carbonel of Aliford*: JUST 1/739, m. 17 (1292 Shropshire eyre); *Roger*

each from six counties. These are Middlesex,[29] Norfolk,[30] Oxfordshire,[31] Cumberland,[32] Cambridgeshire[33] and Cornwall.[34] Nine counties produce only a single case each. They are Sussex,[35] Warwickshire,[36] Northamptonshire,[37] Buckinghamshire,[38] Dorset,[39] Devon,[40] Suffolk,[41] Berkshire[42] and Yorkshire.[43] The counts, as enrolled, generally do not say of whom the land was held or by what specific service, although this is mentioned in a few exceptional examples.[44] Almost all the counts do contain information on two other matters of some importance: when the period of wardship for which an account was being sought commenced, and how long it lasted. From these two facts it is generally possible to deduce a third, that is, how long a time had elapsed between the ending of the wardship and the bringing of the action. In a majority of cases, the period for which an account was claimed commenced after the enactment of the Statute of Marlborough. There is, however, a significant minority in which that period began at a date between the first enactment of the legislation in 1259 and the date of the Statute of Marlborough,[45] and even one case where the period for which an account was sought began prior

son of William Ofthehalle v. Peter Walker of Newport: CP 40/160, mm. 66–66d (Trinity term 1306).

29 *John fitzRoger v. Hugh of Bedford and his wife Joan*: CP 40/45, m. 22 (Easter term 1282); *John le Baud v. Roger of Bedfont*: CP 40/51, m. 75 (Michaelmas term 1283).

30 *Richer son of Nicholas of Docking v. Joan widow of Nicholas of Docking*: CP 40/46, m. 46d (Trinity term 1282); *John son of Geoffrey de Bek v. Richard of Roding and his wife Alphesia* JUST 1/578, m. 52d (1286 Norfolk eyre).

31 *Ranulph de Arderne v. Thomas of Lewknor and his wife Lucy*: CP 40/107, m. 73 (Hilary term 1295); *William Poor v. John de la Chaumbre and his wife Lora*: CP 40/154, m. 225d (Hilary term 1305).

32 *Ranulph son of Robert de Marti v. William de Ponsonby*: CP 40/126, m. 171 (Hilary term 1299); *Thomas de Huthwaite v. prior of St Mary Carlisle*: CP 40/164, m. 291d (Trinity term 1307).

33 *John son of John Elys of Teversham v. Robert Elys and his wife Margaret*: JUST 1/96, m. 14 (1299 Cambridgeshire eyre); *John le Beyre of Ellington v. Richard Clerk of Ellington and his wife Agnes*: JUST 1/96, m. 15d (same).

34 *John of Nanskeval v. Odo de la Roche*: JUST 1/118, m. 3d (1302 Cornwall eyre); *Thomas le Ercedekne v. Serlo de Nansladron and his wife Amice*: CP 40/158, m. 185 (Hilary term 1306).

35 Above, pp. 348–9.

36 *John de Stretlinges and his wife Maud v. Godfrey bishop of Worcester*: CP 40/102, m. 97 (Michaelmas term 1293).

37 *John son of Thomas of Great Doddington v. Simon son of Ralph of Hannington*: CP 40/105, m. 113d (Trinity term 1294).

38 *Thomas le Rutur v. William of Eaton clerk*: CP 40/108, m. 46d (Easter term 1295).

39 *Roger de la Dene v. Walter of Wimborne*: CP 40/129, m. 70d (Trinity term 1299).

40 *Simon fitzGuy v. John fitzGuy*: JUST 1/710, m. 15 (1285 Oxfordshire eyre).

41 *Alexander of Walsham v. prior of Brisett*: CP 40/145, m. 74 (Michaelmas term 1303).

42 *Richard de Louches of Wallingford v. Thomas Hycon*: CP 40/145, m. 168d (Michaelmas term 1303).

43 *John Wyles of Pontefract v. Thomas Chamberlain of Pontefract*: CP 40/163, m. 120 (Easter term 1307).

44 For exceptions see *EELR*, II, 201–4 (Trinity term 1285); CP 40/144, m. 184d (Michaelmas term 1302).

45 For examples (with the date of the beginning of the period in respect of which account was claimed in brackets) see *Orleton v. Attleborough* (above, n. 28) [Easter 1261]; *Doddington v. Hannington* (above, n. 37) [Trinity 1262 (in part)]; *Cleeton v. Carbonel of Aliford* (above, n. 28) [Assumption

to 1259.[46] The shortest period for which an account was sought was two years. This was true of three cases.[47] The longest period, found in four cases, was nineteen years.[48] There are also a further five cases where the period of the wardship for which an account was claimed was in excess of the fourteen years which ought to have been the maximum period for a socage wardship.[49] The average length of the wardships for which an account was sought was just under eleven years. The period of time which elapsed between the ending of the period of wardship for which account was sought and the hearing of the action was less than a year in only two actions, both brought in the eyre.[50] It was also less than two years in a further three actions, two of them brought in the Common Bench.[51] At the opposite extreme are the twenty and twenty-six years which had elapsed before cases were brought in the 1293 Northumberland and 1292 Shropshire eyres.[52] The overall average period of delay in bringing such cases was ten years.

A defendant might manage to have the case dismissed for technical defects in the plaintiff's writ. In 1285 a defendant had a case brought in the Oxfordshire eyre and initiated by a writ of summons addressed to the sheriff of Oxfordshire dismissed on the grounds that the lands for which the account was being sought were all in the county of Devon and the writ was therefore not appropriate.[53] In the Common Bench in 1292 a ward had his guardian summoned to account by a writ addressed to the sheriff of Leicestershire. The parties happily took issue on whether or not the land for which the account was being sought was held in socage or by knight service. However, before a writ could issue to summon the jury someone seems to have noticed that the land concerned was not in Leicestershire. When the plaintiff's attorney confirmed under questioning

of the Virgin 1263]; *Blackwell v. Holbeach* (above, n. 23) [Michaelmas 1266]; *fitzRoger v. Bedford* (above, n. 29) [51 Henry III (1266–7)]; *Ellington v. Ellington* (above, n. 33) [51 Henry III (1266–7)]; *Docking v. Docking* (above, n. 30) [Michaelmas 1267]; *le Baud v. Bedfont* (above, n. 29) [Michaelmas 1267].

46 *De Lisle of Chipchase v. de Lisle of Woodburn* (above, n. 24) [Morrow of the Ascension 1257].

47 *Wooton v. Edlingham* (above, n. 24); *Louches (of Wallingford) v. Hycon* (above, n. 42); *Cleeton v. Carbonel (of Aliford)* (above, n. 28).

48 *FitzGuy v. fitzGuy* (above, n. 40) [but only for part]; *Orleton v. Attleborough* (above, n. 28); *Ellington v. Ellington* (above, n. 33); *Poor v. de la Chaumbre* (above, n. 31). For an explanation of this see below, pp. 359–60.

49 Fifteen years: *Huthwaite v. prior of Carlisle* (above, n. 32); sixteen years: *Blackwell v. Holbeach* (above, n. 23); seventeen years: *de Lisle of Chipchase v. de Lisle of Woodburn* (above, n. 24), *le Rutur v. Eaton* (above, n. 38) and *Pontefract v. Pontefract* (above, n. 43).

50 *Elys v. Elys* (above, n. 33); *Nanskeval v. de la Roche* (above, n. 34).

51 *Brunnesford v. Holte* (above, n. 25); *Poor v. de la Chaumbre* (above, n. 31); *Ditton v. Hormington* (above, n. 25).

52 *Wooton v. Edlingham* (above, n. 24); *Cleeton v. Carbonel (of Aliford)* (above, n. 28).

53 *FitzGuy v. fitzGuy* (above, n. 40).

that the land concerned was in Oxfordshire, the court decided that it could not properly proceed to jury trial on the issue since this required an Oxfordshire jury for which the original writ was not a proper warrant and the plaintiff was given permission to withdraw from his action.[54] In a 1293 case the defendant attempted to have the plaintiff's writ quashed for a different kind of geographical error. The plaintiff's original writ in this action had to specify the village or villages where he claimed the defendant had held the wardship. The writ in this action had specified a number of villages including one named merely as 'Pillardington'. The defendant said there was no such village without a suffix in the county, only an Over and Nether Pillardington, and asked for judgment of the defective writ. After some argument the court told the defendant to answer over since the same precision was not required in this action as would have been required in a land plea.[55]

A different kind of defect in the original writ was the subject of an exception in an action pleaded in Easter term 1296. Here the defendant being sued was a husband and he had only held a socage wardship in right of his wife. The case was dismissed because his wife had not been joined with him in the writ.[56] In a 1292 case a widower had been sued under similar circumstances but after the death of his wife. He asked for judgment whether he was obliged to render account now she was dead, particularly as the plaintiff had failed to bring suit during the wife's lifetime and twelve years had elapsed since the ending of the wardship. Judgment was reserved.[57] It is only from the reports of a 1302 case that we know that under apparently identical circumstances a defendant attempted a rather different argument. He said that his wife's executors ought to have been joined with him as co-defendants. Chief Justice Hengham overruled the objection on the grounds that the husband alone had enjoyed the profits of the wardship during his wife's lifetime. It was he alone therefore who was now accountable for it.[58] The plea roll enrolment is equally silent about a plea made in a Common Bench socage wardship account case of 1303 which is revealed only by the two reports of the same case. These show counsel for the defendant objecting that the tenements for which the account was being claimed were part of the ancient demesne and so the Common Bench was not entitled to jurisdiction over the case.[59] No definitive ruling was made by the court but both Chief Justice Hengham and Justice Bereford seem to have been inclined to think that the matter was one properly for the court, as were actions of debt or trespass arising

[54] *Checkendon v. Nottingham* (above, n. 26). [55] *Stretlinges v. bishop of Worcester* (above, n. 21).
[56] *Walton v. Ripley* (above, n. 25). [57] *Orleton v. Attleborough* (above, n. 28).
[58] *Hagham v. Barton* (above, n. 23). [59] *Houghton v. Daude (of Little Stratton)* (above, n. 26).

there, even if land actions and actions of covenant, wardship or replevin were not.[60]

Even if there were no technical defects in the writ, defendants still had various possible answers to the plaintiff's claim. The defendant might concede that he had been the socage guardian of lands belonging to the plaintiff and that he did owe an account in respect of the time he had held the wardship but claim that he had only held the land concerned for a shorter period of time than alleged by the plaintiff,[61] or had only held lands of lesser extent,[62] or rely on a combination of these two assertions.[63] If not accepted by the plaintiff, the truth of these claims would be tested by jury trial. The reports of one of these cases show why a plaintiff might be wise in practice to compromise with the defendant by accepting an account for a shorter period and for less extensive lands. The general rule was that no account had to be rendered, even in respect of the period admitted and the lands agreed to have been held, until the jury had given its verdict.[64] If the defendant died while jury trial was pending, the plaintiff would never obtain his account and so would recover none of the balance owed him on that account.[65] Alternatively, the defendant might concede that he owed an account for a period of wardship but assert that the plaintiff had subsequently released or quitclaimed all right to demand it. In all three cases where such releases are known to have been pleaded, the plaintiffs denied the validity of the releases. In one case the plaintiff simply denied that the deed proffered was his deed or that he had made any release.[66] In the other two, the plaintiffs asserted that

[60] Note also that in a 1287 case the Common Bench allowed a claim by the bailiffs of Rochester for the jurisdiction of their court of a case relating to tenements in Rochester, *Hugh son of Adam of Gillingham and his brother Geoffrey v. Hugh of Blyth of Rochester* (CP 40/66, m. 1d), but that a report of a case in the 1293 Kent eyre shows the justices in eyre not allowing a claim by the bailiff of Battle abbey for the abbot's court of Wye: *Brunnesford v. Holte* (above, n. 25).

[61] In *Docking v. Docking* (above, n. 30) the defendant admitted nine years and agreed to account for that but a jury was to determine whether an account was owed in respect of a further three years claimed; in *Pontefract v. Pontefract* (above, n. 43) a jury was to determine whether the defendant was to answer for eleven or seventeen years.

[62] In *Norfolk v. Pinchbeck* (above, n. 23) the defendants asserted that no account was owed for half the land as it was held in dower; in *le Rutur v. Eaton* (above, n. 38) just that less land had been held in wardship. For another action where it was asserted that part of the land had been held in dower, not in wardship, see *Frieston v. Wigtoft* (above, n. 23).

[63] *Ellington v. Ellington* (above, n. 33); *Hagham v. Rudde (of Barton)* (above, n. 23); *Houghton v. Daude (of Little Stratton)* (above, n. 26)

[64] But for an early case in which accounting proceeded in respect of the period agreed while jury trial was pending on the disputed period see above, n. 61.

[65] This point is made in the reports of *Hagham v. Rudde (of Barton)* (above, n. 23). This suggests that despite the drafting of a writ for use against the executors of a socage guardian by 1300 (above, p. 350) it was not generally accepted that any action lay against them.

[66] *Blackwell v. Holbeach* (above, n. 23)

although the deed was genuine it was not binding on them because it had been made while they were under age.[67]

The defendant might also, in effect, concede both that the land was held in socage and that the plaintiff was entitled to an account for the period of his minority, but then assert that he was not the appropriate person to render such an account. In a case in the 1292 Shropshire eyre, the defendant claimed to have been only the bailiff of the guardian in socage, whom he named and identified as the uncle of the plaintiff's mother. The plaintiff, however, asserted that the defendant had held the wardship in his own right. A jury confirmed that he had indeed done so and so was liable to render account.[68] Rather more commonly, the defendant asserted that he was only a lessee of the land, not its guardian, and therefore not liable to account for his period of tenure of the land. Sometimes this was all that was said, and it is necessary to supply the corollary, that it was against the lessor (and guardian) that the plaintiff ought to have brought his action,[69] but at least once this was specifically spelled out by the defendant.[70] Jury trial was then joined on these assertions, the plaintiff in two out of the three instances being careful to have placed on the record his assertion that the defendant had enjoyed the wardship not by virtue of a lease but through marriage to the plaintiff's mother, the rightful socage guardian of the land.[71] In a 1305 case the plaintiff did not deny that the defendant had been the lessee of his mother, the rightful guardian, nor that he had paid her a rent equivalent to the value of the land.[72] He still tried, however, to maintain his action on the grounds that it was the defendant only who had held the land and knew best the actual value of the land he had held. The court, however, seems to have been persuaded by the defendant's arguments against maintaining the writ. He argued that the proper remedy lay against the rightful guardian who had already received the value of the land, and that if this action was allowed the plaintiff would then still also be able to bring a second action against his mother for a second accounting. Eventually, the plaintiff was persuaded to seek permission to withdraw from prosecuting his action. The point had earlier been argued in an action in the 1293 Kent eyre, though a report of this case indicates that there was some confusion on the part of the defendant as to whether he was claiming to have been merely the bailiff of the guardian of right or her lessee, rendering to the full the value of the

67 *Frieston v. Wigtoft* (above, n. 23); *le Ercedekne v. Nansladron* (above, n. 34).

68 *Cleeton v. Carbonel (of Aliford)* (above, n. 28).

69 For examples see *fitzRoger v. Bedford* (above, n. 29); *le Baud v. Bedfont* (above, n. 29).

70 See *Doddington v. Hannington* (above, n. 37).

71 In *le Baud v. Bedfont* (above, n. 29); *Doddington v. Hannington* (above, n. 37).

72 In *Ditton v. Hormington* (above, n. 25). The arguments are only recorded in the reports.

land.[73] Again, the plaintiff argued strongly that he should be allowed a remedy against the individual who had been in control of his land during his minority but the court was unsympathetic and the plaintiff was later non-suited. In a third sub-variety of response of this general type, the defendant would agree that the land had been held in wardship but deny that it was he who had held it or that he was answerable for that period. Thus, in a case of 1288, the defendant admitted that the wardship had come into his father's possession, but asserted that his father had then given it to a third party (Ivo the bailiff) to hold until he came of age. The jury, however, found that the defendant's father had only given it to Ivo to hold at will and the defendant had resumed it at his father's death and had then regranted it to Ivo on the same terms.[74] In a case in the 1293 Northumberland eyre the defendant agreed that the plaintiff had held of his father but denied that he had ever had wardship of the land. A jury, however, then found that he had.[75] In a complicated case of 1294 the defendants seem to be saying that a third party (Geoffrey of Stapleford) had held the wardship by his own intrusion until the plaintiff came of age but the plaintiff alleged that Geoffrey held by virtue of their lease and had paid the defendants forty shillings a year for it and so they were answerable for the issues of the land.[76]

In several other cases, the defendant certainly agreed that he had held lands belonging to the plaintiff in wardship but asserted that those lands had been held by a form of tenure which entitled him to a beneficial wardship for which no account was owed to the plaintiff. In all but two of these cases, the claim was that the lands were held by knight service.[77] In the three cases of this kind for which there survive reports (of 1285, 1293 and 1298) we can see that at an early stage each of the defendants denied that this action could be brought against anyone other than the socage guardian and argued that, since they did not claim to have held the land as such, the action ought to fail.[78] In each of the reported cases much the same arguments were made on both sides. The primary argument was that the Statute itself mentioned only the *prochein amy*,

73 In *Brunnesford v. Holte* (above, n. 25).

74 In *Alford v. Rigsby and others* (above, n. 23).

75 *Wooton v. Edlingham* (above, n. 24). For other cases where the defendant seems to be denying ever having held the wardship see *Spalding v. Spalding* (above, n. 23) and *Dene v. Wimborne* (above, n. 39).

76 *Bugge v. Strelley* (above, n. 27).

77 The two exceptions are *Louches (of Wallingford) v. Hycon* (above, n. 42), where the claim was that the land was held by serjeanty of the honour of Wallingford, and *Huthwaite v. prior of Carlisle* (above, n. 32), where the claim was that the land was held by cornage tenure and that under the custom of the cornage tenure of Cumberland the lord was entitled to the beneficial wardship of such land.

78 The reported cases are *de Lisle of Chipchase v. de Lisle of Woodburn* (above, n. 24), *Stretlinges v. bishop of Worcester* (above, n. 21) and *Bugge v. Heriz* (above, n. 27).

the next of kin unable to inherit the land, as liable to account.[79] The standard response to this was that if the next of kin was answerable, so *a fortiori* was a stranger. The 1293 case spelled out the classic argument that the wrongdoing of the defendant should not put him in a more advantageous position than that enjoyed by a rightful guardian who had done no wrong. The second string to the argument was that, even if the lord had usurped the wardship, it was unnecessary to allow the ward to use this action, since the ward already had a remedy or remedies against the lord for doing so: the assize of mort d'ancestor (according to reports of all three cases) and the assize of novel disseisin (according to reports of the 1293 and 1298 cases only). The response to this argument, found only in reports of the 1285 and 1293 cases, was that these remedies were only available while the ward was out of possession of his inheritance and that it was wrong to deprive him of a remedy merely because the inheritance was now in his possession. The 1293 report added that this surrender had taken place while he was still under age and it was wrong that he should be prejudiced by his acceptance of the inheritance while still a minor. It was only after this preliminary argument, and the court's clear decision that the action did lie against a usurping lord, that the parties moved on to what is normally recorded in such cases as the one issue raised in pleading. This is whether the plaintiff held by socage or by knight service or another service which entitled the lord to wardship. When the defendant was the lord of whom the plaintiff held the lands in question, the matter was comparatively simple. The issue could then simply go to a jury for resolution. If the defendant was only a grantee of the wardship, he would normally have to seek aid from the lord concerned and only answer alone if the lord failed to appear to defend his entitlement.[80] Curiously, however, aid was not allowed to a defendant who claimed to have been only the bailiff of the grantee of wardship in a case of 1306.[81]

One final possibility also encountered in the cases of this period was for the defendant to concede that he had held the land or, more commonly, part of the land concerned, during the plaintiff's minority, but claim that he had held it not in wardship but by some other title and in his own

[79] Some of the reports of *Stretlinges v. bishop of Worcester* have a subsidiary argument here: that the guardian by right, the plaintiff's mother, is still alive and can be sued; to which counsel for the plaintiff argued that it would be wrong to charge her with the account when she had never held the wardship.

[80] For examples see *de Lisle of Chipchase v. de Lisle of Woodburn* (above, n. 24) [later complicated by the intervention of counsel acting for the king, as the king also had an interest]; *Otterington v. Cambo* (above, n. 24). But note that aid was not allowed in *Marti v. Ponsonby* (above, n. 32), though the sheriff was told to warn the lord to be present for the jury verdict.

[81] *Ofthehalle v. Walker (of Newport)* (above, n. 28)..

right: as tenant for life;[82] as tenant in frankmarriage;[83] as sole survivor of two joint purchasers (plus second husband);[84] or as doweress.[85]

It is one of the apparently puzzling features of this action that, although the Statute specifically mentions that the guardian was not to give or sell the marriage of the heir other than to the heir's profit, there is not a single action in which the plaintiff's count, as enrolled, mentions the value of a marriage arranged or sold as an element for which an account was being sought. An explanation is provided by a report of a case heard in the 1293 Kent eyre.[86] The report indicates that the initial count in this action did indeed specifically mention the sale of the plaintiff's marriage for twenty pounds as one of the things for which an account was being sought. The objection was immediately taken, however, that the writ spoke only of an account for 'the issues arising out of the lands and tenements' and that the marriage was not such an issue. This was partly because it was a separate profit in itself, partly because its value was already known and so no account as such was required. The count was therefore at variance with the writ. The chief justice of the eyre (John of Berwick) also, however, suggested the opposite of this. He said that the marriage was part of the issues of the land and that by claiming an account of the issues and of the marriage, the plaintiff was claiming the same thing twice over. Eventually the chief justice ordered counsel for the plaintiff to make a second, amended count and it was the count in this form that was enrolled. This case suggests that the omission of any mention of marriage in counts does not mean that plaintiffs did not receive an account of them and their value. It was merely that this was normally part of the accounting process, not something mentioned in the pleading as enrolled in court. There is also a second point of interest about the report of this case. When Berwick instructed the plaintiff's counsel to recount he did so on the basis that counsel could not be disavowed in respect of the count he had already made (or his client penalised for it) because his client was still under age. This suggests that Berwick thought it perfectly proper for a socage heir to bring his action of wardship once he had reached the age when he took possession of his lands (fifteen) even if the heir was still under the common law age of majority of twenty-one.[87]

[82] *Nanskeval v. de la Roche* (above, n. 34).

[83] *Costeyn (of Leicester) v. Quenby* (above, n. 26).

[84] *Elys v. Elys* (above, n. 33) [part only].

[85] *Elys v. Elys* (above, n. 33) [part only]; *Ellington v. Ellington* (above, n. 33) [part only].

[86] The report of *Brunnesford v. Holte* (above, n. 25).

[87] Different considerations would probably have applied in respect of the rendering of account by a guardian out of court: see the theoretical discussion on this point in *YB 20 & 21 EI*, pp. 319–21.

Chapter 14

CONTROLLING THE USE OF DISTRAINT

Several chapters of the Statute of Marlborough were concerned with controlling the use of distraint. We have already looked in detail at the enforcement of chapter 9, whose main concern was with the use of distraint to enforce the performance of suit of court, and which attempted to control it by enacting special rules about when lords were entitled to use distraint for this purpose and by giving tenants a special statutory action to enforce those rules.[1] We have also looked at how in the early fourteenth century those same special rules from chapter 9 came to be applicable also in the common law action of replevin when the tenant was contesting his lord's use of distraint, though only if the tenant wanted to invoke them, and at how the statutory provisions included in the same chapter, restricting lords in the services they could claim from tenants whose charter specified the performance of a fixed service 'for all service', also came around the same time to be enforced through the same action and again in connexion with the lord's use of distraint to enforce the performance of additional services.[2] This chapter will look at the enforcement of the various other chapters of the same Statute which were also concerned with the use and possible abuse of the right of distraint.[3] Chapter 15 had formed part of the original Provisions of Westminster of 1259 and was re-enacted in identical form in 1267; chapters 1–4 were part of the new section added to the Provisions when they were re-enacted as the Statute of Marlborough in 1267.

THE ENFORCEMENT OF CHAPTERS 1–4

As already noted, the first four chapters of the Statute of Marlborough were, in effect, an expanded version of the opening clause of the Dictum of Kenilworth. They were aimed at restating some of the basic rules of the English thirteenth-century legal system in relation to the exercise of

[1] Above, chapter 8. [2] Above, pp. 252–62. [3] But for chapter 21 see below, pp. 381–2.

royal and private jurisdiction and at reaffirming the need for claimants to follow due process when seeking amends for alleged wrongs.

The printed Register of Writs contains a special writ of trespass requiring the defendant to answer why

> whereas the said A. holds and claims to hold no tenement of him and does not belong to his fee, nor does he owe him any service, nor is the same B. our bailiff, as it is said, by which he can or ought make any distraints against the same A. according to the law etc., the said B. has taken animals belonging to the said A. outside his fee at N. and impounded them and still keeps them impounded against the law and custom of our realm of England and against the peace etc. And those animals etc.[4]

The writ looks as though it may have been drafted to give effect to that part of chapter 2 of the Statute of Marlborough which had restated the traditional restrictions on the use of distraint outside the fee or area of the distrainor's jurisdiction. It also occurs in a section of the printed register containing trespassory writs based on Edwardian statutes. What appears to clinch the connexion is a marginal note in the register that specifically refers to chapter 2 of the Statute of Marlborough as though it is the authority for the issuing of the writ. There is, however, one puzzling aspect of it. Other writs in this section contain a preliminary recital of the specific legislation on which they are based. This writ does not. The apparent connexion looks much weaker once we get back to evidence closer in date to 1267. A trespassory writ of very similar form also appears in the early fourteenth-century register of writs printed by de Haas and Hall, and here there is no rubric connecting it with the Statute of Marlborough.[5] The relevant section of the register, moreover, contains non-statutory as well as statutory writs. Further investigation confirms what this suggests: that the writ has little or no connexion with the Statute, despite the overlap in its coverage. The evidence suggests that the writ had evolved gradually through a process of evolution and experimentation with a variety of forms from a trespassory writ first issued well before the Statute of Marlborough.

The starting-point for this process seems to have been a writ enrolled on the Close Rolls in 1255. This ordered the bishop of London to be summoned at the suit of the prior of St Swithin's Winchester to show

[4] *Reg. Omn. Brev.*, fol. 97b: 'ostensurus quare cum prefatus A. nullum tenementum de eo teneat seu tenere clamat neque de feodo suo sit neque servicium aliquod ei debeat nec idem B. ballivus noster sit, ut dicitur, per quod districciones aliquas super ipsum A. facere possit vel debeat secundum legem etc. predictus B. extra feodum suum apud N. averia predicti A. cepit et imparcavit et ea adhuc imparcata detinet contra legem et consuetudinem regni nostri Anglie et contra pacem etc. Et averia illa etc. Teste etc. *vel sic* averia illa diu imparcata detinuit *et tunc non dicatur* et averia etc.'

[5] *Early Registers*, p. 181 (R 322).

'why he had distrained the same prior and his men within the fee of the prior of Cliffe, which he neither holds nor claims to hold of the same bishop, nor does he owe any suit to his court, to answer in the court of the said bishop for certain trespasses alleged against him'.[6] The enrolment specifically notes that the writ form had been authorised by Henry de la Mare, Roger of Thirkleby, Henry of Bracton (all senior royal justices) and others of the royal council, suggesting that the writ was not only being issued for this specific case, but also being authorised for more general use thereafter. It is perhaps this that also explains why the writ was being enrolled. The writ bears no more than a generic resemblance to the eventual standard form. It does, however, share with it the concern to explain in advance in the writ itself why the distraint must have been unjustified. Here the only possibilities mentioned and excluded are tenure of the defendant's fee and obligation to perform suit to his court, and the clause is placed at a different point in the writ. It also differs from the later writ in specifying in a way that the later writ does not the purpose of the distraint. This was to require the prior and his men to answer in the bishop's court. The later writ leaves the purpose of the distraint unclear. A second writ of a generically similar form was used in a Common Bench case enrolled in Easter term 1260. Here the defendant was attached to answer

> why he is distraining the said prior to perform customs and services which he does not owe him and is not accustomed to perform and compels him and his men to pay heavy ransoms, although the same prior neither holds nor claims to hold anything of him, and the same R. has no jurisdiction or lordship over him or his men which would entitle or allow him to make such distraints, as he says.[7]

By 1262 there had been what was to become a permanent change in the form of the writ, placing the allegation that the defendant lacked the necessary power or jurisdiction to distrain the plaintiff as a first element in the writ (and introducing it with a *quare cum*). The first writ of this form noted was used in a Common Bench case enrolled in Easter term 1262. It also added to the claim of a wrongful distraint a second allegation of the distresses having been wrongfully taken out of the county. The defendant was attached to answer

[6] '. . . quare in feodo ipsius prioris de Clyve quod nec de episcopo tenet nec tenere clamat, nec ad curiam ejus sectam aliquam debet, distringit ipsum priorem et homines suos ad respondendum in curia predicti episcopi de quibusdam transgressionibus eis impositis . . .': *CR 1254–6*, pp. 230–1.

[7] '. . . quare distringit ipsum priorem ad faciendum consuetudines et servicia que ei facere non debet nec solet, et ipsum et homines suos ad graves redempciones compellit, desicut idem prior nichil de eo teneat nec tenere clamat nec idem Rogerus jurisdiccionem vel dominium in ipsum vel homines suos habet quare hujusmodi districciones facere debet nec possit ut dicit . . .': *Prior of Thurgarton v. Roger son of Maud Pecche*: KB 26/165, m. 11d.

why, whereas the same R. holds and claims to hold nothing of the said H. the said H. and the others came to the land of the same R. in the county of Westmorland and took the animals of the same R. and his men found there and drove them out of that county into the county of Yorkshire against the law and custom of the realm and detain them there against the peace.[8]

As yet, it will be noted, the *quare cum* clause was still relatively short and simple, mentioning only non-tenure of the defendant and nothing more elaborate. A similarly limited *quare cum* clause is also to be found in a second writ of the same type summarised in a Common Bench enrolment of Michaelmas 1266.[9] But something close to the standard form had emerged by 1272. This was used in a case brought by the royal justice William Weyland. His opponents were attached to answer as to why

whereas the said William holds no tenement of them or their fee and they are not [the king's bailiffs] by which they could make distraints against William according to the law and custom of the realm the said Stephen and the others had taken animals belonging to William within his manor of Oxburgh with force and arms and abducted them and beaten and wounded the men of the same William and committed other enormities against him to William's damage of one hundred pounds and against the peace . . .[10]

There are a series of cases brought by such writs during the reign of Edward I, with considerable variation in detail in the form of the *quare cum* initial clause as well as any additional trespasses mentioned in addition to the basic distraint, but they are all manifestly elaborations, and relatively minor variations, on the basic form as it had developed down to 1272. Thus, although the developed form of this type of trespass writ only came into existence after 1272, the Statute of Marlborough seems to have played little or no part in its evolution. This seems simply to have been the result of a long process of refining and extending a writ form first drafted in 1255.

[8] '. . . quare cum idem Rogerus nichil teneat nec tenere clamat de predicto Henrico, dicti Henricus et alii venerunt ad terram ipsius Rogeri in comitatu Westmerl' et averia [ipsius Rogeri] et hominum suorum ibidem inventa ceperunt et ea extra comitatum illum in comitatum Ebor' fugaverunt contra legem et consuetudinem regni etc. et ea ibidem detinuerunt contra pacem': *Roger de Lascelles v. Henry fitzRannulph et al.*: KB 26/166, m. 15.

[9] *James de Bine and his mother Emma v. John de Polingfaud*: KB 26/176, m. 14d.

[10] '. . . quare . . . cum predictus Willelmus nullum tenementum de eis teneat nec de feodo [eorum], nec ipsi ballivi nostri sint, per quod districciones super ipsum Willelmum secundum legem et consuetudinem regni etc. facere potuerunt, prefati Stephanus et alii averia ipsius Willelmi infra manerium suum de Oxebrigge vi et armis ceperunt et abduxerunt et homines ejusdem Willelmi verberaverunt et vulneraverunt et alia enormia ei intulerunt ad dampnum ipsius Willelmi centum librarum et contra pacem . . .': *William Weyland v. Stephen brother of John le Bracur and others*: JUST 1/238, m. 33d.

A second form of trespassory writ allowed plaintiffs to sue defendants who had driven or taken property they had taken in distraint out of the county where they had taken it into another county. In the Luffield register of writs from the final years of Henry III's reign there is a writ form for attaching the defendant to show 'why he took the animals of such a one in such a county and drove them from that county into such a county against the custom of our realm and against our peace'.[11] Again, the writ says nothing about any statutory basis for the action. Here, too, the writ clearly owed nothing to the Statute, despite the statutory restatement of the rules against driving distresses out of the county where they had been made (in chapter 4 of the Statute of Marlborough), since the writ did not cite the Statute and can be shown to have existed since the early years of the thirteenth century.[12]

There is slightly more evidence to connect these chapters of the Statute of Marlborough with at least one of the new articles of the eyre that appeared in 1278. These asked presentment juries in each hundred in the eyre for information about infractions of certain of the rules about distraint. The rule against excessive distraints contained in chapter 4 of the Statute of Marlborough was re-enacted as part of the *Districciones Scaccarii* in 1275,[13] but when the new article asked for information about excessive distraints, it specifically asked about those made prior to the parliament in 1275 when *Districciones Scaccarii* was enacted as well as after it. It seems likely that this is an indirect reference to the earlier legislation rather than to the existence of a common law rule on the subject.[14] A number of presentments made in response to this article have been noted on the eyre rolls of the 1280s and 1290s.[15] A second new article of the eyre drafted in 1278 asked about 'those who take the animals of others or have them taken in one county and drive them out of that county . . .'[16] There are several presentments made under this article in the eyres of the late 1270s, 1280s and 1290s.[17] There is, however, nothing to connect this article specifically with the Statute of Marlborough, since the rule was of

[11] *Early Registers*, p. 61 (CC 93). [12] Above, p. 194 and note 39.

[13] *SR*, I, 197b. On the date see Plucknett, *Legislation*, p. 60 and note 2.

[14] 'Et similiter de superfluis districcionibus factis tam post parliamentum quam ante . . .': *SR*, I, 238.

[15] For examples see JUST 1/784, m. 31d (1280 Hampshire eyre); JUST 1/924, m. 4 (1288 Sussex eyre); JUST 1/374, m. 10 (1293 Kent eyre); JUST 1/1098, m. 21d (1293–4 Yorkshire eyre).

[16] 'Item de hiis que ceperunt averia aliorum vel capi fecerint in uno comitatu et ea fugaverunt extra comitatum illum . . .': *SR*, I, 237a.

[17] For examples see JUST 1/323, m. 45 (1278 Hertfordshire eyre); JUST 1/371, m. 24d (1279 Kent eyre); JUST 1/784, m. 16d (1280 Hampshire eyre); JUST 1/705, m. 5d (1285 Oxfordshire eyre); JUST 1/827, m. 38 (1286 Suffolk eyre); JUST 1/924, mm. 57d, 72d (1288 Sussex eyre); JUST 1/302, m. 59d (1292 Herefordshire eyre); JUST 1/739, m. 76d (1292 Shropshire eyre); JUST 1/374, m. 12d (1293 Kent eyre).

common law origin and had also been reissued as part of the Statute of Westminster I (as part of ch. 16) in 1275.[18]

There is also evidence for the drafting of at least one special trespass writ after 1267 which does seem to refer directly to a different chapter in this preliminary section, chapter 1. In Easter term 1277 mesne process was enrolled in a case brought by Geoffrey le Bret of Warham against five named individuals as bailiffs of Joan de Lusignan's hundred of North Greenhoe in Norfolk for charging in that hundred court that the plaintiff had committed trespasses against Joan and one of her bailiffs but not allowing him any reply to the charge, for arresting him there without any prior conviction or judgment by the hundred court, and then for taking him and imprisoning him at Winchester for nine days, 'as though obtaining vengeance' against a wrongdoer to the king's contempt and 'in breach of the terms of the king's statutes'.[19] The reference seems to be to chapter 1 of the Statute of Marlborough because it takes up the language of that clause not just in its reference to 'exercising vengeance' but also at an earlier stage in referring to the defendants having acted 'by their own will without the judgment of the king's court' (*per propriam voluntatem absque consideracione curie regis*). No pleading has been found in this case, however, and no other actions of a similar kind have been traced.

Other special trespass writs cite chapter 3 of the Statute. In Trinity term 1269 the sheriff of Yorkshire was instructed to take action in response to a complaint made to the king by the prioress of Nun Appleton.[20] The prioress had recently recovered seisin of an annual rent of forty shillings from a mill in Newton on Wharfe against Lucy, the widow of William of Kyme, in King's Bench by default and the sheriff had been ordered to put the prioress in seisin. Lucy and various other malefactors had taken up position in the mill and prevented the sheriff giving seisin to the prioress. This action was said to be to the damage of the prioress and the contempt of the king and the king's writ to the sheriff went on specifically to cite chapter 3 as having thereby been breached.[21] The sheriff was ordered both to attach Lucy and to make enquiries as to the

[18] *SR*, I, 16.

[19] '. . . de placito quare . . . per propriam voluntatem absque consideracione curie regis imposuerunt predicto Galfrido in pleno hundredo predicto constituto quasdam transgressiones predicte Johanne domine sue et eciam prefato Hugoni intulisse [et] ipsum, nulla habita responsione set de aliquo convictum motu proprio et absque consideracione predicte curie, ibidem arestaverunt et postmodum apud Wynton' duci fecerunt et ipsum ibidem per novem dies imprisonaverunt quasi in transgressorem ulcionem exercendo in contemptum domini regis et contra formam statutorum domini regis et contra pacem': CP 40/19, m. 71d.

[20] KB 26/189, m. 19d.

[21] '. . . unde rex movebatur in mirum si ita esset cum per magnates et per fideles ipsius regis qui sunt de consilio suo nuper ad melioracionem ipsius regni et exhibicionem justicie pleniorem prout regalis dignitas expossit utilitas provisum fuisset et ordinatum quod si aliquis sustinere noluerit

identities of the others offering resistance and have them attached and to ensure the prioress was put in seisin. Only a procedural stage of this action has been found. A second such action is to be found in King's Bench in Trinity term 1274. The writ as enrolled started with a direct citation of chapter 3 of the Statute of Marlborough as authorising ransom as a punishment for those impeding the execution of the judgments of the king's courts. The writ went on to allege that even though the plaintiffs (Walter of Wilbraham and his wife, Elizabeth) had recovered seisin of property at Leeds in Kent in an assize of novel disseisin brought against Roger de Leybourne and Robert de Crevequer in the last Kent eyre (of 1271) and the sheriff had been ordered to put them in seisin, the defendants (William of Leybourne, the son of Roger, and others) had impeded the execution of the judgment and claimed damages for this.[22] The count shows that this had taken place in 1272. The defendants simply denied having impeded the execution and the case went to jury trial. But no later actions of this kind specifically citing the relevant chapter of the Statute of Marlborough have been noted and it clearly did not become a standard form.[23]

The legislation also gave rise to an article of the eyre included in the new articles of 1278 but first drafted as one of the articles of the Hundred Rolls enquiry of 1274. This specifically asked for information about

> lords or their stewards or bailiffs of all kinds or even officials of the lord king who do not allow the execution of the orders of the lord king to be made or also refuse to perform them, or in any way prevent them from being carried out, from the time of the constitutions made at Marlborough in the fifty-second year of the reign of the lord king Henry, the father of the present lord king.[24]

execusiones judiciorum curie ipsius regis fieri puniatur per redempcionem et hoc secundum quantitatem delicti . . .'

[22] '. . . quare cum de communi consilio regni domini Henrici regis patris domini regis nunc provisum fuit quod quicumque execuciones judiciorum curie sue impedire presumpserint et de eo convicti fuerunt redimantur et predicti Walterus et Elizabetha coram justiciariis ultimo itinerantibus in comitatu predicto decem libratas, decem et septem denaratas redditus, ducentas acras bosci et unum vivarium cum pertinenciis in Ledes versus Rogerum de Leyburne patrem predicti Willelmi et Robertum Crevequer per recognicionem assise nove disseisine ibidem inter eos captam, et vicecomiti preceptum fuit quod eisdem Waltero et Elizabet de predicti redditu, bosco et vivario plenam seisinam habere faceret, predicti Willelmus, Johannes et alii execucionem judicii in prefata curia dicti patris nostri pro predictis Waltero et Elizabetha inde redditi fieri non permiserunt sed vi et armis impediverunt quominus execucio fieri potuit in predictorum Walteri et Elyzabethe dampnum non modicum et dicti regis patris nostri contemptum manifestum': KB 27/7, m. 2d. For earlier stages see KB 27/5, m. 9 (Trinity term 1273); KB 27/1, m. 7d (Michaelmas term 1273).

[23] For an action on the complaint of William de la Penne against the sheriff of Buckinghamshire for failure to execute a judgment being brought in 1279 which makes no mention of the Statute see CP 40/30, m. 12.

[24] *SR*, I, 235; H.M. Cam, *The Hundred and the Hundred Rolls: an Outline of Local Government in Medieval England* (London, 1930), p. 250.

Some presentments can be identified with reasonable certainty as having been made in response to this article.[25] There was, however, also an older article of the eyre, which asked specifically about 'those who do not allow the king's bailiffs to enter their lands to make summonses or distraints of the lord king or for other things without a special order of the lord king'.[26] Many more presentments seem to have been made under this article.[27]

Given the fact that these chapters were merely repeating and reinforcing existing norms in the rather special circumstances of the aftermath of a civil war, it is hardly surprising to find that the only original writs created for the enforcement of any of these chapters were so little used, indeed show every sign of having been created only for particular litigants, and never passed into more general use. It is also disappointing, though not surprising, to find that there is so little evidence of the creation of other special mechanisms or procedures for the enforcement of these same chapters.

THE ENFORCEMENT OF CHAPTER 15

There had also been a clause restricting where distraints might be made in the original Provisions of Westminster of 1259. Clause 11 of the Provisions had made it clear that no one other than the king and his officials was allowed to make distraints outside their fee or in the royal or common highway. Although there is some room for doubt about whether or not a version of this clause was included in the Statute of Marlborough, particularly as the subject matter of the clause overlapped significantly with the provisions of chapter 2 of the same Statute, and it is missing from a number of early copies of the Statute, the better opinion is that it was.[28] Also suggestive, but not conclusive, is the fact that within a few years of the enactment of the Statute a trespass writ had been created which specifically cited the legislation and required a defendant to answer for breaching its terms.

The final form of the statutory writ, as included in the printed register, ordered the sheriff to attach the defendant to answer as to

[25] JUST 1/1064, m. 20d (1279–81 Yorkshire eyre); JUST 1/242, m. 69d (1285 Essex eyre); JUST 1/302, m. 56 (1292 Herefordshire eyre).

[26] *SR*, I, 234.

[27] For examples see JUST 1/323, mm. 44d, 53d, 55 (1278 Hertfordshire eyre); JUST 1/371, m. 11 (1279 Kent eyre); JUST 1/645, m. 16 (1279 Northumberland eyre); JUST 1/876, m. 49 (1279 Surrey eyre); JUST 1/915, mm. 5, 24 (1279 Sussex eyre); JUST 1/784, mm. 10d, 27 (1280 Hampshire eyre); JUST 1/486, mm. 1d. 2d, 10, 25d (1281–4 Lincolnshire eyre); JUST 1/457, m. 37d (1284 Leicestershire eyre); JUST 1/619, m. 51d (1285 Northamptonshire eyre); JUST 1/573, m. 98d (1286 Norfolk eyre); JUST 1/278, m. 45 (1287 Gloucestershire eyre); JUST 1/739, m. 82d (1292 Shropshire eyre); JUST 1/543, m. 62 (1294 Middlesex eyre).

[28] Above, p. 189.

why, whereas it has been provided by the common counsel of our kingdom of England that no one is allowed to make distraints for whatever cause outside his fee or in the royal highway or common street, other than the king and his officials, the said B., who is not an official of ours, as is said, took animals belonging to A. at N. outside his fee [or: animals/goods and chattels belonging to the same A. in the royal highway/in the common street at N.] contrary to the terms of the said provision and impounded them and still keeps them impounded against the law and custom of our realm of England and against our peace [or: impounded them and long kept them impounded against the law etc. and against our peace] . . .[29]

A similar writ is found in the early fourteenth-century register of writs printed by de Haas and Hall, with mainly minor variants, but one major and significant difference: the inclusion of an additional phrase in the clause noting the exemption of the king and royal officials from these rules, alleging that they possessed 'special authority to do this'.[30] A note in the printed register observes that this additional clause is included in 'certain registers' but should not be included in the writ because it is not warranted by the Statute.

The plea roll evidence suggests that this new trespassory writ was first drafted and made available to litigants shortly before Easter term 1271.[31] The enrolments also suggest that the additional clause referring to the king and his officials as possessing 'special authority to do this' was added to the writ only in the early 1290s.[32] Throughout the reign it was apparently possible to add to the writ a variety of allegations of other types of related wrongdoing: a subsequent continuation of distraints which have made it impossible for the plaintiff to cultivate his lands;[33] an allegation that the seizure had been made 'with force and arms';[34] an allegation that the animals taken had been harmed by being detained without food,[35] or had been kept so long that they (or a majority of them or some of

[29] *Reg. Omn. Brev.*, fol. 97b. [30] *Early Registers*, pp. 164–5 (R 232).

[31] In that term for the first time there are enrolments of mesne process stages in litigation initiated by such writs both in the Common Bench (KB 26/202, mm. 2d, 36, 37d: *Master Peter of Northampton v. John son of Robert del Estre and others*) and in King's Bench (KB 26/201, m. 9d: *Thomas of Walcott v. Thomas Roscelin and others*).

[32] In King's Bench it appears in an action brought by the chancellor, Robert Burnel, as early as Trinity term 1290: KB 27/124, m. 16 (*Robert bishop of Bath and Wells v. John Purdome*). In the Common Bench the earliest pleaded case enrolled as initiated by a writ containing this clause comes from Michaelmas term 1292: CP 40/96, m. 240d (*Henry of Chadworth v. prior of Hagham*).

[33] *John Sampson v. Philip of Stambourne*: CP 40/27, m. 79 (Michaelmas term 1278).

[34] *Hugh of Culworth v. Simon de Forneus et al.*: CP 40/28, m. 29 (Hilary term 1279) (also made at night); *William of Gilling v. Henry Smith of Egremont and others*: CP 40/108, m. 56 (Easter term 1295); *Abbot of Sawley v. Richard of Wigton et al.*: CP 40/113, m. 92d (Trinity term 1296); *Richard of Bittering of Docking v. John Lovel of Southmere*: CP 40/139, m. 53 (Trinity term 1301).

[35] *Warden of the house of the valley of scholars of Salisbury v. John of Milbourne et al.*: CP 40/95, m. 112d (Trinity term 1292).

them) had died of hunger.[36] They also indicate that during the 1270s the standard writ had an additional clause after the allegation of continued detention claiming that the defendant had not allowed the replevying of the distresses he had taken.

There are only a relatively small number of pleaded actions brought by writs of this kind in the Common Bench during the reign of Edward I: a total of forty-five in all. This overall figure masks a considerable variation in numbers over time. There was one case a year in 1275, 1277 and 1279 and two in 1278. There were no cases at all of this type in the Common Bench during the 1280s. Cases resumed in 1290, with one pleaded case that year and in 1295, 1297, 1302, 1305 and 1306; two in 1291, 1293 and 1296; three in 1292 and 1294; and five in 1301, 1303, 1304 and 1307, but none in either 1298 or 1300. In fifteen of the cases the allegation made in the body of the writ was of a distraint outside the defendant's fee, in twenty-five of a distraint made in the highway, in the remainder of some combination of these.

The enrolled counts show that the most common type of allegation was of a distraint of animals, most commonly of horses. There is, however, one case of 1303 where the plaintiff alleged the seizure of a boat and its contents (wheat and barley) with an overall valuation of fifty pounds.[37] In two further counts what is said to have been taken is a combination of chattels and animals.[38] Most of the counts mention only a single distraint, but not all.[39] There are several cases where pleading took place within a year of the distraint being made and in a majority pleading took place within two years. The longest delay was a period of five years in a case of 1301.[40] Distraints made outside the defendant's fee are normally specified as having been made at a particular location within a named village. Distraints made in the highway normally specify only that the highway was in a particular village, but some give rather more

[36] *Adam son of Thomas of Salthouse v. Roger of Soterley*: CP 40/102, m. 191d (Michaelmas term 1293) and CP 40/103, m. 73 (Easter term 1294); *Abbot of Tewkesbury v. William Franklin of Ampney Crucis and others*: CP 40/115, m. 187 (Michaelmas term 1296); *Robert of Santhorpe parson of Appleton in Ryedale v. John de Bordesden*: CP 40/139, m. 59d (Trinity term 1301); *William of Thoresby v. Philip Chauncy*: CP 40/139, m. 50d (Trinity term 1301); *John Moriz of Cambridge v. William Seygham of Grantchester*: CP 40/150, m. 156 (Hilary term 1304); *William of Thoresby v. Philip de Chauncy et al.*: CP 40/149, m. 337 (Michaelmas term 1304).

[37] *Roger Palmer of London v. Thomas atte Lock*: CP 40/145, m. 245 (Michaelmas term 1303).

[38] *Warden of the house of the valley of scholars of Salisbury v. John of Milbourne et al.*: CP 40/95, m. 112d (Trinity term 1292): a cart laden with wheat, barley and oats plus two horses; *Richer parson of East Wittering v. William de la Hoke of Chichere and Thomas le Bukere clerk*: CP 40/130, m. 100d (Michaelmas term 1299): three horses, an iron cart and a barrel of cider.

[39] The largest number of separate distraints mentioned is the four specified in *Roger de Mar parson of Whixley v. abbot of Fountains et al.*: CP 40/149, m. 141 (Michaelmas term 1304).

[40] *Robert of Bittering of Docking v. John Lovel of Southmere*: CP 40/138, m. 53 (Trinity term 1301).

detail.[41] In one case the 'highway' turns out to be not a road but a navigable river, the Thames at Bray in Berkshire.[42]

In around a quarter of the cases pleaded in the Common Bench, the defendants simply pleaded the general issue, denying having made the distraint concerned. All went to a jury but in none is any kind of verdict recorded. In just under a half of the cases, the defendant denied having taken the distresses at the place assigned by the plaintiff in his count, but claimed to have taken them elsewhere within his fee or within the fee of the lord whose bailiff he claimed to be. The defendant seems invariably to have coupled this with an avowry justifying the making of the distraint, but issue seems always to have been joined on the place of taking alone.

More interesting are those cases where defendants agreed that they had made a distraint at the place alleged by the plaintiff, but claimed that this had been quite proper. The simplest cases are those where the plaintiff had alleged a distraint made outside the defendant's fee, but the defendant claimed that the place concerned was in fact within his own fee or the fee of his lord, an issue which would normally go to jury trial.[43] In one case, the defendant did not make such a claim but did assert that the land where the distraint had been made was part of a tenement on which had been secured an annuity owed to the defendant by final concord, a claim later confirmed by jury verdict.[44] In a second case the defendant claimed to have taken the animals not just in his fee but on his very own land, as he had found them in his corn and he had taken *damage feasant*.[45] In a third case the defendant (the abbot of Fountains) admitted making three distraints outside his fee and on land belonging to the plaintiff, Roger de Mar, parson of Whixley, in Thorp Underwood. He justified the distraints as a commoner of the same village, impounding animals allegedly brought in by the plaintiff from the village of Whixley,

[41] E.g. *John Sampson v. Philip of Stambourne*: CP 40/27, m. 79 (Michaelmas term 1278): outside the house of the Franciscans at Stamford; *William de Brettevile v. John de Hauville and his brother Roger*: CP 40/151, m. 80d (Easter term 1304): in the highway at Clothall leading from 'Ordeswyk' to Baldock.

[42] *Roger Palmer of London v. Thomas atte Lock*: CP 40/145, m. 245 (Michaelmas term 1303).

[43] For examples see *Henry of Berkeley v. Pain of Maresfield*: CP 40/21, m. 17d (Michaelmas term 1277); *Alan fitzRoald v. Peter of Legbourne of Ropley and others*: CP 40/86, m. 125d (Michaelmas term 1290); *Bartholomew Marche of Stanhoe v. John de Fitton of Wiggenhall*: CP 40/102, m. 134 (Michaelmas term 1293); *Agnes widow of John Byde v. John Pulsefund et al.*: CP 40/164, m. 1d (Trinity term 1307). In the first of these cases the defendant claimed the land was held of the earl of Gloucester. The plaintiff's reply was that the land was held of the king. The defendant then admitted this, without awaiting jury trial.

[44] *Hugh of Culworth v. Simon de Forneus et al.*: CP 40/28, m. 29 (Hilary term 1279).

[45] *Abbot of Tewkesbury v. William Franklin of Ampney Crucis*: CP 40/115, m. 187 (Michaelmas term 1296). The jury found that they had in fact been taken on the plaintiff's land.

which did not intercommon with Thorp Underwood.[46] Issue was taken on a related question of fact. Was the plaintiff's land at the time of the distraint lying fallow and thus part of the village common and subject to its commoning regulations? Or were the plaintiff's lands at the relevant time in one of the two years out of three when at that time of year it was the plaintiff's several and he was thus at liberty to plough it and sow it or to graze it with whatever animals he wished? A manuscript note ascribes to Chief Justice Mettingham and his colleague Bereford the doctrine that a man may also be justified in taking animals outside his fee if he has found them on his land *damage feasant* but they have been driven off into another fee before he has had a chance to impound them, provided he has taken them on the other fee while in 'hot pursuit'.[47] This certainly seems to be the assumption underlying the pleading in two ordinary replevin cases of the first half of the 1290s, where the plaintiff was driven to denying that any such damage had been done and into asserting that the taking had, therefore, been malicious.[48]

When the plaintiff's allegation was of a distraint made in the highway, it was also possible for a defendant to admit that the distraint had been made there and to justify it. A defendant might claim that he had made a seizure of the plaintiff's animals while in 'hot pursuit' of animals which had been 'doing damage', such as grazing in his several pasture.[49] Avowries made in ordinary replevin cases suggest that it was also permissible to take animals in 'hot pursuit' on a highway, if they were being driven out of the defendant's fee and the defendant was distraining for arrears of service.[50] Reports of a case of Michaelmas term 1302 suggest that Hengham, CJ also thought it perfectly permissible for a lord who held land on both sides of a highway to seize animals he found grazing on the highway, rather than just passing along it, for any grass there would be in law his several.[51] In a 1291 case Roger of Elmham and his wife,

46 CP 40/149, m. 151 (Michaelmas term 1304): reported in *YB 32 & 33 EI*, pp. 133–7; BL MSS. Additional 31826, fol. 352r and Egerton 2811, fol. 94v; LI MSS. Miscellaneous 738, fol. 26r and Hale 188, fols. 106r–v.

47 BL MS. Additional 37657, fol. 140r.

48 *Prior of Daventry v. John Malore and others*: CP 40/96, m. 215d (Michaelmas term 1292); *Abbot of Fountains v. Henry of Hertlington*: CP 40/110, m. 245 (Michaelmas term 1295).

49 *William Talbot v. Waresius de Valoyns*: CP 40/145, m. 166d (Michaelmas term 1303). For a defendant admitting having taken only some of the animals in this way see *Abbot of Sawley v. Richard of Wigton et al.*: CP 40/113, m. 92d (Trinity term 1296).

50 *Roger de Begthon v. Richard le Furneys*: CP 40/98, m. 26d (Hilary term 1293); *Cecilia widow of Hugh of Lutrington v. Stephen Rabaz*: CP 40/145, m. 161 (Michaelmas term 1303).

51 Hengham's view appears in the reports of *Thomas of Sandwich v. Robert Miriweder* in BL MSS. Additional 31826, fol. 174v, Harley 25, fol. 139r (=Additional 35116, fol. 166r), Harley 25, fol. 6r (=Additional 35116, fol. 151r) and CUL MS. Ee.2.19, fol. 139v. There is also a related note in BL MS. Egerton 2811 at fol. 79r. The enrolment is CP 40/144, m. 94d.

Margaret, and others attempted to justify the seizure of a horse belonging to Robert de Scalers in the royal highway at Barnwell outside Cambridge on the grounds that the burgesses of Cambridge enjoyed the franchise by virtue of charters from the king's predecessors of being able to distrain their clerical debtors belonging to the university anywhere in Cambridge or Barnwell, including the highway, and that they were burgesses of Cambridge and Robert such a debtor.[52] The court proved unsympathetic to this plea. Since the defendants could show no royal charter of a date later than the enactment of the Statute allowing a continuation of the previous practice, the Statute governed and the distraint was therefore unjust. In a second case of the same year, a defendant justified a distraint made in the highway as the bailiff of the lord of the market at Aylesbury. The distraint had been made in order to attach the plaintiff to answer a second defendant on a debt claim.[53] The court and the parties evidently assumed that the distraint would have been justified if the plaintiff had been coming to the market as a merchant intending to trade there, presumably under the law merchant. This was the defendant's claim. The plaintiff asserted that he had not come to Aylesbury to trade but was merely passing through the town on his way back from the fair at Brackley. Thus, even though he was a merchant, he was not subject to the jurisdiction of the Aylesbury fair court on this occasion. A jury confirmed the plaintiff's story. It was also specifically asked whether or not it was the custom of the court to attach those passing through the town as well as those buying and selling there, suggesting that this too was within the range of custom that the court might be willing to accept. On the jury confirming that it was not, judgment was given for the plaintiff. In a 1306 case Walter of Barrow attempted to justify the seizure of a horse belonging to Simon of Barton in the highway at Sudbury in Suffolk as the bailiff of the earl of Gloucester and his wife, Joan.[54] The seizure had been made to enforce payment of a 'common fine' of twenty shillings owed by the town of Sudbury at the Michaelmas session of the view of frankpledge. Simon had been distrained as a member of the community of the town. Only the reports show that Walter's counsel initially justified the seizure as having been made in the market-place of the town, from which Walter's lord received toll and stallage and other dues, and that he claimed that this made it his lord's fee. He soon waived this, however, in favour of an alternative view suggested by Hengham, CJ. This was that since the payment was

[52] CP 40/91, m. 103, reported in *YB 21 & 22 EI*, pp. 55–7.

[53] *Adam Wace v. William atte Hyde et al.*: CP 40/90, m. 115d (Michaelmas term 1291).

[54] CP 40/161, m. 168d (Michaelmas term 1306), reported in *YB 33–35 EI*, pp. 325–7 (and closely related report in BL MS. Harley 2183, fol. 103v) and in BL MSS. Hargrave 375, fol. 172v and Harley 25, fol. 128v (= Additional 35116, fols. 183v–184r).

connected with the view of frankpledge, Walter had in effect been acting as a royal official. He might therefore call in aid the general exception contained in the Statute in favour of royal officials. The court rejected the argument of counsel for the plaintiff, that Walter was a royal bailiff only on the day the leet was held and thus could not take advantage of the statutory exception in respect of a distraint made on a later day. Issue was eventually taken as to whether or not Simon was liable to the payment, or whether he and previous tenants of the tenement he held had enjoyed exemption from it. In a 1295 case the plaintiff alleged the taking of two horses belonging to him in the highway at Egremont in Cumberland.[55] The defendant made a double answer. They claimed that at the death of Thomas of Moulton, late lord of the village (or town), the king's escheator north of the Trent, Thomas de Normanville, had called the tenants of the village together, and they had agreed to pay a fine of five marks for a continuation of their liberties while the village or town was in the king's hands. The plaintiff had then been allotted the sum of three shillings to pay as his share of the fine, but had refused to do so. The defendants had been assigned to levy the fine. By implication at least, they had been acting as royal bailiffs in doing so, and so not subject to the rule about not distraining in the highway. They also, however, added that they had not, in any case, actually taken the horses in distraint. They had asked a man driving the plaintiff's cart for payment of the sum owed and he had voluntarily handed over a single horse. The plaintiff maintained that two horses had been taken and that this had not been for any money owed to the king.

From 1278 onwards there was also a 'new' article of the eyre seeking information on 'those who have taken animals or distresses outside their fee . . .',[56] and a series of presentments were made in response to this article at eyres from 1278 onwards.[57] If, however, this article was drafted with any particular statutory provision in mind it is more likely to have been chapter 16 of the Statute of Westminster I of 1275 than chapter 15 of the Statute of Marlborough, for it shares with the former, but not the latter, a concentration on distraints outside the fee to the exclusion of distraints on the highway. There is also one piece of evidence to suggest that presentments about distraints on the highway may have been sought at the sheriff's tourn.[58]

[55] *William of Gilling v. Henry Smith of Egremont et al.*: CP 40/108, m. 56 (Easter term 1295).

[56] 'De hiis qui ceperunt averia vel districciones extra feodum suum': *SR*, I, 237a.

[57] For some early examples see JUST 1/323, m. 53d (1278 Hertfordshire eyre); JUST 1/371, mm. 19, 24d, 26, 34, 49d (1279 Kent eyre); JUST 1/915, mm. 5, 9, 14 (1279 Sussex eyre).

[58] This is in a conspiracy case brought by Nicholas of Amberden against the jurors of a presentment jury where the alleged conspiracy was to make a false presentment in the sheriff's tourn held in

The fact that there was a statutory action for distraints outside the fee and in the royal highway did not stop plaintiffs making an allegation of distraint outside the fee or in the highway in the course of pleading in common law actions of replevin. An allegation that distresses had been taken in the highway was a common element in plaintiff's counts in such actions. The defendant then probably had the choice either of denying having taken the distresses there[59] or of assigning another location for the taking and making an avowry, justifying the distraint.[60] A plaintiff could perhaps respond either by counterpleading the avowry or by traversing the place assigned by the defendant. They seem in practice normally, or even invariably, to have chosen the latter.[61] There seems to be no evidence, however, that plaintiffs ever mentioned the fact that the distraint they were alleging had been in breach of the Statute and no special awareness on the part of either litigants or the court of that fact.

The count was not the proper place to allege that a distraint had been made outside the defendant's fee. This allegation would normally only emerge once the defendant had in his avowry justified a distraint as made in a particular place. This might or might not be the place assigned for it in the plaintiff's count. Only then could the plaintiff ask for judgment of the avowry on the grounds that the place specified was outside the defendant's fee and issue be joined on whether or not the place in question was within the defendant's fee. This pattern of pleading is encountered most frequently in cases where the defendant was avowing a distraint he had made for arrears of services. It was most common in cases where the plaintiff was the sub-tenant of the tenant whose services were supposedly

the Essex hundred of Lexden that the plaintiff had distrained the prior of Colne twice in the king's highway against the king's peace and in breach of the Statute and thereby procured his amercement: KB 27/156, m. 50. It does not, however, appear among the articles of the tourn included in the Statute of Wales and apparently taken from contemporary English practice (*SR*, I, 57) nor in the lists of articles in *Fleta* (book II, *c.* 52: vol. II, pp. 175–6) and in BL MS. Arundel 310, ff. 116v–119r

59 For examples see *Reginald of Essex v. John Gravassale et al.*.: CP 40/70, m. 2 (Hilary term 1288); *Maud widow of Robert of Caistor v. John of Cockfield et al.*: CP 40/82, m. 48 (Easter term 1290); *Roger son of Master Thomas of Pilson v. Roger son of Jordan of Pilson*: CP 40/95, m. 148 (Trinity term 1292); *John Duket parson of Deene v. John son of Henry of Deene*: CP 40/96, m. 19 (Michaelmas term 1292).

60 For examples see *John of Brinklow v. Thomas son of Henry de Burgh*: CP 40/69, m. 131 (Michaelmas term 1287); *Robert Mariot v. Brother Thomas of Billington master of hospital of Maltby*: CP 40/93, m. 75d (Easter term 1292); *Herbert of Calne v. abbot of Hyde*: CP 40/106, m. 206 (Michaelmas term 1294).

61 For examples see *John of Stanbridge v. John de Boeles et al.*: CP 40/17, m. 42 (Michaelmas term 1276); *Oliver of Ingham v. John de la Mare et al.*: CP 40/19, m. 30 (Easter term 1277); *John of Wimbledon v. Alexander Husee and his wife Isabel*: CP 40/27, m. 137 (Michaelmas term 1278); *Richard Holk of Morton v. abbot of Vaudey*: CP 40/58, m. 8d (Easter term 1285); *William de la Ryvere v. abbot of Abingdon et al.*: CP 40/75, m. 152d (Michaelmas term 1288); *Alan Aldeman v. Ralph bishop of Carlisle et al.*: CP 40/82, m. 99d (Easter term 1290).

in arrears, for lords were entitled to take in distraint animals found on their tenant's holding, whether or not they belonged to that tenant. Denying that the place where the animals had been taken was part of the lord's fee was one of the very few responses allowed such a sub-tenant. Again, it is reasonably clear that plaintiffs who made such a plea did not specifically refer to the Statute when they did so and did not need to do so, for the rule that distraints could only be made within the lord's fee had existed at common law prior to 1259. It was, however, only just prior to the enactment of the initial version of the Provisions of Westminster in 1259 that it first emerged as a possible answer to an avowry for services in the Common Bench.[62]

[62] The earliest case is *Brian de Gouiz v. abbot of Muchelney*: KB 26/160, m. 54 (Michaelmas term 1258).

Chapter 15

REMEDYING ABUSES IN THE OPERATION OF LOCAL COURTS

As has been seen, the longest and most detailed part of the Statute of Marlborough was the chapter dealing with the use of distraint in securing the performance of suit to seignorial courts. This had also been true of the earlier Provisions of Westminster of 1259.[1] Other chapters, too, were concerned with abuses connected with the workings of local, non-royal courts: attempts to enforce attendance at the sheriff's tourn (and at the view of frankpledge) from those who should have been exempt from this;[2] attempts to enforce payment of beaupleder fines from those with a duty to present offences at such sessions;[3] the use of distraint to secure the appearance of defendants to answer in local courts who were not subject to the jurisdiction of those particular courts.[4] There were also a number of other chapters concerned with remedying other perceived abuses in the operation of local courts. These covered sheriffs allowing the release of those convicted of redisseisin in the county court without specific authorisation from the king and payment of the necessary fine (chapter 8); lords hearing pleas of false judgment in their courts (chapter 19); lords and sheriffs compelling those essoined in local courts to warrant their essoins on oath (chapter 20); the failure of sheriffs to secure the release of the animals taken in distraint that were held in franchises after a plaint had been made to them about this (chapter 21); lords forcing their free tenants to answer for their free tenements in their courts without prior authorisation by a royal writ or putting them on oath (as jurors) in their courts against their will without prior royal authorisation (chapter 23). This chapter will look at the evidence for the enforcement and citation of these chapters during the period down to 1307.

[1] Above, chapter 8. [2] Above, pp. 83–7.
[3] Above, pp. 87–90. [4] Above, p. 193.

THE UNAUTHORISED RELEASE OF THOSE IMPRISONED FOR REDISSEISIN

Chapter 8 of the Statute of Marlborough was one of the new chapters which had not been part of earlier versions of the Provisions of Westminster.[5] Those arrested and imprisoned on being convicted of redisseisin were not supposed to be released save on the special order of the king and after making a fine for their offence. This chapter enacted that sheriffs who released such prisoners without such an order were to be heavily amerced and the persons released were still to be punished for their original offence. As already noted, the procedure created by the legislation of 1236 to deal with redisseisin was that the hearing of such cases was delegated to the sheriff and coroners. Its weakness was that no adequate check was kept upon the issue of writs of redisseisin and no attempt made to discover whether or not defendants had been convicted.

There is at least one case from the period after 1267 in which a successful plaintiff in an action of redisseisin sought to invoke the Statute of Marlborough in order to ensure the imprisonment of his opponent and their payment of a fine to the king for release from that imprisonment. This is a case of which only a procedural stage has been found enrolled on the King's Bench plea roll in Hilary term 1278. The defendants were the former sheriff of Kent (William de Valoignes) and the man who had committed the redisseisin (Edmund de Vienne). The release without imprisonment and also without the awarding of damages was characterised as being 'contrary to the terms of the provision of Marlborough in which it is contained that those who are arrested and detained for redisseisin are not to be released without the king's order for this by a fine to be made with the king for their trespass . . .'[6] There is no mention of the Statute in a second case enrolled in King's Bench in Easter term 1270 (of which again only a procedural stage has been found) in which Denis son of Robert and his wife, Clarice, sued Ivo of Kenton, the bailiff of the liberty of St Etheldreda of Ely in Suffolk, for releasing their opponents (Simon Barber and his wife, Katherine, and Abraham de la Fontayne) without any authorisation from the king after they had been handed over to him by the sheriff after a conviction for redisseisin. A further alleged consequence of this premature release was that the plaintiffs had still not managed to gain seisin of the lands they had recovered.[7] A potentially

[5] Above, pp. 195–6.

[6] '. . . contra formam provisionis de Marlebergh' in qua contineatur quod illi qui pro iterata disseisina capti fuerunt et detenti non deliberentur sine precepto regis ad hoc per finem cum regi faciendam pro transgressione sua': *Rex and Thomas Everard v. Edmund de Vienne and William de Valoignes*: KB 27/35, m. 30.

[7] KB 26/198, m. 10.

more effective check, which did not rely on the initiative of individual litigants but used the mechanism of the presentment jury, was the introduction of a new article of the eyre inquiring about sheriffs receiving bribes to release such prisoners. However, no examples of presentments for its breach have been noted.[8] From 1285 onwards (under the provisions of Westminster II, ch. 8) Chancery kept a separate roll recording all writs of redisseisin issued, a copy of which was sent to the Exchequer.[9] In theory at least, this meant that the barons could in future keep some kind of check on what had happened in these cases, though there seems to be no direct evidence to show that they did.

LORDS HEARING PLEAS OF FALSE JUDGMENT IN THEIR COURTS

Chapter 19 of the Statute of Marlborough re-enacted in unaltered form what had been clause 16 of the original Provisions of Westminster.[10] The chapter reiterated what seems to have been a common law rule of long standing that prohibited lords other than the king from exercising jurisdiction over pleas of false judgment relating to pleas originally heard in the courts of their tenants. As already noted, there is no evidence to suggest that there had been any large-scale flouting of the royal monopoly over such cases prior to 1259 and no evidence that the legislation was invoked or cited between 1259 and 1267.[11] There seems to be no evidence for its enforcement after 1267 either. An extended search has found neither litigation brought by aggrieved individual litigants nor any new article of the eyre seeking presentments on the king's behalf for its breach. The most likely explanation is that there continued to be no significant or large-scale breaches of the rule.

REQUIRING THE WARRANTING OF ESSOINS ON OATH

Chapter 20 of the Statute of Marlborough is a second chapter which re-enacted, in unaltered form, one of the clauses of the original Provisions of Westminster, in this case clause 15 of the Provisions.[12] This chapter relaxed the rules for the warranting of essoins in various kinds of local court (county courts, hundred courts and courts baron), insisting that those who ran those courts could no longer require litigants or others to warrant their essoins on oath. The chapter seems generally to have been

[8] *SR*, I. 235a. The same article had been included in the Hundred Rolls enquiry of 1274: Cam, *The Hundred and the Hundred Rolls*, p. 250.

[9] The Chancery redisseisin rolls are now C 69; the Exchequer copy forms part of the originalia rolls (E 371).

[10] Below, pp. 476–7. [11] Above, p. 99. [12] Below, pp. 476–7, 422–3.

observed without the need for the provision of any special mechanism to ensure that it was carried into effect. The only evidence found for its non-observance comes from a presentment made by the wapentake of Morley in the Yorkshire eyre of 1279–81 in response to the general article asking about 'new customs'. According to the jurors, the earl of Warenne's steward of the court of Wakefield (Alexander Lucas) had initiated a custom of making men swear on oath when they appeared to warrant their essoins that they really had fallen ill while actually on their way to the court and amercing them if they refused to take such an oath.[13] The jurors cited three specific individuals who had been amerced in this way. However, interestingly, despite the legislation, his conduct was said by the jurors to be only 'against the custom of the realm', rather than contrary to statute. What the Wakefield court rolls show, however, is that the three men concerned were not amerced but made fine with the steward for being released from the need to warrant their essoins. This is a significant difference since it indicates that they had agreed to pay the sums concerned. They also show that all this had happened some years before, in 1274–5.[14] This suggests that there was no more recent instance to cite and that Lucas may have adopted the practice for a brief period of time only, perhaps even dropping it when he discovered that it was contrary to statute.

THE RETENTION OF DISTRESSES

The following chapter of the Statute of Marlborough (chapter 21) was another clause taken without alteration from the Provisions of Westminster as originally enacted in 1259, of which it had formed clause 17.[15] As has been seen, the clause started by confirming that sheriffs were entitled to secure the release of the animals of anyone who had been distrained once the person who had been distrained had lodged a complaint with them. This seems to have been intended merely to provide the general normative context and justification for the real heart of the legislation.

[13] 'De novis consuetudinibus dicunt quod Alexander Lucas senescallus comitis Warr' in curia de Wakefeld contra consuetudinem regni capit misericordias pro defectu warantizacionis essoniorum, videlicet quod aliquis essoniatus ad proximam apparicionem in curia jurare voluerit quod fuit in eundo versus curiam predictam et quod in eundo egrotavit, per quod ad curiam venire non potuit. Ideo preceptum est vicecomiti quod faciat eum venire. Et juratores dicunt quod cepit tali modo de Thoma de Thornetone una vice et et de eodem ij solidos alia vice; et de Ricardo de Thornhulle dimidiam marcam et de Baldewino de Seyville dimidam marcam': JUST 1/1064, m. 13d.

[14] *Court Rolls of the Manor of Wakefield, vol. I (1274–97)*, ed. W.P. Baildon (Yorkshire Archaeological Society Record Series vol. 29, 1901), pp. 85, 155.

[15] Below, pp. 478–9, 424–5.

This was a second sentence which spelled out that when animals had been taken in distraint within a franchise and the bailiff had failed to secure their release the sheriff was to act instead. This provision was probably intended to provide a general statutory authority for sheriffs to disregard franchises when this was necessary to secure the release of animals taken in distraint. Where an action of replevin was begun by writ a special writ could provide the necessary authorisation; this legislation provided a standing authorisation when the action was begun by plaint.

Had there been surviving county court rolls for this period, it might have been possible to trace in detail the application of this legislation. As there are none, it is not possible to do this. Nor have any other incidental mentions of the legislation been found in other surviving records for this period. If the legislation worked as intended there is no reason why there should have been.

FORCING FREE TENANTS TO ANSWER FOR THEIR FREE TENEMENTS WITHOUT AUTHORISATION

Chapter 22 of the Statute of Marlborough was yet another clause taken without alteration from the original Provisions of Westminster of 1259, of which it had formed clause 18. The first part of this chapter restated the traditional rule against lords distraining their free tenants to answer in their courts for their free tenements or for anything belonging to their free tenements unless the lords had the authority of a royal writ for holding the litigation.[16] There is comparatively little evidence of the rule being specifically invoked after 1267. This may perhaps indicate that infraction of the rule itself remained comparatively uncommon. Such evidence as there is takes three different forms: presentments of breaches of the rule, the existence of writs prohibiting breaches and the invocation of the rule in individual proceedings.

In the Hundred Rolls enquiry of 1274–5 a presentment was made against the bailiffs of the earl of Gloucester in Norfolk for holding a court 'in which they plead several pleas which ought not be pleaded without the king's writ'.[17] This is most probably to be construed as a reference to breaches of this rule. In the Kent eyre of 1293 two bailiffs of the hundred of Milton were presented for holding 'pleas concerning free tenement without writ'.[18] In neither case, however, is it specifically said that the bailiffs concerned were doing this without the consent of the tenants or

[16] Below, pp. 478–9, 424–5.

[17] '. . . in qua placitant plura placita que non debent placitari sine brevi domini regis': *RH*, I, 584.

[18] '. . . placita de libero tenemento sine brevi . . .': JUST 1/374, m. 61d.

defendants concerned and in neither case is the legislation mentioned. In the 1281 Wiltshire eyre the presentment jury of the hundred of Alderbury presented that William of Monkton, while steward of John Giffard, had taken forty shillings of John de la Forde, presumably as an amercement or fine, because he held four acres which Walter de la Forde had claimed as his right in John's Giffard's court without a writ, although he was not obliged to answer for the holding without a writ. The implication seems to be that John de la Forde had refused to answer for his holding without a writ but that his exception or objection had been overruled. The presentment was marked for judgment but none is recorded.[19]

Registers of writs suggest that it remained possible for those impleaded without a writ to go to Chancery to obtain a writ addressed to the appropriate local sheriff ordering him to see the rule enforced. Although some changes were made to the wording of the writ between the time of the pre-Mertonian register and that of the Luffield register those changes did not reflect the fact that during the intervening period legislation had also been passed on this subject and the prohibition continued to cite no special authority of any kind for the rule the sheriff was being required to enforce.[20]

It is possible to see litigants acquiring and using such prohibitions in at least two cases dating from the reign of Edward I. In a false judgment case heard in the Common Bench in Michaelmas term 1279 four suitors from Edmund of Lancaster's ancient demesne court of Godmanchester, Huntingdonshire, bearing the record of the court, attested that a tenant (William de Boneville of Huntingdon) had appealed to the rule in court in a land case about a five-acre holding at Godmanchester when impleaded there without a writ by Andrew Butcher (le Mascegref) and his wife, Nicholaa.[21] After the case had been adjourned William had purchased a royal writ to the sheriff of Huntingdonshire to secure its observance. When again forced to appear he had made a renewed challenge to proceedings, arguing that he should only be impleaded by the

[19] 'Juratores presentant quod Willelmus de Monketon' quondam senescallus Johannis Gyffard cepit et extorsit de Johanne de la Ford xl solidos eo quod tenuit quatuor acras terre quas Walterus de la Forde peciit in curia Johannis Gyffard ut jus suum sine brevi cum inde respondere non debuit nisi cum brevi. Ideo ad judicium de eo': JUST 1/1005, m. 147. In the margin of the entry is written *'Ad judicium'* but this has later been deleted.

[20] '*Quod nullus inplacitetur sine speciali precepto regis.* Rex vicecomiti salutem. Precipimus tibi quod non inplacites vel inplacitari permittas A. de libero tenemento suo in tali villa sine speciali precepto nostro vel capitalis justiciarii nostri. Teste etc.': *Early Registers*, p. 68 (CC 117). A virtually identical form is found in the early fourteenth-century register: *Early Registers*, p. 207 (R411). A similar form of writ had also been included in the post-Mertonian register CB: Maitland, *Collected Papers*, II, 146 (CB79).

[21] '. . . respondens quod non debet respondere de libero tenemento suo sine speciali mandato domini regis vel capitalis justiciarii sui': CP 40/31, m. 137.

little writ of right and would then have the appropriate opportunities for delay.[22] It had been the sheriff himself, however, who had threatened that, if he did not answer at once, he would be adjudged undefended and so he had unwisely agreed to a jury. He had then left the court when he was not allowed his proper challenges to the jurors. It had also been the sheriff alone who had then awarded seisin to the claimants without even securing a judgment from the suitors and despite his lack of any proper position or standing in the court. Not surprisingly the court before whom the record was recited gave judgment quashing this purported 'judgment'. The procedural irregularities alone would have sufficed for this, even without the overriding of the 'free tenement' rule.

The rule was again invoked apparently during the second half of the 1280s in a case relating to land at Willesden in Middlesex heard in the court of Robert of Drayton, a canon of St Paul's cathedral in London who held the prebend of East Twyford.[23] Thomas le Fayrsire and Hugh le Lorimer and his wife, Gunnilda, had been claiming the land against Roger of Cornhill of Edmonton. Roger had refused to answer for his free tenement without a writ. He had then reinforced this by getting the king's writ of prohibition reciting the rule and ordering the sheriff of Middlesex to ensure the rule was enforced. The sheriff had duly prohibited further proceedings in the case. This had led to the proceedings being suspended for a year. The case had then been resummoned. Roger had then obtained a second writ of prohibition reciting the rule. This time the case had proceeded after some kind of consultation with the royal justices Ralph of Hengham, Solomon of Rochester and John de Lovetot. He had eventually lost the land. Roger subsequently brought an assize of novel disseisin against the lord of the court and his bailiff and the successful claimants. In Easter term 1293 he recovered on the grounds that the court proceedings had been void because the court had ignored the king's prohibition and given judgment despite the defendant's objection to answering the case without a writ.

PUTTING FREE TENANTS ON OATH AGAINST THEIR WILL WITHOUT AUTHORISATION

The second half of chapter 23, also re-enacting part of clause 18 of the Provisions of Westminster, restated a second traditional restriction on

[22] '. . . statum suum viriliter calumpnians, petens quod parvum breve de recto clausum secundum consuetudinem manerii legi et audiri, ac super hoc debitas et consuetas dilaciones haberi prout moris fuit in eadem curia . . .'

[23] CP 40/100, m. 132.

lords and their courts: against lords putting their free tenants on oath against their will unless they had royal authorisation for doing this.[24] This rule was enforced during the forty years after 1267 mainly through presentments under the pre-existing article of the eyre which had asked for presentments against sheriffs and 'other bailiffs' who breached the rule, but which also continued to attract presentments against lords as well. The period also saw the drafting of a Chancery writ for the enforcement of the rule and to secure damages for its breach, but this was used only very infrequently.

Many of the presentments mention only the breach of the rule by stewards and bailiffs without noting the context of that breach.[25] These include one from the Kent eyre of 1279 in which the bailiff of the earl of Gloucester was presented for such an offence. He was amerced for doing this even though it was attested 'that this was before the Statute', an obvious reference to the Statute of Marlborough. This was a clear recognition that the rule had existed at common law before the Statute.[26] Other presentments give some context. The jurors of Strafforth wapentake in the 1268 Yorkshire eyre associated a breach of this rule by the sheriff of Yorkshire with his holding inquisitions into robberies and thefts,[27] while in the Cambridgeshire eyre of 1272 the same man, Robert de Estre, was presented as sheriff of that county for compelling free men to take oaths 'for all kinds of complaints and demands made to him' without 'the order of the lord king', presumably a reference to litigation initiated without writ.[28] At the Worcestershire eyre of 1275 breach of the rule by the abbot of Pershore in the hundred of Pershore was associated with inquests into the shedding of blood.[29] In the Gloucestershire eyre of 1287 a breach of the rules by the bailiffs of the earl of Gloucester was associated with their exercise of a forest jurisdiction in the form of inquests on vert and venison.[30] Several other presentments associate breaches of the rule with the wrongful holding of pleas of replevin.[31]

[24] Below, pp. 478–9.

[25] E.g. JUST 1/323, m. 50 (1278 Hertfordshire eyre: the stewards of the earl of Gloucester); JUST 1/915, m. 11 (1279 Sussex eyre: the bailiff of the Earl Warenne); JUST 1/573, m. 16d (1286 Norfolk eyre: the bailiff of Diss); JUST 1/924, m. 52 (1288 Sussex eyre: the steward of Pevensey); JUST 1/374, m. 61d (1293 Kent eyre: the bailiffs of the hundred of Milton).

[26] 'Hoc fuit ante statuta . . .': JUST 1/371, m. 4. [27] JUST 1/1051, m. 13d.

[28] '. . . ad omnimodas querelas et exactiones sibi factas sine precepto domini regis': JUST 1/85, m. 7.

[29] JUST 1/1026, m. 38d. [30] JUST 1/278, m. 43d.

[31] For examples see JUST 1/85, m. 6 (1272 Cambridgeshire eyre: the bailiffs of the Lord Edward of Babraham); JUST 1/780, m. 23d (1272 Hampshire eyre: the steward of the countess of Devon's hundred of East Medina); JUST 1/923, m. 21 (1279 Sussex eyre: the steward of Arundel, who was also sheriff, 'non quia vicecomes sed quia senescallus').

For some time there seems to have been considerable doubt as to whether sheriffs and franchise officials could compel free men to take oaths and serve as jurors even at the tourn or view of frankpledge. A presentment was made in the Essex eyre of 1272 by the hundred of Tendring against a former sheriff because he forced 'free men of this hundred to swear at his tourn without the order of the lord king' and he was even duly amerced for doing this.[32] Similar presentments were made in the Middlesex eyre of 1274 against Edmund, earl of Cornwall, in connexion with a view of frankpledge and against the sheriffs of the county in connexion with the tourn,[33] and in the Bedfordshire eyre of 1276 against the abbot of Waltham and the prior of Dunstable in connexion with the holding of views of frankpledge.[34] In a case in the court *coram rege* in Michaelmas 1274 the defendants were accused of impeding the sheriff of Leicestershire (Osbert de Bereford) in his tourn.[35] The verdict revealed that when the sheriff had come to the hundred and ordered the defendants, on the king's behalf, 'that they should swear to tell the truth on the customary articles which ought to be and usually are the subject of enquiry at the said sheriff's tourn', Thomas and the others had 'said they are free men and neither ought nor wished to take an oath on the bible except by the special order of the lord king'. So the said sheriff had gone away without holding the tourn.[36] The case was then adjourned for judgment. Any lingering doubts seem, however, to have been resolved by 1279 when twenty-six men were amerced in the Sussex eyre for refusing to take an oath in the sheriff's tourn at Lewes without the king's special command 'although the same sheriff has power to put free men on oath in his tourn for the preservation of the peace of the lord king'.[37] In both *Britton* and *Fleta* the sheriff's tourn and the view of frankpledge are noted as among exceptions to the general rule.[38] They also feature among the contexts in which the requirement of a specific royal authorisation is said to be waived in an undated early fourteenth-century note in BL MS. Egerton 2811, which

32 '. . . liberos homines istius hundredi jurare ad turnum suum sine precepto domini regis': JUST 1/238, m. 57.

33 JUST 1/538, mm. 12, 17d.

34 JUST 1/7, mm. 28d, 34d.

35 *Rex v. Thomas de Hotot et al.*: KB 27/12, m. 20d.

36 '. . . quod jurarent de veritate dicenda de articulis consuetis que debent et solent inquiri ad turnum vicecomitis predictum, ipsi Thomas et alii dixerunt quod sunt liberi homines nec debent nec voluerunt prestare sacramentum super librum nisi per speciale mandatum domini regis, propter quod predictus vicecomes recessit'.

37 '. . . cum idem vicecomes potestatem habeat ponere libere homines ad sacramentum in turno suo pro pace domini regis observanda': JUST 1/923, m. 7. Note, however, that in the Sussex eyre of 1288 the queen mother's bailiffs were again presented for putting free men on oath 'without the special order of the lord king' ('sine speciali precepto domini regis') at two lawdays: JUST 1/924, m. 53d.

38 *Britton*, I, ii, 2 (I, 9); *Fleta*, lib. 2, cap. 52 (II, 176–7).

also mentions the coroner's inquest and *ex officio* enquiries held by the escheator.[39]

In 1286 Gilbert of Pinchbeck and Richard son of William of Spalding brought a special action in the Common Bench based on this general rule and accusing the prior of Spalding of having breached both it and a prior prohibition.[40] His action was said to have been 'against the law and custom of the king's realm' but not against the Statute. A report of the case does, however, indicate that the Statute was mentioned in pleading by counsel for the plaintiffs. The prior justified his action on the grounds that he possessed the franchise of trying thieves taken with stolen goods (mainour) in his liberty and that a thief had been arrested and had stood trial at the suit of the victim and put himself on a jury. Gilbert and Richard had been told to take oaths to serve on that jury and had refused and had then been distrained for their contempt. The enrolment notes the judgment of the Common Bench that this, too, was a situation where a free man could be made to take an oath and serve on a jury if so chosen and that the court ordered the return of the animals taken in distraint. There is also evidence from registers of writs of this period to suggest that a prohibition of similar form to this was issued in at least one other case, for two registers have a prohibition writ addressed not to the prior of Spalding but to the bailiffs of the prior of the Hospitallers at 'M'.[41]

39 'Qe home seit tenu jurer saunz le comandement le rey en office de coroner, en tour de vesconte, en view de fraunk plegge a jour de lete, en office de eschetour le roy, en presence du roy ou de son seneschale ou en bref de justice': BL MS. Egerton 2811, fol. 91r.

40 *EELR*, II, 258–60 (1286.11).

41 '. . . *quod nemo distringatur ad corporale sacramentum prestandum sine precepto domini regis.* Rex ballivis prioris hospitalis sancti Johannis Jerlm' in Anglia de M. salutem. Monstraverunt nobis A. et B. et alii in brevi quod cum ipsi liberi homines sint et tenementa sua libere teneant vos ipsos distringitis ad corporale sacramentum prestandum sine precepto [fol. 208v] nostro contra legem et consuetudinem regni nostri. Et quia nolumus quod illis vel aliis in hujusmodi casibus injurietur vobis precipimus quod predictos A. etc. non distringetis ad hujusmodi sacramentum contra legem et consuetudinem regni coram vobis prestandum. Et districcionem si quam eis ea occasione feceritis sine dilacione relaxetis eidem. T. etc.': BL MS. Additional 32085, fols. 208r–v. There is a similar writ in BL MS. Harley 748, fol. 60r.

CONCLUSIONS

THE LEGAL AND SOCIAL CONTEXT OF THE LEGISLATION

One of the main purposes of this study has been to place the legislation of 1259–67 in its proper contemporary context. That has meant looking at the individual clauses within the broader context of the development of the English common law and the English legal system during the period prior to its enactment. It has also meant placing the legislation within its more specific context, that of the political events and developments of the years between 1258 and 1267.

The pioneering work of T.F.T. Plucknett on the legal and social context of the legislation of Edward I (which, for his purposes, was taken to include the Statute of Marlborough) was hampered by his exclusive reliance on the sources in print at the time he was writing *Legislation of Edward I*. This meant that he knew nothing of what was on the plea rolls of the king's courts after 1222 other than the cases copied into *Bracton's Note Book*. His acquaintance with the manuscript material for the reign of Edward I was limited to the selected King's Bench cases printed by Sayles and the reported cases printed in the Rolls Series Year Books edited by Horwood. This study has attempted to show what can be done by using a much wider range of unprinted as well as printed sources. Setting the legislation in its proper contemporary context has proved particularly important for understanding the significance of the legislation on suit of court.[1] As has been shown, this legislation needs to be located within the context of wider developments affecting the nature and importance of seignorial courts and transforming the nature of the lord–tenant relationship as well as of developments in the law relating to the obligation to perform suit of court prior to 1259. These indicate that suit of court was very much *sui generis* as an obligation and raised quite specific problems, very different from those raised by other kinds of tenant obligation. They also suggest that suit of court was important primarily as a symbolic issue

[1] Above, pp. 43–51. Contrast Plucknett's discussion of the same topic in chapter 3 of *Legislation of Edward I*.

for lords and tenants in 1259. Tracing the prior history and development of mesne process and the system of adjournments also proved to be an essential requirement for understanding the various clauses authorising changes in process and the adjustment of the system of adjournments made in this period to see what they were attempting to achieve, why they were necessary and how genuinely innovative they were.[2] Investigation demonstrated that requiring the guardians of land held in socage to account for their stewardship was not a novelty in 1259 but had long been a feature of Kent and London local custom and possibly of other areas too.[3] All that the legislation did was to turn this into the general, common law rule. Other parts of the legislation turned out on investigation merely to be codification of existing common law rules. This was clearly true of the legislation prohibiting the making of distraints outside a lord's fee or in the highway and of the various rules about distraints being moderate and proportionate and not being driven out of the county where they had been taken.[4] Clause 17 of the Provisions (chapter 21 of the Statute) also turned out to be misleading in its implication that it was providing authority for actions of replevin to be commenced without writ.[5] Any innovation it may have been making was in providing standing authorisation for the sheriff to release distresses taken within franchises where the bailiff of the franchise refused to act and when litigation was initiated by plaint. Investigation also revealed that a number of other problems tackled by the legislation were of relatively recent origin. These included the problems posed by charters of exemption from jury service;[6] the extension of penalties for the failure of villages to attend inquests to encompass failure to attend in full;[7] the penalisation of the sureties of clerics if they claimed benefit of clergy;[8] and the amercement of absent vouchees to warranty at the eyre if they were resident in the county.[9] Much the same appears to be true of attendance at the sheriff's tourn. There appears to have been a fairly concerted attempt in many counties to diminish or abolish the customary exemptions during the years prior to 1259.[10] The legislation on tourn attendance also needs to be seen against the background of an Exchequer judgment *c.* 1258 which had already confirmed the exemption of the heads of religious houses from the duty of attendance.[11] As far as they were concerned the legislation was merely giving greater publicity to a decision of principle recently made in a royal court. Investigation of the background to chapter 6 of the

[2] Above, pp. 69–75. [3] Above, pp. 66–9. [4] Above, pp. 94–5, 194.
[5] Above, pp. 96–8. [6] Above, pp. 75–6. [7] Above, pp. 81–2.
[8] Above, pp. 82–3. [9] Above, pp. 91–2. [10] Above, pp. 83–5.
[11] Above, pp. 84–5.

Statute of Marlborough has discovered that it was not, as has been previously suggested, a well thought-out response to a general problem of the evasion of wardship by tenants but an immediate (and in some respects ill-considered) response to a case then pending in the courts and a single earlier case brought to the attention of the king's council in part because it involved the king's chancellor, Walter de Merton.[12] I have done some work of a similar kind on a few of the Edwardian statutes or individual chapters or clauses in them,[13] but much still remains to be done before we can produce a satisfactory revision of Plucknett's pioneering work that is based on an adequate range of primary sources. This study has shown how important it is as a corrective to otherwise ill-informed conclusions about the significance of legislation and its effects.

THE POLITICAL AND ADMINISTRATIVE CONTEXT OF THE LEGISLATION

This book has also attempted to place not only the Provisions of Westminster as originally enacted in 1259 and revised and reissued in 1263 and 1264 but also their final revision and reissue in 1267 as the Statute of Marlborough within their immediate political and administrative context. The original Provisions of Westminster of 1259 were one of the most significant achievements of the baronial council which took power in the summer of 1258. They were also in part a specific response to the complaints of various groups of the king's subjects produced at the Oxford parliament (and known to us as the 'Petition of the Barons'),[14] and possibly to other local grievances collected by the four knights in each county.[15] They were thus distinctly not a 'normal' product of the king's governmental machinery. It is their non-royal origin that helps to explain why at least seven out of the twenty-four clauses of the Provisions of Westminster were drafted and enacted in response to the grievances of his subjects against the king, his justices or his local officials.[16] What is more striking and impressive about the legislation, though, is just how little it reflects the specifically magnate domination of the king's council in 1258–9. The largest element in the legislation, clauses 1–3 on suit of court, were of little obvious benefit to them since none of them owed suit to the court of their main lord, the king. The legislation was, however, potentially disadvantageous to all of them as holders of courts. The same is true of clauses 9 and 10 providing additional protection for tenants at

[12] Above, pp. 196–203. [13] Brand, *MCL*, pp. 233–44, 287–324.

[14] Above, pp. 20–4, 28–9, 34–5. [15] Above, pp. 24, 30, 35.

[16] Clauses 4, 5, 13 and 21–4: above, pp. 83–7, 87–90, 93–4, 81–2, 77–80, 90–3, 82–3. See also clause 8: above, pp. 75–6.

succession. These did not apply to the relationship of the magnates with their most important lord, the king,[17] but did apply to their own tenants' relationship with them. Even more obviously against their interest, and all the more surprising in the context of magnate domination of the council and royal weakness, are the four clauses (clauses 11, 16, 17 and 18) which favoured and protected the king and royal judicial monopolies as against lords and more particularly magnates.[18] The only parts of the legislation which do look at all favourable to the magnates are that part of clause 4 on attendance at the tourn which exempted them from attendance,[19] clause 19 allowing the use of imprisonment as the initial process in the action of account against landless bailiffs,[20] and clause 14 requiring seignorial consent for alienations in mortmain to the religious.[21] However, the magnates were only one of a number of groups exempted from attendance at the sheriff's tourn,[22] and clause 14 was of greater use to lesser lords who were least able to protect their own interests by vigorous self-help than to the magnates.[23] There is an obvious contrast in this repect between the Provisions of Westminster and Magna Carta. Magna Carta in all its different versions was primarily a concession to magnates and tenants-in-chief by the king and only to a lesser extent a concession by the king to his other subjects. Its form (as a charter of grant by the king to his subjects) specifically reflects that fact. It is only as an afterthought that clause 60 of Magna Carta provided that the king's concessions in respect of his tenants were also to apply to the tenants of other lords. The magnates are equally prominent in the groups whose interests seem to lie behind the composite text known as the Provisions of Merton. Clause 4 is specifically stated to have been enacted in response to a magnate request. It seems probable that clause 5 (stopping the accumulation of interest on debts during a minority) was also the product of pressure from magnates. It revived a clause which had been included in the original 1215 issue of Magna Carta but had been dropped from subsequent reissues. Although there is nothing in their wording to suggest this, clauses 6 and 7 (on wardship and marriage) may also have been enacted in response to requests for legislation on the part of lords since such legislation was very clearly in their interests. One of the two abortive clauses for legislative change (clause 11) also records a specifically magnate demand.

It looks, moreover, as though king and magnates were both keen to take credit for the Provisions. The tussle between them about claiming credit for reforms began as early as February 1259 when the king issued

[17] Above, pp. 190–1. [18] Above, pp. 94–5, 99, 98, 99–103.
[19] Above, pp. 83–7. [20] Above, pp. 65–6. [21] Above, pp. 57–62.
[22] Above, pp. 83–7. [23] Above, pp. 60–1.

a document giving his side of things, pointing out how he had long ago made various concessions but that it was only now that the magnates were beginning to make their own parallel ones.[24] The Provisions of Westminster as originally enacted made plain the role the magnates claimed to have played in the enacting of the legislation and even staked out for them an equal role in the publication of the legislation.[25] The magnate role in the legislative process was also spelled out in the various statutory writs drafted and issued in the immediate aftermath of the enactment of the Provisions.[26] These provided a continuing reminder to litigants acquiring such writs of the part they had played in producing the legislation from which they were now benefiting, a constant prompting for gratitude and support.

Henry III and his advisers were equally careful to claim credit for the Provisions when they reissued them in a revised form in 1263. There is no hint in the revised Provisions that they were anything other than new legislation and care was taken when redrafting the preamble to remove all references to the part the magnate members of the council had played in the making and publication of the legislation, insisting that the legislation had been issued of the king's own free will and that it was the king alone who was commanding obedience to the Provisions.[27] After the reissue there was a revision of the statutory writs based on the legislation to ensure they reflected the king's view of the legislative process and to claim for the king much greater credit for the making of the Provisions.[28] The 1264 reissue was evidently a hasty one. No attempt was made to revise the body of the text. This time, however, the preamble did acknowledge on its face that the text which followed was a reissue of earlier legislation and that the chief concern was to ensure that existing legislation hitherto poorly observed was better observed for the future.[29] The Statute of Marlborough marks a return to the earlier royal policy of deliberately ignoring the earlier legislation of which it was a revised reissue.[30] It appeared to claim that all the legislation was a studied response to the specific conditions of recent disorder. It ultimately succeeded in claiming for the king and his advisers in 1267 sole responsibility for the legislative text known to later generations as the Statute of Marlborough.

THE EVOLUTION OF THE FINAL TEXT OF THE LEGISLATION

This study has also looked in some detail at the process of drafting and amendment which lies behind the emergence of the final text of the

[24] Above, pp. 31–2. [25] Above, pp. 15–16. [26] Above, pp. 109–20.
[27] Above, pp. 145–6. [28] Above, pp. 169, 170–1, 172–3.
[29] Above, p. 163. [30] Above, p. 188.

revised reissue of the Provisions of Westminster as the Statute of Marlborough in 1267. This is not normally possible for thirteenth-century legislation. Something of the same can be done with Magna Carta, tracing the evolution of the final text of 1225 from the initial 1215 text and looking at the Articles of the Barons and other texts which lie behind the 1215 text.[31] We do also have at least a draft text of the Statute of Acton Burnel of 1283 with various amendments to the original draft text interlined in it.[32] Our discussion has indicated how some of the clauses included in the composite 'Petition of the Barons' of the summer of 1258 seem to have acted as the starting-points for the drafting of legislation, but only as starting-points. In general the drafters of the legislation did considerably more than simply turn those clauses of complaint into the corresponding remedial legislation and the final clauses reflect further consideration and discussion.[33] The clauses on suit of court and on amercements for default of the common summons, it has been seen, may have been suggested by the complaints made at a clerical council held at the same time.[34] It has also been suggested, though it cannot be proved, that some of the legislation may have arisen from the grievances collected locally by the four knights assigned to collect grievances or from complaints made to the baronial justiciar, Hugh Bigod.[35] Other evidence suggests a role for royal justices and other legal experts in suggesting as well as drafting legislation.[36] It seems likely that the clauses on the reform of legal procedure and possibly others are the product of their suggestions.

The various surviving documents deriving from the drafting process provide evidence of the process of elaboration and of the resolution of conflicting ideas that took place between the summer of 1258 and the autumn of 1259. Conflicting ideas about the proper basis for the obligation of suit of court and of exemption from attendance at the tourn are shown particularly clearly by these documents and indicate that the eventual legislation was not the product of a consensus but of a continuing clash of conflicting ideas.[37] The process of elaboration and generalisation is shown by the legislation about hereditary succession which started from a complaint relating only to the case of adult succession but came as a result of subsequent discussion to cover the case of heirs who had been in wardship to their lords as well;[38] by the way in which a complaint about the effect of jury exemptions on grand assizes led after discussion to legislation which allowed a more general overriding of such charters of

[31] Most are printed in *SSC* at pp. 285–304 and 336–51. [32] E 175/11, no. 4.
[33] Above, pp. 28–9, 34–5. [34] Above, pp. 49, 93.
[35] Above, pp. 30, 35. [36] Above, p. 30.
[37] Above, pp. 85–7. [38] Above, pp. 56–7.

exemption when this was required in the interests of justice;[39] by the way in which a complaint about the injustice of very specific circumstances leading to imposition of a *murdrum* fine led to more general legislation preventing the fine being imposed in respect of any kind of accidental death;[40] and by the way in which a specific complaint about the levying of the beaupleder fine in the eyre led to more general legislation prohibiting the fine being levied in all kinds of courts.[41]

It seems clear that it is the special circumstances of 1258–9 that explain why there survives so much documentation relating to the drafting process. What is rather less clear is whether the drafting process we can observe through this documentation is itself atypical or whether, if we had more surviving documentation from the preliminary drafting stage of other thirteenth-century legislation, we would be able to observe something not dissimilar. What is also a little unclear is just who the main participants in the drafting process were. Some of the evidence certainly points to the participation of members of the judiciary and other legal experts in the drafting process.[42] There is also some evidence to suggest that the magnate members of the council may have played some part in it.[43] But for the most part we remain in the dark. Sometimes we can see the different positions taken but not who was taking them. Often we can see the changes made in the draft legislation but do not know why the changes were made or what arguments were advanced before they were made.

For the reissues of 1263, 1264 and 1267 we have only the final product, those reissues themselves, and it is only from the changes that went in to each reissue and the contemporary political situation that we can deduce much about the factors that must have influenced the redrafting. It would not be wholly fanciful to see the hand of Henry III himself in the redrafting of the preamble to the reissues of 1263. If it is not his own work, it probably closely reflects his own view of his central significance in the process of the making, publication and enforcement of legislation. But there is little substantive change to the body of the legislation that reflects the fact that this is a 'royalist' reissue of the Provisions. Only the modification of the beaupleder clause to allow the continuation of fines fixed since 1230 obviously falls into that category.[44] It does, however, looks as though there was also some kind of organised lobbying by the major religious houses prior to this reissue. This is reflected not just in the dropping of the clause requiring the consent of the lord of whom land was held for alienations in mortmain to religious houses,[45] but also in the

[39] Above, pp. 75–6. [40] Above, p. 80. [41] Above, p. 90.
[42] Above, pp. 26–7, 41. [43] Above, pp. 25, 31, note 57. [44] Above, pp. 147–8.
[45] Above, pp. 146–7.

addition of a clause allowing the heads of religious houses new forms of action to recover damages for movables of their houses taken during the time of their predecessors and also for the recovery of lands taken from their houses during a vacancy.[46] It is, perhaps, the king's overall resumption of control that explains why this lobbying by religious houses was so successful. Other amendments and additions made to the legislation for this reissue seem to reflect the continuing input of the legal experts into the legislative process and the essentially uncontroversial nature of much of the reform. Raising the target number of adjournments in dower actions, reducing the number of stages in mesne process in personal actions and allowing jury trial by default after joinder of issue in personal actions were all simply intended to make the royal courts more efficient.[47] Even the new clause allowing the drafting of writs of entry outside the degrees was probably uncontroversial.[48] It revived an idea discussed in 1258–9 and probably dropped then owing to pressure of time or the difficulty in drafting a suitable writ form or writ forms rather than from any major objections in principle or obstruction. Much less care was taken for the reissue of 1264, which was simply a further reissue of the Provisions as revised and reissued in 1263. All the care, as we have seen, went into the new preamble and the new final clause on enforcement which envisaged this as primarily a local matter.[49]

It is unfortunate that we have no preliminary material from the drafting process that preceded the final reissue of the Provisions of Westminster as the Statute of Marlborough in 1267. It is none the less plain that the drafters of the Statute started work from a text of the Provisions as they had been reissued in 1263 and decided this time to make their additions not in the body and at the end of the text but at the very beginning.[50] This helps to disguise just how much of the legislation was taken (with only minor verbal changes) from the earlier legislation. As with the 1263 reissue, but with much less reason, there is also no open avowal in the preamble that any of what follows is a reissue of earlier legislation. It seems plain that the drafters decided that there needed to be a grand restatement about the place of the king's courts and royal justice in the English polity and excluding vengeance and the unjustified use of distraint at the very beginning of the Statute, even if this did not entirely fit with the more detailed prescriptions and less high-flown language of the remainder of the Statute.[51] In purely legal terms, chapters 1–4 were probably quite unnecessary, but the Statute was evidently seen as providing a good opportunity for a restatement and reinforcement of traditional royal ideology. We have

[46] Above, pp. 149–50. [47] Above, pp. 148–9. [48] Above, pp. 151–60.
[49] Above, pp. 162–4. [50] Above, p. 188. [51] Above, pp. 192–4.

already noted the probable origins of the new chapter 6 in recent and pending litigation.[52] Chapter 7 (allowing judgment by default in the action of wardship) attests to the continued interest in procedural reform and a continued desire to experiment with ways of doing this that also provided adequate safeguards against abuse.[53] Two of the amendments were clearly in the interests of the crown. However, only the amendment of the clause relating to attendance at inquests into crown pleas to exclude the coroner's inquest into homicides from its scope clearly claws back for the crown a minor source of revenue it had lost.[54] The addition specifically reserving the crown's right of primer seisin at the succession of tenants-in-chief seems merely to have made specific something already tacitly understood.[55] The most surprising of the amendments was that made to chapter 9, apparently intended to allow *pro omni servicio* clauses in charters of enfeoffment to be pleaded in bar of all claims to service beyond that specified in the charter.[56] This took up an idea first mentioned in 1258–9 in respect of demands for suit of court only and dropped in the course of drafting, now reviving it and extending it to other services as well.[57]

ENFORCEMENT AND USE OF THE LEGISLATION

The other main concern of this study has been with the enforcement of the Provisions of Westminster and Statute of Marlborough between 1259 and 1307. Here, too, Plucknett was the pioneer. His *Legislation of Edward I* also provides an overall view of the ways in which Edwardian legislation (including the Statute of Marlborough) was subsequently used and interpreted. Again, however, Plucknett's exclusive reliance on printed sources was a major handicap. For the reign of Edward I, the only material available to him was the selected enrolments from the King's Bench plea rolls printed by Sayles and the law reports printed by Horwood in the Rolls Series edition of the Year Books of Edward I. It is thus hardly surprising that often his main interest seems to be in the later interpretation of the legislation by the courts in the reigns of Edward II and Edward III for which there existed Selden Society editions and the less satisfactory Maynard edition and (for the early years of the reign of Edward III) the Rolls Series edition by Horwood and Pike. This study has been largely confined to the period down to 1307 but it is based on a thorough reading of the surviving plea rolls of the king's courts (Common Bench, King's Bench, eyre, assizes), of the printed and unprinted records of the Chancery and

[52] Above, pp. 196–203. [53] Above, pp. 203–4. [54] Above, p. 191.
[55] Above, pp. 190–1. [56] Above, pp. 189–90. [57] Above, p. 36.

the Exchequer, and of unprinted as well as printed reports of cases heard in the king's courts for this period.

Enforcement and use between 1259 and 1267

Even though the surviving evidence is somewhat patchy, it is possible to demonstrate conclusively the effectiveness of the Provisions of Westminster during at least part of the period between 1259 and 1267. During the initial period of their operation (between the time of the promulgation of the first version of the Provisions in October 1259 and the first revised reissue of the Provisions in January 1263) the tangled political history of the period is to some extent mirrored in the evidence for enforcement which the surviving legal records of the period provide. The initial period, when the baronial council was still in firm control of the governmental apparatus, saw the drafting of a number of new writs to give effect to the new legislation. Three forms of writ based on the Provisions were made available to complainants within six months of their enactment. Writs of *contra formam feoffamenti* remained available throughout 1260 and for at least part of 1261 but seem to have ceased to be available not long after Walter of Merton took over the Chancery in the summer of 1261, perhaps because the very wording of the writ made it objectionable to the king and his royalist chancellor.[58] Writs to ensure exemption from attendance at the tourn for those whom the legislation had freed from that requirement, by contrast, continued to be issued into 1262, though the writs issued after late 1261 deliberately ceased to mention the Provisions as the authority for the exemption they were intended to enforce.[59] At least two different kinds of writ of *monstravit de compoto*, one for initiating litigation in the London city courts and the other initiating litigation in the Common Bench, were also issued in 1260–1.[60] Enforcement of the legislation on beaupleder fines and on attendance at the tourn by means of plaints is also a phenomenon found only in 1260 and 1261.[61] However, the citation and enforcement of various different clauses of the legislation in the course of civil proceedings not themselves specifically based on the legislation can be found in 1260, 1261 and 1262 and as late as 1262 an award of damages was justified by specific reference to the Provisions.[62] Some clauses of the legislation may have been more objectionable to the king than others. An amercement imposed by virtue of clause 8 of the Provisions (which effectively challenged the king's right to grant unqualified exemptions from jury service) was being quashed as early as May

58 Above, pp. 109–11. 59 Above, pp. 115–17. 60 Above, pp. 117–19.
61 Above, pp. 120–2. 62 Above, pp. 123–6.

1261.[63] There seems to be no readily discernible pattern to the courts' treatment of clause 22 limiting the imposition of *murdrum* fines to felonious homicides.[64] The legislation was ignored in at least two eyres, those held in Berkshire in February and March of 1261 and in Sussex late in 1262, although both groups of justices are known to have observed the same legislation in other counties they visited, even when not specifically reminded of it by the counties themselves. The Sussex eyre of 1262 is, moreover, also the eyre in which the justices seem to have deliberately ignored clause 21 (on the amercement of villages who did not attend inquests fully) and the same group of justices did the same thing in its next eyre in Surrey.[65] This may suggest that this group of justices had ceased by late 1262 to feel themselves bound by the Provisions. The legislation clearly also had some impact on the mesne process ordered by the courts in the new statutory actions and in *quare impedit* even if it was certainly not followed in detail in every case.[66] The length of adjournments in many, if not all, actions of dower *unde nichil habet* and actions relating to vacant churches was also clearly shortened by the legislation, even if its prescriptions were not followed quite to the letter.[67] In neither case is there any real evidence to suggest a falling-off in compliance over time.

The evidence for the second period of operation of the Provisions (between the first royalist revised reissue of the Provisions in January 1263 and the final revised reissue of the Provisions as the Statute of Marlborough in 1267) is much more fragmentary. For a significant part of this period the courts were not in operation and the surviving record evidence is seriously deficient. Most of the evidence for the enforcement of the legislation comes from 1263 although there is at least some evidence to suggest it was being applied during the succeeding period as well. The legislation on suit of court was enforced in 1263 both through a specially drafted writ and through two writs of *contra formam feoffamenti*, of which only procedural stages survive, but there is no further evidence for the issuing of such writs until after the reissuing of the Provisions as the Statute of Marlborough in 1267.[68] From 1263 there is also evidence from the Exchequer of writs of prohibition being issued citing the legislation on exemptions from attendance at the tourn. Similar prohibitions were issued there in 1264 and in 1265 (both before and after the battle of Evesham) though not thereafter.[69] There are no known examples of litigation based on the writ of *monstravit de compoto* during this period but the Exchequer records do show the issuing in 1263 of a writ based on

[63] Above, pp. 127–8. [64] Above, pp. 128–32.
[65] Above, pp. 132–3. [66] Above, pp. 134–6.
[67] Above, pp. 136–9. [68] Above, pp. 168–9. [69] Above, pp. 170–2.

the same clause of the legislation allowing the imprisonment of landless bailiffs who absconded before rendering their account but authorising this as part of the mesne process rather than the initial process of an action of account.[70] Litigants can also be found during 1263 taking advantage of the additional clause authorising the issuing of a writ for the head of a religious house to recover land of which his predecessor had been seised at the time of his death, and (in the 1263 Rutland eyre) of the clause authorising the drafting and issuing of writs of entry in the *post*.[71] Another writ of entry in the *post* used in litigation in 1267 came under legal challenge as not being properly authorised, but it is unclear whether or not this was also a challenge to the validity of the Provisions themselves.[72] The Provisions were also applied and cited in 1263 in pre-existing forms of action, as authorising the awarding of damages against lords in the assize of mort d'ancestor and as imposing special rules about entitlement to suit of court in the lord's action of customs and services.[73] Damages were still being awarded against lords in the assize in November 1267 on the eve of the enactment of the Statute of Marlborough.[74] The repealed legislation on mortmain alienations requiring the consent of the lord of whom land was held was also cited in 1264 shortly before the Montfortian reissue and as though the legislation was still in force.[75] There was also a partial, but not total, compliance with the legislation during 1263 and again in 1266–7 both in respect of changes in mesne process and in terms of length of adjournments in action of dower and relating to vacant churches.[76] Two other pieces of information about the enforcement of the legislation during this period are more difficult to evaluate. Prohibitions against beaupleder fines were issued during 1265 but were based on Magna Carta or without any specific basis.[77] There is also evidence to indicate that at some unknown date between 1263 and 1266 Chancery drafted a writ to give force to the rule laid down by clause 2 of the Provisions against lords demanding more than one suit from a divided tenement.[78] Both point in their different ways to further enforcement of the Provisions during this period.

Enforcement and use between 1267 and 1307

There could be no doubt after 1267 that the Statute of Marlborough was a valid statute and accepted as such by all the king's subjects and all the king's courts. What now becomes interesting is to see how much the

[70] Above, pp. 172–3. [71] Above, pp. 182–3, 181. [72] Above, pp. 181–2.
[73] Above, pp. 174–5. [74] Above, p. 174. [75] Above, pp. 183–4.
[76] Above, pp. 176–8. [77] Above, p. 173. [78] Above, pp. 178–9.

legislation is used and cited in practice and also how the courts dealt with the various problems of interpretation the legislation posed.

Remedies specifically citing their statutory basis

The clauses about suit of court which had become chapter 9 of the Statute of Marlborough remained the longest and most detailed single element in the legislation. They provide an interesting contrast in effectiveness between that part of the chapter which authorised a lord's action to enforce suit of court and the tenant's action to challenge the lord's distraint for suit of court (*contra formam feoffamenti*). The former remained a paper creation, for which even the writ to commence litigation was never drafted.[79] The latter had been drafted in 1260 and remained in regular, but not frequent, use between 1267 and 1307, with some ninety-five pleaded cases or an average of about three a year.[80] The overwhelming majority of these cases were heard in the Common Bench and a quite disproportionate number came from Yorkshire.[81] It cannot, however, be said that the statutory action was entirely a success, if the object of the drafters was to ensure that it became the sole mechanism for determining questions of entitlement to suit of court raised by seignorial distraints. For a variety of reasons tenants more often preferred to litigate about this in the common law action of replevin and it was not until 1305 that they even gained the choice of invoking the statutory rules about the obligation to perform suit in the common law action.[82] Among the other defects in the drafting of the legislation raised by the cases, and only partly catered for by the continuing availability of replevin to challenge distraints made for suit of court, was its failure to cater for the common situation where the person distrained was a sub-tenant of the person from whom suit was being claimed (the courts eventually decided that neither tenant nor sub-tenant could under these circumstances bring *contra formam feoffamenti*) and its unrealistic assumption that a lord might be able to base his claim to suit on a specific provision in the tenant's charter of feoffment when it provided no mechanism to compel the tenant to produce that charter in court.[83] The courts sometimes proved cavalier in their interpretation of the legislation. Throughout the period under review they refused to give any special status to charters granting land for a fixed service *pro omni servicio* in this action, regularly holding that the tenant's entitlement to be free of suit was voided by the lord's subsequent seisin of that suit. The one contrary example was in an action initiated by

79 Above, pp. 251–2. 80 Above, p. 218 and appendix to chapter 8 at pp. 242–9.
81 Above, pp. 218, 240. 82 Above, pp. 219–23, 252–62.
83 Above, pp. 220–1, 230–1.

a special writ in 1288 and later litigants who tried to cite this precedent had no success when they attempted to do so.[84] The specific mesne process authorised for this action was commonly ignored in practice as were the provisions authorising the awarding of judgment by default. In the latter case we know that it was up to the litigant to claim judgment by default and the court would not award it if he failed to do so.[85] Even the originating process authorised by the Statute (immediate attachment) was abandoned in the early 1270s in favour of attachment only after a prior, disregarded prohibition or, in a smaller number of cases, in favour of an originating summons. This change must have been made by Chancery, which issued original writs, but the surviving evidence suggests that it was not challenged in or by the courts.[86] Chancery also took the initiative in 1277 in changing the date limitation cited in *contra formam feoffamenti* so as to allow lords to justify distraint for suit if they could show seisin since 1242 rather than since 1230, under the mistaken impression that this was a limitation date intended to be changed by chapter 39 of the Statute of Westminster I. Here, however, a successful later challenge to the original writ in the case of *Seyville v. prior of Pontefract* did lead in 1303 to a reversion to the date specified in the legislation.[87] Nothing specific was said in the legislation about the creation of actions to give effect to what had been clause 2 of the original Provisions (also part of chapter 9 of the Statute) dealing with the consequences of the division of a tenement between coheirs or between feoffees or between a combination of the two for the obligation to perform suit of court. The first writs based on the legislation for the use of tenants against a lord distraining for more than one suit seem to have been drafted prior to 1267, although the first direct evidence for such an action comes from 1271.[88] The earliest writs based on the legislation for the eldest coheir to use against younger coheirs when seeking a contribution to the performance of suit of court is later (from 1279–80) and the variant for the use of a feoffee against his fellow feoffees comes from around the same date.[89] There is no evidence from this period for the drafting of a writ for the younger coheirs to use against a lord distraining them for the suit owed by the eldest coheir.[90] None of these actions seems ever to have been in common use but the evidence from this period does seem to indicate that Chancery and the courts found no difficulty in extending the statutory rules which only covered the division of tenements which owed suit to seignorial courts to cover communal courts (hundred and county courts) as well.[91]

[84] Above, pp. 234–8. [85] Above, pp. 217–18. [86] Above, pp. 213–14.
[87] Above, pp. 208–12. [88] Above, pp. 263–8. [89] Above, pp. 268–71.
[90] Above, p. 271. [91] Above, pp. 267–8.

Writs giving effect to the legislation about the exemption of various status groups as well as non-resident free men from attendance at the tourn clearly went on being issued after 1267 by both Exchequer and Chancery, but the latter at least are normally impossible to trace in the surviving records since they were not in general enrolled and did not give rise to litigation.[92] Chancery seems to have had no difficulty in extending this legislation well beyond its specific terms by issuing writs to cover attendance at the corresponding franchisal institution, the view of frankpledge, and these did give rise to occasional pleaded cases in the Common Bench.[93] There is no evidence that litigants ever challenged this extension of the legislation. The legislation on beaupleder fines was also enforced partly through prohibitions enrolled in the Exchequer and partly through writs issued by Chancery which could lead to litigation in the Common Bench (from at least 1277 onwards). The evidence seems to indicate, however, that they remained comparatively infrequent and gave rise to only a single pleaded case.[94]

The two forms of writ of *monstravit de compoto*, initiating ordinary actions of account in London and in the Common Bench but with a particularly stringent initial process, both continued in use after 1267.[95] The post-1267 evidence shows that there was a special procedure in Chancery for obtaining the writ which required the plaintiff to affirm on oath the requirements for the issuing of the writ before Chancery would issue it.[96] The identities of those using such writs prior to 1280 also suggest, however, that the writ was only available in practice during that period as a matter of special favour to prominent magnates and royal servants.[97] It seems to have become more widely available only during the period after 1280. It was fairly clear that the writ authorised the use of arrest and imprisonment as the first stage of process but neither the courts nor Chancery seem to have reached any settled conclusion as to whether or not the sheriff could or should accept mainprise after the initial arrest and the wording of the legislation offered no particular guidance on this point.[98] The legislation authorised the use of the writ only against those sued for an account as bailiffs but Chancery and the courts seem to have found no difficulty about issuing and upholding writs brought against men sued as receivers from 1277 onwards. There was good reason for them to do so since those being sued as receivers would earlier simply have been sued as bailiffs. The change was only a change of nomenclature and not an expansion of the remedy.[99] An important development of the

[92] Above, pp. 286–8. [93] Above, pp. 288–93. [94] Above, pp. 295–7.
[95] Above, p. 313. [96] Above, pp. 313–14. [97] Above, p. 314.
[98] Above, pp. 318–20. [99] Above, pp. 322–3.

second half of the reign was the creation of an action of deception (in 1294) for bailiffs and receivers to use against lords who used *monstravit de compoto* against them when they did possess lands and so should only have been sued in the ordinary action of account.[100] It was also possible for a period between 1303 and 1305 (and again under Edward II) for the bailiff or receiver to except to the writ in the action of *monstravit de compoto* itself on the grounds of his posession of lands and tenements and, if successful, drive his lord to bring the ordinary action of account instead.[101] Both actions raised difficult questions about the interpretation of the legislation which vexed the courts down to the end of the reign and beyond.[102] Was it necessary for the bailiff or receiver to be entirely landless before the lord could use this remedy or could he use it if the bailiff or receiver had merely a small quantity of land against which distraint was likely to be ineffective as a means of securing his attendance in court? Did the lands have to be in the same county as that where the account was being claimed or was the possession of land anywhere in the country enough to bar the action?

All these were writs specifically based on the legislation and first issued prior to 1267. Rather surprisingly there are also at least two forms of action of that same type (specifically based on the legislation) that are based on clauses included in the original legislation of 1259 which were also included in the Statute of Marlborough and that are first found only some years after 1267. The first of these (an action of trespass alleging distraint either in the highway or outside the defendant's fee) is first found (in King's Bench and the Common Bench) in 1271.[103] The pleading in the relatively small number of recorded Common Bench cases indicates that rules banning distraint in the highway or outside the fee were both qualified rather than absolute rules, to which there were a number of exceptions. Since both rules were also enforced in other ways and had existed before the statutory confrmation of them the discussion and decisions on these points in the statutory actions probably reflect existing and well-recognised exceptions to the rules rather than innovatory decisions that helped create a new jurisprudence in this area.[104] The second of these actions is the action of account against guardians in socage.[105] This seems to have come into existence only around 1278. There is evidence to suggest that this existed in both a returnable and a non-returnable form: the first initiating litigation in the Common Bench or the eyre, the second initiating litigation in the county court. This may mean that the forty-six Common Bench and eyre cases are only the tip of a much

[100] Above, pp. 323–33. [101] Above, pp. 327–8. [102] Above, pp. 329–32.
[103] Above, pp. 369–70. [104] Above, pp. 372–5. [105] Above, p. 348.

larger iceberg, since there is no means of knowing how many such cases may have been heard and determined in county courts.[106] The lands for which an account was claimed in the cases that did reach the king's courts could be worth as much as a hundred pounds a year and the period for which accounting was sought went back in a number of cases to before 1267 and in at least one case to before 1259. In four cases the period for which an account was sought was as long as nineteen years and the average period was eleven years; the average delay in initiating litigation claiming an account was ten years (and the maximum was as much as twenty-six).[107] The main points of legal interest concerned who were proper parties to such litigation. If a husband and wife held a wardship in right of the wife she needed to be joined, if still alive, but action still lay against her widower after her death and he had to answer alone without assistance from her executors. No action lay against the bailiff or lessee of the socage guardian of right even though he or she was in the best position to account for the actual profits of the land, because the bailiff or lessee would have paid over the value of the land to the guardian of right and the chief purpose of the action was to ensure this value was then paid over to the heir. Despite the wording of the Statute and the objections of defendants the courts did allow the use of the action from at least 1285 onwards against a lord who wrongfully took the wardship of land where he was not entitled to it.[108]

Even more surprising is evidence for the creation and occasional use after 1267 of a writ based on clause 14 of the original Provisions of Westminster requiring the consent of the lord of whom land was held for any alienation in mortmain to the religious. This clause had been dropped from the reissue of 1263 and not reinstated for the final revised reissue of the Provisions as the Statute of Marlborough in 1267. There were at least three such actions prior to the enactment of the Statute of Mortmain in 1279.[109] One in 1277 specifically claimed to be based on a clause in the Statute of Marlborough. A second in 1279 recited the rule but did not explain its status. A third, also in 1279, asserted a statutory origin for the rule but did not specify the relevant statute. The defendant's objections to this writ may well have given rise to the discussion that led on to the enactment of the Statute of Mortmain in November 1279. Even after the enactment of this Statute, with its provisions for forfeiture for alienations in mortmain and the introduction shortly afterwards of a scheme for licensing such alienations, the occasional litigant continued to get writs from the king's Chancery to seek damages for breach of a

[106] Above, pp. 348–50.
[107] Above, pp. 352–5.
[108] Above, pp. 356–60.
[109] Above, pp. 277–80.

statutory rule purportedly requiring the consent of the lord of the fee (or of the lord of the fee and of the king) for an alienation into mortmain. The writ seems to have ceased to be available only when a defendant in 1291 objected to the form of the writ as unwarranted by conciliar consent.[110]

Remedies authorised by Statute but not citing the Statute

Other writs that were specifically authorised by the legislation bore no marks on their face that this was the case. There is nothing at all in the various standard forms of writs of entry in the *post* to show that they had been issued only as a result of the statutory authorisation offered by one of the additional clauses in the revised reissue of 1263 that was repeated as chapter 29 of the Statute of Marlborough. This provision was perhaps that which had the greatest effect, simply in terms of the number of writs issued under its provisions, of all the clauses of the legislation. Within five years of 1267 it is possible to find examples of every type of writ of entry in the *post*.[111] Their introduction appears, moreover, to have had a dramatic effect in reducing the number of litigants compelled to bring writs of right in order to bring their claims within a form of action available in the king's court.[112] By contrast, the new remedies for ecclesiastical tenants authorised by the additional clause of 1263 that became chapter 28 of the Statute remained little used. Only one example of the writ of trespass authorised by the Statute has been found prior to 1307, though there may be others lurking unnoticed in the rolls, and the factual situation lying behind it seems quite different from that envisaged by the legislation.[113] The land actions were used a little more often but only in a handful of cases.[114] Only a single example has been found of an action of waste against a lessee apparently based on the Statute but not citing it before the provisions of the Statute of Marlborough were effectively superseded by the provisions of the Statute of Gloucester. There are, however, also three actions of waste against tenants for life and by curtesy pre-1278 that do purport to be based on statute and must refer to the Statute of Marlborough as extended by analogy, since neither this Statute nor any other directly authorised their issue.[115]

Application of the legislation in common law actions

The legislation was also commonly invoked and applied in pre-existing common law actions. It was this legislation that was the warrant for the awarding of damages against lords in the assize of mort d'ancestor

[110] Above, pp. 280–1. [111] Above, pp. 336–7. [112] Above, pp. 337–9.
[113] Above, pp. 339–41. [114] Above, pp. 343–5. [115] Above, pp. 345–6.

down to 1278 when the Statute of Gloucester effectively superseded its provisions by allowing the recovery of damages against all types of defendants. Between 1267 and 1278 the courts followed the precedent created prior to 1267 of allowing the recovery of damages against lords not just in the two situations envisaged by the legislation (where the lord held on to the land after taking primer seisin and after the ending of a wardship) but also in a third situation (where a lord usurped a wardship) that was not envisaged by the legislation but where the awarding of damages seemed equally merited.[116] Interestingly, this extension of the Statute's provisions preceded, but was closely related to, the later decision to extend the coverage of the action of account for socage wardships to cover similar usurpations.[117] No new actions were created to give effect to chapter 6 of the Statute of Marlborough; indeed the second part of the chapter specifically envisaged that its provisions would be applied in the existing action of wardship. It seems to have been the first part of the chapter which was the more commonly invoked in litigation, both in actions of wardship initiated by lords and in assizes of novel disseisin initiated by their tenants. The cases indicate that the type of arrangement mentioned by the Statute was often, perhaps normally, intended not to defraud lords of their rights of wardship but to facilitate inter-familial agreements about the settlement of property at marriage. That such settlements often granted rights not just to the heir but also to his future wife created real difficulties for the courts in interpreting the provisions of the Statute. Even in the simpler type of arrangement envisaged by the Statute it was a real defect in its drafting that it did not make plain whom the lord should sue.[118] The smaller number of cases where the second part of the chapter was invoked raised fewer problems of interpretation, but they also demonstrate that defrauding the lord of his wardship might well not be the the main goal of those making 'feigned feoffments'.[119]

Certain parts of the legislation were invoked in common law actions even where there already existed a statutory action to enforce the statutory rules. The legislation on exemptions from attendance at the sheriff's tourn (and, by extension, at view of frankpledge) was invoked by way of defence against claims for acquittal made by those distrained against their mesne lords in actions of mesne and fin fet and also as an answer to avowries made in actions of replevin.[120] The legislation on beaupleder fines was also invoked and applied in actions of replevin.[121] The legislation extending the availability of the actions available to ecclesiastics was also cited (by way of analogy) in actions of detinue and annual rent.[122] It seems more

[116] Above, pp. 271–2. [117] Above, pp. 359–60. [118] Above, pp. 272–5.
[119] Above, pp. 275–7. [120] Above, pp. 293–5. [121] Above, pp. 300–1.
[122] Above, pp. 341–3.

dubious, however, whether the plaintiff was specifically invoking the Statute in an action of covenant when he asserted the existence of a legal rule requiring a lessee to have written permission to commit waste since this was probably also the general older rule.[123] Complaints in replevin pleas of distraints made in the highway and pleas made by plaintiffs in answer to avowries alleging that distraints had been made outside the lord's fee never cite the Statute as the basis for asserting that such distraints were wrong and seem likewise to have relied on existing pre-statutory norms against such distraints.[124] It was only in the early fourteenth century (as a result of *Auney's case*) that the Common Bench decided that it was permissible for a tenant to invoke the statutory rules about the obligation to suit of court in the common law action of replevin. A year or so earlier the same court had also decided that tenants could invoke the protection of the statutory rule (from chapter 9) on *pro omni servicio* charters barring any claim to services in excess of those specified in the charter in replevin cases irrespective of whether or not the lord had been seised of those additional services after the making of the charter.[125]

Enforcement through plaints and presentments

Various clauses of the legislation were enforced through presentments (mainly at the eyre) and through plaints. The clause on beaupleder fines, which was also enforced through specific prohibitions and in common law actions, was enforced in both these ways as well.[126] The chapters confirming the existing common law rule against excessive distraints and condemning resistance to the execution of judgments were enforced through presentments made in response to specific articles of the eyre; the clause prohibiting the requirement to warrant essoins on oath through presentments made in answer to a more general article of the eyre.[127] Presentments also continued to enforce the older rules prohibiting compulsion to answer for a free tenement without royal authorisation or against free men to take an oath (to serve on a jury).[128]

Observance of the legislation on changes in process

The evidence of the plea rolls suggests that in general the prescriptions of the legislation requiring significantly briefer adjournments to be made in actions of dower *unde nichil habet* were observed and that this meant that such litigation passed through the legal system at twice the speed of most other litigation.[129] It is less easy to be confident about the success of the legislative requirement of briefer adjournments in litigation

[123] Above, pp. 346–7. [124] Above, pp. 376–7. [125] Above, pp. 255–6, 259–62.
[126] Above, pp. 297–9. [127] Above, pp. 366–7, 368–9, 380–1.
[128] Above, pp. 382–3, 385. [129] Above, pp. 302–4.

relating to vacant churches. Many cases of darrein presentment and *quare impedit* did pass through the system at the required speed. Many others did not. There is no way of being certain that all the latter were cases relating to churches no longer vacant.[130] With minor exceptions, the prescriptions of the legislation about the abbreviation of mesne process were also complied with.[131] The authorisation of judgment by default in actions of *quare impedit* seems also to have been a success and was even extended by judicial interpretation from 1292 to cover continued default after appearance as well as before it. One problem not catered for by the legislation was continued default by a defendant who had no lands or chattels in the relevant county to distrain. The courts adopted a number of different ways of dealing with this.[132] The story was a very different one in the case of the action of wardship. It is possible to find judgments by default in this action and, rather more commonly, the preliminary stages to awarding judgment by default. The evidence suggests, however, that renewed use of the grand distress without any judgment by default remained much the more common procedure.[133] The plea roll evidence shows the successsful application of the legislative rules allowing jury trial to proceed and judgment to be given in the absence of a contumacious defendant.[134] The surviving evidence has less to tell about the application of the legislation allowing the overriding of charters of exemption from jury service, though it is known that this continued. The courts continued, however, to have problems in the smaller counties in producing the necessary numbers of eligible and suitable knights for grand assizes and had to adopt various *ad hoc* solutions for this problem.[135]

Fines and amercements in criminal and civil pleas

For the most part the legislation restricting the imposition of *murdrum* fines to cases of felonious homicide worked after 1267, with the solitary exception of a single case in the 1279 Sussex eyre where such a fine was imposed for an accidental and non-felonious death.[136] The evidence indicates, however, that this made very little practical difference. Most of the communities who were liable for *murdrum* fines continued to have to pay them and there is every reason to suppose that the legislation made no difference to the amount that they paid.[137] The amended legislation about the penalisation of villages for not attending inquests 'fully', which allowed them to continue being penalised for not attending coroner's inquests into homicides 'fully', seems in effect to have allowed the

[130] Above, pp. 304–6. [131] Above, pp. 306–7. [132] Above, pp. 307–9.
[133] Above, pp. 309–11. [134] Above, p. 312. [135] Above, pp. 333–4.
[136] Above, pp. 282–4. [137] Above, pp. 284–5.

continuation of the levying of these fines.[138] However, the two relatively recent but vexing practices of amercing the sureties of criminous clerks who appeared but then pleaded benefit of clergy and amercing absent warrantors in the eyre if they were resident in the county both disappeared.[139] The clause restricting those with power to amerce for default of the common summons seems also to have been generally observed.[140]

THE BEGINNINGS OF LARGE-SCALE LEGISLATION

The first half of the thirteenth century was not, in general, a period of large-scale legislative reform of the common law. With the one obvious exception of Magna Carta, almost all the legislation enacted was on a small scale and was generally concerned with no more than a single topic. The one other apparent exception to this, the Provisions of Merton of 1236, consists in its 'standard' text of eleven clauses.[141] Of these, two clauses (9 and 11) do no more than record abortive discussions about proposed legislation. Only the first five of the remaining nine clauses represent legislation actually enacted at Merton in January 1236. The other clauses all come from legislation enacted on other occasions. Thus the 'standard' text of the Provisions of Merton is a composite of different pieces of legislation conflated with each other only in later collections of statutes.[142] The Jewish legislation of 1253 also consists of eleven clauses. It really is a single piece of legislation. It is, however, for the most part solely concerned with regulating the conduct of members of the Jewish community in England and possessed little or no relevance to the wider world of the king's subjects and the king's common law courts.[143] The Provisions of Westminster of 1259 and the various reissues of those Provisions culminating in the Statute of Marlborough of 1267 thus marked a significant break with recent legislative tradition. They effectively created the idea of large-scale legislative reform and acted as a curtain-raiser for the large-scale legislative activity associated with the reign of Edward I. They were also pioneering pieces of legislation in other respects. Clauses 1–3 of the Provisions (chapter 9 of the Statute) represent the first attempt to take a particular area of the law (suit of court to seignorial courts) and create a network of rules to determine the existence of obligation and what was to happen to it on the division of a tenement, and also

138 Above, p. 285.
139 Above, pp. 285, 334.
140 Above, pp. 334–5.
141 *SR*, I, 1–4.
142 The origins and dates of the various clauses are discussed by G.D.G. Hall in footnote 7 to p. ciii of his introduction to *Early Registers*.
143 *CR 1251–1253*, pp. 312–13.

to create a new action to allow tenants to enforce the new rules against their lords, employing an improved and accelerated version of the existing procedures for this type of action, abbreviating the normal mesne process and allowing judgment by default. There was also an attempt to create a matching action for lords, though this action was still-born and never used in practice. The Provisions and the Statute seem also to have been pioneering legislation in at least one other respect. They seem to have been the first legislation deliberately to alter existing procedures in the king's courts: authorising the giving of shorter adjournments in certain types of litigation (dower and actions about vacant benefices); abbreviating process and introducing judgment by default in *quare impedit*; introducing judgment by default in the action of wardship.

The end result of the co-operative efforts of barons, justices and the king in the legislative process between 1259 and 1267 was to produce genuinely innovative legislation and to create an impressive model of large-scale legislative improvement in the common law. This clearly influenced Edward I and his advisers when they began their programme of legislation in 1275. But the legislation of 1259–67 is worth studying in its own right, not just for its influence on the Edwardian programme of legislation. The importance of its individual clauses varied, as did the skill with which they were drafted, but the legislation as a whole made a significant and lasting contribution to the continuing development of the medieval common law.

Appendixes

Appendix I

THE PROVISIONS OF WESTMINSTER OF 1259

Sources

a) E 164/2 (Red Book of the Exchequer), fols. 181r–182r (numbered in modern pencil fols. 284r–285r but the original foliation has been followed here): here taken as the main text.

b) C 54/75 (Close Roll, 44 Henry III), m. 17d: printed in *Close Rolls, 1259–61*, pp. 146–61; *SR*, 1, 8–11; *SSC*, pp. 390–4. Re-examined for this text and significant differences from the Red Book noted in the footnotes.

c) Worcester Dean and Chapter Muniments, A.2, fols. 163r–168r: printed in *Registrum Prioratus Beate Marie Wigorniensis*, ed. W.H. Hale (Camden Society original series, vol. 91, 1865), pp. 163a–168a: significant differences from the Red Book are noted in the footnotes.

Appendix I

TEXT

PREAMBLE

Anno ab incarnacione Domini millesimo ducentesimo quinquagesimo nono, regni autem regis Henrici filii regis Johannis quadragesimo tercio, convenientibus apud Westm' in quindena sancti Michaelis ipso domino rege et magnatibus suis, de comuni consilio et consensu dictorum regis et magnatum facte sunt provisiones subscripte <et>[1] per ipsos regem et magnates[2] puplicate in hunc modum.

CLAUSE I

De sectis faciendis ad curias magnatum et aliorum dominorum ipsarum curiarum provisum est et concorditer statutum quod nullus, qui per cartam feofatus est, distringatur <ad sectam de cetero>[3] faciendam ad curiam domini sui, nisi per formam carte sue specialiter teneatur ad sectam faciendam, hiis tantum exceptis quorum antecessores vel ipsimet hujusmodi sectam facere consueverunt ante primam transfretacionem <predicti>[4] domini H[enrici] regis in Britanniam, a tempore cujus transfretacionis elapsi <fuerant>[5] viginti et novem anni et dimidius tempore quo hec constitucio facta fuit. Et similiter nullus feofatus sine carta a tempore Conquestus vel alio antiquo feofamento distringatur[6] ad hujusmodi sectam faciendam nisi ipse vel antecessores sui eam facere consueverunt ante primam transfretacionem <predicti>[7] domini regis <supradictam.>[8]

CLAUSE 2

Et, si hereditas aliqua, de qua <una tantum secta>[9] debebatur, ad plures heredes participes ejusdem devolvatur, ille qui habet eyneciam hereditatis illius unicam faciat sectam pro se et participibus suis, et <alii>[10] participes sui pro porcione sua contribuant ad sectam illam faciendam. Similiter eciam, si plures feofati fuerint de hereditate aliqua, de qua secta unica debebatur, dominus illius feodi unicam sectam inde habeat, nec possit de predicta hereditate nisi unicam sectam exigere sicut prius fieri consuevit. Et, si feofati illi warantum vel medium non habeant qui eos inde acquietare debeat, tunc omnes feofati contribuant pro porcione sua ad sectam illam faciendam.

[1] This word is omitted from the Close Roll text.
[2] The Close Roll text wrongly adds 'et' at this point.
[3] The Close Roll and Worcester texts read 'de cetero ad sectam'.
[4] The Close Roll and Worcester texts read 'dicti'.
[5] The Close Roll text reads 'fuerunt'; the Worcester text reads 'fuerint'.

TRANSLATION

PREAMBLE

In the year of the Incarnation 1259 and the forty-third regnal year of King Henry the son of King John, the same lord king and his magnates meeting together at Westminster at the quindene of Michaelmas, by the common counsel and consent of the said king and magnates the provisions written below were made and published by the king and the magnates in the following terms.

CLAUSE 1

Concerning the performance of suits to the courts of magnates and other lords of courts it has been provided and decreed by common agreement that no one who has been enfeoffed by charter is to be distrained in future to perform suit to the court of his lord unless he is specifically obliged by the terms of his charter to perform suit, except only for those whose ancestors or who themselves customarily performed such suit before the first voyage of the said lord King Henry to Brittany, from the time of which crossing twenty-nine and a half years had elapsed at the time this constitution was made. And likewise no one enfeoffed without a charter from the time of the Conquest or by some other ancient feoffment is to be distrained to perform such suit unless he or his ancestors customarily performed it before the said first voyage of the said lord king.

CLAUSE 2

And, if any inheritance for which only one suit is owed devolves on several heirs as parceners of the same inheritance, the one who has the share of the eldest coheir is to perform that one suit on behalf of himself and his parceners and his other parceners are to contribute proportionately to the performance of that suit. Likewise also, if several are enfeoffed of any inheritance from which one suit only is owed, the lord of that fee is to have only one suit from it, nor may he demand from that inheritance any more than the one suit that used previously to be performed for it. And, if those feoffees do not have a warrantor or mesne who is obliged to acquit them of it, then all the feoffees are to contribute proportionately to the performance of that suit.

[6] The Worcester text adds 'de cetero' at this point.
[7] The Close Roll and Worcester texts read 'dicti'.
[8] The Close Roll and Worcester texts read 'in Britanniam'.
[9] The Close Roll text reads 'tantum una secta'; the Worcester text reads 'unica secta tantum'.
[10] The Close Roll text omits this word.

CLAUSE 3

Si autem contingat quod domini <curiarum>[11] tenentes suos contra hanc provisionem pro hujusmodi secta distringant, tunc ad querimoniam tenencium illorum attachientur quod ad curiam regis veniant ad brevem diem inde responsuri, et unicum habeant essonium si fuerint in regno; et incontinenti deliberentur conquerenti averia sive districciones alie hac occasione facte et deliberata remaneant donec placitum inter eos inde terminetur. Et, si domini curiarum qui districciones hujusmodi fecerint ad diem ad quem attachiati fuerint non venerint vel diem per essonium sibi datum non observaverint, tunc mandetur vicecomiti quod eos ad diem <alium>[12] venire faciat; ad quem diem, si non venerint, mandetur vicecomiti quod distringat eos per omnia que habent in balliva sua, ita quod regi respondeat de exitibus, et quod habeat eorum corpora ad <certum>[13] diem prefigendum; ita quod, si die illo non venerint, pars conquerens eat sine die inde et averia sive alie districciones deliberata remaneant donec ipsi domini sectam illam recuperaverint per considera [f. 181v]cionem curie regis, et cessent interim districciones hujusmodi, salvo dominis curiarum jure suo de sectis illis perquirendis in forma juris cum inde loqui voluerint. Et cum domini curiarum venerint responsuri conquerentibus de hujusmodi districcionibus, si super hoc convincantur, tunc per consideracionem curie recuperent conquerentes versus eos dampna sua que sustinuerunt occasione districcionis predicte.

Simili autem modo, si tenentes post hanc constitucionem subtrahant dominis suis sectas quas facere debent et quas ante tempus supradicte transfretacionis et hactenus facere consueverunt, per eandem justiciam et celeritatem quoad dies prefigendos et districciones adjudicandas consequantur domini curiarum justiciam de sectis illis una cum dampnis suis quemadmodum tenentes dampna sua recuperant. Et hoc, scilicet de dampnis recuperandis, intelligatur de <subtraccionibus sibi factis et non de>[14] subtraccionibus factis predecessoribus ipsorum. Verumptamen domini curiarum versus tenentes suos seisinam de sectis hujusmodi recuperare non poterunt per defaltam, sicut nec hactenus fieri consuevit. De sectis autem que ante tempus <supradictum>[15] subtracte fuerunt currat lex communis sicut prius currere consuevit.

[11] The Worcester text (here and elsewhere in this clause) reads 'curie'.

[12] The Close Roll text reads 'illum'. [13] The Worcester text reads 'tercium'.

[14] This passage is written in the margin of the Close Roll text and marked for insertion here.

[15] The Close Roll text substitutes 'supradicte transfretacionis'.

CLAUSE 3

If, however, it should happen that the lords of courts distrain their tenants for such suit contrary to this provision, then on the complaint of those tenants they are to be attached to appear at the king's court to answer for this without delay and they are to have no more than one essoin, if they are within the kingdom; and the animals or other distresses taken for this reason are to be released to the complainant immediately and they are to remain released until the plea between them on this is determined. And if the lords of courts who have made such distraints do not appear on the day for which they were attached or do not keep the day given them by the essoin, then the sheriff is to be instructed to produce them on another day; on which day, if they do not appear, the sheriff is to be instructed to distrain them by everything they have in his bailiwick, so that he answer the king for the issues, and that he produce their bodies at a certain day to be fixed; so that, if they do not appear on that day, the complainant is to go without a day on the plea and the animals or other distresses are to remain delivered until those lords have recovered that suit by the judgment of the court of the lord king and in the interim such distraints are to cease, but without prejudice to the lords of the courts recovering those suits by way of law when they wish to do this. And when the lords of courts appear to answer the complainants for such distraints, if they are convicted of this, then the complainants are to recover against them by judgment of the court their damages which they sustained by reason of the said distraint.

Likewise, if tenants after this constitution withdraw from their lords the suits which they are obliged to perform and which they customarily performed before the time of the aforesaid voyage and hitherto, the lords of courts are to get justice in respect of those suits together with damages by the same process and speed in making adjournments and adjudging distraints as tenants recover their damages. And this, that is on the recovery of damages, is to be understood in relation to withdrawals made from them and not withdrawals made from their predecessors. But the lords of courts may not recover seisin of such suits against their tenants by default, just as it has not been the custom hitherto. Concerning suits which were withdrawn before the said time the common law is to apply as it has applied hitherto.

CLAUSE 4

De turno vicecomitis provisum est ut necesse non habeant ibi venire archiepiscopi, episcopi, abbates, priores, comites, barones, nec aliqui religiosi seu mulieres, nisi specialiter eorum presencia exigatur, set teneatur turnus sicut temporibus predecessorum domini regis teneri consuevit. Et si qui in hundredis diversis habeant tenementa non habeant necesse ad hujusmodi turnos venire nisi in ballivis ubi fuerint conversantes. Et teneantur turni secundum formam Magne Carte regis et sicut temporibus regum Johannis et <Ricardi>[16] teneri consueverunt.

CLAUSE 5

Provisum est eciam quod nec in itinere justiciariorum nec in comitatibus <aut hundredis>[17] nec in curiis baronum decetero ab aliquibus recipiantur fines pro pulcro placitando neque per sic quod non occasionentur.

CLAUSE 6

In placito vero dotis quod dicitur 'unde nichil habet' dentur decetero quatuor dies per annum ad minus et plures si comode fieri <possit.>[18]

CLAUSE 7

In assisis ultime presentacionis et in placito 'quare impedit' de ecclesiis vacantibus detur dies de quindena in quindenam vel de tribus septimanis in tres septimanas, prout locus propinquus fuerit vel remotus.

Et in placito 'quare impedit', si ad primum diem ad quem summonitus fuerit non veniat nec essonium mittat <impeditor, tunc attachietur ad diem alium; quo die si non veniat nec essonium>[19] mittat, distringatur per magnam districcionem superius dictam. Et, si tunc non venerit, per ejus defaltam scribatur episcopo quod reclamacio impeditoris illa vice conquerenti non obsistat, salvo impeditori alias jure suo cum inde loqui <velit.>[20]

[16] The Worcester text reads 'Henrici'. [17] The Close Roll text omits these words.

[18] The Close Roll text reads 'posset'; the Worcester text reads 'potest'.

[19] This passage is written in the margin of the Close Roll text and marked for insertion here.

[20] The Close Roll text reads 'voluerit'; the Worcester text 'valeat et velit'.

CLAUSE 4

Concerning the sheriff's tourn it has been provided that archbishops, bishops, abbots, priors, earls, barons, the religious and women should have no need to appear there unless their presence was specially required, but the tourn was to be held as it used to be held in the reigns of the predecessors of the lord king. Those who have tenements in different hundreds are not to have to appear at such tourns other than in the bailiwicks where they are living. And tourns are to be held according to the terms of the king's Magna Carta and as they used to be held in the reigns of kings John and Richard.

CLAUSE 5

It has been provided also that neither in the eyre of the justices nor in county courts nor in hundred courts nor in courts baron are fines to be received in future from anyone for beaupleder or for not being harmed.

CLAUSE 6

In pleas of dower *unde nichil habet* four days are to be given within a year at least and more if this can conveniently be done.

CLAUSE 7

In assizes of darrein presentment and pleas of *quare impedit* relating to vacant churches adjournments of a fortnight or three weeks are to be given in accordance with whether the place is close or distant.

And in pleas of *quare impedit*, if the impedient does not appear or send an essoin on the first day for which he has been summoned, then he is to be attached for another day. If he does not appear on that day or send an essoin he is to be distrained by the grand distress mentioned above. And, if he does not then appear, the bishop is to be told on the basis of his default that the claim of the impedient is not to obstruct the complainant on this occasion, but without prejudice to the impedient's right on another occasion when he wishes to pursue it.

CLAUSE 8

De cartis vero exempcionum et libertatis ne ponantur impetrantes in assisis, juratis vel recognicionibus provisum est ut, si adeo sit necessarium eorum juramentum quod sine eo justicia exhiberi non possit, veluti in magna assisa, in perambulacionibus et ubi in cartis vel in scripturis convencionum fuerint testes nominati aut in attinctis vel casibus aliis consimilibus, jurare cogantur, salva sibi alias libertate et exemptione sua predicta.

CLAUSE 11[21]

Nulli de cetero liceat ex quacumque causa districciones facere extra feodum suum neque in regia aut communi strata nisi domino regi et ministris suis.

CLAUSE 9

Si heres aliquis post mortem sui antecessoris infra etatem extiterit et dominus suus custodiam terrarum suarum habuerit, si dominus ille dicto heredi, cum ad legitimam etatem pervenerit, terram suam sine placito reddere noluerit, heres ipse terram suam ut de morte sui antecessoris recuperabit una cum dampnis que sustinuerit per illam detentionem a tempore quo legittime fuerit etatis.

CLAUSE 10

Quod si heres in morte sui antecessoris plene fuerit etatis et heres ille apparens et pro herede cognitus inventus sit in hereditate illa, capitalis dominus ejus eum non ejiciat vel aliquid ibi capiat vel amoveat, set <tantum>[22] simplicem seisinam inde faciat pro recognicione dominii sui.[23] <Et si capitalis dominus hujusmodi heredem extra seisinam maliciose teneat, per quod per accionem mortis antecessoris vel consanguinitatis oporteat ipsum placitare, tunc dampna sua recuperet sicut in accione nove disseisine.>[24]

[21] Clause 11 appears at this point in the Red Book and Worcester texts.

[22] The Worcester text reads 'tamen'.

[23] Stubbs' break between clauses 9 and 10 comes at this point.

[24] This passage is written in the margin of the Close Roll text and marked for insertion here.

CLAUSE 8

Concerning charters of exemption and freedom whose holders are freed from being put on assizes, juries and recognitions it has been provided that, if their oath is so essential that without it justice cannot be done, as in case of the grand assize and in perambulations and where they are the witnesses named in charters or in deeds of agreement or in attaints or in like cases, they are to be compelled to take the oath, without prejudice to their said liberty and exemption on another occasion.

CLAUSE 11

No one in future is to be allowed for whatever reason to make distraints outside his fee nor in the king's or common highway other than the lord king and his officials.

CLAUSE 9

If any heir at the death of his ancestor is below age and his lord has wardship of his lands and that lord refuses to hand over his land without a plea to the said heir when he comes of lawful age that heir will recover his land as of the death of his ancestor together with the damages which he has sustained by that detention from the time he was of lawful age.

CLAUSE 10

But if the heir was of full age at the death of his ancestor and heir apparent and known as heir and found in that inheritance, his chief lord is not to eject him or take or remove anything there but merely to take a simple seisin for the acknowledgement of his lordship. And if the chief lord keeps such an heir out of seisin maliciously, so that it is necessary to implead him by an action of mort d'ancestor or cosinage, then he is to recover his damages as in the action of novel disseisin.

CLAUSE 12

Provisum est eciam quod, si terra que tenetur in sokagium sit in custodia parentum heredis eo quod <heres infra etatem fuerit,>[25] custodes illi vastum facere non <possint>[26] neque vendicionem nec aliquam destruccionem de hereditate illa, set salvo eam custodiant ad opus dicti heredis. ita tamen quod, cum [f. 182r] ad etatem pervenerit, sibi respondeant per legitimam computacionem de exitibus dicte hereditatis, salvis ipsis custodibus racionabilibus misis suis. Nec eciam possunt dicti custodes maritagium dicti heredis dare vel vendere nisi ad commodum ipsius heredis.

CLAUSE 13

Nullus escaetor aut inquisitor vel justiciarius ad assisas aliquas capiendas specialiter assignatus <vel>[27] ad querelas aliquas <specialiter>[28] audiendas et terminandas de cetero potestatem <habeat>[29] amerciandi pro defalta summonicionis comunis nisi capitalis justiciarius vel justiciarii itinerantes in itineribus suis.

CLAUSE 14

Viris <autem>[30] religiosis non liceat ingredi feodum alicujus sine licencia capitalis domini de quo, scilicet, res ipsa immediate tenetur.

CLAUSE 15

De essoniis autem provisum est quod in comitatibus, hundredis aut curiis baronum vel alibi nullus habeat <necesse>[31] jurare pro essonio suo warantizando.

CLAUSE 16

Nullus decetero excepto rege placitum teneat in curia sua de falso judicio facto in curia tenencium suorum, quia hujusmodi placita ad coronam specialiter pertinent et dignitatem regis.[32]

[25] The Close Roll text reads 'heredes infra etatem fuerint'.

[26] The Close Roll and Worcester texts read 'possunt'.

[27] This word is interlined in the Close Roll text.

[28] This word is omitted from the Close Roll text.

[29] The Close Roll text wrongly reads 'habeant'; the Worcester text adds 'aliquos' at this point.

[30] The Worcester text omits this word.

[31] This word is interlined in the Close Roll text.

[32] The whole of this clause is written in a blank space after clause 18 in the Close Roll text but it is marked for transfer to this position.

CLAUSE 12

It has also been provided that, if land which is held in socage is in the wardship of the kinsmen of the heir because the heir is under age, those guardians may not make waste or sale or any destruction of that inheritance but are to keep it safely for the benefit of the said heir, so that when he shall come of age, they are to answer him through a lawful accounting for the issues of the said inheritance with due allowance made to those guardians of their reasonable expenses. Nor may the said guardians give or sell the marriage of the said heir other than for the benefit of the same heir.

CLAUSE 13

No escheator or inquirer or justice specially assigned to take any assizes or to hear and determine any complaints is in future to have power to amerce for default of the common summons except for the chief justiciar and the justices itinerant in their eyres.

CLAUSE 14

The religious are not to be allowed to enter the fee of anyone without the permission of the chief lord, namely the lord of whom that property is immediately held.

CLAUSE 15

Concerning essoins, moreover, it has been provided that in county courts, hundred courts and courts baron and elsewhere no one is to be required to warrant his essoin on oath.

CLAUSE 16

No one in future other than the king is to hold a plea in his court about a wrongful judgment made in the court of his tenants, because such pleas belong specially to the crown and dignity of the king.

CLAUSE 17

Provisum est <eciam>[33] quod, si averia alicujus capiantur et injuste detineantur, vicecomes post querimoniam inde sibi factam ea sine impedimento vel contradiccione ejus qui dicta averia cepit diliberare possit, si extra libertates capta fuerint. Et si infra libertates hujusmodi averia capiantur et ballivi libertatum ea deliberare noluerint tunc vicecomes <per defectum>[34] <dictorum>[35] ballivorum ea faciat deliberari.

CLAUSE 18

Nullus decetero distringere possit libere tenentes suos ad respondendum de libero tenemento suo neque de aliquibus ad liberum tenementum suum spectantibus sine brevi regis. Nec jurare faciat libere tenentes suos contra voluntatem suam, desicut nullus hoc facere potest sine precepto regis.

CLAUSE 19

Provisum est eciam quod, si ballivi qui compotum dominis suis reddere tenentur se subtraxherint et terras vel tenementa non habuerint per que distringi possint, tunc per eorum corpora atachientur, ita quod vicecomites in quorum ballivis invenientur eos venire faciant ad compotum suum reddendum.

CLAUSE 20

Item firmarii tempore suarum firmarum vastum, vendicionem vel exilium non faciant de boscis, domibus, hominibus, nec de aliquibus aliis ad tenementa que ad firmam habuerint spectantibus, nisi specialem habeant concessionem per scripturam sue convencionis mencionem habentis quod <hec>[36] facere possint. Et si <facerint>[37] et de hoc convincantur dampna plene refundant.

CLAUSE 21

Justiciarii itinerantes decetero non amercient villatas in itinero suo pro eo quod singuli xij annorum non venerint coram vicecomite et coronatoribus ad inquisiciones de morte hominis aut aliis ad coronam pertinentibus, dum tamen de villis illis veniant sufficienter per quos inquisiciones hujusmodi plene fieri possint.

[33] The Worcester text omits this word.
[34] The Worcester text reads 'pro defectu'.
[35] This word is interlined in our main text.
[36] The Close Roll and Worcester texts read 'hoc'.
[37] This word has been altered from 'facerent'; the Close Roll and Worcester texts read 'fecerint'.

CLAUSE 17

It has also been provided that if anyone's animals are taken and unjustly kept, the sheriff, after a complaint made to him about this, may release them without the impediment or obstruction of the person who took the said animals, if they were taken outside franchises. If such animals are taken within franchises and the bailiffs of the franchises refuse to release them then the sheriff is to have them released by virtue of the failure of the said bailiffs.

CLAUSE 18

No one may in future distrain his free tenants to answer for their free tenement or anything relating to their free tenement without the king's writ. Nor is he to make his free tenants take oaths against their will, since no one may do this without the king's authorisation.

CLAUSE 19

It has also been provided that, if bailiffs who are obliged to render account to their lords flee from them and do not have lands and tenements by which they may be distrained, then they are to be attached by their bodies, so that the sheriffs in whose bailiwicks they are found are to make them come to render their account.

CLAUSE 20

Also lessees during the period of their leases are not to make waste or sale or exile of the woods, houses, men or of anything else belonging to the tenements which they have on lease, unless they have a specific concession in the writing of their agreement mentioning that they may do these things. And if they do this and are convicted of doing so they are to refund the damages in full.

CLAUSE 21

The justices itinerant are not in future to amerce townships on their eyre because everyone aged twelve and over did not appear before the sheriff and coroners for inquisitions into homicides or other matters belonging to the crown, provided there was a sufficient attendance from those villages to allow such inquisitions to be properly held.

CLAUSE 22

Murdrum decetero non adjudicetur coram justiciariis ubi infortunium tantummodo adjudicatum est, set locum habeat murdrum in interfectis per feloniam et non aliter.

CLAUSE 23

Provisum est insuper quod nullus, qui coram justiciariis itinerantibus vocatur ad warantum de placito terre vel tenementi, amercietur decetero pro eo quod presens non fuerit, excepto primo die adventus ipsorum justiciariorum. Set, si warantus ille sit infra comitatum, tunc injungatur vicecomiti quod ipsum infra diem tercium vel quartum secundum locorum distanciam faciat venire, sicut in itinere justiciariorum fieri consuevit. Et, si extra comitatum maneat, tunc racionabilem habeat summonicionem xv dierum ad minus secundum discrecionem justiciariorum et legem communem.

CLAUSE 24

Si clericus aliquis pro crimine aliquo vel retto quod ad coronam pertineat arestatus fuerit et postmodum de precepto regis in ballium traditus vel replegiatus extiterit, ita quod hii quibus traditur in ballium eum habeant coram justiciariis, non amercientur decetero illi quibus traditus fuit in ballium vel alii plegii sui, si corpus suum habeant coram justiciariis, licet coram eis propter privilegium clericale respondere nolit vel non possit.

Note

I have in general followed Stubbs' numbering of the individual clauses, except for a readjustment of the break between the related clauses 9 and 10 where Stubbs' break is a positive impediment to the sense. I have not always followed Stubbs' punctuation or that of the editor of the published Close Roll text, but have punctuated for sense.

CLAUSE 22

The *murdrum* fine is not in future to be adjudged as due before the justices where only death by misadventure has been adjudged but is to apply only to those killed feloniously.

CLAUSE 23

It has also been provided that no one who is vouched to warranty before the justices itinerant in a plea relating to land or a tenement is to be amerced in future because he was not present other than on the first day of the visitation of the same justices. But, if that warrantor is within the county, the sheriff is to be enjoined to make him come by the third or the fourth day depending on the distance, as has been customary in the eyre of the justices. And, if he is living outside the county, then he is to have a proper summons of at least fifteen days according to the discretion of the justices and common law.

CLAUSE 24

If any clerk is arrested for any crime or offence which belongs to the crown and is subsequently by the king's order released on bail or replevied, so that those to whom he is bailed produce him before the justices, those to whom he is bailed or his other sureties are not in future to be amerced if they have his body before the justices even if he refuses or is unable to answer before them because of clerical privilege.

Note

This is my own independent original translation of the Provisions. It is a relatively free rendering of the original, intended to convey the sense of the original, but not following the exact wording of the original literally.

Appendix II

THE PROVISIONS OF WESTMINSTER AS REISSUED IN 1263 AND 1264

Sources

For the 1263 reissue

a) C 66/79 (Patent Roll, 47 Henry III), m. 14 schedule: taken here as the main text for both reissues. Although stained with gall it remains legible. A seventeenth-century hand has added the heading *Statutum de Marlebrig' incipiend' ad caput nonum'*.

b) Bodleian MS. Bodley 91, fols. 133r–135r: significant variants are noted in the footnotes.

c) Bodleian MS. Douce 139, fols. 103v–105r: significant variants are noted in the footnotes.

For the 1264 reissue

a) E 164/24 (Malmesbury Cartulary), fols. 33v–37r: printed in *Registrum Malmesburiense*, I, 42–50: main text of 1264 preamble and concluding clause; otherwise only significant variants noted in footnotes.

b) BL MS. Cotton Claudius D. ii, fols. 128v–131r: significant variants are noted in the footnotes.

There is also a text of this reissue in Philadelphia Free Library, Hampton L. Carson Collection MS. LC 14.3, fols. 173v–175v but it has not been collated for this edition.

Appendix II

TEXT

PREAMBLE

i) to the 1263 reissue

Anno Domini M°CC sexagesimo secundo, <regni autem domini H[enrici] regis filii regis Johannis xlvij,>[1] de mera et libera voluntate ipsius domini regis <et>[2] in plena et libera potestate ipsius, interveniente consilio fidelium suorum, edite sunt per ipsum dominum regem constituciones subscripte ad reformacionem et melioracionem regni sui et per ipsum publicate ac observacioni <generaliter sua auctoritate>[3] demandate.

ii) to the 1264 reissue

H[enricus] dei gracia rex Anglie, <dominus Hybernie et dux Aquitannie>[4] archiepiscopis, <episcopis, abbatibus, prioribus, comitibus, baronibus, militibus, liberis hominibus>[5] et omnibus aliis <comitatus Devon'>[6] salutem. Cum [dudum][7] ad reformacionem et melioracionem regni nostri provisiones et constituciones subscriptas per vicecomites nostros singulorum comitatuum nostrorum per Angliam publicari et per totum regnum nostrum firmiter observari <preceptum erat,>[8] eedem provisiones et constituciones occasione turbacionis nuper habite in regno ipso nondum fuerint observate, nos eas iterato presentibus duximus inserendas et per totum regnum nostrum predictum publicandas sub hac forma.

1 Douce 139 reads 'et regni regis Henrici filii Johannis xlvij ad festum sancti Hillarii apud Westm' '.
2 Bodley 91 omits this word.
3 Bodley 91 reads 'auctoritate sua generaliter'; Douce 139 reads 'auctoritate sua fideliter'.
4 Cotton Claudius abbreviates to 'etc.'
5 Cotton Claudius reads 'etc'.
6 Cotton Claudius reads 'de comitatu Midd' '.
7 Supplied from Cotton Claudius.
8 Cotton Claudius reads 'precepimus ac'.

TRANSLATION

PREAMBLE

i) to the 1263 reissue

In the year of the Lord 1262, in the forty-seventh regnal year of the lord King Henry the son of King John, of the mere and free will of the same lord king and in the full and free power of the same, with the stimulus of the counsel of his subjects, the constitutions that follow were issued by the same lord king for the reformation and improvement of his kingdom and published by him and ordered to be observed generally by his authority.

ii) to the 1264 reissue

Henry by the grace of God king of England, lord of Ireland and duke of Aquitaine to the archbishops, bishops, abbots, priors, earls, barons, knights, free men and all others of the county of Devon greetings. Whereas some time ago it was ordered for the reformation and improvement of our kingdom that the provisions and constitutions written below should be published by our sheriffs of each of our counties throughout England and firmly observed throughout our whole realm, and the same provisions and constitutions have not yet been observed because of the disturbance that recently occurred in the same kingdom, we have decided again to insert them in what follows and to publish them throughout our whole realm in the terms that follow.

CLAUSE 1

De sectis faciendis ad curias magnatum et aliorum dominorum ipsarum curiarum **decetero <sic>**[9] **observandum est** quod **<scilicet>**[10] nullus qui per cartam feofatus est distringatur de cetero ad sectam faciendam ad curiam domini sui nisi per formam carte sue specialiter teneatur ad sectam[11] faciendam **<ad curiam domini sui,>**[12] hiis <tantum>[13] exceptis quorum antecessores vel ipsimet hujusmodi sectam facere consueverint ante primam transfretacionem <dicti domini regis>[14] in Britanniam, a tempore cujus transfretacionis[15] elapsi fuerunt **triginta et duo anni** [et dimidius][16] tempore quo hec constitucio facta fuit. Et similiter nullus feofatus sine carta a tempore Conquestus vel alio antiquo feofamento distringatur ad hujusmodi sectam faciendam, nisi ipse vel antecessores sui eam facere consueverunt ante primam transfretacionem <dicti domini regis **in Britanniam.**>[17]
[1259 Provisions, clause 1]

CLAUSE 2[18]

Et, si hereditas aliqua de qua <tantum>[19] unica secta debebatur ad plures heredes participes ejusdem hereditatis devolvatur, ille qui habet eyneciam illius hereditatis unicam faciat sectam pro se et participibus suis, et alii participes sui pro porcione sua contribuant ad sectam illam faciendam. Similiter eciam, si plures feofati fuerint <de hereditate aliqua,>[20] de qua unica secta debebatur, dominus illius feodi unicam habeat inde sectam, nec possit de predicta hereditate nisi unicam sectam exigere sicut prius fieri consuevit. Et, si feofati illi warantum vel medium non habeant qui eos inde acquietare debeat, tunc omnes feofati contribuant pro porcione sua ad sectam illam faciendam.
[1259 Provisions, clause 2]

[9] Douce 139 omits this word.
[10] Douce 139 omits this word.
[11] Malmesbury adds 'illam' here.
[12] Douce 139 and Malmesbury omit.
[13] Cotton Claudius reads 'tamen'.
[14] Malmesbury and Cotton Claudius substitute 'nostram'.
[15] Malmesbury adds here 'nostre'.
[16] Supplied from Douce 139, Cotton Claudius and Malmesbury.
[17] Malmesbury reads 'nostram predictam'; Cotton Claudius reads 'predictam in Britanniam'.
[18] There is no new paragraph heading at this point in the Patent Roll text, suggesting that the scribe thought that clauses 1 and 2 were a single clause.
[19] This word is interlined in the Patent Roll text. It is omitted from Bodley 91.
[20] Malmesbury reads 'ex aliqua hereditate'.

CLAUSE 1

Concerning the performance of suits to the courts of magnates and other lords of courts **in future the following is to be observed, namely** that no one who has been enfeoffed by charter is to be distrained in future to perform suit to the court of his lord unless he is specifically obliged by the terms of his charter to perform suit **to the court of his lord,** except only for those whose ancestors or who themselves customarily performed such suit before the first voyage of the said lord king to Brittany, from the time of which crossing **thirty-two and a half years** had elapsed at the time this constitution was made. And likewise no one enfeoffed without a charter from the time of the Conquest or by some other ancient feoffment is to be distrained to perform such suit unless he or his ancestors customarily performed it before the first voyage of the said lord king to Brittany.
[1259 Provisions, clause 1]

CLAUSE 2

And, if any inheritance for which only one suit is owed devolves on several heirs as parceners of the same inheritance, the one who has the share of the eldest coheir is to perform that one suit on behalf of himself and his parceners and his other parceners are to contribute proportionately to the performance of that suit. Likewise also, if several are enfeoffed of any inheritance from which one suit only is owed, the lord of that fee is to have only one suit from it, nor may he demand from that inheritance any more than the one suit that used previously to be performed for it. And, if those feoffees do not have a warrantor or mesne who is obliged to acquit them of it, then all the feoffees are to contribute proportionately to the performance of that suit.
[1259 Provisions, clause 2]

CLAUSE 3

Si autem contingat quod domini curiarum tenentes suos contra hanc provisionem pro hujusmodi secta distringant, tunc ad querimoniam tenencium illorum attachientur quod ad curiam <regis>[21] veniant ad brevem diem inde responsuri, et unicum habeant essonium si fuerint in regno; et incontinenti deliberentur conquerenti averia[22] sive districciones alie hac occasione facte et <deliberata>[23] remaneant donec placitum[24] inter eos terminetur. Et, si domini curiarum qui districciones hujusmodi fecerint ad diem ad quem attachiati fuerint non venerunt vel diem per essonium sibi datum non observaverint, tunc mandetur vicecomiti <quod eos ad diem alium venire faciat; ad quem diem, si non venerint, mandetur vicecomiti>[25] quod distringat eos per omnia que habent in balliva sua, ita quod **vicecomes** <regi>[26] respondeat de exitibus, et quod habeat eorum corpora ad certum diem prefigendum; ita quod, si die illo non venerint, pars conquerens eat <inde>[27] sine die et averia sive alie districciones deliberata remaneant donec ipsi domini sectam illam recuperaverint per consideracionem curie <domini regis,>[28] et cessent interim districciones hujusmodi, salvo dominis curiarum jure suo de sectis illis <perquirendis>[29] in forma juris cum inde loqui voluerunt. Et cum domini curiarum venerint responsuri conquerentibus de hujusmodi districcionibus, **et** super hoc convincantur, tunc per consideracionem curie <**domini regis**>[30] recuperent versus eos conquerentes eos dampna sua que sustinuerunt occasione districcionis predicte.[31]

Simili autem modo, si tenentes post hanc constitucionem subtrahant dominis suis sectas quas facere debent et quas ante tempus supradicte transfretacionis et hactenus facere consueverunt, per eandem justiciam et celeritatem quoad dies prefigendos et districciones adjudicandos <**prosequantur**>[32] domini curiarum justiciam de sectis illis una cum dampnis suis quemadmodum tenentes sua dampna recuperant. Et hoc, scilicet de dampnis recuperandis, intelligatur de subtraccionibus sibi factis et non de subtraccionibus factis predecessoribus ipsorum. Verumptamen domini curiarum versus tenentes suos seisinam de hujusmodi sectis recuperare non poterunt per defaltam, sicut nec hactenus fieri consuevit.[33] De sectis autem que ante tempus supradictum subtracte fuerint currat lex comunis sicut prius currere consuevit.

[1259 Provisions, clause 3]

[21] Cotton Claudius and Malmesbury read 'nostram'.

[22] Douce 139 adds 'sua'. [23] Cotton Claudius reads 'liberate'.

[24] Bodley 91, Douce 139, Cotton Claudius and Malmesbury add 'inde'.

[25] Douce 139 omits this passage. [26] Cotton Claudius and Malmesbury read 'nobis'.

[27] This word is interlined in the Patent Roll text.

[28] Cotton Claudius and Malmesbury read 'nostre'.

CLAUSE 3

If, however, it should happen that the lords of courts distrain their tenants for such suit contrary to this provision, then on the complaint of those tenants they are to be attached to appear at the king's court to answer for this without delay and they are to have no more than one essoin, if they are within the kingdom; and the animals or other distresses taken for this reason are to be released to the complainant immediately and they are to remain released until the plea between them is determined. And if the lords of courts who have made such distraints do not appear on the day for which they were attached or do not keep the day given them by the essoin, then the sheriff is to be instructed to produce them on another day; on which day, if they do not appear, the sheriff is to be instructed to distrain them by everything they have in his bailiwick, so that **the sheriff** answer the king for the issues, and that he produce their bodies at a certain day to be fixed; so that, if they do not appear on that day, the complainant is to go without a day on the plea and the animals or other distresses are to remain delivered until those lords have recovered that suit by the judgment of the court of the lord king and in the interim such distraints are to cease, but without prejudice to the lords of the courts recovering those suits by way of law when they wish to do this. And when the lords of courts appear to answer the complainants for such distraints, if they are convicted of this, then the complainants are to recover against them by judgment of the court of the lord king their damages which they sustained by reason of the said distraint.

Likewise, if tenants after this constitution withdraw from their lords the suits which they are obliged to perform and which they customarily performed before the time of the aforesaid voyage and hitherto, the lords of courts are to get justice in respect of those suits together with damages by the same process and speed in making adjournments and adjudging distraints as tenants recover their damages. And this, that is on the recovery of damages, is to be understood in relation to withdrawals made from them and not withdrawals made from their predecessors. But the lords of courts may not recover seisin of such suits against their tenants by default, just as it has not been the custom hitherto. Concerning suits which were withdrawn before the said time the common law is to apply as it has applied hitherto. [1259 provisions, clause 3]

29 Douce 139 reads 'recuperandis'. 30 Cotton Claudius omits.

31 The Patent Roll marks a new paragraph at this point, suggesting that the scribe thought that what followed was a separate clause.

32 Partially changed back to 'consequantur' on the Patent Roll. This is the reading of the other texts.

33 The Patent Roll text marks a further paragraph break at this point.

CLAUSE 4

De turnis <vicecomitis>[34] provisum est ut necesse non habeant ibi venire archiepiscopi, episcopi, abbates, priores, comites, barones, vel aliqui religiosi **viri** seu mulieres, nisi eorum presencia specialiter exigatur, set teneatur turnus sicut temporibus predecessorum **<nostrorum>**[35] teneri consuevit. Et si qui in hundredis diversis habeant tenementa non habeant necesse ad hujusmodi turnos venire nisi in ballivis ubi fuerint conversantes. Et teneantur turni secundum formam Magne Carte **<nostre>**[36] et sicut temporibus regum Johannis et Ricardi teneri consueverunt.
[1259 Provisions, clause 4]

CLAUSE 5

Provisum est eciam quod nec in itinere justiciariorum nec in comitatibus, hundredis nec in curiis baronum decetero ab aliquibus recipiantur fines pro pulcre placitando nec per sic quod non occasionentur. **Et sciendum quod per istam constitucionem non tolluntur fines certi seu prestaciones arentate a tempore quo primo <dominus rex transfretavit>**[37] **in Britanniam usque nunc.**
[1259 Provisions, clause 5]

CLAUSE 6

In placito vero dotis <quod dicitur>[38] 'unde nichil habet' dentur decetero quatuor dies per annum <ad minus>[39] et plures si commode fieri possit; **ita quod habeantur sex dies per annum vel quinque ad minus.**
[1259 Provisions, clause 6]

[34] Bodley 91 reads 'vicecomitum'.
[35] This word is interlined above 'domini regis' (which is marked for deletion) in the Patent Roll text.
[36] This word is interlined in the Patent Roll text above 'regis' which is marked for deletion.
[37] These words have been partially changed to 'transfretavimus' in the Patent Roll text; 'transfretavimus' is the reading of the Cotton Claudius and Malmesbury.
[38] Douce 139 omits. [39] Bodley 91 omits.

CLAUSE 4

Concerning the sheriff's tourn it has been provided that archbishops, bishops, abbots, priors, earls, barons, and religious men and women should have no need to appear there unless their presence was specially required, but the tourn was to be held as it used to be held in the reigns of **our** predecessors. Those who have tenements in different hundreds are not to have to appear at such tourns other than in the bailiwicks where they are living. And tourns are to be held according to the terms of **our** Magna Carta and as they used to be held in the reigns of kings John and Richard.
[1259 Provisions, clause 4]

CLAUSE 5

It has been provided also that neither in the eyre of the justices nor in county courts nor in hundred courts nor in courts baron are fines to be received in future from anyone for beaupleder or for not being harmed. **And it is to be known that this constitution does not abolish those fines which have been fixed since the lord king's first voyage into Brittany or regular payments made ever since then.**
[1259 Provisions, clause 5]

CLAUSE 6

In pleas of dower *unde nichil habet* four days are to be given within a year at least and more if this can conveniently be done; **so that there should be six days each year or five at the least.**
[1259 Provisions, clause 6]

CLAUSE 7

In assisa ultime presentacionis et in placito 'quare impedit' de ecclesiis vacantibus detur dies de quindena in quindenam vel de tribus septimanis in tres septimanas, prout locus fuerit propinquus vel remotus.

Et in placito 'quare impedit', si ad primum diem ad quem summonitus fuerit non veniat nec essonium mittat impeditor, tunc attachietur ad diem alium; quo die si non venerit nec essonium mittat, distringatur per magnam districcionem superius dictam. Et, si tunc non venerit, per ejus defaltam scribatur episcopo quod reclamacio impeditoris illa vice conquerenti non obsistat, salvo impeditori alias jure suo cum inde loqui voluerit.
[1259 Provisions, clause 7]

CLAUSE 8

Eadem lex de attachiamentis faciendis in omnibus brevibus ubi attachiamenta jacent decetero quo ad districciones firmiter observetur, ita tamen quod secundum attachiamentum <fit>[40] per meliores plegios et postmodum ultima districcio.
[new clause]

CLAUSE 9

Et sciendum quod <cum>[41] aliquis posuerit se in inquisicionem aliquam que emergit vel que emergere potest in hujusmodi brevibus non habebit nisi unicum essonium vel unicam defaltam; ita scilicet quod, si ad diem sibi datum per essonium suum non venerit <aut secundam defaltam fecerit,>[42] tunc inquisicio illa per defaltam ipsius capiatur et secundum inquisionem illam ad judicium <procedatur.>[43] Si vero inquisicio illa capta fuerit in comitatu coram coronatoribus vel <justiciario domini regis>[44] ad certum diem remittenda et pars rea non venerit ad diem illum, tunc propter defaltam ipsius assingnetur ei secundum discrecionem justicariorum alius dies et mandetur vicecomiti quod ad diem illum faciat ipsum venire ad audiendum judicium suum <si velit secundum inquisicionem illam;>[45] <ad quem diem, si non venerit, <procedatur ad judicium per defaltam suam.>[46] Eodem modo fiat si non venerit>[47] ad diem datum sibi per essonium suum.
[new clause]

[40] Cotton Claudius and Malmesbury read 'sit'.
[41] Bodley 91, Cotton Claudius and Malmesbury read 'postquam'. [42] Bodley 91 omits.
[43] Malmesbury reads 'producatur'.
[44] Cotton Claudius and Malmesbury read 'justiciariis nostris'.
[45] These words are interlined in the Patent Roll text. [46] Bodley 91 omits.
[47] Cotton Claudius omits through homoeoteleuton.

CLAUSE 7

In the assize of darrein presentment and plea of *quare impedit* relating to vacant churches adjournments of a fortnight or three weeks are to be given in accordance with whether the place is close or distant.

And in pleas of *quare impedit*, if the impedient does not appear or send an essoin on the first day for which he has been summoned, then he is to be attached for another day. If he does not appear on that day or send an essoin he is to be distrained by the grand distress mentioned above. And, if he does not then appear, the bishop is to be told on the basis of his default that the claim of the impedient is not to obstruct the complainant on this occasion, but without prejudice to the impedient's right on another occasion when he wishes to pursue it.
[1259 Provisions, clause 7]

CLAUSE 8

The same procedure in regard to the making of attachments is to be firmly observed in respect of distraints in all writs where attachments lie, so that the second attachment be made by better sureties and then the final distraint.
[new clause]

CLAUSE 9

And it is to be known that when someone has put himself on any inquisition that has arisen or might arise in such writs he will not have more than a single essoin or single default, so that if he does not appear on the day given him by his essoin or makes a second default then the inquisition is to be taken by his default and judgment is to be given on the basis of that inquisition. If, however, that inquisition shall be taken in the county before the coroners or a justice of the lord king to be reported back for a certain day and the defendant does not appear on that day then another day is to be assigned to him by virtue of his default according to the discretion of the justices and the sheriff is to be instructed to produce him on that day to hear his judgment, if he wishes, in accordance with that inquisition, and if he does not appear on that day judgment is to be given by his default. The same procedure is to be followed if he does not appear on the day given him by his essoin.
[new clause]

CLAUSE 10

Nulli de cetero liceat ex quacumque causa districciones facere extra feodum suum neque in regia aut communi strata nisi <domino regi>[48] <et>[49] ministris <suis.>[50]
[1259 Provisions, clause 11]

CLAUSE 11

Si heres <aliquis>[51] post mortem sui antecessoris infra etatem extiterit et dominus suus custodiam terrarum suarum habuerit, si dominus ille predicto heredi, cum ad legitimam etatem pervenerit, terram suam sine placito reddere noluerit, heres ille terram suam <ut de morte sui>[52] antecessoris recuperabit una cum dampnis suis que sustinuerit propter illam detencionem a tempore quo fuerit legittime etatis.

<Quod>[53] si heres aliquis <in morte>[54] sui antecessoris plene fuerit etatis et heres ille apparens et pro herede cognitus inventus fuerit in hereditate illa, capitalis dominus ejus eum non ejiciat nec aliquid <ibi>[55] capiat vel ammoveat, set tantum simplicem seisinam inde faciat pro recognicione dominii sui. Et si capitalis dominus heredem hujusmodi extra seisinam maliciose teneat, per quod per accionem mortis antecessoris vel consanguinitatis oporteat ipsum placitare, tunc dampna sua <recuperet>[56] sicut in accione nove disseisine.
[1259 Provisions, clauses 9 and 10]

CLAUSE 12

Provisum est <eciam>[57] quod, si terra que tenetur in soccagio sit in custodia parentum heredis eo quod heres infra etatem <**extiterit,**>[58] custodes illi vastum facere non <possint>[59] neque vendicionem nec aliquam destruccionem de hereditate illa, set salvo eam custodiant ad opus dicti heredis ita quod, cum ad etatem pervenerit, sibi respondeant per legittimam computacionem de exitibus dicte hereditatis, <salvis ipsis custodibus racionabilibus misis suis. Nec eciam possint dicti custodes maritagium dicti heredis dare vel vendere nisi ad commodum dicti heredis.>[60]
[1259 Provisions, clause 12]

[48] Cotton Claudius reads 'nobis'.
[49] Bodley 91 and Douce 139 read 'aut'.
[50] Cotton Claudius reads 'nostris'.
[51] Douce 139 reads 'alicujus'.
[52] Douce 139 reads 'per breve de morte'.
[53] Douce 139 reads 'et'.
[54] Douce 139 reads 'post mortem'.
[55] Cotton Claudius reads 'sibi'.
[56] Douce 139 reads 'recuperabit'.
[57] Bodley 91 reads 'insuper'.
[58] Bodley 91 and Douce 139 read 'fuerit'.
[59] Douce 139 reads 'debent'.
[60] Douce 139 omits.

CLAUSE 10

No one in future is to be allowed for whatever reason to make distraints outside his fee nor in the king's or common highway other than the lord king and his officials.
[1259 Provisions, clause 11]

CLAUSE 11

If any heir at the death of his ancestor is below age and his lord has wardship of his lands and that lord refuses to hand over his land without a plea to the said heir when he comes of lawful age that heir will recover his land as of the death of his ancestor together with the damages which he has sustained by reason of that detention from the time he was of lawful age. But if the heir was of full age at the death of his ancestor and heir apparent and known as heir and found in that inheritance, his chief lord is not to eject him or take or remove anything there but merely to take a simple seisin of it for the acknowledgement of his lordship. And if the chief lord keeps such an heir out of seisin maliciously, so that it is necessary to implead him by an action of mort d'ancestor or consanguinity, then he is to recover his damages as in the action of novel disseisin.
[1259 Provisions, clauses 9 and 10]

CLAUSE 12

It has also been provided that, if land which is held in socage is in the wardship of the kinsmen of the heir because the heir is under age, those guardians may not make waste or sale or any destruction of that inheritance but are to keep it safely for the benefit of the said heir, so that when he shall come of age, they are to answer him through a lawful accounting for the issues of the said inheritance with due allowance made to those guardians of their reasonable expenses. Nor may the said guardians give or sell the marriage of the said heir other than for the benefit of the same heir.
[1259 Provisions, clause 12]

CLAUSE 13

Nullus escaetor aut inquisitor vel justiciarius ad assisas aliquas capiendas specialiter assignatus vel ad querelas aliquas audiendas et terminandas de cetero potestatem habeat aliquem amerciandi pro <defalta>[61] communis summonicionis nisi capitalis justiciarius vel justiciarii itinerantes in itineribus suis.
[1259 Provisions, clause 13]

CLAUSE 14

De essoniis autem provisum est quod in comitatibus, hundredis[62] aut curiis baronum vel alibi nullus habeat necesse jurare pro essonio suo warantizando.
[1259 Provisions, clause 14]

CLAUSE 15

Nullus <decetero>[63] <excepto rege>[64] placitum teneat in curia sua de falso judicio facto in curia tenencium suorum, quia hujusmodi placita <specialiter pertinent>[65] ad coronam et dignitatem <domini regis.>[66]
[1259 Provisions, clause 16]

CLAUSE 16

Provisum est eciam quod, si averia alicujus capiantur et injuste detineantur, vicecomes post querimoniam inde sibi factam ea sine impedimento vel contradiccione ejus qui dicta averia cepit deliberare possit, si extra libertates fuerint capta. Et si infra libertates hujusmodi averia capiantur et ballivi libertatum ea deliberare noluerint tunc vicecomes <per defectum>[67] dictorum ballivorum ea faciat deliberari.
[1259 Provisions, clause 17]

CLAUSE 17

Provisum est eciam quod, si ballivi qui compotum dominis suis reddere <tenentur>[68] se subtraxerint et terras vel tenementa non habuerint per que distringi possint, tunc <per>[69] eorum corpora attachientur, ita quod vicecomites in quorum ballivis invenientur eos venire faciant ad compotum suum reddendum.
[1259 Provisions, clause 19]

[61] Bodley 91 reads 'defectu'.
[62] Douce 139 adds 'wapentakiis'. [63] Douce 139 reads 'autem'.
[64] Douce 139 reads 'excepto domino rege'; Cotton Claudius and Malmesbury read 'exceptis nobis'.
[65] Douce 139 reads 'spectant specialiter'. [66] Cotton Claudius and Malmesbury read 'nostram'.

CLAUSE 13

No escheator or inquirer or justice specially assigned to take any assizes or to hear and determine any complaints is in future to have power to amerce anyone for default of the common summons except for the chief justiciar and the justices itinerant in their eyres.
[1259 Provisions, clause 13]

CLAUSE 14

Concerning essoins, moreover, it has been provided that in county courts, hundred courts and courts baron and elsewhere no one is to be required to warrant his essoin on oath.
[1259 Provisions, clause 15]

CLAUSE 15

No one in future other than the king is to hold a plea in his court about a wrongful judgment made in the court of his tenants, because such pleas belong specially to the crown and dignity of the king.
[1259 Provisions, clause 16]

CLAUSE 16

It has also been provided that if anyone's animals are taken and unjustly detained, the sheriff, after a complaint made to him about this, may release them without the impediment or obstruction of the person who took the said animals, if they were taken outside franchises. If such animals are taken within franchises and the bailiffs of the franchises refuse to release them then the sheriff is to have them released by virtue of the failure of the said bailiffs.
[1259 Provisions, clause 17]

CLAUSE 17

It has also been provided that, if bailiffs who are obliged to render account to their lords flee from them and do not have lands and tenements by which they may be distrained, then they are to be attached by their bodies, so that the sheriffs in whose bailiwicks they are found are to make them come to render their account.
[1259 Provisions, clause 19]

[67] Cotton Claudius reads 'pro defectu'. [68] Douce 139 reads 'debeant'.
[69] Cotton Claudius omits.

CLAUSE 18

Item firmarii tempore suarum firmarum vastum, vendicionem seu exilium non faciant <**in**>[70] boscis, domibus, hominibus, neque de aliquibus ad tenementa que ad firmam habent <spectantibus,>[71] nisi specialem habeant <concessionem>[72] per <scripturam>[73] sue convencionis mencionem habentis quod hec facere possint. Et si fecerint et de hoc convincantur dampna plene refundent.
[1259 Provisions, clause 20]
[schedule dorse]

CLAUSE 19

Justiciarii itinerantes decetero non amercient villatas in itinero suo pro eo quod singuli xij annorum non venerint coram **vicecomitibus** et coronatoribus ad inquisiciones de morte hominis aut aliis ad coronam <pertinentibus,>[74] dum tamen <de>[75] <villis>[76] illis veniant sufficienter per quos hujusmodi inquisiciones fieri plene possint.
[1259 Provisions, clause 21]

CLAUSE 20

Murdrum decetero non adjudicetur coram justiciariis ubi infortunium tantummodo adjudicatum est, set locum habeat murdrum in interfectis per feloniam et non aliter.
[1259 Provisions, clause 22]

CLAUSE 21

Provisum est **eciam** quod nullus, qui coram justiciariis itinerantibus vocatur ad warantum de placito terre vel tenementi, amercietur decetero pro eo quod presens non fuerit <**quando**>[77] **vocatur ad warantum,** excepto primo die adventus ipsorum justiciariorum. Set, si warantus ille sit infra comitatum, tunc injungatur vicecomiti quod ipsum infra tercium diem vel quartum secundum locorum distanciam faciat venire, sicut in itinere justiciariorum fieri consuevit. Et, si extra comitatum maneat, tunc racionabilem habeat summonicionem xv dierum ad minus secundum discrecionem justiciariorum et legem communem.
[1259 Provisions, clause 23]

[70] Cotton Claudius and Malmesbury read 'de'. [71] Cotton Claudius reads 'pertinentibus'.
[72] Malmesbury reads 'convencionem'; Douce 139 adds here 'aut'.
[73] Bodley 91 and Douce 139 read 'scripta'; Cotton Claudius reads 'scripturas'.
[74] Cotton Claudius and Malmesbury read 'spectantibus'.
[75] Douce 139 reads 'pro'. [76] Douce 139 reads 'villatis'. [77] Douce 139 reads 'qui'.

CLAUSE 18

Also lessees during the period of their leases are not to make waste, sale or exile **in** the woods, houses, men or of anything else belonging to the tenements which they have on lease, unless they have a specific concession in the writing of their agreement mentioning that they may do these things. And if they do this and are convicted of doing so they are to refund the damages in full.
[1259 Provisions, clause 20]

CLAUSE 19

The justices itinerant are not in future to amerce townships on their eyre because everyone aged twelve and over did not appear before the sheriffs and coroners for inquisitions into homicides or other matters belonging to the crown, provided there was a sufficient attendance from those villages to allow such inquisitions to be properly held.
[1259 Provisions, clause 21]

CLAUSE 20

The *murdrum* fine is not in future to be adjudged as due before the justices where only death by misadventure has been adjudged but is to apply only to those killed feloniously.
[1259 Provisions, clause 22]

CLAUSE 21

It has also been provided that no one who is vouched to warranty before the justices itinerant in a plea relating to land or a tenement is to be amerced in future because he was not present **when he was vouched to warranty** other than on the first day of the visitation of the same justices. But, if that warrantor is within the county, the sheriff is to be enjoined to make him come by the third or the fourth day depending on the distance, as has been customary in the eyre of the justices. And, if he is living outside the county, then he is to have a proper summons of at least fifteen days according to the discretion of the justices and common law.
[1259 Provisions, clause 23]

CLAUSE 22

Si clericus aliquis <pro crimine aliquo vel retto quod ad coronam pertineat arestatus>[78] fuerit et postmodum de precepto <regis>[79] in ballium traditus vel replegiatus extiterit, ita quod hii quibus traditur in ballium eum habeant coram justiciariis, non amercientur decetero illi quibus traditus fuit in ballium vel alii plegii sui, si corpus suum habeant coram justiciariis, licet coram eis propter privilegium clericale respondere nolit vel non possit.
[1259 Provisions, clause 24]

CLAUSE 23[80]

Nullus decetero distringere possit libere tenentes suos ad respondendum de libero tenemento suo neque de aliquibus ad liberum tenementum suum spectantibus <sine brevi domini regis.>[81] Nec jurare faciat libere tenentes suos contra voluntatem suam, desicut nullus hoc facere potest sine precepto <domini regis.>[82]
[1259 Provisions, clause 18]

CLAUSE 24

Provisum est eciam quod, si depredaciones vel rapine alique fiant abbatibus aut aliis prelatis ecclesiasticis et ipsi jus suum de hujusmodi depredacionibus prosequentes morte preveniantur antequam inde justiciam fuerunt assecuti, successores eorum accionem habeant ad bona ecclesie sue <de manibus hujusmodi transgressorum repetenda. Similem insuper accionem habeant successores de hiis que domui <et>[83] ecclesie sue>[84] recenter ante obitum predecessorum suorum per hujusmodi violenciam fuerint <subtracta,>[85] licet predicti predecessores jus suum prosecuti non fuerint in vita sua.

Si autem in terras et tenementa hujusmodi religiosorum de quibus eorum prelati obierunt seisiti ut de jure ecclesie sue aliqui se intrudant tempore vacacionis, eorum successores breve habeant de recuperanda seisina sua et adjudicentur eis dampna sicut in nova disseisina adjudicari <consueverunt.>[86]
[New clause]

[78] Douce 139 reads 'qui aliquo retto criminis ad coronam pertinente attachiatus'.
[79] Cotton Claudius and Malmesbury read 'nostro'.
[80] This clause is omitted from Douce 139; in Cotton Claudius and Malmesbury it comes immediately after clause 16.
[81] Cotton Claudius and Malmesbury omit. [82] Cotton Claudius and Malmesbury read 'nostro'.
[83] Cotton Claudius reads 'vel'. [84] Malmesbury omits.
[85] Bodley 91 reads 'abstracta'. [86] Bodley 91 reads 'consuevit'.

CLAUSE 22

If any clerk is arrested for any crime or offence which belongs to the crown and is subsequently by the king's order released on bail or replevied, so that those to whom he is bailed produce him before the justices, those to whom he is bailed or his other sureties are not in future to be amerced if they have his body before the justices even if he refuses or is unable to answer before them because of clerical privilege.
[1259 Provisions, clause 24]

CLAUSE 23

No one may in future distrain his free tenants to answer for their free tenement or anything relating to their free tenement without the lord king's writ. Nor is he to make his free tenants take oaths against their will, since no one may do this without the lord king's authorisation.
[1259 Provisions, clause 18]

CLAUSE 24

It has also been provided that if any depredations or forcible seizures are made from abbots or other ecclesiastical prelates and, while prosecuting justice in respect of such depredations, death overcomes them before they have received justice, their successors are to have an action to recover the goods of their church from the hands of such offenders. Their successors are, moreover, to have a like action for those things taken from their house and church shortly before the death of their predecessors by such violence, even if the said predecessors did not initiate action in their lifetimes.

If, moreover, anyone intrudes into lands and tenements belonging to such men of religion of which their prelates died seised as of the right of their church during a vacancy their successors are to have a writ to recover their seisin and damages are to be adjudged to them as are customarily adjudged in novel disseisin.
[new clause]

CLAUSE 25

Provisum est eciam quod [si][87] alienaciones ille de quibus breve de ingressu dari consuevit per tot gradus fiant quod breve illud in forma prius usitata haberi non possit habeat breve conquerens ad [recuperandum][88] seisinam suam sine mensione graduum ad cujuscumque manus per hujusmodi alienaciones res illa devenerit per originalia per consilium <regis>[89] inde providenda.
[New clause]

CLAUSE 26[90]

De cartis vero <exempcionis>[91] et libertatis ne ponantur impetrantes in assisis, juratis vel recognicionibus provisum est ut, si adeo necessarium sit eorum juramentum quod sine eo justicia exhiberi non possit, veluti in magna assisa, in perambulacionibus et ubi in cartis vel scriptis convencionum fuerint testes nominati aut in attinctis vel aliis <casibus>[92] aliis consimilibus, jurare cogantur, salva sibi alias libertate et <exempcione>[93] predicta.
[1259 Provisions, clause 8]

87 Supplied from Cotton Claudius and Malmesbury.
88 MS. reads 'recipiendum'; 'recuperandum' is the reading of Bodley 91, Douce 139, Cotton Claudius and Malmesbury.
89 Cotton Claudius and Malmesbury read 'nostrum'.
90 This clause appears immediately after clause 9 in Bodley 91, Douce 139, Cotton Claudius and Malmesbury.
91 Bodley 91 and Malmesbury read 'excepcionis'.
92 Cotton Claudius reads 'causis'.
93 Bodley 91 and Malmesbury read 'excepcione'.

CLAUSE 25

It has also been provided that, [if] alienations for which the writ of entry is customarily given have passed through so many degrees that this writ is unavailable in the form previously in use, the complainant is to have a writ to recover his seisin without mention of degrees to whomsoever's hands that property has come by original writs that are to be provided for this purpose by the king's council.
[New clause]

CLAUSE 26

Concerning charters of exemption and freedom whose holders are freed from being put on assizes, juries and recognitions it has been provided that, if their oath is so essential that without it justice cannot be done, as in case of the grand assize and perambulations and where they are the witnesses named in charters or deeds of agreement or in attaints or in like cases, they are to be compelled to take the oath, without prejudice to their said liberty and exemption on another occasion.
[1259 Provisions, clause 8]

Appendix II

CONCLUDING CLAUSE ADDED FOR THE 1264 REISSUE

Et quia nolumus quod aliquis <sub>[94] observacione premissorum decetero se possit per ignoranciam excusare, seu quod dicte provisiones et constituciones tantummodo verbales ab aliquibus ulterius reputentur, sed quod universa et singula predicta opere compleantur, de consilio prelatorum et magnatum nostrorum precipimus, firmiter injungentes, quod eedem provisiones et constituciones per vicecomites nostros de mense in mensem in comitatibus, hundredis et wapentachiis suis, <et>[95] curiis baronum publicentur et ad utilitatem tocius communitatis Anglie[96] de cetero firmiter observentur. Et si aliqui dictis provisionibus et constitucionibus contraire presumpserint,volumus quod ipsi per vicecomites nostros predictos, tanquam precepti nostri contemptores et earundem provisionum et constitucionum transgressores, graviter puniantur. Quod si dicti vicecomites ad hoc non sufficiant, tunc nomina eorum nobis scire faciant, ut ipsos et prefatos vicecomites, si in premissis negligentes fuerint et remissi, puniri faciamus, prout de jure fuerit faciendum. In cujus rei testimonium has literas nostras fieri fecimus patentes. Teste me ipso apud <Wygorn'. Anno regni nostri quadragesimo nono. Quartodecimo die Decembris.>[97]

Note

The enumeration of the clauses is my own. The passages where this text differs materially from the 1259 Provisions are marked in bold type.

94 Cotton Claudius reads 'super'.
95 Cotton Claudius reads 'necnon in'.
96 Cotton Claudius adds 'sub omnibus' here.
97 Cotton Claudius reads 'Wygorniam xiij^{o} die Decembris anno regni nostri quadragesimo nono et anno domini millesimo cc lxiiij^{to}'.

CONCLUDING CLAUSE ADDED FOR THE 1264 REISSUE

And because we do not wish that anyone can in future excuse himself from the observance of the foregoing by ignorance, or that the said provisions and constitutions be reputed by anyone hereafter as mere words, but that all and each be put into execution, on the advice of our prelates and magnates we order and firmly enjoin that the same provisions and constitutions be published by our sheriffs each month in their county courts, hundred courts and wapentake courts and also in courts baron and in future be firmly observed for the benefit of the whole community of England. And if anyone presumes to go against the said provisions and constitutions we wish that they be heavily punished by our said sheriffs as being in contempt of our order and as offenders against the same provisions and constitutions. But if the said sheriffs are unable to do this they are to let us know their names, so that we may have them punished and the said sheriffs, if they shall be negligent and remiss in the foregoing, as is rightfully to be done. In witness of which we have had made these our letters patent. Witness myself at Worcester on 14 December in the forty-ninth year of our reign.

Note

This is my own independent original translation of the Provisions. It is a relatively free rendering of the original, intended to convey the sense of the original, but not following the exact wording of the original literally.

Appendix III

THE STATUTE OF MARLBOROUGH OF 1267

Sources

a) E 164/2 (Red Book of the Exchequer), fols. 243r–244v (new pencil foliation makes 349r–350v): printed *SR*, I, 19–25: checked against the original for this text.

b) ff. 147v–153v: printed in *Liber de Antiquis Legibus* (*LAL*), pp. 227–34: only significant differences noted in the footnotes (here abbreviated as *LAL*).

Appendix III

TEXT

HEADING[1]

Provisiones facte apud Marleberg' presentibus domino rege H[enrico] et R[icardo] rege Alemannie et domino Edward filio <ejusdem H[enrici]>[2] regis primogenito et domino Octobuono tunc legato in Anglia.

PREAMBLE

Anno <gracie>[3] M°CC° LX° septimo, regni autem <domini>[4] H[enrici] regis filii regis Johannis quinquagesimo secundo, in octabis sancti Martini, providente ipso domino rege ad regni sui Anglie melioracionem et exhibicionem justicie, prout regalis officii exposcit utilitas, meliorem, convocatis discrecioribus ejusdem regni tam ex majoribus quam minoribus, <provisum est et statutum ac concorditer ordinatum ut, cum regnum Anglie multis tribulacionibus et dissensionum incomodis nuper depressum reformacione legum et jurium, quibus pax et tranquillitas incolarum conservetur, indigeat, ad quod remedium salubre per ipsum regem et suos fideles oportuit adhiberi, provisiones, ordinaciones et statuta subscripta ab omnibus regni ipsius incolis, tam majoribus quam minoribus,>[5] firmiter ac inviolabiliter temporibus perpetuis observentur.
[new]

[1] This heading is found in the Red Book text only. [2] These words are interlined.
[3] *LAL* reads 'Domini'. [4] *LAL* omits. [5] *LAL* omits through homoeoteleuton.

Text of the Statute of Marlborough

TRANSLATION

HEADING

Provisions made at Marlborough in the presence of lord King Henry and Richard king of Germany and the lord Edward the eldest son of the same King Henry and Lord Ottobuono then legate in England.

PREAMBLE

In the year of grace 1267, and in the fifty-second regnal year of the lord King Henry the son of King John, at the octaves of Martinmas, with the same lord king making provision for the amelioration of his kingdom of England and the better administration of justice, as the nature of the king's office requires, having called together the wiser men of the same kingdom from both the great men and the lesser men of the same kingdom, it has been provided and decreed and ordained by common agreement that whereas the kingdom of England, having recently been brought low by many tribulations and the inconveniences of dissensions, requires a reform of laws and rights by which the peace and tranquillity of the inhabitants might be preserved, for which it was necessary that a salutary remedy be provided by the same king and his faithful subjects, the provisions, ordinances and statutes below written were to be observed by all the inhabitants of the same kingdom, both great men and lesser, firmly and inviolably for all time.
[new]

CHAPTER I

Cum igitur tempore turbacionis nuper in regno suborte et deinceps multi magnates et alii justiciam non dignati fuerint recipere per dominum regem et curiam ejus, prout debuerunt et consueverunt temporibus predecessorum ipsius domini regis et eciam tempore suo, set de vicinis et aliis per seipsos graves ulciones fecerint et graves districciones quousque redempciones receperint ad voluntatem suam, et preterea quidam eorum se justiciari non permittant per ministros domini regis nec sustineant quod per eos liberentur districciones quas auctoritate propria fecerunt ad voluntatem suam, provisum est et concorditer concessum quod tam majores quam minores justiciam faciant et recipiant in curia domini regis et nullus de cetero ulciones aut districciones faciat per propriam voluntatem suam absque consideracione curie domini regis si forte dampnum vel injuria sibi fiat unde emendas habere voluerit de vicino suo, sive majore sive minore.

Super articulo autem supradicto provisum est et concessum ut, si quis de cetero ulcionem hujusmodi capiat per voluntatem suam propriam sine consideracione curie domini regis et inde convincatur, puniatur per redempcionem et hoc secundum quantitatem delicti; et similiter, si super vicinum suum faciat districciones sine consideracione curie <domini regis>[6] per quod dampnum habeat, puniatur eodem modo et hoc secundum delicti sui qualitatem et nichilominus fiant emende plene et sufficientes eis qui dampnum sustinuerunt per hujusmodi districcionem.

[new chapter]

[6] *LAL* omits.

CHAPTER I

Whereas, therefore, during the period of recent disturbances in the kingdom and since, many magnates and others have not deigned to receive justice at the hands of the lord king and his court, as they ought to do and customarily did in the reigns of the predecessors of the same lord king and in his own reign, but have taken heavy revenge against their neighbours and others themselves and have made heavy distraints until they have received ransoms at their own pleasure, and moreover some of them have refused to submit to the actions of the officials of the lord king as part of the judicial system nor allowed the distresses which they have taken on their own authority and as they pleased to be released by them, it has been provided and conceded by common agreement that both great and lesser men are to do and receive justice in the court of the lord king and that no one in future is to take revenge or make distraints at their own pleasure without a judgment of the court of the lord king, if perhaps some harm or wrong has been done to him for which he wishes to have compensation from his neighbour, whether a great man or a lesser man.

It has also been provided and conceded, moreover, in relation to the above article that, if anyone in future takes this kind of revenge on his own authority without a judgment of the court of the lord king and is convicted of this, he is to be punished by a ransom and that in proportion to the gravity of the offence. Likewise, if he make distraints against his neighbour without the judgment of the court of the lord king and thereby causes loss, he is to be punished in the same way and in proportion to the nature of his offence and in addition full and sufficient compensation is to be paid to those who have sustained loss by such a distraint.

[new chapter]

CHAPTER 2

Nullus insuper major vel minor distringat aliquem ad veniendum ad curiam suam qui non sit de feodo suo aut super ipsum habeat jurisdiccionem per hundredum vel ballivam que sua sit; <nec districciones faciat extra feodum suum seu locum ubi ballivam habeat seu jurisdiccionem.>[7] Et qui contrafecerit puniatur eodem modo et hoc secundum delicti quantitatem.
[new chapter]

CHAPTER 3

Si quis autem major vel minor permittere noluerit liberari per ministros domini regis et secundum legem et consuetudinem regni districciones quas fecerit, aut eciam si sustinere noluerit execuciones judiciorum curie domini regis fieri aut eciam sustinere noluerit summoniciones et athachiamenta fieri secundum legem et consuetudinem regni, puniatur modo predicto, tanquam se justiciari non permittens, et hoc secundum delicti quantitatem.[8]

Quod si quis major vel minor districciones faciat super tenentem suum pro serviciis aut consuetudinibus que sibi deberi dicat vel pro re altera unde ad dominum feodi pertineat facere districciones et postea convincatur quod tenens ejus ea sibi non debeat, non ideo puniatur dominus per redempcionem, sicut in casibus supradictis, si permittat districciones liberari secundum legem et consuetudinem regni set amercietur velud hactenus fieri consueverit et tenens dampna sua recuperet plene versus eum.
[new chapter]

[7] *LAL* omits.
[8] *LAL* marks the break between its chapters 2 and 3 at this point.

CHAPTER 2

No one, moreover, whether a great or a lesser man, is to distrain anyone to appear at his court who does not belong to his fee or who does not come under his jurisdiction by virtue of a hundred or bailiwick which he holds; nor is he to make distraints outside his fee or the area where he has a bailiwick or jurisdiction. Anyone who breaches this is to be punished in the same way and in proportion to the gravity of his offence.
[new chapter]

CHAPTER 3

If anyone, whether a great or a lesser man, refuses to allow the distresses which he has made to be released by the officials of the lord king and in accordance with the law and custom of the realm or refuses to permit the execution of the judgments of the court of the lord king or refuses to permit the making of summonses and attachments in accordance with the law and custom of the realm, he is to be punished in the same way as of one refusing to allow the judicial system to operate against him and that in proportion to the gravity of his offence.

But if anyone, whether a great or a lesser man, makes distraints against his tenant for services or customary dues which he says are owed to him or for some other matter for which the lord of the fee is allowed to make distraints and subsequently it is found that his tenant does not owe them to him, the lord is not as a result to be punished by ransom, as in the foregoing situations, provided he allows the distresses to be released in accordance with the law and custom of the realm, but he is to be amerced as has hitherto been customary and the tenant is to recover his damages in full against him.
[new chapter]

CHAPTER 4

Nullus decetero ducere faciat districciones quas fecerit extra comitatum in quo fuerint; et si vicinus hoc fecerit supra vicinum per voluntatem suam et sine judicio puniatur per redempcionem ut supra, veluti de re contra pacem; verumptamen si dominus hoc supra tenentem suum facere presumpserit castigetur per gravem misericordiam.[9] **Districciones insuper sint racionabiles et non nimis graves et, si quis districciones fecerit inracionabiles et indebitas, graviter amercietur propter excessum districcionum ipsarum.**
[new chapter]

CHAPTER 5

Magna Carta in singulis suis articulis teneatur tam in hiis que ad regem pertinent quam ad alios. Et hoc justiciariis in itineribus suis et vicecomitibus in suis comitatibus cum opus fuerit demandetur. Et brevia versus eos qui contravenerint gratis concedantur coram rege vel coram Banco vel coram justiciariis itinerantibus cum venerint ad partes illas.
[new chapter]

[9] *LAL* marks the break between its chapters 4 and 5 at this point.

CHAPTER 4

No one is in future to take distresses which he has taken outside the county where they have been made. If a neighbour does this against a neighbour at his own pleasure and without a judgment he is to be punished by a ransom, as above, as of an offence against the peace; but if a lord presume to do this against his tenant he is to be disciplined by a heavy amercement. Distresses are, moreover, to be reasonable and not too harsh and, if anyone makes unreasonable and improper distraints, he is to be heavily amerced for the excessive nature of those distraints.

[new chapter]

CHAPTER 5

Magna Carta is to be observed in every article, both in those relating to the king and those relating to others. And this is to be required of both the justices on their eyres and sheriffs in their counties, whenever needed. And writs against those who breach its provisions are to be granted freely for hearing before the king or the Bench or before the justices itinerant when they come to those parts.

[new chapter]

CHAPTER 6

De hiis autem qui primogenitos et heredes suos infra etatem existentes feoffare solent de hereditate sua, ut per hoc amitterent domini feodorum custodias suas, provisum est et concorditer concessum ut occasione hujusmodi feoffamenti nullus capitalis dominus custodiam suam amittat.[10]

De hiis insuper qui de terris suis, quas tradere volunt ad terminum annorum, et ut domini feodorum amittant custodias suas, falsa confingunt feoffamenta continencia quod eis satisfactum est de summa servicii in illis contenti usque ad terminum aliquem et quod post dictum terminum solvere teneantur huiusmodi feoffati summam aliquam valorem terrarum illarum in multo excedentem, ut sic post terminum illum terra eorum revertatur ad ipsos, eo quod nemo eas pro tanto tenere currat, provisum est et concessum, ut per hujusmodi fraudem nullus capitalis dominus amittat custodiam suam. Verumptamen non licebit eis hujusmodi feoffatos sine judicio disseisire set breve capiant de hujusmodi custodia sibi reddenda. Et per testes in cartis [fol. 243v] de hujusmodi feoffamentis contentos, una cum aliis liberis et legalibus de patria, et per quantitatem valoris tenementi et per quantitatem summe que reddi debet post terminum predictum attingatur utrum hujusmodi feoffamentum bona fide factum sit vel in fraudem ad auferendum capitalibus dominis custodiam suam. Si tamen capitales domini per judicium curie recuperent in hujusmodi casibus custodiam suam, salva sit nichilominus hujusmodi feoffatis accio sua ad terminum seu ad feodum suum recuperandum cum heres ad legitimam etatem pervenerit.[11] **Quod si aliqui capitales domini feoffatos aliquos maliciose implacitaverint fingentes casum istum, ubi feoffamenta legitime et bona fide facta fuerint, tunc adjudicentur feoffatis dampna sua et mise sue quas fecerint occasione placiti predicti, et ipsi actores per misericordiam graviter puniantur.**
[new chapter]

10 *LAL* marks the break between its chapters 7 and 8 at this point.

11 *LAL* marks the break between its chapters 8 and 9 at this point.

CHAPTER 6

As for those who have been accustomed to enfeoff their eldest sons and heirs while they are still under age of their inheritance, so that the lords of fees should thereby lose their wardships, it has been provided and conceded by common agreement that no chief lord is to lose his wardship by reason of such a feoffment. As for those, moreover, who, wishing to lease their lands for a term of years and to ensure that the lords of the fee lose their wardships, make false feoffments stating that they have been satisfied in advance for the total service they contain up to a certain date and that after that date these feoffees are obliged to pay an amount much in excess of the value of those lands, so that after that date their land should revert to them, as no one would care to hold them for so much, it has been provided and conceded that no chief lord is to lose his wardship by such a trick. However, they are not to be allowed to disseise such feoffees without judgment but are to get a writ for the recovery of such a wardship, and through the witnesses contained in the charters of such feoffments with other free and respectable men of the area and by considering the value of the tenement and the total payable after the said date it is to be ascertained whether such a feoffment has been made in good faith or as a trick to defraud chief lords of their wardship. None the less, even if chief lords recover their wardships in such cases by judgment of the court, this is to be without prejudice to the right of action of such feoffees to recover their term or fee when the heir comes of age. But if any chief lords maliciously implead any feoffees falsely asserting this to be the case but where the feoffments have been made properly and in good faith the feoffees are to be adjudged their damages and the expenses which they have had to sustain by reason of the said plea and the plaintiffs are to be heavily punished by amercement.

[new chapter]

CHAPTER 7

In placito vero communi de custodiis si ad magnam districcionem non venerint deforciantes, tunc bis vel ter iteretur breve predictum ad terminos quibus poterit fieri infra medietatem anni sequentis, ita quod singulis vicibus legatur breve in pleno comitatu <ubi>[12] inventus fuerit deforciator et ibi pupblice denuncietur ut veniat ad diem sibi prefixum. Quod si ipse se subtraxerit, ita quod infra predictam medietatem anni responsurus non venerit, nec vicecomes illum invenire possit, per quod corpus suum habere possit coram justiciariis ad respondendum secundum legem et consuetudinem regni, tunc tanquam rebellis et se justiciari non permittens amittat seysinam hujusmodi custodie, salva sibi alias accione sua si forte jus habeat ad eandem. In casibus autem ubi custodie pertinent ad custodes heredum infra etatem existencium et versus custodes ipsos petuntur custodie que accidunt heredibus illis tanquam pertinentes ad eorum hereditatem non amittant hujusmodi heredes infra etatem existentes per negligenciam seu rebellionem sui custodis, sicut in casu supradicto, sed currat <lis>[13] eodem modo quo prius consuevit.

[new chapter]

CHAPTER 8

Illi autem qui pro iterata disseysina capti fuerint et detenti non deliberentur sine speciali precepto regis et hoc per finem cum domino rege faciendam pro hujusmodi transgressione sua. Et si compertum fuerit quod vicecomes eos aliter deliberavit graviter propter hoc amercietur et nichilominus illi qui per vicecomitem sine precepto regis deliberantur pro sua transgressione puniantur.

[new chapter]

[12] *LAL* reads 'nisi prius'

[13] *LAL* reads 'lex'.

CHAPTER 7

In the common plea of wardship, if the defendants do not appear at the grand distress, then the said writ is to be repeated two or three times within the following half year at whatever terms are possible, so that each time the writ is to be read in a full session of the county court in the county where the defendant is to be found and a public announcement be made there that he should appear on the day appointed for his appearance. But if he goes missing, so that he does not appear to answer within that said half year and the sheriff is unable to find him so that he may produce his body before the justices to answer in accordance with the law and custom of the realm, then as a rebel and one refusing to sumit to the judicial system, he is to lose seisin of the wardship, but without prejudice to his right of action on another occasion if by chance he is entitled to it. But in cases where wardships belong to the guardians of heirs who are under age and the wardships which have come to those heirs as appurtenant to their inheritances are claimed against those guardians, such heirs who are under age are not to lose through the negligence or rebellion of their guardian, as in the above case, but the case is to follow the existing procedure.
[new chapter]

CHAPTER 8

Those, moreover, who have been arrested and imprisoned for redisseisin are not to be released without the specific order of the king obtained in return for a fine agreed with the lord king for their offence. And if it should be found that a sheriff has released them in any other way he is to be heavily amerced for this and those who have been released by the sheriff without the king's authorisation are none the less to be punished for their offence.
[new chapter]

CHAPTER 9

De sectis **siquidem** faciendis ad curias magnatum et aliorum dominorum ipsarum curiarum decetero sic observandum est, scilicet quod nullus qui per cartam feoffatus est distringatur de cetero ad hujusmodi sectam faciendam ad curiam domini sui nisi per formam carte sue specialiter teneatur ad sectam faciendam, hiis tantum exceptis quorum antecessores vel ipsimet hujusmodi sectam facere consueverunt ante primam transfretacionem domini regis in Britanniam, a tempore cujus transfretacionis elapsi fuerant **triginta et novem anni et medietas unius anni** tempore quo **hujusmodi constituciones fuerant statute.**[14] Et similiter nullus feoffatus sine carta a tempore Conquestus vel alio antiquo feofamento distringatur **de cetero** ad hujusmodi sectam faciendam, nisi ipse vel antecessores sui eam facere consueverunt ante transfretacionem domini regis supradictam.[15] **Qui autem per cartam pro certo servicio, veluti pro libero servicio tot solidorum annuatim pro omni servicio solvendorum, feoffati sunt ad sectam vel aliud ultra formam sui feoffamenti non teneantur.**[16]

Et, si hereditas aliqua de qua unica tantum secta debebatur ad plures heredes participes ejusdem hereditatis devolvatur, ille qui habet eyneciam ejusdem hereditatis unicam faciat sectam pro se et participibus suis, et alii participes sui pro porcione sua contribuant ad sectam illam faciendam.[17] Similiter si plures feoffati fuerint de hereditate aliqua, de qua unica secta debebatur, dominus feodi illius unicam inde habeat sectam, nec possit de hereditate illa nisi unicam sectam exigere sicut prius fieri consuevit. Et, si feoffati illi warantum vel medium non habeant qui eos inde acquietare debeat, tunc omnes feoffati **illi** contribuant <pro porcione sua>[18] ad sectam illam faciendam.[19]

Si autem contingat quod domini curiarum tenentes suos contra hanc provisionem pro hujusmodi secta distringant, tunc ad querimoniam tenencium illorum atthachientur quod ad curiam regis veniant ad brevem diem inde responsuri, et unicum habeant essonium si fuerint in regno; et incontinenti deliberentur averia conquerenti sive alie districciones hac occasione facte et deliberata remaneant donec placitum inde inter eos terminetur. Et, si domini curiarum qui hujusmodi districciones fecerint ad diem ad quem atthachiati fuerint non venerint vel diem sibi datum per essonium non observaverint, tunc mandetur vicecomiti quod eos ad

[14] *LAL* marks the break between its chapters 13 and 14 at this point.
[15] *LAL* marks the break between its chapters 14 and 15 at this point.
[16] *LAL* marks the break between its chapters 15 and 16 at this point.
[17] *LAL* marks the break between its chapters 16 and 17 at this point.
[18] *LAL* reads 'proporcionem suam'.
[19] *LAL* marks the break between its chapters 17 and 18 at this point.

CHAPTER 9

Concerning the performance of suits to the courts of magnates and other lords of courts in future the following is to be observed, namely that no one who has been enfeoffed by charter is to be distrained in future to perform suit to the court of his lord unless he is specifically obliged by the terms of his charter to perform suit, except only for those whose ancestors or who themselves customarily performed such suit before the first voyage of the said lord king to Brittany, from the time of which voyage **thirty-nine and a half years** had elapsed at the time **these constitutions were** made. And likewise no one enfeoffed without a charter from the time of the Conquest or by some other ancient feoffment is to be distrained **in future** to perform such suit unless he or his ancestors customarily performed it before the first voyage of the said lord king to Brittany. **Those, moreover, who have been enfeoffed by charter for a fixed service, such as the free service of so many shillings a year for all service, are not to be obliged to perform suit or anything else beyond the terms of their feoffment.**

And, if any inheritance for which only one suit is owed devolves on several heirs as parceners of the same inheritance, the one who has the share of the eldest coheir is to perform that one suit on behalf of himself and his parceners and his other parceners are to contribute proportionately to the performance of that suit. Likewise also, if several are enfeoffed of any inheritance from which one suit only is owed, the lord of that fee is to have only one suit from it, nor may he demand from that inheritance any more than the one suit that used previously to be performed for it. And, if those feoffees do not have a warrantor or mesne who is obliged to acquit them of it, then all **those** feoffees are to contribute proportionately to the performance of that suit.

If, however, it should happen that the lords of courts distrain their tenants for such suit contrary to this provision, then on the complaint of those tenants they are to be attached to appear at the king's court to answer for this without delay and they are to have no more than one essoin, if they are within the kingdom; and the animals or other distresses taken for this reason are to be released to the complainant immediately and they are to remain released until the plea between them is determined. And if the lords of courts who have made such distraints do not appear on the day for which they were attached or do not keep the day given them by the essoin, then the sheriff is to be instructed to produce them on another day; on which day, if they do not appear, the sheriff is to be instructed to distrain them by everything they have in his bailiwick, so that the sheriff answer the king for the issues, and that he produce

alium diem venire faciat; ad quem diem, si non venerint, mandetur vicecomiti quod distringat eos per omnia que habent in balliva sua, ita quod vicecomes domino regi respondeat de exitibus, et quod habeat corpora eorum ad certum diem prefigendum; ita quod, si die illo non venerint, pars conquerens eat sine die et averia sive alie districciones deliberate remaneant donec ipsi domini sectam illam recuperaverint per consideracionem curie domini regis, et cessent interim districciones hujusmodi, salvo dominis curiarum jure suo de sectis illis perquirendis in forma juris cum inde loqui voluerint. Et cum domini curiarum venerint responsuri conquerentibus de hujusmodi districcionibus, si super hoc convincantur, tunc per consideracionem curie recuperent versus eos conquerentes dampna sua que sustinuerunt occasione districcionis predicte.

Simili autem modo, si tenentes post hanc constitucionem subtrahant dominis suis sectas quas facere debent et quas ante tempus supradicte transfretacionis et hactenus facere consueverunt, per eandem justiciam et celeritatem quoad dies prefigendos et districciones adjudicandos consequantur domini curiarum justiciam de sectis illis una cum dampnis suis quemadmodum tenentes dampna sua recuperant. Et hoc, scilicet de dampnis recuperandis, intelligatur de subtraccionibus sibi factis et non de subtraccionibus factis predecessoribus ipsorum. Verumptamen domini curiarum versus tenentes suos seisinam de sectis hujusmodi recuperare non poterunt per defaltam, sicut nec hactenus fieri consuevit.[20] [fol. 244r] De sectis autem que ante tempus supradictum subtracte fuerunt currat lex communis sicut prius currere consuevit.
[1263–4 Provisions, clauses 1–3]

CHAPTER 10

De turnis <vicecomitis>[21] provisum est ut necesse non habeant ibi venire archiepiscopi, episcopi, abbates, priores, comites, barones, nec aliqui viri religiosi seu mulieres, nisi eorum presencia specialiter exigatur, set teneatur turnus sicut temporibus predecessorum **domini regis** teneri consuevit. Et si qui in hundredis diversis habeant tenementa non habeant necesse ad hujusmodi turnos venire nisi in ballivis ubi fuerint conversantes. Et teneantur turni secundum formam Magne Carte **regis** et sicut temporibus regum Ricardi et Johannis teneri consueverunt.
[1263–4 Provisions, clause 4]

[20] *LAL* marks the break between its chapters 18 and 19 at this point.
[21] *LAL* reads 'vicecomitum'.

their bodies at a certain day to be fixed; so that, if they do not appear on that day, the complainant is to go without a day on the plea and the animals or other distresses are to remain delivered until those lords have recovered that suit by the judgment of the court of the lord king and in the interim such distraints are to cease, but without prejudice to the lords of the courts recovering those suits by way of law when they wish to do this. And when the lords of courts appear to answer the complainants for such distraints, if they are convicted of this, then the complainants are to recover against them by judgment of the court of the lord king their damages which they sustained by reason of the said distraint.

Likewise, if tenants after this constitution withdraw from their lords the suits which they are obliged to perform and which they customarily performed before the time of the aforesaid voyage and hitherto, the lords of courts are to get justice in respect of those suits together with damages by the same process and speed in making adjournments and adjudging distraints as tenants recover their damages. And this, that is on the recovery of damages, is to be understood in relation to withdrawals made from them and not withdrawals made from their predecessors. But the lords of courts may not recover seisin of such suits against their tenants by default, just as it has not been the custom hitherto. Concerning suits which were withdrawn before the said time the common law is to apply as it has applied hitherto.

[1263–4 Provisions, clauses 1–3]

CHAPTER 10

Concerning the sheriff's tourn it has been provided that archbishops, bishops, abbots, priors, earls, barons, and religious men and women should have no need to appear there unless their presence was specially required, but the tourn was to be held as it used to be held in the reigns of **the lord king's** predecessors. Those who have tenements in different hundreds are not to have to appear at such tourns other than in the bailiwicks where they are living. And tourns are to be held according to the terms of **the king's** Magna Carta and as they used to be held in the reigns of kings John and Richard.

[1263–4 Provisions, clause 4]

CHAPTER 11

Provisum est eciam quod nec in itinere justiciariorum nec in comitatibus, hundredis nec in curiis baronum decetero capiantur fines pro pulcre placitando neque per sic quod non occasionentur. Et sciendum [est][22] quod per istam constitucionem non tolluntur fines certi seu prestaciones arentate a tempore quo primo transfretavit rex in Britanniam usque nunc.
[1263–4 Provisions, clause 5]

CHAPTER 12

In placito vero dotis quod dicitur 'unde nichil habet' dentur decetero quatuor dies per annum <ad minus>[23] et plures si comode fieri possit; ita quod habeantur sex dies vel quinque ad minus per annum.[24]

In assisa autem ultime presentacionis et in placito 'quare impedit' de ecclesiis vacantibus detur dies de quindena in quindenam vel de tribus septimanis in tres septimanas, prout locus propinquus fuerit vel remotus.

Et in placito 'quare impedit', si ad primum diem ad quem summonitus fuerit non veniat nec essonium mittat impeditor, tunc athachietur ad diem alium; quo die, si non veniat nec essonium mittat, distringatur per magnam districcionem superius dictam. Et, si tunc non venerit, per ejus defaltam scribatur episcopo quod reclamacio inpeditoris illa vice conquerenti non obsistat, salvo impeditori alias jure suo cum inde loqui voluerit.[25]

Eadem lex de athachiamentis faciendis in omnibus brevibus ubi attachiamenta jacent decetero quo ad districciones faciendis firmiter observetur, ita tamen quod secundum attachiamentum sit per meliores plegios et postmodum ultima [districcio].[26]
[1263–4 Provisions, clauses 6–8]

[22] Supplied from *LAL*. [23] *LAL* omits.
[24] *LAL* marks the break between its chapters 22 and 23 at this point.
[25] *LAL* marks the break between its chapters 23 and 24 at this point.
[26] MS. reads 'restriccio'; 'districcio' is the reading of *LAL*.

CHAPTER 11

It has been provided also that neither in the eyre of the justices nor in county courts nor in hundred courts nor in courts baron are fines to be received in future from anyone for beaupleder or for not being harmed. And it is to be known that this constitution does not abolish those fines which have been fixed since the lord king's first voyage into Brittany or regular payments made ever since then.
[1263–4 Provisions, clause 5]

CHAPTER 12

In pleas, moreover, of dower *unde nichil habet* four days are to be given within a year at least and more if this can conveniently be done; so that there should be six days each year or five at the least.

In the assize of darrein presentment and plea of *quare impedit* relating to vacant churches adjournments of a fortnight or three weeks are to be given in accordance with whether the place is close or distant.

And in pleas of *quare impedit*, if the impedient does not appear or send an essoin on the first day for which he has been summoned, then he is to be attached for another day. If he does not appear on that day or send an essoin he is to be distrained by the grand distress mentioned above. And, if he does not then appear, the bishop is to be told on the basis of his default that the claim of the impedient is not to obstruct the complainant on this occasion, but without prejudice to the impedient's right on another occasion when he wishes to pursue it.

The same procedure in regard to the making of attachments is to be firmly observed in respect of distraints in all writs where attachments lie, so that the second attachment be made by better sureties and then the final distraint.
[1263–4 Provisions, clauses 6–8]

CHAPTER 13

Et sciendum quod **postquam** aliquis posuerit se in inquisicionem aliquam que **emersit** vel emergere potest in hujusmodi brevibus non habebit nisi unicum essonium vel unicam defaltam; ita scilicet quod, si ad diem sibi datum per essonium suum non venerit aut secundam defaltam fecerit, tunc inquisicio illa per defaltam ipsius capiatur et secundum inquisionem d judicium procedatur. Si vero inquisicio illa capta fuerit in comitatu coram coronatoribus vel justiciario regis ad certum diem remittenda et pars [rea][27] non venerit ad diem illum, tunc propter defaltam ipsius assignetur ei alius dies secundum discrecionem justicariorum <et mandetur vicecomiti quod ad diem illum ipsum venire faciat ad audiendum judicium suum si velit secundum inquisicionem illam;>[28] ad quem diem, si non venerit, procedatur ad judicium propter defaltam suam. Eodem modo fiat si non veniat ad diem datum sibi per essonium suum.
[1263–4 Provisions, clause 9]

CHAPTER 14

De cartis vero exempcionis et libertatis ne ponantur impetrantes in assisis, juratis vel recognicionibus provisum est quod, si adeo necessarium sit eorum juramentum quod sine eo justicia exhiberi non possit, veluti in magna assisa et in perambulacionibus et ubi in cartis vel scriptis convencionum fuerint testes nominati aut in attinctis vel aliis casibus consimilibus, jurare cogantur, salva sibi alias libertate et exempcione sua predicta.
[1263–4 Provisions, clause 26]

CHAPTER 15

[Nulli de cetero liceat ex quacumque causa districciones facere extra feodum suum neque in regia aut communi strata nisi domino regi et ministris suis.][29]
[1263–4 Provisions, clause 11]

[27] MS. reads 'ea'; 'rea' is the reading of *LAL*. [28] *LAL* omits.
[29] This chapter is missing from the Red Book and *LAL* texts but is included in most other early texts of the Statute: see above, p. 189.

CHAPTER 13

And it is to be known that **after** someone has put himself on any inquisition that **has arisen** or might arise in such writs he will not have more than a single essoin or single default, so that if he does not appear on the day given him by his essoin or makes a second default then the inquisition is to be taken by his default and judgment is to be given on the basis of that inquisition. If, however, that inquisition shall be taken in the county before the coroners or a justice of the lord king to be reported back for a certain day and the defendant does not appear on that day then another day is to be assigned to him by virtue of his default according to the discretion of the justices and the sheriff is to be instructed to produce him on that day to hear his judgment, if he wishes, in accordance with that inquisition, and if he does not appear on that day judgment is to be given by his default. The same procedure is to be followed if he does not appear on the day given him by his essoin.
[1263–4 Provisions, clause 9]

CHAPTER 14

Concerning charters of exemption and freedom whose holders are freed from being put on assizes, juries and recognitions it has been provided that, if their oath is so essential that without it justice cannot be done, as in case of the grand assize and perambulations and where they are the witnesses named in charters or deeds of agreement or in attaints or in like cases, they are to be compelled to take the oath, without prejudice to their said liberty and exemption on another occasion.
[1263–4 Provisions, clause 26]

CHAPTER 15

No one in future is to be allowed for whatever reason to make distraints outside his fee nor in the king's or common highway other than the lord king and his officials.
[1263–4 Provisions, clause 11]

CHAPTER 16

Si heres aliquis post mortem sui antecessoris infra etatem exstiterit et dominus suus custodiam terrarum suarum habuerit, si dominus ille dicto heredi, cum ad legitimam etatem pervenerit, terram suam sine placito reddere noluerit, heres ille terram suam <ut per mortem>[30] antecessoris sui recuperabit una cum dampnis que sustinuerit <per>[31] illam detencionem a tempore quo legittime fuerit etatis.[32]

Quod si heres **aliquis** in morte sui antecessoris plene fuerit etatis et heres ille apparens et pro herede cognitus inventus sit in hereditate illa, capitalis dominus ejus eum non ejiciat nec aliquid ibi capiat vel amoveat, set tantum inde simplicem seysinam faciat pro recognicione dominii sui. Et si capitalis dominus heredem hujusmodi extra seysinam maliciose teneat, per quod per <accionem>[33] mortis antecessoris vel consanguinitatis oporteat ipsum placitare, tunc dampna sua recuperet sicut in accione nove disseisine.[34]

De hereditatibus autem que de domino rege tenentur in capite sic observandum est, ut dominus rex liberam inde habeat seysinam, sicut prius consuevit, nec heres vel alius in hereditatem illam se intrudat [priusquam][35] illam de manibus domini regis recipiat, prout hujusmodi hereditates de manibus ipsius et antecessorum suorum recipi consueverint. Et hic intelligatur de terris et feodis [que][36] racione servicii militaris vel serjantie seu jure patronatus[37] in manu regis esse consueverunt.

[1263–4 Provisions, clause 11]

30 *LAL* reads 'ni per accionem mortis'.

31 *LAL* reads 'propter'.

32 *LAL* marks the break between its chapters 27 and 28 at this point.

33 *LAL* reads 'breve'.

34 *LAL* marks the break between its chapters 28 and 29 at this point.

35 MS. reads 'postquam'; 'priusquam' is the reading of *LAL*.

36 MS. reads 'in'; 'que' is the reading of *LAL*.

37 Followed in MS. (but not in *LAL*) by 'que'.

CHAPTER 16

If any heir at the death of his ancestor is below age and his lord has wardship of his lands and that lord refuses to hand over his land without a plea to the said heir when he comes of lawful age that heir will recover his land as of the death of his ancestor together with the damages which he has sustained by reason of that detention from the time he was of lawful age. But if the heir was of full age at the death of his ancestor and heir apparent and known as heir and found in that inheritance, his chief lord is not to eject him or take or remove anything there but merely to take a simple seisin of it for the acknowledgement of his lordship. And if the chief lord keeps such an heir out of seisin maliciously, so that it is necessary to implead him by an action of mort d'ancestor or cosinage, then he is to recover his damages as in the action of novel disseisin.

But for inheritances which are held in chief of the lord king the following is to apply: the king is to have unimpeded seisin, as was previously the case, and neither the heir nor anyone else is to intrude himself into that inheritance before he receives it from the hands of the lord king, as such inheritances have been customarily received from the hands of himself and his ancestors. And this is to be understood of lands and fees which have customarily been in the hands of the lord king by reason of knight service or serjeanty or by right of patronage.

[1263–4 Provisions, clause 11]

CHAPTER 17

Provisum est eciam quod, si terra que tenetur in socagio sit in custodia parentum heredis eo quod heres infra etatem exstiterit, custodes illi vastum facere non possint neque vendicionem nec aliquam destruccionem de hereditate, set salvo eam custodiant ad opus dicti heredis ita quod, cum ad etatem pervenerit, sibi respondeant per legitimam computacionem de exitibus dicte hereditatis, salvis ipsis custodibus racionabilibus misis suis. Nec eciam possunt dicti custodes maritagium dicti heredis dare vel vendere nisi ad comodum ipsius heredis. **Sed parentes propinquiores qui hujusmodi custodiam habuerint a toto tempore illo a quo brevia inplacitandi non conceduntur hujusmodi custodias habeant ad comodum heredis, ut predictum est, sine vasto, exilio vel destruccione faciendo.**
[1263–4 Provisions, clause 12]

CHAPTER 18

Nullus escaetor aut inquisitor vel justiciarius ad assisas aliquas capiendas[38] assignatus vel ad querelas aliquas audiendas et [fol. 244v] terminandas de cetero potestatem habeant aliquem amerciandi pro defalta comunis summonicionis nisi capitalis justiciarius vel justiciarii itinerantes in itineribus suis.
[1263–4 Provisions, clause 13]

CHAPTER 20

De essoniis autem provisum est quod in comitatibus, hundredis aut curiis baronum vel aliis nullus habeat necesse jurare pro essonio suo warantizando.
[1263–4 Provisions, clause 14]

CHAPTER 19

Nullus decetero excepto **domino** rege teneat placitum in curia sua de falso judicio facto in curia tenencium suorum, quia hujusmodi placita specialiter pertinent ad coronam et dignitatem **domini** regis.
[1263–4 Provisions, clause 15]

[38] *LAL* adds here 'specialiter'.

CHAPTER 17

It has also been provided that, if land which is held in socage is in the wardship of the kinsmen of the heir because the heir is under age, those guardians may not make waste or sale or any destruction of the inheritance but are to keep it safely for the benefit of the said heir, so that when he shall come of age, they are to answer him through a lawful accounting for the issues of the said inheritance with due allowance made to those guardians of their reasonable expenses. Nor may the said guardians give or sell the marriage of the said heir other than for the benefit of the same heir. **But the closest kinsmen who have held such a wardship from all that time when writs for impleading were not granted are to hold such wardships for the benefit of the heir, as is said, without committing waste, exile or destruction.**
[1263–4 Provisions, clause 12]

CHAPTER 18

No escheator or inquirer or justice assigned to take any assizes or to hear and determine any complaints is in future to have power to amerce for default of the common summons except for the chief justiciar and the justices itinerant in their eyres.
[1263–4 Provisions, clause 13]

CHAPTER 20

Concerning essoins, moreover, it has been provided that in county courts, hundred courts and courts baron and elsewhere no one is to be required to warrant his essoin on oath.
[1263–4 Provisions, clause 14]

CHAPTER 19

No one in future other than the **lord** king is to hold a plea in his court about a wrongful judgment made in the court of his tenants, because such pleas belong specially to the crown and dignity of the **lord** king.
[1263–4 Provisions, clause 15]

CHAPTER 21

Provisum est eciam quod, si averia alicujus capiantur et injuste detineantur, vicecomes post querimoniam sibi inde factam ea sine impedimento vel contradiccione ejus qui dicta averia ceperit deliberare possit, si extra libertates capta fuerint. Et si infra libertates hujusmodi averia capiantur et ballivi libertatum ea deliberare noluerint tunc vicecomes pro defectu eorumdem ballivorum ea faciat deliberari.
[1263–4 Provisions, clause 16]

CHAPTER 22

Nullus decetero distringere possit libere tenentes suos ad respondendum de libero tenemento suo neque de aliquibus ad liberum tenementum suum spectantibus, nec jurare faciat libere tenentes suos contra voluntatem suam, desicut nullus hoc facere potest sine precepto domini regis.
[1263–4 Provisions, clause 23]

CHAPTER 23

Provisum est eciam quod, si ballivi qui dominis suis compotum reddere tenentur **et** se subtraxerint et terras vel tenementa non habuerint per que distringi possint, tunc per eorum corpora atthachientur, ita quod vicecomites in quorum ballivis inveniantur eos venire faciant ad compotum suum reddendum.[39]

Item firmarii tempore firmarum suarum vastum, vendicionem seu exilium non faciant <in>[40] domibus, boscis, hominibus, neque de aliquibus ad tenementa que ad firmam habent spectantibus, nisi specialem habuerint concessionem[41] per scripturam [sue][42] convencionis mencionem habentis quod hoc facere possint. Et si fecerint et super hoc convincantur dampna plene refundent, **et graviter per misericordiam puniantur**.
[1263–4 Provisions, clauses 17 and 18]

[39] *LAL* marks the break between its chapters 26 and 27 at this point. [40] *LAL* reads 'de'.
[41] *LAL* adds here 'et'. [42] MSS. read 'sive'.

CHAPTER 21

It has also been provided that if anyone's animals are taken and unjustly detained, the sheriff, after a complaint made to him about this, may release them without the impediment or obstruction of the person who took the said animals, if they were taken outside franchises. If such animals are taken within franchises and the bailiffs of the franchises refuse to release them then the sheriff is to have them released by virtue of the failure of the said bailiffs.
[1263–4 Provisions, clause 16]

CHAPTER 22

No one may in future distrain his free tenants to answer for their free tenement or anything relating to their free tenement, nor is he to make his free tenants take oaths against their will, since no one may do this without the lord king's authorisation.
[1263–4 Provisions, clause 23]

CHAPTER 23

It has also been provided that, if bailiffs who are obliged to render account to their lords flee from them and do not have lands and tenements by which they may be distrained, then they are to be attached by their bodies, so that the sheriffs in whose bailiwicks they are found are to make them come to render their account.

Also lessees during the period of their leases are not to make waste, sale or exile in the woods, houses, men or of anything else belonging to the tenements which they have on lease, unless they have a specific concession in the writing of their agreement mentioning that they may do these things. And if they do this and are convicted of doing so they are to refund the damages in full **and to be heavily punished by amercement**.
[1263–4 Provisions, clauses 17 and 18]

CHAPTER 24

Item justiciarii itinerantes non amercient de cetero villatas in itinero suo pro eo quod singuli <duodecim>[43] annorum non venerint coram vicecomiti et coronatoribus ad inquisiciones de **robberiis et incendiis** aut aliis ad coronam spectantibus faciendas, dum tamen de <villis>[44] illis veniant sufficienter per quos hujusmodi inquisiciones plene fieri possint; **exceptis inquisicionibus de morte hominis faciendis ubi omnes <duodecim>[45] annorum venire debent nisi racionabilem causam absencie sue habeant**.
[1263–4 Provisions, clause 19]

CHAPTER 25

Murdrum decetero non adjudicetur coram justiciariis ubi infortunium tantummodo adjudicatum est, set locum habeat murdrum in interfectis per feloniam et non aliter.
[1263–4 Provisions, clause 20]

CHAPTER 26

Provisum est insuper quod nullus coram justiciariis itinerantibus vocatus ad warantum in placito terre vel tenementi, amercietur decetero pro eo quod presens non fuerit quando vocatur ad warantum, excepto primo die adventus justiciariorum. Set, si warantus ille sit infra comitatum, tunc injungatur vicecomiti quod ipsum infra diem tercium vel quartum, secundum locorum distanciam, faciat venire, sicut in itinere justiciariorum fieri consuevit. Et, si extra comitatum maneat, tunc racionabilem habeat summonicionem quindecim dierum ad minus secundum discrecionem justiciariorum et legem communem.
[1263–4 Provisions, clause 21]

CHAPTER 27

Si clericus aliquis pro crimine aliquo vel [retto][46] quod ad coronam pertineat arestatus fuerit et postmodum de precepto regis in ballium traditus vel replegiatus exstiterit, ita quod hii quibus **traditus fuerit** in ballium eum habeant coram justiciariis, non amercientur decetero illi quibus traditus fuit in ballium vel alii plegii sui, si corpus suum habeant coram justiciariis, licet coram eis propter privilegium clericale respondere nolit vel non possit.
[1263–4 Provisions, clause 22]

[43] *LAL* reads 'xxi' [44] *LAL* reads 'villatis'. [45] *LAL* reads 'xxj'. [46] MSS. read 'recto'.

CHAPTER 24

Also the justices itinerant are not in future to amerce townships on their eyre because everyone aged twelve and over did not appear before the sheriff and coroners for inquisitions into **robberies and arsons or** other matters belonging to the crown, provided there was a sufficient attendance from those villages to allow such inquisitions to be properly held. **This excludes inquisitions into homicides where all aged twelve years and over ought to appear unless they have a reasonable cause for their absence.**
[1263–4 Provisions, clause 19]

CHAPTER 25

The *murdrum* fine is not in future to be adjudged as due before the justices where only death by misadventure has been adjudged but is to apply only to those killed feloniously.
[1263–4 Provisions, clause 20]

CHAPTER 26

It has also been provided that no one who is vouched to warranty before the justices itinerant in a plea relating to land or a tenement is to be amerced in future because he was not present when he was vouched to warranty other than on the first day of the visitation of the same justices. But, if that warrantor is within the county, the sheriff is to be enjoined to make him come by the third or the fourth day depending on the distance, as has been customary in the eyre of the justices. And, if he is living outside the county, then he is to have a proper summons of at least fifteen days according to the discretion of the justices and common law.
[1263–4 Provisions, clause 21]

CHAPTER 27

If any clerk is arrested for any crime or offence which belongs to the crown and is subsequently by the king's order released on bail or replevied, so that those to whom he is bailed produce him before the justices, those to whom he is bailed or his other sureties are not in future to be amerced if they have his body before the justices even if he refuses or is unable to answer before them because of clerical privilege.
[1263–4 Provisions, clause 22]

CHAPTER 28

Provisum est eciam quod, si depredaciones vel rapine alique fiant abbatibus aut aliis prelatis ecclesiasticis et ipsi jus suum de hujusmodi depredacionibus prosequentes morte preveniantur antequam inde justiciam fuerunt assecuti, successores eorum acciones habeant ad bona ecclesie sue de manibus hujusmodi transgressorum repetenda. [Similem insuper accionem habeant successores <de hiis que>[47] domui et ecclesie sue recenter ante obitum predecessorum suorum per hujusmodi violenciam fuerint subtracta, licet predicti predecessores jus suum prosecuti non fuerint in vita sua.][48]

Si autem in terras et tenementa hujusmodi religiosorum de quibus eorum prelati obierunt seisiti ut de jure ecclesie sue aliqui se intrudant tempore vacacionis, eorum successores **<litteras>**[49] habeant ad recuperandum seisinam suam et adjudicentur eis dampna sicut in nova disseysina **fieri** consuevit.
[1263–4 Provisions, clause 24]

CHAPTER 29

Provisum est eciam quod si alienaciones ille de quibus breve de ingressu dari consuevit per tot gradus fiant quod breve illud in forma prius usitata haberi non possit habeat breve conquerens **de recuperanda seysina** sine mencione graduum ad cujuscumque manus per hujusmodi alienaciones res illa devenerit per originalia per consilium regis inde providenda.
[1263–4 Provisions, clause 25]

Note

The numbering of the chapters is that of *SR*. Chapters 19 and 20 are printed in reverse order since that is the order in which they are found in the Red Book and also in *SR* itself. I have repunctuated for sense. The passages or words marked in bold show additions and changes to the text of the Provisions of 1263 made for this reissue, but I have not marked minor changes of word order or very minor substitutions of equivalent words.

47 *LAL* reads 'qui'.

48 MS. omits but supplied from *LAL* and a similar sentence is found in most other texts of the Statute. *LAL* marks the break between its chapters 42 and 43 at this point.

49 *LAL* reads 'breve'.

CHAPTER 28

It has also been provided that if any depredations or forcible seizures are made from abbots or other ecclesiastical prelates and, while prosecuting justice in respect of such depredations, death overcomes them before they have received justice, their successors are to have an action to recover the goods of their church from the hands of such offenders. Their successors are, moreover, to have a like action for those things taken from their house and church shortly before the death of their predecessors by such violence, even if the said predecessors did not initiate action in their lifetimes.

If, moreover, anyone intrudes into lands and tenements belonging to such men of religion of which their prelates died seised as of the right of their church during a vacancy their successors are to have **letters** to recover their seisin and damages are to be adjudged to them as are customarily adjudged in novel disseisin.
[1263–4 Provisions, clause 24]

CHAPTER 29

It has also been provided that, if those alienations for which the writ of entry is customarily given have passed through so many degrees that this writ is unavailable in the form previously in use, the complainant is to have a writ to **recover his seisin** without mention of degrees to whomsoever's hands that property has come by original writs that are to be provided for this purpose by the king's council.
[1263–4 Provisions, clause 25]

Note

I have repunctuated for sense. The passages or words marked in bold show additions and changes to the text of the Provisions of 1263 made for this reissue, but I have not marked minor changes of word order or very minor substitutions of equivalent words. The translation is a relatively free one of my own, intended to convey the sense of the Statute, rather than a literal one, mimicking the exact phrasing of the original.

BIBLIOGRAPHY

MANUSCRIPT SOURCES

1 IN LONDON

British Library (BL)

ADDITIONAL MSS.

5762 Legal manuscript of *c.* 1300 containing a register of writs and a variety of shorter legal treatises. For a discussion of its contents see Dorothea Oschinsky, *Walter of Henley and Other Treatises on Estate Management and Accounting* (Oxford, 1971), p. 15

5925 Legal manuscript of the early fourteenth century containing only law reports. For a discussion of its contents see *EELR*, I, lvii–lxi

15668 Cartulary of the priory of Newent. For a description of its contents see *Catalogue of the Additions to the Manuscripts in the British Museum in the Years MDCCCXLVI–MDCCCXLVIII* (London, 1864), pp. 1–2

31826 Legal manuscript of the early fourteenth century containing statutes, legal treatises, notes on matters of legal interest and law reports. For a discussion of its contents see *EELR*, I, lxi–lxx

32085 Composite, but mainly legal, manuscript of the early fourteenth century. For a discussion of its contents see Oschinsky, *Walter of Henley*, pp. 16–17

34194 Legal manuscript of the later thirteenth century containing only a register of writs

35116 Legal manuscript of the early fourteenth century containing only law reports and associated materials. For a discussion of its contents and its relationship with BL MS. Harley 25 see *EELR*, I, xlvii–lvii

37657 Legal manuscript of the early fourteenth century containing mainly law reports but also a text of *Novae Narrationes*. For a discussion of its contents see *EELR*, I, lxx–lxxvi

38821 Mainly legal manuscript of the last quarter of the thirteenth century containing a register of writs, legal and other treatises, some law reports and other miscellaneous material. For a discussion of its contents see *EELR*, I, xci–xcv

ARUNDEL MSS.

310 Manuscript of *c.* 1300 compiled for St Augustine's abbey, Canterbury containing legal materials (some with specifically Kent connexions), material relating to the abbey's possessions and list of popes and emperors, etc. For a brief

description see *Catalogue of Manuscripts in the British Museum, New Series, volume I, part 1: The Arundel Manuscripts* (London, 1840), pp. 90–1

COTTONIAN MSS.

Claudius D ii Composite manuscript of antiquarian and legal material assembled by Sir Robert Cotton. Much of it comes from two London manuscripts of the fourteenth century, on which see Neil Ker, '*Liber Custumarum* and other manuscripts formerly at the Guildhall', *Guildhall Miscellany* 3 (1954), 37–45

Cleopatra C vi Composite manuscript of which fols. 60–204 are a register of leases and other deeds associated with Merton priory to *c.* 1352. For a discussion of this part of its contents see G.R.C. Davis, *Medieval Cartularies of Great Britain: a Short Catalogue* (London, 1958), p. 75 (no. 662)

Nero D i The *Liber Additamentorum* of Matthew Paris. Its contents are listed in *Matthaei Parisiensis Chronica Majora*, VI, Appendix III at 491–523 and discussed by Richard Vaughan in *Matthew Paris* (Cambridge, 1958), chapter 5

EGERTON MSS.

656 Legal manuscript of the early fourteenth century containing a register of writs, statutes and shorter legal treatises

2811 English legal manuscript of the second quarter of the fourteenth century containing law reports. Originally two separate manuscripts, only combined in the sixteenth century. The first part contains mainly reports of the reign of Edward II with a few reports of the reign of Edward I. For a discussion of its contents see *The Eyre of Northamptonshire, 3–4 Edward III (AD 1329–1330)*, vol. I, ed. Donald W. Sutherland (Selden Society vol. 97, 1983)

2823 Cartulary of the abbey of Byland. For a discussion of its contents see Davis, *Medieval Cartularies*, p. 18 (no. 142)

HARGRAVE MSS.

375 Legal manuscript of the early fourteenth century containing mainly law reports and associated material but also a short pleading treatise. For a discussion of its contents see *EELR*, I, civ–cvi

HARLEIAN MSS.

25 Legal manuscript of the early fourteenth century consisting solely of law reports and associated materials. For a discussion of its contents and its relationship with BL MS. Additional 35116 see *EELR*, I, xlvii–lvii

79 Composite manuscript perhaps associated with Osney abbey with an initial section (at fols. 2–26) of statutes, probably written not long after 1285. For a list of its contents see *A Catalogue of the Harleian Manuscripts in the British Museum* (4 vols., London, 1808–12), I, 21

323 Composite manuscript of the first half of the thirteenth century including a text of *Glanvill*, a register of writs and a text of Magna Carta. For a list of its contents see *Catalogue of Harleian MSS.*, I, 198

395 Legal manuscript of *c.* 1300 containing statutes and various of the shorter treatises. It formerly contained a register as well. For a list of its contents see *Catalogue of Harleian MSS.*, I, 232

409 Legal manuscript of the last quarter of the thirteenth century, containing a register of writs, statutes (up to 1278) and shorter treatises. For a list of its contents see *Catalogue of Harleian MSS.*, I, 236

489 Legal manuscript of the end of the thirteenth century, containing statutes, short legal treatises and a text of *Britton*. For a list of its contents see *Catalogue of Harleian MSS.*, I, 326–7

493 A and B Originally a single, fat legal manuscript of the second decade of the fourteenth century, divided into two separate volumes in 1876. A legal manuscript containing statutes, legal treatises and material arranged by form of action including writs, possible exceptions and related plea roll enrolments and law reports: see *EELR*, I, lxxviii–lxxxii

529 Legal manuscript of the last decade of the thirteenth century with various statutes and an incomplete text of *Britton*. For a list of its contents see *Catalogue of Harleian MSS.*, I, 341

572 Legal manuscript of the second decade of the fourteenth century, consisting solely of law reports and associated materials. For a discussion of its contents see *EELR*, I, cviii

673 Legal manuscript of the early fourteenth century, consisting mainly of short treatises and statutes. For a list of its contents see *Catalogue of Harleian MSS.*, I, 404

746 Legal manuscript of the late thirteenth century with much twelfth-century legal material, an early thirteenth-century register of writs, some thirteenth-century statutes and some miscellaneous material. For a discussion of its contents see Bruce R. O'Brien, *God's Peace and King's Peace: the Laws of Edward the Confessor* (Philadephia, 1999), pp. 144–5

748 Legal manuscript of the late thirteenth century, consisting of a register of writs, statutes and legal treatises. For a list of its contents see *Catalogue of Harleian MSS.*, I, 431–2

1033 Legal manuscript of the last decade of the thirteenth century with some later fourteenth- and fifteenth-century additions containing mainly statutes and analogous material, short treatises and a register of writs. For a list of its contents see *Catalogue of Harleian MSS.*, I, 514–15

1120 Legal manuscript of the late thirteenth century, consisting of statutes, legal treatises and a register of writs. For a list of its contents see *Catalogue of Harleian MSS.*, I, 556–7

1208 Legal manuscript of the early fourteenth century consisting mainly of statutes but also containing various legal and administrative treatises and a short section of law reports. For a discussion of its contents see *EELR*, I, cviii and for a list of its contents see *Catalogue of Harleian MSS.*, I, 597–8

1259 Legal manuscript of *c.* 1300 consisting mainly of statutes and analogous material and a few short treatises. For a list of its contents see *Catalogue of Harleian MSS.*, I, 637

1690 Legal manuscript of the final decade of the thirteenth century consisting mainly of statutes and analogous material, short treatises and a register of writs, with many losses of individual folios. For a list of its contents see *Catalogue of Harleian MSS.*, II, 174

2183 Legal manuscript written towards the end of the second decade of the fourteenth century, consisting of law reports and related material. For a discussion of its contents see *EELR*, I, xcvii–xcviii

4975 Legal manuscript apparently written shortly before 1290 with statutes and short treatises, and with material from the last decade of the thirteenth century and earlier added in a later hand.

LANSDOWNE MSS.

467 Legal manuscript of *c.* 1300, containing statutes, a register of writs, a brief section of law reports and legal treatises. For a discussion of its contents see *EELR*, I, c–ci

472 Legal manuscript originally compiled *c.* 1290 but with fourteenth-century additions, containing statutes and analogous material and a fragment of *Britton*. For a list of its contents see *A Catalogue of the Lansdowne Manuscripts in the British Museum* (London, 1819), pp. 130–1

564 Mainly legal manuscript of the late thirteenth century, consisting of legal treatises, registers of writs, statutes, law reports and other miscellaneous material. For a discussion of its contents see *EELR*, I, lxxxvii–xci

ROYAL MSS.

10.A.V Legal manuscript of *c.* 1300 consisting of statutes, treatises and reports. For a discussion of its contents see *EELR*, I, xxxviii–xlii

STOWE MSS.

386 Legal manuscript of second decade of fourteenth century consisting of statutes, legal treatises and law reports and related material. For a discussion of its contents see *EELR*, I, cii–civ

Corporation of London Records Office (CLRO)
class

Husting of Common Pleas, Rolls

Inner Temple Library (IT)
MS. Miscellaneous 1 Legal manuscript of early fourteenth century containing mainly law reports and related notes. For a discussion of its contents see *Catalogue of Manuscripts in the Library of the Honourable Society of the Inner Temple*, ed. J. Conway Davies (3 vols., London, 1972), III, 1151–2; *EELR*, I, cx and note

Lincoln's Inn Library (LI)

HALE MSS.

188 Legal manuscript of the first decade of the fourteenth century, consisting entirely of reports and related materials. For a discussion of its contents see *EELR*, I, xlii–xlvii

MISCELLANEOUS MSS.

87 Legal manuscript of the early fourteenth century, consiting mainly of reports plus a fragment of *Britton*. For a discussion of its contents see *EELR*, I, xxxiv–xxxviii

738 Legal manuscript of the first decade of the fourteenth century, consisting almost entirely of law reports. For a discussion of its contents see *EELR*, I, lxxxi–lxxxv

Public Record Office (Kew) (PRO)
classes

CHANCERY

C 54 Close Rolls
C 60 Fine Rolls
C 66 Patent Rolls
C 69 Redisseisin Rolls
C 133 Inquisitions Post Mortem, Edward I
C 143 Inquisitions Ad Quod Damnum

COMMON PLEAS

CP 25(1) Feet of Fines, Series I
CP 40 Common Bench Plea Rolls, 1273 onwards
CP 52 Common Bench Writ Files

EXCHEQUER

E 40 Treasury of Receipt, Ancient Deeds, Series A
E 152 King's Remembrancer, Enrolments of Inquisitions
E 159 King's Remembrancer, Memoranda Rolls
E 164 King's Remembrancer, Miscellaneous Books, Series I
E 175 King's Remembrancer, Parliamentary and Council Proceedings
E 198 King's Remembrancer, Documents Relating to Serjeanties, Knights' Fees etc.
E 210 King's Remembrancer, Ancient Deeds, Series D
E 326 Augmentation Deeds, Series B
E 368 Lord Treasurer's Remembrancer, Memoranda Rolls
E 371 Originalia Rolls

JUSTICES ITINERANT, ETC.

JUST 1 Eyre, Assize and other Plea Rolls
JUST 2 Coroners' Rolls
JUST 4 Eyre, Assize and other Writ Files

KING'S BENCH, ETC.

KB 26 'Curia Regis Rolls' (Common Bench and King's Bench Plea Rolls pre-1273)
KB 27 King's Bench Plea Rolls, 1273 onwards
KB 136 King's Bench Writ Files

SPECIAL COLLECTIONS

SC 8 Ancient Petitions
SC 9 Parliament Rolls (Exchequer Series)

2 IN CAMBRIDGE

Cambridge University Library (CUL)

Dd.7.14 Mainly legal manuscript written around 1295 but with some later additions, consisting of legal treatises, statutes and law reports and related material. For discussions of its contents see *EELR*, I, xxviii–xxxiv; J.H. Baker and J.S. Ringrose, *A Catalogue of English Legal Manuscripts in Cambridge University Library* (Woodbridge, 1996), pp. 69–83

Ee.2.19 English legal manuscript of *c.* 1300 containing mainly statutes and treatises. For a discussion of its contents see Baker and Ringrose, *English Legal MSS.*, pp. 176–80

Ee.6.18 Legal manuscript of the early fourteenth century containing instructional material and law reports and related material. For discussions of its contents see *EELR*, I, cvii; Baker and Ringrose, *English Legal MSS.*, pp. 231–3

Ll.4.17 Legal manuscript of the early fourteenth century consisting of statutes, legal treatises and a register of writs. For discussion of its contents see Baker and Ringrose, *English Legal MSS.*, pp. 454–63

Ll.4.18 Legal manuscript originally written in the last decade of the thirteenth century but with some later additions, consisting of statutes, a register of writs, legal treatises and a sequence of copies of plea roll enrolments that includes a few law reports. For discussions of its contents see *EELR*, I, cix; Baker and Ringrose, *English Legal MSS.*, pp. 463–8

ADDITIONAL MSS.

3022 Legal manuscript of the late thirteenth century consisting of a register of writs, statutes and short legal treatises. For a discussion of its contents see Baker and Ringrose, *English Legal MSS.*, pp. 549–57

3129 Legal manuscript written after 1317 containing statutes, treatises and a register and a small number of reports. For a discussion of its contents see Baker and Ringrose, *English Legal MSS.*, pp. 567–75

Trinity College Cambridge

O.3.45 Legal manuscript of *c.* 1300 consisting of a register of writs, statutes, short treatises and two short sections of law reports.

3 IN OXFORD

Oxford Bodleian Library

ADDITIONAL MSS.

A 228 Legal manuscript apparently of the late thirteenth century containing only statutes to 1286, but with many losses

C 188 Legal manuscript of the last decade of the thirteenth century containing statutes, legal treatises and a register of writs

BODLEY MSS.

91 A composite volume whose contents are discussed further at pp. 142–3 above

DOUCE MSS.

139 Legal manuscript associated with Coventry cathedral priory, whose contents are discussed further at pp. 140–2 above

HOLKHAM MSS.

Misc. 30 Legal manuscript of *c.* 1310 consisting of some short treatises and law reports. For a discussion of its contents see *EELR*, I, lxxxv–lxxxvii

RAWLINSON MSS.

C 668A Legal manuscript of the last decade of the thirteenth century, consisting of statutes and associated material. For a list of its contents see *Catalogi Codicum Manuscriptorum Bibliothecae Bodleianae partis quinte*, ed. W.D. Macray (Oxford, 1878), columns 339–41

C 820 Legal manuscript of the last decade of the thirteenth century consisting of statutes and short treatises. For a list of its contents see *Catalogi . . . partis quinte*, columns 424–6

Trinity College

MS. 27 Legal manuscript of the later thirteenth century consisting only of a register of writs of which the beginning is now lost

4 IN WORCESTER CATHEDRAL

Dean and Chapter Muniments, A.2 A rental of Worcester cathedral priory from 1240 with other material relating to the priory and copies of Magna Carta and the Forest Charter, the Provisions of Westminster of 1259, the Provisions of Merton, the Assize of Arms. Edited by W.H. Hale in *Registrum Prioratus Beate Marie Wigorniensis* (Camden Society, original series 91: 1865)

5 IN THE UNITED STATES OF AMERICA

Harvard Law School Library

33 Legal manuscript of the early fourteenth century containing statutes, treatises and older register of writs. For a listing of its contents see Baker, *English Legal MSS. in the USA, part 1*, p. 22

206 Legal manuscript of the second quarter of the fourteenth century containing an amalgam of a register of writs and a treatise on counting and various law reports. For a listing of its contents (under its previous reference of Hale-Rogers MS. 106) see Baker, *English Legal MSS. in the USA, part 1*, p. 36

Philadelphia Free Library

HAMPTON L. CARSON COLLECTION

LC 14.3 Mainly legal manuscript of *c.* 1300 with some later additions containing legal treatises and statutes and a text of *Britton*. For discussions of its contents see Brand, *MCL*, p. 337; Baker, *English Legal MSS. in the USA, part 1*, pp. 57–8

Bibliography

University of Chicago

Bacon MS. I Court roll of the Manor of Redgrave, Suffolk for 1260

OFFICIAL PUBLICATIONS

Calendar of Charter Rolls (6 vols., London, 1903–27).

Calendar of Liberate Rolls (6 vols., London, 1917–64).

Catalogue of Ancient Deeds preserved in the Public Record Office (6 vols., London, 1890–1915).

Excerpta e Rotulis Finium in Turri Londinensi asservati, Henry III, 1216–72, ed. C. Roberts (2 vols., London, 1835–6).

Foedera, Conventiones, Litterae etc.; or Rymer's Foedera, 1066–1383, ed. Adam Clarke and others (4 vols. (vols. I–III in two parts each), London, 1816–69).

Placita de Quo Warranto, ed. W. Illingworth and J. Caley (London, 1818).

Rotuli Chartarum in Turri Londinensi asservati, 1199–1216, ed. T.D. Hardy (London, 1837).

Rotuli Litterarum Clausarum in Turri Londinensi asservati, ed. T.D. Hardy (2 vols., London, 1833–44).

Rotuli Parliamentorum (6 vols., London, 1783).

OTHER PRINTED PRIMARY SOURCES

Annales Monastici, ed. H.R. Luard (5 vols., Rolls Series, London, 1864–9).

The Beauchamp Cartulary: Charters 1100–1268, ed. Emma Mason (Pipe Roll Society new series vol. 43, 1980).

Borough Customs, ed. Mary Bateson (2 vols., Selden Society vols. 18 and 21, 1904 and 1906).

Brevia Placitata, ed. G.J. Turner and completed by T.F.T. Plucknett (Selden Society vol. 66, 1951).

The Cartulary of Cirencester Abbey, ed. C. Ross (vols. I–II) and M. Devine (vol. III) (3 vols., Oxford, 1974–7).

Casus Placitorum and Reports of Cases in the King's Courts (1272–8), ed. W.H. Dunham, jr. (Selden Society vol. 69, 1952).

Chronicles, Edward I and Edward II, ed. W. Stubbs (2 vols., Rolls Series, London, 1882–3).

Councils and Synods with Other Documents Relating to the English Church vol. II (in two parts) (1205–1313), ed. F.M. Powicke and C.R. Cheney (Oxford, 1964).

Court Rolls of the Abbey of Ramsey and of the Honor of Clare, ed. W.O. Ault (New Haven, 1928).

Court Rolls of the Manor of Wakefield, vol. I (1274–97), ed. W.P. Baildon (Yorkshire Archaeological Society Record Series vol. 29, 1901).

De Antiquis Legibus Liber: Cronica Maiorum et Vicecomitum Londoniarum, ed. Thomas Stapleton (Camden Society original series vol. 34, 1846).

Dialogus de Scaccario, ed. A. Hughes, C.G. Crump and C. Johnson (Oxford, 1902).

Feet of Fines for the County of York 1272–1300, ed. F.H. Slingsby (Yorkshire Archaeological Society, Record Series vol. 112, 1956).

Feet of Fines for Essex, ed. R.E.G. Kirk and E.F. Kirk (vols. I–III) and P.H. Reaney and Marc Fitch (vol. IV) (4 vols., Essex Archaeological Society, 1899–1964).

Final Concords of the County of Lincoln, 1244–1272, ed. C.W. Foster (Lincoln Record Society vol. 17, 1920).
Flores Historiarum, per Matthaeum Westmonasteriensem collecti, ed. H.R. Luard (3 vols., Rolls Series, London, 1890).
Die Gesetze der Angelsachsen, ed. Felix Liebermann (3 vols., Halle, 1898–1916).
The Great Roll of the Pipe for the thirty-first year of the reign of King Henry the Second, AD 1184–1185 (Pipe Roll Society original series vol. 34, 1913).
Leges Henrici Primi, ed. L.J. Downer (Oxford, 1972).
Liber Memorandorum Ecclesie de Bernewell, ed. J. Willis Clark (Cambridge, 1907).
The London Eyre of 1244, ed. H.M. Chew and M. Weinbaum (London Record Society vol. 6, 1970).
Matthaei Parisiensis Chronica Majora, ed. H.R. Luard (7 vols., Rolls Series, London, 1872–84).
Memoranda de Parliamento: Records of the Parliament holden at Westminster on the Twenty-Eighth Day of February, in the Thirty-Third Year of the Reign of Edward I (AD 1305), ed. F.W. Maitland (Rolls Series, London, 1893).
Memoranda Roll 10 John etc., ed. R. Allen Brown (Pipe Roll Society new series vol. 31, 1957).
The Mirror of Justices, ed. W.J. Whittaker and F.W. Maitland (Selden Society vol. 7, 1893).
Pleas of the Crown for the County of Gloucester before the Justices Itinerant, 1221, ed. F.W. Maitland (London, 1884).
Red Book of the Exchequer, ed. H. Hall (3 vols., Rolls Series, London, 1897).
The Register of John le Romeyn, lord archbishop of York, 1286–1296, ed. W. Brown (2 vols., Surtees Society vols. 123 and 128, 1913 and 1917).
The 'Registrum Antiquissimum' of the Cathedral Church of Lincoln, ed. C.W. Foster (8 vols., Lincoln Record Society vols. 27–9, 32, 34, 41, 42 and 46, 1931–53).
Registrum Malmesburiense: the Register of Malmesbury Abbey, ed. J.S. Brewer and C.T. Martin (2 vols., Rolls Series, London, 1879–80).
Rolls of the Justices in Eyre for Lincolnshire (1218–1219) and Worcestershire (1221), ed. D.M. Stenton (Selden Society vol. 53, 1934).
Royal Letters, Henry III, ed. W.W. Shirley (2 vols., Rolls Series, London, 1862–6).
Select Cases from the Coroners' Rolls (1265–1413), ed. Charles Gross (Selden Society vol. 9, 1895).
Select Cases of Procedure Without Writ under Henry III, ed. H.G. Richardson and G.O. Sayles (Selden Society vol. 60, 1941).
Select Charters and Other Illustrations of English Constitutional History, ed. W. Stubbs, 9th edition revised by H.W.C. Davis (Oxford, 1913).
Select Pleas of the Forest, ed. G.J. Turner (Selden Society vol. 13, 1901).
Select Pleas in Manorial and other Seignorial Courts, vol. 1, ed. F.W. Maitland (Selden Society vol. 2, 1888).
Sir Christopher Hatton's Book of Seals, ed. L.C. Loyd and D.M. Stenton (Northamptonshire Record Society vol. 15, 1950).
State Trials of the Reign of Edward the First, 1289–1293, ed. T.F. Tout and Hilda Johnstone (Camden 3rd Series vol. 9, 1906).
Year Books 2 & 3 Edward II (1308–10), ed. F.W. Maitland (Selden Society vol. 19, 1904).
Year Books 3 Edward II (1309–10), ed. F.W. Maitland (Selden Society vol. 20, 1905).

Year Books 4 Edward II (1310–11), ed. G.J. Turner (Selden Society vol. 26, 1911).
Year Books 4 Edward II (1311), ed. G.J. Turner (Selden Society vol. 42, 1925).
Year Book 5 Edward II (1312), ed. W.C. Bolland (Selden Society vol. 33, 1916).
Year Book 7 Edward II (1313–1314), ed. W.C. Bolland (Selden Society vol. 39, 1922).
Year Book 8 Edward II (1314–1315), ed. W.C. Bolland (Selden Society vol. 41, 1924).
Year Book of the Eyre of London, 14 Edward II (AD 1321), ed. H.M. Cam (2 vols., Selden Society vols. 85–6, 1968–9).
Year Books 11–12 Edward III: Year Books of the Reign of King Edward the Third: Years XI and XII, ed. A.J. Horwood and L.O. Pike (Rolls Series, London, 1883).
Year Books 16 Edward III – II: Year Books of the Reign of King Edward the Third: Year XVI (Second Part), ed. L.O. Pike (Rolls Series, London, 1900).

SECONDARY WORKS

Baker, J.H., *English Legal Manuscripts in the United States of America, part 1: Medieval and Renaissance* (Selden Society, 1985).
Readers and Readings in the Inns of Court and Chancery (Selden Society Supplementary series vol. 13, 2000).
Barton, J.L., 'The Mystery of Bracton', *Journal of Legal History* 14, no. 3 (1993), 1–142.
Bean, J.M.W., *The Decline of English Feudalism, 1215–1540* (Manchester, 1968).
Beckerman, John S., 'The Forty-Shilling Jurisdictional Limit in Medieval English Personal Actions' in *Legal History Studies, 1972*, ed. Dafydd Jenkins (Cardiff, 1975), pp. 110–17.
Biancalana, Joseph, 'For Want of Justice: Legal Reforms of Henry II', *Columbia Law Review* 88 (1988), 484–514.
Brand, Paul, 'The Beginnings of English Law Reporting' in *Law Reporting in England*, ed. Chantal Stebbings (London, 1995), pp. 1–14.
'English Thirteenth Century Legislation' in '. . . *Colendo iustitiam et iura condendo . . .': Federico II Legislatore del Regno di Sicilia nell'Europa del Duecento*, ed. A. Romano (Rome, 1997), pp. 325–44.
'Oldcotes v. d'Arcy' in *Medieval Legal Records edited in Memory of C.A.F. Meekings*, ed. R.F. Hunnisett and J.B. Post (London, 1978), pp. 63–118.
'"Time out of Mind": the Knowledge and Use of the Eleventh and Twelfth-Century Past in Thirteenth-Century Litigation', *Anglo-Norman Studies* 16 (1994), 37–54.
Cam, H.M., *The Hundred and the Hundred Rolls: an Outline of Local Government in Medieval England* (London, 1930).
Carpenter, D.A., 'What Happened in 1258?' in *War and Government in the Middle Ages: Essays in Honour of J.O. Prestwich* (Woodbridge, 1984), pp. 106–19.
Clanchy, M.T., 'The Franchise of Return of Writs', *Transactions of the Royal Historical Society* 5th series 17 (1967), 59–82.
Cokayne, G.E., *Complete Peerage of England, Scotland, Ireland, Great Britain and United Kingdom, extant, extinct, or dormant*, new edition by Vicary Gibbs and others (13 vols. (in 14), London, 1910–59).
Crook, David, *Records of the General Eyre* (Public Record Office Handbooks 20, 1982).

Davis, G.R.C., *Medieval Cartularies of Great Britain: a Short Catalogue* (London, 1958).
Denholm-Young, Noel, *Collected Papers* (Cardiff, 1969).
Douie, D.L., *Archbishop Pecham* (Oxford, 1952).
Dugdale, William, *Monasticon Anglicanum*, revised by J. Caley and others (6 vols. (in 8), London, 1817–30).
Fitzherbert, Anthony, *La Graunde Abridgement* (London, 1577).
The New Natura Brevium, 9th edition (London, 1794).
Gray, J.W., 'The Ius Praesentandi in England from the Constitutions of Clarendon to Bracton', *English Historical Review* 67 (1952), 481–509.
Hall, G.D.G., 'The Early History of Entry Sur Disseisin', *Tulane Law Review* 42 (1968), 584–602.
Hamil, F.C.,'The Presentment of Englishry and the Murder Fine', *Speculum* 12 (1937), 285–98.
Hershey, Andrew N., 'Success or Failure? Hugh Bigod and Judicial Reform during the Baronial Movement, June 1258–February 1259' in *Thirteenth Century England V*, ed. P.R. Coss and S.D. Lloyd (Woodbridge, 1995), pp. 65–87.
Holt, J.C., *Magna Carta*, 2nd edition (Cambridge, 1992).
Magna Carta and Medieval Government (London, 1985).
Hunnisett, R.F., *The Medieval Coroner* (Cambridge, 1961).
Ibbetson, David J., 'Words and Deeds: the Action of Covenant in the Reign of Edward I', *Law and History Review* 4, no. 1 (1986), 71–94.
Jacob, E.F., *Studies in the Period of Baronial Reform and Rebellion, 1258–1267* (Oxford Studies in Social and Legal History 8, 1925).
Ker, N.R., '*Liber Custumarum* and Other Manuscripts Formerly at the Guildhall', *Guildhall Miscellany* 3 (1954), 37–45.
Medieval Manuscripts in British Libraries, I: London (Oxford, 1969).
Knowles, C.H., 'The Resettlement of England after the Barons' War, 1264–67', *Transactions of the Royal Historical Society* 5th series 32 (1982), 25–41.
Knowles, D. and R.N. Hadcock, *Medieval Religious Houses: England and Wales* (London, 1972).
Maddicott, J.R., *Simon de Montfort* (Cambridge, 1994).
Milsom, S.F.C., *Historical Foundations of the Common Law*, 1st edition (London, 1969); 2nd edition (London, 1981).
The Legal Framework of English Feudalism (Cambridge, 1976).
O'Brien, Bruce, 'From *Mordor* to *Murdrum*: the Preconquest Origin and Norman Revival of the Murder Fine', *Speculum* 71 (1996), 321–57.
Palmer, Robert C., *The County Courts of Medieval England, 1150–1350* (Princeton, 1982).
'The Origins of Property in England', *Law and History Review* 3 (1985), 24–50.
Plucknett, T.F.T., *The Medieval Bailiff* (London, 1953).
Statutes and their Interpretation in the First Half of the Fourteenth Century (Cambridge, 1922).
Powicke, F.M., *King Henry III and the Lord Edward: the Community of the Realm in the Thirteenth Century* (Oxford, 1966).
Raban, Sandra, *Mortmain Legislation and the English Church, 1279–1500* (Cambridge, 1982).
Richardson, H.G., 'Glanville Continued', *Law Quarterly Review* 54 (1938), 381–99.

Richardson, H.G. and G.O. Sayles, 'The Provisions of Oxford: a Forgotten Document and Some Comments', *Bulletin of the John Rylands Library* 17 (1933), 291–321 and reprinted (with different pagination) in *The English Parliament in the Middle Ages* (London, 1981) as III.

'The Early Statutes', *Law Quarterly Review* 50 (1934), 201–23 and 540–71 and reprinted (with different pagination) in *The English Parliament in the Middle Ages* as XXV.

Skemer, Don C., 'Reading the Law: Statute Books and the Private Transmission of Legal Knowledge in Late Medieval England' in *Learning the Law: Teaching and the Transmission of Law in England, 1150–1900*, ed. Jonathan A. Bush and Alain Wijffels (London, 1999), pp. 113–31.

Stubbs, William, *The Constitutional History of England*, 2nd edition (3 vols., Oxford, 1874–8).

Sutherland, Donald W., *The Assize of Novel Disseisin* (Oxford, 1973).

A Summary Catalogue of Western Manuscripts in the Bodleian Library Oxford (7 vols. (in 8), Oxford, 1897–1953).

Thompson, Faith, *The First Century of Magna Carta: Why It Persisted as a Document* (Minneapolis, 1925).

Magna Carta: Its Role in the Making of the English Constitution, 1300–1629 (Minneapolis, 1948).

Treharne, R.F., *The Baronial Plan of Reform, 1258–1263* (Manchester, 1932).

Turner, G.J., 'Some Thirteenth Century Statutes', *Law Magazine and Review* 4th series 21 (1896), 300–16 and 22 (1897), 240–50.

Wood, Susan, *English Monasteries and Their Patrons in the Thirteenth Century* (Oxford, 1955).

INDEX

Index

Index

Index

Index

Cambridge Studies in Medieval Life and Thought
Fourth series

Titles in series

1 The Beaumont Twins: The Roots and Branches of Power in the Twelfth Century
D. B. CROUCH

2 The Thought of Gregory the Great*
G. R. EVANS

3 The Government of England Under Henry I*
JUDITH A. GREEN

4 Charity and Community in Medieval Cambridge*
MIRI RUBIN

5 Autonomy and Community: The Royal Manor of Havering, 1200–1500*
MARJORIE KENISTON MCINTOSH

6 The Political Thought of Baldus de Ubaldis
JOSEPH CANNING

7 Land and Power in Late Medieval Ferrara: The Rule of the Este, 1350–1450*
TREVOR DEAN

8 William of Tyre: Historian of the Latin East*
PETER W. EDBURY AND JOHN GORDON ROWE

9 The Royal Saints of Anglo-Saxon England: A Study of West Saxon and East Anglian Cults
SUSAN J. RIDYARD

10 John of Wales: A Study of the Works and Ideas of a Thirteenth-Century Friar*
JENNY SWANSON

11 Richard III: A Study of Service*
ROSEMARY HORROX

12 A Marginal Economy? East Anglian Breckland in the Later Middle Ages
MARK BAILEY

13 Clement VI: The Pontificate and Ideas of an Avignon Pope
DIANA WOOD

14 Hagiography and the Cult of Saints: The Diocese of Orléans, 800–1200
THOMAS HEAD

15 Kings and Lords in Conquest England
ROBIN FLEMING

16 Council and Hierarchy: The Political Thought of William Durant the Younger*
CONSTANTIN FASOLT

17 Warfare in the Latin East, 1192–1291*
CHRISTOPHER MARSHALL

18 Province and Empire: Brittany and the Carolingians
JULIA M. H. SMITH

19 A Gentry Community: Leicestershire in the Fifteenth Century, *c.* 1422–*c.* 1485
ERIC ACHESON

20 Baptism and Change in the Early Middle Ages, *c.* 200–1150
PETER CRAMER

21 Itinerant Kingship and Royal Monasteries in Early Medieval Germany, *c.* 936–1075*
JOHN W. BERNHARDT

22 Caesarius of Arles: The Making of a Christian Community in Late Antique Gaul
WILLIAM E. KLINGSHIRN

23 Bishop and Chapter in Twelfth-Century England: A Study of the *Mensa Episcopalis*
EVERETT U. CROSBY

24 Trade and Traders in Muslim Spain: The Commercial Realignment of the Iberian Peninsula, 900–1500*
OLIVIA REMIE CONSTABLE

25 Lithuania Ascending: A Pagan Empire Within East-Central Europe, 1295–1345
S. C. ROWELL

26 Barcelona and Its Rulers, 1100–1291*
STEPHEN P. BENSCH

27 Conquest, Anarchy and Lordship: Yorkshire, 1066–1154*
PAUL DALTON

28 Preaching the Crusades: Mendicant Friars and the Cross in the Thirteenth Century*
CHRISTOPH T. MAIER

29 Family Power in Southern Italy: The Duchy of Gaeta and Its Neighbours, 850–1139
PATRICIA SKINNER

30 The Papacy, Scotland and Northern England, 1342–1378*
A. D. M. BARRELL

31 Peter des Roches: An Alien in English Politics, 1205–1238*
NICHOLAS VINCENT

32 Runaway Religious in Medieval England, *c.* 1240–1540*
F. DONALD LOGAN

33 People and Identity in Ostrogothic Italy, 489–554
PATRICK AMORY

34 The Aristocracy in Twelfth-Century León and Castile*
SIMON BARTON

35 Economy and Nature in the Fourteenth Century: Money, Market Exchange and the Emergence of Scientific Thought*
JOEL KAYE

36 Clement V
SOPHIA MENACHE

37 England's Jewish Solution, 1262–1290: Experiment and Expulsion*
ROBIN R. MUNDILL

38 Medieval Merchants: York, Beverley and Hull in the Later Middle Ages*
JENNY KERMODE

39 Family, Commerce and Religion in London and Cologne: A Comparative Social History of Anglo-German Emigrants, *c.* 1000–*c.* 1300
JOSEPH P. HUFFMAN

40 The Monastic Order in Yorkshire, 1069–1215
JANET BURTON

41 Parisian Scholars in the Early Fourteenth Century: A Social Portrait
WILLIAM J. COURTENAY

42 Colonisation and Conquest in Medieval Ireland: The English in Louth, 1170–1330
BRENDAN SMITH

43 The Early Humiliati
FRANCES ANDREWS

44 The Household Knights of King John
S. D. CHURCH

45 The English in Rome, 1362–1420: Portrait of an Expatriate Community
MARGARET HARVEY

46 Restoration and Reform: Recovery from Civil War in England, 1153–1165
GRAEME J. WHITE

47 State and Society in the Early Middle Ages: The Middle Rhine Valley, 400–1000
MATTHEW INNES

48 Brittany and the Angevins: Province and Empire, 1157–1203
JUDITH EVERARD

49 The Making of Gratian's *Decretum*
ANDERS WINROTH

50 At the Gate of Christendom: Jews, Muslims and 'Pagans' in Medieval Hungary, *c.* 1000–*c.* 1300
NORA BEREND

51 Making Agreements in Medieval Catalonia: Power, Order, and the Written Word, 1000–1200
ADAM J. KOSTO

52 The Making of the Slavs: History and Archaeology of the Lower Danube Region, *c.* 500–700
FLORIN CURTA

53 Literacy in Lombard Italy, *c.* 568–774
NICHOLAS EVERETT

54 Philosophy and Politics in the Thought of John Wyclif
STEPHEN E. LAHEY

55 Envoys and Political Communication in the Late Antique West, 411–533
ANDREW GILLETT

56 Kings, Barons and Justices: The Making and Enforcement of Legislation in Thirteenth-Century England
PAUL BRAND

**Also published as a paperback*

For EU product safety concerns, contact us at Calle de José Abascal, 56–1°,
28003 Madrid, Spain or eugpsr@cambridge.org.

www.ingramcontent.com/pod-product-compliance
Lightning Source LLC
LaVergne TN
LVHW090255210926
848480LV00001B/27
* 9 7 8 0 5 2 1 0 2 5 8 5 0 *